POLITICS
IN
STATES
AND
COMMUNITIES
▲

POLITICS
IN
STATES
AND
COMMUNITIES

▲

EIGHTH EDITION

THOMAS R. DYE
Florida State University

PRENTICE HALL, Englewood Cliffs, New Jersey 07632

Dye, Thomas R.
  Politics in states and communities / Thomas R. Dye. — 8th ed.
    p. cm.
  Includes bibliographical references and index.
  ISBN 0-13-042714-4
  1. State governments—United States. 2. Local government—United
States. I. Title.
JK2408.D82 1994
320.8'0973—dc20   93–19487
                                    CIP

Acquisitions editor: Charlyce Jones Owen
Editorial/production supervision: Marina Harrison
Cover and interior design: Jerry Votta
Production coordinator: Mary Ann Gloriande
Photo research: Rhoda Sidney
Photo editor: Lorinda Morris-Nantz
Cover photo: Comstock

© 1994, 1991, 1988, 1985, 1981, 1977, 1973, 1969 by Prentice-Hall, Inc.
A Paramount Communications Company
Englewood Cliffs, New Jersey 07632

Printed in the United States of America
10 9 8 7 6 5 4 3 2 1

ISBN 0-13-042714-4

Prentice-Hall International (UK) Limited, *London*
Prentice-Hall of Australia Pty. Limited, *Sydney*
Prentice-Hall Canada Inc., *Toronto*
Prentice-Hall Hispanoamericana, S.A., *Mexico*
Prentice-Hall of India Private Limited, *New Delhi*
Prentice-Hall of Japan, Inc., *Tokyo*
Simon & Schuster Asia Pte. Ltd., *Singapore*
Editora Prentice-Hall do Brasil, Ltda, *Rio de Janeiro*

To Joann

CONTENTS

▲

PREFACE

Since its first edition, *Politics in States and Communities* has maintained certain distinguishing features:

Its focus on *politics*
Its *comparative* approach
Its concern with *explanation*
Its interest in *policy*

The Eighth Edition continues the development of each of these themes. The focus remains on conflicts in states and communities and the structures and processes designed to manage conflict. This "conflict management" theme emphasizes the sources and nature of conflict in society, how conflict is carried on, how key decision makers in states and communities act in conflict situations, how public policies emerge and determine "who gets what."

POLITICS

The *political conflict* theme guides the discussion of formal governmental structures: federalism, state constitutions, parties and primaries, apportionment, legislative organization, gubernatorial powers, court procedures, nonpartisanship, mayor and manager government, metropolitan government, community power, school boards and superintendents, tax systems, budget making, and so on.

This theme also guides the discussion of *illustrative studies* in state and local politics:

Tax Limitation Initiatives
Term Limit Battles
Congress Raises the Drinking Age
The States and ERA
Money in Politics
The Great Incumbency Machine
Impeachment: Arizona's Evan Mecham
The Lawyering of America
The Rejection of Rose Bird
The War on Drugs
Political Corruption
"Reinventing Government"
The Radical Style: Politics in Berkeley
Minorities in Local Politics

Machine and Reform Politics in Chicago
Top Bananas in the Big Apple
Busing and Racial Balancing in Schools
The Battle over Abortion
The Inner City: Racial Tensions and Rioting
Wilder of Virginia: Putting Race to Rest
Educational Reform
Revolting Against Taxes
"No-Growth" Politics and the Nimby Syndrome

The timely case studies are designed to both improve understanding and stimulate interest in state and local politics.

COMPARISON

In each chapter, *comparative analysis* is used both to describe and to explain differences among states and communities in governmental structures, political processes, and public policy. Students observe the relative ranking of their own state on such measures as

Income
Education
Urbanization
Growth
Black and ethnic populations
Liberalism and conservatism
Reliance and Federal Aid
Party competition
Political participation
Interest groups
Black representation in legislatures
Professionalism in legislatures
Governors' powers
Governors' Fiscal Conservatism
Judicial selection
Crime rates
Police protection
Prison populations
Drop out rates
Educational spending
Income inequality
Welfare spending
Tax burdens

"Rankings of the states" are presented in clear bar graphs and plots. They enable students and instructors to assess their own state's position in relation to all fifty states.

EXPLANATION

We want to know "what" is happening in American politics, but we also want to know "why." *Comparative analysis* lays the groundwork for explanation. In each chapter, recent systematic research in the social sciences is summarized for undergraduate students. Difficult theoretical questions are presented clearly and concisely for undergraduates:

Direct versus representative Democracy
Politics and the popular initiative
Why federalism?
How money shifted power to Washington
Are protests effective?
The effects of party competition
Apportionment, districting, and gerrymandering
Are legislators responsible policy makers?
Governors versus Legislatures
Are school boards responsible policy makers?
Are council members responsible policy makers?
Crime and deterrence
Types of cities and forms of government
Privatization as Reform
Reformism and public policy
Models of community power
How to study community power
Metropolitan government as marketplace
Explaining educational policies in the states
Explaining welfare policies in the states
Explaining state tax systems
Explaining the tax revolt

The most recent systematic social science research of these topics is presented in the Eighth Edition.

POLICY

Public *policy* is what governments do, and state and local governments in America do many things that touch the lives of all of us. This text is divided roughly into three parts: federalism and state politics, local politics and community power, and public policy. Specific attention is devoted to policy questions in

Crime in the states

Police and law enforcement

State correctional policies

The death penalty

Abortion

The states and school desegregation

Affirmative action

The politics of higher education

The politics of "no-growth"

Housing and development policy

Poverty in America

Health care in the states

The tax revolt

The politics of budgeting

Fiscal stress and cutback management

The Eighth Edition reflects the changing dynamics of conflict in states and communities, including debates over term limits and incumbency advantages, battles over abortion restrictions following *Planned Parenthood v. Casey,* controversies over the privatization of governmental services, fights over educational performance and its measurement, and disputes over welfare and health care reform. It describes increased minority representation in state legislatures and city councils, following recent redistricting under federal court supervision. It focuses new attention on conflicts between governors and legislatures and the "gridlock" resulting from divided party control of state government. It reports on conditions in the nation's inner cities and racial tensions and rioting in Los Angeles and elsewhere. It describes the evolution of governmental reform, including the "reinventing government" movement supported by Bill Clinton in Arkansas. It focuses anew on local battles over the control of land use and the conflicting interests of developers, landowners, "no-growthers," environmentalists, and "Nimbys."

If this book has a theme, it is that states and communities in America play an important role in the political life of the nation. State and local governments do more than merely provide certain services such as education, road building, or fire protection. They also perform a vital political function by helping to resolve conflicts of interests in American society.

THOMAS R. DYE

1

POLITICS IN STATES AND COMMUNITIES

▲

A POLITICAL APPROACH TO STATES AND COMMUNITIES

The management of conflict is one of the basic purposes of government. Two hundred years ago, James Madison wrote that the control of "factions" was the principal function of government. He defined a faction as a number of citizens united by common interests that opposed the interests of other citizens "or to the permanent and aggregate interests of the community." He thought that regulating such conflict was "the principal task of modern legislation."[1] To paraphrase Madison, the management of conflict is "the principal task" of state and local government.

Politics is the management of conflict. An understanding of "politics" in American states and communities requires an understanding of the major conflicts confronting society and an understanding of political processes and governmental organizations designed to manage conflict. State and local governments do more than provide public services such as education, highways, police and fire protec-

---

[1] James Madison, *The Federalist*, Number 10. New York: Modern Library, 1958.

1

tion, sewage disposal, and garbage collection. These are important functions of government to be sure; but it is even more important that government deal with racial tensions, school disputes, growth problems, economic stagnation, minority concerns, poverty, drugs, crime, and violence. These problems are primarily *political* in nature; that is, people have different ideas about what should be done, or if government should do anything at all.

Moreover, many of the service functions of government also engender political conflict. Even if "there is only one way to pave a street," political questions remain. Whose street will get paved? Who will get the paving contract? Who will pay for it? Why not build a school gym instead of paving the street?

So it is appropriate that a book on *politics* in states and communities deals not only with the structure and organization of state and local government, but also with many of the central policy questions confronting American society. It is true that these problems are national in scope, but they occur in our communities and our states. And much of this book is devoted to describing how these questions arise in state and local settings, and how state and local governments confront them.

A COMPARATIVE APPROACH TO STATES AND COMMUNITIES

The task of political science is not only to *describe* politics and public policy in American states and communities, but also to *explain* differences encountered from state to state and community to community through comparative analysis. We want to know *what* is happening in American politics, and we want to know *why*. In the past, the phrase "comparative government" applied to the study of foreign governments, but American states and communities provide an excellent opportunity for genuine comparative study, which is *comparing political institutions and behaviors from state to state and community to community in order to identify and explain similarities or differences.*

Comparison is a vital part of explanation. Only by comparing politics and public policy in different states and communities with different socioeconomic and political environments can we arrive at any comprehensive explanations of political life. Comparative analysis helps us answer the question *why*.

American states and communities provide excellent "laboratories" for applying comparative analysis. States and communities are not alike in social and economic conditions, in politics and government, or in their public policies. These differences are important assets in comparative study because they enable us to search for relationships between different socioeconomic conditions, political system characteristics, and policy outcomes. For example, if differences among states and communities in educational policies are closely associated with differences in economic resources or in party politics, then we may assume that economic resources or party politics help "explain" educational policies.

State politics are often affected by unique historical circumstances. (See Figure 1-1, Table 1-1.) Louisiana is distinctive because of its French–Spanish colonial background, and the continuing influence of this background on its politics today.

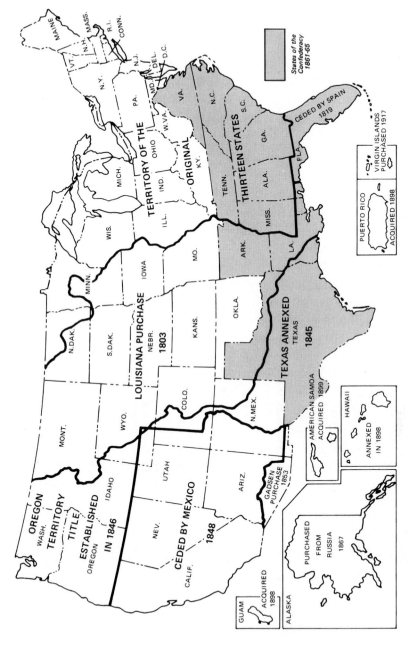

FIGURE 1–1 State Histories

3

TABLE 1-1   THE STATES OF THE UNION—HISTORICAL DATA

State or Other Jurisdiction	Capital	Source of State Lands	Date Organized as Territory	Date Admitted to Union	Chronological Order of Admission to Union
Alabama	Montgomery	Mississippi Territory, 1798[a]	March 3, 1817	Dec. 14, 1819	22
Alaska	Juneau	Purchased from Russia, 1867	Aug. 24, 1912	Jan. 3, 1959	49
Arizona	Phoenix	Ceded by Mexico, 1848[b]	Feb. 24, 1863	Feb. 14, 1912	48
Arkansas	Little Rock	Louisiana Purchase, 1803	March 2, 1819	June 15, 1836	25
California	Sacramento	Ceded by Mexico, 1848	(c)	Sept. 9, 1850	31
Colorado	Denver	Louisiana Purchase, 1803[d]	Feb. 28, 1861	Aug. 1, 1876	38
Connecticut	Hartford	Royal charter, 1662[e]		Jan. 9, 1788[f]	5
Delaware	Dover	Swedish charter, 1638; English charter 1683[e]		Dec. 7, 1787[f]	1
Florida	Tallahassee	Ceded by Spain, 1819	March 30, 1822	March 3, 1845	27
Georgia	Atlanta	Charter, 1732, from George II to Trustees for Establishing the Colony of Georgia[e]		Jan. 2, 1788[f]	4
Hawaii	Honolulu	Annexed, 1898	June 14, 1900	Aug. 21, 1959	50
Idaho	Boise	Treaty with Britain, 1846	March 4, 1863	July 3, 1890	43
Illinois	Springfield	Northwest Territory, 1787	Feb. 3, 1809	Dec. 3, 1818	21
Indiana	Indianapolis	Northwest Territory, 1787	May 7, 1800	Dec. 11, 1816	19
Iowa	Des Moines	Louisiana Purchase, 1803	June 12, 1838	Dec. 28, 1846	29
Kansas	Topeka	Louisiana Puchase, 1803[d]	May 30, 1854	Jan. 29, 1861	34
Kentucky	Frankfort	Part of Virginia until admitted as State	(c)	June 1, 1792	15
Louisiana	Baton Rouge	Louisiana Purchase, 1803[g]	March 26, 1804	April 30, 1812	18
Maine	Augusta	Part of Massachusetts until admitted as State	(c)	March 15, 1820	23
Maryland	Annapolis	Charter, 1632, from Charles I to Calvert[e]		April 28, 1788[f]	7
Massachusetts	Boston	Charter to Massachusetts Bay Company, 1629[e]		Feb. 6, 1788[f]	6
Michigan	Lansing	Northwest Territory, 1787	Jan. 11, 1805	Jan. 26, 1837	26
Minnesota	St. Paul	Northwest Territory, 1787[h]	March 3, 1849	May 11, 1858	32
Mississippi	Jackson	Mississippi Territory[i]	April 7, 1798	Dec. 10, 1817	20
Missouri	Jefferson City	Louisiana Purchase, 1803	June 4, 1812	Aug. 10, 1821	24
Montana	Helena	Louisiana Purchase, 1803[j]	May 26, 1864	Nov. 8, 1889	41
Nebraska	Lincoln	Louisiana Purchase, 1803	May 30, 1854	March 1, 1867	37
Nevada	Carson City	Ceded by Mexico, 1848	March 2, 1861	Oct. 31, 1864	36
New Hampshire	Concord	Grants from Council for New England, 1622 and 1629. Made royal province, 1679[e]		June 21, 1788[f]	9

State/Area	Capital	Source of land	Date organized as territory	Date admitted to Union	Chronological order of admission to Union
New Jersey	Trenton	Dutch settlement, 1618; English charter, 1664[e]		Dec. 18, 1787[f]	3
New Mexico	Santa Fe	Ceded by Mexico, 1848[b]	Sept. 9, 1850	Jan. 6, 1912	47
New York	Albany	Dutch settlement, 1623; English control, 1664[e]		July 26, 1788[f]	11
North Carolina	Raleigh	Charter, 1663, from Charles II[e]		Nov. 21, 1789[f]	12
North Dakota	Bismarck	Louisiana Purchase, 1803[k]	March 2, 1861	Nov. 2, 1889	39
Ohio	Columbus	Northwest Territory, 1787	(c)	March 1, 1803	17
Oklahoma	Oklahoma City	Louisiana Purchase, 1803	May 22, 1890	Nov. 16, 1907	46
Oregon	Salem	Settlement and treaty with Britain, 1846	Aug. 14, 1848	Feb. 14, 1859	33
Pennsylvania	Harrisburg	Grant from Charles II to William Penn, 1681[e]		Dec. 12, 1787[f]	2
Rhode Island	Providence	Charter, 1663, from Charles II[e]		May 29, 1790[f]	13
South Carolina	Columbia	Charter, 1663, from Charles II[e]		May 23, 1788[f]	8
South Dakota	Pierre	Louisiana Purchase, 1803	March 2, 1861	Nov. 2, 1889	40
Tennessee	Nashville	Part of North Carolina until admitted as State	(c)	June 1, 1796	16
Texas	Austin	Republic of Texas, 1845	(c)	Dec. 29, 1845	28
Utah	Salt Lake City	Ceded by Mexico, 1848	Sept. 9, 1850	Jan. 4, 1896	45
Vermont	Montpelier	From lands of New Hampshire and New York	(c)	March 4, 1791	14
Virginia	Richmond	Charter, 1609, from James I to London Company[e]		June 25, 1788[f]	10
Washington	Olympia	Oregon Territory, 1848	March 2, 1853	Nov. 11, 1889	42
West Virginia	Charleston	Part of Virginia until admitted as State	(c)	June 20, 1863	35
Wisconsin	Madison	Northwest Territory, 1787	April 20, 1836	May 29, 1848	30
Wyoming	Cheyenne	Louisiana Purchase, 1803[d,j]	July 25, 1868	July 10, 1890	44
American Samoa	Pago Pago		Became a territory 1899		—
Guam	Agana	Ceded by Spain, 1898	Aug. 1, 1950		—
Puerto Rico	San Juan	Ceded by Spain, 1898		July 25, 1952[l]	—
TTPI	Saipan	Administered as trusteeship for the United Nations, July 18, 1947			
Virgin Islands	Charlotte Amalie	Purchased from Denmark, January 17, 1917			—

a By the Treaty of Paris, 1783, England gave up claim to the thirteen original Colonies, and to all land within an area extending along the present Canadian border to the Lake of the Woods, down the Mississippi River to the 31st parallel, east to the source of the Chattahoochie, down that river to the mouth of the Flint, east to the source of the St. Mary's, down that river to the ocean. Territory west of the Alleghenies was claimed by various states but was eventually all ceded to the nation. Thus, the major part of Alabama was acquired by the Treaty of Paris, but the lower portion was acquired from Spain in 1813.

b Portion of land obtained by Gadsden Purchase, 1853.

c No territorial status before admission to Union.

d Portion of land ceded by Mexico, 1848.

e One of the original Thirteen Colonies.

f Date of ratification of U.S. Constitution.

g West Feliciana District (Baton Rouge) acquired from Spain, 1810, added to Louisiana, 1812.

h Portion of land obtained by Louisiana Purchase, 1803.

i See footnote (a). The lower portion of Mississippi was also acquired from Spain in 1813.

j Portion of land obtained from Oregon Territory, 1848.

k Portion of land acquired by the Treaty of Paris, but the lower portion was acquired from Spain in 1813.

l The northern portion and the Red River Valley were acquired by treaty with Great Britain in 1818.

l On this date Puerto Rico became a self-governing Commonwealth by compact approved by the United States Congress and the voters of Puerto Rico as provided in U.S. Public Law 600 of 1950.

Source: The Book of the States 1978-79 (Lexington, KY: Council of State Governments, 1978).

For nine years Texas was an independent republic (1836–1845) before it was annexed as a state by Congress. Eleven southern states were involved in a bloody war against the federal government from 1861 to 1865. Hawaii has a unique history and culture, combining the influence of Polynesian, Chinese, Japanese, and haole civilizations. Alaska's rugged climate and geography and physical isolation set it apart. Wisconsin and Minnesota reflect the Scandinavian influences of their settlers, and Utah reflects the religious influences of its Mormon settlers. The states of the Deep South—South Carolina, Georgia, Alabama, Mississippi, Louisiana—still reflect their plantation cultures. Four states—Pennsylvania, Massachusetts, Kentucky, and Virginia—call themselves "commonwealth," but this title has no legal meaning. Life in Florida is more tourist oriented than anywhere else. Michigan is the home of the automobile industry. West Virginia is noted for its mountains and its coal mines. For many years Nevada was the only state that permitted legalized casino gambling.

These unique historical and cultural settings help to shape state political systems and public policies. However, the mere identification of unique traits or histories does not really "explain" why politics or public policy differs from state to state. Ad hoc explanations do not help very much in developing general theories of politics. For example, only Texas has the Alamo and only New York has the Statue of Liberty, but these characteristics do not explain why New York has a state income tax and Texas does not. Students of state politics must search for social and economic conditions that appear most influential in shaping state politics over time in all the states. Despite the uniqueness of history and culture in many of our states, we must *search for generalizations* that will help to explain why state governments do what they do.

Since it is impossible to consider all the conditions that might influence state politics, we must focus our attention on a limited number of variables. Economic development is one of the most influential variables affecting state politics. Economic development is defined broadly to include three closely related components: population growth and urbanization, income, and education.

Growth and Urbanization   *Growth and urbanization* are a part of economic development. The population of the United States has grown about 1 percent per year over the past few decades. But population growth is spread unevenly among the fifty states; over the last decade, Nevada, Arizona, and Florida grew by more than 30 percent, while Iowa, West Virginia, North Dakota, and Wyoming actually lost population (see Figure 1–2). The standard Census Bureau definition of urbanization is the percentage of population living in urban areas, that is, in incorporated cities of 2500 or more or the urban fringe of cities of 50,000 or more. In 1790 the urban population of the United States was only 5 percent of the total population. By 1900 this figure had grown to 40 percent, and in 1990, 77.5 percent of the population lived in urban areas. Yet not all the states share this high degree of urbanization. Idaho has the smallest proportion of urban residents of any state in the nation, and New Jersey has the highest proportion.

Income   Rising *income* is also a component of economic development. An industrial economy means increased worker productivity and the creation of more

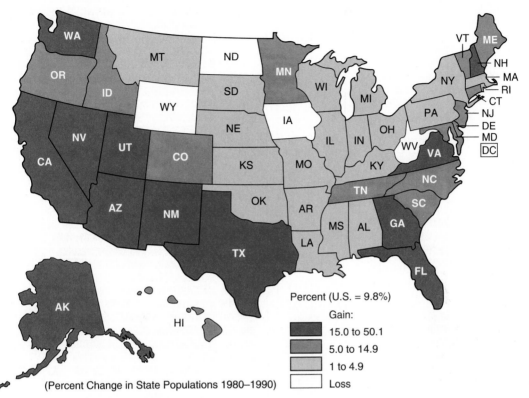

FIGURE 1-2   Population Growth in the States: Percent Change in State Population, 1980-1990

Source: Chart prepared by U.S. Bureau of the Census.

wealth. Per capita personal income in the United States grew from $3,996 in 1970 to nearly $18,000 in 1990. This wealth was not evenly distributed throughout the states (see Figure 1-3). Per capita personal income in 1990 in Connecticut was $24,683, but it was only $11,724 in Mississippi.

Education   An economically developed society requires educated workers. Many economists have asserted that economic growth involves an upgrading in the work force, the development of professional managerial skills, and an increase in the volume of research. These developments obviously involve a general increase in the *educational levels* of the adult population. In 1970 about 11 percent of the adult population of the United States had completed four years or more of college; by 1990 that figure had risen to over 21 percent. But high levels of educational attainment do not prevail uniformly throughout the states (see Figure 1-3).

The extent to which economic development—growth and urbanization, income, and education—affects the politics of the states is an important question, which we will return to again in the chapters that follow.

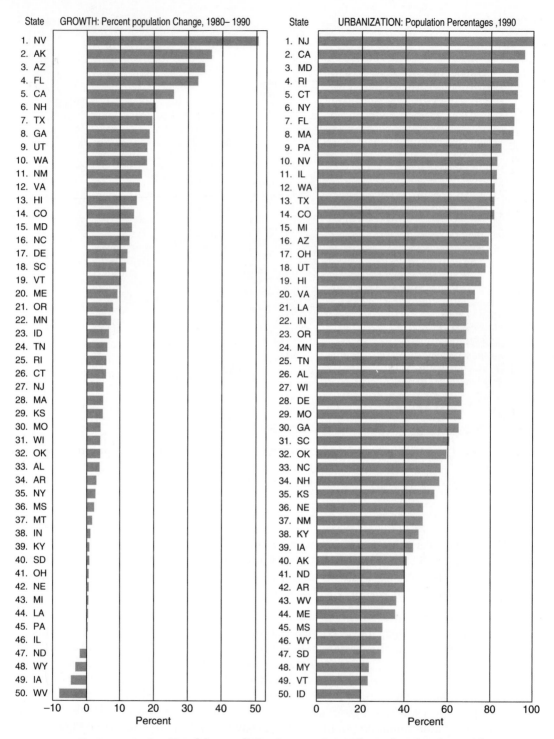

State	GROWTH: Percent population Change, 1980–1990		State	URBANIZATION: Population Percentages ,1990
1. NV			1. NJ	
2. AK			2. CA	
3. AZ			3. MD	
4. FL			4. RI	
5. CA			5. CT	
6. NH			6. NY	
7. TX			7. FL	
8. GA			8. MA	
9. UT			9. PA	
10. WA			10. NV	
11. NM			11. IL	
12. VA			12. WA	
13. HI			13. TX	
14. CO			14. CO	
15. MD			15. MI	
16. NC			16. AZ	
17. DE			17. OH	
18. SC			18. UT	
19. VT			19. HI	
20. ME			20. VA	
21. OR			21. LA	
22. MN			22. IN	
23. ID			23. OR	
24. TN			24. MN	
25. RI			25. TN	
26. CT			26. AL	
27. NJ			27. WI	
28. MA			28. DE	
29. KS			29. MO	
30. MO			30. GA	
31. WI			31. SC	
32. OK			32. OK	
33. AL			33. NC	
34. AR			34. NH	
35. NY			35. KS	
36. MS			36. NE	
37. MT			37. NM	
38. IN			38. KY	
39. KY			39. IA	
40. SD			40. AK	
41. OH			41. ND	
42. NE			42. AR	
43. MI			43. WV	
44. LA			44. ME	
45. PA			45. MS	
46. IL			46. WY	
47. ND			47. SD	
48. WY			48. MY	
49. IA			49. VT	
50. WV			50. ID	

Percent — Growth axis: −10 0 10 20 30 40 50

Percent — Urbanization axis: 0 20 40 60 80 100

FIGURE 1–3 **Rankings of the States: Growth, Urbanization, Education, and Income**

Source: Statistical Abstract of the United States, 1992

FIGURE 1-3 *(continued)*

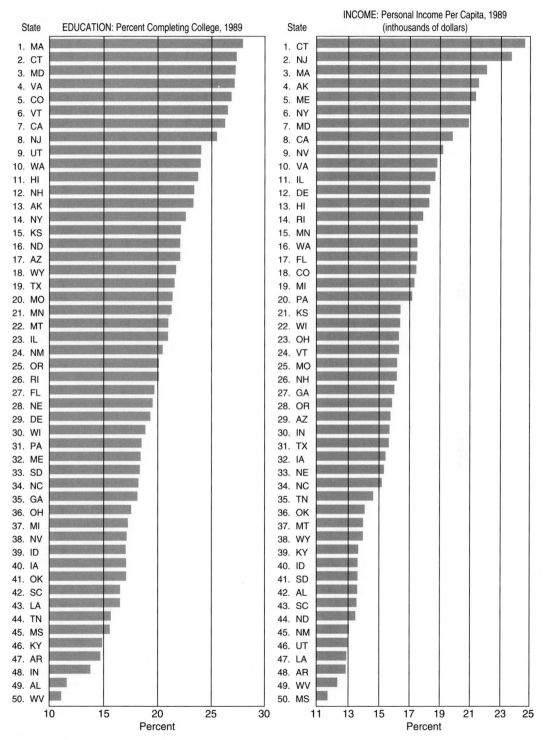

EDUCATION: Percent Completing College, 1989

State	
1.	MA
2.	CT
3.	MD
4.	VA
5.	CO
6.	VT
7.	CA
8.	NJ
9.	UT
10.	WA
11.	HI
12.	NH
13.	AK
14.	NY
15.	KS
16.	ND
17.	AZ
18.	WY
19.	TX
20.	MO
21.	MN
22.	MT
23.	IL
24.	NM
25.	OR
26.	RI
27.	FL
28.	NE
29.	DE
30.	WI
31.	PA
32.	ME
33.	SD
34.	NC
35.	GA
36.	OH
37.	MI
38.	NV
39.	ID
40.	IA
41.	OK
42.	SC
43.	LA
44.	TN
45.	MS
46.	KY
47.	AR
48.	IN
49.	AL
50.	WV

Percent: 10 15 20 25 30

INCOME: Personal Income Per Capita, 1989 (in thousands of dollars)

State	
1.	CT
2.	NJ
3.	MA
4.	AK
5.	ME
6.	NY
7.	MD
8.	CA
9.	NV
10.	VA
11.	IL
12.	DE
13.	HI
14.	RI
15.	MN
16.	WA
17.	FL
18.	CO
19.	MI
20.	PA
21.	KS
22.	WI
23.	OH
24.	VT
25.	MO
26.	NH
27.	GA
28.	OR
29.	AZ
30.	IN
31.	TX
32.	IA
33.	NE
34.	NC
35.	TN
36.	OK
37.	MT
38.	WY
39.	KY
40.	ID
41.	SD
42.	AL
43.	SC
44.	ND
45.	NM
46.	UT
47.	LA
48.	AR
49.	WV
50.	MS

Percent: 11 13 15 17 19 21 23 25

SOURCES OF DATA ON STATES AND COMMUNITIES IN THE UNITED STATES

Standard sources of data on American states and communities in tables throughout this volume include: U.S. Bureau of the Census, *Statistical Abstract of the United States*, published annually by the U.S. Government Printing Office, Washington, DC; U.S. Bureau of the Census, *Census of Governments*, published after each five-year governmental census (1982, 1987, 1992, etc.) by the U.S. Government Printing Office, Washington, DC; U.S. Bureau of the Census, *Census of Population 1990*, including individual state volumes on "Numbers of Inhabitants," "General Population Characteristics," and "General Social and Economic Characteristics," as well as individual reports on Standard Metropolitan Statistical Areas, published by the U.S. Government Printing Office, Washington, DC, *The Book of the States*, published biennially by the Council of State Governments, Lexington, KY; *Municipal Yearbook*, published annually by the International City Managers Association, Washington, DC; U.S. Bureau of the Census, *City–County Data Book*, published every five years by the U.S. Government Printing Office, Washington, DC. Unless otherwise indicated, the social, economic, governmental, and electoral data presented in this volume are drawn from these sources.

STATE POLITICAL "CULTURES" AND ETHNIC INFLUENCES

Anthropologists define *culture* as customary "ways of life," including designs for living, shared values, and guides to appropriate behavior.[2] We know that states have different histories, economies, climates, and rates of growth, but can the states also be distinguished by their dominant political cultures? If so, can the different political cultures of the states help explain diversity in politics and public policy? Actually, the term *culture* applies to a whole society, so we must search for important variations, or *subcultures*, that may account for political differences among the states.

One theory of American political subcultures, set forth initially by political scientist Daniel J. Elazar, attempts to identify variations in shared political values and appropriate guides to political activity.[3] These cultural differences arise among the states primarily because of different patterns of early migration and settlement

---

[2] Clyde Kluckholm, "The Concept of Culture," in *The Science of Man in the World*, Ralph Linton, ed. (New York: Columbia University Press, 1945). For an explanation of the idea of *political* culture, see Michael Thompson, Richard Ellis, and Aaron Wildavsky, *Cultural Theory* (Boulder, CO: Westview Press, 1990).

[3] Daniel Elazar, *American Federalism: A View from the States* (New York: Thomas Y. Crowell, 1966), Chapter 4.

and the resulting dominance of different religious and ethnic groups in a state's society. Elazar labeled these political subcultures as moralistic, individualistic, and traditionalistic (shown as M, I, and T, and combinations thereof in Figure 1–4).

Moralistic   A *moralistic* political subculture emphasizes a common public interest—honesty in government, selflessness, and a commitment to the public welfare by those who govern. Every citizen has a duty to participate in political affairs, and office-holding is looked upon as public service demanding high moral obligations. Politics should be concerned with general issues and programs, not narrow special interests or selfish office-seeking. Nonpartisanship is preferred over party politics, and citizen (amateur) officeholders are preferred over professional politicians. The moralistic political subculture allows a great deal of government intervention into the social and economic life of the state or community in order to promote the "common good."

Individualistic   In contrast, the *individualistic* political subculture emphasizes politics as a means of advancing the social and economic interests of groups and individuals. Political activity is undertaken for personal benefit or group advancement. Politics is based primarily on group obligations rooted in personal relationships; general political issues or public service motives are secondary. Professional politicians who look after the material interests of their own constituents are preferred to moralizing amateurs. Government intervention in private life should be minimal, although large public bureaucracies may result from efforts to give jobs (patronage) to large numbers of people.

Traditionalistic   In a *traditionalistic* political culture, a paternalistic elite plays a special and dominant role in government. The political community is ordered in a hierarchical fashion with those at the top of the social structure using government to maintain and preserve the social and economic system and their dominant role in it. Real political power is confined to a relatively small and self-perpetuating elite who generally inherit their position from family ties, social position, and wealth. *Nonelites* are not expected to be politically active; indeed, they may not even be expected to vote. Political parties have little importance; competition is usually limited to factional alignments centered around individuals or geographical areas. The primary political values are the maintenance and encouragement of traditional social and religious values. Government services are often provided on a personal, first-name basis.

Culture and Ethnicity   The location of these political subcultures throughout the American states is largely determined by the migration patterns of different ethnic and religious groups. Indeed, it appears that the *moralistic* subculture is a product of northern European, English, and German liberal Protestantism; the *individualistic* subculture is a product of southern and eastern European and Irish Catholicism; and the *traditionalist* subculture is a product of fundamentalist white Protestantism in potential conflict with large black populations.[4]

---

[4] A genealogy of American political culture based on waves of very early colonial migration is developed in David Hackett Fischer, *Albion's Seed* (New York: Oxford University Press, 1989).

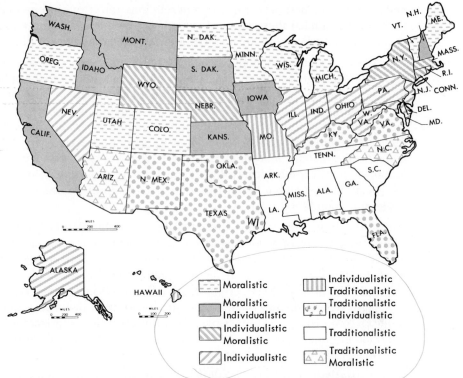

FIGURE 1–4   Regional Distribution of Political Culture in the United States

Source: Daniel Elazar, *American Federalism: A View from the States,* 3rd ed. (New York: Harper & Row, 1984) p. 135. Copyright © 1984 by Harper & Row Publishers, Inc. Reprinted by permission of Harper Collins Publishers, Inc.

Over time, subcultures tend to blur, owing to continued mobility of the nation's population and the impact of national cultural media—particularly television, movies, and music. Efforts to test Elazar's theory about the political effects of subcultures have produced only mixed results.[5] There is little empirical evidence that people actually think about politics in individualistic, moralistic, or traditionalistic terms.[6]

Nonetheless, America is indeed a nation of immigrants, and patterns of immigration in the states have left their mark. A serious examination of the political

---

[5] Ira Sharkansky, "The Utility of Elazar's Political Culture," *Polity,* 2 (Fall 1969), 66–83; Leonard G. Ritt, "Political Cultures and Political Reform," *Publius,* 4 (Winter 1974), 131–34; Charles A. Johnson, "Political Culture in American States," *American Journal of Political Science,* 20 (August 1976), 491–509; Eric B. Herzik, "The Legal–Formal Structuring of State Politics: A Cultural Explanation," *Western Political Quarterly,* 85 (September 1985), 413–23.

[6] Peter F. Nardulli, "Political Subcultures in the American states," *American Politics Quarterly,* 18 (July 1990), 287–315.

effects of ethnicity might begin by observing the current distribution of people with foreign-born parentage. This distribution is shown in Table 1–2. It should come as no surprise that Canada is the leading country of origin for the states on our northern border, and Mexico is the leading country of origin for the states on our southern border. The Spanish heritage in Texas, New Mexico, Arizona, and southern California is important politically as well as culturally. Likewise the Cuban heritage in southern Florida creates the cultural background for politics in that state. Recent scholarly work on ethnicity-based political cultures throughout the nation suggests distinctive patterns based on the prevalence of "Anglo," "Germanic," "Nordic," "Hispanic," "Mormon," and other cultural influences.[7]

State Political Cultures   Do the states exhibit separate and identifiable political cultures? That is, are there political differences among the states that cannot be accounted for by demographic characteristics, for example, race, religion, income, education? It does appear that some states have developed historical traditions of Democratic and Republican party affiliation, as well as cultural patterns of liberal and conservative politics, that are independent of any demographic features of their populations.[8] For example, Minnesota has developed a liberal and Democratic tradition, Indiana a conservative and Republican tradition, and neither can be explained by the racial, religious, or socioeconomic composition of their populations. Historical traditions stemming from the Civil War and Reconstruction can help explain the Democratic political cultures of the southern states. But the liberal politics of Massachusetts, Rhode Island, Vermont, and West Virginia, as well as the conservative politics of Idaho, North Dakota, and Utah, are not fully explained by characteristics of these states' populations or by specific historical events. So we attribute to "political culture" the unexplained variation in partisan affiliations and ideological predispositions that we cannot explain by social or economic factors.

LIBERALISM AND CONSERVATISM IN THE STATES

State political cultures may differ in their ideological predispositions—that is, whether they are predominantly "liberal" or "conservative." There are various ways of defining and measuring ideological predispositions. Liberal and conservative states might be identified in terms of their policy enactments. For example, "policy liberalism" might be defined as the adoption of relaxed eligibility standards for receipts of welfare and medical benefits, decriminalization of marijuana possession and an absence of the death penalty, extensive regulation of business, state ratification of the Equal Rights Amendment, and the adoption of progressive state income taxes; "policy conservatism" would be defined as the opposite of these enactments. Or liberal and conservative states might be defined in terms of their voters' self-identification in opinion surveys as "liberal," "moderate," or "conser-

---

7 Joel Liske, "Political Subcultures of the United States." Paper delivered at the American Political Science Association Annual Meeting, Washington, DC, 1991.

8 Robert S. Erikson, John P. McIver, and Gerald C. Wright, "State Political Culture and Public Opinion," *American Political Science Review,* 81 (September 1987), 797–813.

TABLE 1–2 RACE AND ETHNICITY IN THE STATES, 1990

	Foreign-born %	Leading Country of Origin	Black Population %	American Indian, Eskimo, Aleut	Asian, Pacific Islander	Hispanic origin
New England						
ME	19.4	Canada	0.4	0.5	0.5	0.6
NH	23.2	Canada	0.6	0.2	0.8	1.0
VT	18.2	Canada	0.3	0.3	0.6	0.7
MA	33.3	Canada	5.0	0.2	2.4	4.8
RI	32.8	Italy	3.9	0.4	1.8	4.6
CT	32.0	Italy	8.3	0.2	1.5	6.5
Middle Atlantic						
NY	32.9	Italy	15.9	0.3	3.9	12.3
NJ	30.1	Italy	13.4	0.2	3.5	9.6
PA	18.1	Italy	9.2	0.1	1.2	2.0
DE	11.9	Italy	16.9	0.3	1.4	2.4
Central						
OH	12.3	Germany	16.9	0.3	1.4	2.4
IN	6.8	Germany	7.8	0.2	0.7	1.8
IL	19.8	Germany	14.8	0.2	2.5	7.9
MI	19.0	Canada	13.9	0.6	1.1	2.2
WI	16.9	Germany	5.0	0.8	1.1	1.9
MN	18.6	Germany	2.2	1.1	1.8	1.2
IA	10.5	Germany	1.7	0.3	0.9	1.2
MO	6.7	Germany	10.7	0.4	0.8	1.2
ND	23.6	Norway	0.6	4.1	0.5	0.7
SD	16.4	Germany	0.5	7.3	0.4	0.8
NE	13.8	Germany	3.6	0.8	0.8	2.3
KS	7.8	Germany	5.8	0.9	1.3	3.8

Southeastern						
MD	11.6	Germany	24.9	0.3	2.9	2.6
VA	5.4	Germany	18.8	0.2	2.6	2.6
WV	4.2	Italy	3.1	0.1	0.4	0.5
NC	1.9	Germany	22.0	1.2	0.8	1.2
SC	1.9	Germany	29.8	0.2	0.6	0.9
GA	2.4	Germany	27.0	0.2	1.2	1.7
FL	18.2	Cuba	13.6	0.3	1.2	12.2
KY	2.3	Germany	7.1	0.2	0.5	0.6
TN	1.7	Germany	16.0	0.2	0.7	0.7
AL	1.9	Germany	25.3	0.4	0.5	0.6
MS	1.4	Germany	35.6	0.3	0.5	0.6
Southwestern						
AR	1.9	Germany	15.9	0.5	0.5	0.8
LA	3.8	Italy	30.8	0.4	1.0	2.2
OK	3.6	Germany	7.4	8.0	1.1	2.7
TX	10.7	Mexico	11.9	0.4	1.9	25.5
NM	8.8	Mexico	2.0	8.9	0.9	38.2
AZ	16.8	Mexico	3.0	5.6	1.5	18.8
Mountain						
MT	17.6	Canada	0.3	6.0	0.5	1.5
ID	10.4	Canada	0.3	1.4	0.9	5.3
WY	11.4	Germany	0.8	2.1	0.6	5.7
CO	12.7	Germany	4.0	0.8	1.8	12.9
UT	12.5	United Kingdom	0.7	1.4	1.9	4.9
NV	13.9	Italy	6.6	1.6	3.2	10.4
Pacific						
WA	18.7	Canada	3.1	1.7	4.3	4.4
OR	14.1	Canada	1.6	1.4	2.4	4.0
CA	25.0	Mexico	7.4	0.8	9.6	25.8
AK	11.0	Canada	4.1	15.6	3.6	3.2
HI	33.4	Japan	2.5	0.5	61.8	7.3
U.S. Totals	16.5		12.1	0.8	2.9	9.0

vative." A common question on opinion polls is: "How would you describe your views on most political matters? Generally do you think of yourself as liberal, moderate, or conservative?" One study collected the results of national opinion polls over six years (1976–1982) and then observed the responses of voters in each state.[9] Nationwide during this period 32 percent of respondents identified themselves as "conservative," 40 percent, "moderate," and 21 percent, "liberal." Figure 1–5 shows the "conservative" responses in each state: The most conservative state in terms of voter self-identification was Utah (45 percent conservative, 37 percent moderate, 13 percent liberal) followed by Indiana (42 percent conservative, 39 percent moderate, 13 percent liberal). The most liberal states were Massachusetts (26 percent conservative, 42 percent moderate, 26 percent liberal), New York (29 percent conservative, 39 percent moderate, 26 percent liberal), and New Jersey (28 percent conservative, 40 percent moderate, 26 percent liberal). It is interesting to note that ideological identification of the voters in the states correlates very closely with measures of policy liberalism and conservatism.

RACE AND ETHNICITY

States differ in the racial and ethnic composition of their populations. These differences account for much of the variation in the politics of states and cities throughout the nation. Later we will be examining racial and ethnic cleavages in voting behavior and political participation (Chapter 4), state legislative politics (Chapter 6), community politics (Chapter 11), and civil rights policy (Chapter 14).

African-Americans   In 1900, most blacks (89.7 percent) were concentrated in the South. But World Wars I and II provided job opportunities in large cities of the Northeast and Midwest. Blacks could not cast ballots in most southern counties, but they could "vote with their feet." The migration of blacks from the rural South to the urban North was one of the largest internal migrations in our history. By 1990 only 53 percent of the nation's 30 million blacks lived in the South—still more than any other region but less of a concentration than earlier in American history. Blacks comprise 12.1 percent of the total population of the United States. The distribution of blacks among the fifty states is shown in Table 1–2.

Black candidates have been increasingly successful in winning city and county offices and state legislative seats in the southern states and in big cities throughout the nation. (See Chapter 4 for a discussion of voting rights laws.) The largest number of black elected officials are found in the southern states. In 1989 the nation's first elected black governor, Douglas Wilder, moved into Virginia's statehouse, once the office of Jefferson Davis, president of the Confederacy (see Chapter 14). Black candidates have also been increasingly successful in winning

---

[9] Gerald C. Wright, Robert S. Erikson, and John P. McIver, "Public Opinion and Policy Liberalism in the American States," *American Journal of Political Science,* 31 (November 1987), 980–1001.

FIGURE 1–5   Liberalism and Conservatism

election in large cities throughout the nation. On the whole, blacks are still under-represented in city councils (see Chapter 11) and in state legislatures (see Chapter 6), but black mayors in the nation's major cities testify to the growing political clout of urban black voters (see Chapter 14).

Hispanics   The term *Hispanics* refers to persons of Spanish-speaking ancestry and culture, regardless of race and includes Mexican-Americans, Cuban-Americans, and Puerto Ricans. In 1990 there were an estimated 22 million Hispanics or 9 percent of the U.S population. The largest subgroup are Mexican-Americans, some of whom are descendants of citizens living in Mexican territory that was annexed to the United States in 1848 (see Figure 1–1), but most of them have come to the United States in accelerating numbers in recent years. The largest Mexican-American populations are found in Texas, Arizona, New Mexico, and California (see Table 1–2). The second largest subgroup are the Puerto Ricans, many of whom retain ties to the Commonwealth and move back and forth from the island to the mainland, especially New York City. The third largest subgroup are Cubans, most of whom have fled from Castro's Cuba. They live mainly in the Miami metropolitan area. While these groups have different experiences, they share a common language and culture, and they have encountered similar difficulties in making government responsive to their needs (see Chapter 14).

Native Americans   It is estimated that 10 million Native Americans once inhabited the North American continent. By 1900 the Native American population had been reduced to barely a half million by wars, diseases, and forced privations inflicted upon them. Today Native Americans number about 2 million or slightly less than 1 percent of the U.S. population. Approximately half live on semiautonomous reservations in 280 federally recognized tribes, and in hundreds of native villages in Alaska. The largest concentrations of Native Americans are found in New Mexico, Oklahoma, South Dakota, Montana, and Arizona, as well as Alaska.

THE "NATIONALIZATION" OF THE STATES

We know that states differ in their histories, economies, growth rates, and ethnic and racial compositions. Yet over time these differences are diminishing—a process that has been labeled the "nationalization" of states.

Over time the states have become more similar in levels of economic development. Income differences among the states have diminished. As industry, people, and money moved from the Northeast and Midwest to the South, the historic disadvantage of the South gradually diminished (see Figure 1–6).

Americans are the most mobile people in the world. Four out of every ten people move within a five-year period! Nearly one in ten moves to a different state. As people move about the country, distinct cultural and ethnic differences of the regions diminish. Even regional accents become less pronounced. The impact of national television, motion pictures, and record industries adds to the "homogenization" of state and regional cultures.

The political systems of the states are no longer as distinct as they were historically. Years ago the Democratic party could count on "the Solid South" in national elections. The Democrats can still count on winning most state and local offices in southern and border states, but these states are now swing states in presidential elections and occasionally elect Republican governors and U.S. senators. Historically, voter participation in the southern states was very low and it is still lower there than in the rest of the nation. However, one important effect of the civil rights movement was to increase black voter participation in the South. Today, voter turnout in the South is both higher than in previous decades and closer to the national average.

Nonetheless, even though the states are gradually becoming more similar over time, in many respects there is still "enough" variation to merit comparative analysis. Interestingly, many important policy differences between the states are *not* diminishing.[10] Throughout this book we will make comparisons among the states, and also among cities, in order to better understand politics, economics, and public policy throughout the nation.

---

[10] See Kathleen A. Kemp, "Nationalization of the American States," *American Politics Quarterly,* 6 (April 1978), 237–47; Harvey J. Tucker, "Interparty Competition in the American States," *American Politics Quarterly,* 10 (January 1982), 93–116; Philip W. Roeder, *Stability and Change in the Determinants of Public Expenditures* (Beverly Hills, CA: Sage Publications, Inc., 1976).

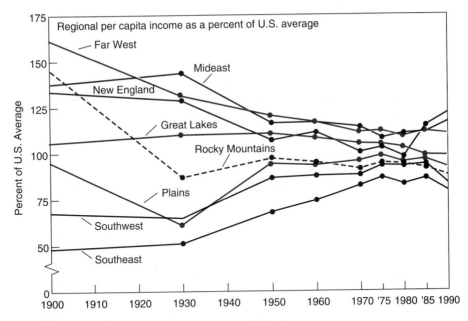

FIGURE 1-6   The Nationalization of the States

Reprinted with the permission of The American Enterprise Institute for Public Policy Research, Washington, D.C. Note: Bureau of Economic Analysis regional groupings: *New England* = Maine, New Hampshire, Vermont, Massachusetts, Connecticut, Rhode Island. *Mideast* = New York, Pennsylvania, New Jersey, Delaware, Maryland, District of Columbia. *Southeast* = Virginia, West Virginia, North Carolina, South Carolina, Georgia, Florida, Kentucky, Tennessee, Alabama, Mississippi, Arkansas, Louisiana. *Southwest* = Oklahoma, Texas, Arizona, New Mexico. *Rocky Mountain* = Colorado, Wyoming, Montana, Idaho, Utah. *Far West* = Nevada, California, Oregon, Washington. *Plains* = Minnesota, Iowa, Missouri, North Dakota, South Dakota, Nebraska, Kansas. *Great Lakes* = Ohio, Michigan, Indiana, Wisconsin, Illinois. Not classified, Alaska, Hawaii.

POLICY RESPONSIBILITIES OF STATES AND COMMUNITIES

States and communities in America operate the world's largest public school system and highway network. They operate most of the nation's judicial, welfare, police, health, correctional, and recreational facilities. Most regulation of industry, banking, commerce, utilities, labor, and protection of public safety is in the hands of state and local governments. Their programs in conservation, sanitation, social work, housing, and urban planning are vital to the day-to-day lives of all Americans. Even when the national government is involved in these programs, states and communities must often decide whether or not to participate in national programs, and if they participate, they must administer the programs within their jurisdictions.

Despite the glamour of national politics, states and communities carry on the greatest volume of public business, settle the greatest number of political conflicts, make the majority of policy decisions, and direct the bulk of public programs. They have the major responsibility for maintaining domestic law and order, for educating the children, for moving Americans from place to place, and for caring for the poor and the ill. They regulate the provision of water, gas, electric, and other public utilities, share in the regulation of insurance and banking enterprise, regulate the use of land, and supervise the sale of ownership of property. Their courts settle by far the greatest number of civil and criminal cases. In short, states and communities are by no means unimportant political systems.

Education   Education is the most important responsibility of state and local governments and the most costly of all state–local functions (see Figure 1–7). States and communities are responsible for decisions about what should be taught in the public schools, how much should be spent on the education of each child, how many children should be in each classroom, how much teachers should be paid, how responsibilities in education should be divided between state and local governments, what qualifications teachers must have, what types of rates and taxes shall be levied for education, and many other decisions that affect the life of every child in America. Support for higher education, including funds for state and community colleges and universities, is now a major expenditure of state governments. The federal government has never contributed more than 10 percent of the nation's total expenditures for education.

Transportation   Transportation—more particularly, highways—is the second most costly function of state and local governments. There are over 3 million miles of surfaced roads in America, and over 180 million registered motor vehicles in the nation. States and communities must make decisions about the allocation of money for streets and highways, sources of funds for highway revenue, the extent of gasoline and motor vehicle taxation, the regulation of traffic on the highways, the location of highways, the determination of construction policies, the division of responsibility between state and local governments for highway financing administration, the division of highway funds between rural and urban areas, and other important issues in highway politics. While the federal government is deeply involved in highway construction, federal grants for highways amount to less than 30 percent of all expenditures for highways.

Health and Welfare   States and communities continue to carry a heavy burden in the field of health and welfare—despite an extensive system of federal grants-in-aid for this purpose. States and communities must make decisions about participation in federal programs and allocate responsibilities among themselves for health and welfare programs. While the federal government itself administers Social Security and Medicare, state governments administer the largest public assistance programs—Aid to Families with Dependent Children (AFDC), Medicaid, and food stamps, as well as unemployment compensation. Within the broad outlines of federal policy, states and communities decide the amount of money appropriated for health and welfare purposes, the benefits to be paid to recipients, the rules of eligibility, and the means by which the programs will be administered. States and communities may choose to grant assistance beyond the limits supported by the national government, or they may choose to have no welfare programs at all.

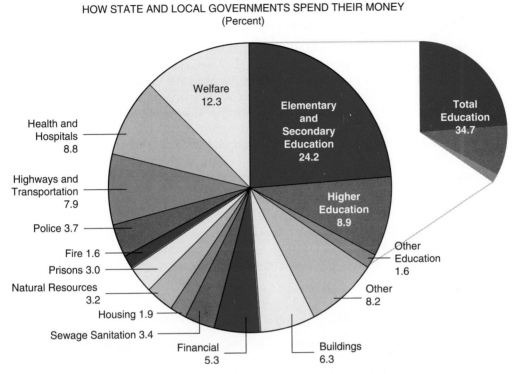

HOW STATE AND LOCAL GOVERNMENTS SPEND THEIR MONEY
(Percent)

Welfare 12.3

Health and Hospitals 8.8

Highways and Transportation 7.9

Police 3.7

Fire 1.6

Prisons 3.0

Natural Resources 3.2

Housing 1.9

Sewage Sanitation 3.4

Financial 5.3

Buildings 6.3

Elementary and Secondary Education 24.2

Higher Education 8.9

Other Education 1.6

Other 8.2

Total Education 34.7

FIGURE 1–7   How State and Local Governments Spend Their Money

Crime   States and communities have the principal responsibility for public safety in America. The federal government, through the Federal Bureau of Investigation, has limited jurisdiction over certain crimes, such as kidnapping, bank robbery, and espionage. State police have important highway safety responsibilities and cooperate with local authorities in the apprehension of criminals. However, community police forces continue to be the principal instrument of law enforcement and public safety. Local governments employ over a quarter of a million police in the United States today, and almost as many firefighters. Sheriffs and their deputies are still the principal enforcement and arresting officers in rural counties. States and communities also have the principal responsibility for maintaining prisons and correctional institutions. Each year over 2 million Americans are prisoners in jails, police stations, juvenile homes, or penitentiaries. More than 90 percent of these prisoners are at state and local rather than federal institutions.

Civil Rights   The national government has defined a national system of civil rights, but these rights cannot become realities without the support of state and local authorities. States and communities must deal directly with racial problems, such as racial isolation in the public schools, job discrimination, and the existence of segregated housing patterns or ghettos in the cities. They must also deal directly with the consequences of racial tension, including violence.

Physical Environment   Local governments have the principal responsibility for our physical environment. They must plan streets, parks, and commercial, residential, and industrial areas and provide essential public utilities for the community. The waste materials of human beings—rubbish, garbage, and sewage—exceed one ton every day per person. The task of disposal is an immense one; the problem is not only collecting it, but finding ways to dispose of it. If it is incinerated, it contributes to air pollution; and if it is carried off into streams, rivers, or lakes, it contributes to water pollution. Thus, communities are largely responsible for two of the nation's most pressing problems—air and water pollution.

Taxation   To pay for these programs, states and communities must make important decisions about taxation: They must decide about levels of taxation and what tax burdens their citizens can carry. They must determine how much to rely upon income, sales, or property taxation. States and communities must raise over $600 billion per year and at the same time compete with one another to attract industry and commerce.

"STATES," "DISTRICTS," AND "TERRITORIES"

How did the states become states? The original thirteen states did so by ratifying the U.S. Constitution. The first new states to be admitted were Vermont in 1791 and Kentucky in 1792. States that sought admission began by petitioning Congress to allow them to elect delegates and draw up a state constitution. The Congress granted this permission in a series of enabling acts. Later, when the territorial voters approved the new constitution, the territory formally applied for admission and presented its constitution to Congress for approval. Congress accepted the application by a joint resolution of both houses, and a new star was added to the flag. The last admissions were Alaska and Hawaii in 1959.

Of course, from a political perspective, admission was not always an easy process. Long before the Civil War (or "The War Between the States" as it is still called in parts of the Old South), states were admitted roughly in pairs of free and slave states, so as not to upset the delicate balance in the U.S. Senate. Iowa and Wisconsin were admitted as free states in 1846 and 1848, while Florida and Texas were admitted in 1845 as slave states. When California was admitted as a free state in the famous Compromise of 1850, the balance was tilted toward the free states. The balance was further tipped when Minnesota was admitted in 1858 and Oregon in 1859. The Civil War followed in 1861.

Eleven states seceded from the Union that year—Alabama, Arkansas, Florida, Georgia, Louisiana, Mississippi, North Carolina, South Carolina (December 1860), Tennessee, Texas, and Virginia. Although the Supreme Court later voided the acts of secession as unconstitutional, Congress required all of these states to reapply for admission to the Union. These states were under military occupation by United

States troops. The military governments drew up new state constitutions, registered black voters, and sent black representatives to Congress. Congress required these governments to ratify the Thirteenth, Fourteenth, and Fifteenth Amendments in order to be readmitted to the Union. The "reconstructed" southern state governments did so, and all were readmitted by 1870.

When Texas was admitted in 1845, Congress granted it a special privilege: The state might, if it wished, divide itself into four states. This provision recognized that Texas was a separate nation when it chose to become a state. A conservative Congress initially rejected Arizona's constitution because it included the progressive notion of popular recall of judges; the state obligingly changed its constitution, was admitted in 1912, and then promptly amended the constitution to put recall back in. Once admitted, there was nothing the Congress could do about Arizona's recalcitrance.

The District of Columbia   The U.S. Constitution, Article I, Section 8, specified in 1787 that "the seat of the government of the United States" shall be in a "district not exceeding ten square miles" ceded to the federal government by the states (Maryland and Virginia). The District of Columbia was to be governed by the Congress. In defense of a separate district, Alexander Hamilton wrote:

> [Congressional control] of the seat of government . . . is an indispensable necessity. Without it not only the public authority may be insulted and its proceedings interrupted with impunity, but a dependence of the members of the general government of the state comprehending the seat of government . . . might bring the national councils an imputation of awe or influence . . . dishonorable to the government.[11]

Hamilton's language is stiff and formal, but his meaning is clear: Making Washington a state would generate undue local pressure on Congress.

Politically, Washington is heavily Democratic, liberal, and black. Its 607,000 residents are likely to support larger social welfare programs, an expanded bureaucracy, and increased federal spending. Opponents of these policies are not likely to be enthusiastic about DC representation in Congress.

The Twenty-third Amendment, ratified in 1961, gives Washington full participation in presidential elections. Congress has also granted by law full home rule to the city so it has its own elected mayor and city council. In 1978, Congress passed another constitutional amendment that would grant the District full congressional representation and the right to vote on ratification of future constitutional amendments. In short, the District of Columbia would have all the powers of a state. However, the necessary three-quarters of the states failed to ratify this amendment. So while DC residents can vote in presidential elections, they are not represented by voting members in the U.S. Senate or House of Representatives.

---

[11]Alexander Hamilton, *The Federalist,* Number 43.

The Commonwealth of Puerto Rico   Over 3 million people live on the Caribbean island of Puerto Rico. They are American citizens, and the government of Puerto Rico resembles a state government, with a constitution and an elected governor and legislature. However, Puerto Rico has no voting members of the Congress and no electoral votes in presidential elections.

The population of Puerto Rico is greater than that of twenty states; over 1 million Puerto Ricans have migrated over the years to the U.S. mainland, particularly to New York City. Median family income in Puerto Rico is the highest in the Caribbean, but it is only half that of the poorest state in the United States. The population is largely Spanish-speaking; as citizens they can move anywhere in the United States; and they have been subject to the draft in wartime. The United States seized Puerto Rico in 1898 in the Spanish-American War. In 1950, its voters chose to become a "commonwealth," and self-governing commonwealth status was officially recognized in 1952. In a 1967 plebiscite, 60 percent of Puerto Ricans voted to remain a commonwealth, 39 percent voted for statehood, and less than 1 percent voted for independence. Recent efforts to schedule another plebiscite have floundered over the specifics of each option—commonwealth, statehood, or independence.

Under "commonwealth" status Puerto Ricans pay no U.S. income tax, although local taxes are substantial. Yet, they receive all of the benefits that U.S. citizens are entitled to—Social Security, public assistance, food stamps, Medicaid, Medicare, and so forth. If Puerto Rico chose to become a state, its voters could participate in presidential and congressional elections; but its taxpayers would not enjoy the same favorable cost-benefit ratio they enjoy under commonwealth status. Some Puerto Ricans fear that statehood would dilute the island's cultural identity and force English upon them as the national language.

Statehood would grant two U.S. senators and perhaps six U.S. representatives to the island. Most of these new members would be Democrats; the island's majority party, the Popular Democratic party, is closely identified with the Democratic party. But the island's New Progressive party, identified with the Republican party, supports statehood, and many GOP leaders believe their party should appeal to Hispanic voters. If Puerto Ricans were to choose independence, a new constitution for the Republic of Puerto Rico would be drawn up by the islanders themselves.

U.S. Territories   The U.S. Virgin Islands were purchased from Denmark in 1917. Residents of the beautiful islands in the Caribbean are predominantly black, English-speaking, and poorer than most Americans on the mainland. The United States acquired Samoa and Guam from Spain in 1898; and after World War II, the United States held Wake, Midway, and the United Nations Trusteeships of the Caroline, Marianas, and Marshall Islands (the locations of some of the heaviest fighting in the Pacific). In 1903 the United States encouraged a revolution and secession of Panama from Columbia, so that the new Panamanian nation would conclude an agreement to build a canal and govern a zone five miles wide on both sides of the canal. U.S. "Canal Zone" governance was ended by a new treaty with Panama in 1978.

WHAT'S IN A NAME: THE AMERICAN STATES

Alabama—Indian for tribal town, later a tribe (Alabamas or Alibamons) of the Creek confederacy.

Alaska—Russian version of Aleutian (Eskimo) word, *alakshak*, for "peninsula," "great lands," or "land that is not an island."

Arizona—Spanish version of Pimo Indian word for "little spring place," or Aztec *arizuma*, meaning "silver-bearing."

Arkansas—French variant of Kansas, a Sioux Indian name for "south wind people."

California—bestowed by the Spanish conquistadors (possibly by Cortez). It was the name of an imaginary island, and earthly paradise, in "Las Serges de Esplandian," a Spanish romance written by Montalvo in 1510. Baja California (Lower California, in Mexico) was first visited by the Spanish in 1533. The present U.S. state was called Alta (Upper) California.

Colorado—Spanish, red, first applied to Colorado River.

Connecticut—From Mohican and other Algonquin words meaning "long river place."

Delaware—Named for Lord De La Warr, early governor of Virginia; first applied to river, then to Indian tribe (Lenni-Lenape), and the state.

District of Columbia—For Columbus, 1791.

Florida—Named by Ponce de Leon on Pascua Florida, "Flowery Easter," on Easter Sunday, 1513.

Georgia—For King George II of England by James Oglethorpe, colonial administrator, 1732.

Hawaii—Possibly derived from native word for homeland, Hawaiki or Owhyhee.

Idaho—A coined name with an invented Indian meaning: "gem of the mountains," originally suggested for the Pike's Peak mining territory (Colorado), then applied to the new mining territory of the Pacific Northwest. Another theory suggests Idaho may be a Kiowa Apache term for the Comanche.

Illinois—French for Illini or land of Illini, Algonquin word meaning men or warriors.

Indiana—Means "land of the Indians."

Iowa—Indian word variously translated as "one who puts to sleep" or "beautiful land."

Kansas—Sioux word for "south wind people."

Kentucky—Indian word variously translated as "dark and bloody ground," "meadow land," and "land of tomorrow."

Louisiana—Part of territory called Louisiana by Sieur de La Salle for French King Louis XIV.

Maine—From Maine, ancient French province. Also: descriptive, referring to the mainland in distinction to the many coastal islands.

Maryland—For Queen Henrietta Maria, wife of Charles I of England.

Massachusetts—From Indian tribe named after "large hill place" identified by Capt. John Smith as near Milton, MA.

Michigan—from Chippewa words *mici gama,* meaning "great water," after the lake of the same name.

Minnesota—From Dakota Sioux word meaning "cloudy water" or "sky-tinted water" of the Minnesota River.

Mississippi—Probably Chippewa; *mici zibi,* "great river" or "gathering-in of all the waters." Also: Algonquin word, "Messipi."

Missouri—Algonquin Indian tribe named after Missouri River, meaning "muddy water."

Montana—Latin or Spanish for "mountainous."

Nebraska—from Omaha or Otos Indian word meaning "broad water" or "flat river," describing the Platte River.

Nevada—Spanish, meaning snow-clad.

New Hampshire—Named 1629 by Capt. John Mason of Plymouth Council for his home county in England.

New Jersey—The Duke of York, 1664, gave a patent to John Berkeley and Sir George Carteret to be called Nova Caesaria, or New Jersey, after England's Isle of Jersey.

New Mexico—Spaniards in Mexico applied term to land north and west of Rio Grande in the sixteenth century.

New York—For Duke of York and Albany who received patent to New Netherland from his brother Charles II and sent an expedition to capture it, 1664.

North Carolina—In 1619 Charles I gave a large patent to Sir Robert Heath to be called Province of Carolana, from Carolus, Latin name for Charles. A new patent was granted by Charles II to Earl of Clarendon and others. Divided into North and South Carolina, 1710.

North Dakota—Dakota is Sioux for friend or ally.

Ohio—Iroquois word for "fine or good river."

Oklahoma—Choctaw coined word meaning red man, proposed by Rev. Allen Wright, Choctaw-speaking Indian.

Oregon—Origin unknown. One theory holds that the name may have been derived from that of the Wisconsin River shown on a 1715 French map as "Ouaricon-sint."

Pennsylvania—William Penn, the Quaker, who was made full proprietor by King Charles II in 1681, suggested Sylvania, or woodland, for his tract. The king's government owed Penn's father, Admiral William Penn, £16,000, and the land being granted in part settlement, the king added the Penn to Sylvania, against the desires of the modest proprietor, in honor of the admiral.

Puerto Rico—Spanish for Rich Port.

Rhode Island—Exact origin is unknown. One theory notes that Giovanni de Verazano recorded an island about the size of Rhodes in the Mediterranean in 1524, but others believe the state was named Roode Eylandt by Adriaen Block, Dutch explorer, because of its red clay.

South Carolina—See North Carolina.

South Dakota—See North Dakota.

Tennessee—Tanasi was the name of Cherokee villages on the Little Tennessee River. From 1784 to 1788 this was the State of Franklin, or Frankland.

Texas—Variant of word used by Caddo and other Indians meaning friends or allies, and applied to them by the Spanish in eastern Texas. Also written texias, tejas, teysas.

Utah—From a Navajo word meaning upper, or higher up, as applied to a Shoshone tribe called Ute. Spanish form is Yutta, English Uta or Utah. Proposed name Deseret, "land of honeybees," from Book of Mormon, was rejected by Congress.

Vermont—From French words *vert*/green, and *mont*/mountain. The Green Mountains were said to have been named by Samuel de Champlain. The Green Mountain Boys were Gen. Stark's men in the Revolution. When the state was formed, 1777, Dr. Thomas Young suggested combining *vert* and *mont* into Vermont.

Virginia—Named by Sir Walter Raleigh, who fitted out the expedition of 1584, in honor of Queen Elizabeth, the Virgin Queen of England.

Washington—Named after George Washington. When the bill creating the Territory of Columbia was introduced in the 32d Congress, the name was changed to Washington because of the existence of the District of Columbia.

West Virginia—So named when western counties of Virginia refused to secede from the United States, 1863.

Wisconsin—An Indian name, spelled Quisconsin and Mesconsing by early chroniclers. Believed to mean "grassy place" in Chippewa. Congress made it Wisconsin.

Wyoming—The word was taken from Wyoming Valley, PA, which was the site of an Indian massacre and became widely known by Campbell's poem "Gertrude of Wyoming." In Algonquin it means "large prairie place."

Source: By permission of The Smithsonian Institution Press, Smithsonian Institution, Washington, DC.

2

Democracy
and Constitutionalism
in the States

▲

Constitutional Government in the States

Constitutions govern governments. They set forth the structure and organization of government; they distribute powers among branches of government; they prescribe the rules by which decisions will be made. Most important, constitutions limit the powers of government and protect the rights of citizens. All fifty states have written constitutions.

Limited Government   The true meaning of constitutionalism is limited government. Today most of the world's governments, including even the most authoritarian regimes, have written constitutions that describe the formal structure of government. But the constitutions of authoritarian regions rarely place any restrictions on the powers of government. In the English and American political heritage, constitutionalism means that the power of government over the individual is clearly limited, that there are some aspects of life that even democratic majorities cannot regulate, and that government itself is restrained by a higher law. Constitutional government places individual liberty beyond the reach of governments, even democratic governments. Thus if a majority of voters wanted to prohibit communists, or atheists, or racists, from writing or speaking or organizing themselves, they could not do so under a constitutional government that protected free speech and press and assembly.

All fifty state constitutions limit the powers of state government and protect individual liberty. While we have come to rely principally on the U.S. Constitution for the protection of individual liberty, every state constitution also contains a bill of rights that protects individuals in each state from deprivations of personal liberty by their state government. Most of these state constitutional guarantees merely reiterate rights guaranteed to all Americans in the U.S. Constitution, but some state documents extend rights beyond the federal guarantees.

Legal Status   State *constitutions* are the supreme law of the state. They take precedence over any state *law* in conflict with them. Since constitutions govern the activities of governments themselves, they are considered more fundamental than the ordinary laws passed by governments.

The U.S. Constitution is the supreme law of the nation. State constitutions take precedence over state law, but they are subordinate to the U.S. Constitution and the laws of the United States. The U.S. Constitution mentions state constitutions only once, and it does so to assert the supremacy of the U.S. Constitution and the laws and treaties of the United States. Article VI states:

> This constitution, and the laws of the United States which shall be made in pursuance thereof; and all treaties made, or which shall be made, under the authority of the United States, shall be the supreme law of the land; and the judges in every state shall be bound thereby, anything in the constitution or laws of any state to the contrary notwithstanding.

Origins of Written Constitutions   Probably no other people in the world are more devoted to the idea of written constitutions than are Americans. This devotion has deep roots in national traditions. In 1215 a group of English lords forced King John to sign a document, later known as the Magna Carta, that guaranteed them certain feudal rights and set a precedent for constitutional government. Although the British political tradition eventually rejected formal written constitutions, the idea of a written constitution was strongly reinforced by the experience in the American colonies. The colonies were legally established by charters given to companies establishing settlements in America. These charters became more elaborate as the colonial ventures succeeded, and depending upon a written code for the regulation of government organization and operation became strongly entrenched in the American colonies.

Colonial History   The charters, or "constitutions," were granted by royal action, either by recognizing proprietary rights, as in Maryland, Delaware, and Pennsylvania, or by granting royal commissions to companies to establish governments, as in Virginia, Massachusetts, New Hampshire, New York, New Jersey, Georgia, and North and South Carolina. Only in Connecticut and Rhode Island was there much popular participation in early constitution making. In these two colonies, royal charters were granted directly to the colonists themselves, who participated in drawing up the charter for submission to the Crown. The important point is that these charters, whatever their origin, were present in all the colonies, and many political traditions and expectations grew up around them.

All the colonies were subject to royal control. Yet colonists looked to their charters for protection against British interference in colonial affairs. This was particularly true in Connecticut and Rhode Island, which had elected governors and legislatures whose acts were not subjected to a royal governor's veto, nor sent to England for approval. The political importance of these early charters is illustrated by the conflict over the Fundamental Orders of Connecticut. In 1685 King James issued an order for the repeal of Connecticut's charter. In 1687 Sir Edmund Androse went to Hartford and in the name of the Crown declared the government dissolved. The charter was not surrendered, however, but hidden by Captain John Wadsworth in an oak tree, which is now displayed for sightseers. Immediately after the English revolution of 1688, the document was taken out of the "Charter Oak" and used again as the fundamental law of the colony. Succeeding British monarchs silently permitted this colonial defiance. After the Declaration of Independence, new constitutions were written in eleven states; Connecticut retained its charter as the fundamental law until 1818, and Rhode Island kept its charter until 1842. The colonial experience, together with the earlier English heritage, firmly implanted the tradition of written constitutions.

State Constitutional Politics   Theoretically, constitutional decision making is deciding *how to decide*. It is deciding on the rules for policy making; it is not policy making itself. Policies are to be decided later, according to the rules set forth in a constitution.

Constitutional Policy Making   But realistically, all state constitutions not only specify organizations and processes of decision making, they also undertake to determine many substantive policy questions. Unlike the U.S. Constitution, state constitutions contain many policy mandates on topics as diverse as tax rates, utility regulation, labor–management relations, insurance regulation, debt limits, educational funding, gambling, and a host of other policy matters. In nearly every election, voters are asked to decide on proposed amendments to their state constitutions. Most of these amendments deal with policy questions about which the voters have little knowledge or information. The result, of course, is that most state constitutions have become ponderous tomes that look more like law books than constitutions. While the U.S. Constitution contains only about 8,700 words, the average state constitution contains 26,000, and some run to over 100,000 (see Table 2–1). Length itself is not the problem, but rather that these constitutions are laden with detailed policy decisions.

Interest Group Influence   Why have so many policy mandates crept into state constitutions? Inasmuch as constitutions govern the actions of governors, legislators, executive agencies, and courts, many special interest groups as well as citizen movements have sought to place their own policy preferences in constitutions. This places these preferences beyond the immediate reach of government officials, who are bound by constitutional mandates. If a policy preference is enacted into state law, it can be changed by ordinary actions of the legislature and governor. But if a policy preference is written into the state constitution, it can be changed only by extraordinary procedures—for most states a two-thirds vote in both houses of the legislature and majority approval of the voters in a statewide referendum. So interest groups frequently strive to "constitutionalize" their policy preferences.[1]

Citizens' Movements   Moreover, grass-roots citizen movements in the United States have frequently displayed a distrust of elected officials. Citizens have frequently sought to bind officials by constitutional mandates. Indeed, referenda on proposed state constitutional amendments confront voters in many states in almost every election. Over the years, specific constitutional amendments seeking to tell legislatures and governors what they can and cannot do have been accumulated in lengthy documents. The more detailed and specific a state's constitution, the more likely it is to require more amendments to meet changing circumstances over time, thus leading to an even longer document.

Reformers' Influence   Constitutional reformers and "good government" groups have sought for many years to take policy matters out of the state constitution. They argue that governors and legislators should not be bound by constitutional details, that they need flexibility in confronting new challenges, that state government should be strengthened, not weakened, in the modern era. These reform efforts have met with some success; newer state constitutions tend to be shorter than older ones.

Growth of State Constitutional Law   Along with interest groups and citizens' movements, lawyers and judges have also contributed to the growth of state constitutional law. In a significant number of cases, state court judges have interpreted their own constitutions independently of the U.S. Constitution regarding civil rights and other controversies (see "The New Judicial Federalism" in Chapter 8). An emerging body of state constitutional law is a reminder of the legal importance of state constitutions.[2]

---

[1] Lewis A. Froman, "Some Effects of Interest Group Strength in State Politics," *American Political Science Review,* 60 (December 1966), 956–94.

[2] Advisory Commission on Intergovernmental Relations, *State Constitutional Law: Cases and Materials* (Washington, DC: ACIR, 1988).

TABLE 2–1   GENERAL INFORMATION ON STATE CONSTITUTIONS

State or Other Jurisdiction	Number of Constitutions	Dates of Adoption	Effective Date of Present Constitution	Estimated Length (Number of Words)	Number of Amendments Proposed	Number of Amendments Adopted
Alabama	6	1819; 1861; 1865; 1868; 1875; 1901	1901	174,000	759	538
Alaska	1	1956	1959	13,000	32	23
Arizona	1	1911	1912	28,876a	204	111
Arkansas	5	1836; 1861; 1864; 1868; 1874	1874	40,720a	167	77b
California	2	1849; 1879	1879	33,350	800	480
Colorado	1	1876	1876	45,679	243	118
Connecticut	4	1818c; 1965	1965	9,564	27	26
Delaware	4	1776; 1792; 1831; 1897	1897	19,000	(d)	121
Florida	6	1839; 1861; 1865; 1868; 1886; 1968	1969	25,100	83	57
Georgia	10	1777; 1789; 1798; 1861; 1865; 1868; 1877; 1945; 1976; 1982	1983	25,000	44e	32
Hawaii	1f	1950	1959	17,453a	98	82
Idaho	1	1889	1890	21,500	188	108
Illinois	4	1818; 1848; 1870; 1970	1971	13,200	12	7
Indiana	2	1816; 1851	1851	9,377a	70	38
Iowa	2	1846; 1857	1857	12,500	51	48g
Kansas	1	1859	1861	11,865	116	88g
Kentucky	4	1792; 1799; 1850; 1891	1891	23,500	62	30
Louisiana	11	1812; 1845; 1852; 1861; 1864; 1868; 1879; 1898; 1913; 1921; 1974	1975	36,146a	74	46

State		Constitutions				
Maine	1	1819	1820	13,500	188	158[h]
Maryland	4	1776; 1851; 1864; 1867	1867	41,134	235	202
Massachusetts	1	1780	1780	36,690[a,i]	144	117
Michigan	4	1835; 1850; 1908; 1963	1964	20,000	47	16
Minnesota	1	1857	1858	9,500	207	113
Mississippi	4	1817; 1832; 1869; 1890	1890	23,500	140	108
Missouri	4	1820; 1865; 1875; 1945	1945	42,000	119	76
Montana	2	1889; 1972	1973	11,866[a]	27	16
Nebraska	2	1866; 1875	1875	20,048[a]	289	193
Nevada	1	1864	1864	20,770	178	111[g]
New Hampshire	2	1776; 1784	1784	9,200	277[j]	143[j]
New Jersey	3	1776; 1844; 1947	1948	17,086	53	40
New Mexico	1	1911	1912	27,200	236	121
New York	4	1777; 1822; 1846; 1894	1895	80,000	277	210
North Carolina	3	1776; 1868; 1970	1971	11,000	34	27
North Dakota	1	1889	1889	31,000	231[k]	127[k]
Ohio	2	1802; 1851	1851	36,900	248	147
Oklahoma	1	1907	1907	68,800	287[l]	141[l]
Oregon	1	1857	1859	25,965	375	192
Pennsylvania	5	1776; 1790; 1838; 1968[m]	1968[m]	21,675	25[m]	19[m]
Rhode Island	2	1842[c]	1843	19,026[a,i]	99	53
South Carolina	7	1776; 1778; 1790; 1861; 1865; 1868; 1895	1896	22,500[n]	648[o]	463[o]
South Dakota	1	1889	1889	23,300	190	98
Tennessee	3	1796; 1835; 1870	1870	15,300	55	32
Texas	5	1845; 1861; 1866; 1869; 1876	1876	62,000	499	339
Utah	1	1895	1896	17,500	128	79
Vermont	3	1777; 1786; 1793	1793	6,600	208	50
Virginia	6	1776; 1830; 1851; 1869; 1902; 1970	1971	18,500	27	22

TABLE 2-1 (*Continued*)

State or Other Jurisdiction	Number of Constitutions	Dates of Adoption	Effective Date of Present Constitution	Estimated Length (Number of Words)	Number of Amendments	
					PROPOSED	ADOPTED
Washington	1	1889	1889	29,400	156	86
West Virginia	2	1863; 1872	1872	25,600	107	62
Wisconsin	1	1848	1848	13,500	169	125g
Wyoming	1	1889	1890	31,800	101	61
American Samoa	2	1960; 1967	1967	6,000	14	7
Puerto Rico	1	1952	1952	9,281a	6	6

* The constitutions referred to in this table include those Civil War documents customarily listed by the individual states.

a Actual word count.

b Eight of the approved amendments have been superseded and are not printed in the current edition of the constitution. The total adopted does not include five amendments that were invalidated.

c Colonial charters with some alterations served as the first constitutions in Connecticut (1638, 1662) and in Rhode Island (1663).

d Proposed amendments are not submitted to the voters in Delaware.

e The new Georgia constitution eliminates the need for local amendments, which have been a long-term problem for state constitution makers.

f As a kingdom and republic, Hawaii had five constitutions.

g The figure given includes amendments approved by the voters and later nullified by the state supreme court in Iowa (three), Kansas (one), Nevada (six), and Wisconsin (two).

h The figure does not include one amendment approved by the voters in 1967 that is inoperative until implemented by legislation.

i The printed constitution includes many provisions that have been annulled. The length of effective provisions is an estimated 24,122 words (12,490 annulled) in Massachusetts and 11,399 words (7,627 annulled) in Rhode Island.

j The constitution of 1784 was extensively revised in 1792. Figures show proposals and adoptions since the constitution was adopted in 1784.

k The figures do not include submission and approval of the constitution of 1889 itself and of Article XX; these are constitutional questions included in some counts of constitutional amendments and would add two to the figure in each column.

l The figures include five amendments submitted to, and approved by the voters which were, by decisions of the Oklahoma or U.S. Supreme Court, rendered inoperative or ruled invalid, unconstitutional or illegally submitted.

m Certain sections of the constitution were revised by the limited constitutional convention of 1967–68. Amendments proposed and adopted are since 1968.

n Of the estimated length, approximately two-thirds is of general statewide effect; the remainder is local amendments.

o Of the 626 proposed amendments submitted to the voters, 130 were of general statewide effect and 496 were local; the voters rejected 83 (12 statewide, 71 local). Of the remaining 543, the General Assembly refused to approve 100 (22 statewide, 78 local), and 443 (96 statewide, 347 local) were finally added to the constitution.

Source: Book of the States, 1992–1993 (Lexington, KY: Council on State Governments, 1992). Data as of January 1, 1992.

State Constitutions: an Overview

Bill of Rights   All state constitutions have a bill of rights, which asserts the basic freedoms of speech, press, religion, and assembly. There are frequent references to basic procedural rights, such as the writ of habeas corpus, trial by jury, protection against double jeopardy and self-incrimination, prohibitions against ex post facto laws, imprisonment for debt, unreasonable searches and seizures, and excessive bail. Most of these protections merely duplicate the guarantees of the U.S. Constitution. However, frequently one finds in the state constitutions interesting "rights," which are not found in the national Constitution. For example, the Rhode Island Constitution prohibits discrimination on the grounds of gender, race, or handicap; Mississippi guarantees the right of victims of crime to speak in court and receive restitution; Indiana prohibits "unnecessary rigor" in punishment for crime. Seventeen state constitutions have "little ERAs"—equal rights amendments, guaranteeing sexual equality under law. Moreover, a *state* supreme court may place a different interpretation on a state constitutional right than the *federal* courts place on the same guarantee in the U.S. Constitution.

Separation of Powers   All state constitutions reflect the American political tradition of separation of powers, with separate legislative, executive, and judicial articles establishing these separate branches of government. Generally, however, state constitutions emphasize legislative power over executive power. The historical explanation for this is that governors were appointed by the king in most colonies and the early constitutions reflected the colonists' distaste for executive authority. Yet the fact that constitutions are usually written by legislatures, legislative commissions, or constitutional conventions that resemble legislatures may also explain why legislative power is emphasized. Finally, the curtailment of executive power may reflect the desires of important interest groups in the states, who would prefer to deal with independent boards and commissions in the executive branch rather than a strong governor. (See Chapter 7 for further discussion.)

Weak Governors   Whether the reasons are historical or political, the executive branches of most state governments are weakened and divided by state constitutions. Executive powers are divided between the governor and many separately elected executive officers—attorney general, secretary of state, treasurer, auditor, lieutenant governor, state school superintendent, and others. State constitutions also curtail executive authority by establishing a multitude of boards or commissions to head executive departments. Membership on these boards and commissions is generally for long overlapping terms, which are not coextensive with the term of the governor.

Legislative Powers   Only the Nebraska Constitution provides for a unicameral legislature. All other state legislatures are divided into an upper and a lower chamber—making a total of ninety-nine state legislative bodies. In many states the basis for apportioning these bodies is set forth in the state constitution. However, since the guarantee of the U.S. Constitution that no state shall deny to any person the "equal protection of the laws" takes precedence over state constitutions, federal courts require state legislative apportionment to meet the constitutional standard of one person, one vote. (See Chapter 6.)

Local Governments   All state constitutions have provisions regarding the organization and powers of local government. Local governments are really subdivisions of state governments; they are not independent governmental bodies. State constitutions generally describe the organization of counties, cities, towns, townships, boroughs, school districts, and special districts. They may delegate responsibilities to them for public safety, police, fire, sanitation, sewage and refuse disposal, hospitals, streets, and public health. State constitutions may establish tax and debt limits for local governments, describe the kinds of taxes they may levy, and prescribe the way in which their funds may be spent. In the absence of constitutional provisions governing local governments, these subordinate units must rely upon state legislatures for their organization and powers. In recent years there has been a movement toward greater home rule for communities. More than half the states have provided for some semblance of home rule, which removes some of the internal affairs of communities from the intervention of state legislatures. Of course, when a "home rule" charter is granted to a community by an act of the legislature, it can be readily withdrawn or revised by the legislature. Constitutional home rule is a more secure grant of power to communities than legislative home rule. (See Chapter 9 for further discussion.)

Interest Group Regulation   Since state constitutions take precedence over state laws and are more difficult to amend, interest groups prefer to see special protections written into the state's fundamental document. This prevents legislatures from meddling in important business affairs each legislative session. Even reformers sometimes support the inclusion of regulatory language in the state's constitution, out of fear that later lobbying efforts by business could easily change state laws. So most state constitutions include long sections on regulation of insurance, utilities, corporations, alcoholic beverages, railroads, mining, medicine, real estate, the state bar association, and so forth.

Taxation and Finance   All state constitutions have articles on taxation and finance. Frequently these place severe restrictions on the taxing power of state and local governments. Taxpayer groups distrust state legislatures and wherever possible seek to restrict taxing powers by constitutional mandate. Many referenda votes are designed to amend the state's constitution to limit tax burdens. (See Chapter 18.) Local governments may also be limited in state constitutions to specific tax sources and upper limits or "caps" on local taxation. Certain classes of property may be protected, such as that devoted to religious, educational, or charitable uses; government property; some agricultural or forestry land; and even "homesteads," that is, low-priced, owner-occupied homes. Some constitutions may grant tax exemptions to new industries in order to attract industrial development. Constitutions may "earmark" certain tax revenues for specific purposes; for example, gasoline taxes may be earmarked for highway use only.

Debt Limitation   Most state constitutions limit debt that can be incurred by the state only or by local governments. Many states *must* have a balanced operating budget. (Although such a constitutional command does not always succeed, on the whole, state governments are less burdened by debt than is the federal government.) Local governments are frequently limited to a debt that cannot exceed a fixed percentage of the value of property in the community. Moreover, state constitutions generally require a local referendum to approve any increase in local debt. Occasionally, however, state and local governments devise ways to get around constitutional debt limits; for example, they may pledge the revenues of a new project ("revenue bonds") to pay off the debt, rather than taxes ("full faith and credit bonds"). (See Chapter 18.)

Trivia   According to the Vermont Constitution: "Every sect or denomination of Christians ought to observe the Sabbath or Lord's Day, and keep some sort of religious worship, which to them seem most agreeable to the revealed will of God." There are many old phrases and clauses like this in state constitutions. Commentators enjoy rummaging through state constitutions and laws to find antique provisions that have little more than symbolic meaning.

CONSTITUTIONAL CHANGE IN THE STATES

The U.S. Constitution has been amended only twenty-six times in 200 years (and the first ten amendments, the Bill of Rights, were really part of the process of ratifying the original document). But state constitutions are so detailed and restrictive that they must be amended frequently. Nearly every year state voters must consider constitutional amendments on the ballot.

Throughout the fifty states, there are now four methods of constitutional change:

1. *Legislative proposal:* Amendments are passed by the state legislature and then submitted to the voters for approval in a referendum. This method is available in all states. (However, in Delaware amendments passed by the legislature need not be submitted to the voters.)
2. *Popular initiative:* A specific number of voters petition to get a constitutional amendment on the ballot for approval by the voters in a referendum. This method is available in seventeen states.
3. *Constitutional convention:* Legislatures submit to the voters a proposal for calling a constitutional convention, and if voters approve, a convention convenes, draws up constitutional revisions, and submits them again for approval by the voters in a referendum. This method is available in at least forty-one states.
4. *Constitutional commission:* Constitutional commissions may be created by legislatures to study the constitution and recommend changes to the state legislature, or in the case of Florida (only) to submit its recommendations directly to the voters in a referendum.

Legislative Proposal   The most common method of amending state constitutions is by *legislative proposal.* Many states require that a constitutional amendment receive a two-thirds vote in both chambers of the legislature before submission to the voters; a few states require a three-fifths majority in both houses, while others

Table 2–2   State Constitutional Amendment by Legislatures

	Legislative Vote Required for Proposal	Consideration by Two Sessions Required	Referendum Vote Required for Ratification
Alabama	3/5	No	Majority vote on amendment
Alaska	2/3	No	Majority vote on amendment
Arizona	Majority	No	Majority vote on amendment
Arkansas	Majority	No	Majority vote on amendment
California	2/3	No	Majority vote on amendment
Colorado	2/3	No	Majority vote on amendment
Connecticut	(c)	(a)	Majority vote on amendment
Delaware	2/3	Yes	Not required
Florida	3/5	No	Majority vote on amendment
Georgia	2/3	No	Majority vote on amendment
Hawaii	(b)	(b)	Majority vote on amendment
Idaho	2/3	No	Majority vote on amendment
Illinois	3/5	No	(c)
Indiana	Majority	Yes	Majority vote on amendment
Iowa	Majority	Yes	Majority vote on amendment
Kansas	2/3	No	Majority vote on amendment
Kentucky	3/5	No	Majority vote on amendment
Louisiana	2/3	No	Majority vote on amendment
Maine	2/3	No	Majority vote on amendment
Maryland	3/5	No	Majority vote on amendment
Massachusetts	Majority	Yes	Majority vote on amendment
Michigan	2/3	No	Majority vote on amendment
Minnesota	Majority	No	Majority vote in election
Mississippi	2/3	No	Majority vote on amendment
Missouri	Majority	No	Majority vote on amendment
Montana	2/3	No	Majority vote on amendment
Nebraska	3/5	No	Majority vote on amendment
Nevada	Majority	Yes	Majority vote on amendment
New Hampshire	3/5	No	2/3 vote on amendment
New Jersey	(d)	(d)	Majority vote on amendment
New Mexico	Majority	No	Majority vote on amendment
New York	Majority	Yes	Majority vote on amendment
North Carolina	3/5	No	Majority vote on amendment
North Dakota	Majority	No	Majority vote on amendment
Ohio	3/5	No	Majority vote on amendment
Oklahoma	Majority	No	Majority vote on amendment
Oregon	Majority	No	Majority vote on amendment
Pennsylvania	Majority	Yes	Majority vote on amendment
Rhode Island	Majority	No	Majority vote on amendment
South Carolina	2/3	Yes	Majority vote on amendment
South Dakota	Majority	No	Majority vote on amendment
Tennessee	2/3	Yes	Majority vote in election

TABLE 2–2   *(Continued)*

Texas	⅔	No	Majority vote on amendment
Utah	⅔	No	Majority vote on amendment
Vermont	Majority	Yes	Majority vote on amendment
Virginia	Majority	Yes	Majority vote on amendment
Washington	⅔	No	Majority vote on amendment
West Virginia	⅔	No	Majority vote on amendment
Wisconsin	Majority	Yes	Majority vote on amendment
Wyoming	⅔	No	Majority vote in election

[a] ¾ vote at one session, or majority vote in two sessions between which an election has intervened.

[b] ⅔ vote at one session or majority vote in two sessions.

[c] Majority voting in election or ⅗ voting on amendment.

[d] ⅗ vote at one session or majority vote in two sessions.

Source: Book of the States, 1992–93.

require only simple legislative majorities. Some states require that a constitutional amendment be passed by two successive legislative sessions before being submitted to the voters. Every state except Delaware requires constitutional amendments proposed by the legislature to be submitted to the voters for approval in a referendum. (See Table 2–2.)

Popular Initiative   *Popular initiative* for constitutional revision was introduced during the Progressive Era at the beginning of the twentieth century. These states usually require that an initiative petition be signed by 5, 10, or 15 percent of the number of voters in the last governor's election. (See Table 2–3.) The petition method allows citizens to get an amendment on the ballot *without the approval of the state legislature.* It is not surprising that measures designed to reduce the powers of legislators—for example, *tax limitation* measures and *term limits* for legislators— have come about as a result of citizen initiatives.

Constitutional Convention   While there has been only one national Constitutional Convention, in 1787, there have been over 230 state constitutional conventions. State constitutional conventions are generally proposed by state legislatures, and the question of whether or not to have a convention is generally submitted to the state's voters. (Some state constitutions require periodic submission to the voters of the question of calling a constitutional convention.) The legislature usually decides how convention delegates are to be elected and the convention organized. More important, the legislature usually decides whether the convention's work is to be *limited* to specific proposals or topics, or *unlimited* and free to write an entire new constitution.

Voters are often wary of calling a constitutional convention. Over the years voters have rejected as many constitutional convention calls as they have approved. This is true despite the fact that voters always have the option of later voting on the constitutional changes proposed by the conventions. Voters are very reluctant to approve unlimited conventions; most of these calls are rejected. Ap-

TABLE 2-3   INITIATIVE, REFERENDA, AND RECALL IN THE STATES

Initiative for Constitutional Amendment (Signatures Required to Get on Ballot)[a]	Initiative for State Legislation (Signatures Required to Get on Ballot)[a]	Referendum on State Legislation[b]	Recall (Signatures Required to Force a Recall Election)[c]
Arizona (15%)	Alaska (10%)	Alabama	Alaska (25%)
Arkansas (10%)	Arizona (10%)	Alaska	Arizona (25%)
California (8%)	Arkansas (8%)	Arizona	California (25%)
Colorado (5%)	California (5%)	Arkansas	Colorado (25%)
Florida (8%)	Colorado (5%	California	Georgia (15%)
Illinois (8%)	secretary	Hawaii	Idaho (20%)
Massachusetts (10%)	of state election)	Idaho	Kansas (40%)
Michigan (10%)	Idaho (10%)	Kentucky	Louisiana (33%)
Missouri (8%)	Maine (10%)	Maine	Michigan (25%)
Montana (10%)	Massachusetts (3%)	Maryland	Montana (15%)
Nebraska (10%)	Michigan (8%)	Massachusetts	Nevada (25%)
Nevada (10%)	Missouri (5%)	Michigan	North Dakota (25%)
North Dakota (4% of state population)	Montana (5% total qualified elections)	Missouri	Oregon (15%)
Ohio (10%)	Nebraska (7%)	Montana	Washington (25%)
Oklahoma (15%)	Nevada (10%)	Nebraska	Wisconsin (25%)
Oregon (8%)	North Dakota (2% of state population)	Nevada	
South Dakota (10%)	Ohio (3% electors)	New Mexico	
	Oklahoma (8%)	North Dakota	
	Oregon (6%)	Ohio	
	South Dakota (5%)	Oklahoma	
	Utah (10%)	Oregon	
	Washington (8%)	South Dakota	
	Wyoming (15%, general election)	Utah	
		Washington	
		Wyoming	

[a] Figures expressed as percentage of vote in last governor's election unless otherwise specified; some states also require distribution of votes across counties and districts.

[b] Some state legislatures are required by state constitutions to submit certain questions, such as debt authorization, to the voters. Other states allow citizens to petition for a referendum.

[c] Figures are percentages of voters in last general elections of the official sought to be recalled.

Source: Council of State Governments, *The Book of the States, 1992–93.*

parently they are suspicious of "reform" and fearful about "runaway" conventions changing things too much. Only one new constitution has been approved by voters in over a decade—that in Georgia in 1982.

Constitutional Commissions   Constitutional commissions are supposed to "study and recommend" constitutional changes. These commissions are established by the legislatures and report their recommendations back to the legislature. (Only in Florida do the recommendations of the Constitutional Revision Commission go directly to the voters for ratification and so far all of their proposals have been defeated.) Legislatures generally prefer constitutional commissions to a constitutional convention, because a commission can only study and report to the legislature. A commission can relieve the state legislature of a great deal of work. The typical commission is appointed by an act of the legislature, and its membership usually includes legislators, executive officials, and prominent citizens. Its recommendations are usually handled in the legislature like regular constitutional amendments, although they may be more sweeping than ordinary amendments.

DEMOCRACY IN THE STATES

Democracy means popular participation in government. (The Greek root of the word means "rule by the many.") But popular participation can have different meanings. To our nation's Founders, who were quite ambivalent about the wisdom of democracy, it meant that the voice of the people would be *represented* in government. "Representational democracy" means the selection of government officials by vote of the people in periodic elections open to competition in which candidates and voters can freely express themselves. (Note that "elections" in which only one party is permitted to run candidates, or where candidates are not free to express their views, do not qualify as democratic.) The Founders believed that government rests ultimately on the consent of the governed. But their notion of "republicanism" envisioned decision making by representatives of the people, rather than direct decision making by the people themselves. The U.S. Constitution has no provision for direct voting by the people on national policy questions.

"Direct democracy" means that the people themselves can initiate and decide policy questions by popular vote. The Founders were profoundly skeptical of this form of democracy. They had read about direct democracy in the ancient Greek city-state of Athens, and they believed that "the follies" of direct democracy far outweighed any virtues it might possess. It was not until over one hundred years after the U.S. Constitution was written that widespread support developed in the American states for direct voter participation in policy making. Direct democracy developed in states and communities, and it is to be found today *only* in state and local government.

Historical Development in the States   At the beginning of the twentieth century, a strong populist movement in the midwestern and western states attacked railroads, banks, corporations, and the political institutions that were said to be in their hands. The populists were later joined by progressive reformers who attacked "bosses," "machines," and parties as corrupt. The populists believed that their elected representatives were ignoring the needs of farmers, debtors, and laborers. They wished to bypass governors and legislatures and directly enact popular laws for railroad rate regulation, relief of farm debt, and monetary expansion. They believed that both the Democratic and Republican parties of their era were controlled by the trusts and monopolies. The progressives and reformers viewed politics as distasteful. They did not believe that government should be involved in resolving conflicts among competing interests or striving for compromises in public policy. Instead, government should serve "the public interest"; it should seek out the "right" answer to public questions; it should replace politicians with managers and administrators. The progressive reform movement was supported by many upper-middle-class, white, Anglo-Saxon, Protestant groups, who felt that political "machines" were catering to the votes of recent immigrants such as the Irish, Italians, eastern and southern Europeans, working-class people, Catholics, and Jews.[3] The progressive reform movement brought about many changes in the structure of municipal government. (See "Reformers and Do-Gooders" in Chapter 10.) The movement also brought about some interesting innovations in state government.

In order to reduce the influence of "politics," "parties," and "politicians," the populists and progressives advocated a wide range of devices designed to bypass political institutions and encourage direct participation by voters in public affairs. They were largely responsible for replacing party conventions with the primary elections we use today. They were also successful in bringing about the Seventeenth Amendment to the U.S. Constitution requiring that U.S. senators be directly elected by the voters, rather than chosen by state legislatures. They also supported women's suffrage, civil service, and restrictive immigration laws.

The populists and progressives were also responsible for the widespread adoption of three forms of direct democracy—the initiative, referendum, and recall. These reforms began in the farm states of the Midwest and the mining states of the West. The populists provided much of the early support for these devices, and the progressives and reformers carried them to fruition. President Woodrow Wilson endorsed the initiative, referendum, and recall, and most adoptions occurred prior to World War I.[4]

Initiative   The *initiative* is a device whereby a specific number or percent of voters, through the use of a petition, may have a proposed state constitutional amendment or a state law placed on the ballot for adoption or rejection by the electorate of a state. This process bypasses the legislature and allows citizens to both propose and adopt laws and constitutional amendments. Table 2–3 lists the states that allow popular initiatives for constitutional amendments, and those that allow popular initiatives for state law.

Referendum   The *referendum* is a device by which the electorate must approve decisions of the legislature before these become law or become part of the state constitution. As we noted earlier, most states require a favorable referenda vote for a state constitutional amendment (see Table 2–3). Referenda on state laws may be submitted by the legislature (when legislators want to shift decision-making responsibility to the people), or referenda may be demanded by popular petition (when the people wish to change laws passed by the legislature).

Recall   Recall elections allow voters to remove an elected official before his or her term expires. Usually a recall election is initiated by a petition. The number of signatures required is usually expressed as a percentage of votes cast in the last

[3] See Richard Hofstadter, *The Age of Reform* (New York: Knopf, 1955).

[4] See Thomas E. Cronin, *Direct Democracy: The Politics of Initiative, Referendum and Recall* (Cambridge, MA: Harvard University Press, 1989).

election for the official being recalled (frequently 25 percent). Currently fifteen states provide for recall election for some or all of their elected officials (see Table 2–3). Although officials are often publicly threatened with recall, rarely is anyone ever removed from office through this device. A recall of a state elected official requires an expensive petition drive as well as a campaign against the incumbent. Perhaps the mere existence of recall provisions in a state constitution makes public officials more responsive to popular moods.

DIRECT VERSUS REPRESENTATIVE DEMOCRACY

The U.S. Constitution has no provision for national referenda. Americans as a nation cannot vote on federal laws or amendments to the national constitution. But voters in the *states* can express their frustrations directly in popular initiatives and referenda voting.

Arguments for Direct Democracy   Proponents of direct democracy make several strong arguments on behalf of the initiative and referendum devices:[5]

- Direct democracy enhances government responsiveness and accountability. The threat of a successful initiative and referendum drive—indeed sometimes the mere circulation of a petition—encourages officials to take the popular actions.
- Direct democracy allows citizen groups to bring their concerns directly to the public. Taxpayer groups, for example, who are not especially well represented in state capitols, have been able through initiative and referendum devices to place their concerns on the public agenda.
- Direct democracy stimulates debate about policy issues. In elections with important referendum issues on the ballot, campaigns tend to be more issue-oriented. Candidates, newspapers, interest groups, and television news are all forced to directly confront policy issues.
- Direct democracy stimulates voter interest and improves election-day turnout. Controversial issues on the ballot—the death penalty, abortion, gun control, taxes, gay rights, English only, and so on—bring out additional voters. There is some limited evidence that elections with initiatives on the ballot increase voter turnout by three to five percentage points over elections with no initiatives on the ballot.[6]
- Direct democracy increases trust in government and diminishes alienation. While it is difficult to substantiate such a claim, the opportunity to directly affect issues should give voters an increased sense of power.

Arguments for Representative Democracy   Opponents of direct democracy, from our nation's Founders to the present, argue that representative democracy offers far better protection for individual liberty and the rights of minorities than

---

[5] For a balanced summary and evaluation of direct democracy in the states, see Cronin, *Direct Democracy.*

[6] Ibid., p. 227.

direct democracy. The Founders constructed a system of checks and balances not so much to protect against the oppression of a ruler, but to protect against the tyranny of the majority. Opponents of direct democracy echo many of the Founders' arguments:

- Direct democracy encourages majorities to sacrifice the rights of individuals and minorities. This argument supposes that voters are generally less tolerant than elected officials, and there is some evidence to support this supposition. However, there is little evidence that public policy in states with the initiative and referendum is any more oppressive than public policy in states without these devices. Nonetheless, the potential of majoritarian sacrifice of the liberty of unpopular people is always a concern.
- Direct democracy facilitates the adoption of unwise and unsound policies. Although voters have rejected many bad ideas, frequently initiatives are less well drafted than legislation.
- Voters are not sufficiently informed to cast intelligent ballots on many issues. Many voters cast their vote in a referendum without ever having considered the issue before going into the polling booth.
- A referendum does not allow consideration of alternative policies or modifications or amendments to the proposition set forth on the ballot. In contrast, legislators devote a great deal of attention to writing, rewriting, and amending bills, and seeking out compromises among interests.
- Direct democracy enables special interests to mount expensive initiative and referendum campaigns. Although proponents of direct democracy argue that these devices allow citizens to bypass special-interest-group-dominated legislatures, in fact only a fairly well-financed group can mount a statewide campaign on behalf of a referendum issue. And the outcomes of the vote may be heavily influenced by paid television advertising. So money is important in both "representational" and "direct" democracy.

◀ TAX LIMITATION INITIATIVES

What issues in state politics tend to be decided by popular initiatives and referenda? In the late 1970s the "tax revolt" placed propositions to limit taxes on the ballot in many states. Initially many of these tax limitation propositions were approved, including Proposition 13 in California in 1978. But in the early 1980s the "tax revolt" seemed to subside; fewer tax limitation initiatives got on state ballots, and many of those that appeared on ballots were defeated by the voters. Environmentalists succeeded in getting "bottle bills" on the ballot in a number of states, but voters rejected most of these efforts to prohibit beer and soft drink cans. Legalization of state lotteries became popular in 1984. Most lottery propositions were approved, but casino gambling propositions were defeated. Vermont surprised observers in 1986 by voting down an equal rights amendment to the state constitution. In 1988, voters in Arizona, Colorado, and Florida all followed California's lead in declaring English to be their official language. (See Table 2–4.)

Public funding of abortions has been voted on in a number of states with varying outcomes. In 1992 Colorado voted to deny homosexuals preferential

TABLE 2–4   STATE VOTING ON SELECTED PROPOSITIONS

		For (%)	Against (%)
Tax Limitations			
Oregon (1982)	Limit property taxes to 1.5%	49.2	50.8
Michigan (1984)	Require voter approval of new taxes	40.3	59.7
Nevada (1984)	Exempt food from sales tax	83.3	16.7
California (1986)	New local taxes require ⅔ vote	57.9	42.1
Nevada (1988)	Prohibits state income tax	81.2	17.8
Colorado (1992)	Require elections for tax increases	54.0	46.0
Civil Rights			
Maine (1984)	Equal Rights Amendment	36.9	63.1
North Dakota (1984)	Guarantee right to bear arms	80.2	19.8
Vermont (1986)	Equal Rights Amendment	48.4	51.6
Arizona (1988)	Make English official language	50.5	49.5
Colorado (1988)	Make English official language	61.1	38.9
Florida (1988)	Make English official language	83.9	16.1
Iowa (1992)	Equal Rights Amendment	48.0	52.0
Colorado (1992)	Deny homosexuals preferential treatment or protections against discrimination	53.0	47.0
Oregon	Require government to discourage homosexuality	43.0	57.0
Crime			
Oregon (1984)	Reinstate death penalty	55.6	44.4
Massachusetts (1982)	Legalize death penalty	60.1	39.9
Arizona (1982)	Prohibit bail for dangerous felons	81.0	19.0
Illinois (1982)	Prohibit bail for dangerous felons	85.3	14.7
Georgia (1988)	Compensate crime victims	52.7	47.3
Gambling			
Arkansas (1984)	Allow casino gambling	29.6	70.4
Colorado (1984)	Allow casino gambling	33.2	66.8
California (1984)	Authorize state lottery	57.9	42.1
Florida (1986)	Allow casino gambling	31.7	68.3
Florida (1986)	Authorize state lottery	63.6	36.4
South Dakota (1992)	Repeal video lottery	37.0	63.0
Abortion			
Colorado (1984)	Prohibit state funds for abortion	50.4	49.6
Washington (1984)	Prohibit state funds for abortion	46.5	53.5
Rhode Island (1986)	Prohibit state funds for abortion	31.0	69.0
Arkansas (1988)	Prohibit state funds for abortion	51.9	48.1
Colorado (1988)	Prohibit state funds for abortion	39.8	61.2
Maryland (1992)	Ease restrictions on abortion	62.0	38.0
Arizona (1992)	Eliminate public funding of abortion	31.0	69.0
Other			
New Hampshire (1982)	Change all references in state laws from "man" and "men" to "person" and "people"	16.4	83.6
California (1986)	Quarantine persons with AIDS	29.0	71.0
New Mexico (1986)	Guarantee right to bear arms	61.7	38.3
Oregon (1986)	Allow possession of marijuana	26.5	73.5

Note: These are selected proposition votes from recent years. For information, see *Public Opinion,* February–March, 1981; December–January, 1983; January–February, 1985; January–February, 1987; January–February, 1989.

treatment or special protection against discrimination. But a citizen initiative in Oregon to require the government to discourage homosexual behavior lost.

California's Proposition 13   California has a history of citizen initiatives for constitutional change. So in 1978, in the wake of popular frustration over inflation and taxes, a Los Angeles real estate developer, Howard Jarvis, found the state's voters more than willing to support a constitutional amendment initiative to reduce property taxes. He succeeded in collecting over 1.2 million signatures, the largest number ever to sign an initiative in California history! His effort was funded by real estate developers, business, and agricultural interests, but he also succeeded in organizing a statewide, grass-roots United Organization of Taxpayers to support his initiative.

Opposition to Proposition 13 was led by public officials who believed the amendment would cripple public services. The political establishment was joined by the League of Women Voters, the PTA, public employee unions, teachers, and environmental groups, in making dire predictions about the impact of the amendment. They argued that it would "drastically reduce" police and fire protection, raise insurance costs, "slash" funding for parks and beaches, and "penalize" school children.

Voter turnout on election day was a record for a California June primary. Over 6.7 million California voters went to the polls to give overwhelming approval to Proposition 13 by better than a two-to-one margin. The publicity surrounding the success of Proposition 13 gave the impression that this citizen initiative was the beginning of a national tax revolt. By 1980 Democrats and Republicans across the nation were campaigning as "tax cutters." Later President Ronald Reagan would interpret it as part of a general mandate for lower taxes and less government, and as a forerunner to his own federal income tax cuts. But the reality of the "tax revolt" has proven far more complex. In the years since Proposition 13, almost as many states *defeated* tax limitation referenda as passed them. (In Chapter 18 we will devote more discussion to the politics of taxation.)

Facilitating Citizen Preferences   The citizen initiative facilitates the enactment of citizen preferences into public policy. In the years after Proposition 13, scholars tried to distinguish between states in which the tax revolt was successful and those where it was not. It turned out that the states *with constitutional provisions for citizen initiatives* were far more likely to join the "tax revolt"—that is, to pass tax limitation constitutional amendments—than states without provisions for citizen initiatives.[7] Thus, the constitutional framework of state government has important consequences for public policy.

---

[7] Susan Hansen reports that "Of the 21 states that permit voter initiatives, 11 (or 52 percent) passed tax or expenditure limitations between 1976 and 1980; 4 others in this group had them on the ballot although they were defeated. But of the 29 states that do not permit initiatives, only 6 (21 percent) passed tax or expenditure limitations during this period—a pattern highly unlikely to arise by chance." Susan B. Hansen, *The Politics of Taxation* (New York: Praeger, 1983), p. 233.

TERM LIMIT BATTLES

Increasing distrust of politicians and declining confidence in the ability of government to confront national problems have fueled grass-roots movements in many states to limit the terms of public officials—both Congress members and state legislators. National opinion polls show widespread popular support for term limits for members of Congress:

How long should members of the House and Senate serve?

	1991	1992
A maximum of 12 years	61%	67%
As long as they get elected	37	31

Limiting the terms of *state* legislators is equally popular. But the enthusiasm of the general public for term limits is seldom matched by legislators themselves—either in Washington or state capitals. It is not likely that Congress members or state legislators would ever agree to limit their own legislative careers. Hence, citizens in states with the popular initiative and referenda have turned to these instruments of direct democracy.

Arguments for Term Limits   Proponents of term limits argue that "citizen-legislators" have largely been replaced by career "professional politicians." People who have held legislative office for many years become isolated from the lives and concerns of average citizens. Career politicians respond to the media, to polls, to interest groups, but they have no direct feeling for how their constituents live. Term limits, proponents argue, would force politicians to return home and live under the laws that they make.

Proponents also argue that term limits would increase competition in the electoral system. By creating "open seat" races on a regular basis, more people would be encouraged to seek public office. Incumbents do not win so often because they are the most qualified people in their districts, but rather because of the many electoral advantages granted by incumbency itself—name recognition, campaign contributions from special interests, pork barrel and casework, office staff, and so on (see "The Great Incumbency Machine" in Chapter 6). These incumbent advantages discourage good people from challenging officeholders.

Arguments Against Term Limits   Opponents of term limits argue that they infringe on the voters' freedom of choice. If voters are upset with the performance of their state legislators, they can always "throw the rascals out." If they want to limit a legislator's term, they can do so simply by not reelecting him or her. But if voters wish to keep popular, able, experienced, and hard-working legislators in office, they should be permitted to do so. Experience is a valuable asset in state capitals; voters may legitimately desire to be represented by senior legislators with knowledge and experience in public affairs.

TABLE 2-5   Voting on Term Limits in the States

State	Term Limit	Vote Percent	
		Yes	No
1990			
Oklahoma	Limit state legislators	67	33
Colorado	Limit Congress and state legislators	71	29
California	Limit state legislators	52	48
1991			
Washington	Limit Congress and state legislators	46	54
1992			
Arizona	Limit Congress and state legislators	74	26
Arkansas	Limit Congress and state legislators	60	40
California	Limit Congress and state legislators	63	37
Florida	Limit Congress and state legislators	77	23
Michigan	Limit Congress and state legislators	59	41
Missouri	Limit Congress and state legislators	74	26
Montana	Limit Congress and state legislators	67	33
Nebraska	Limit Congress and state legislators	68	32
North Dakota	Limit Congress	55	45
Ohio	Limit Congress and state legislators	66	34
Oregon	Limit Congress and state legislators	69	31
South Dakota	Limit Congress and state legislators	63	37
Washington	Limit Congress and state legislators	52	48
Wyoming	Limit Congress and state legislators	77	23

Opponents argue that inexperienced legislators would be forced to rely more on the policy information supplied to them by bureaucrats, lobbyists, and staff people. Term limits, they argue, would weaken the legislature, leaving it less capable of checking the power of the special interests. But proponents counter this argument by observing that the closest relationships in state capitals develop between lobbyists and senior legislators who have interacted professionally and socially over the years, and that most powerful lobbying groups strongly oppose term limits.

A constitutional question arises as to whether voters in the states can limit the terms of Congress members without amending the U.S. Constitution. The U.S. Constitution places no restrictions on congressional terms. Can states place term limits on U.S. senators or representatives by amending only *state* constitutions? This question must ultimately be decided by the U.S. Supreme Court.

Popular Approval of Term Limits   Term limits have won by landslide margins whenever they have appeared on referenda ballots. (The only state electorate that appears ambivalent about term limits is Washington. In 1991, when Speaker of the House Tom Foley returned to his state to lead a fight against a retroactive measure that threatened to oust him, voters rejected it by a narrow margin. The following year they approved a term limit measure that would allow Foley and his other

House colleagues an additional six years only.) Most of these referenda measures specify 12 year term limits for Senators and 6 years for House members. None of these count prior service against the new limits, so the earliest any of these limits will take effect is 1998. Despite their approval of term limits, voters in these states continue to reelect incumbents.

POLITICS IN CONSTITUTIONAL CONVENTIONS

State constitutional conventions generally come into being in response to demands by reform-oriented "good-government" interest groups, often with the assistance of aspiring politicians who are seeking higher office and want to use the convention as a stepping stone. But the activities of constitutional reformers usually spark counteractivities from interests desiring to preserve the status quo—political officeholders, party politicians, bureaucrats, and business interests, particularly those subject to state regulation.

Interest Groups   Important political interests are at stake in constitutional revision. Legislatures are understandably hesitant about calling constitutional conventions. A "runaway" convention may rearrange the balance of political power in the state. It may strengthen the governor at the expense of the legislature, authorize new taxes, eliminate the earmarking of certain revenues, or allocate greater power over urban affairs to cities. In other words, a constitutional convention may seriously alter the status quo. Interest groups that presently enjoy special privileges or exemptions from taxation in the state constitution have reason to fear a constitutional convention. They may stress the expense involved in such a convention or the danger that "radical reformers" may foist their dangerous ideas upon an unsuspecting public. Taxpayer groups may fear that constitutional limitations on taxing powers may be removed. Public officials may be concerned that their offices will be abolished. In other words, constitutional revision is a political thicket that discourages all but the most courageous of individuals.

Reformers   Reform interests—good-government groups, the League of Women Voters, and political science professors—argue that the constitution and the structure of state and local government should be simple, brief, and understandable. It should permit the legislature and the governor to make public policy. It should allocate power to the governor and the legislature commensurate with their responsibilities, and it should enable the voters to hold elected officials clearly accountable for public decisions. It should permit local governmental consolidation and community home rule. The need for frequent amendment should be eliminated.

Delegates   Membership in constitutional conventions is generally weighted in the direction of reform, since the calling of the convention itself indicates the strength of reformers in the state political system. There is a relationship, however, between the type of election for delegate and the type of delegate selected. Partisan elections (delegates run under party labels) with small-size districts maximize the selection of party activists, current officeholders, and bureaucrats interested in preserving the status quo. Nonpartisan elections (delegates run without party designation) with at-large or multimember constituencies maximize the number of "reformer," "good-government" types.[8] The basic division within most conventions is between reformers versus preservers of the status quo. This line of division is often more pronounced than the division between Republicans versus Democrats, urban versus rural, a governor's supporters versus opponents, and so forth.[9]

POLITICS OF STATE CONSTITUTIONAL RATIFICATION

Despite the influence of reformers at constitutional conventions, the final outcome of constitutional revision through the convention method has been mixed. While new constitutions have generally moved states closer to the "reform model," the extent of change has not been very great. Since new constitutions must go to the voters for approval, reform-oriented constitution makers must be careful not to offend voters with controversial innovations. They must also try to satisfy all major blocs at the convention in order to avoid future additional work against ratification. New constitutions are very vulnerable at the polls. Voters who are offended by a single provision may vote no even when all other provisions are acceptable. Different voters may be voting no for different reasons, but a cumulation of specific no votes on separate provisions may spell defeat for the whole document.

Generalizations about factors affecting voter support or opposition to new constitutions are difficult to derive, even on close examination of voting results.[10] There is some evidence that higher socioeconomic groups give greater support to ratification than lower socioeconomic groups. But special circumstances may explain ratification outcomes more successfully than socioeconomic factors. In the successful states, partisanship was carefully avoided, the changes proposed were very modest, and state leaders of both parties publicly supported the document. Moreover, some of the less popular items proposed were separated from the main document for separate voting.

Of course, reform interests have not yet succeeded in simplifying state constitutions or in eliminating the special privileges and exemptions contained in them. Newer constitutions, however, are somewhat shorter and more streamlined than the average state constitution. All the newer documents tend to strengthen the executive, provide for more equitable apportionment, and remove limitations

---

[8] See Elmer E. Cornwell, Jr., Jay S. Goodman, and Wayne R. Swanson, "State Constitutional Conventions: Delegates, Roll Calls and Issues," *Midwest Journal of Political Science,* 14 (February 1970), 105–30; Jack R. Van Der Sik et al., "Patterns of Partisanship in a Nonpartisan Representational Setting: The Illinois Constitutional Convention," *American Journal of Political Science,* 18 (February 1974), 95–116; Cal Clark, Janet Clark, and Albert K. Karnig, "Voting Behavior of Chicago Democrats at the Illinois Constitutional Convention," *American Politics Quarterly,* 6 (July 1978), 325–44.

[9] Indeed, convention delegates do not usually behave in the fashion of politicians "ambitious" for higher office. See William H. Thompson, "An Analysis of the Legislative Ambitions of State Constitutional Convention Delegates," *Western Political Quarterly,* 39 (August 1976), 425–39.

[10] See Jay S. Goodman et al., "Public Responses to State Constitutional Revision," *American Journal of Political Science,* 17 (August 1973), 511–96.

TABLE 2–6   THE SUCCESS OF STATE CONSTITUTIONAL AMENDMENTS BY METHOD OF INITIATION

	Number of States				Total Proposals			
	1984–85	1986–87	1988–89	1990–91	1984–85	1986–87	1988–89	1990–91
All Methods	45	47	45	41	238	275	267	226
Legislative Proposal	45	46	45	41	211	243	246	197
Popular Initiative	10	9	11	10	17	18	21	29
Constitutional Convention	1	1	—	—	10	14	—	—
Constitutional Commission	—	—	—	—	—	—	—	—

	Percent Adopted			
	1984–85	1986–87	1988–89	1990–91
All Methods	65.5	74.3	74.0	63.3
Legislative Proposal	67.3	77.7	75.6	67.0
Popular Initiative	47.1	27.7	55.0	37.9
Constitutional Convention	60.0	57.1	—	—
Constitutional Commission	—	—	—	—

Source: Book of the States 1992–93.

on legislative power. However, there is not much hope that state constitutions will be simplified in the near future or that special exemptions and privileges will be eliminated.

Voter approval of new state constitutions is by no means assured. Over the years, the record of voters' response to state constitutional amendment (Table 2–6) shows that voters are more accepting of individual amendments submitted to them by *state legislatures* than any other method of constitutional change. In contrast, most popular initiatives are defeated at the polls, as are most amendments proposed by constitutional conventions. These figures suggest the key role that state legislatures play in constitutional change. While it is true that many legislative proposals are merely "editorial," voters seem to prefer limited, step-by-step, constitutional change, rather than sweeping reform initiated by citizens.[11]

---

[11] For a current assessment of state constitutional revision, see Janice C. May, "State Constitutions and Constitutional Revision," in Council of State Governments, *The Book of the States 1992–93* (Lexington, KY: Council of State Governments, 1992).

From the Vital to the Trivial

One of the less important, yet sometimes very heated, issues that confront state legislatures is the selection of official nicknames for their state as well as official birds, flowers, trees, songs, and the like. If you think you know about the American states (or if you pass your driving time reading license plates), try to match the state with its official nickname without looking at the answers.

Easy Ones	*Answers*
Heart of Dixie	Alabama
Grand Canyon State	Arizona
Golden State	California
Centennial State	Colorado
Peach State, Empire State of the South	Georgia
Sunshine State	Florida
Aloha State	Hawaii
Hawkeye State	Iowa
Hoosier State	Indiana
Bluegrass State	Kentucky
Bay State, Old Colony	Massachusetts
Great Lake State, Wolverine State	Michigan
Show Me State	Missouri
Cornhusker State	Nebraska
Empire State	New York
Tar Heel State	North Carolina
Buckeye State	Ohio
Sooner State	Oklahoma
Beaver State	Oregon
Little Rhody	Rhode Island
Volunteer State	Tennessee
Lone Star State	Texas
Old Dominion	Virginia
Mountain State	West Virginia
Badger State	Wisconsin

Hard Ones	*Answers*
Land of Opportunity	Arkansas
Constitution State, Nutmeg State	Connecticut
First State, Diamond State	Delaware
Gem State	Idaho
Prairie State	Illinois
Sunflower State	Kansas
Pelican State	Louisiana
Pine Tree State	Maine
Old Line State, Free State	Maryland

North Star State, Gopher State	Minnesota
Magnolia State	Mississippi
Treasurer State	Montana
Silver State	Nevada
Granite State	New Hampshire
Garden State	New Jersey
Land of Enchantment	New Mexico
Sioux State, Flickertale State	North Dakota
Keystone State	Pennsylvania
Palmetto State	South Carolina
Coyote State	South Dakota
Beehive State	Utah
Green Mountain State	Vermont
Evergreen State	Washington
Equality State	Wyoming
None (only state with no official nickname)	Alaska

Source: Book of the States 1988–89.

3

STATES, COMMUNITIES, AND AMERICAN FEDERALISM

▲

WHAT IS FEDERALISM?

Virtually all nations of the world have some units of local government—states, republics, provinces, regions, cities, counties, or villages. Decentralization of the administrative burdens of government is required almost everywhere. But not all nations have federal systems of government.

Federalism is a system of government in which power is divided between national and subnational governments with both exercising separate and autonomous authority, both electing their own officials, and both taxing their own citizens for the provision of public services. Moreover, federalism requires that the powers of the national and subnational governments be guaranteed by a constitution that cannot be changed without the consent of both national and subnational populations.[1]

---

[1] Other definitions of federalism in American political science include: "Federalism refers to a political system in which there are local (territorial, regional, provincial, state, or municipal) units of

The United States, Canada, Australia, India, the Federal Republic of Germany, and Switzerland are generally regarded as federal systems. But Great Britain, France, Italy, and Sweden are not. While these nations have local governments, they are dependent on the national government for their powers. They are considered *unitary* rather than federal systems, because their local governments can be altered or even abolished by the national governments acting alone. In contrast, a system is said to be *confederal* if the power of the national government is dependent upon local units of government. While these terms—unitary, and confederal—can be defined theoretically, in the real world of politics it is not so easy to distinguish between governments that are truly federal and those that are not. Indeed, as we shall see in this chapter, it is not clear whether the U.S. government today retains its federal character.

Why Federalism?

Why have state and local governments anyway? Why not have a centralized political system with a single government accountable to national majorities in national elections—a government capable of implementing uniform policies throughout the country?

"Auxiliary Precautions" Against Tyranny   The nation's Founders understood that "republican principles," while they should be nurtured and cherished, would not be sufficient in themselves to protect individual liberty. Periodic elections, party competition, voter enfranchisement, and political equality may function to make governing elites more responsive to popular concerns. But these processes do not protect minorities or individuals, "the weaker party or an obnoxious individual," from government deprivations of liberty or property. Indeed, according to the Founders, "the great object" of constitution writing was to both preserve popular government and protect individuals from "unjust and interested" *majorities.* "A dependence on the people is, no doubt, the primary control of government, but experience has taught mankind the necessity of auxiliary precautions."

Among the most important "auxiliary precautions" devised by the Founders to control government are federalism—dividing powers between the national and state governments—and *separation of powers*—the dispersal of power among the separate executive, legislative, and judicial branches of government.

> In the compound republic of America, the power surrendered by the people is first divided between two distinct governments, and then the portion allotted to each subdivided among distinct and separate departments. Hence a double security arises

government as well as a national government, that can make final decisions with respect to at least some governmental authorities and whose existence is especially protected." James Q. Wilson, *American Government,* 4th ed. (Lexington, MA: D.C. Heath, 1989), p. 47; "Federalism is the mode of political organization that unites smaller polities within an overarching political system by distributing power among general and constituent units in a manner designed to protect the existence and authority of both national and subnational systems enabling all to share in the overall system's decision-making and executing processes." Daniel J. Elazar, *American Federalism: A View from the States* (New York: Thomas Y. Crowell, 1966), p. 2.

to the rights of the people. The different governments will control each other, at the same time that each will be controlled by itself.[2]

Dispersing Power   Decentralization distributes power more widely among different sets of leaders. Multiple leadership groups are generally believed to be more democratic than a single set of all-powerful leaders. To the extent that pluralism exists in America, state and local governments have undoubtedly contributed to it. Robert Dahl observes that

> state and local governments have provided a number of centers of power whose autonomy is strongly protected by Constitutional and political traditions. A governor of a state or the mayor of a large city may not be the political equal of a president (at least not often); but he is most assuredly not a subordinate. In dealing with a governor or mayor, a president rarely if ever commands; he negotiates; he may even plead. Here then is a part of the intermediate stratum of leadership that Tocqueville looked to as a barrier to tyranny.[3]

It should be added that state and local governments provide a political base of offices for the opposition party when it has lost national elections. In this way state and local governments contribute to party competition in America by helping to tide over the losing party after electoral defeat so that it may remain strong enough to challenge incumbents at the next election. And finally, of course, state and local governments provide a channel of recruitment for national political leaders. National leaders can be drawn from a pool of leaders experienced in state and local politics.

Increasing Participation   Decentralization allows more people to participate in the political system. There are over eighty thousand governments in America—states, counties, townships, municipalities, towns, special districts, and school districts. Nearly a million people hold some kind of public office. The opportunity to participate doubtlessly contributes to popular support of the political system. Many people are given the opportunity to exercise political leadership; moreover, state and local governments are widely regarded as being "closer to the people." Thus, by providing more opportunities for direct citizen involvement in government, state and local governments contribute to the popular sense of political effectiveness and well-being.

Improving Efficiency   Decentralization makes government more manageable and efficient. Imagine the bureaucracy, red tape, and confusion if every government activity in every local community in the nation—police, schools, roads, fire fighting, garbage collection, sewage disposal, and so forth—were controlled by a centralized administration in Washington. If local governments did not exist, they would have to be invented. Government becomes arbitrary when a bureaucracy far from the scene directs a local administrator to proceed with the impossible—local conditions notwithstanding. Decentralization softens the rigidity of law.

---

[2] James Madison, Alexander Hamilton, and John Jay, *The Federalist*, 51 (New York: Modern Library, 1958).

[3] Robert A. Dahl, *Pluralist Democracy in America* (Chicago: Rand McNally, 1967), p. 189.

(5) **Ensuring Policy Responsiveness**   Decentralized government encourages policy responsiveness. Multiple competing governments are more sensitive to citizen views than monopoly government. The existence of multiple governments offering different packages of benefits and costs allows a better match between citizen preferences and public policy. People and businesses can "vote with their feet" by relocating to those states and communities that most closely conform to their own policy preferences. Americans are very mobile. About four of every ten Americans moves in any five-year period: One in five moves to a different county, and one in ten to a different state. Business and industry are also increasingly mobile. Mobility not only facilitates a better match between citizen preferences and public policy, it also encourages competition between states and communities to offer improved services at lower costs.

Encouraging Policy Innovation   Decentralization encourages policy experimentation and innovation. Federalism may be perceived today as a "conservative" idea, but it was once viewed as the instrument of "progressivism." A strong argument can be made that the groundwork for the New Deal was built in state policy experimentation during the Progressive Era. Federal programs as diverse as the income tax, unemployment compensation, countercyclical public works, Social Security, wage and hour legislation, bank deposit insurance, and food stamps all had antecedents at the state level. Indeed, much of the current "neo-liberal" policy agenda—mandatory health insurance for workers, child care programs, notification of plant closing, government support of industrial research and development —has been embraced by various states. Indeed, the compelling phrase "laboratories of democracies" is generally attributed to the great progressive jurist, Supreme Court Justice Louis D. Brandeis, who used it in defense of state experimentation with new solutions to social and economic problems.[4] But the states cannot serve as "laboratories," and the innovative potential of federalism cannot be realized, if the states are not free to pursue a wide range of policies. Competition among governments provides additional incentives for inventiveness and innovation in public policy.[5]

Managing Conflict   Political decentralization frequently reduces the severity of conflict in a society. Decentralization is a classic method by which different peoples can be brought together in a nation without engendering irresolvable conflict. Conflicts between geographically defined groups in America are resolved by allowing each to pursue its own policies within the separate states and communities; this avoids battling over a single national policy to be applied uniformly throughout the land.

---

[4] David Osborne, *Laboratories of Democracy* (Cambridge, MA: Harvard Business School, 1988).

[5] The arguments for "competitive federalism" are developed at length in Thomas R. Dye, *American Federalism: Competition Among Governments* (Lexington, MA: Lexington Books, 1990). The book argues that competitive decentralized government has many advantages over centralized "monopoly" governments: greater overall responsiveness to citizen preferences; incentives for government to become efficient and provide quality services at lowest costs; restraints on the overall burdens of taxation and nonproportional taxes; encouragement of economic growth; and innovation in policies designed to improve the well-being of citizens.

FEDERALISM'S FAULTS

Federalism is not without its faults. Federalism can obstruct action on national issues. Although decentralization may reduce conflict at the national level, it may do so at the price of "sweeping under the rug" some serious, national injustices.

Protecting Slavery and Segregation   Federalism in America remains tainted by its historical association with slavery, segregation, and discrimination. An early doctrine of "nullification" was asserted by Thomas Jefferson in the Virginia and Kentucky Resolution of 1798, giving states the right to nullify unconstitutional laws of Congress. Although the original use of this doctrine was to counter congressional attacks on a free press in the Alien and Sedition Acts, the doctrine was later revived to defend slavery. John C. Calhoun of South Carolina argued forcefully in the years before the Civil War that slavery was an issue for states to decide and that under the Constitution of 1787, Congress had no power to interfere with slavery in the southern states or in the new western territories.

In the years immediately following the Civil War the issues of slavery, racial inequality, and black voting rights were *nationalized*. The Thirteenth, Fourteenth, and Fifteenth Amendments to the Constitution were enforced with federal troops in the southern states during Reconstruction. But following the Compromise of 1876 federal troops were withdrawn from the southern states and legal and social segregation of blacks became a "way of life" in the region. Segregation was *denationalized;* this reduced national conflict over race, but the price was paid by black Americans. Not until the 1950s and 1960s were questions of segregation and equality again made into national issues. The civil rights movement asserted the supremacy of national law, especially the U.S. Supreme Court's decision in *Brown v. Topeka,* 1954, that segregation violated the Fourteenth Amendment's guarantee of equal protection of the law, and later the national Civil Rights Act of 1964. Segregationists asserted the states' rights argument so often in defense of racial discrimination that it became a code word for racism.

Indeed, only now that *national* constitutional and legal guarantees of equal protection of the law are in place is it possible to reassess the true values of federalism. Having established that federalism will not be allowed to justify racial inequality, we are now free to explore the values of decentralized government.

Obstructing National Policies   Federalism allows state and local officials to obstruct action on national problems. It allows local leaders and citizens to frustrate national policy, to sacrifice the national interest to local interests. Decentralized government provides an opportunity for local "NIMBYs" (not in my back yard) to obstruct airports, highways, waste disposal plants, public housing, and many other projects in the national interest.

Allowing Inequalities   Finally, under federalism the benefits and costs of government are spread unevenly across the nation. For example, some states spend over twice as much on the education of each child in the public schools as other states (see Chapter 15). Welfare benefits in some states are over twice as high as in other states (see Chapter 17). Taxes in some states are over twice as high per capita as in other states (see Chapter 18). Competition among states may keep welfare benefits low in order not to encourage an immigration of poor people. Federalism allows these differences in policy to develop. Federalism is the opposite of uniformity.

THE STRUCTURE OF AMERICAN FEDERALISM

In deciding in 1869 that a state had no constitutional right to secede from the union, Chief Justice Salmon P. Chase described the legal character of American federalism:

> The preservation of the states and the maintenance of their governments, are as much within the design and care of the constitution as the preservation of the union and the maintenance of the national government. The constitution, in all of its provisions, looks to an indestructible union, composed of indestructible states.[6]

What is meant by "an indestructible union, composed of indestructible states"? American federalism is an indissoluble partnership between the states and the national government. The Constitution of the United States allocated power between two separate authorities, the nation and the states, each of which was to be independent of the other. Both the nation and the states were allowed to enforce their laws directly on individuals through their own officials and courts. The Constitution itself was the only legal source of authority for the division of powers between the states and the nation. The American federal system is a strong national government, coupled with a strong state government, in which authority and power are shared, constitutionally and practically.

The framework of American federalism is determined by (1) the powers delegated by the Constitution of the national government, and the supremacy of the government; (2) the constitutional guarantees reserved for the states; (3) the powers denied by the Constitution to both the national government and the states; (4) the constitutional provisions giving the states a role in the compositions of the national government; and (5) the subsequent constitutional and historical development of federalism.

Delegated Powers and National Supremacy   Article I, Section 8, of the U.S. Constitution lists eighteen grants of power to Congress. These "delegated" or "enumerated" powers include authority over matters of war and foreign affairs, the power to declare war, raise armies, equip navies, and establish rules for the military. Another series of delegated powers is related to control of the economy, including the power to coin money, to control its value, and to regulate foreign and interstate commerce. The national government has been given independent powers of taxation "to pay the debts and provide for the common defense and general welfare of the United States." It has the power to establish its own court system, to decide cases arising under the Constitution and the laws and treaties of the United States and cases involving certain kinds of parties. The national government

---

[6] *Texas* v. *White*, 7 Wallace 700 (1869).

was given the authority to grant copyright patents, establish post offices, enact bankruptcy laws, punish counterfeiting, punish crimes committed on the high seas, and govern the District of Columbia. (See Table 3–1.) Finally, after seventeen grants of express power, came the power "to make all laws which shall be necessary and proper for carrying into execution the foregoing powers, and all other powers vested by this constitution in the government of the United States or in any department or officer thereof." This is generally referred to as the Necessary and Proper Clause.

These delegated powers, when coupled with the National Supremacy Clause of Article VI, ensured a powerful national government. The National Supremacy Clause was quite specific regarding the relationship between the national government and the states. In questions involving conflict between the state laws and the Constitution, laws, or treaties of the United States:

> This constitution, and the laws of the United States which shall be made in pursuance thereof; and all treaties made or which shall be made under the authority of the United States shall be the supreme law of the land; and the judges in every state shall be bound thereby, anything in the constitution or laws of any state to the contrary notwithstanding.

Reserved Powers   Despite these broad grants of power to the national government, the states retained a great deal of authority over the lives of their citizens. The Tenth Amendment reaffirmed the idea that the national government had only certain delegated powers and that all powers not delegated to it were retained by the states:

> The powers not delegated to the United States by the constitution, nor prohibited by it to the states, are reserved to the states respectively, or to the people.

The states retained control over the ownership and use of property; the regulation of offenses against persons and property (criminal law and civil law); the regulation of marriage and divorce; the control of business, labor, farming, trades, and professions; the provision of education, welfare, health, hospitals, and other social welfare activities; and provision of highways, roads, canals, and other public works. The states retained full authority over the organization and control of local government units. Finally, the states, like the federal government, possessed the power to tax and spend for the general welfare.

Powers Denied to the Nation and States   The Constitution denies some powers to both national and state governments; these denials generally safeguard individual rights. Both nation and states are forbidden to pass ex post facto laws or bills of attainder. The first eight amendments to the Constitution, "the Bill of Rights," originally applied to the federal government, but the Fourteenth Amendment, passed by Congress in 1866, provided that the states must also adhere to fundamental guarantees of individual liberty. "No state shall make or enforce any law which shall abridge the privileges or immunities of the citizens of the United States; nor shall any state deprive any person of life, liberty or property without due process of law; nor deny to any person within its jurisdiction equal protection of the laws."

TABLE 3–1   THE CONSTITUTIONAL DISTRIBUTION OF POWERS

(Article and Section numbers of the U.S. Constitution shown in parentheses)

National powers
Military affairs and defense
  Provide for the common defense (I–8)
  Declare war (I–8)
  Raise and support armies (I–8)
  Provide and maintain a navy (I–8)
  Define and punish piracies (I–8)
  Define and punish offenses against the law of nations (I–8)
  Make rules for the regulation of military and naval forces (I–8)
  Provide for calling forth the militia to execute laws, suppress insurrections, and repel invasions (I–8)
  Provide for organizing, arming, and disciplining militia (I–8)
  Declare the punishment of treason (III–3)

Economic matters
  Regulate commerce with foreign nations, among the several states, and with Indian tribes (I–8)
  Establish uniform laws on bankruptcy (I–8)
  Coin money and regulate its value (I–8)
  Regulate value of foreign coin (I–8)
  Fix standards of weights and measures (I–8)
  Provide for patents and copyrights (I–8)
  Establish post offices and post roads (I–8)

Taxing powers
  Levy taxes (I–8)
  Contract and pay debts (I–8)

Governmental organization
  Constitute tribunals inferior to the Supreme Court (I–8, III–1)
  Exercise exclusive legislative power over the seat of government and over certain military installations (I–8)
  Admit new states (IV–3)
  Dispose of and regulate territory or property of the United States (IV–3)
  Make rules for appointments (II–2)

Implied powers
  Make necessary and proper laws for carrying expressed powers into execution (I–8)

Reserved powers of the states
All powers not delegated to the national government by the Constitution, nor prohibited by the Constitution to the states, are reserved to the states "or to the people." (Amendment X)

Restrictions on national power
Economic matters
  No preference to ports of any state (I–9)
  No tax or duty on articles exported from any state (I–9)

Fiscal matters
  No direct tax except by apportionment among states on population bases (I–9), now superseded as to income tax (Amendment XVI)
  No money to be drawn from Treasury except by appropriation (I–9)

TABLE 3–1   *Continued*

Social classes

No title of nobility to be granted (I–9)

Civil and political rights

Congress not to establish religion or prohibit free exercise of religion (Amendment I)

Congress not to abridge freedom of speech, press, assembly, or right of petition (Amendment I)

Right to bear arms protected (Amendment II)

Restriction on quartering of soldiers in private homes (Amendment III)

No unreasonable searches or seizures (Amendment IV)

Guarantees of fair trials (Amendment V, Amendment VI, Amendment VII)

No excessive bail or cruel or unusual punishments (Amendment VIII)

No taking of life, liberty, or property without due process (Amendment V)

Voting not to be denied because of race, color, previous servitude (Amendment XV), or sex (Amendment XIX), or age if 18 or over (Amendment XXVI)

Voting not to be denied because of nonpayment of any tax (Amendment XXIV)

Suspension of habeas corpus limited (I–9)

No bills of attainder (I–9)

No ex post facto laws (I–9)

 Restrictions on the powers of the states

Foreign affairs

States not to enter into treaties, alliances, or confederation (I–10)

No compact with a foreign state, except by congressional consent (I–10)

Military affairs

No letters of marque and reprisal (I–10)

No standing military forces in peace without congressional consent (I–10)

No engagement in war, without congressional consent, except in imminent danger or when invaded (I–10)

Economic matters

No legal tender other than gold or silver coin (I–10)

No separate state coinage (I–10)

No impairment of the obligation of contracts (I–10)

No emission of bills of credit (I–10)

No levying of import or export duties, except reasonable inspection fees, without consent of Congress (I–10)

Civil and political rights

No slavery (Amendment XIII)

No bills of attainder (I–10)

No ex post facto laws (I–10)

No denial of life, liberty, or property by state without due process of law (Amendment XIV)

No denial by state of the equal protection of the laws (Amendment XIV)

No abridgment by state of privileges and immunities of national citizenship (Amendment XIV)

No abridgment of voting rights because of race, color, or previous condition of servitude (Amendment XV)

No abridgment of voting rights because of sex (Amendment XIX)

No poll or other taxes required for voting in federal elections (Amendment XXIV)

TABLE 3–1   *Continued*

Social restrictions
   No titles of nobility (I–10)
General restrictions
   Federal law supreme (VI)
   No payment of debts for rebellion against United States or for emancipated slaves
   (Amendment XIV)
National obligations to the states
   Territorial integrity (IV–3)
   Guarantee of a republican form of government (IV–4)
   Protection against foreign invasion and domestic violence (IV–4)
   Equal representation in the Senate (V)

Some powers were denied only to the states, generally as a safeguard to national unity, including the powers to coin money, enter into treaties with foreign powers, interfere with the obligations of contracts, levy duties on imports or exports without congressional consent, maintain military forces in peacetime, engage in war, or enter into compacts with foreign nations or other states.

The National Government's Obligations to the States   The Constitution imposes several obligations on the national government in its relations with the states. First of all, the states are guaranteed *territorial integrity:* No new state can be created by Congress out of the territory of an existing state without its consent. (Nonetheless, Congress admitted West Virginia to the Union in 1863 when the western counties of Virginia separated from that state during the Civil War. Later a "reconstructed" Virginia legislature gave its approval.) The national government must also guarantee to every state *"a republican form of government."* A republican government is a government by democratically elected representatives. Presumably this clause in the Constitution means that the national government will ensure that no authoritarian or dictatorial regime will be permitted to rule in any state. Apparently this clause does *not* prohibit popular initiatives, referenda, town meetings, or other forms of direct democracy. The Supreme Court has never given any specific meaning to this guarantee. Each state is also guaranteed *equal representation in the U.S. Senate.* Indeed, the Constitution, Article V, prohibits any amendments that would deprive the states of equal representation in the Senate. Finally, the national government is required to *protect each state against foreign invasion and domestic violence.* The protection against foreign invasion is unequivocal, but the clause dealing with domestic violence includes the phrase "upon application of the legislature or the Executive (when the legislature cannot be convened)." Governors have called upon the national government to intervene in riots to maintain public order. But the national government has also intervened *without* "application" by state officials in cases where federal laws are being violated.

State Role in National Government   The states also play an important role in the composition of the national government. U.S. representatives must be appor-

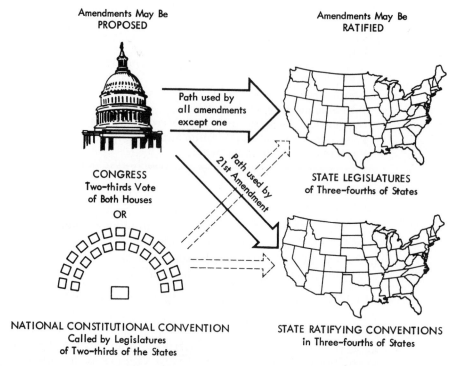

THE STATES' ROLE IN
CONSTITUTIONAL AMENDMENT

Amendments May Be
PROPOSED

Amendments May Be
RATIFIED

Path used by
all amendments
except one

Path used by
21st Amendment

CONGRESS
Two-thirds Vote
of Both Houses

OR

STATE LEGISLATURES
of Three-fourths of States

NATIONAL CONSTITUTIONAL CONVENTION
Called by Legislatures
of Two-thirds of the States

STATE RATIFYING CONVENTIONS
in Three-fourths of States

FIGURE 3–1   The States' Role in Constitutional Amendment

tioned among the states according to their population every ten years. Governors
have the authority to fill vacancies in Congress, and every state must have at least
one representative regardless of population. The Senate of the United States is composed of two senators from each state regardless of the state's population. The
times, places, and manner of holding elections for Congress are determined by the
states. The president is chosen by electors, allotted to each state on the basis of its
senators and representatives. Finally, amendments to the U.S. Constitution must be
ratified by three-fourths of the states. (See Figure 3–1.)

AMENDING THE U.S. CONSTITUTION: THE STATES AND ERA

The power of the states in the American federal system was demonstrated in the
struggle over the Equal Rights Amendment (ERA) to the U.S. Constitution.[7] According to Article V, *the U.S. Constitution cannot be amended without the approval of*

---

[7] For another example of national-state relations in the constitutional amendment process, see
David C. Nice, "State Support for Constitutional Balanced Budget Requirements," *Journal of Politics*, 48
(February 1986), 134–42.

three-fourths of the states, either by the state legislatures or state constitutional ratifying conventions. When Congress proposed ERA to the states in 1972, it did so by more than the necessary two-thirds vote of both the Senate and the House of Representatives. Indeed, Republicans and Democrats, Presidents Nixon, Ford, and Carter (but not Reagan), and most national political leaders endorsed the simple language of the amendment: "Equality of rights under law shall not be denied or abridged by the United States or by any State on account of sex."

Battle in the States   ERA won quick ratification in about half of the states, but by 1975, a growing "Stop ERA" movement slowed progress in the states and threatened to defeat the amendment itself. By 1978, thirty-five state legislatures had ratified ERA. (See Figure 3–2.) (However, five states voted to rescind their earlier ratification. While there is some disagreement about the validity of these "rescissions," most constitutional scholars do not believe a state can rescind its earlier ratification of a constitutional amendment; there is no language in the Constitution referring to rescissions of constitutional amendments.) Leaders of the ERA movement called upon Congress to grant an unprecedented extension of time beyond the traditional seven years to continue the battle for ratification. (The Constitution, Article V, does not specify how long states can consider a constitutional amendment.) In 1978, Congress (by simple majority vote) granted ERA an unprecedented additional three years for state ratification; the new limit was 1982, a full ten years after Congress proposed the original ERA.

Three States Short   Three-quarters of the states *must* concur in a constitutional amendment. This is a powerful tool of the states in our federal system. The wording of the Constitution cannot be altered without the approval of the states, regardless of how much support such a change in wording may have in Washington. Despite national support for ERA, the amendment fell three states short of ratification by the necessary thirty-eight states. Last-ditch attempts to pass ERA in states where the battle was close (Florida, Illinois, and North Carolina) failed in 1982. Unlike his predecessors in the Oval Office, President Reagan opposed ERA, although he did not take an active role in defeating it.

Ladies in Pink   While writers have devoted a great deal of attention to the leaders of the feminist movement in America,[8] less has been said about the active group of women who successfully lobbied *against* ERA in state legislatures. In spite of overwhelming support for ERA from Democratic and Republican presidents and congresses, leading celebrities from television and films, and even a majority of Americans surveyed by national polling organizations, the "ladies in pink" were influential in the defeat of ERA. (The phrase "ladies in pink" refers to a common practice of anti-ERA women lobbyists wearing pink, dressing well, baking apple pies for legislators, and otherwise adopting the traditional symbols of femininity.) Most of the lobbying against ERA in state legislatures was done by women's

---

[8] See J. Freeman, *The Politics of Woman's Liberation* (New York: David McKay Co., Inc., 1975); K. Amundsen, *The Selected Majority* (Englewood Cliffs, NJ: Prentice Hall, 1971); Karen DeCrow, "Who Are We? Survey of N.O.W.'s Membership" (New York: National Organization for Women, 1974).

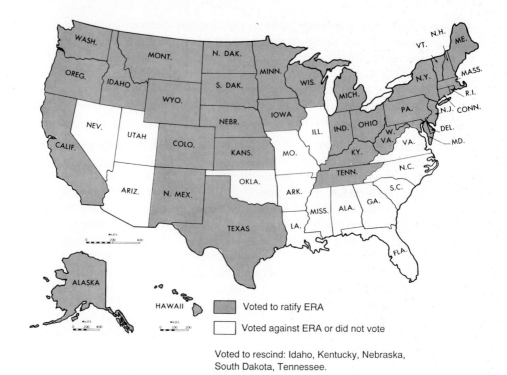

Voted to ratify ERA

Voted against ERA or did not vote

Voted to rescind: Idaho, Kentucky, Nebraska, South Dakota, Tennessee.

FIGURE 3–2   ERA in the States

groups. While not as well organized as the leading feminist groups (NOW, the League of Women Voters, the Women's Political Caucus, and so on), the "ladies in pink" were very much in evidence when state legislatures considered ratification of ERA.

One interesting study comparing pro-ERA and anti-ERA lobbyists revealed the following differences:[9]

Occupation: Nearly three-quarters of the pro-ERA women were employed outside of the home, while nearly three-quarters of the "ladies in pink" were homemakers.

Education and Income: The pro-ERA women were drawn from higher socioeconomic class groups than the anti-ERA women.

Age: A majority of the pro-ERA women lobbyists were under thirty-five, while a majority of the anti-ERA women were over thirty-five.

Religion: Fully 98 percent of the "ladies in pink" were church members, compared to only 48 percent of the pro-ERA women.

In addition to being younger, employed, more educated and affluent, and less religious, the pro-ERA women were decidedly more liberal in their political ideology

---

[9] See Kent L. Tedin et al., "Social Background and Political Differences Between Pro- and Anti-ERA Activists," *American Politics Quarterly,* 5 (July 1977), 395–408.

than were the anti-ERA women. The "ladies in pink" tended to share moderate to conservative ideas on varieties of political issues. The pro-ERA women were more active in politics generally and displayed greater interest in, and information about, public affairs. The surprise is that the "ladies in pink"—mostly homemakers, middle-aged, religious, less educated and less affluent, politically conservative, and less active and knowledgeable about politics—were so effective in halting the Equal Rights Amendment.[10]

CONSTITUTIONAL AND HISTORICAL DEVELOPMENT OF FEDERALISM

The importance of formal constitutional arrangements should not be underestimated. However, the American federal system is a product of more than formal constitutional provisions. It is also shaped by court interpretations of constitutional principles and the history of disputes over state and national authority.

Federal Court Authority   The real meaning of American federalism has emerged in the heat of political conflict between states and nation. In the formative days of the new Republic, Chief Justice John Marshall, who presided over the Supreme Court from 1801 to 1835, became a major architect of American federalism. Under John Marshall, *the Supreme Court assumed the role of arbiter in disputes between state and national authority*. It was under John Marshall that the Supreme Court in *Marbury* v. *Madison* assumed the power to interpret the U.S. Constitution authoritatively. Nothing in the Constitution explicitly gave the Supreme Court the power to render authoritative interpretations of the Constitution. However, John Marshall argued forcefully that Article III of the Constitution, which says that "the judicial power of the United States shall be vested in one Supreme Court," made the Court the final arbiter in conflicts over the meaning of the Constitution. Marshall argued that "the judicial power" historically meant the power to interpret the meaning of the law, and since the Constitution was the supreme *law* of the land, it was the legitimate duty of the Supreme Court to interpret the law. This meant that the Supreme Court assumed the role of umpire of the federal system and referee of conflicts between nation and states.

The fact that the referee of disputes between state and national authority has been the *national* Supreme Court has had a profound influence on the development of American federalism. Since the Supreme Court is a *national* institution, one might say that in disputes between nation and states, one of the members of the two contending teams is also serving as umpire. Constitutionally speaking then, there is really *no* limitation on national as against state authority *if* all three branches of the national government—the Congress, the president, and the Court—act together to override state authority. The Constitution and the laws of the United States "made in pursuance thereof" are the supreme laws of the land, "anything in the constitution or laws of any state to the contrary notwithstanding."

---

[10] See Val Burris, "Who Opposed the ERA? An Analysis of the Social Basis for Antifeminism," *Social Science Quarterly,* 64 (June 1983), 305–17.

Moreover, the Supreme Court, a national institution, through its "judicial power" interprets the Constitution and decides what laws are "made in pursuance thereof." Thus, *Marbury* v. *Madison* paved the way for the development of national power.

Implied Federal Powers   Chief Justice John Marshall was also responsible for making the *Necessary and Proper Clause* the most significant grant of constitutional power to the national government. Political conflict over the scope of national power arose before the new Republic had been in operation for a year. In 1790 Alexander Hamilton, as secretary of the treasury, proposed the establishment of a national bank. Congress acted on Hamilton's suggestion in 1791, establishing a national bank to serve as a depository for national money and to facilitate federal borrowing. Jeffersonians considered the national bank dangerous centralization in government and objected that the power to establish a national bank was nowhere to be found in the enumerated powers of Congress. Thomas Jefferson contended that Congress had no constitutional authority to establish a bank because a bank was not "indispensably necessary" in carrying out its delegated functions. Hamilton replied that Congress could easily deduce the power to establish a bank from grants of authority in the Constitution relating to currency and other aspects of national finance, backed by the clause authorizing Congress "to make all laws which will be necessary and proper for carrying into execution the foregoing powers." Jefferson interpreted the word "necessary" to mean "indispensable," but Hamilton argued that the national government had the right to choose the manner and means of performing its delegated functions and was not restricted to employing only those means considered indispensable in the performance of its functions. The question eventually reached the Supreme Court in 1819 when Maryland levied a tax on the national bank, and the bank refused to pay it. In the case of *McCulloch* v. *Maryland,* Chief Justice John Marshall accepted the broader Hamiltonian version of the Necessary and Proper Clause:

> Let the end be legitimate, let it be within the scope of the Constitution, and all means which are appropriate, which are plainly adopted to the end, which are not prohibited but consistent with the letter and the spirit of the Constitution, are constitutional.[11]

The *McCulloch* case firmly established the principle that the Necessary and Proper Clause gives Congress the right to choose its means for carrying out the enumerated powers of the national government. Today, Congress can devise programs, create agencies, and establish national laws on the basis of long chains of reasoning from the most meager phrases of the constitutional text because of the broad interpretation of the Necessary and Proper Clause.

Secession and Civil War   The Civil War was, of course, the greatest crisis of the American federal system. Did a state have the right to oppose national law to the point of secession? In the years preceding the Civil War, John C. Calhoun argued

---

[11] *McCulloch* v. *Maryland,* 4 Wheaton 316 (1819).

that the Constitution was a compact made by the *states* in a sovereign capacity rather than by the *people* in their national capacity. Calhoun contended that the federal government was an agent of the states, that the states retained their sovereignty in this compact, and that the federal government must not violate the compact, under the penalty of state nullification or even secession. Calhoun's doctrine was embodied in the Constitution of the Confederacy, which begins with the words "We, the people of the Confederate States, each state acting in its sovereign and independent character, in order to form a permanent federal government . . ." This wording contrasts with the preamble of the United States Constitution, "We, the people of the United States, in order to form a more perfect union . . ." The difference emphasizes Calhoun's thesis that the central government should be an agency of the states rather than of the people.

The issue was decided in the nation's bloodiest war. What was decided on the battlefield between 1861 and 1865 was confirmed by the Supreme Court in 1869: "Ours is an indestructible union, composed of indestructible states."[12] Yet the states' rights doctrines, and political disputes over the character of American federalism, did not disappear with Lee's surrender at Appomattox. The Thirteenth, Fourteenth, and Fifteenth Amendments, passed by the Reconstruction Congress, were clearly aimed at limiting state power in the interests of individual freedom. The Thirteenth Amendment eliminated slavery in the states; the Fifteenth Amendment prevented states from discriminating against blacks in the right to vote; and the Fourteenth Amendment declared that "No State shall make or enforce any law which shall abridge the privileges or immunities of citizens of the United States; nor shall any state deprive any person of life, liberty, or property without due process of law; nor deny to any person within its jurisdiction the equal protection of the laws." These amendments delegated to Congress the power to secure their enforcement. Yet for several generations these amendments were narrowly construed and added little, if anything, to national power. By tacit agreement, after southern states demonstrated their continued political importance in the disputed presidential election of 1876, the federal government refrained from using its power to enforce these civil rights.

Civil Rights   However, after World War II, the Supreme Court began to build a national system of civil rights based upon the Fourteenth Amendment. In early cases, the Court held the Fourteenth Amendment prevented states from interfering with free speech, free press, or religious practices. Not until 1954, in the Supreme Court's desegregation decision in *Brown* v. *Board of Education* in Topeka, Kansas, did the Court begin to call for the full assertion of national authority on behalf of civil rights.[13]

The Supreme Court's use of the Fourteenth Amendment to ensure a national system of civil rights supported by the power of the federal government is an important step in the evolution of the American federal system. The controversy over

---

[12] *Texas* v. *White,* 7 Wallace 700 (1869).

[13] *Brown* v. *Board of Education of Topeka, Kansas,* 347 U.S. 483 (1954).

federally imposed desegregation in the southern states renewed the debate over states' rights versus national authority. Despite the clear mandate of the Supreme Court in the *Brown* case, the southern states succeeded in avoiding all but token integration for more than ten years. (See Chapter 14.) Governor Faubus used the Arkansas National Guard to prevent the desegregation of Little Rock Central High School in 1957, but this opposition was ended quickly when President Eisenhower ordered the National Guard removed and sent units of the United States Army to enforce national authority. In 1962 President Kennedy took similar action when Governor Ross Barnett of Mississippi personally barred the entry of a black student to the University of Mississippi, despite a federal court order requiring his admission. Governor George Wallace of Alabama "stood in the doorway" to prevent desegregation but left his post at the doorway several hours later when federal marshals arrived. These actions reinforced the principle of national supremacy in the American federal system.

Interstate Commerce   The growth of national power under the *Interstate Commerce Clause* is also an important development in the evolution of American federalism. The Industrial Revolution in America created a *national* economy with a nationwide network of transportation and communication and the potential for national economic depressions. In response to the growth of the national economy, Congress progressively widened the definition of "interstate commerce." Industrialization created interstate businesses, which could be regulated by the national government.

Yet for a time, the Supreme Court placed obstacles in the way of national authority over the economy, and by so doing created a "crisis" in American federalism. For many years, the Court narrowly construed interstate commerce to mean only the movement of goods and services across state lines, and until the late 1930s, the Supreme Court insisted that agriculture, mining, manufacturing, and labor relations were outside the reach of the delegated powers of the national government. However, when confronted with the depression of the 1930s and the threat of presidential attack on the membership of the Court itself, the Court yielded. In *National Labor Relations Board* v. *Jones and Laughlin Steel Corporation* in 1937, the Court recognized the principle that production and distribution of goods and services for a national market could be regulated by Congress under the Interstate Commerce Clause. The effect was to give the national government effective control over the national economy, and today few economic activities are not within the reach of congressional power.

HOW MONEY SHIFTED POWER TO WASHINGTON

Over the years the national government has acquired much greater power in the federal system than the Founders originally envisioned. The growth of power in Washington has not necessarily meant a reduction in the powers of states and local governments—in fact, *all* governments have vastly increased their powers and responsibilities in the twentieth century. Nevertheless, today the national government is no longer really a government with only "delegated" or "enumerated" powers. The delegated powers of the national government are now so broadly defined—particularly the power to tax and spend for the general welfare —that the government in Washington is involved in every aspect of American life. There are really no segments of public activity "reserved" to the states or the people.

The Earliest Federal Aid   It is possible to argue that even in the earliest days of the Republic, the national government was involved in public activities that were not specifically delegated to it in the Constitution.[14] The first Congress of the United States in the famous Northwest Ordinance, providing for the government of the territories to the west of the Appalachian Mountains, authorized grants of federal land for the establishment of public schools, and by so doing, showed a concern for education, an area "reserved" to the states by the Constitution. Again, in 1863 in the Morrill Land Grant Act, Congress provided grants of land to the states to promote higher education.

Money, Power, and the Income Tax   The date 1913, when the Sixteenth Amendment gave the federal government the power to tax income directly, marked the beginning of a new era in American federalism. Congress had been given the power to tax and spend for the general welfare in Article I of the Constitution. However, the Sixteenth Amendment helped to shift the balance of financial power from the states to Washington, when it gave Congress the power to tax the incomes of corporations and individuals on a progressive basis. The income tax gave the federal government the power to raise large sums of money, which it proceeded to spend for the general welfare as well as for defense. It is no coincidence that the first major grant-in-aid programs (agricultural extension in 1914, highways in 1916, vocational education in 1917, and public health in 1918) all came shortly after the inauguration of the federal income tax.

Financial Centralization   At the beginning of the twentieth century, most government activity in America was carried on at the local level. Table 3–2 reveals that local governments once made about 59 percent of all government expenditures in the United States, compared to 35 percent for the federal government and 6 percent for state governments. But the Great Depression of the 1930s and World War II in the 1940s helped bring about centralization in the American federal system. In recent decades, federal spending has amounted to 55 to 60 percent of all government spending in the United States.

The extent of centralization of government activity in the American federal system varies widely according to policy area (see Table 3–3). In the fields of national defense, space research, and postal service, the federal government assumes almost exclusive responsibility. In all other fields, state and local governments share responsibility and costs with the federal government. State and local governments assume the major share of the costs of education, highways, health and hospitals, sanitation, and fire and police protection. Welfare costs are shared, and the

---

[14] See Daniel J. Elazer, *The American Partnership: Inter-Governmental Cooperation in Nineteenth-Century United States* (Chicago: University of Chicago Press, 1962).

TABLE 3–2   A COMPARISON OF THE EXPENDITURES OF FEDERAL, STATE, AND LOCAL GOVERNMENTS OVER EIGHT DECADES

	Percentages of Total General Expenditures of Governments in the U.S.		
	FEDERAL[a]	STATE[b]	LOCAL[b]
1902	35	6	59
1927	31	13	56
1936	50	14	36
1944	91	3	7
1950	60	16	24
1960	60	15	25
1970	62	10	28
1980	64	9	27
1985	65	10	25
1990	64	11	25

[a] Figures include Social Security and trust fund expenditures.

[b] State payments to local governments are shown as local government expenditures; federal grants-in-aid shown as federal expenditures.

Source: Statistical Abstract of the United States, 1992, p. 279.

federal government assumes the major share of the costs of natural resource development and housing and community development.

CONGRESS RAISES THE DRINKING AGE

Nowhere among Congress's enumerated powers in the U.S. Constitution do we find the power to regulate the consumption of alcoholic beverages. Traditionally, the "reserved" powers of the states included the protection of the health, safety, and well-being of their own citizens. And every state set minimum drinking age laws of its own.

In the early 1970s most states lowered their drinking age to eighteen, influenced perhaps by the Twenty-sixth Amendment giving eighteen-year-olds the right to vote. But in the early 1980s, the states individually began to raise the drinking age, as part of a national movement against drunk driving. By 1984 about half of the states had changed the legal drinking age to twenty-one (such as California); other states chose nineteen (including New York, Florida, and Texas) or twenty (such as Massachusetts and Connecticut); and still other states allowed eighteen-year-olds to buy beer and wine but required a person to be twenty-one in order to buy "distilled spirits" (such as Colorado, Kansas). Only a few states (Vermont, Rhode Island, Louisiana, Hawaii) retained a general eighteen-year-old drinking age.

The minimum drinking age became a national issue largely as a result of emotional appeals by groups such as Mothers Against Drunk Driving (MADD). Po-

TABLE 3–3 FEDERAL AND STATE-LOCAL SHARES OF EXPENDITURES BY POLICY AREAS, 1927–1990

	1927		1938		1970		1990	
	FEDERAL[a]	STATE AND LOCAL	FEDERAL[a]	STATE AND LOCAL	FEDERAL[a]	STATE AND LOCAL	FEDERAL[a]	STATE AND LOCAL
National defense	100%	0%	100%	0%	100%	0%	100%	0%
Space research	100	0	100	0	100	0	100	0
Postal service	100	0	100	0	100	0	100	0
Education	1	99	6	94	15	85	14	86
Highways	1	99	23	77	23	77	19	81
Welfare	6	94	13	87	41	59	40	60
Health and hospitals	18	82	19	81	34	66	19	81
Police	7	93	5	95	8	92	15	85
Natural resources	31	69	81	19	77	23	73	27
Housing and community development	—	—	—	—	56	44	52	48

[a] Federal grants-in-aid shown as federal expenditures.

Source: U.S. Statistical Abstract of the United States 1992, p. 280

73

litically these appeals were more effective than any scientific studies of alcohol-related deaths. Nonetheless, statistical evidence presented to Congress by the National Transportation Safety Board showed that teenagers were more likely to be involved in alcohol-related traffic deaths than nonteenagers. Indeed, drunk driving was the leading cause of death among teenagers.[15] The National Student Association, restaurant owners, and liquor industry countered that teenagers were no worse offenders than those in the twenty-one to twenty-five age group and that the selection of all teenagers for special restrictions was age discrimination. But the tragic stories told at televised committee hearings by grieving mothers of dead teenagers swept away the opposition.

Federalism arguments were also swept away. Several senators argued that a national drinking age infringed on the powers of the states in a matter traditionally under state control. However, the new law did not *directly* mandate a national drinking age. Instead, it ordered the withholding of 10 percent of all federal highways funds from any state that failed to raise its minimum drinking age to twenty-one. States retained the right to ignore the national drinking age and give up a significant portion of their highway funds. This was the same approach taken by Congress in 1974 in establishing a national 55-mile-per-hour speed limit. Opponents of this device labeled it "federal blackmail" and a federal intrusion into state responsibilities. For some state officials the issue was not teen drinking but rather the preemption of state authority.

But proponents of the legislation cited the national interest in a uniform minimum drinking age. They argued that protecting the lives of young people outweighed the states' interest in preserving their authority. Moreover, teens were crossing state lines to go to states which lower drinking ages. New York, for example, with a minimum drinking age of nineteen was attracting teenagers from Pennsylvania and New Jersey, where the drinking age was twenty-one. Reports of "bloody borders" justified national action to establish a uniform drinking age. While the Reagan White House had pledged to return responsibilities to the states, it did not wish to offend the nation's mothers on such an emotional issue. Despite initial reservations, President Reagan supported the bill and signed it into law in 1984.

Constitutionally, Congress was exercising its powers to spend money for the general welfare. Congress was not *directly* legislating in an area "reserved" to the states—protection of health, safety, and well-being. Instead, Congress was threatening to withhold some *federal* highway grant monies from states that did not meet a federal requirement. Technically states remain free to set their own minimum drinking age. Despite heated arguments in many state legislatures, all but Wyoming adopted the twenty-one-year-old national drinking age by 1988. Money is power; this axiom holds true in the American federal system as in politics generally.

---

[15] Congressional Quarterly, *Weekly Report,* June 30, 1984, p. 1557.

FEDERAL GRANTS-IN-AID: PROS AND CONS

The federal "grant-in-aid" has been the principal instrument in the expansion of national power. Recent growth of federal grants is depicted in Figure 3–3. Approximately one-sixth of all state and local government revenues are from federal grants. This money is paid out through a staggering number and variety of programs. Federal grants may be obtained to assist in everything from the preservation of historic buildings, the development of minority-owned businesses, and aid for foreign refugees, to the drainage of abandoned mines, riot control, and school milk.

Pros   There are several reasons for this growth of federal aid. First of all, these grants permit the federal government to single out and support those states and local government services in which it has a particular interest. Grants permit the government to set national goals and priorities in all levels of government without formally altering the federal structure. Thus, as problems of public assistance, urban renewal, highway construction, education, and poverty acquire national significance, they can be dealt with by the application of national resources.

Second, the grant-in-aid system adds to state–local revenue resources. States and communities must raise revenue and at the same time carry on interstate and interlocal competition for industry and wealth. Although the influence of tax considerations on industrial location decisions may be overstated by most lawmakers, this overstatement itself is part of the political lore at statehouses and courthouses and operates to impede revenue raising.

Finally, grants-in-aid provide an opportunity for the national government to ensure a uniform level of public service throughout the nation—for example, federal grants-in-aid help ensure a minimum level of existence for the poverty stricken regardless of where they live. This aspect of federal policy assumes that in some parts of the nation, state and local governments are unable, or perhaps unwilling, to devote their resources to raising public service levels to minimum national standards.

Cons   Whenever the national government contributes financially to state or local programs, state and local officials are left with less freedom of choice than they would have had otherwise. Federal grants-in-aid are invariably accompanied by federal standards or "guidelines," which must be adhered to if states and communities are to receive their federal money.

No state is required to accept a federal grant-in-aid. Thus, states are not required to meet federal standards or guidelines, set forth as conditions. However, it is very difficult for states and communities to resist the pressure to accept federal money. It is sometimes said that states are "bribed and blackmailed" into federal grant-in-aid programs. They are "bribed" by the temptation of much-needed federal money, and they are "blackmailed" by the thought that other states and communities will get the federal money if they do not, money contributed in part by their own citizens through federal taxation.

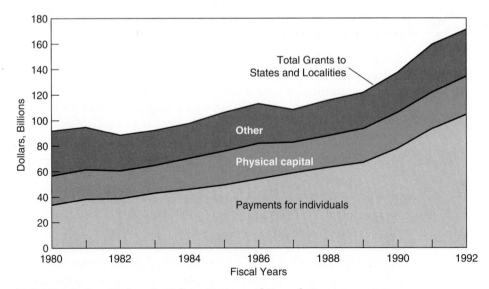

FIGURE 3–3   Federal Aid to State and Local Governments
Source: The budget of the United States Government Fiscal Year, 1992

Cities are sometimes pressured to apply for funds for projects they do not really need, simply because federal funds are available, while they may receive little or no federal assistance for more vital programs. Federal grant money is frequently provided for "new" or "innovative" or "demonstration" programs, when the real problems facing states and communities may be in traditional public services such as police, sewage, and sanitation.

The maze of separate federal grant programs creates an administrative quagmire. State and local officials spend a great deal of time in "grantsmanship"— learning where to find federal funds, how to apply, and how to write applications to meet purposes and guidelines.

Finally, the grant-in-aid system assumes that federal officials are better judges of goals and priorities at all levels of government than are state or local officials. State and local officials do not determine what activities in their states and communities will receive federal money—federal officials determine these priorities. Moreover, in many grant programs federal officials must approve each funded project—a housing project in Des Moines, an airport in Denver, a new set of welfare regulations in California, a sewage disposal system in Baton Rouge, an urban renewal project in Alabama, or a highway in North Dakota. Whether federal officials or state and local officials are better judges of public goals and priorities is, of course, a political question.

Grant Purposes   The largest portion of federal grant-in-aid money is devoted to welfare (especially Aid to Families with Dependent Children) and health (especially Medicaid's health care for the poor). In 1992, over 64 percent of total grant money was used for these purposes. Less than 12 percent was used for highways and tran-

TABLE 3–4   FEDERAL GRANT OUTLAYS BY FUNCTION

Function	1990	1992	1996[a]
(In billions of dollars)			
National defense	0.2	0.1	0.1
Energy	0.5	0.4	0.3
Natural resources and environment	3.7	3.8	2.9
Agriculture	1.3	1.4	1.7
Transportation	19.2	20.2	23.3
Community and regional development	5.0	4.3	3.6
Education, training, employment and social services	23.1	27.6	28.9
Health	43.9	63.4	103.7
Income security	37.0	46.3	55.6
Veterans benefits and services	0.1	0.2	0.2
Administration of justice	0.6	0.8	0.7
General government	2.3	2.2	2.3
Total outlays	136.9	171.0	223.2

[a] Estimated

Source: Budget of the United States Government, 1992, Part II–164.

sit, and only about 16 percent for education. Given the skyrocketing costs of health care in the United States, it is estimated that by 1996 federal grants to the states for Medicaid alone will rise to over $100 billion—nearly half of all federal aid money (see Table 3–4). Rising federal aid for Medicaid is not really a sign of how much the federal government is helping the states, but rather a sign of how it is causing them to bear a very heavy fiscal burden. On the average, state and local governments pay 43 percent of the cost of Medicaid, while the federal government pays 57 percent. Over time the federal government has mandated expanding Medicaid services and new eligibility groups. Hence, federal aid is actually helping to drive up the costs of Medicaid to state and local governments.

Grantsmanship   Federal money flows unevenly among the states. While about 18 percent of all state and local government revenue comes in the form of federal aid, the percentage is much higher in some states than others. (See Figure 3–4.)

The federal grant system is not neutral in its impact on the states, nor is it intended to be. Many grant programs are based upon formulas that incorporate various indications of need and financial ability. Federal aid is supposed to be "targeted" on national problems.[16] The effect of differential grant allocations among the states, combined with differences among state populations in federal tax collections, is to *redistribute* federal money throughout the nation. The Tax Foundation regularly estimates the extent of this redistribution by calculating the taxes paid by

---

[16] Robert M. Stein, "The Allocation of Federal Aid Monies: The Synthesis of Demand-Side and Supply-Side Explanations," *American Political Science Review,* 75 (June, 1981), 334–43.

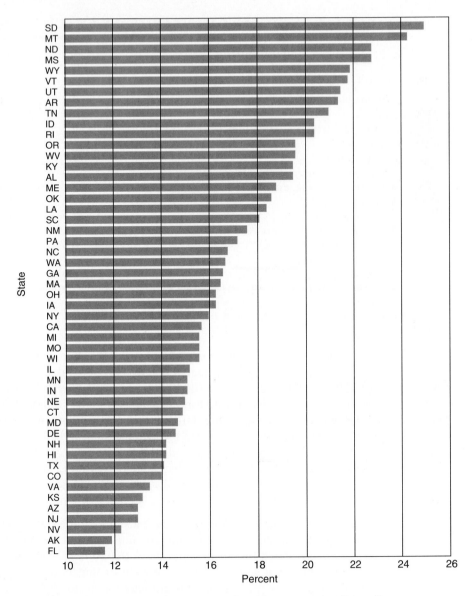

FIGURE 3–4 **Reliance on Federal Aid—Percent of Total State–Local Revenue from Federal Aid**

Source: National Abstract of the United States 1992, p. 286.

residents of each state to finance federal grants, and then subtracting the total federal grant money that comes to the state. In this fashion, the Tax Foundation estimates whether a state receives more or less from the federal government than it contributes in taxes. The results of these calculations are shown in Figure 3–5. Note

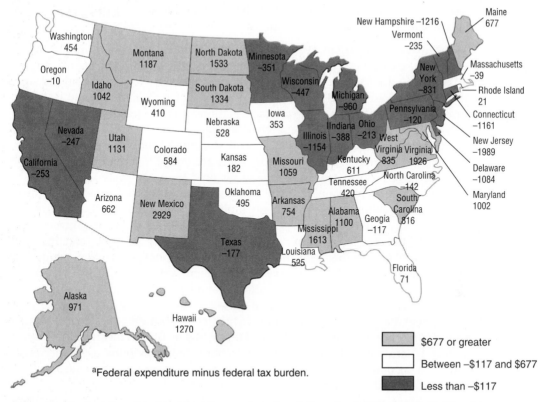

FIGURE 3–5   Per Capita Net Flow of Federal Funds, 1988–1990 (dollars)*

*Note: The District of Columbia is not included.

Source: ACIR computations based on data from the U.S. Department of Commerce, Bureau of the Census, *Federal Expenditures by State for Fiscal Year 1990,* Table 11; and Tax Foundation, "Federal Tax Burden by State," May 1990, and *Facts and Figures on Government Finance,* 1991 Edition, p. 146.

that the big winners in the federal grant game are generally rural states; the losers are the urban states.

FEDERALISM: VARIATIONS ON THE THEME

Dual Federalism (1787–1913)   For the nation's first hundred years, the pattern of federal–state relations has been described as *dual federalism.* Under this pattern, the states and the nation divided most governmental functions. The national government concentrated its attention on the "delegated" powers—national defense, foreign affairs, tariffs, commerce crossing state lines, coining money, establishing standard weights and measures, maintaining a post office and building post roads, and admitting new states. State governments decided the important domestic policy issues—slavery (until the Civil War), education, welfare, health, and criminal justice. This separation of policy responsibilities was once compared to a "layer cake,"[17] with local governments at the base, state governments in the middle, and the national government at the top.

Cooperative Federalism (1913–1964)   The Industrial Revolution and the development of a national economy, the income tax which shifted financial resources to the national government, and the challenges of two world wars and the Great Depression, all combined to end the distinction between national and state concerns. The new pattern of federal–state relations was labeled *cooperative federalism.* Both the nation and the states exercised responsibilities for welfare, health, highways, education, and criminal justice. This merging of policy responsibilities was compared to a "marble cake." "As the colors are mixed in a marble cake, so functions are mixed in the American federal system."[18]

The Great Depression of the 1930s forced states to ask for federal financial assistance in dealing with poverty, unemployment, and old age. Governors welcomed massive federal public works projects. In addition, the federal government intervened directly in economic affairs, labor relations, business practices, and agriculture. Through the grant-in-aid device, the national government cooperated with the states in public assistance, employment services, child welfare, public housing, urban renewal, highway building, and vocational education.

Yet even in this period of shared national–state responsibility, the national government emphasized cooperation in achieving common national and state goals. Congress generally acknowledged that it had no direct constitutional authority to regulate public health, safety, or welfare. Congress relied primarily on its powers to tax and spend for the general welfare, and to provide financial assistance to state and local governments to achieve shared goals.

Centralized Federalism (1964–1980)   Over the years it became increasingly difficult to maintain the fiction that the national government was merely assisting the states in performing their domestic responsibility. By the time President Lyndon B. Johnson launched the "Great Society" in 1964, the federal government clearly set forth its own "national" goals. Virtually all problems confronting American society—from solid-waste disposal and water and air pollution to consumer safety, home insulation, noise abatement, and even metric conversion—were declared to be national problems. Congress legislated directly on any matter it chose, without regard to its "enumerated powers" and without pretense to financial assistance. The Supreme Court no longer concerned itself with the "reserved" powers of the states; the Tenth Amendment lost most of its meaning. The pattern of national–state relations became centralized. As for the cake analogies, one commentator observed: "The frosting had moved up to the top, something like a pineapple upside-down cake."[19]

---

[17] Morton Grodzins, *The American System* (Chicago: Rand McNally, 1966), pp. 8–9.

[18] Ibid., p. 265.

[19] Charles Press, *State and Community Governments in the Federal System* (New York: John Wiley, 1979), p. 78.

THE *NEW FEDERALISM*

Efforts to reverse the flow of power to Washington and return responsibilities to state and local government have been labeled the *New Federalism*. The phrase originated in the administration of President Richard M. Nixon, who used it to describe General Revenue Sharing—federal sharing of tax revenues with state and local governments with few strings attached. More recently, however, New Federalism was used by President Ronald Reagan to describe a series of proposals designed to reduce federal involvement in domestic programs and encourage states and cities to undertake greater policy responsibilities themselves. According to President Reagan:

> Our citizens feel they have lost control of even the most basic decisions made about the essential services of government, such as schools, welfare, roads, and even garbage collection. They are right. A maze of interlocking jurisdictions and levels of government confronts the average citizen in trying to solve even the simplest of problems. They do not know where to turn to for answers, who to hold accountable, who to praise, who to blame, who to vote for or against. The main reason for this is the overpowering growth of federal grants-in-aid programs during the past few decades.[20]

General Revenue Sharing   Although the Reagan administration ended General Revenue Sharing (GRS) in implementing *its* definition of New Federalism, the original GRS legislation in 1972 was designed as a conservative alternative to categorical grants by federal agencies for specific projects. It was argued that unrestricted federal money grants to state and local government was preferable to centralized bureaucratic decision making in Washington. GRS promised to reverse the flow of power to federal bureaucrats, end excessive red tape, and revitalize state and local governments. GRS was strongly supported by state and local government officials, who were happy to have the federal government collect tax money and then turn it over to them to spend. The history of GRS shows that these monies were used for common state and local government functions—police, fire, sewage, waste disposal, or transportation.[21] But revenue sharing never really replaced the hundreds of categorical grant programs; it was simply an added source of state and local government revenue.[22]

The Reagan administration, confronting high federal deficits and wanting to reduce Washington's role in domestic policy, undertook a long and eventually successful effort to end General Revenue Sharing. The president argued that it was unreasonable to expect the federal government, which was running deep deficits, to

---

[20] President Ronald Reagan, State of the Union Address, January, 1982.

[21] Richard P. Nathan et al., *Monitoring Revenue Sharing* (Washington, DC: Brookings Institution, 1975).

[22] See Diel S. Wright and Alfred R. Light, "The Indeterminants of State Revenue Sharing," *Journal of Politics,* 37 (February 1977), 457–63.

turn over revenues to state and local governments, which had no deficits. (Most state and local governments are prohibited by their own constitutions and charters from having deficits in their operating budgets; bond issues for capital improvement must usually be approved by local residents in referenda.) Most GRS funds went for traditional services which local taxpayers should fund themselves. For several years, state and local government officials successfully lobbied Congress to restore GRS funds cut from the president's budget. But deficit pressures finally ended GRS in 1986.

Block Grants   Another approach to cutting federal strings in grant-in-aid programs is the *block grant*. Block grants may be used by states and communities for projects decided at the local level within a broad category—"community development" or "law enforcement," for example. Federal agencies still supervise block grants, but specific projects are supposed to be decided at the local level. Obviously, block grants do not give states and communities the same freedom as revenue sharing money. But block grants provide greater flexibility than traditional project grants. State and local officials may use block-grant funds for their stated purpose without seeking the approval of federal agencies for specific projects. Congress endorsed these block grants, but the struggle between categorical grant interest (liberals and Democrats) and the consolidationists (Reagan and the Republicans) was really a draw. Many categorical grant programs were merged (notably in health services; alcohol, drug abuse, and mental health; social services; maternal and child health; community services; community development; and education), but many others remained independent.

Reducing State–Local Dependence on Federal Grants   Perhaps the most important accomplishment of the Reagan administration's New Federalism was a reversal of the historical trend of the greater dependence of state and local governments on federal money. In the years prior to 1980, state and local governments had become increasingly dependent on federal grants as sources of revenue. Federal grants rose to over one-quarter of all state–local expenditures in 1980 (see Table 3–5). Total federal aid dollars continued to rise during the Reagan years, but not at the same rate as in previous years. Many state and local officials sought to blame "cutbacks in federal aid" for various troubles they encountered. It is true, of course, that federal aid declined somewhat in relative terms: as a percentage of GNP, as a percentage of total federal outlays, and most importantly as a percentage of state–local revenue. But this occurred because grants did not rise as fast as these denominators, not because of any overall "cutbacks."

However, it is not likely that presidents or Congress members or candidates for these national offices will ever be moved to restrain national power. Congress is not likely to pass constitutional amendments limiting its own powers over the states, nor can the states likely muster the political support necessary to initiate such amendments themselves. People expect federal officials to "do something" about virtually every problem that confronts individuals, families, communities, or the nation. Politicians gain very little by telling their constituents that a particular problem is not a federal problem.

TABLE 3–5   TRENDS IN FEDERAL GRANTS-IN-AID

	Total Federal Grants (Billion Dollars)	Federal Grants as a Percent of:		
		Total Federal Spending	State and Local Expenditures	Gross National Product
1950	2.3	5.3	10.4	0.8
1960	7.0	7.6	14.6	1.4
1970	24.1	12.3	19.2	2.4
1975	49.8	15.0	22.7	3.3
1980	91.5	15.5	25.8	3.4
1985	105.9	11.2	21.1	2.7
1990	136.9	11.0	18.0	3.0

Source: U.S. Office of Management and Budget, *Special Analysis of the Budget 1992,* Part II–166.

COERCIVE FEDERALISM

Can Congress *directly* regulate the traditional functions of state and local governments? We know that Congress can influence the actions of state and local governments by offering them grants of money and then threatening to withdraw them if they do not meet federal rules, regulations, or "guidelines." But can Congress, in the exercise of its broad constitutional powers, legislate directly about traditional functions of state and local governments—schools, streets, police and fire protection, water and sewers, refuse disposal? Can the national government by law treat the states as administrative units required to carry out the mandates of Congress?

Certainly the historical answer to this question was "No." A typical nineteenth-century description of federalism by the U.S. Supreme Court asserted that the federal government could not intrude or interfere with the independent powers of state governments and vice versa:

> There are within the territorial limits of each state two governments [state and national], restricted in their spheres of action, but independent of each other, and supreme within their respective spheres. Each has its separate departments, each has its distinct laws, and each has its own tribunes for their enforcement. Neither government can intrude within the jurisdiction of the other or authorize any interference therein by its judicial officers with the action of the other.[23]

---

[23] *Tarbels Case,* 13 Wall. 397 (1872). Also cited and discussed in Deil S. Wright, *Understanding Intergovernmental Relations* (Boston: Duxberg Press, 1978), p. 22.

Perhaps this separation and independence never really characterized relations between the national government and the state governments. But at least state governments were viewed as independent authorities which could not be directly coerced by the national government in their traditional functions. Indeed, in 1976 the U.S. Supreme Court ruled that Congress did *not* have the authority to require state and local governments to observe federal wage and hour laws for their own employees.[24] But this decision, hailed as a reaffirmation of American federalism, was soon reversed by the Supreme Court itself.

Direct Congressional Regulation of State and Local Governments
Ordinarily, Congress is careful not to give direct orders to state or local governments. Instead, Congress involves itself in state and local affairs by granting or withholding federal dollars depending on whether states and cities do what Congress wishes. (For example, Congress did not directly enact the 55-mile-an-hour speed limit; instead Congress threatened to withhold federal highway money from states that did not pass such a speed limit themselves.) In theory at least, states and cities remain independent; they *could* forgo the federal government's money and conduct their own affairs as they please. But in 1974 in amending its Fair Labor Standards Act, Congress decided to directly order state and local governments to obey minimum wage and hour legislation for all public employees. When the League of Cities, acting on behalf of all state and local governments, challenged the constitutionality of this law, the U.S. Supreme Court first ruled (five to four) that Congress could *not* order the states to do anything in matters traditionally reserved to the states.

However, in its 1985 *Garcia* decision, the U.S. Supreme Court reversed itself and removed all barriers to direct congressional legislation in matters traditionally "reserved" to the states.[25] The Court dismissed the argument that the nature of American federalism and the reserved powers clause of the Tenth Amendment prevented Congress from directly legislating in state and local affairs. The Court held that it would no longer intervene to protect state powers, that judicial intervention was "unworkable," and that Congress itself should decide how far its own powers extended to state and local affairs.

Congressional Regulation of State Taxes   Nearly a century ago, the U.S. Supreme Court held that Congress could not levy taxes on the states or on their bonds or notes.[26] Intergovernmental tax immunity was believed to be an integral part of the Tenth Amendment's guarantee of the reserved powers of the states. The states could not tax federal bonds and the nation could not tax state bonds. But in 1987 the U.S. Supreme Court shocked state and local officials and the municipal bond

---

[24] *National League of Cities* v. *Usery,* 426 U.S. 833 (1976).

[25] *Garcia* v. *San Antonio Metropolitan Transit Authority,* 105 U.S. 1005 (1985).

[26] *Pollock* v. *Farmers Loan and Trust Company,* 157 U.S. 429 (1895).

market by holding that Congress could if it wished levy taxes on the interest received from state and local bonds. In a dissent, Justice Sandra Day O'Connor observed that "the Court has failed to enforce the constitutional safeguards of state autonomy and self-sufficiency that may be found in the Tenth Amendment and the Guarantee Clause, as well as in the principles of federalism implicit in the Constitution."[27]

Federal Preemptions   The supremacy of federal laws over those of the states, spelled out in the Supremacy Clause of the Constitution, permits Congress to decide whether or not state laws in a particular field are preempted by federal law. *Total preemption* refers to the federal government's assumption of all regulatory powers in a particular field—for example, copyrights, bankruptcy, railroads, and airlines. No state regulations in a totally preempted field are permitted. *Partial preemption* stipulates that a state law on the same subject is valid as long as it does not conflict with the federal law in the same area. For example, the Occupational Safety and Health Act of 1970 specifically permits state regulation of any occupational safety or health issue on which the federal Occupational Safety and Health Administration (OSHA) has *not* developed a standard; but once OSHA enacts a standard, all state standards are nullified. Yet another form of the partial preemption, the *standard partial preemption*, permits states to regulate activities in a field already regulated by the federal government, as long as state regulatory standards are at least as stringent as those of the federal government. Usually states must submit their regulations to the responsible federal agency for approval; the federal agency may revoke a state's regulating power if it fails to enforce the approved standards. For example, the federal Environmental Protection Agency (EPA) permits state environmental regulations that meet or exceed EPA standards. Occasionally Congress grants preemptive relief to states in response to protests that federal regulations are incompatible with state or local conditions. For example, Congress permits states to petition the U.S. Department of Transportation to limit the size of commercial tractor-trailers on interstate highways within a state.

Federal Mandates   Federal mandates are orders to state and local governments to comply with federal laws. Federal mandates occur in a wide variety of areas—from civil rights and voter rights laws to conditions of jails and juvenile detention centers, minimum wage and worker safety regulations, air and water pollution controls, and requirements for access for disabled people. State and local governments frequently complain that compliance with federal government mandates imposes costs on them that are seldom reimbursed. President Bush voiced this complaint in his 1992 State of the Union message: "If Congress passes a mandate, it should be forced to pay for it and to balance the cost with savings elsewhere. After all, a mandate just increases someone else's burden, and that means higher taxes at

---

[27] *South Carolina v. Barker*, 485 U.S. 505 (1988).

the state and local level." True, but neither Congress nor the president is likely to act on these sentiments in an era of high federal deficits.[28]

REPRESENTATIONAL FEDERALISM

What is left of federalism today? If there are no real constitutional restraints on the powers of the national government, if people look primarily to the national government to solve their problems, if the national government's superior fiscal resources give it powerful leverage over states and communities, what remains of the federal division of power between states and nation? Are there any guarantees of state power remaining in our federal system?

The notion of "representational federalism" denies that there is any constitutional division of powers between states and nation and asserts that federalism is defined by the role of the states in electing members of Congress and the president. The United States is said to retain a federal system because national officials are selected from subunits of government—the president through the allocation of electoral college votes to the states, and the Congress through the allocation of two Senate seats per state and the apportionment of representatives to states based on population. Whatever protection exists for state power and independence must be found in the national political process—in the influence of state and district voters on their senators and congress members. Representational federalism does not recognize any constitutionally protected powers of the states.

Federalism in the *Garcia* Decision   The U.S. Supreme Court appears to have adopted this notion of representational federalism, especially in its *Garcia* decision in 1985. The Court declared that there were *no* "a priori definitions of state sovereignty," *no* "discrete limitations on the objects of federal authority," and *no* protection of state powers in the U.S. Constitution. According to the Court: "State sovereign interests . . . are more properly protected by procedural safeguards inherent in the structure of the federal system than by judicially created limitations on federal power." The Court rhetorically endorsed a federal system, but left it up to the national Congress, rather than the Constitution or the courts, to decide what powers should be exercised by the states and the national government.

In a strongly worded dissenting opinion in the *Garcia* case, Justice Lewis Powell argued that if federalism is to be retained, the Constitution must divide powers, not the Congress. "The states' role in our system of government is a matter of constitutional law, not legislative grace." And the Court must interpret the Constitution, protecting the powers of the states and defining the powers of the national government. In the words of the Supreme Court's dissenting members,

> the extent to which the states may exercise their authority . . . henceforth is to be determined by political decision made by members of the federal government,

---

[28] See Timothy J. Conlan, "Intergovernmental Mandates and Preemption in an Era of Deregulation," *Publius,* 21 (Summer 1991), 43–57.

decision the Court says will not be subjected to judicial review. It does not seem to have occurred to the Court that *it*—an unelected majority of five justices—today rejects almost 200 years of the understanding of the constitutional status of federalism.[29]

Federalism and the "Clear Statement"   However, the Supreme Court may be unwilling to jettison altogether the notion of federalism as the division of power between nation and states. Justice Sandra Day O'Connor, a former Arizona legislator and appellate court judge, has been a staunch defender of federalism on the Supreme Court. Quoting from the *Federalist* and citing the Tenth Amendment, Justice O'Connor wrote the majority opinion in a case considering whether Congress's Age Discrimination Employment Act invalidated a provision of the Missouri Constitution requiring judges to retire at age 70.[30] She cited the "constitutional balance of federal and state powers" as a reason for upholding the Missouri Constitution. Only a "clear statement" by Congress of its intent to override a traditional state power would justify doing so. This "clear statement" rule presumably governs federal laws that may be in conflict with state laws or constitutions. The rule does not prevent Congress from directly regulating state government activity, but it requires Congress to say unambiguously that this is its intent.

CENTRALIZATION WITHIN THE STATES: ERODING LOCAL AUTONOMY

Accompanying the growth of power at the national level has been a centralization of power *within* states in state capitals. Local governments are gradually losing power in relation to state governments. This centralizing tendency continues today.

State vary in their degree of centralization. Centralization can be measured by financial responsibility (the percentage of state–local expenditures paid at the state level; by responsibility for governmental services (the number of major functions performed by the state rather than by local governments); and by work force (the percentage of total state–local public workers employed by the state.[31] These measures are closely interrelated, and it is possible to construct a composite index of centralization in the states. Such an index is shown in Table 3–6. Highly centralized states such as Hawaii have higher percentages of state expenditures, more state services, and proportionately larger state bureaucracies than the decentralized states such as New York and California. Note that there is some tendency for larger states to be decentralized, while smaller states are more centralized.

---

[29] *Garcia* v. *San Antonio Metropolitan Transit Authority* 469 U.S. 528 (1985).

[30] *Gregory* v. *Ashcraft,* 11 S.Ct. 2395 (1991).

[31] See G. Ross Stephens, "State Centralization and the Erosion of Local Autonomy," *Journal of Politics,* 36 (February 1974), 44–76.

TABLE 3–6   CENTRALIZATION WITHIN THE STATES[a]

1957	1986	
CENTRALIZED		
1. Hawaii	1. Hawaii	11. New Mexico
2. Delaware	2. Vermont	12. Massachusetts
3. New Mexico	3. Delaware	13. South Dakota
4. West Virginia	4. Alaska	14. Connecticut
	5. Rhode Island	15. New Jersey
	6. North Dakota	16. Arkansas
	7. Maine	17. Indiana
	8. West Virginia	18. Maryland
	9. South Carolina	19. Oklahoma
	10. Kentucky	20. Montana
PARTLY CENTRALIZED		
5. Alaska	21. Alabama	28. Mississippi
6. Louisiana	22. Louisiana	29. Washington
7. North Carolina	23. Utah	30. Wyoming
8. Arkansas	24. New Hampshire	31. Oregon
9. Oklahoma	25. Virginia	32. Ohio
	26. Pennsylvania	33. Indiana
	27. North Carolina	34. Iowa
BALANCED		
10. Connecticut	35. Wisconsin	42. New York
11. Kentucky	36. Michigan	43. California
12. Maine	37. Missouri	44. Georgia
13. South Carolina	38. Nevada	45. Kansas
14. Vermont	39. Illinois	46. Texas
15. Montana	40. Minnesota	47. Arizona
16. Oregon	41. Tennessee	48. Nebraska
17. Rhode Island		
18. Alabama		
19. Mississippi		
20. New Hampshire		
21. Nevada		
22. Virginia		
23. North Dakota		
24. Washington		
25. South Dakota		
26. Utah		
27. Indiana		
28. Wyoming		
29. Arizona		

TABLE 3–6 *Continued*

1957	1986
PARTLY DECENTRALIZED	
30. Pennsylvania	49. Florida
31. Missouri	50. Colorado
32. Georgia	
33. Florida	
34. Michigan	
35. Tennessee	
36. Maryland	
37. Kansas	
DECENTRALIZED	
38. Iowa	NONE
39. Indiana	
40. Massachusetts	
41. Texas	
42. Colorado	
43. Ohio	
44. Minnesota	
45. Illinois	
46. Nebraska	
47. California	
48. Wisconsin	
49. New Jersey	
50. New York	

[a] Composite rankings based upon state vs. local proportions of financial resources, services, and work force.
Source: Derived from data provided by G. Ross Stephens, University of Missouri, Kansas City.

INTERSTATE RELATIONS—HORIZONTAL FEDERALISM

Full Faith and Credit   The U.S. Constitution provides that "full faith and credit shall be given in each state to the public acts, records, and judicial proceedings of every other state." As more Americans move from state to state, it becomes increasingly important that the states recognize each other's legal instruments. This constitutional clause is intended to protect the rights of individuals who move from one state to another, and it is also intended to prevent individuals from evading their legal responsibilities by crossing state lines. Courts in Illinois must recognize decisions made by courts in Michigan. Contracts entered into in New York may be enforced in Florida. Corporations chartered in Delaware should be permitted to do business in North Dakota. One of the more serious problems in interstate relations today is the failure of the states to meet their obligations under the Full Faith and Credit Clause in the area of domestic relations, including divorce, alimony, child support, and custody of children. The result is now a complex and confused situation in domestic relations law.

Privileges and Immunities   The Constitution also states: "The citizens of each state shall be entitled to all privileges and immunities of citizens in the several states." Apparently the Founding Fathers thought that no state should discriminate against citizens from another state in favor of its own citizens. To do so would seriously jeopardize national unity. This clause also implies that citizens of any state may move freely about the country and settle where they like, with the assurance that as newcomers they will not be subjected to unreasonable discrimination. The newcomer should not be subject to discriminatory taxation; nor barred from lawful occupations under the same conditions as other citizens of the state; nor prevented from acquiring and using property; nor denied equal protection of the laws; nor refused access to the courts. However, states have managed to compromise this constitutional guarantee in several important ways. States establish residence requirements for voting and holding office, which prevent newcomers from exercising the same rights as older residents. States often require periods of residence as a prerequisite for holding a state job or for admission into professional practice such as law or medicine. States discriminate against out-of-state students in the tuition charged in public schools and colleges. Finally, some states are now seeking ways to keep "outsiders" from moving in and presumably altering the "natural" environment.

Extradition   The Constitution also provides that "A person in any state with treason, felony, or other crime who shall flee from justice and be found in another state, shall on the demand of the executive authority from the state from which he fled, be delivered up, to be removed to the state having jurisdiction of the crime." In other words, the Constitution requires governors to extradite fugitives from another state's justice.

Governors have not always honored requests for extradition, but since no state wants to harbor criminals of another state, extradition is seldom refused. Among reasons advanced for the occasional refusals are (1) the individual has become a law-abiding citizen in his new state; (2) a northern governor did not approve of the conditions in Georgia chain gangs; (3) a black returned to a southern state would not receive a fair trial; (4) the governor did not believe that there was sufficient evidence against the fugitive to warrant his conviction in the first place.

Interstate Compacts   The Constitution provides that "No state shall without the consent of Congress . . . enter into any agreement or compact with another state." Over one hundred interstate compacts now serve a wide variety of interests, such as interstate water resources; conservation of natural resources, including oil, wildlife, fisheries; the control of floods; the development of interstate toll highways; the coordination of civil defense measures; the reciprocal supervision of parolees; the coordination of welfare and institutional care programs; the administration of interstate metropolitan areas; and the resolution of interstate tax conflicts. In practice, Congress has little to do with these compacts; the Supreme Court has held that congressional consent is required only if the compact encroaches upon some federal power.

Conflicts Between States   States are not supposed to make war on each other, although they did so from 1861 to 1865. They are supposed to take their conflicts to the Supreme Court. The Constitution gives the Supreme Court the power to settle all cases involving two or more states. In recent years the Supreme Court has heard disputes between states over boundaries, the diversion of water, fishing rights, and the disposal of sewage and garbage.

POLITICS OF FEDERALISM

What political interests are likely to support the rights of states in contrast to national authority?

Interests that constitute a majority at the national level assert the supremacy of the national government and praise the virtues of national regulation. Interests that are minorities in national politics, but comprise local or statewide majorities in one or more states, continue to see merit in the preservation of the powers of states.

Generally, liberals seek to enhance the power of the *national* government. Liberals believe that people's lives can be changed by the exercise of governmental power—to end discrimination, abolish poverty, eliminate slums, ensure employment, uplift the downtrodden, educate the masses, and cure the sick. The government in Washington has more power and resources than state and local governments have, and the liberals have turned to it rather than to state and local governments to cure America's ills. State and local governments are regarded as too slow, cumbersome, weak, and unresponsive. The government in Washington is seen as the principal instrument for liberal social and economic reform. Thus, liberalism and centralization are closely related in American politics.

The liberal argument for national authority can be summarized as follows:

1. There is insufficient awareness of social problems by state and local governments. The federal government must take the lead in civil rights, equal employment opportunities, care for the poor and aged, the provision of adequate medical care for all Americans, and the elimination of urban poverty and blight.
2. It is difficult to achieve change when reform-minded citizens must deal with fifty state governments or 83,000 local governments. Change is more likely to be accomplished by a strong central government.
3. State and local governments contribute to inequality in society by setting different levels of service in education, welfare, health, and other public functions. A strong national government can ensure uniformity of standards throughout the nation.

4. A strong national government can unify the nation behind principles and ideals of social justice and economic progress. Extreme decentralization can foster local or regional "special" interests at the expense of the general "public" interest.

Generally, conservatives seek power to return power to *state and local* governments. Conservatives are more skeptical about the "good" that government can do. Adding to the power of the national government is not an effective way of resolving society's problems. On the contrary, conservatives argue that "government is the problem, not the solution." Excessive government regulation, burdensome taxation, and inflationary government spending combine to restrict individual freedom, penalize work and saving, and destroy incentives for economic growth. Government should be kept small, controllable, and close to the people.

The conservative argument for state and local autonomy can be summarized as follows:

1. Grass-roots government promises a sense of self-responsibility and self-reliance.
2. State and local governments can better adapt public programs to local needs and conditions.
3. State and local governments promote participation in politics and civic responsibility by allowing more people to become involved in public questions.
4. Competition between states and cities can result in improved public programs and services.
5. The existence of multiple state and local governments encourages experimentation and innovation in public policy, from which the whole nation may gain.
6. State and local governments reduce the administrative workload on the national government, as well as reduce the political turmoil that results when one single policy must govern the entire nation.

Americans are divided over the merits of these arguments. Most national opinion surveys reveal general support for the notion of federalism, greater trust and confidence in state and local government than the federal government, a belief that the federal government has too much power, and a greater concern about waste, inefficiency, and unfairness at the federal level (see Table 3–7). But, paradoxically, many Americans want the federal government to assume even greater responsibility in specific policy areas, including areas traditionally thought to be state or local government responsibilities. For example, majorities favor having a *national* policy for registration and voting, setting penalties for murder, establishing factory safety standards, and setting minimum wages. There is no way to settle these arguments about federalism, which have been heard for over 200 years in American politics.

TABLE 3–7   PUBLIC OPINION AND FEDERALISM

General

Trust and Confidence
In which of the following people in government do you have the most trust and confidence?

Federal government   19[a]
State government   22
Local government   37

Power
Overall, do you feel that the federal government has too much power, the right amount of power, or too little power over the activities of state and local government today?

Too much power   46
The right amount of power   37
Too little power   7

Efficiency
From which level of government do you feel you get the most for your money—federal, state, or local?

Federal   28
State   22
Local   29

Waste
Which government do you feel wastes the most of your tax money—federal, state, or local?

Federal   66
State   14
Local   8

Specific

Should there be one national policy set by the federal government or should the fifty states make their own rules?

	FEDERAL	STATES
in controlling pollution	49	46
in setting penalties for murder	62	34
on the issue of registration and voting	64	31
in selecting textbooks for public schools	35	61
in establishing safety standards for factories	65	31
in setting highway speed limits	42	56

[a] All figures in percentages of U.S. public in national opinion surveys. No Opinions and Don't Knows not shown.

Sources: General responses from Advisory Commission on Intergovernmental Relations *Changing Public Attitudes on Governments and Taxes* (Washington, DC: Advisory Commission on Intergovernmental Relations, 1987); specific responses from *New York Times,* May 26, 1987, p. 10.

4

PARTICIPATION
IN STATE POLITICS

▲

THE NATURE OF POLITICAL PARTICIPATION

Popular participation in politics is the very definition of democracy. Individuals can participate in politics in many ways. They may run for, and win, public office; participate in marches, demonstrations, and sit-ins; make financial contributions to political candidates or causes; attend political meetings, speeches, and rallies; write letters to public officials or to newspapers; wear a political button or place a bumper sticker on a car; belong to organizations that support or oppose particular candidates or take stands on public issues; attempt to influence friends while discussing candidates or issues; vote in elections; or merely follow an issue or a campaign in the media.

This listing probably constitutes a ranking of the forms of political participation in their ascending order of frequency. (See Figure 4–1.) Less than 1 percent of the American adult population runs for public office. Only about 5 percent are active in parties and campaigns, and about 10 percent make financial contributions. About 15 percent wear political buttons or display bumper stickers. Less than 20 percent ever write their congressional representatives or contact any other public official. About one-third of the population belongs to organizations that could be

Essay

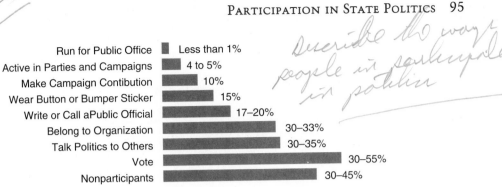

Describe the ways people in participate in politics

FIGURE 4–1   **Political Participation**

classified as interest groups, and only a few more ever try to convince their friends to vote for a certain candidate. Only about half of the voting age population vote in presidential elections. Far fewer vote in state and local elections. Over one-third of the population is politically apathetic: They do not vote at all, and they are largely unaware of the political life of the nation.

   Sustained political participation—voting consistently in election after election for state and local offices as well as Congress and the president—is very rare. One study of voter participation over ten elections (including presidential, congressional, gubernatorial, and state and local legislative elections) showed that only 4 percent of the voting age population voted in nine or all ten of the elections; only 26 percent voted in half of the ten elections; and 38 percent did not vote in any election.[1] Age is the best predictor of sustained political activity; older citizens are more likely than young people to be regular voters.

EXPLAINING VOTER TURNOUT

A sign of the times: A bumper sticker reads, "DON'T VOTE. IT JUST ENCOURAGES THEM." Nearly half of America's eligible voters stay away from the polls, even in a presidential election. Voter turnout is even lower in congressional elections, where turnout falls to 35 percent of the voting age population in the off-years (when presidential candidates are not on the ballot). Turnouts in gubernatorial elections are roughly similar to turnouts for congressional races, rising and falling depending on whether the election is held simultaneously with a presidential election (see Figure 4–2). Turnout for city and county elections, when they are held separately from national elections, usually produces turnouts of 25 to 35 percent.

Is Voting Rational?   Why is voter turnout so low? Actually, we could reverse the question and ask why people vote at all. A "rational" voter (one who seeks to maximize personal benefits and minimize costs) should vote only if the costs of voting (the time and energy spent first in registering, then in informing oneself

---

[1] Lee Sigelman et al., "Voting and Nonvoting: A Multi-Election Perspective," *American Journal of Political Science,* 29 (November 1985), 749–65.

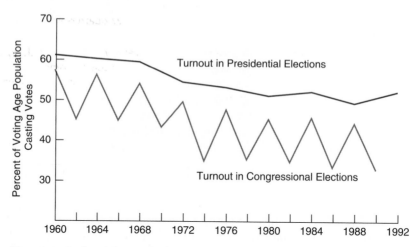

FIGURE 4–2   The Trend in Voter Turnout

about the candidates, and finally going to the polls on election day) are exceeded by the expected value of having the preferred candidate win (the personal benefits to be received from the winner) multiplied by the probability that one's own vote will be the deciding vote.[2] But under this "rational" notion, not many people would vote: Few Americans receive direct personal and tangible benefits from the election of one candidate versus another. And most Americans know that the likelihood of one vote determining the outcome of the election is very remote. Yet millions of Americans vote anyway.

In order to rescue the "rational" model, political theorists have added "the intrinsic rewards of voting" to the equation.[3] These rewards include the ethic of voting, patriotism, a sense of duty, and allegiance to democracy. In other words, people get psychic rewards from voting itself rather than tangible benefits, and these psychic rewards do not depend on who wins or whether a single vote determines the outcome. So more people vote out of a sense of civic duty and commitment to democracy than on a purely rational basis.

Why People Stay at Home   Nonetheless, millions of Americans stay at home on election day. We can apply some of the rational theorizing to understanding nonvoting in the states:

1. Registration requirements that are restrictive increase the costs of voting.
   By making it easier to register, states can increase voter turnout. Of the peo-

---

[2] William H. Riker and Peter C. Ordeshook, "A Theory of the Calculus of Voting," *American Political Science Review*, 62 (March 1968), 25–42.

[3] J. A. Ferejohn and Morris Fiorina, "The Paradox of Voting," *American Political Science Review*, 18 (March 1974), 525–36.

ple who are registered in the nation, about three-quarters will vote in presidential elections.

2. Competition increases turnout. If a political contest appears close, more people believe that their vote might determine the outcome. Active campaigning by the candidates may not change people's minds, but it mobilizes supporters to get to the polls on election day.

3. Civic attachments and education increase voter turnout. People who believe they have a stake in the political system are more likely to vote than those who do not. Nonvoting may indicate a lack of faith in one's own power, a feeling of political impotency, or a lack of faith in the political system— a belief that it is too corrupt or too large for any single individual to make a difference.

Who Fails to Vote?   Political alienation involves a feeling that voting is useless, that nothing is really decided in an election, and that the individual cannot personally influence the outcome of political events. Political alienation explains the failure to vote by many people. Various socioeconomic factors also help to explain alienation and nonvoting (see Table 4–1). Blacks vote less frequently than whites. Hispanic-Americans vote less frequently than either blacks or whites, suggesting that language differences may be a barrier to political participation. People who are working vote more frequently than the unemployed. Young people vote less often than older people. But the greatest differences in voter turnout are found among people with different educational backgrounds. Education apparently increases one's sense of civic responsibility and attachment to democratic norms.[4]

Policy Implications of Nonvoting   Do nonvoters differ significantly from voters on major policy questions? If so, then we might expect changes in government policy with a sustained increase in voter turnout. But the available evidence suggests that nonvoters generally hold policy views similar to those of voters.[5] Opinion surveys reveal that nonvoters and voters do *not* differ much on civil liberties and civil rights issues, or foreign or domestic policy issues, with the exception of a slight bias among nonvoters toward greater government spending and guaranteed jobs programs. Nonvoters are no more liberal or conservative than voters. However, nonvoters are much less informed about politics and government than voters; for example, when asked which party controlled the U.S. House and Senate, 62 percent of voters knew the Democrats had more seats in both houses, while only 31 percent of nonvoters answered correctly. In brief, despite a class bias in voting turnout, it is unlikely that nonvoting skews public policy in any particular direction.

---

[4] See John R. Bauer, "Patterns of Voter Participation in the American States," *Social Science Quarterly,* 71 (December 1990), 824–34; education is even more important in determining voter turnout in states with restrictive registration laws and lower competition levels.

[5] See Stephen Earl Bennett and David Resnick, "The Implications of Nonvoting for Democracy in the United States," *American Journal of Political Science,* 34 (August 1990), 771–802.

TABLE 4–1   CHARACTERISTICS OF VOTERS

Percent Reporting They Voted[a]

Total	57.4
Sex	
Male	56.4
Female	58.3
Race	
White	59.1
Black	51.5
Hispanic	28.8
Age	
18–20	33.2
21–24	38.3
25–34	48.0
35–44	61.3
45–64	67.9
65 and over	68.8
Employment	
Employed	58.4
Unemployed	38.6
Education	
8 years	36.7
High school	54.7
College	77.6

[a] Figures are for the 1988 presidential election. Some people tell pollsters that they voted when they really did not. While 59.9 percent of the voting age population reported that they voted, the actual number of votes cast was only 53.3 percent of the voting age population.

Source: Statistical Abstract of the United States, 1991, p. 257.

VOTING IN THE STATES

There is a great deal of variation among the states in voter participation rates (see Figure 4–3). The turnout in presidential elections ranges from less than 45 percent of the voting population to over 70 percent. The states with the lowest turnouts are the Deep South states; the next lowest are found in the border states. Midwestern, New England, and Mountain states rank very high in voter turnout. The urban industrial states, with large metropolitan populations, tend to cluster around the middle of the rankings.

Socioeconomic Explanations   Much of the variation among the states in voter turnout can be explained by *socioeconomic characteristics* of their population. Indeed, educational level, urbanization, median family income, and percentage black, considered together, can explain about 85 percent of the variation in voter turnout in presidential elections.[6] This means that most of the differences among states in voter turnout are explained by the socioeconomic characteristics of individuals living in the states.

Legal Explanations   However, *legal factors* also affect voter turnout. Turnout is affected by laws of the states, which define registration procedures, residency requirements, voting hours, absentee-ballot rules, and so on. Indeed, some political scientists have cited these legal factors as paramount: "Differences in the turnout for elections are to a large extent related to local differences in registration, and these in turn reflect to a considerable degree local differences in the rules governing . . . and . . . handling . . . the registration of voters.[7] However, these legal factors themselves may be a product of the socioeconomic character of the state; wealthy urban states with well-educated adult populations have generally placed fewer barriers to voting than poorer, rural states with ill-educated populations. More important, in recent years, the influence of legal factors has been diminished by federal legislation and constitutional amendments, which have eliminated most of these local barriers to voting.

Registration   Nevertheless, voter *registration* itself is a major obstacle to voting. Not only must citizens care enough to go to the polls on election day, they must also expend time and energy, weeks or months before the election, to register. Registration occurs at a time when interest in the campaign is far from its peak; registration may require a trip to the county courthouse and a more complicated procedure than voting itself. (However, most states continue to carry the names of voters on registration lists if these voters vote at least once every two or four years; reregistration is generally not required unless individuals change residence or fail to vote regularly. Moreover, most states allow periodic mobile registration booths at shopping centers and other central locations to encourage registration.) It is estimated that liberalizing or eliminating registration requirements would increase turnout and change the composition of the electorate somewhat.[8] Voters in the aggregate would be slightly less educated, poorer, blacker, and younger. These changes would probably increase Democratic party voting, and hence Democrats are usually more supportive of liberal registration laws than Republicans. Registration is supposed to prevent fraud: Voters must identify themselves on election day and show that they have previously registered in their districts as voters; once they have voted, their names are checked off and they cannot vote again. Maine, Minnesota, and Wisconsin allow same-day registration at the polls; voters present

---

[6] For a discussion of the factors affecting voter turnout in the states, see Jae-On Kim et al., "Voter Turnout in the American States: Systemic and Individual Components," *American Political Science Review,* 69 (March 1975), 107–23.

[7] Stanley Kelley et al., "Registration and Voting: Putting First Things First," *American Political Science Review,* 61 (June 1967), 359–77.

[8] For a discussion of the consequences of registration changes, see Steven J. Rosentone and Raymond E. Wolfinger, "The Effect of Registration Laws on Voter Turnout," *American Political Science Review,* 72 (March 1978), 22–45.

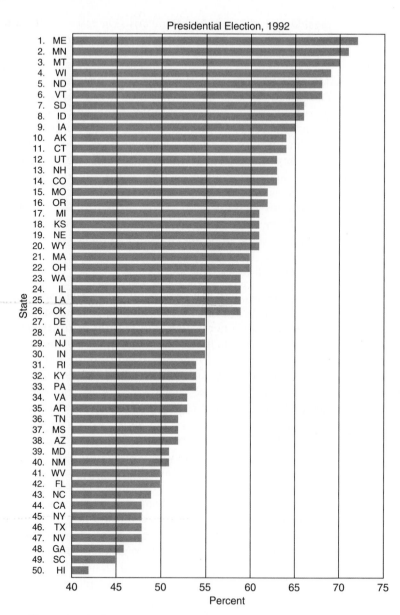

FIGURE 4-3   Ranking of the States: Voter Participation

proof of residence and certify that they have not already voted. North Dakota is the only state that does not require citizens to register before they can vote.

Democrats in Congress recently passed a national voter registration law in 1993 that would require states to register voters at the same time that they apply for a driver's license (i.e., a ''motor voter'' law), and when they apply for welfare benefits.

Competition   Voter participation rates can also be affected by the degree of *interparty competition* in a state. The more vigorous the competition between the parties, the greater the interest of citizens in elections, and the larger the voter turnout. When parties and candidates compete vigorously, they make news and are given a large play via the mass media. Thus, a setting of competitive politics tends to have a greater amount of political stimuli available in the environment than does a setting with weak competition. People are also more likely to perceive that their votes count in a close, competitive contest, and thus they are more likely to cast them. Moreover, when parties are fighting in a close contest, their workers tend to spend more time and energy campaigning and getting out the vote.[9]

Indeed, some political scientists argue that *political mobilization* can explain most of the variation among the states in voter turnout for gubernatorial elections.[10] Political mobilization is measured by a combination of party competition, the closeness of the race, the amount of money spent campaigning, and whether or not a U.S. Senate seat was being decided in the same election.

Region   Some scholars have cited *region* as an explanation of differences among the states in voter turnout.[11] This notion is supported by the southern states which are usually at the bottom of voter turnout figures. On the other hand, to cite "region" as an explanation of voter turnout begs the question: What characteristics of various regions explain the electoral behavior of their populations? For the most part, the lower voter turnout of the southern states is explained by their lower educational levels, lower income levels, and larger black populations. While turnout in most states has declined since 1960, turnout has actually increased in Alabama, Arkansas, Florida, Georgia, Louisiana, Mississippi, South Carolina, Tennessee, Texas, and Virginia.[12] Federal civil rights laws, northern in-migration, and greater Republican competition may all combine to help explain why voter participation has increased in these states. Nonetheless, these states continue to rank near the bottom of the fifty states in participation.

History   Finally, voter behavior in some states is a product of *unique political history.* West Virginia has experienced considerable poverty in recent years—its adult educational level is one of the lowest in the nation and its registration and voting laws are similar to those of most states. Yet voter turnout in West Virginia is close to the national average. For many years this apparent inconsistency defied political analysis. However, an intensive study of West Virginia politics suggests that the

---

[9] Studies of voter turnout *within* states (e.g., studies of voter turnout by county) confirm the importance of competition in increasing turnout. See C. Richard Hofstetter, "Inter-Party Competition and Electoral Turnout: The Case of Indiana," *American Journal of Political Science,* 17 (May 1973), 351–66.

[10] Samuel C. Patterson and Gregory A. Caldeira, "Getting Out to Vote: Participation in Gubernatorial Elections," *American Political Science Review,* 77 (September 1983), 675–89.

[11] Robert H. Blank, "Socioeconomic Determination of Voting Turnout," *Journal of Politics,* 36 (August 1974), 731–52.

[12] See Norman R. Lutbeg, "Differential Voting Turnout Decline in the American States," *Social Science Quarterly,* 65 (March 1984), 60–73.

bloody history of organizing miners' unions in that state established a tradition of active political participation among West Virginians. "Contrary to what was taking place in other border and southern states, in West Virginia that group that was least likely to participate in politics—the lower socioeconomic status group, the 'working man'—was being motivated and 'organized' to participate [by the United Mine Workers]."[13]

SECURING THE RIGHT TO VOTE

The only mention of voting requirements in the Constitution of the United States as it was originally adopted is in Article I: "The electors in each state shall have the qualifications requisite for electors for the most numerous branch of the state legislature." Of course, "electors" (voters) for the most numerous branch of the state legislature are determined by *state* laws and constitutions. The effect of this constitutional provision was to leave to the states the power to determine who is eligible to vote in both state and federal elections. Over the years, however, a combination of constitutional amendments, congressional actions, and Supreme Court decisions has largely removed control over voting from the states and made it a responsibility of the national government.

Elimination of Property Qualifications   Early in American history, voting was limited to males over twenty-one years of age, who resided in the voting district for a certain period and owned a considerable amount of land or received a large income from other investments. So great was the fear that "the common man" would use his vote to attack the rights of property that only 120,000 people out of 2 million were permitted to vote in the 1780s. Men of property felt that only other men of property had sufficient "stake in society" to exercise their vote in a "responsible" fashion. Gradually, however, Jeffersonian and Jacksonian principles of democracy, including confidence in the reason and integrity of the common man, spread rapidly in the new Republic. Most property qualifications were eliminated by the states themselves in the early nineteenth century.

Fifteenth Amendment   The first important limitation on state powers over voting came with the ratification of the Fifteenth Amendment: "The right of the citizens of the United States to vote shall not be denied or abridged by the United States or any state on account of race, color, or previous condition of servitude." The object of this amendment, passed by the Reconstruction Congress and adopted in 1870, was to extend the vote to former black slaves and prohibit voter discrimination on the basis of race. The Fifteenth Amendment also gives Congress the power to enforce black voting rights "by appropriate legislation." Thus, the states retained their right to determine voter qualifications, *as long as they do not practice racial discrimination,* and Congress was given the power to pass legislation ensuring black voting rights.

---

[13] Gerald W. Johnson, "Research Note on Political Correlates of Voter Participation: A Deviant Case Analysis," *American Political Science Review,* 65 (September 1971), 768–76.

Nineteenth Amendment   Following the Civil War many of the women who had been active Abolitionists seeking to end slavery, turned their attention to the condition of women in America. They had learned to organize, conduct petition campaigns, and parade and demonstrate, as abolitionists, and later they sought to improve the legal and political rights of women. In 1869 the Wyoming territory adopted women suffrage; later several other western states followed suit. But it was not until the Nineteenth Amendment to the U.S. Constitution in 1920 that women voter rights were constitutionally guaranteed.

The "White Primary"   For almost 100 years after the adoption of the Fifteenth Amendment, white politicians in the southern states were able to defeat its purposes. Social and economic pressures and threats of violence were used to intimidate many thousands of would-be voters. There were also many "legal" methods of disenfranchisement.

For many years the most effective means of banning black voting was a technique known as the "white primary." So strong was the Democratic party throughout the South that the Democratic nomination for public office was tantamount to election. This meant that *primary* elections to choose the Democratic nominee were the only elections in which real choices were made. If blacks were prevented from voting in Democratic primaries, they could be effectively disenfranchised. Thus southern state legislatures resorted to the simple device of declaring the Democratic party in southern states a private club and ruling that only white people could participate in its elections, that is, in *primary* elections. Blacks would be free to vote in "official," general elections, but all whites tacitly agreed to support the Democratic, or "white man's" party, in general elections, regardless of their differences in the primary. Not until 1944, in *Smith* v. *Allright,* did the Supreme Court declare this practice unconstitutional.[14]

Discrimination   Black voting in the South increased substantially after World War II. From an estimated 5 percent of voting age blacks registered in southern states in the 1940s, black registration rose to an estimated 20 percent in 1952, 25 percent in 1956, 28 percent in 1960, and 39 percent in 1964. This last figure was a little more than half of the comparable figure for white registration in the South. Most of this increase in black registration occurred in urban areas of the South. Prior to 1965, in hundreds of rural counties throughout the South, no blacks were permitted to vote. Despite the Fifteenth Amendment, local registrars in the South succeeded in barring black registration by means of an endless variety of obstacles, delays, and frustrations. Application forms for registration were lengthy and complicated; even a minor error would lead to rejection, like underlining rather than circling in the "Mr.–Mrs.–Miss" set of choices as instructed. Literacy tests were the most common form of disenfranchisement. Many a black college graduate failed to interpret "properly" the complex legal documents that were part of the test. White applicants for voter registration were seldom asked to go through these lengthy procedures.

---

[14] *Smith* v. *Allright,* 321 U.S. 649 (1944).

Civil Rights Act of 1964   The Civil Rights Act of 1964 made it unlawful for registrars to apply unequal standards in registration procedures or to reject applications because of immaterial errors. It required that literacy tests be in writing and made a sixth-grade education a presumption of literacy.

Twenty-fourth Amendment   The Twenty-fourth Amendment to the Constitution was ratified in 1964, making poll taxes unconstitutional as a requirement for voting in national elections. In 1965 the Supreme Court declared poll taxes unconstitutional in state and local elections as well.[15]

Voting Rights Act of 1965   In Selma, Alabama, in early 1965, civil rights organizations effectively demonstrated that local registrars were still keeping large numbers of blacks off the voting rolls. Registrars closed their offices for all but a few hours every month, placed limits on the number of applications processed, went out to lunch when black applicants appeared; delayed months before processing applications from blacks, and discovered a variety of other methods to keep blacks disenfranchised. In response to the Selma march, Congress enacted a strong Voting Rights Act in 1965. The U.S. attorney general, upon evidence of voter discrimination, was empowered to replace local registrars with federal registrars, abolish literacy tests, and register voters under simplified federal procedures.[16] However, it turned out that federal registrars were sent to only a small number of southern counties. Many southern counties that had previously discriminated in voting registration hurried to sign up black voters just to avoid the imposition of federal registrars. The Voting Rights Act of 1965 proved to be very effective and Congress voted to extend it indefinitely. The key provisions of the voting Rights Act are as follows:

1. *The Triggering Mechanism.* The act applies to states and counties in which half the voting-age population fails to register or fails to vote in the preceding presidential election. Entire states covered are Alabama, Alaska, Arizona, Georgia, Louisiana, Mississippi, South Carolina, Texas, and Virginia. Various counties throughout the nation are also covered including most of the counties in North Carolina.

2. *Preclearance.* The U.S. Department of Justice must give prior approval to any changes in election laws (for example, laws relating to voter registration, at-large or district elections, candidate eligibility, or drawing of election district lines). Approval would be denied if the *effect* of the change would be to dilute minority voting. In 1975 the act was amended to add protection for members of "language minority groups," including Hispanics.

3. *Federal Intervention.* Upon evidence of voter discrimination, the U.S. Justice Department is empowered to send federal poll watchers, and if needed, to replace local election officials with federal registrars.

Diluting Minority Votes   In recent years, conflict over voting rights has centered on the effects of various institutional arrangements on minority influence in government. In 1982, Congress strengthened the Voting Rights Act by outlawing

---

[15] *Harper v. Virginia State Board of Elections,* 383 U.S. 663 (1966).

[16] *South Carolina v. Katzenbach,* U.S. 301 (1966).

any electoral arrangements that had the *effect* of weakening minority voting power. This "effects" test replaced the earlier "intent" test which required black plaintiffs to prove that a particular arrangement was adopted with the specific intent of reducing black voting power.[17] (An "intent" test invalidates laws or practices only if they are designed to discriminate; an "effects" test invalidates laws or practices that adversely affect racial minorities regardless of the original intent.) For example, at-large elections or multimember districts for city councils, county commissions, or state legislative seats may have the effect of weakening black voting power if a white majority in such districts prevents blacks from winning office. Congress stopped short of directly outlawing such districts but established a "totality of circumstances" test to be used to determine if such districts had a discriminatory effect. The "circumstances" to be considered by the courts include whether or not there has been a history of racial polarization in voting and whether black candidates have ever won election to office in the district.[18]

Affirmative Racial Gerrymandering   The U.S. Supreme Court requires states and cities to provide minorities with "a realistic opportunity to elect officials of their choice." In the key case of *Thornburg* v. *Gingles,*[19] the Court interpreted the Voting Rights Act Amendments of 1982 to require state legislatures to draw election district boundary lines in a way that guarantees that minorities can elect minority representatives to governing bodies. The burden of proof was shifted *from* minorities to show that district lines diluted their voting strength *to* state lawmakers to show that they have done everything possible to maximize minority representation. The effect of the Court's decision was to require affirmative racial gerrymandering—the creation of predominately black and minority districts wherever possible.

Racial gerrymandering dominated the redistricting process in all of the large states following the 1990 census. In many states Republican legislators allied themselves with black and Hispanic groups in efforts to create minority districts; Republicans understood that "packing" minority (usually Democratic) voters into selected districts would reduce Democratic votes in many other districts. The U.S. Justice Department also pressed state legislatures to maximize the number of "majority-minority" congressional and state legislative districts. Debate centered on the appropriate standard for these minority-dominated districts. Federal courts ruled that a 50 percent minority population in a district was insufficient to guarantee minority representation; the most common standards were 65 percent minority of the total population and 55 percent minority of the population registered to vote. With the assistance of sophisticated computer models, state legislatures and federal courts drew many odd-shaped minority congressional and state legislative districts.

---

[17] *Mobile* v. *Bolden,* 446 U.S. 50 (1980).

[18] See Susan A. MacManus, "Racial Representation Issues," *PS Quarterly of the American Political Science Association,* 18 (Fall 1985), 759–69.

[19] *Thornburg* v. *Gingles* 478 U.S. 30 (1986).

TABLE 4–2   GROWTH IN NUMBERS OF BLACK ELECTED OFFICIALS

	1970	1980	1991
U.S. Congress	10	17	38[e]
State government[a]	169	309	450
City and county government[b]	719	2,871	4,493
Judicial and law enforcement[c]	213	534	847
Education[d]	368	1,232	1,629
Total	1,479	4,963	7,445

[a] Includes elected state administrators.

[b] County commissioners and council members, mayors, vice-mayors, city council members, regional officials, and other.

[c] Judges, magistrates, constables, marshals, sheriffs, justices of the peace, and other.

[d] Members of state education agencies, college boards, school boards, and other.

[e] Figures for 1993 all others in column for 1991.

Source: Joint Center for Political Studies, Washington, DC

Increased Black Representation   Black representation in state and local government, as well as in the U.S. Congress, has risen dramatically in recent years. Afro-American members of the U.S House of Representatives rose from 26 to 38 following the 1992 elections, and one Afro-American was elected to the U.S. Senate, Carol Moseley-Braun of Illinois. The numbers of blacks elected to state and local office nearly doubled between 1980 and 1991 (see Table 4–2), and new minority districts in many states boosted black representation in state legislatures. We will return to the question of minority representation in state legislatures in Chapter 6 and on city councils in Chapter 11.

Racial Polarization   Increases in the number of African-American officeholders in state and local government are primarily the result of the creation of more black majority districts in cities and states. Few blacks win office in majority white city council or state legislative districts. And the federal Voting Rights Act has been responsible for the creation of more black majority districts. In legislative districts where the black population is 65 percent or more, black candidates win 98 percent of the legislative seats. Majority white districts elect black candidates to about 2 percent of their legislative seats. While a few notable black political leaders have won electoral support across racial lines (see "Wilder of Virginia: Putting Race to Rest" in Chapter 14), racial polarization in voting remains a fact of life.[20]

Hispanic Power   The progress of Hispanics in state and local politics in recent years is reflected in the election of several governors and increasing numbers of

---

[20] Bernard Grofman and Lisa Handley, "The Impact of the Voting Rights Act on Black Representation in Southern State Legislatures," *Legislative Studies Quarterly,* 16 (February 1991), 111–28.

TABLE 4–3   GROWTH IN NUMBER OF HISPANIC ELECTED OFFICIALS

	1984	1990
U.S. Congress	9	17[a]
State government	110	133
City and county government	1,276	1,724
Judicial and law enforcement	495	575
Education	1,173	1,341
Total	3,063	3,783

[a] Figure for 1993, all other figures in column for 1990.

Source: National Association of Latino Elected and Appointed Officials. Washington DC: *National Roster of Hispanic Elected Officials.*

state legislators, city and county commission members, and school board members (see Table 4–3).

However, Hispanic political influence in the states is still very limited. Hispanic voter turnout is much lower than that for other ethnic groups in America. Many Hispanics are resident aliens and therefore not eligible to vote. Language barriers may also present an obstacle to full participation. Finally, Hispanic voters divide their political loyalties. Cuban-Americans and other political refugees from Marxist guerilla wars in Central and South America tend to vote Republican. These groups are economically very successful; they are concentrated in the Miami area, and they are now a force in city and state politics in Florida. The largest Hispanic group, Mexican-Americans, tends to vote Democratic; their power is concentrated in California, Texas, Arizona, and New Mexico.

VOTING AND AMERICAN YOUTH

Before 1970 only three of the fifty states permitted residents eighteen to twenty-one years of age to vote—Georgia, Kentucky, and Alaska. All other states, in the exercise of their constitutional responsibility to determine the qualifications of "electors," had set the voting age at twenty-one. The movement for eighteen-year-old voting received its original impetus in Georgia in 1944 under the leadership of Governor Ellis Arnall, who argued successfully that eighteen-year-olds were then being called upon to fight and die for their country in World War II and, therefore, deserved to have a voice in the conduct of government. However, this argument failed to convince adult voters in other states; qualifications for military service were not regarded as the same as qualifications for rational decision making in elections. In state after state, voters rejected state constitutional amendments designed to extend the vote to eighteen-year-olds.

Congress intervened on behalf of eighteen-year-old voting with the passage of the Twenty-sixth Amendment to the Constitution in 1971.[21] The states quickly ratified this amendment, during a period of national turbulence over the Vietnam War. Many supporters of the amendment believed that protests on the campuses and streets could be reduced if youthful protesters were given the vote. Moreover, Democrats believed that their party would gain from the youth vote, and liberal candidates believed that idealistic young voters would spark their campaigns.

It turns out that young people vote less often than older people. (See Table 4–1.) Moreover, young people do *not* vote as a bloc. Young voters cast their votes for most political candidates in the same proportions as older voters. The image of the idealistic, activist student is not an accurate image of the young voter in America. Less than one-third of people aged eighteen to twenty-four are in college. More than half of this age group are working and either living with their parents or are married and living in their own households. College students may achieve greater visibility in the news media than young working people, but the bulk of young voters are not on the campus.

WOMEN IN STATE POLITICS

Traditionally women did not participate in politics as much as men. Women were less likely than men to contribute money, lobby elected officials, and run for or win public office.

Why was this so? Several explanations have been offered: (1) Women were socialized into more "passive" roles from childhood; (2) women with children and family responsibilities could not fully participate in politics; and (3) women did not have educations, occupations, and incomes equivalent to those of men. Perhaps all of these factors were at work in reducing female political participation.

Women in State Offices   Women have made impressive political gains in state politics in recent years. Today over 1500 of the nation's 7500 state legislators (20 percent) are women. Several women served as governors of their state in the 1980s: Martha Layne Collins (D.) of Kentucky, Kay A. Orr (R.) of Nebraska, and Madeleine M. Kunin (D.) of Vermont.[22] (In the 103rd Congress—1993–1995—47 women are serving in the House and 6 in the Senate.) While these figures are modest indeed, they represent significant advances over the recent past. In 1969 only 4 percent of the nation's state legislators were women. Until the election of Ella Grasso (D.–Connecticut) and Dixie Lee Ray (D.–Washington) in the late 1970s, no woman had

---

[21] Congress had earlier passed the Voting Rights Act of 1970 which (1) extended the vote to eighteen-year-olds regardless of state law; (2) abolished residency requirements in excess of thirty days; and (3) prohibited literacy tests. However, there was some constitutional debate about the power of Congress to change state laws on voting age. While Congress can end *racial* discrimination, extending the vote to eighteen-year-olds was a different matter. All previous extensions of the vote had come by constitutional amendment. Hence, Congress quickly passed the Twenty-sixth Amendment.

[22] Governors in the 1990s include Joan Finney (D) of Kansas, Barbara Roberts (D) of Oregon, and Ann Richards (D) of Texas.

won election to that office on her own; earlier women governors had succeeded their husbands to that office. Women are making even more rapid gains in city and county offices. The total number of women officeholders in local government has more than tripled over the last decade. This influx of women at the grass-roots level over the last decade is now contributing to the success of women in running for and winning higher state and national offices.

Election Challenges Confronting Women   The National Women's Political Caucus points out that women continue to confront special challenges when running for office.[23] In general, female candidates enjoy a slight advantage over male candidates in public perceptions of honesty, sincerity, and caring. However, women candidates are often perceived as "not tough enough" to deal with hard issues like drugs and crime. When women candidates seek to prove that they are "tough," they risk being branded with adjectives like "strident" or "abrasive." Moreover, according to the Women's Political Caucus, men in public office are presumed to be competent, while women in public office must prove their competency.

Women and Policy Making   Do greater numbers of women in state and local elected offices make any significant difference in public policy? Political scientists have attempted to learn whether or not increases in female elected officials actually bring about any significant policy changes. The evidence on this question is mixed. Male legislators support feminist positions on ERA, abortion, employment, education, and health just as often as female legislators. However, there is some evidence that women legislators give higher *priority* to these issues. Women are more likely than men to have as their "top legislative priority" bills focusing on women's and children's issues. However, state legislatures with larger percentages of women do *not* pass feminist legislation any more often than state legislatures with fewer women legislators.[24] Women's priority issues are discussed in Chapter 14.

INTEREST GROUPS IN STATE POLITICS

Interest groups arise when individuals with a common interest decide that by banding together and by consolidating their strength they can exercise more influence over public policy than they could as individuals acting alone. The impulse toward organization and collective action is particularly strong in a society of great size and complexity. As societies become more urban and industrial, individual action in politics gives way to collective action by giant organizations of business-people, farmers, professionals, and laborers, as well as racial, religious, and ideological groups.

---

[23] *New York Times,* August 8, 1989.

[24] Sue Thomas, "The Impact of Women on State Legislative Policies," *Journal of Politics,* 53 (November 1991), 958–76. See also Michelle A. Saint-Germain, "Does Their Difference Make a Difference?" *Social Science Quarterly,* 70 (December 1989), 956–68.

Organized Interests   Groups may be highly organized into formal organizations with offices and professional staffs within the capitals of every state: The U.S. Chamber of Commerce, the National Association of Manufacturers, the AFL–CIO, and the National Education Association are examples of highly organized interest groups that operate in every state. Other groups have little formal organization and have been unable to organize themselves very effectively for political action: An example of such a group would be parents opposed to busing for racial integration. Interest groups may be organized around *occupational or economic interests* (for example, the American Farm Bureau Federation, the National Association of Real Estate Boards, the National Association of Broadcasters, the Bankers Association, the Automobile Dealers Association, the Cattleman's Association, the Home Builders Association, the Insurance Council, the Association of Trial Lawyers, etc.), or on *racial or religious* bases (for example, the National Association for the Advancement of Colored People, the National Council of Churches, the Anti-Defamation League of B'nai B'rith), or around *shared experiences* (for example, the American Legion, the Veterans of Foreign Wars, the League of Women Voters, the Automobile Association of America), or around *ideological positions* (for example, Americans for Democratic Action, Common Cause, Americans for Constitutional Action). *Government officials* and governments themselves organize and help exert pressure on higher levels of government (for example, the National Governors' Conference, the Council of State Governments, the National League of Cities, U.S. Conference of Mayors, the National Association of Chiefs of Police, and National Association of Counties). Even the *recipients of government services* are organizing themselves (for example, the American Association of Retired Persons, the National Welfare Rights Organization).

Many scholars believe that economic interests tend to exercise more influence in American politics than noneconomic interests. But certainly the proliferation of active noneconomic groups in America, from the American Legion to the Sierra Club, the League of Women Voters, and the liberal-oriented Common Cause, testifies to the importance of organization in all phases of political life. Particularly active at the state level are the businesses subject to extensive regulation by state governments. The banks, truckers, railroads, insurance companies, utilities, and liquor interests are consistently found to be among the most highly organized groups in state capitals. Chapters of the National Education Association are also active in state capitals, presenting the demands of educational administrators and teachers. Even local governments and local government officials organize themselves to present their demands at state capitals.

A national survey of interest group activity in all fifty state capitals identified groups that were present and continually active in almost all of the states (column 1 in Table 4–4) as well as those that were intermittently active in all or only some of the states. As much as 75 percent of all state-level lobbying can be attributed to the eighteen interests in the continually active group.

Lobby Registration   It is very difficult to get a comprehensive picture of interest group activity in state capitals. Many organizations, businesses, legal firms, and individuals engage in interest group activity of one kind or another, and it is difficult to keep track of their varied activities. Most states require the registration of "lobbyists" and the submission of reports about their membership and finances. These laws do not restrain lobbying (that would probably violate the First Amendment freedom to "petition" the government for "redress of grievances"). Rather, they are meant to spotlight the activities of lobbyists. However, many hundreds of lobbyists never register under the pretext that they are not *really lobbyists,* but, instead, businesses, public relations firms, lawyers, researchers, or educational people. Thus, only the larger, formal, organized interest groups are officially registered as lobbyists in the states.

FUNCTIONS AND TACTICS OF INTEREST GROUPS

Both interest groups and political parties organize individuals to make claims upon government, but these two forms of political organizations differ in several respects. An interest group seeks to influence specific policies of government—not to achieve control over government as a whole. A political party concentrates on winning public office in elections and is somewhat less concerned with policy questions. An interest group does not ordinarily run candidates for public office under its own banner, although it may give influential support to party candidates. Finally, the basic function of a political party in a two-party system is to organize a *majority* of persons for the purpose of governing. In contrast, an interest group gives political expression to the interests of *minority* groups.

Interest group techniques are as varied as the imaginations of their leaders. Groups are attempting to advance their interests when a liquor firm sends a case of bourbon to a state legislator; when NOW marches on the state capital in support of the Equal Rights Amendment; when the League of Women Voters distributes biographies of political candidates; when an insurance company argues before a state insurance commission that rates must be increased; when the National Education Association provides state legislators with information comparing teachers' salaries in the fifty states; when railroads ask state highway departments to place weight limitations upon trucks; when the American Civil Liberties Union supplies lawyers for civil rights demonstrators; or when outdoor theater owners testify in legislative committee hearings against the adoption of daylight savings time. Let us try to classify the many techniques of interest groups under three major headings —public relations, campaign financing, and lobbying.

Public Relations   Most people think of interest group tactics as direct attempts to influence decision makers, but many groups spend more of their time, energy, and resources in general public relations activities than anything else. The purpose of a continuing public relations campaign is to create an environment favorable to the interest group and its program. It is hoped that a reservoir of public goodwill can be established, which can be relied on later when a critical issue arises. Generally, business interests have a distinct advantage over nonbusiness interests in public relations since they already have at their disposal public relations departments. The cost of business public relations campaigns is tax-deductible.

TABLE 4–4   TYPES OF INTERESTS AND THEIR FREQUENCY OF PRESENCE IN THE FIFTY STATES

Present in Over 40 States	Present in 20 to 40 States	Present in Less than 20 States
CONTINUALLY ACTIVE		
Individual business corporations[a]	Manufacturing companies	Latino groups
Local government units (cities, districts, etc.)	Tourism groups	Gaming (Race tracks/casinos/lotteries)
State departments, boards and commissions	Manufacturers' associations	
Business trade associations[b]	Railroads	
Utility companies and associations (public and private)	Agri-business corporations	
Banks and financial institutions/associations	Sportsmen's groups (especially hunting and fishing)	
Insurance companies/associations	Commercial fishermen	
Public employee unions/associations (state and local)	Health care corporations	
Universities and colleges (public and private)	Mining companies	
School teachers' unions/associations		
Local government associations		
Farmers' organizations/commodity associations		
Traditional labor unions		
Labor associations (mainly AFL-CIO)		
Environmentalists		
Oil and gas companies/associations		
Hospital associations		
Contractors/builders/developers		

Campaign Financing   Political campaigns are very expensive, and it is always difficult for a candidate to find enough money to finance a campaign. This is true for officeholders seeking reelection as well as new contenders. It is perfectly legal for an interest group to make a contribution to a candidate's campaign fund. Ordinarily, a respectable lobbyist would not be so crude as to exact any specific pledges from a candidate in exchange for a campaign contribution. He or she simply makes a contribution and lets the candidate figure out what to do when in office to assure further contributions to the candidate's next campaign. (For further discussion, see "Money in Politics," Chapter 5.)

TABLE 4–4 *Continued*

Present in Over 40 States	Present in 20 to 40 States	Present in Less than 20 States
INTERMITTENTLY ACTIVE		
Doctors	Black American groups	Native American groups
Trial lawyers/state bar associations	Groups for the physically and mentally handicapped	Animal rights groups
Retailers' associations	Student groups	Welfare rights groups
Real estate interests	Nurses	Foreign businesses (especially from Japan)
Liquor interests	Chiropractors	Children's rights groups
Communication interests (telecommunications, cable TV, etc.)	Taxpayers groups	
	Gay rights groups	
Nursing home operators	Parent teachers associations	
Truckers	Media associations	
Women's groups	Consumer groups	
Groups for the arts	Veterans' groups	
Pro and anti-abortion groups	Moral Majority	
Religious groups	Community groups	
Senior citizens	Pro and anti-smoking interests	
Social service groups and coalitions	Pro and anti-gun control groups	
Good government groups (League of Women Voters, Common Cause)		
American Civil Liberties Union		
Federal agencies		

a An unavoidably broad category. It includes manufacturing and service corporations with the exception of those listed separately, such as private utilities and oil and gas companies. These and other business corporations were listed separately because of their frequency of presence across the states.

b Another unavoidably broad category. It includes chambers of commerce as well as specific trade associations, such as the Tobacco Institute, Air Carriers, Manufacturers' Associations, etc.

Source: From *Politics in the American States: A Comparative Analysis,* 5/e, by Virginia Gray, et al. Copyright © 1985 by Virginia Gray, Herbert Jacob, and Robert B. Albritton. Reprinted by permission of Harper Collins Publishers.

PACs IN THE STATES

Interest groups, operating through political action committees or PACs, are becoming the major source of campaign funding for state office. As campaign costs increase, reliance on PAC money increases. In large urban states such as California and New York, where campaigns for state legislature may cost $50,000 to $100,000 or more, PAC contributions are the largest source of campaign funding (see Table 4–5).

Lobbying   *Lobbying* is defined as any communication, by someone acting on behalf of a group, directed at a government decision maker with the hope of influencing that person. Direct persuasion is usually more than just a matter of

TABLE 4–5 INTEREST GROUP CAMPAIGN CONTRIBUTIONS: FUNDING THE FLORIDA SENATE PRESIDENT

As president of the Florida state senate, Democrat Pat Thomas was a favored recipient of PAC contributions in his 1992 reelection campaign. Florida law limits contributions to $500 for each election. The following is a partial list of Thomas's contributors.

Contributor	Business/trade	Contributor	Business/trade
Agents PAC	Insurance	Professional Fire Fighters of Fla.	Firefighters
Accredited Bond Agencies, Inc.	Bail-bond	Funeral Directors	Funerals
American Cyanamid	Chemical	Florida Asphalt Contractors	Construction
American Family Corp.	Insurance	Florida Associated Services Inc.	Computer
American Family Life	Insurance	Florida Assn. of Surety Agents	Bail bonds
Anesthesiology PAC	Physicians	Florida Bankpac-State	Bank
Anheuser Bush Companies	Beer	Florida Beer Wholesalers	Beer
AFSCME	Public employees	Florida Business Forum Inc.	Business
American Publishers Assn.	Book publishers	Florida Chiropractic Association	Chiropractors
Associated Industries of Florida	Manufacturers	Florida CPA	CPAs
AT&T PAC–Florida	Telephone	Florida Dairy Farmers Association	Dairy farmers
Barnett People for Better Gov't	Bank	Florida Dental PAC	Dentists
Lewis Bear Co.	Wholesale	Florida Employers Insurance	Insurance
Ronnie Bergeron	Road construction	Florida Engineers	Engineers
Blue Cross/Blue Shield	Health insurance	Florida Farm Bureau	Agriculture
Calder Race Course, Inc.	Horse track	Florida Fruit and Vegetable Assn.	Agriculture
Cargill Poultry Products	Poultry	Florida Greyhound Track Owners	Dog tracks
Carson Farms	Farms	Florida Hearing Aid Society	Manufacturers
CAR PAC	Car dealers	Florida Hospital League	Hospital
Carlton, Fields PAC	Attorneys/lobbyists	Florida Medical PAC	Doctors
Centel Corp.	Telephone	Florida Osteopathic Medical Assn.	Osteopaths
Champion International Corp.	Paper	Florida Phosphate Committee	Phosphate industry
Citizens & Southern	Bank	Florida Podiatry PAC	Podiatrists
Clark, Roumelis and Associates	Engineering	Florida Premium Finance Assn.	Financial services
Coastal States Mgmt.	Energy	Florida Propane PAC	Propane gas
Coca-Cola Bottling Co.	Bottler	Florida Restaurant Assn.	Restaurants
CSX Transportation	Rail transportation	Florida RV Trade Assn.	Recreational vehicles
Eastern Airlines PAC	Airlines	Florida Shopping Center	Commercial
E. I. DuPont DeNemours & Co.	Chemical	Florida Transportation	Truckers
Everglades Agriculture PAC	Agricultural	Florida Trucking Assn.	Truckers
Exxon Corp. 500	Oil	GTE State PAC	Telephone

Source: Florida, Office of the Secretary of State

argument or emotional appeal to the lawmaker. Often it involves the communication of useful technical and political information. Many public officials are required to vote on, or decide about, hundreds of questions each year. It is impossible for them to be fully informed about the wide variety of the bills and issues they face. Consequently, many decision makers depend upon skilled lobbyists to provide technical information about matters requiring action, and to inform them of the policy preferences of important segments of the population.

The behavior of lobbyists depends on the interests they represent and the characteristics of the state political system in which they function. Some interests hire full-time lobbyists; others rely on attorneys or firms who lobby on behalf of more than one group. Still other interests rely on volunteers. Some maintain active contact with legislators or make campaign contributions. Some formulate a legislative agenda each session and trace the progress of bills in which they are interested. Indeed, one study of lobbying on behalf of the aging in four separate states revealed much variation in lobbying activity even on the same issues.[25]

Most state lobbying activity is undertaken by economic interests—finance, insurance, and real estate industries; wholesale and retail business; mining and agriculture; transportation and utilities.[26] The professions—physicians, lawyers, teachers, and others—follow next in lobbying activity. They are closely matched by governmental bodies—from cities, counties, and school districts to state bureaucracies. Public interest groups, consumer groups, and environmentalists follow, together with labor unions. Single interest and ideological groups are only intermittently active in state capitals.

COMPARING INTEREST GROUPS IN THE STATES

How do interest group systems in the states differ? Why do some states have strong influential interest groups shaping public policy, while in other states the influence of interest groups is moderated by group competition, party rivalry, and electoral politics?

We might define overall interest group influence in a state as "the extent to which interest groups as a whole influence public policy when compared to other components of the political system, such as political parties, the legislature, the governor, etc."[27] Using this definition researchers have attempted to categorize the states as having a "dominant," "complementary," or "subordinate" interest group system, in terms of its policy impact relative to the parties and the branches of government (see Table 4–6).

Over time interest group influence appears to be increasing in all of the states. A major factor in this strengthening of interest groups is their increasing role in

[25] See, for example, William P. Browne, "Variations in the Behavior and Style of State Lobbyists and Interest Groups," *Journal of Politics,* 47 (May 1985), 450–68.

[26] See Kenneth G. Hunter, Laura Ann Wilson, and Gregory G. Brunk, "Societal Complexity and Interest Group Lobbying in the American States," *Journal of Politics,* 53 (May 1991), 488–503.

[27] Thomas and Hrebenar "Interest Groups in the States," p. 141.

TABLE 4-6 CLASSIFICATION OF THE FIFTY STATES ACCORDING TO THE OVERALL IMPACT OF INTEREST GROUPS

	States Where the Overall Impact of Interest Groups Is			
Dominant (9)	Dominant/ Complementary (18)	Complementary (18)	Complementary/ Subordinate (5)	Subordinate (0)
Alabama	Arizona	Colorado	Connecticut	
Alaska	Arakansas	Illinois	Delaware	
Florida	California	Indiana	Minnesota	
Louisiana	Hawaii	Iowa	Rhode Island	
Mississippi	Georgia	Kansas	Vermont	
New Mexico	Idaho	Maine		
South Carolina	Kentucky	Maryland		
Tennessee	Montana	Massachusetts		
West Virginia	Nebraska	Michigan		
	Nevada	Missouri		
	Ohio	New Jersey		
	Oklahoma	New Hampshire		
	Oregon	New York		
	Texas	North Carolina		
	Utah	North Dakota		
	Virginia	Pennsylvania		
	Washington	South Dakota		
	Wyoming	Wisconsin		

Source: From *Politics in the American States: A Comparative Analysis,* 5/e by Virginia Gray, et al. Copyright © 1985 by Virginia Gray, Herbert Jacob, and Robert B. Albritton. Reprinted by permission of Harper Collins Publishers.

campaign finance. The more money coming from interest groups to political candidates, the greater is the influence of the interest group system.

Yet interest group influence in some states is greater than in other states and our task is to search for explanations.

The Economic Diversity Explanation   Wealthy urban industrial states (Connecticut, Massachusetts, Michigan, New Jersey, New York, Rhode Island) have weaker interest group systems because of the diversity and complexity of their economies. No single industry can dominate political life. Instead, multiple competing interest groups tend to balance each other, and this cancels the influence of interest groups generally. In contrast, in rural states with less economic diversity, a single dominant industry (oil in Alaska, oil and gas in Louisiana, coal in West Virginia) appears to have more influence. The reputation for influence for particular industries in these states causes them to be viewed as strong pressure group states.

The Party Explanation   According to political scientist Sarah McCally Morehouse, "Where parties are strong, pressure groups are weak or moderate; where parties are weak, pressure groups are strong enough to dominate the policy-making process.''[28] Where competitive political parties are strong—where the parties actively recruit candidates, provide campaign support, and hold their members accountable after the election—interest groups are less powerful. Policy makers in these states look to the party for policy guidance rather than to interest groups. Interest group influence is channeled through the parties; the parties are coalitions of interest groups; no single interest group can dominate or circumvent the party. Strong party states (Connecticut, Illinois, New York, Minnesota, North Dakota, Rhode Island, Wisconsin, Massachusetts, Colorado) have weak interest group systems. Weak party states (primarily the one-party southern states) have strong interest group systems. We will discuss party competition in Chapter 5.

Strong governors and strong legislative leadership, exercising their influence as party leaders, can provide a check on the lobbying efforts of interest groups. When the special interests lose, it is usually on issues on which the governor and the party leadership have taken a clear stand.[29]

The Professionalism Explanation   State legislatures are becoming more professional over time. In Chapter 6 we define a *professional* legislature as a well-paid, full-time, well-staffed body, as opposed to an amateur legislature which meets only a few weeks each year, pays its members very little, and has few research or information services available to it. Professional legislatures have less turnover in members and more experience in lawmaking. Clearly, these characteristics of legislatures affect the power of interest groups. Interest groups are more influential when legislatures are *less* professional. When members are less experienced, paid less, and have little time or resources to research issues themselves, they must depend more on interest groups, and interest groups gain influence. But in more professional legislatures, we should expect members to be less dependent on interest groups for information and technical expertise.

The Governmental Fragmentation Explanation   It is also likely that states with weak governors, multiple independently elected state officials, and numerous independent boards and commissions have strong interest group systems. In states with fragmented executive power (Florida, Mississippi, South Carolina), interest groups have additional points of access and control, and executive officials do not have counterbalancing power. Strong governors (as in New York, Massachusetts, New Jersey, Connecticut, Delaware, and Minnesota) are better able to confront the influence of interest groups when they choose to do so. (We will discuss governors' powers in Chapter 7.)

Fortunately, we do not have to choose one explanation to the exclusion of others. Economic diversity, party strength, professionalism, and governmental fragmentation all contribute to the explanation of interest group strength in the states.

---

[28] Sarah McCally Morehouse, *State Politics, Parties and Policy* (New York: Holt, Rinehart, & Winston, 1981), p. 118.

[29] See Charles W. Wiggins, Keith E. Harmun, and Charles G. Bell, "Interest-Group and Party Influence Agents in the Legislative Process: A Comparative State Analysis," *Journal of Politics* 54 (February 1992), 82–100.

PROTEST AS POLITICAL PARTICIPATION

Organized protests—marches, demonstrations, disruptions, civil disobedience—are important forms of political activity. Protest marches and demonstrations are now nearly as frequent at state capitols and city halls as in Washington.

It is important to distinguish between *protest, civil disobedience,* and *violence,* even though all may be forms of political activity. Most *protests* do *not* involve unlawful conduct and are protected by the constitutional guarantee of the First Amendment to "peaceably assemble and petition for redress of grievances." A march on city hall or the state capitol, followed by a mass assembly of people with speakers, sign-waving, songs, and perhaps the formal presentation of grievances to whichever brave official agrees to meet with the protesters is well within the constitutional guarantees of Americans.

Protest   *Protest* refers to direct, collective activity by persons who wish to obtain concessions from established power-holders. Often the protest is a means of acquiring bargaining power by those who would otherwise be powerless. The protest may challenge established groups by threatening their reputations (in cases in which they might be harmed by unfavorable publicity), their economic position (in cases in which noise and disruption upset their daily activity), or their sense of security (when the threat exists that the protest may turn unruly or violent). The strategy of protest may appeal especially to powerless minorities who have little else to bargain with except the promise to stop protesting.

Protests may also aim at motivating uncommitted "third parties" to enter the political arena on behalf of the protesters. The object of the protest is to call attention to the existence of some issue and urge others to apply pressure on public officials. Of course, this strategy requires the support and assistance of the news media. If protests are ignored by television and newspapers, they can hardly be expected to activate support. However, the news media seldom ignore protests with audience interest; protest leaders and journalists share an interest in dramatizing "news" for the public.

Civil Disobedience   *Civil disobedience* is a form of protest that involves breaking "unjust" laws. Civil disobedience is not new: It has played an important role in American history, from the Boston Tea Party to the abolitionists who illegally hid runaway slaves, to the suffragettes who demonstrated for women's voting rights, to the labor organizers who picketed to form the nation's major industrial unions, to the civil rights workers of the early 1960s who deliberately violated segregation laws. The purpose of civil disobedience is to call attention, or to "bear witness," to the existence of injustice. In the words of Martin Luther King, Jr., civil disobedience "seeks to dramatize the issue so that it can no longer be ignored."[30] There should be no violence in true civil disobedience, and only "unjust" laws are bro-

---

[30] For an inspiring essay on "nonviolent direct action" and civil disobedience in a modern context, read Martin Luther King, Jr., "Letter From Birmingham City Jail," April 16, 1963.

ken. Moreover, the law is broken "openly, lovingly" with a willingness to accept the penalty. Punishment is actively sought rather than avoided, since punishment will help to emphasize the injustice of the law. The object is to stir the conscience of an apathetic majority and win support for measures that will eliminate injustices. By willingly accepting punishment for the violation of an unjust law, people who practice civil disobedience demonstrate their sincerity. They hope to shame public officials and make them ask themselves how far they are willing to go to protect the status quo.

As in all protest activity, the participation of the news media, particularly television, is essential to the success of civil disobedience. The dramatization of injustice makes news; the public's sympathy is won when injustices are spotlighted; and the willingness of demonstrators to accept punishment is visible evidence of their sincerity. Cruelty or violence directed *against* the demonstrators by police or others plays into the hands of the protesters by further emphasizing injustices.[31]

Violence   *Violence* can also be a form of political participation. To be sure, it is criminal, and it is generally irrational and self-defeating. However, political assassination, bombing and terrorism, and rioting, burning, and looting have occurred with uncomfortable frequency in American politics.

It is important to distinguish violence from protest. Peaceful protest is constitutionally guaranteed. One careful study of protest activity in American cities estimates that only 6 percent of the reported protests involved violence of any kind.[32] Occasionally there is an implicit *threat* of violence in a protest—a threat that can be manipulated by protesters to help gain their ends. However, most protests harness frustrations and hostilities and direct them into constitutionally acceptable activities. Civil disobedience should also be distinguished from violence. The civil disobedient breaks only "unjust" laws, openly and without violence, and willingly accepts punishment without attempting escape. Rioting, burning, and looting—as well as bombing and assassination—are clearly distinguishable from peaceful protest and even civil disobedience.

News Media   The real key to success in protest activity is found in the support or opposition of the news media to protest group demands. Virtually all of the studies of protest activity have asserted that it is the response of "third parties," primarily the news media, and not the immediate response of public officials, that is essential to success.[33] "As an indirect process, the communications and reference publics—not the targets—play crucial roles in determining the response of local political

---

[31] For more detailed examination of the purposes, functions, and rationale of civil disobedience, see Paul F. Power, "Civil Disobedience as Functional Opposition," *Journal of Politics,* 34 (February 1972), 37–55; and "On Civil Disobedience in Recent American Thought," *American Political Science Review,* 64 (March 1970), 35–47.

[32] Peter K. Eisinger, "The Conditions of Protest Behavior in American Cities," *American Political Science Review,* 67 (March 1973), 11–29.

[33] Michael Lipsky, *Protest in City Politics* (Chicago: Rand, McNally, 1970); Eisinger, "The Conditions of Protest Behavior in American Cities"; Paul D. Schumaker, "Policy Responsiveness to Protest Group Demands," *Journal of Politics,* 37 (May 1975), 488–521.

systems."[34] This is a plausible finding, because, after all, if protesters could persuade public officials directly there would be no need to protest. Indeed, one might even distinguish between "interest groups," which have a high degree of continuous interaction with public officials, and "protest groups," which do not regularly interact with public officials and must engage in protest to be heard. Furthermore, to be heard, reports of their protests must be carried in newspapers and on television.

Explaining Protest Activity   Protest activity in the fifty states is associated with income, urbanization, and education.[35] Student and antiwar demonstrations occurred more frequently in states with higher incomes, greater urbanization, and more educated populations. Racial demonstrations occurred more frequently in states with larger black population percentages and lower voter participation rates. There is no convincing evidence that *state* policies (educational spending, for example) had any direct effect on this protest activity, although scholars disagree on this point. Nor is there any convincing evidence that protest activity was successful in achieving much more than *symbolic* gains. At best, governments may adopt a "policy" statement designed to meet the demands of protesters. However, it is very difficult for protest activity to ensure "implementation" of long-run goals or any real lasting "impact" on conditions that concern protesters.

THE EFFECTIVENESS OF PROTESTS

Several conditions must be present if protest is to be effective.[36] First of all, there must be a clear goal or objective of the protest. Protesters must aim at specific concessions or legislation they desire; generally, complex problems or complaints that cannot readily be solved by specific governmental action are not good targets for protest activity. Second, the protest must be directed at some public officials who are capable of granting the desired goal. It is difficult to secure concessions if no one is in a position to grant them. Third, the protest leaders must not only organize their masses for protest activity, but they must also simultaneously bargain with public officials for the desired concessions. This implies a division of labor between "organizers" and the "negotiators."[37]

---

[34] Schumaker, "Policy Responsiveness," p. 513.

[35] Ira M. Wasserman, "State Policy Outputs and Collective Behavior," *Social Science Quarterly,* 59 (September 1978), 379–85; Dean Jaros and Michael A. Baer, "Political Disaffection in the American States: Substantive and Symbolic Policy Determinants," *Social Science Quarterly,* 57 (December 1976), 579–88.

[36] See Michael Lipsky, "Protest as a Political Resource," *American Political Science Review,* 62 (December 1968), 1144–58.

[37] For an example of how protest leaders and established bargainers worked in tandem to desegregate public facilities in Atlanta in 1960, see Jack L. Walker, "Protest and Negotiation: A Case Study of Negro Leadership in Atlanta," *Midwest Journal of Political Science* (May 1963), 99–124.

The effectiveness of protest activity can be measured in a variety of ways:[38]

"Access"—Will officials listen to the concerns of the protesters?

"Agenda"—Will officials agree to vote on a proposal by the protesters?

"Policy"—Will officials pass a law desired by the protesters?

"Implementation"—Will officials enforce the law passed as a result of the protests?

"Impact"—Will the law actually improve the conditions that led to the protest?

Obviously these measures of success move from the easiest to achieve, "Access," to the most difficult, "Impact."

Finally, we might note in this discussion the strategies available to public officials who are faced with protest activity. They may greet the protesters with smiles and reassurances that they agree with their objectives. They may dispense *symbolic* satisfaction without actually granting any tangible payoffs. Once the "crisis" is abated, the bargaining leverage of the protest leaders diminishes considerably. Public officials may dispense *token* satisfactions by responding, with much publicity, to one or more specific cases of injustice, while doing little of a broad-based nature to alleviate conditions. Or public officials may *appear to be constrained* in their ability to grant protest goals by claiming that they lack the financial resources or legal authority to do anything—the "I-would-help-you-if-I-could-but-I-can't" pose. Another tactic is to *postpone action* by calling for further study while offering assurances of sympathy and interest. Finally, public officials may try to *discredit* protesters by stating or implying that they are violence-prone or unrepresentative of the real aspirations of the people they seek to lead. This tactic is especially effective if the protest involves violence or disruption or if protest leaders have "leftist" or criminal backgrounds.

---

[38] Schumaker, "Policy Responsiveness."

5

PARTIES AND CAMPAIGNS
IN THE STATES

AMERICAN POLITICAL PARTIES IN DISARRAY

Once upon a time, political parties were the central features on the American political landscape. Party loyalties were a way of life, passed on in families like religion.
People identified themselves as Republicans or Democrats and usually voted for
their party's nominees. Scholars wrote that parties were indispensable to democracy: "Political parties created modern democracy and modern democracy is un-
thinkable save in terms of parties."[1]

The Responsible Party Model   The parties were viewed as the principal instrument of majority control of public policy. "Responsible parties" were supposed to
(1) develop and clarify alternative policy positions for the voters; (2) educate the
people about the issues and simplify choices for them; (3) recruit candidates for
public office who agreed with the parties' policy positions; (4) organize and direct
their candidates' campaigns to win office; (5) hold their elected officials responsible
for enacting the parties' policy positions after they were elected; and (6) organize

---

[1] E. E. Schattschneider, *Party Government* (New York: Rinehart, 1942), p. 1.

legislatures to ensure party control of policy making. In carrying out these functions, responsible parties were supposed to modify the demands of special interests, build a consensus that could win majority support, and provide simple and identifiable, yet meaningful, choices for the voters on election day. In this way, disciplined, issue-oriented, competitive parties would be the principal means by which the people would direct public policy.

Problems with the Model   Over the years, this "responsible party" model fell into disarray, if indeed it ever accurately described American political parties. There are fundamental problems with the responsible model itself:

1. *The parties do not offer the voters clear policy alternatives.* Instead, each tries to capture the broad center of most policy dimensions, where it believes most Americans can be found. There is no incentive for parties to stand on the far right or far left when most Americans are found in the center. So the parties echo each other, and critics refer to them as Tweedledee and Tweedledum.

2. *Voter decisions are not motivated primarily by policy considerations.* Most voters cast their votes on the basis of candidate "image," the "goodness" or "badness" of the times, and traditional voting habits. This means there is little incentive for either parties or candidates to concentrate on issues. Party platforms are seldom read by anyone. Modern campaign techniques focus on the image of the candidate—compassion, warmth, good humor, experience, physical appearance, ease in front of a camera, and so forth—rather than positions on the issues.

3. *American political parties have no way to bind their elected officials to party positions or even their campaign pledges.* Parties cannot really discipline members of Congress or state legislatures for voting against the party position. Party cohesion, where it exists, is more a product of likemindedness among Democratic or Republican legislators than it is of party control.

In addition to these underlying problems, today's parties face new challenges:

4. *The rise of primary elections.* Party organizations cannot control who the party's nominee shall be. Nominations are won in primary elections. The progressive reformers who introduced primary elections at the beginning of the twentieth century wanted to undercut the power of party machines in determining who runs for office, and the reformers succeeded in doing so. Nominees now establish personal organizations in primary elections and campaign for popular votes; they do not have to negotiate with party leaders. Of course, the party organization may endorse a candidate in a primary election, but this is no guarantee of success with the party's voters.

5. *The decline of party identification.* Democratic and Republican party loyalties have been declining over the years. Most people remain registered as Democrats or Republicans in order to vote in party primary elections, but increasing numbers of people identify themselves as "independent" and cast their vote in general elections without reference to party. Split-ticket voting (where a single voter casts his or her vote for a Democrat in one race and a Republican in another) is also increasing.

6. *The influence of the mass media, particularly television.* Candidates can come directly into the voter's living room via television. Campaigning is now

largely a media activity. Candidates no longer need party workers to carry their message from block to block

7. *The decline of patronage.* Civil service reforms, at the national, state, and even city levels, have reduced the tangible rewards of electoral victory. Party "professionals"—who work in political campaigns to secure jobs and favors for themselves and their friends—are now being replaced by political "amateurs"—who work in political campaigns for the emotional satisfaction of supporting a "cause." Amateurs work intensely during campaigns, but professionals once worked year-round, off-years and election years, building party support with small personal favors for the voters. These party "regulars" are disappearing.

8. *The rise of single-issue interest groups and PACs.* Parties have always coexisted with broad-based interest groups, many of whom contribute money to both Democratic and Republican candidates in order to ensure access regardless of who wins. But many of the more militant single-issue groups require a "litmus test" of individual candidates on single issues—abortion, gun control, ERA, and so forth. Their support and money hinge on the candidate's position on a single issue. Most PAC (political action committee) money goes directly to candidates, not to party organizations. Increasingly, parties have less and less to do with campaign financing.

Continuing Party Role in Selecting Candidates   Despite these problems, the American political parties survive. They are important in the selection of *personnel* for public office, if not for the selection of public policy. Very few independents are ever elected to high political office. Only three governors in recent years, James Longley of Maine, Walter Hickel of Alaska, and Lowell Weicker of Connecticut, were elected as independents; there are fewer than a dozen independent state legislators in the nation; the Nebraska legislature is the nation's only nonpartisan state legislative body.

Party Structures   We might view political parties as three separate structures. The first is the *party-in-the-electorate:* the voters who identify themselves as Democrats or Republicans, and who tend to vote for the candidates of their party. It is this party-in-the-electorate that appears to be in decline today. Party loyalties are weakening; more people identify themselves as "independents"; "crossover" and "ticket splitting" have increased, and more voters cast their ballots without regard to the party affiliation of the candidates. The second is the *party-in-the-government:* state and local elected officials who won party nominations and appeared on the ballot as Democratic or Republican candidates. This party has weakened also: More party nominations are won through primary elections; party leaders have less influence over the nomination process; candidates communicate to the voters by television rather than through party workers; and parties have no way to bind elected officials to party positions. Nonetheless, party identification and loyalty among elected officeholders (the party-in-the-government) is generally stronger than party identification and loyalty among voters (the party-in-the-electorate). (We will examine the role of parties in state legislatures in Chapter 6 and in the governorship in Chapter 7.) Finally, there is *the party organization:* party officials and workers, committee members and convention delegates, and other party activists. Years ago, many American cities were dominated by party "machines" and "bosses," but the reformers succeeded in bringing nonpartisan elections to local government in a majority of the nation's cities (see Chapter 9). Nonetheless, party organizations still flourish at the state and county level, as we will see later in this chapter.

PARTIES IN THE FIFTY STATES

The Democratic and Republican parties are highly visible in state politics. But the assertion that parties are the "single most important factor in state politics"[2] is more an expression of hope than a description of reality. Years ago, when parties were more important than they are today, political scientist V. O. Key, Jr., was careful to distinguish between a "few" states in which the parties resembled the responsible model and the many states in which the party labels were meaningless.

The party systems in each state differ. According to Key, "The institutions developed to perform [party] functions in each state differ markedly in form from the national parties. It is an error to assume that the political parties of each state are but miniatures of the national party system. In a few states that condition is approached, but . . . each state has its own pattern of action and often it deviates markedly from the forms of organization commonly thought of as constituting party systems."[3]

How do the fifty state party systems differ?

1. *Partisan success.* The Democratic party has long dominated American state politics (Table 5–1). Nationwide, Democratic state legislators outnumber Republicans by more than three to two, and there are usually more Democratic governors than Republican governors. (See section, "Republican and Democratic Party Fortunes.")

2. *Party competition.* Some states are "one-party" states, where winning the dominant party's nomination is a guarantee of election to office. The opposition party is so weak that it may not even nominate candidates in many elections, and when it does, these candidates have little chances of success. (See section, "Party Competition in the States.")

3. *Class-based party constituencies.* In some states the Democratic and Republican parties represent separate social and economic groups within the state: The Democratic party may be composed of central-city, low-income, ethnic, and black constituencies; the Republican party may represent middle-class, suburban, small-town, and rural constituencies. However, in other states both parties may attempt to represent the same groups, and it is difficult to detect any socioeconomic differences between the Democratic and Republican parties. (See section, "The Effects of Party Competition.")

---

2 Sarah McCally Morehouse, *State Parties, Politics and Policy* (New York: Holt Rinehart, & Winston, 1981), p. 29.

3 V. O. Key, Jr., *Politics, Parties and Pressure Groups,* 4th ed. (New York: Thomas Y. Crowell, 1958), p. 311.

TABLE 5–1   DEMOCRATIC AND REPUBLICAN GOVERNORS AND LEGISLATORS

	Governors[a]		Upper Houses[c]			Lower Houses[c]		
	DEM	REP	DEM	REP	TIE	DEM	REP	TIE
1992	30	18[a]	31	16	2	34	14	1
1990	28	20[a]	35	12	2	38	11	0
1988	28	22[a]	32	17	0	36	12	1
1986	26	24	31	16	2	35	13	1
1984	34	16	32	16	1	33	15	1
1982	34	16	33	15	1	38	11	0
1980	27	23	32	17	0	31	18	0
1978	31	19	35	14	0	32	15	2
1976	37	12[b]	38	9	2	40	8	1
1974	36	24	35	14	0	41	8	0

[a] Two Independent governors, Hickel of Alaska and Weicker of Connecticut.
[b] Maine elected an Independent governor in 1974 and 1976.
[c] Nebraska has a nonpartisan legislature; therefore, legislative chambers in this listing total forty-nine.

REPUBLICAN AND DEMOCRATIC PARTY FORTUNES

In recent years, the Democratic party has held a decided edge in American state government. Table 5–1 shows the number of upper and lower houses in state legislatures controlled by Democrats and Republicans in recent years, along with the total number of Democratic and Republican governors and legislators. Throughout this period the Democratic party has controlled a majority of state legislatures and governorships.

Presidential Elections   A state's political coloration in national politics may be quite different from its statewide political affiliation. In presidential elections the eleven southern states have been a partisan battleground. Democrat Bill Clinton won four southern states in 1992. (Arkansas, Tennessee, Georgia, and Louisiana). But Republican Ronald Reagan swept the South in both 1980 and 1984, and Republican George Bush swept the South in 1988. In 1976, the Democratic presidential candidate, former Georgia Governor Jimmy Carter, pulled all but one of the southern states into the Democratic column. In 1968, Republican Richard Nixon won five southern states (Florida, North Carolina, South Carolina, Tennessee, and Virginia); independent candidate George C. Wallace won five southern states (Alabama, Arkansas, Georgia, Louisiana, and Mississippi); and the Democratic nominee Hubert Humphrey won only Texas. This continuing battle for the electoral votes of the southern states in presidential races really began in 1964 when five traditionally Democratic states of the Old Confederacy (Alabama, Georgia, Louisiana, Mississippi, and South Carolina) voted for Republican Barry Goldwater.

TABLE 5–2   PARTY IDENTIFICATION AMONG ALL AMERICAN ADULTS

	1960	1964	1968	1972	1976	1980	1984	1986	1990	1992
Democrats	47	52	43	41	40	41	42	37	39	37
Independents	32	23	28	35	36	25	28	29	30	30
Republicans	31	24	29	23	23	34	30	34	31	32

Figures may not add to 100 because of rounding.

Sources: Harold W. Stanley and Richard G. Niemi, *Vital Statistics on American Politics,* 3rd ed. (Washington, DC: CQ Press, 1992), p. 158; updated by author.

State and Local Elections   In state and local elections the southern states have remained heavily Democratic. However, Republicans have succeeded over time in increasing their representation in every southern state legislature, even though they have yet to capture majority control of either the house or the senate in any southern state. Moreover, Republican governors have been elected at one time or another in recent decades in every southern state except Georgia. Nonetheless, it is likely that the southern states will remain heavily Democratic in state and local politics for some time to come.

Party Identification   Not only has the Democratic party been the dominant party-in-the-government in the American states, it has also enjoyed greater support in the national electorate. More Americans identify with the Democratic party than the Republican party (Table 5–2). This Democratic party preference persists even in years when Republican presidents win landslide elections.

In most states, Democratic party identifiers outnumber Republican party identifiers. It is estimated that Republican identifiers outnumber Democratic identifiers in only eight states—Indiana, Iowa, Kansas, Nebraska, New Hampshire, North Dakota, Utah, and Vermont.[4] All other states polls tend to report a plurality of Democratic party identifiers.

Party Registration   In states that register voters by party, the Democratic party does even better in registration figures than it does in opinion polls.[5] The tendency for many independents and even some Republicans to register as Democrats is not confined to the South. (In Florida 1992 polls showed party identifications as 32 percent Democratic, 32 percent Republican, and 36 percent independent; yet official registration figures showed 52 percent Democratic, 41 percent Republican, and 7 percent independent.) Of course, independents are spurred in many states to register with one party or another in order to participate in primary elections that are

---

[4] Robert S. Erikson, Gerald C. Wright, and John P. McIver, "Political Parties, Public Opinion, and State Policy," *American Political Science Review* 83 (September 1989), 729–50.

[5] See Steven E. Finkel and Howard A. Scarrow, "Party Identification and Party Enrollment," *Journal of Politics,* 47 (May 1985), 620–42.

closed to all but party registrants. (See "Parties and Primaries" later in this chapter.) Voters chose to register in the dominant party for several reasons: perhaps because the dominant party's primary is more interesting insofar as the winner is more likely to go on to win office; or perhaps because people seeking political favors (like jobs, contracts, zoning decisions) wish to be identified publicly with the dominant party; or perhaps because of social pressures and a desire to be seen as a member of the dominant party. Because the Democratic party is the dominant party in most states, registration figures are even more heavily skewed toward the Democrats than actual party identification or voting.

PARTY COMPETITION IN THE STATES

The ideal "responsible" party system is said to be one in which *competitive parties* present alternative programs in election campaigns, and the party winning the majority of votes captures all the power it needs to write its program into law. Moreover, in the responsible party system, the elected officials act cohesively so the voters can hold the party collectively responsible at the end of its term of office. The key to this ideal party system is the existence of competitive parties that are roughly balanced in strength.

How Much Party Competition?   In reality, however, party competition throughout the fifty states is limited. The dominance of the Democratic party in so many states precludes any real competition for control of upper or lower chambers of state legislatures in these states and renders most gubernatorial races noncompetitive as well. Table 5–3 groups states according to the percentage of times between 1968 and 1992 Republicans captured control of the governorship and upper and lower houses of the state legislature. Note that twenty-one states fall into the category of Democratic dominance, wherein fewer than 20 percent of the institutional wins went to the Republican party. In contrast, in only three states did the GOP win control of these institutions over 80 percent of the time. Only six states are genuinely competitive in the sense that the Democratic and Republican parties have won control of these governing institutions between 41 and 60 percent of the time. Modified Democratic dominance characterizes 12 states, and modified Republican dominance characterizes eight states.

Party Labels   There are several important differences between competitive or two-party states and noncompetitive or one-party states. Voters in *two-party* states can use party labels to help them identify the politics of candidates. The fact that candidates run under the Republican or Democratic banner does not guarantee their stand on every public issue, but it indicates with which broad coalition in American politics candidates have associated themselves. Party labels carry meaning for most voters, even though individual candidates may be "disloyal" to their party on occasion. At the very least, a party label in a two-party state tells more about a candidate's politics than a strange name on a ballot with no party affiliation indicated. Even if policy differences between the parties are vague, there is at least an "in party" and an "out party," which can be identified at election time. However, in *one-party* states the minority party often fails to run candidates for many

TABLE 5–3   PARTY COMPETITION FOR CONTROL OF STATE GOVERNMENT

Percentage of Republican Wins 1968–1992[a]

DEMOCRATIC DOMINANCE	MODIFIED DEMOCRATIC DOMINANCE	COMPETITIVE	MODIFIED REPUBLICAN DOMINANCE	REPUBLICAN DOMINANCE
0–20	21–40	41–60	61–80	81–100
Alabama	California	Alaska	Arizona	Indiana
Arkansas	Connecticut	Delaware	Colorado	New Hampshire
Florida	Illinois	Iowa	Idaho	South Dakota
Georgia	Maine	Nebraska[b]	Kansas	
Hawaii	Michigan	New York	North Dakota	
Kentucky	Minnesota	Ohio	Utah	
Louisiana	Montana		Vermont	
Maryland	New Jersey		Wyoming	
Massachusetts	Oregon			
Mississippi	Pennsylvania			
Missouri	Washington			
Nevada	Wisconsin			
New Mexico				
North Carolina				
Oklahoma				
Rhode Island				
South Carolina				
Tennessee				
Texas				
Virginia				
West Virginia				

[a] The governorship, control of the lower chamber, and control of the upper chamber are figured separately. That is, if in a given year the Republicans won the governorship and control of one chamber, they had two wins and Democrats one win.

[b] Results are for the governorship only because the legislature is nonpartisan.

Source: Stanley and Niemi, *Vital Statistics on American Politics,* p. 38; updated by author.

offices. Under these circumstances, the party out of office is unable to perform the important role of criticizing officeholders. The existence of a competitive party *outside* of government, a party that has a real chance of replacing officeholders at the next election, can help to make officeholders more aware of their responsibilities to the voters.

Factions   One-party states may have "liberal" and "conservative" factions of some durability. However, in two-party states, the party label can be seen by every voter on election day. A party label is not so obscure as an alignment with a liberal or conservative faction. Most students of state politics believe that it is more difficult to hold factions responsible. Factions are even more fluid and change personality and policies more frequently than parties. V. O. Key argued that the southern factional system obscured politics for most citizens and permitted conservative interests to manipulate the voters.[6] A large number of people who know little about the policies of various factions are easily misled. This does not mean that many voters are not confused about party policies in competitive states or that competitive parties can always hold their legislators responsible, but it does mean that party competition is more likely to clarify things for the voter than one-party factional politics.

THE EFFECTS OF PARTY COMPETITION

What difference does it make in public policy whether a state has competitive or noncompetitive parties? Do states with a competitive party system differ in their approach to education, welfare, health, taxation, or highways from states with noncompetitive party systems? This is not an easy question to answer. Since competitive states tend to be wealthy, urban, and industrialized, and noncompetitive states poorer, rural, and agricultural, it is difficult to sort out the effects of party competition from those other socioeconomic variables. Some scholars assert that a competitive party system leads to more liberal education, welfare, and taxation policies and that one-partyism strengthens conservative views. However, available evidence indicates that education, welfare, taxation, and highway programs appear to be *more closely related* to socioeconomic factors in the states than to the degree of party competition itself.[7]

Policy Effects of Competition   The thesis that party competition produced liberal welfare programs was suggested many years ago by V. O. Key, Jr.:

> In the two-party states the anxiety over the next election pushes political leaders into serving the interests of the have-less elements of society, therefore putting the party into the countervailing power operation.
>
> . . . [i]n the one-party states it is easier for a few powerful interests to manage the government of the state without party interference since the parties are not rep-

---

[6] V. O. Key, Jr., *Southern Politics in State and Nation* (New York: Knopf, 1949). See also Alan P. Sindler, "Bifactional Rivalry as an Alternative to Two-Party Competition in Louisiana," *American Political Science Review,* 46 (1955), 641.

[7] The traditional assumption that party competition had an important liberalizing effect on public policy is found in V. O. Key, Jr., *American State Politics: An Introduction* (New York: Knopf, 1956); Duane Lockard, *The Politics of State and Local Government* (New York: Macmillan, 1963); John H. Fenton, *People and Parties in Politics* (Glenview, IL: Scott, Foresman, 1966). The effect of party competition on public policy was shown in statistic analysis to be *less* influential than economic condition in Thomas R. Dye, *Politics, Economics, and the Public* (Chicago: Rand McNally, 1966); Richard E. Dawson and James A. Robinson, "Inter-Party Competition, Economic Variables, and Welfare Policies in the American States," *Journal of Politics,* 25 (May 1963), 265–89; Richard I. Hofferbert, "The Relation Between Public Policy and Some Structural and Environmental Variables in the American States," *American Political Science Review* 60 (March 1966), 78–82. However, party competition combined with voter participation was found to have some effect on certain welfare policies in Ira Sharkansky and Richard I. Hofferbert, "Dimensions of State Politics, Economics and Public Policy," *American Political Science Review,* 63 (September 1969), 867–79.

resentative of the particular elements that might pose opposition to the dominant group.

... [o]ver the long run the have-nots lose in a disorganized politics.[8]

When these assertions were tested, however, it turned out that there were few significant *independent* relationships between party competition and levels of public taxing and spending in the American states. Once the effects of income, urbanization, and education are controlled, the initial relationships between competition and participation and public policy largely disappear. Competition and participation are dependent upon levels of economic development, and so are levels of public taxing and spending; the associations between competitive politics and public policies turned out to be largely spurious. Or, as Thomas R. Dye explains:

> Economic development shapes both political systems and policy outcomes, and most of the association that occurs between system characteristics and policy outcomes can be attributed to the influence of economic development. Differences in the policy choices of states with different types of political systems turn out to be largely a product of differing socioeconomic levels rather than a direct product of political variables.[9]

Why Competition May Not Produce Policy Differences   Party competition itself does not necessarily cause more liberal welfare policies. If there is a *unimodal* distribution of voters' preferences in a state, and if the state parties are devoid of strong organizations and ideologically motivated activists, then the party system will have little meaning for public policy. This notion can be diagrammed as follows:

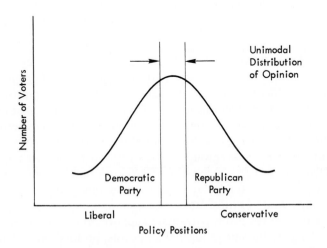

---

[8] Key, *Southern Politics*, p. 307.

[9] Dye, *Politics, Economics, and the Public*, p. 293.

where there is a unimodal distribution of opinion (most voters are found in the center) and the parties move toward the middle position to capture the greatest number of voters.

However, the party system can be policy-relevant if there is a *bimodal* distribution of voters' preferences in a state; and if the parties have strong organization and ideologically motivated activists, then the parties in that state will offer clear policy alternatives. This notion can be diagrammed as follows:

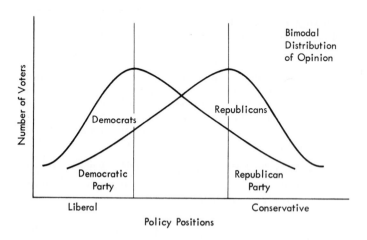

where there is a bimodal distribution of opinion (voters divide into liberals and conservatives) and the parties take the policy positions of their different groups of constituents.

Policy Relevance of the Parties   Does this mean that there are no real differences between Republican and Democratic parties in the states? Certainly at the national level, it is not difficult to see the different coalitions that comprise the two parties. While the moderate viewpoints of American parties ensure that major social groups are seldom wholly within one party or another, differences between the Democratic and Republican parties at the national level are revealed by different proportions of votes given by major groups in the electorate to the two major political parties. The Democratic party receives a disproportionate amount of support from Catholics, Jews, blacks, less educated and lower-income groups; younger people; skilled, semiskilled, and unskilled laborers; union members; big-city residents. The Republican party receives disproportionate support from Protestants, whites, better educated and higher-income groups; older people; professional, managerial, and other white-collar workers; nonunion members; and rural and small-town residents. (See Table 5–4.)

These differences between the Democratic and Republican parties at the national level can be observed in the politics of some states but not in others. *State Republican and Democratic parties resemble the national Republican and Democratic parties*

TABLE 5-4 VOTE BY GROUPS IN PRESIDENTIAL ELECTIONS

	1980			1984		1988		1992		
	DEM CARTER	REP REAGAN	IND ANDERSON	DEM MONDALE	REP REAGAN	DEM DUKAKIS	REP BUSH	DEM CLINTON	REP BUSH	IND PEROT
National	41%	51%	7%	41%	59%	46%	54%	43%	38%	19%
Sex										
Men	38	53	7	37	61	41	57	41	38	21
Women	44	49	6	42	57	49	51	46	37	17
Race										
White	36	56	7	34	66	40	59	39	41	20
Nonwhite	86	10	2	90	9	86	12	82	11	7
Education										
College	35	53	10	40	59	31	62	44	39	18
High school	43	51	5	39	60	49	50	43	36	20
Grade school	54	42	3	49	50	56	43	55	28	17
Age										
Under 30 years	47	41	11	41	58	47	52	44	34	22
30–49 years	38	52	8	40	59	45	54	42	38	20
50 years and older	41	54	4	37	62	46	54	41	40	19
Religion										
Protestants	39	54	6	26	73	33	66	33	46	21
Catholics	46	47	6	44	55	47	52	44	36	20
Politics										
Republicans	8	86	5	7	92	8	92	10	73	17
Democrats	69	26	4	73	26	82	17	77	10	13
Independents	29	55	14	35	63	43	55	38	32	30
Region										
East	43	47	9	47	52	49	50	47	35	18
Midwest	41	51	7	38	61	47	52	42	37	21
South	44	52	3	36	63	41	58	42	43	16
West	35	54	9	40	49	46	52	44	34	22
Members of Labor Union Families	50	43	5	53	45	57	42	55	24	21

Sources: Gallup Opinion Surveys for 1980–88; The New York Times, November 5, 1992, for 1992.

only in those states where each party represents separate socioeconomic constituencies.[10] Party conflict over policy questions is most frequent in those states in which the Democratic party represents central-city, low-income, ethnic, and racial constituencies, and the Republican party represents middle-class, suburban, small-town, and rural constituencies. In these larger urban industrialized states, the Democratic and Republican parties will tend to disagree over taxation and appropriations, welfare, education, and regulation of business and labor—that is, the major social and economic controversies that divide the national parties.

Party and Policy in the States   We have tried to classify the states on the basis of *both* party competition and the policy-relevance of their party systems. The results are shown in Table 5–5. *Party competition* is measured here by the average closeness of the vote in governors' races over the past thirty years. *Policy-relevance* is determined by whether or not a change in party control of state government (the governor's office and one or both houses of the legislature) was associated with changes in state welfare spending. If Democratic control of a state government was associated with significant increases in state welfare spending, and Republican control was associated with only modest increases or no increases in welfare spending, then the state party system is classified as policy-relevant.[11]

Only twenty-one states have had truly policy-relevant party systems over the past thirty years. (These are the states listed in the left column of Table 5–5.) In these states, the party systems conform to the national party model; electing Democratic governors and legislatures in these states resulted in increased welfare spending, while the election of Republicans held down welfare spending. But in twenty-nine states the election of Democratic or Republican governors or legislatures had *no* significant effect on welfare spending.

PARTY ACTIVISTS AND POLITICAL IDEOLOGY

While state parties are pushed toward the ideological center in order to win elections, the activists in the parties tend to be strong ideologues—people who take consistently "liberal" or "conservative" positions on the issues. Republican party activists in most states are more conservative than Democratic party activists. Indeed, Republican party activists tend to be more conservative than the general public, and Democratic party activists tend to be more liberal than the general public. This is true even though activists in both parties will tend to be more conser-

[10] See Edward T. Jennings, "Competition Constituencies and Welfare Politics in American States," *American Political Science Review,* 73 (June 1979), 414–29; Thomas A. Flinn, "Party Responsibility in the States; Some Causal Factors," *American Political Science Review,* 58 (1964), 60–71; Duncan McRae, Jr., "The Relation Between Roll Call Votes and Constituencies in the Massachusetts House of Representatives," *American Political Science Review,* 46 (1952), 1046–55.

[11] See Thomas R. Dye, "Party and Policy in the States," *Journal of Politics,* 46 (November 1984), 1097–1116.

TABLE 5–5   PARTY AND POLICY IN THE STATES

Competitive States

POLICY-RELEVANT PARTIES	NON-POLICY-RELEVANT PARTIES
California	Alaska
Hawaii	Connecticut
Iowa	Illinois
Maine	Indiana
Michigan	New York
Minnesota	
Nebraska	
New Jersey	
North Dakota	
Ohio	
Oregon	
Pennsylvania	
South Dakota	
Wisconsin	
Wyoming	

Modified Competitive States

POLICY-RELEVANT PARTIES	NON-POLICY-RELEVANT PARTIES
Idaho	Colorado
Massachusetts	Kansas
Montana	New Hampshire
Nevada	Vermont
Utah	Washington

Noncompetitive States

POLICY-RELEVANT PARTIES	NON-POLICY-RELEVANT PARTIES	
Rhode Island	Alabama	Mississippi
	Arizona	Missouri
	Arkansas	New Mexico
	Delaware	North Carolina
	Florida	Oklahoma
	Georgia	South Carolina
	Kentucky	Tennessee
	Louisiana	Texas
	Maryland	Virginia
		West Virginia

vative in a conservative state and more liberal in a liberal state. We might represent the ideological positions of party activists in the states in the following diagram:

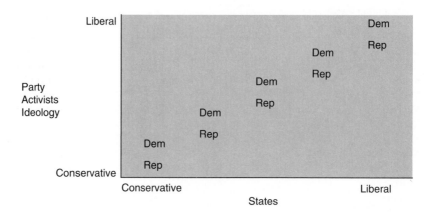

In conservative states, both Democratic and Republican activists are more conservative than their counterparts in liberal states. But in each state Democratic party activists are more liberal than Republican party activists. In the most liberal states, the Republican activists are more liberal than the Democratic activists in the most conservative states. According to this theory, we expect the Republican party activists in New York and Connecticut (liberal states according to Figure 1–5) to be more liberal than Democratic party activists in Arizona, Utah, or Mississippi. Some evidence to support this theory has been gleaned from public opinion polls and surveys of party leaders in the states.[12]

In short, we know that party control of state government is not a good predictor of public policy. But this does not necessarily mean that there are no differences between the parties. *Party activists* may differ over the issues, yet the parties in the government may be obliged to respond to public opinion in the states.

STATE PARTY ORGANIZATIONS

State party organizations are "highly variable, elusive to find, difficult to define, and frustrating to study."[13] Indeed, both Democratic and Republican party organizations at the state and local level are ill defined, fluid, and very often "unoccupied." As many as half of the official party positions in the nation may be vacant. Moreover, many people who hold party positions do little or nothing to help their parties or its candidates.

---

[12] Erikson et al., "Political Parties."

[13] Robert J. Huckshorn, *Party Leadership in the States* (Amherst: University of Massachusetts Press, 1976), p. 1.

Impact of Federalism   American political parties are decentralized in their organization. It is not really surprising in the American system of federalism—when only the president and vice-president have *national* constituencies, and senators, representatives, governors, state legislators, county and city officials all have *state and local* constituencies—that the American parties are decentralized.

At the national level, the Democratic and Republican parties consist of a national committee; a House and Senate party conference; various national clubs, such as Young Democrats and Young Republicans, and Democratic and Republican Women's Federations. There are also *fifty state parties,* which are composed of state committees and county and city organizations. This structure is tied together very loosely. State parties are not very responsive to national direction, and in most states, city and county organizations operate quite independently of the state committees. State committees are generally involved in important statewide elections —governors, U.S. senators, and representatives in the smaller states. City and county committees are generally responsible for county and municipal offices, state legislative seats, and congressional seats in the larger states. The Democratic and Republican National Committees exist primarily for the purpose of holding national conventions every four years to select the party's presidential candidate. Since each level of party organization has "its own fish to fry," each operates quite independently of the other levels.

State Laws Govern Parties   Party affairs are governed largely by the laws of the states. Each state sets forth the conditions that an organization must meet to qualify as a political party and to get its candidates' names printed on the official election ballots. Each state sets the qualifications for membership in a party and the right to vote in the party's primary election. State laws determine the number, method of selection, and duties of various party officials, committees, and conventions. The states, rather than the parties themselves, decide how the parties shall nominate candidates for public office. Most states require that party nominations be made by direct primaries, but several states still nominate by party caucuses or conventions. Most states also attempt to regulate party finances, although with little success.

State Committees   State party organizations officially consist of a "state committee," a "state chairman," or "chairwoman," and perhaps a small office staff working at the state capitol. Democratic and Republican state committees vary from state to state in composition, organization, and function. Membership on the state committee may range from about a dozen up to several hundred. The members may be chosen through party primaries or by state party conventions. Generally, representation on state committees is allocated to counties, but occasionally other units of government are recognized in state party organization. A state party chairman or chairwoman generally serves at the head of the state committee; these people are generally selected by the state committee, but their selection is often dictated by the party's candidate for governor.

State committees are supposed to direct the campaigns for important statewide elections—governors and U.S. senators, and congressional representatives in the smaller states. They are supposed to serve as central coordinating agencies for these election campaigns and to serve as the party's principal fund-raising organization in the state. However, the role of the state committee very often depends upon the preferences of the party's statewide candidates regarding the handling of their campaigns. Today, most candidates have their own campaign organizations to plan and execute campaign strategy. State party organizations seldom play a major role in the candidate's campaign.

State committees are not very responsive to the direction of the national committee, and in most states, city and county party organizations operate quite independently of the state committees. In other words, there is no real hierarchy of authority in state party systems.[14]

County Committees   Party organizations at the city and county level are probably the most cohesive organizations within the parties. Yet these organizations are far from disciplined, cohesive groups. Frank Sorauf describes the "average" city or county party organization as follows:[15]

1. An active chairperson and executive committee, plus a few associated activists, who in effect make most of the decisions in the name of the party, who raise funds, who seek out and screen candidates (or approve the candidates who select themselves), and who speak locally for the party
2. A ward and precinct organization in which only a few local committee members are active and in which there is little door-to-door canvassing or other direct voter contact
3. The active participation in organizational matters of some of the party's elected public officials, who may share effective control of the organization with the official leadership of the party organization
4. A distinctly periodic calendar of activities marked by a watchful waiting or general inactivity at other than election times

Nonetheless, Republican and Democratic county chairpersons probably constitute the most important building blocks in party organization in America. City and county party officers and committees are chosen locally and cannot be removed by any higher party authority. City and county committees are elected by the voters in their constituency, and they cannot be removed by state committees or national committees of their party, even if they decide to campaign for the opposition party. In short, authority is not concentrated in any single statewide organization but is divided among many city and county party organizations.

State Party Chairpersons   Although state party organizations are weakened by decentralization, state party chairpersons are by no means political hacks. Most state chairpersons have been successful business people, lawyers, or public officials who serve in their posts without salaries to satisfy their interest in politics and

---

[14] Key, *Politics, Parties, and Pressure Groups,* p. 316.

[15] Frank J. Sorauf, *Party Politics in America,* 2nd ed. (Boston: Little, Brown, 1972), p. 72.

public affairs.[16] Republican chairpersons are more likely to have held important positions in business and management, while Democratic chairpersons are more likely to be lawyers who have held political office previously.

State party chairpersons can play different roles from state to state. Some see themselves as mere "political agents" of their governor; others are independently powerful. In general, chairpersons of the party out of power have more independence and power than those of the party in power. The latter are overshadowed by their governor. Party chairpersons do not hold on to their jobs very long—the average is less than three years.[17]

State Organizations   While party attachment among voters has weakened over the years, state party organizations have strengthened.[18] Today most state party organizations maintain a permanent party headquarters in the state capital. Most have full-time staffs, including an executive director; a budget official; and public relations, fund-raising, and research people. These state party organizations help to raise campaign funds for their candidates, conduct registration drives, provide advice and services to their nominees, and even recruit candidates to run in districts and for offices where the party would otherwise have no names on the ballot. Services to candidates may include advertising and media consulting, advice on election law compliance, polling, research (including research on opponents), registration and voter identification, mailing lists, and even seminars on campaign techniques.

Local Organizations   City and county (rather than state) party organizations are the most active and cohesive levels of organization. (City "machines" and "bosses" are discussed at length in Chapter 10, together with the reform movements that have severely reduced their power.) Yet very few local organizations have a full-time staff, or a permanent headquarters, or even a telephone listing.[19] Most rely upon volunteers—precinct and county committee members—who seldom meet in nonelection years. Few local organizations have any budget. Yet most report election year efforts at distributing campaign literature, organizing campaign events, putting up posters and lawn signs, conducting registration drives, and even some door-to-door canvassing.

Strong city and county party organizations were traditionally found in the big cities of the Northeast. While these "machines" have lost most of their "clout," local party organizations are still more visible in New York, New Jersey, and Pennsylvania than in the southern or border states (see Table 5–6).

---

[16] See Charles W. Wiggins and Willian L. Turk, "State Party Chairmen: A Profile," *Western Political Quarterly,* 23 (June 1970), 321–32.

[17] Huckshorn, *Party Leadership,* p. 46.

[18] See James L. Gibson et al., "Assembling Party Organization Strength," *American Journal of Political Science,* 27 (May 1983), 193–222.

[19] James L. Gibson et al., "Whither the Local Parties?" *American Journal of Political Science,* 29 (February 1985), 139–60.

TABLE 5-6 RANKING OF THE STATES: STRENGTH OF LOCAL PARTY ORGANIZATIONS

Democrats		Republicans	
RANK	STATE	RANK	STATE
1	New Jersey	1	New Jersey
2	Pennsylvania	2	New York
3	New York	3	Indiana
4	Delaware	4	Pennsylvania
5	Indiana	5	Maryland
6	Rhode Island	6	Arizona
7	Ohio	7	Ohio
8	New Hampshire	8	California
9	Connecticut	9	New Mexico
10	Illinois	10	Connecticut
11	Maryland	11	Delaware
12	Michigan	12	Illinois
13	Hawaii	13	Washington
14	Idaho	14	Michigan
15	Washington	15	Hawaii
16	Maine	16	Rhode Island
17	Florida	17	Iowa
18	North Dakota	18	Minnesota
19	Alaska	19	North Dakota
20	Utah	20	Wisconsin
21	Minnesota	21	Wyoming
22	New Mexico	22	Nevada
23	Tennessee	23	North Carolina
24	California	24	West Virginia
25	North Carolina	25	Maine

Source: James L. Gibson et al., "Whither the Local Parties?" *American Journal of Political Science,* 29 (February 1985), 154–55.

PARTIES AND PRIMARIES

Party *primary* elections nominate most candidates for public office in America. For the nation's first century, candidates were nominated by party conventions, not primary elections, and as a result party organizations were far more influential than they are today. Primary elections were a key reform in the progressive movement of the early twentieth century. Primaries "democratized" the nomination process and reduced the power of party bosses.

Filing   Primary elections are governed by state law; anyone can *file* a petition with a minimum number of voter signatures, pay a small fee, and have his or her name placed on the primary ballot of either party for practically any public office. A candidate does *not* have to have experience in the party, or even the support of party officials, in order to file for elective office.

TABLE 5-6   *Continued*

Democrats		Republicans	
RANK	STATE	RANK	STATE
26	Wisconsin	26	Idaho
27	Iowa	27	Virginia
28	Oregon	28	Colorado
29	Vermont	29	Oregon
30	Arizona	30	Tennessee
31	Colorado	31	New Hampshire
32	Virginia	32	South Carolina
33	West Virginia	33	South Dakota
34	South Dakota	34	Alaska
35	Wyoming	35	Montana
36	South Carolina	36	Kansas
37	Missouri	37	Oklahoma
38	Massachusetts	38	Massachusetts
39	Montana	39	Mississippi
40	Oklahoma	40	Arkansas
41	Kentucky	41	Texas
42	Nevada	42	Missouri
43	Alabama	43	Utah
44	Arkansas	44	Nebraska
45	Kansas	45	Vermont
46	Georgia	46	Louisiana
47	Mississippi	47	Alabama
48	Texas	48	Kentucky
49	Nebraska	49	Florida
50	Louisiana	50	Georgia

Source: James L. Gibson et al., "Whither the Local Parties?" *American Journal of Political Science,* 29 (February 1985), 154–55.

Endorsements   Primaries, then, reduce the influence of party organizations in the political process. It is possible, of course, for party organizations at the city, county, or state levels to *endorse,* officially or unofficially, candidates in primary elections. The importance of endorsements varies with the strength and unity of party organizations. Where party organizations are strong at the city or county level, the word can be passed down to precinct committee members to turn out the party's faithful for the endorsed candidate. Party endorsement in a statewide race appears to have less value.

Closed and Open Primaries   Primary elections in most states are *closed*—that is, only voters who have *previously* registered as members of a party may vote in that party's primary. Only registered Democrats vote in the Democratic primary, and only registered Republicans vote in the Republican primary. Semiclosed primaries allow voters to change party registration on election day. Primaries in other states are *open*—voters can choose when they enter the polling place which party primary they wish to vote in. Alaska and Washington have *blanket* primaries in which voters can vote in *both* party primaries simultaneously. Party leaders generally prefer the closed primary because they fear *crossovers* and *raiding: Crossovers* are voters who choose to vote in the primary of the party that they usually do not support in the general election; *Raiding* is an organized attempt to cross over and try to defeat an attractive candidate running for the opposition party's nomination. However, there is no evidence that large numbers of voters connive in such a fashion. Louisiana is unique in its *nonpartisan* statewide elections: All candidates run in the same primary election. If a candidate gets over 50 percent of the vote, he or she wins the office; otherwise, the top two vote-getters run again in the general election. (See Table 5–7.)

Run-off Primaries   In most states, the *plurality* winner of the party's primary election—the candidate receiving the most votes, whether a majority or not—becomes the party's nominee. But in ten southern states, a candidate must win a *majority* of votes in a primary election to become the party's nominee. If no candidate succeeds in winning a majority in the first primary, a *run-off primary* is held between the top two vote-getters in the first primary.

Run-off primaries are linked to the traditional one-party politics of the southern states. Run-off primaries present a candidate with a minority of party voters from capturing the nomination in a race with three or more contenders. Presumably the run-off primary strengthens interparty factional competition. It encourages candidates to seek majority support and prevents extremist candidates from winning nominations. No one can win a nomination by relying on splits among multiple opponents.

First primary front-runners have a better than even chance of winning the run-off. Overall, front-runners win about two-thirds of run-off primaries for state legislature seats, although they win only slightly more than half of the run-offs for governor and U.S. senator.[20]

Run-off primaries have been attacked as racially discriminatory. In districts where there is a large but less than majority black population and a history of racial block voting, black candidates who win a plurality of votes in the first primary may be defeated in the run-off if white voters unite behind the white runner-up. (It is possible, of course, for the reverse to occur in a majority black district.) A study of local run-off primaries in Georgia suggests that black plurality winners in the first primary are somewhat less likely to win a run-off against a white runner-up (50 percent black run-off victories) than white plurality winners against a black runner-up (84 percent white run-off victories).[21]

Conventions   State conventions continue in a handful of states. In New York and Connecticut, statewide party conventions nominate candidates; however, candidates can ''challenge'' the convention nominee to a primary election if the chal-

---

[20] See Charles S. Bullock and Lock K. Johnson, ''Sex and the Second Primary,'' *Social Science Quarterly,* 66 (December 1985), 933–42.

[21] Charles S. Bullock and A. Brock Smith, ''Black Success in Local Run-off Elections,'' *Journal of Politics,* 52 (November 1990), 1205–20.

TABLE 5-7 PRIMARY ELECTIONS IN THE STATES

Closed: Prior Party Registration Required	Semiclosed: Voters may register or change party on election day	Semiopen: Voters request party ballot	Open: Voter decides in which primary to vote in voting booth	Blanket	Nonpartisan	Run-off
Arizona	Colorado[a]	Alabama	Hawaii	Alaska	Louisiana	Alabama
California	Iowa[b]	Arkansas	Idaho	Washington		Arkansas
Connecticut	Kansas[a]	Georgia	Michigan			Florida
Delaware	Maine[a]	Illinois	Minnesota			Georgia
Florida	Massachusetts[c]	Indiana	Montana			Louisiana
Kentucky	New Hampshire[c]	Mississippi	North Dakota			Mississippi
Maryland	New Jersey[a]	Missouri	Utah			North Carolina
Nebraska	Ohio[b]	South Carolina	Vermont			Oklahoma
Nevada	Rhode Island[a]	Tennessee	Wisconsin			South Carolina
New Mexico	Wyoming[b]	Texas				Texas
New York		Virginia				
North Carolina						
Oklahoma						
Oregon						
Pennsylvania						
South Dakota						
West Virginia						

[a] Persons not previously voting in a party primary may register with a party on election day.

[b] Party registration may be changed on election day.

[c] Independents are permitted to change registration on election day.

lenger receives a specified share of the convention vote (25 percent in New York, 20 percent in Connecticut).

The failure of statewide organizations to have much influence over primary outcomes is due in part to changes in the styles of political activity in recent years. First of all, party organizations are weak or nonexistent in many counties: There are *no* ward or precinct-level workers. (Reasons for the decline of city and county party organizations are discussed in Chapter 10.) More important, traditional grass-roots efforts—telephoning, canvassing, driving voters to the polls—which are usually handled by party organizations, have given way to mass media techniques. Television appearances, radio commercials, and mass mailings permit candidates to take their case directly to the voters.

PROFESSIONAL MASS MEDIA CAMPAIGNS

Mass media campaigns, directed by professional public relations specialists, have replaced the party organizations' role in elections. Few candidates for governor or senator rely exclusively on the party organization to handle their campaigns. Most statewide candidates create their own campaign organizations, and increasingly these candidates are relying on professional public relations firms or consultants to manage their mass media campaigns. Only state legislative races and local politics remain "amateurish" today. A whole new "image industry" has gradually replaced the traditional role of party organizations in campaigns.

"Marketing" Candidates   If marketing, advertising, and public relations firms can sell toothpaste, why not political candidates? Indeed, today marketing and media specialists have largely taken over political campaigns for most important offices. Modern professional campaign management involves techniques that strongly resemble those employed in commercial product marketing, including the following:

1. Computerized mailing lists for fund raising and the preparation and mailing of slick brochures to the voters.
2. Computerized voter lists that include occupation, age, race, interests, memberships, and so on, of each voter, so that special statements by the candidate can be delivered to special groups of voters.
3. Public opinion polling on a regular basis throughout the campaign which enables candidates to identify their opponents' weaknesses as well as their own and to assess the voters' moods and opinion shifts throughout the campaign.
4. The preparation of videotapes, radio broadcasts, signs, bumper stickers, and so on, which emphasize the candidate's "theme."
5. Developing "media events" that will attract the attention of television and newspapers, for example, walking across the state, working a day in the lettuce fields, and so forth.

Public Relations Firms   Professional public relations firms come in different sizes and shapes. Some are all-purpose organizations that plan the whole campaign; select a theme; monitor the electorate with continuous polling; produce television tapes for commercials, newspaper advertisements, and radio spots; select clothing and hair styles for their candidates; write speeches and schedule appearances (or avoid them if the candidates cannot speak well); and even plan the victory party. Other organizations limit themselves to particular functions, such as polling or television production. Some firms specialize by party, handling only Democratic or Republican candidates; a few firms specialize by ideology, handling liberal or conservative clients. Still other firms are strictly professional, providing services to any candidate who can afford them.

Polling   Frequently, *polling* is at the center of strategic campaign decision making. At the beginning of the campaign, polls test the "recognition factor" of the candidate and assess what political issues are uppermost in the minds of voters. Special polling techniques can determine what a "winning candidate profile" looks like in a district. The results of these polls will be used to determine a general strategy—developing a favorable "image" for the candidate and focusing on a popular campaign "theme." Early polls can also detect weaknesses in the candidate, which can then be overcome in advertising (too rich—then show him in blue jeans digging ditches; too intellectual—then show him in a hog-calling contest; and so on). Polls can tell whether the party is stronger than the candidate (then identify the candidate as loyal to the party) or whether the candidate is stronger than the party (then stress the candidate's independent thinking). During the campaign the polls can chart the progress of the candidate and even assess the effectiveness of specific themes and "media events." A "media event" is an activity generated to attract news coverage, for example, walking the entire length of the state to show "closeness to the people," or carrying around a broom to symbolize "house cleaning," or spending occasional days doing manual work on a factory or farm. Finally, polls can identify the undecided vote toward the end of the campaign and help direct the time and resources of the candidate.

Name Recognition   The first objective in a professional campaign is to increase the candidate's *name recognition* among the voters. Years ago, name recognition could only be achieved through years of service in minor public or party offices (or owning a well-known family name). Today, expert media advisors (and lots of money) can create instant celebrity. "Exposure" is the name of the game, and exposure requires attracting the attention of the news media. (As one commentator observed: "To a politician there is no such thing as indecent exposure. Obscurity is a dirty word and almost all exposure is decidedly decent.") A millionaire land developer (former Governor and now U.S. Senator Bob Graham of Florida) attracted attention by simply working a few days as ditch-digger, busboy, bulldozer operator, and so on, to identify with the "common people" and receive a great deal of news coverage.

Campaign Themes   The emphasis of the professional public-relations campaign is on simplicity: a few themes, brief speeches, uncluttered ads, quick and catchy spot commercials. Finding the right theme or slogan is essential; this effort is not greatly different from that of launching an advertising campaign for a new detergent. A campaign theme should not be controversial; indeed, it should not even focus on a specific issue. It might be as simple as "A leader you can trust"; the candidate would then be "packaged" as competent and trustworthy.

Personality, not Policy   A professional media campaign generally focuses on the personal qualities of the candidate rather than his or her stand on policy issues. Professional campaigns are based on the assumption that a candidate's image is the most important factor affecting voter choice. This image is largely devoid of issues, except in very general terms, for example, "tough on crime," "stands up to the special interests," "fights for the taxpayer."

"Grass-roots" Campaigning   Door-to-door campaigning by candidates or party workers has all but disappeared from American politics. Perhaps in small towns, candidates for local office still walk through neighborhoods handing out their brochures. But grass-roots campaigning has largely been replaced with media campaigning.

Media Campaigning   Media campaigning concentrates on obtaining the maximum "free" exposure on the evening news, as well as saturating television and newspapers with paid commercial advertising. To win favorable news coverage, candidates and their managers must devise attractive media events with visuals and sound bites too good for the television news to ignore. News coverage of a candidate is more creditable than paid commercials. So candidates must do or say something interesting and "newsworthy" as often as possible during the campaign.

Television "spot" advertisements incur costs in both production and broadcast time. Indeed, television may consume up to three-quarters of all campaign costs; about one-third of TV costs go for production of ads and two-thirds to buying time from television stations. The Federal Communication Commission requires broadcasters to make available broadcast time to political candidates at the same rates charged to product advertisers.

Negative Ads   Professional media campaigns have increasingly turned to the airing of television commercials depicting the opponent in negative terms. The original negative TV ad is generally identified as the 1964 "daisy-picking" commercial, aired by the Lyndon B. Johnson presidential campaign, which portrayed Republican opponent Barry Goldwater as a nuclear warmonger. Over time the techniques of negative ads have been refined; weaknesses in opponents are identified and dramatized in emotionally forceful thirty-second spots.

While reformers bemoan "mudslinging," negative advertising can be very effective. Such advertising seeks to "define" an opponent in negative terms. Many voters cast their ballots *against* candidates they have come to dislike. Research into the opponent's public and personal background provides the data for negative campaigning. Previous speeches or writings can be mined for embarrassing statements, and previous voting records can be scrutinized for unpopular policy positions. Personal scandals can be exposed as evidence of "character." Victims of negative ads can be expected to counterattack on charges of "mudslinging" and "dirty" politics. If candidates fear that their personal attacks on opponents might backfire, they may "leak" negative information to reporters and hope that the media will do their dirty work for them.

Free Air Time   Candidates also seek free air time on public service programs and televised debates. Underfunded candidates are more dependent upon these opportunities than their more affluent opponents. Thus, well-funded and poorly funded candidates may argue over the number and times of public debates.

MONEY IN POLITICS

Running for public office costs money. Running for statewide offices in large states may cost millions; but even running for local school boards can cost thousands. Candidates who do not have enough personal wealth to finance their own campaigns must find contributors. Fund raising is one of the least pleasant aspects of politics.

What Money Can Do   Can money buy elections? Not always, but money can make a significant difference in the outcome. Let us summarize what research has shown about the effects of campaign spending:

1. Campaign spending is more important in primary elections than general elections. David Adamany writes: "From the candidate's perspective, money may be more important in the nominating process than in the general election. In primaries there is no party label voting and less early voter decision; the electorate is more easily influenced by the kinds of campaigning that money can buy."[22]

2. Campaign spending is more important in larger jurisdictions, where face-to-face campaigning is not possible and mass media appeals are essential.

3. After a certain level of campaign spending is reached, additional expenditures do not produce the same effect. A law of diminishing returns seems to operate to reduce the impact of very heavy campaign spending.[23]

4. Incumbent officeholders have a very strong advantage over challengers in soliciting and receiving campaign contributions.[24]

5. However, the advantage of incumbency itself is greater than the advantage of heavy campaign spending. While it is true that incumbents have an easier time obtaining campaign contributions than challengers, only part of the advantage of being an incumbent derives from easier access to money. Most of the incumbent's advantage is in name recognition and greater news media coverage.[25]

6. Candidates who outspend their opponents win in two out of three elections. Of course, the higher-spending candidates are usually incumbents, and in-

---

[22] David Adamany, *Financing Politics* (Madison: University of Wisconsin Press, 1969), p. 268.

[23] W. P. Welch, "The Effectiveness of Expenditures in State Legislative Races," *American Politics Quarterly*, 4 (July 1976), 333–56.

[24] Frank J. Sorauf, *Money in American Elections* (Boston: Scott Foresman, 1988).

[25] Welch, "State Legislative Races."

cumbents tend to win even when they are outspent. But in elections in which there is no incumbent seeking reelection, the candidate who spends the most money can be expected to win two of every three of these open-seat contests.[26]

Fund Raising   The need to raise millions of dollars for political campaigns, especially for costly television advertising, has stimulated the development of many new fund-raising techniques. Campaign financing has moved beyond the small, face-to-face, circle of contributing friends, supporters, and partisans. An important source of campaign money now are the political action committees, or PACs, which mobilize group financial support for candidates. PACs have been organized by corporations, unions, trade and professional associations, environmental groups, and liberal and conservative ideological groups. It is estimated that PAC contributions now account for over 40 percent of all congressional campaign financial support.[27] The wealthiest PACs are based in Washington, but PAC contributions are becoming increasingly important in state gubernatorial and legislative campaigns as well. (See Table 4–5, p. 114.)

Individual contributions are now sought through a variety of solicitation techniques, including direct mail to persons designated by computer programs to be likely contributors, direct telephone solicitation with recorded messages by the candidates, and live appeals by workers at telephone banks. These efforts have increased the *number* of political contributions in recent years as well as the *total amount* of political contributions.[28] About 7 percent of the population now claims to have contributed to candidates running for public office. However, contributors disproportionately represent high-income, well-educated, older, political partisans. There are, indeed, networks of contributors.[29] Some candidates have been able to tap into these networks through specialized mailing lists and telephone directories.

These specialized techniques supplement the more traditional fund-raising dinners, barbecues, fish frys, and cocktail parties. A successful fund-raising dinner usually includes an appearance by a national political figure, perhaps even the president, or an appearance by a show business celebrity. Tickets are sold in blocks to PACs and to well-heeled, individual contributors. Successful techniques may vary with the political culture of the state, for example, celebrity rock concerts in California versus barbecues in Texas.

Campaign Spending in the States   Campaign spending in state elections varies enormously from state to state. A gubernatorial campaign in a small state may cost

---

[26] Larry Sabato, *Goodbye to Good-time Charlie,* 2nd ed. (Washington, DC: Congressional Quarterly Press, 1983), p. 152.

[27] Michael J. Walbin, *Money and Politics in the United States* (Washington, DC: American Enterprise Institute, 1984).

[28] Ruth S. Jones and Warren E. Miller, "Financing Campaigns," *Western Political Quarterly,* 38 (June 1985), 187–210.

[29] Ruth S. Jones and Ann H. Hopkings, "State Campaign Fund Raising," *Journal of Politics,* 47 (May 1985), 427–49.

only $2 to $5 million, but campaigns in California, New York, and Texas cost real money—$10 to $25 million or more.

State legislative campaigns may range in cost from $10,000 to over $300,000 (see Table 5–8). Political scientist Frank Sorauf reports that California leads in campaign spending, not only because of its size, but also because of its influence and sophisticated political culture.[30] Media consultants, pollsters, campaign strategists, and slick television advertising have become the political norm in the Golden State.

Campaign Finance Laws   Many states, as well as the federal government, have laws designed to bring greater "ethics" into political campaigning and reduce the importance of large campaign contributions. Generally these laws attempt to do one or more of the following:

1. Limit the size of campaign contributions and limit the overall spending of candidates and parties
2. Require financial disclosure of a candidate's personal finances as well as campaign contributions and expenditures—"Who gave it? Who got it?"
3. Establish public funding of campaign expenses
4. Establish regulatory agencies, or "commissions," to oversee campaign practices

The model for state laws in this area was the Federal Election Campaign Act of 1974, which placed limits on campaign contributions in presidential elections, required disclosure of campaign finances, provided for public funding of presidential elections through a tax checkoff on federal income tax returns, and established a Federal Elections Commission to supervise presidential elections and distribute public funds to candidates.

The Constitutional Right to Campaign   However, reformers in the states and in Washington were surprised by the important U.S. Supreme Court decision in *Buckley* v. *Valeo* in 1976.[31] James L. Buckley, former U.S. Senator from New York and brother of William F. Buckley, the well-known conservative commentator, argued successfully in court that laws which limited an individual's right to participate in political campaigns, financially or otherwise, violated First Amendment freedoms. Specifically, the U.S. Supreme Court held that no government could limit an individual's right to spend money to publish or broadcast his or her own views on issues or elections. Candidates can spend as much of their own money as they wish on their own campaigns. Private individuals can spend as much as they wish to circulate their own views on elections (although their contributions to candidates and parties can still be limited). The Court, however, permitted government limitations on parties and campaign organizations and allowed the use of federal funds for financing campaigns.

---

[30] Sorauf, *Money in American Elections,* pp. 262–64.

[31] *Buckley* v. *Valeo,* 424 U.S. 1 (1976).

Table 5-8 Expenditures of Candidates for Lower Houses of Six State Legislatures, 1978-1984[a]

	1978-80			1982-1984		
	Expendi-tures	Cost/Seat	Expends/Resident	Expendi-tures	Cost/Seat	Expends/Resident
California	$24,845,619	$310,570	$1.05	$30,752,440	$384,406	$1.20
Florida	4,336,209	36,150	.44	7,634,878	63,624	.70
Minnesota	1,818,225	13,569	.45	3,104,182	23,166	.75
Missouri	1,479,406	9,076	.30	1,707,016	10,472	.34
New Jersey	2,532,268	63,307	.34	2,671,499	66,787	.36
Wisconsin	1,307,570	13,208	.28	2,178,591	22,006	.46

[a] The data are inevitably not fully comparable.

Source: From *Money in American Elections* by Frank J. Sorauf. Copyright © 1988 by Frank J. Sorauf. Reprinted by permission of Harper Collins Publisher.

This decision struck down laws of many states (as well as portions of the Federal Election Campaign Act) limiting campaign contributions by individuals. Any candidate can spend unlimited personal wealth on his or her own election campaign, and individuals can spend any amount to advertise their own personal views, as long as they do not spend their money through a party or campaign organization. If anything, the personal wealth of the candidate has become an even more important qualification for successful campaigning.

Who Gave It? Who Got It? All states now have some form of campaign finance reporting. Almost everyone agrees that the public should know who is contributing to a candidate's campaign and how the candidate is spending the money. The press was largely responsible for pushing these laws through the legislatures of the states, and the success of these laws largely depends on the press's publishing these campaign reports. Half of the states have assigned collection of reports to an existing state official, usually the secretary of state. These officials ordinarily cannot bring enforcement actions against violators themselves but must instead turn over suspected cases to state law enforcement agencies such as the attorney general. Enforcement may be weakened if the attorney general's office does not wish to embarrass fellow state officials, or if elections law enforcement is assigned a low priority relative to more serious crimes.[32] Half the states have created independent commissions resembling the Federal Elections Commission. Appointments to these commissions are usually made by the governor, or the governor and the legislature, and membership is usually divided between the parties. Staff members perform much of the filing, auditing, and investigating for these commissions which are empowered to investigate election law violations and turn over evidence of

---

[32] See Robert J. Huckshorn, "Who Gave It? Who Got It?," *Journal of Politics*, 47 (August 1985), 773-89.

wrongdoing to law enforcement officials. In addition, some commissions have the power to levy civil fines on their own authority. Examples of these strong enforcement commissions include the Connecticut State Election Commission, the New Jersey Election Law Enforcement Commission, the Florida Election Commission, and the California Fair Political Practices Commission. In most states the success of these laws depends heavily on press reporting.

Regulating PACs   The Federal Election Commission prohibits PACs from contributing more than $5,000 per election to any candidate *for federal office.* Federal law preempts state laws in regulating PACs in federal elections, but states can regulate PAC contributions in state elections. Indeed, several states currently do so, with limits varying from $1,000 to $5,000 per statewide candidate per election.

Personal Financial Disclosure   Most states now require candidates for public office to disclose their financial assets and sources of income. Financial disclosure laws have been upheld by the courts, although opponents of these laws have argued that such laws are an "invasion of privacy." These laws vary regarding the degree of detail required and whether or not the finances of the candidate's immediate family must also be disclosed. A glance at these required financial statements will convince anyone that candidates greatly understate their assets and income.

Public Campaign Financing   Some states provide some public funds for candidates or parties.[33] New Jersey was the first state to undertake major financial support for candidates for governor. The arguments for such public financing are that it (1) permits less affluent candidates to run for office, (2) removes some of the advantages of wealth in office seeking, and (3) reduces the dependency of candidates on large financial contributors.[34] But there is very little evidence to support or refute these arguments.

State public campaign finance laws differ from each other and from the federal model:

1. *Check-offs* versus *add-ons:* Most state campaign finance laws allow taxpayers to check off one dollar of their state income tax payments with no additional tax liability, but some states have an add-on feature that increases liability. Experience indicates that about 20 percent of state taxpayers will contribute to campaign financing if there is no additional cost to them, but only 1 to 3 percent will do so if it adds to their taxes.[35]

2. Party funds or general funds: Some state campaign finance laws allow contributors to designate which party should receive their dollar, while other state laws (like federal law) provide that all contributions go to a general

---

[33] Including Hawaii, Idaho, Iowa, Kentucky, Michigan, Minnesota, New Jersey, North Carolina, Rhode Island, Utah, Wisconsin.

[34] See James M. Penning and Corwin Smith, "Public Funding of Gubernatorial Elections," *American Politics Quarterly,* 10 (July 1982), 315–32.

[35] Jack L. Noragon, "Political Finance and Political Reform: The Experience with State Income Tax Checkoffs," *American Political Science Review,* 75 (September 1981), 667–87.

fund for direct distribution to candidates.[36] Allowing party preference favors the Democratic party because of its majority status.

3. General elections or general election plus primary elections: Most states with campaign finance laws limit funding to general elections, probably because of the added costs of funding primaries.

4. Distribution of money to parties or directly to candidates: States that permit taxpayers to designate which party is to receive their contribution give these funds to party organizations. But states with general campaign funds can distribute them either to the parties or directly to the candidates.

5. Gubernatorial elections only or elections for all constitutional officers and legislators: Some states subsidize only the gubernatorial election, while others subsidize all statewide elections and even state legislative campaigns.

The real stimulus to public campaign funding schemes arises from the distaste with which most politicians approach the task of soliciting contributions. Many complain that fund raising takes more time and effort than campaigning itself. Moreover, limits on campaign spending help protect incumbents by denying their opponents the funds to overcome the advantages of incumbency.

Federal Tax Laws   Finally, the U.S. Internal Revenue Service plays an overseer role in political finance. It is a violation of federal tax laws for a candidate to use campaign contributions for personal expenses. Indeed, serious legal consequences for office-seekers occur when campaign funds are directed to personal use.

---

[36] See Ruth S. Jones, "State Campaign Finance: Implications for Partisan Politics," *American Journal of Political Science,* 25 (May 1981), 342–61.

6

Legislators in State Politics

▲

Functions of State Legislatures

If you were to ask state legislators what the job of the legislature is, they might say: "Our job is to pass laws," or "We have to represent the people," or "We have to make policy." All the answers are correct, but none by itself tells the whole story.

Enacting Laws   It is true that, from a *legal viewpoint*, the function of state legislatures is to "pass laws," that is, the enactment of statutory law. Legislatures may enact more than a thousand laws in a single legislative session. The average legislator introduces ten to twelve bills each year. Many are never expected to pass. They are introduced merely as a favor to a constituent or an interest group, or to get a headline in a newspaper back home.

The range of subject matter of bills considered by a legislature is enormous. A legislature may consider the authorization of $10 billion of state spending, or it may debate the expansion of the hunting season on raccoons, or it may increase teachers' salaries, or it may argue whether or not inscribing license plates with "The Poultry State" would cause the state to be called "chicken." Obviously, these considerations range from the trivial to the vital.

153

Approving Budgets   In addition to the enactment of statutory law, legislatures share in the process of state constitutional revision, approve many of the governor's appointments, establish U.S. congressional districts, and consider amendments to the U.S. Constitution. Perhaps their single most important legal function is the passage of the appropriation and tax measures in the state budget. No state monies may be spent without a legislative appropriation, and it is difficult to think of any governmental action that does not involve some financial expenditure. Potentially, a legislature can control any activity of the state government through its power over appropriations.

Serving Constituents   Legislators spend a great deal of time answering requests from constituents—"servicing the district." Many letters and phone calls will come from interest groups in their districts—business, labor, agriculture, school teachers, municipal employees, and so on. These communications may deal with specific bills or with items in the state budget. Other communications may come from citizens who want specific assistance or favors—help with getting a state job, help with permits or licenses, voicing an opinion about whom the state university should hire as a new football coach, and so forth.[1]

Overseeing State Agencies   Legislative "oversight" of state agencies and programs is another important function. Legislators frequently challenge state administrators to explain why they are doing what they do. Frequently, committee hearings and budget hearings, in particular, provide opportunities for legislators to put administrators "through the wringer" about programs and expenditures. Often embarrassed administrators feel harassed at these meetings, but the true purpose is to remind state administrators that elected representatives of the people are the final legal authority.

THE MAKING OF A STATE LEGISLATOR

State legislators are not "representative" of the population of their states in the sense of being typical cross sections of them. On the contrary, the nation's 7461 state legislators are generally selected from the better-educated, more prestigiously employed, middle-class segments of the population.

Status   Social background information on state legislators also indicates that legislators tend to come from the "upwardly mobile" sectors of the population. This places many of them among the "second-rung" elites in the status system rather than the established wealth. Although the sons and grandsons of distinguished old families of great wealth frequently enter presidential and gubernatorial politics in the states, they seldom run for the state legislature. In contrast, state legislators have tended to take up occupations with more prestige than their fathers. Legislators are frequently among the middle status groups for whom politics is an avenue of upward mobility.

---

[1] See Patricia K. Freeman and Lilliard E. Richardson, "Casework in State Legislatures," Knoxville: Department of Political Science, University of Tennessee, 1993.

Occupation   Legislators must come from occupational groups with flexible work responsibility. The lawyer, the farmer, or the business owner can adjust his or her work to the legislative schedule, but the office manager cannot. The overrepresented occupations are those involving extensive public contact. The lawyer, insurance agent, farm implement dealer, salesperson, tavern owner, and merchant establish in their business the wide circle of friends necessary for political success. In short, the legislator's occupation should provide free time, public contacts, and social respectability. (See Figure 6–1.)

Mobility   Legislators are far less mobile than the population as a whole. They tend to have deep roots in their constituencies. One study reported that 83 percent of the state legislators of New Jersey had been born in the district they represented or had lived there over thirty years. Even in California, one of the states with the highest population mobility, 56 percent of the legislators had been born in their district or had lived there thirty years.[2]

Education   State legislators are generally well educated. More than three-quarters of them have attended college, compared to only 37 percent of the general population.

Race and Ethnicity   African-Americans have made impressive gains in state legislatures in recent years. Black voter mobilization, stemming from the Voting Rights Act of 1965, and federal court enforcement of later amendments to that law, have resulted in the election of substantial numbers of black state legislators. Most African-American legislators are elected from majority black districts. Southern states, with larger black populations, have the largest numbers and percentages of black state legislatures (see Table 6–1).

Black legislators in the states have had a significant impact on legislative voting. Their voting on civil rights and welfare issues is clearly distinguishable in southern states.[3] White legislators, even those with substantial numbers of black constituents, are not as strong in support of these issues as black legislators.

Hispanic membership in state legislators has also increased significantly in a number of states. The largest Hispanic delegations are found in those states with the largest Hispanic populations—New Mexico, Texas, Arizona, Colorado, and California.

Gender   About 20 percent of the members of all state legislatures are women.[4] This is a significant increase over the scant 4 percent female legislators in 1969. (See Figure 6–1.) Like their male counterparts, female legislators tend to come from politically active families, to have lived in their communities for a long time, to be representative of their district in race and ethnicity, and to enjoy somewhat higher social status than most of their constituents. Women are somewhat better

---

[2] John C. Wahlke et al., *The Legislative System* (New York: John Wiley, 1962), p. 488.

[3] Mary Herring, "Legislative Responsiveness to Black Constituents in Three Southern States," *Journal of Politics,* 52 (August 1990), 740–58.

[4] The Center for the American Woman in Politics at Rutgers University.

TABLE 6–1 BLACK REPRESENTATION IN STATE LEGISLATURES

	PERCENT BLACK POPULATION	Percent Black State Legislators[a]	
		1991	1993
Nation	**12.1**	**5.8**	**6.8**
Georgia	26.9	18.2	16.1
Alabama	25.6	17.1	17.1
Maryland	26.1	16.0	16.5
Louisiana	30.6	13.2	20.8
South Carolina	30.1	12.4	15.3
Mississippi	35.6	11.5	24.1
Michigan	14.6	10.8	9.5
Illinois	16.1	10.7	12.4
North Carolina	22.1	10.6	14.1
Tennessee	16.3	9.8	11.4
Ohio	11.0	9.5	11.4
New York	16.1	9.5	13.7
Arkansas	15.9	8.9	8.9
Florida	14.2	8.8	11.9
Texas	11.9	7.5	8.8
California	8.2	7.5	7.5
Virginia	19.0	7.1	8.6
Missouri	10.8	7.1	7.6
Pennsylvania	9.4	6.7	7.1

[a] Unlisted states below 6 percent.

Source: Data supplied by National Conference on State Legislatures, Denver, CO.

represented in the New England and western states with less "professional" legislatures; the large urban industrial states with more "professional" legislatures have fewer female representatives.[5] Southern states also tend to have fewer female legislators. Among the factors associated with increased representation of women are the female percentage of the labor force and the proliferation of active women's organizations in the states.[6]

Women candidates are just as successful in primary and general elections as men.[7] Voters are *not* predisposed to cast ballots either for or against female candi-

[5] See Emmy F. Werner, "Women in State Legislatures," *Western Political Quarterly,* 21 (March 1968), 40–50; Paula J. Dubeck, "Women and Access to Political Office," *Sociological Quarterly,* 17 (March 1976), 42–52; Susan Welch, "The Recruitment of Women to Public Office," *Western Political Quarterly* (June 1978), 372–80.

[6] Wilma Rule, "Why More Women Are State Legislators," *Western Political Quarterly,* 43 (June 1990), 437–48.

[7] Susan Welch et al., "The Effect of Gender on Electoral Outcomes in State Legislative Races," *Western Political Quarterly,* 38 (September 1985), 464–75.

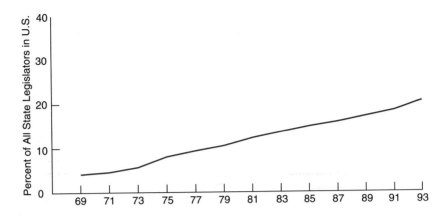

The ten states with the highest percentages of women state legislators are:

State	% Women	State	% Women
Washington	39.5	Maine	31.2
Arizona	35.6	Idaho	30.5
Colorado	34.0	Kansas	28.5
New Hampshire	33.96	Nevada	27.4
Vermont	33.9	Wisconsin	27.3

The ten states with the lowest percentages of women state legislators are:

State	% Women	State	% Women
Kentucky	4.3	Pennsylvania	9.9
Alabama	5.7	Mississippi	10.9
Louisiana	6.9	Virginia	11.4
Oklahoma	9.4	Tennessee	12.1
Arkansas	9.6	New Jersey	12.5

FIGURE 6–1   Women in State Legislatures

Source: Data supplied by Center for the American Woman in Politics, Eagleton Institute of Politics, Rutgers University.

dates.[8] Incumbency gives all officeholders an electoral advantage; since more males held office in the past, women challengers have faced the obstacle of incumbency. But women and men fare equally in races for open seats. So why are women underrepresented in state legislatures?

Fewer women than men run for state legislative seats. Scholars frequently cite women's traditional family roles of wife and mother as obstacles to a political career. Female legislative candidates with young children are very rare; newly elected women legislators are four years older on the average than newly elected male legislators—a fact generally attributed to women waiting until their children

---

[8] Susan Welch and Lee Sigelman, "Changes in Public Attitudes Toward Women in Politics," *Social Science Quarterly,* 63 (June 1982), 321–22.

are older.[9] Many women who confront conflicts between family life and political activity choose in favor of their families. One study found that more women serve in the legislatures of states whose capitals are located close to the major population centers than in the legislatures of states whose capitals are isolated and require long commutes from home.[10]

Personal Wealth   Legislators frequently claim that public service is a financial burden. While this may be true, legislators are generally recruited from among the more affluent members of society, and they become even more affluent during their tenure. Indeed, there is evidence that (1) the average net worth of new legislators is increasing over time, and (2) the average legislator increases his or her net worth while serving in the legislature. (Net worth is the total value of all assets—houses, autos, stocks, bonds, property, etc.—after subtracting the total value of all outstanding debts—mortgages, loans, etc.) For example, in Florida in 1980 the average net worth of newly elected legislators was about $180,000, but the average net worth of newly elected legislators in 1986 had grown to $380,000. More important, perhaps, persons who serve in the legislature generally increase their own net worth by large amounts during their tenure. In Florida, the average state senator increased his or her net worth from $329,000 to $1,100,000 over a ten-year period, and the average house member increased his or her net worth from $124,000 to $433,000. In short, the average legislator more than *tripled* his or her net worth in ten years of legislative service. Asked to explain these increases in personal wealth, one legislator said, "Maybe they do well because they're achievers. That's why they win when they run for office and that's why they make money."[11] But it's more likely that legislative service, and the public name recognition that comes with it, enhances one's legal practice, real estate or insurance business, as well as investment opportunities.

Lawyers   The overrepresentation of lawyers among state legislators is particularly marked. It is sometimes argued that the lawyer brings a special kind of skill to politics. The lawyer's occupation is the representation of clients, so he or she makes no great change in occupation when going from representing clients in private practice to representing constituents in the legislature. Lawyers are trained to deal with public policy as it is reflected in the statute books, so they may be reasonably familiar with public policy before entering the legislature. Moreover, service in the legislature can help a lawyer's private practice through free public advertising and opportunities to make contacts with potential clients.

There are also important structural advantages for lawyers to enter state politics—specifically, the availability of a large number of highly valued "lawyers-only" posts in state government, such as judge and prosecuting attorney. Lawyers

---

[9] Virginia Shapiro, "Private Costs of Public Commitments: Family Roles Versus Political Ambition," *American Journal of Political Science,* 26 (May 1982), 265–79.

[10] Carol Nechemias, "Geographic Mobility and Women's Access to State Legislatures," *Western Political Quarterly,* 38 (March 1985), 119–31.

[11] *Tampa Tribune,* July 27, 1987.

are eligible for many elective and appointive public jobs from which nonlawyers are excluded. State legislative seats are viewed by lawyers as stepping stones to these posts—appellate court judge, Supreme Court justice, attorney general, regulatory commissioner, and so on. Examination of post legislative careers of lawyers shows that over half go on to other public offices, compared to less than one-third of the nonlawyer legislators.[12] Moreover, available evidence suggests that lawyers in the legislature are more likely to entertain conscious aspirations for advancement than nonlawyers.

Do lawyers behave any differently from nonlawyers in the legislature? Several studies suggest that lawyers do *not* vote any differently from nonlawyers on most issues; that lawyers are neutral "contractors" for parties, interest groups, constituents, and others; and that lawyers do not vote together as a bloc.[13]

Nevertheless, lawyers do act together in legislatures to protect the legal profession. The first systematic study to demonstrate this point focused on "no-fault" insurance proposals in Congress and state legislatures.[14] No-fault insurance threatens to take away a great deal of legal business from practicing attorneys. Much larger percentages of lawyers than nonlawyers in state legislatures vote against no-fault.

In recent years the opposition of trial lawyers to insurance reform has become a national scandal. Reforming the nation's liability laws, or "tort reform" (a tort is a civil wrong that results in damages), has been a major item on the agenda of state legislatures. Reform proposals include capping "pain and suffering" awards at $250,000 or $500,000; restricting the fees a trial lawyer can take from a victim's award; and ending the rule of "joint and several liability" which forces wealthy defendants to pay the total award even if they are only partially at fault. Businesses, doctors, hospitals, municipalities, and insurance companies have all lobbied heavily at state capitals for liability law reform. But they have generally been defeated in state legislatures. The reason: Lawyers are disproportionately represented in these bodies. And it is certainly not in the financial interest of lawyers themselves to limit jury awards or restrict their fees or prevent them from suing the deepest pockets. (See "The Lawyering of America" in Chapter 8.)

Amateurs   Most state legislatures are still part-time bodies. There are constitutional limits to the length of legislative sessions in most states; the most common limit is sixty days per year. Most state legislatures put in fewer than 100 working days a year.[15] It is true that interim committee meetings and other legislative re-

---

[12] See Paul J. Hain and James E. Pierson, "Lawyers and Politics Revisited: Structural Advantages of Lawyer-Politicians," *American Journal of Political Science,* 19 (February 1975), 41–51.

[13] David Brady, John Schmidhauser, and Larry Berg, "House Lawyers Support for the Supreme Court," *Journal of Politics,* 35 (August 1973), 724–29; Heinz Eulau and John Sprague, *Lawyers in Politics,* (New York: Bobbs-Merrill, 1964).

[14] James A. Dyer, "Do Lawyers Vote Differently: A Study of Voting on No-Fault Insurance," *Journal of Politics,* 38 (May 1976), 452–56.

[15] Wayne L. Francis, "Costs and Benefits of Legislative Service in the American States," *American Journal of Political Science,* 29 (August 1985), 626–42.

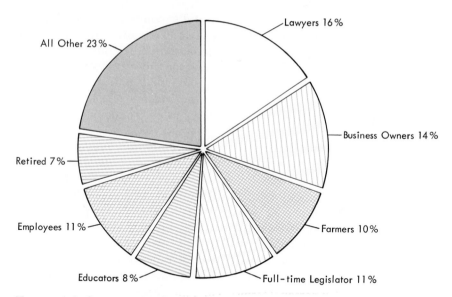

FIGURE 6–2   Legislators' Careers
Source: National Conference of State Legislatures, *New York Times,* June 4, 1989.

sponsibilities may add to the duties of legislators, and over the years sessions have grown longer. But most state legislators have other occupations, and few rely on their legislative compensation alone.

In recent years, however, an increasing number of state legislators are full-time representatives. The "citizen legislator" who spends two months in the state capitol and then returns home to his or her own business or profession still predominates in the states, but the proportion of full-time legislators is now 11 percent (see Figure 6–2). Full-time legislators are even more frequent in large states with better-paid legislatures, such as California, New York, and Michigan.

Psychology   We know, then, that legislators differ from their constituents in certain *socioeconomic* background characteristics—social class, education, occupation. But are there *psychological* differences between legislators and their constituents that are independent of these socioeconomic differences? Years ago, political scientist John B. McConaughy succeeded in getting South Carolina state legislators to submit to extensive psychological testing.[16] The results suggested that legislators were more self-sufficient, more self-confident, more extroverted, slightly more dominant, and less neurotic than the average American. Another study of Iowa state legislators found that legislators are generally more tolerant toward others, less authoritarian, and more favorably disposed toward minority groups than a

---

[16] John B. McConaughy, "Some Personality Factors of State Legislators," in *Legislative Behavior: A Reader in Theory and Research,* eds. John C. Wahlke and Heinz Eulau (Glencoe, IL: Free Press, 1959).

cross section of Iowa voters, even when the effects of socioeconomic backgrounds are controlled.[17] In short, there is some evidence that psychological predispositions—self-confidence, gregariousness, tolerance toward others—operate as self-selective factors in determining who will choose to make a career in political life.

GETTING TO THE STATE CAPITOL

The state legislature is a convenient starting place for a political career. About one-half of the state legislators in the nation never served in public office before their election to the legislature, and a greater percentage of new members are in the lower rather than upper chambers. The other half had only limited experience on city councils, county commissions, and school boards.

Getting into Politics   Why does a legislator decide to run for office in the first place? It is next to impossible to determine the real motivations of political office seekers—they seldom know themselves. Legislators will usually describe their motivations in highly idealistic terms: "I felt that I could do the community a service"; "I considered it a civic duty." Only seldom are reasons for candidacy expressed in personal terms: "Oh, I just think it's lots of fun." Gregariousness and the desire to socialize no doubt contribute to the reasons for some office seekers. Politics can have a special lure of its own: "It gets into your blood and you like it." Particular issues may mobilize a political career, but ideological involvement occupies a relatively unimportant place in a candidate's motives. Activity in organizations that are deeply involved in politics also leads to candidacy: "When I decided to run, I was quite active in the union." There is some evidence that political activists, including legislators, from middle- and upper-class districts are more *ideologically motivated* (running for office to correct perceived wrongs, do good, resolve issues, and so on) than political activists from working-class districts, who are more *personally motivated* (running to achieve prestige, recognition, or material rewards).[18]

Political Experience   States with stronger parties are more likely to nominate people who have worked for the party in some previous appointed or elective office.[19] States with weaker parties are more likely to elect "amateurs" with no previous political experience. The stronger the party organization, the more likely a legislative candidate will have to serve a political apprenticeship in some local or party offices. However, as party organizations weaken, the easier it becomes for individuals with little or no prior governmental experience to win legislative seats.

---

[17] Ronald W. Hedlund, "Psychological Predispositions: Political Representatives and the Public," *American Journal of Political Science,* 19 (August 1973), 489–505.

[18] Quotations from state legislators interviewed by Wahlke et al., *Legislative System,* pp. 95–134. See also David J. Webber, "The Contours and Complexities of Legislator Objectives," *Western Political Quarterly,* 39 (March 1986), 93–103.

[19] Richard J. Tobin, "The Influence of Nominating Systems on the Political Experience of State Legislators," *Western Political Quarterly,* 28 (September 1975), 553–66.

Raising Campaign Money   The first challenge that an aspiring legislator faces is raising money to finance the campaign. In some states with small legislative districts, nonprofessional legislatures, and largely rural constituencies, a state legislative race may cost only $5,000 to $10,000. But large urban state legislative races may cost $50,000 to $100,000 or more. On the average, senate contests cost more than house contests, and winners spend more than losers. Money allows a candidate to produce commercials, buy television and radio time, buy newspaper ads, travel around the district, and distribute bumper stickers and campaign buttons. Some state legislative candidates employ professional campaign management firms. Most state legislative campaigns are relatively amateurish, but they still cost money. When campaigns are relatively inexpensive, the candidate and his or her friends contribute most of the money. But in more expensive races, candidates may turn to PACs. Corporate, labor, environmental, and ideological PACs are becoming increasingly active in state capitals, particularly in the larger states. (See Campaign Financing in Chapter 4.)

Facing the Primaries   Candidates face two important obstacles when they decide to run for the state legislature: the primary and the general election. A seat in the legislature depends on how much competition a candidate encounters in these elections. First, let us consider competition in the primary elections. Available evidence indicates that more than half of the nation's state legislators are *unopposed* for their party's nomination in primary elections. Many legislators who do face primary competition have only token opposition. Most primary competition occurs in a party's "sure" districts, some competition occurs in "close" districts, and there is a distinct shortage of candidates in districts where the party's chances are poor. In other words, primary competition is greater where the likelihood of victory in the general election is greater. Specifically, one study of primary competition for state legislative seats reported the following findings:[20]

1. Over 60 percent of state legislators face no primary opposition.
2. Democrats (who hold a three-to-two edge in legislative seats across the country) are more likely to face primary opposition than Republicans.
3. There is greater likelihood of competition in a primary if the incumbent is not running. Strong incumbents discourage competition.

Some states require runoff elections when no candidate wins a majority in the first primary. Thus, some candidates face three elections on their way to the legislature —a first primary, a runoff primary, and the general election.

The General Election   The culmination of the recruitment process is in the general election, yet in many legislative constituencies one party is so entrenched that the voters have little real choice at the general election. In many districts, the mi-

---

[20] Craig Grau, "Competition in State Legislative Primaries," *Legislative Studies Quarterly,* 6 (February 1981), 35–54.

nority party is so weak that it fails to run candidates for legislative seats. In the southern and border states where the legislatures are heavily Democratic, there are often no Republican candidates in the general election for legislative seats. More seats are contested in states with close two-party competition, but even in a hotly contested state such as Pennsylvania, some nominations to the state legislature will go unfilled because of a collapse in local party organization in certain districts.

"Competition" implies more than a name filed under the opposition party label. Generally a competitive election is one in which the winning candidate wins by something less than two to one. In light of this more realistic definition of competition, the absence of truly competitive politics in state legislative elections is striking. Overall, more than half of the nation's legislatures are elected in *noncompetitive* general elections, where their opponents are either nonexistent or receive less than one-third of the vote. In the southern states more than three-quarters of all legislators are elected in these noncompetitive elections. But even in competitive states, such as California, Michigan, Minnesota, New York, Pennsylvania, and Wisconsin, over half the state legislators face only token opposition in the general election.[21] Moreover, competition is *declining* over time, as more legislators are winning by lopsided margins.[22]

Turnover   Turnover in state legislatures is fairly high. About one-third of all state legislators are newcomers at any legislative session. However, turnover rates vary by state, ranging from below 20 percent to above 50 percent.[23] Interestingly, it is *not* party competition that increases turnover; far more legislators voluntarily quit than are defeated for reelection. A careful study of factors affecting turnover indicates that the frequency of elections is the most important factor. The more often one has to go through the work and expense of a campaign for reelection, the more likely one is to voluntarily give up the seat. Reapportionment also contributes to turnover, but this should occur only after each ten-year census. There is *less* turnover in the larger states, which have longer legislative sessions and pay their legislators more money. In other words, more "professional" legislatures have lower turnover rates than the "amateur" legislatures.

Over time turnover in state legislatures is diminishing. More legislators are becoming careerists. Higher pay, greater prestige, more professional staff assistance, and increased perquisites of office reduce voluntary retirements, even though sessions are longer and more work is required.[24] An increasing percentage

---

[21] David Ray and John Havick, "A Longitudinal Analysis of Party Competition in State Legislative Elections," *American Journal of Political Science,* 25 (February 1981), 119–28.

[22] Ronald Weber, Harvey Tucker, and Paul Brace, "Vanishing Marginals in State Legislative Elections," *Legislative Studies Quarterly,* 16 (February 1991), 29–47.

[23] Alan Rosenthal, "Turnover in State Legislatures," *American Journal of Political Science,* 18 (August 1974), 609–16.

[24] David Ray, "Membership Stability in Three State Legislatures: 1893–1969," *American Political Science Review,* 68 (March 1974), 106–12; and "Voluntary Retirement and Electoral Defeat in Eight State Legislatures," *Journal of Politics,* 38 (May 1976), 426–33.

of legislators are seeking reelection in urban, industrial states; and despite greater party competition, these incumbents are remaining in office. It is still an open question, however, whether increased experience and seniority lead to more effective legislatures.

The high turnover clearly is *not* a product of competition for the job; only a very small proportion of state legislators are rejected at the polls. Most simply do not seek reelection and quit because of dissatisfaction: "Being in the legislature has hurt my law practice and cost me money"; "Any way you look at it, the job means a sacrifice to you, your home, and your business."

THE GREAT INCUMBENCY MACHINE

Legislators who choose to run for reelection are seldom defeated. Indeed, they are usually unopposed in the primary election, and sometimes unopposed in the general election. Potential challenges are discouraged by the record of success of incumbents.[25] *Over 90 percent of incumbent state legislators who seek reelection are successful.* As *The New York Times* observed, "Few things in America are as safe as a seat in the New York state legislature."[26] (The reelection rate of incumbents in New York is over 98 percent, the highest in the nation.) Aspiring newcomers in politics are advised to wait for incumbents to leave office voluntarily. Redistricting also opens up legislative seats and occasionally forces incumbents to run against each other. The likelihood of defeating an incumbent in either the primary or general election is very low.

Incumbents' Vote Advantage   Incumbency itself, apart from any other characteristic of a legislator, is a major advantage in state legislative elections. This can be demonstrated by vote margins that reveal a "retirement slump" in a party's vote following the retirement of an incumbent; when incumbents do not seek reelection, their party's share of the district vote declines measurably from the previous election. Additional evidence of incumbent advantage is found in the "sophomore surge": When freshmen incumbents run for reelection they increase their vote margins significantly over their initial election.[27]

Visibility   Why do incumbents win? First of all, they enjoy greater visibility and name recognition in their districts: "The reason I get 93 percent victories is what I do back home. I stay highly visible. No grass grows under my feet. I show I haven't

---

[25] It is not uncommon in southern states for 40 to 50 percent of incumbent legislators who seek reelection to be unopposed in both the primary and general elections. See Malcolm Jewell and David Breaux, "Southern Primary and Electoral Competition," *Legislative Studies Quarterly,* 16 (February 1991), 129–43.

[26] Kevin Sack, "The Great Incumbency Machine," *New York Times Magazine,* September 27, 1992, p. 47.

[27] See David Breaux, "Specifying the Impact of Incumbency on State Legislative Elections," *American Politics Quarterly,* 18 (July 1990), 270–86.

forgot from whence I came."[28] Incumbents spend a major portion of their time throughout their term of office campaigning for reelection: "I have the feeling that the most effective campaigning is done when no election is near. During the interval between elections you have to establish every personal contact you can." Legislators regularly appear at civic clubs, social and charitable events, churches, and many other gatherings: "Personally, I will speak on any subject. I talk on everything whether it deals with politics or not." Indeed, many legislators spend more time campaigning for reelection than lawmaking. Few challengers can afford to spend two or four years campaigning.

Professionalism   As legislatures become more professional over time—employing large professional staffs; providing offices, expense accounts, and travel budgets to legislators; and increasing their pay—incumbents acquire greater resources to assist them in servicing constituents. Constituents' services or "casework" is growing in state legislatures; legislators are increasingly involved in assisting constituents in dealing with state bureaucracies, providing information, and doing small favors at the capital. Legislators may help constituents get food stamps, sign up for unemployment compensation, obtain driver's licenses, or apply for state jobs. Over time this form of "retail" politics gradually builds a network of grateful voters.

It is no accident that the most professional state legislatures in the nation (California, Illinois, Massachusetts, Michigan, New York, Ohio, Pennsylvania, and Wisconsin) have the lowest turnover. Their legislators are given large sums to subsidize what are really campaign activities—printing and mailing of newsletters; press rooms and video studios; travel reimbursement; and aides, assistants, and secretaries who spend much of their time on constituent services.

Money   Finally, and perhaps most importantly, incumbents attract much more in the way of campaign contributions than challengers. Interest group contributions go overwhelmingly to incumbents. (See "Money in Politics" in Chapter 5.) These groups are seeking access and influence with decision makers, so they direct their contributions to people in office. (For example, see the list of contributions to the reelection of the Florida senate president, Table 4–5.) Moreover, group leaders know that incumbents are rarely defeated and they do not want to antagonize incumbents by contributing to challengers. Incumbents can build a "war chest" over time; often the size of the war chest itself is enough to discourage potential challengers from entering races against them.

LEGISLATIVE APPORTIONMENT AND DISTRICTING

Legislative apportionment refers to the allocation of seats to specific populations. Malapportionment occurs when there are differing numbers of people in legislative districts that receive the same number of seats. Malapportionment creates in-

---

[28] Quotations of legislators from William J. Keefe and Morris S. Ogue, *The American Legislative Process: Congress and the States,* 8th ed. (Englewood Cliffs, NJ: Prentice Hall, 1993).

equality of representation: If one single-member district has twice the population of another, the value of a vote in the larger district is only half the value of a vote in the smaller district. Prior to 1962, malapportionment was common in American state legislatures. Small minorities of the population could elect a majority of the house or senate or both in most of the states. Generally, it was the rural voters in a state who controlled a majority of legislative seats, and it was the urban voters who were discriminated against in the value of their vote.

Supreme Court Intervention   After years of avoiding the issue of malapportionment, the U.S. Supreme Court finally acted in 1962 in the landmark case of *Baker* v. *Carr*.[29] This case involved the complaint of urban residents in Tennessee where the largest district in the lower house was twenty-three times larger than the smallest district. The Supreme Court decided that such inequalities in state apportionment laws denied voters "equal protection of the laws" guaranteed by the Fourteenth Amendment and that the federal courts should grant relief from these inequalities. The Supreme Court did not decide on any firm mathematical standard of correct apportionment, holding only that "as nearly as practicable, one man's vote should be equal to another's."[30] The Supreme Court required that *both* houses of the state legislature be apportioned on the basis of population; the Court rejected the federal analogy of a senate based upon geographic units: "Legislators represent people, not trees or acres. Legislators are elected by voters, not farms or cities or economic interests."[31] State after state was forced to reapportion its legislature under the threat of judicial intervention. In addition to requiring population equality in legislative districting, the Supreme Court also required population equality in congressional districting by state legislatures. The philosophy underlying these decisions was expressed by the Court: "The conception of political equality from the Declaration of Independence to Lincoln's Gettysburg Address, to the Fourteenth, Fifteenth, Seventeenth, and Nineteenth Amendments, can mean only one thing— one person, one vote."[32]

The Impact of Reapportionment   The reapportionment revolution of the 1960s significantly increased the representation afforded urban interests in state legislatures. Reapportionment also seemed to bring younger, better-educated, more prestigiously employed people into the legislature. It also brought many "new" people into legislative politics—people who have had little or no previous experience in public office.

Scholars disagree over whether or not any significant policy changes occurred as a result of reapportionment. In the first place, even before *Baker* v. *Carr*, there was no evidence that the policy choices of well-apportioned states differed

---

[29] *Baker* v. *Carr*, 369 U.S. 186 (1962).

[30] *Reynold* v. *Sims*, 84 S. Ct. 1362 (1964).

[31] *Wesberry* v. *Sanders*, 84 S. Ct. 526 (1964).

[32] *Gray* v. *Sanders*, 83 S. Ct. 801 (1963), p. 809.

significantly from the policy choices of malapportioned states.[33] Expenditures for schools, welfare, health, cities, and so on, were increasing rapidly in the states in the 1960s, without regard to reapportionment. Many political scientists maintain that the long-term effect of reapportionment has been to: (1) increase party competition in state legislatures; (2) distribute more educational and highway funds to urban areas; (3) produce more environmental regulation.[34]

Standards of Equality Among Districts   Today there is very little inequality among legislative districts in any state, and "one person, one vote" is the prevailing form of representation. But federal courts have not always been consistent or precise in determining exactly *how equal* congressional and state legislative districts must be. In several early cases, federal courts calculated an "ideal" district by dividing the total population of the state by the number of legislative seats and then comparing all district populations to this ideal district. Variations of more than 2 percent in any district from the ideal often led to federal court invalidation of a state's redistricting plan. Later the federal courts began calculating an "overall range" by adding the deviations of the largest district and the smallest district from the ideal, disregarding the plus and minus signs. (Thus if the largest district was 2 percent larger than the ideal, and the smallest district 1 percent smaller than the ideal, the "overall range" would be 3 percent.)

With regard to *congressional* districts, the U.S. Supreme Court has required strict standards of equality. Indeed, no population inequality that "could practicably be avoided" is permitted in congressional districts; a New Jersey plan with an overall range of 0.70 percent was struck down upon presentation of evidence that the legislature could have reduced the range to 0.45.[35]

However, the U.S. Supreme Court has been somewhat more lenient in considering *state legislative* districting plans. The Court has refused to set any specific mathematical standards of equality for legislative districts. Nonetheless, districting plans with an overall range of more than 10 percent "create a prima facie case of discrimination and therefore must be justified by the state."[36] Federal courts will allow some deviations from absolute equality in order to recognize political subdivision boundaries.

Districting   Districting refers to the drawing of boundary lines for legislative districts. While malapportionment refers to inequality in representation, *gerryman-*

---

[33] Thomas R. Dye, "Malapportionment and Public Policy in the States," *Journal of Politics,* 27 (August 1965), 586–601; Herbert Jacob, "The Consequences of Malapportionment: A Note of Caution," *Social Forces* (Winter 1965), 256–61; Douglas G. Feig, "Expenditures in the American States: The Impact of Court-Ordered Reapportionment," *American Politics Quarterly,* 6 (July 1978), 309–24; Robert E. Firestine, "The Impact of Reapportionment Upon Local Government Aid," *Social Science Quarterly,* 54 (September 1973), 394–402.

[34] See Michael A. Maggiotto et al., "The Impact of Reapportionment in Public Policy," *American Politics Quarterly,* 13 (January 1985), 101–21.

[35] *Karchev* v. *Daggett,* 462 U.S. 725 (1983).

[36] *Brown* v. *Thompson,* 462 U.S. 835 (1983).

dering refers to the drawing of district lines for political advantage. The population of districts can be equal, yet the districts drawn in such a fashion as to give advantage to one party or group over another. Consider a very simple example:

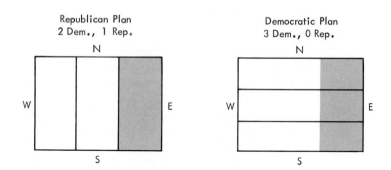

For a city that is entitled to three representatives, the eastern third of the city is Republican while the western two-thirds is Democratic. If the Republicans draw the district lines, they will draw them along a north-south direction to allow them to win in one of the three districts; if Democrats draw the district lines, they will draw them along an east-west direction to allow them to win all three districts by diluting the Republican vote. Often, gerrymandering is not as neat as our example; district lines may twist and turn and create grotesque geographic patterns.

Gerrymandering can be accomplished by the combined methods of *splintering* and *packing.* Splintering involves dividing up and diluting a strong minority to deny it the power to elect a representative (see accompanying diagram). Packing involves the concentration of partisan voters in a single district in order to "waste" their votes in large majorities for a single representative and thereby protect modest majorities in other districts (see box, "The Original Gerrymander").

As long as districts are equal in population, partisan gerrymandering does *not* violate federal court standards for "equal protection" under the Fourteenth Amendment of the U.S. Constitution. There is no constitutional obligation to allocate seats "to the contending parties in proportion to what their anticipated statewide vote will be."[37] However, the federal courts may intervene in political gerrymandering if it "consistently degrades a voter's or a group of voters' influence on the political process as a whole." This vague standard set forth by the U.S. Supreme Court opens the door to judicial intervention in particularly grievous cases of political gerrymandering.

Incumbent gerrymandering sometimes supplements traditional partisan gerrymandering. The object of incumbent gerrymandering is to protect the seats of incumbents. Often if party control of state government is divided, thus preventing the passage of a partisan gerrymander, legislators will agree to protect themselves.

---

[37] *Davis v. Bandemer,* 106 S. Ct. 2797 (1986).

THE ORIGINAL GERRYMANDER

The term *gerrymander* immortalizes Governor Elbridge Gerry (1744–1814) of Massachusetts, who in 1812 redistricted the state legislature to favor Democrats over Federalists. A district north of Boston was designed to concentrate and thus waste Federalist votes. The district was portrayed in a political cartoon in the *Boston Gazette* on March 26, 1812, as a "gerrymander."

The Seats–Votes Relationship   One way to determine whether partisan gerrymandering has short-changed a party is to compare the total statewide vote compiled by all of the party's candidates with the proportion of legislative seats it won.[38] For example, if a party's candidates won 55 percent of the total votes cast in all legislative elections, but won only 45 percent of the seats, we might conclude that partisan gerrymandering was to blame. This comparison is not always valid, however, especially when it is understood that a party that wins a slight majority of votes would normally be expected to win a much larger proportion of seats. For example, a party that wins 52 percent of total votes cast in all legislative elections might win 65 percent of the seats; theoretically it could win 100 percent of the

---

[38] See Harry Basehart, "The Seats/Vote Relationship and the Identification of Partisan Gerrymandering in State Legislature," *American Politics Quarterly,* 15 (October 1987), 484–98. See also Gerard S. Gryski, Bruce Reed, and Euel Elliot, "The Seats–Vote Relationship in State Legislative Elections," *American Politics Quarterly* 18 (April 1990), 141–57, for an estimate of bias for each state prior to 1990 redistricting.

seats in the unlikely event that its 52 percent of the votes was spread evenly in every legislative district. The U.S. Supreme Court has held that "a mere lack of proportionality in results in one election" cannot prove an unconstitutional gerrymander; however the Court said that it might intervene when there is "a history of disproportionate result."[39] It is important to remember that the United States does not employ proportional representation as do many European democracies. Hence we cannot expect proportionality in the seats–votes relationship. However, extreme and persistent differences in this relationship may signal the existence of partisan gerrymandering.

Affirmative Racial Gerrymandering   Gerrymandering designed to *dis*advantage blacks is a violation of the Equal Protection Clause of the Fourteenth Amendment of the U.S. Constitution, and it is a violation of the federal Voting Rights Act of 1965.[40] In 1982 Congress strengthened the Voting Rights Act by outlawing any electoral arrangements that had the *effect* of weakening minority voting power (see "Securing the Right to Vote" in Chapter 4). The U.S. Supreme Court obliges the states to create predominately black and minority districts whenever possible in order to maximize opportunities for blacks and minority candidates to win election.[41] This mandate for affirmative racial gerrymandering governed redistricting following the 1990 census and resulted in a significant increase in black and minority representation in many state legislatures.

Multimember Districts   Multimember legislative districts were once very common (seventeen states had multimember districts in at least one of their legislative chambers before 1990). But court challenges and complaints by minority parties and racial minorities have restricted their use. The U.S. Supreme Court has never held multimember to be unconstitutional per se, as long as the population representation is equal.[42] (A two-member district, for example, should have twice the ideal district population.) However, multimember district plans that discriminate against racial minorities are unconstitutional.[43] Multimember districts provide additional opportunities for partisan gerrymandering. (In our previous example, the Democrats could simply declare the entire city a three-member district and ensure the dilution of Republican votes.) Single-member districts are strongly preferred by minorities—minority parties as well as racial minorities.

Who Draws the Lines?   Traditionally, legislatures drew up their own district lines. In most states this continues to be the case. Many legislatures employ private consultants to assist in the task, and computer mapping is now common. Legislatures generally try to protect incumbents, and the majority party frequently tries to

---

[39] *Davis* v. *Bandemer*, 106 S. Ct. 2797 (1986).

[40] *Fortson* v. *Dorsey*, 179 U.S. 433 (1965).

[41] *Thornbury* v. *Gingles*, 478 U.S. 30 (1986).

[42] *Conner* v. *Johnson*, 407 U.S. 640 (1971).

[43] *White* v. *Regester*, 412 U.S. 755 (1973).

maximize its advantages over the minority party. But in recent years, because of court challenges over apportionment (equality of population in districts) and racial gerrymandering, most legislative districting plans must be approved by courts. Reformers (Common Cause, National Municipal League, League of Women Voters) have urged state legislatures to turn over redistricting to independent nonpartisan commissions, and some states have done so. Reformers argue that gerrymandering devalues voter participation because the results are predetermined, reduce competition for legislative seats, and reduce the responsiveness of legislators by creating "sure" seats.

LEGISLATIVE ORGANIZATION AND PROCEDURE

The formal rules and procedures by which state legislatures operate are primarily designed to make the legislative process fair and orderly. Without established customs, rules, and procedures, it would be impossible for 50, 100, or 200 people to arrive at a collective decision about the thousands of items submitted to them at a legislative session. State legislatures follow a fairly standard pattern in the formal process of making laws. Figure 6–3 provides a brief description of some of the more important procedural steps in lawmaking.

Procedures Have Consequences   What are the political consequences of the legislative procedures described in Figure 6–2? Obviously, it is a very difficult process for a bill to become a law—legislative procedures offer many opportunities to defeat legislation. Formal rules and procedures of state legislatures lend themselves easily to those who would delay or obstruct legislation. Figure 6–2 illustrates the deliberative function of legislatures and the consequent procedural advantages given to those who would defend the status quo. Moreover, these procedures imply that the legislature is structured for deliberation and delay in decision making, rather than speed and innovation. This suggests that the legislature functions as an arbiter, rather than an initiator, of public policy, since its procedures are designed to maximize deliberation, even at the expense of granting advantage to those who oppose change.

Disorderliness   As experienced legislators are fond of saying: "There are two things in the world you do not want to watch being made—sausages and laws." Lawmaking is a disorderly process, in spite of the formal procedures listed in Figure 6–2. Students often express shock and dismay when they spend some time watching or working in their legislature. After studying the formal rules, they may be unprepared for the "actual" haste, disorganization, log rolling, informality, infighting, petty jealousies, vote trading, ignorance, and ineptitude that they encounter.

Workload   Fewer than one in four bills introduced in a legislative session actually makes its way through the whole process and becomes law. In large states such as California and New York, nearly 10,000 bills may be introduced in a single legislative session, and 2000 may be enacted into law. In smaller states a typical legislative session may produce 300 to 500 laws. Most bills die in committee. Many bills

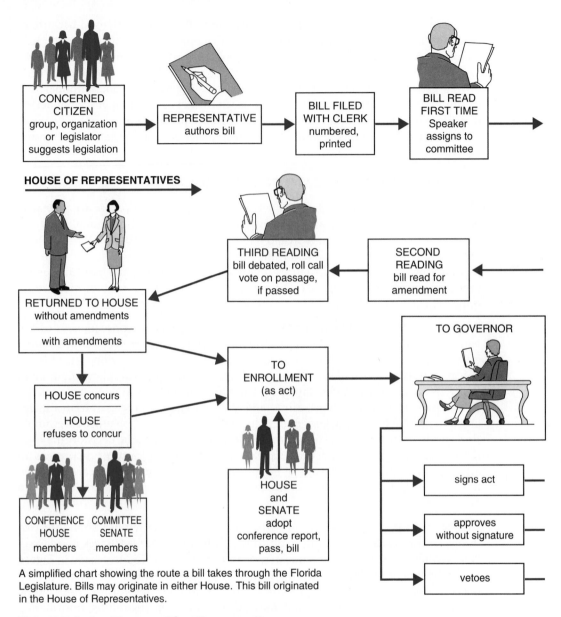

A simplified chart showing the route a bill takes through the Florida Legislature. Bills may originate in either House. This bill originated in the House of Representatives.

FIGURE 6-3   How an Idea Becomes Law

are introduced with no real expectation they will pass; legislators simply seek to "go on record" as working for a particular goal.

Logjams   The end-of-session logjam is typically the most disorderly phase of law making. In the closing days of a legislative session, hasty efforts are made to win approval for many bills and amendments which are still languishing somewhere in

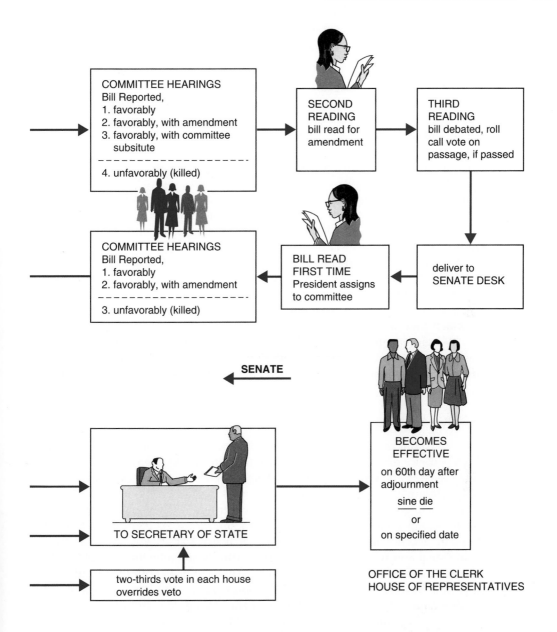

COMMITTEE HEARINGS
Bill Reported,
1. favorably
2. favorably, with amendment
3. favorably, with committee subsitute
- - - - - - - - - - - - - - - - - - -
4. unfavorably (killed)

SECOND READING
bill read for amendment

THIRD READING
bill debated, roll call vote on passage, if passed

COMMITTEE HEARINGS
Bill Reported,
1. favorably
2. favorably, with amendment
- - - - - - - - - - - - - - - - - - -
3. unfavorably (killed)

BILL READ FIRST TIME
President assigns to committee

deliver to SENATE DESK

SENATE

TO SECRETARY OF STATE

BECOMES EFFECTIVE
on 60th day after adjournment
sine die
or
on specified date

two-thirds vote in each house overrides veto

OFFICE OF THE CLERK
HOUSE OF REPRESENTATIVES

the legislative process. Legislative chambers sometimes become scenes of noisy confusion, with legislators voting blindly on bills described only by number. Most reformers condemn the end-of-session logjam as a source of inferior quality legislation. Other observers consider it an inevitable product of workload. For still others, the logjam is a strategy to enhance the power of legislative leaders. These leaders control the daily agenda and grant recognition to members seeking the floor; these decisions in a confused end-of-session logjam can determine whose bills get passed and whose do not. In some states in some sessions, over half of all the bills passed will be pushed through in the last few days of the session.[44]

Sessions   Traditionally state constitutions limited legislative sessions to thirty or sixty days once every two years. These limits reflected the "citizen" nature of state legislatures, in contrast to the "professional" full-time congressional model of a legislature. Many observers still argue that the predominant occupation of members should *not* be "legislator," and that legislative sessions should be kept short so that citizens with other occupations can serve in the legislature. But the growing demands of legislative business have led to longer sessions.

Most states now hold annual legislative sessions; only a few are limited to biennial sessions (see Table 6–2 on p. 176). Twelve states place no limit on the length of sessions while thirty-two states have constitutional limits, and six states have statutory limits. The most common limit is sixty days; most legislatures convene in January and adjourn in March.

Frequently legislatures convene in "special sessions" in addition to those regularly scheduled. Special sessions may be called by the governor, or in some states by the legislative leadership, to consider special topics, for example, projected budget deficits or reapportionment. Usually these sessions are limited to the topic for which they were called.

We should remember that legislators have many duties between sessions; their work does not end when the session adjourns. Often legislative committees meet between sessions, and constituents continue to contact legislators for services.

INFORMAL RULES OF THE GAME

Partly to counteract the impact of formal rules and procedures, legislatures have developed a number of informal "rules of the game." These unwritten rules are not merely quaint and curious folkways. They support the purposes and functions of the legislature by helping to maintain the working consensus among legislators so essential to legislative output. Some rules contribute to the legislative task by promoting group cohesion and solidarity. In the words of legislators themselves: "Support another member's local bill if it doesn't affect you or your district"; "Don't steal another's bill"; "Accept the author's amendments to a bill"; "Don't make personal attacks on other members." Other informal rules promote predictability of behavior: "Keep your word"; "Don't conceal the real purpose of bills or amendments"; "Notify in advance if you cannot keep a commitment." Other rules try to put limits on interpersonal conflict: "Be willing to compromise"; "Accept half a loaf"; "Respect the seniority system"; "Respect committee jurisdiction." Finally, other rules are designed to expedite legislative business: "Don't talk too much"; "Don't fight unnecessarily"; "Don't introduce too many bills and amend-

[44] Harvey J. Tucker, "Legislative Logjams: A Comparative State Analysis," *Western Political Quarterly,* 38 (September 1985), 432–46.

ments''; ''Don't point out the absence of a quorum''; ''Don't be too political.''[45] (See also Table 6–3 on p. 178.)

A most important informal device is unanimous consent for the suspension of formal rules; this permits a legislature to consider bills not on the calendar, pass bills immediately without the necessary three readings, dispense with time-consuming formalities, permit nonmembers to speak, and otherwise alter procedure. Another informal rule is the practice in many states of passing ''local bills'' that would affect only one area of a state without debate or opposition when the delegation in that area unanimously supports the bill.

Most of these rules are enforced by informal sanctions. The most frequently mentioned sanction involves obstructing the bills of errant legislators by abstaining or voting against them, keeping their bills in committee, and amending their bills; or more personal sanctions, such as using the ''silent treatment,'' not trusting the legislator, and removing patronage and good committee assignments. Other sanctions include denial of legislative courtesies and occasionally even overt demonstrations of displeasure, such as ridicule, hissing, or laughing. The observance of rules, however, is not obtained primarily through fear of sanction so much as the positive recognition by legislators of the usefulness of rules in helping the legislature perform its chores.

LEGISLATIVE COMMITTEES

While it is most convenient to study legislative decision making by observing floor actions, particularly the division of ayes and nays, the floor is not the only locus of important legislative decisions. Many observers and legislators feel that committee work is essential to the legislative process. It is here that public hearings are held, policies pleaded and debated, legislation amended and compromised, bills rushed to the floor or pigeonholed. Harmon Zeigler writes: ''The committee hearing is generally the most important source of information for legislators, and lobbyists tend to flock to the committee rooms as the focal point of their contact with legislators.[46] The function of the committee system is to reduce legislative work to manageable proportions by providing for a division of labor among legislators. However, by so doing the committees themselves often come to exercise considerable influence over the outcome of legislation. Another opportunity is provided for delay and obstruction by less than the majority of legislators, sometimes by a single committee chairperson.

Functions   A typical legislative chamber will have between twenty and thirty standing committees that consider all bills in a particular area, such as revenue, appropriations, highways, welfare, education, labor, judiciary, or local government. Typically, a legislator will serve on three, or four, or five committees. In most state

---

[45] Quotations from state legislators interviewed by Wahlke, *Legislative System,* pp. 146–61.

[46] Harmon Zeigler and Michael Baer, *Lobbying: Interaction and Influence n American State Legislatures* (Belmont, CA: Wadsworth, 1969), p. 126.

TABLE 6-2   THE STATE LEGISLATURES

| State | Official name | Senate | | House | | Salaries, 1990 | Regular Sessions |
		NUMBER	TERM	NUMBER	TERM	(+ INDICATES ADDED PER DIEM)	
Alabama	Legislature	35	4	105	4	Per diem	Annual
Alaska	Legislature	20	4	40	2	$22,140+	Annual
Arizona	Legislature	30	2	60	2	15,000+	Annual
Arkansas	General Assembly	35	4	100	2	7,500+	Odd
California	Legislature	40	4	80	2	40,816+	Odd/Even
Colorado	General Assembly	35	4	65	2	17,500+	Annual
Connecticut	General Assembly	36	2	151	2	16,760+	Annual
Delaware	General Assembly	21	4	41	2	23,282+	Annual
Florida	Legislature	40	4	120	2	21,684+	Annual
Georgia	General Assembly	56	2	180	2	10,376+	Annual
Hawaii	Legislature	25	4	51	2	27,000+	Annual
Idaho	Legislature	42	2	84	2	Per diem	Annual
Illinois	General Assembly	59	4	118	2	35,661+	Annual
Indiana	General Assembly	50	4	100	2	11,600+	Annual
Iowa	General Assembly	50	4	100	2	16,600+	Annual
Kansas	Legislature	40	4	125	2	Per diem	Annual
Kentucky	General Assembly	38	4	100	2	Per diem	Even
Louisiana	Legislature	39	4	105	4	16,800+	Annual
Maine	Legislature	35	2	151	2	10,500+	Even/Odd
Maryland	General Assembly	47	4	141	4	25,000+	Annual
Massachusetts	General Court	40	2	160	2	30,000+	Annual
Michigan	Legislature	38	4	110	2	45,450+	Annual

Minnesota	Legislature	67	4	134	2	26,395+	Odd
Mississippi	Legislature	52	4	122	4	10,000+	Annual
Missouri	General Assembly	34	4	163	2	22,414+	Annual
Montana	Legislature	50	4	100	2	Per diem	Odd
Nebraska	Legislature	49	4	Unicameral		12,000+	Annual
Nevada	Legislature	21	4	42	2	Per diem	Odd
New Hampshire	General Court	24	2	400	2	100	Annual
New Jersey	Legislature	40	4	80	2	35,000	Annual
New Mexico	Legislature	42	4	70	2	Per diem	Annual
New York	Legislature	61	2	150	2	57,500+	Annual
North Carolina	General Assembly	50	2	120	2	11,124+	Odd
North Dakota	Legislative Assembly	53	4	106	2	Per diem	Odd
Ohio	General Assembly	33	4	99	2	38,482	Annual
Oklahoma	Legislature	48	4	101	2	32,000+	Annual
Oregon	Legislative Assembly	30	4	60	2	11,868+	Odd
Pennsylvania	General Assembly	50	4	203	2	47,000	Annual
Rhode Island	General Assembly	50	2	100	2	Per diem	Annual
South Carolina	General Assembly	46	4	124	2	10,000+	Annual
South Dakota	Legislature	35	2	70	2	4,267+	Annual
Tennessee	General Assembly	33	4	99	2	16,500+	Odd
Texas	Legislature	31	4	150	2	7,200+	Odd
Utah	Legislature	29	4	75	2	Per diem	Annual
Vermont	General Assembly	30	2	150	2	6,750+	Odd
Virginia	General Assembly	40	4	100	2	18,000+	Annual
Washington	Legislature	49	4	98	2	17,900+	Annual
West Virginia	Legislature	34	4	100	2	6,500+	Annual
Wisconsin	Legislature	33	4	99	2	32,239+	Annual
Wyoming	Legislature	30	4	64	2	Per diem	Annual

Source: Book of the States 1990–91, various tables.

177

TABLE 6–3   INFORMAL LEGISLATIVE NORMS[a]

"Highly Undesirable" Legislative Behavior

1. Concealing the real purpose(s) of a bill or purposely overlooking some portion of it in order to assure its passage.
2. Dealing in personalities in debate or in other remarks made on the floor of the chamber.
3. Being a thorn to the majority by refusing unanimous consent, etc.
4. Talking about decisions that have been reached in private to the press or anyone else.
5. Seeking as much publicity as possible from the press back home.
6. Being generally known as a spokesperson for some special-interest group.
7. Introducing as many bills and amendments as possible during any legislative session.
8. Talking on a subject coming before the legislature about which you are not completely informed.
9. Giving first priority to your reelection in all of your actions as a legislator.

[a] Items which at least 40 percent of Iowa House and Senate members checked as "highly undesirable." See F. Ted Hebert and Lelan E. McLemore, "Character and Structure of Legislative Norms," *American Journal of Political Science,* 17 (August 1973), 506–27.

legislatures, committee assignments, including the assignment of chairpersons, are made by the speaker of the house and the president of the senate in their respective bodies. This power of appointment gives these leaders some control over the actions of committees.

Committees may decide to hold early hearings on a bill, send it to the floor with little or no revision, and recommend it favorably. Or committees may simply ignore a bill ("pigeonholing"), fail to schedule hearings on it, allow hostile witnesses to testify against it, write extensive revisions and amendments into it, and so forth. Some states reduce the power of committees by allowing bills to be considered on the floor even though they have not been reported out of committee, or by requiring that all bills be reported out either favorably or unfavorably.

Influence   The importance of committee systems seems to vary from state to state. Studies suggest the following explanations for variations among the several states in the strength of their committee systems:

1. Committees exercise less independent influence over legislation in two-party states where party discipline is high.
2. Committees exercise less influence in states where the governor is strong and the legislature is of the same party as the governor, but exercise more influence under divided government.
3. In states where the governor, the party, or a faction exercises strong influence over the legislature (for example, by appointing committee chairpersons), committees are not likely to play an independent role.
4. In contrast, committees are more likely to be influential in one-party states where the governor does not exert strong leadership.
5. Committees are more effective when they are fewer in number and characterized by a more rational division of labor.

6. Committees are more influential in more "professional" legislative settings.[47]

Personnel   Committee assignments in most legislatures are made by the leadership. Occupational background frequently determines a legislator's committee assignments. Thus, lawyers are frequently assigned to committees on the judiciary and civil and criminal law, educators to education committees, farmers to agricultural committees, bankers to banking committees, and so on.[48] The effect of these assignments is to further strengthen the power of special interests in the legislative process. Legislators with occupational ties to various interests dominate the committees that consider legislation dealing with those same interests.

LEGISLATIVE INSTITUTIONALIZATION

Over time political bodies develop their own rules, organizational structures, and patterns of behavior. Social scientists refer to this process as "institutionalization." In legislative bodies, institutionalization is said to occur when (1) membership stabilizes and legislators come to look upon their service as a career, (2) staffs are added, salaries increased, and internal operations expanded, and (3) rules of procedure become more complex.[49]

State legislatures have gradually become more institutionalized. We have already observed that membership turnover, while still fairly high, with one-third of the numbers new to each session, has diminished from even higher levels a few decades ago. Legislative salaries and perks are increasing over time, and incumbents enjoy a heavy advantage in seeking reelection. And we have observed that more legislators are coming to see their jobs as full-time occupations. Now we shall observe increasing institutionalization in the internal functioning of state legislatures.

Professionalism   Some state legislatures are highly professional, while others are not. By *professional* we mean that in some legislatures the members are well paid and tend to think of their jobs as full-time ones; members and committees are well staffed and have good informational services available to them; and a variety of legislative services, such as bill drafting and statutory revision, are well supported and maintained. In other legislatures, members are poorly paid and regard their legislative work as part-time; there is little in the way of staff for legislators or committees; and little is provided in the way of legislative assistance and services. Table 6–4 groups the states by the professionalism of their legislatures.

---

[47] See Alan Rosenthal, "Legislative Committee Systems," *Western Political Quarterly,* 26 (June 1973), 252–62.

[48] Keith E. Hamm and Ronald D. Hedlund, "Occupational Interests and State Legislative Committees." Paper delivered at the Midwest Political Science Association, Chicago, 1989.

[49] The "institutionalization" theme was first developed to understand changes in the U.S. House of Representatives by Nelson Polsby, "The Institutionalization of the U.S. House of Representatives," *American Political Science Review,* 62 (March 1968), 144–68.

TABLE 6-4   PROFESSIONALISM IN STATE LEGISLATURES

PROFESSIONAL—Full-time, large staff, high pay, low turnover

California	Michigan	Pennsylvania
Illinois	New York	Wisconsin
Massachusetts	Ohio	

PROFESSIONAL–CITIZEN—Moderate pay, staff, turnover, and time

Alabama	Indiana	Oklahoma
Alaska	Iowa	Oregon
Arizona	Kansas	South Carolina
Colorado	Kentucky	Tennessee
Connecticut	Maryland	Texas
Delaware	Minnesota	Virginia
Florida	Missouri	Washington
Georgia	Nebraska	
Hawaii	New Jersey	

CITIZEN—Part-time, low pay, small staff, high turnover

Arkansas	New Hampshire	Vermont
Idaho	New Mexico	West Virginia
Louisiana	North Carolina	Wyoming
Maine	North Dakota	
Mississippi	Rhode Island	
Montana	South Dakota	
Nevada	Utah	

Reform   Reform organizations (for example, the Advisory Commission on Inter-governmental Relations, the Council on State Governments, the Eagleton Institute, and the Citizens Conference on State Legislatures) generally argue that state legislatures should be:

Small in size. This is supposed to enhance the prestige of legislative service, improve public accountability, and recruit more qualified people. The recommended size is no more than 100 members total in both upper and lower chambers. However, currently only eight state legislatures (Alabama, Arizona, Delaware, Hawaii, Nebraska, Nevada, Oregon, and Wyoming) have fewer than 100 total members. New Hampshire has 400 house members and 24 senators. Most states have between 150 and 200 legislators. (See Table 6–2.)

Well paid. Annual salaries vary a great deal from state to state. The large urban industrial states generally pay their legislators more than small, rural states. (See Table 6–2.) Reformers argue that better pay would make legislators full-time professional representatives, rather than part-time amateurs who must spend time on their private business interests in order to make a living.

Well staffed. Reformers argue that experienced, knowledgeable staffs are required to provide information, draft bills, analyze the potential impact of proposed legislation, study the governor's budget proposals, and evaluate the impact of existing programs. Less professional legislatures have only a single small "reference service" for the entire legislature; this service is mainly concerned with drafting bills with only minimal research. However, most legislatures provide professional staff for their major committees and for leadership. Twenty-two states now provide each house and senate member with year-round personal staff.

Flexible. Reformers generally argue that legislatures should be free from constitutional restrictions, for example, restrictions on the maximum number of days they can meet annually or biennially, and restrictions on budget powers through constitutional earmarking of revenues for special purposes.

Functional. Reformers argue that legislatures should have clear and simple procedures, well-defined committee responsibilities, published schedules for testimony, committee consideration, and floor debate, and a smooth flow of bills through the legislation process. Yet most legislatures suffer the traditional "end-of-session logjam" when many bills are passed in haste without careful consideration of their merits and other important pieces of legislation are lost in the shuffle. Most abuses of the legislative process occur in this last-minute frenzied period of lawmaking.

Well policed. Reformers have put forward a variety of proposals to ensure the integrity of the legislation process:

1. Public financing of all state elections (only Hawaii and Minnesota provide public funds for *legislative* candidates)
2. Limitations on campaign contributions
3. Reporting of all campaign contributions
4. Registration of lobbyists and regulation of lobbying activity
5. Creation of ethics commissions
6. Sunshine laws that open all legislative activity to the media

Professionalism and Careerism Professionalism in state legislatures encourages careerism. It encourages people who view politics as a career to seek and win a seat in the state legislature. Higher pay makes the job more attractive and allows legislators to devote all their time to politics and policy making. Year-round sessions discourage people who cannot take leave from their business or profession. Greater resources available to legislators allow them to perform more casework for constituents and to build a personal organization devoted to keeping themselves in office. Additional resources make life at the state capital more comfortable. There is less voluntary turnover in professional legislatures, and less likelihood that an incumbent will be defeated. Political scientist Alan Rosenthal writes, "One quality that distinguishes the new breed of full-time, professional politicians from the old breed of part-time, citizen legislators is ambition. The latter were content to spend a few years in legislative office and then return to private careers. The former, by contrast, would like to spend most of their careers in government and politics. They find public office appealing and the game of politics exhilarating."[50]

Careerism fosters individualism among legislators. With their own careers paramount in their calculations, professional legislators are less likely to follow the lead of the governor or party leaders. They have their own agendas to pursue. Professionalism grants some advantage to liberals and Democrats in state politics. Liberals are more likely to view government as a career, conservatives view government service as a sacrifice of business or professional time. Republicans have more difficulty finding business people willing to meet the demands of running for office and serving full time.

Professionalism and Public Policy   Does it make any difference in public policy whether a legislature is "professional" or not? Reformers generally *assume* that "professionalism" will result in legislatures that are "generally innovative in many different areas of public policy, generous in welfare and educational spending and services, and 'interventionist' in the sense of having powers and responsibilities of broad scope."[51] Does legislative reform, however, *really* have any policy consequences?

Unfortunately there is no systematic evidence that legislative professionalism has any direct effect on public policy. While it is true that professional legislatures spend more per person on welfare and more per pupil on education than nonprofessional legislatures, professional legislatures are found in the wealthier, urban states with well-educated populations, and these states spend more on welfare and education anyway. (See Chapter 15, "The Politics of Education," and Chapter 17, "The Politics of Poverty and Welfare.") In other words, there is no evidence that legislative professionalism *causes* increased spending for welfare and education. Instead, both legislative professionalism *and* spending for welfare and education are caused by income, urbanization, and education.[52]

Of course, reformers are disappointed with findings that legislative procedures and legislative professionalism do not directly affect the content of public policy. Many political scientists would like to believe that tinkering with the system or improving the efficiency of government will produce different policies. It rarely turns out that way.

Legislative Staffing   Years ago, state legislatures employed only a few clerks and secretaries to handle the clerical chores and a few lawyers in a small "legislative reference service" to draft bills at the request of lawmakers. Today, the movement

---

[50] Alan Rosenthal, *Governors and Legislatures: Contending Powers* (Washington: CQ Press, 1990), p. 63.

[51] Citizens Conference on State Legislatures, *The Sometimes Governments* (New York: Bantam Books, 1971), p. 77.

[52] See Albert K. Karnig and Lee Sigelman, "State Legislative Reform: Another Look," *Western Political Quarterly,* 28 (September 1975), 548–52.

toward professionalism in state legislatures has created large professional staffs to serve the needs of the leadership and the standing committees. Some more "professional" legislatures have full-time professional staffs—lawyers, researchers, and speechwriters, as well as secretaries—for the house speaker, senate president, majority and minority leaders, and all standing committees; and many states now even provide full-time, year-round staff for each house and senate member. Only the less "professional" rural, small-state legislatures still depend on a small legislative reference service to serve all legislators in drafting bills and doing research.

Legislative staffs have grown rapidly over the last decade, so that today this new "legislative bureaucracy" is itself becoming an important political force.[53] Staff members are political appointees, and they are supposed to reflect the political views of their legislator-bosses in their work. However, some "staffers" become so knowledgeable about state government, or about the state budget, or about their aspects of legislative work, that they are kept on in their jobs even when their original sponsor leaves the capital.

The staffs are expected to research issues, find out what other states are doing, assist in analyzing the budget, schedule legislative hearings, line up experts and interest groups to testify, keep abreast of the status of bills and appropriation items as they move through the legislature, maintain contact with state agencies and the governor's staff, make coffee and fetch doughnuts, write and rewrite bills, and perform other assorted chores and errands. As legislators come to rely on trusted "staffers," the "staffers" themselves become more powerful. Their advice may kill a bill or an appropriation item, or their work may amend a bill or alter an appropriation, without the legislator becoming directly involved. Often "staffers" are young, and they exercise a great deal of influence in policy making.

ROLE PLAYING IN LEGISLATURES

Roles are expectations about the kind of behavior people ought to exhibit. Expectations are placed upon a legislator by fellow legislators, the legislator's party, the opposition party, the governor, constituents, interest groups, and by friends, as well as by legislators themselves.

Leadership Roles   Perhaps the most distinctive roles in the legislative process are those of the leadership. A typical legislative chamber has a presiding officer (usually a house "speaker" and a senate "president"), a majority and a minority floor leader, a number of committee chairpersons, and a steering committee. These leaders perform functions similar to the functions of rules. First of all, leaders are expected to help make the legislative system stable and manageable. They are expected to maintain order, to know the rules and procedures, to follow the rules, and to show fairness and impartiality. Leaders are also expected to help focus the issues and resolve conflict by presenting issues clearly, narrowing the alternatives, organizing public hearings, and promoting the party or administrative point of view

---

[53] J. J. Heaphey and A. P. Balutis, eds. *Legislative Staffing* (New York: Halstead Press, 1975).

on bills. The majority leader is supposed to "get the administrative program through," while the minority leader develops a "constructive opposition."

Leaders are also expected to administer the legislature and expedite business. This includes "promoting teamwork," "being accessible," starting the sessions on time, keeping them on schedule, and distributing the workload. It involves communication, coordination, and liaison with the governor, the administrative departments, and the other chambers.

The role of legislative leaders varies from state to state, and there appears to be a relationship between "professionalism" and leadership roles. In more professional legislatures, there is less turnover in legislative leadership; the leaders serve a longer apprenticeship before becoming leaders; there is more likely to be an established line of succession to leadership positions (from party whip, to floor leader, to speaker); and there are fewer open contests for leadership positions.[54]

Expert Roles   Another set of legislative roles that are commonly encountered and make important contributions to the legislative process are the "subject-matter experts." Unlike leadership roles, the roles of subject-matter experts are not embodied in formal offices. The committee system introduces specialization into the legislature, and the seniority system places at the head of the committee those persons longest exposed to the information about the committee's subject matter. Thus, subject-matter experts emerge among legislators in the fields of law, finance, education, agriculture, natural resources, local government, labor, transportation, and so on. There is some evidence to support the view that subject-matter experts exercise more influence over bills within their fields than nonexperts.[55]

Trustees and Delegates   Another way of describing characteristic behaviors in a legislature is to discover the legislators' orientations toward the expectations of constituents. Legislators have been classified as *trustees* (those who are guided in legislative affairs solely by their personal conscience) and *delegates* (those who are guided by instructions or wishes of their constituents).[56] Despite the concern of many political scientists with the classic question of whether legislators should represent their constituency or their own conscience, few legislators actually exhibit in their behavior a firm commitment to either of these. Most legislators when facing specific issues do not see any conflict between the wishes of their constituents, their party, and their own judgment. Even when such conflict is perceived, most legislators attempt to find a compromise between conflicting demands rather than choose one role or the other exclusively. One legislator even denied that such a question would ever arise: "A representative's judgment should arise from knowing the needs and wants of his district and state."[57] Of course, if legislators are

---

[54] See Douglas Camp Chaffey and Malcolm E. Jewell, "Selection and Tenure of State Legialstive Party Leaders: A Comparative Analysis," *Journal of Politics,* 34 (November 1972), 1278–86.

[55] William Buchanan et al., "The Legislator as Specialist," *Western Political Quarterly,* 13 (1960), 636–51.

[56] Sorauf, *Party and Representation,* pp. 121–46; and Wahlke et al., *Legislative System,* New York: Athertan Press, 1963, pp. 281–86.

[57] Sorauf, *Party and Representation,* p. 125.

asked how they make their decisions, they *claim* to be guided solely by their own conscience. However, this is little more than a verbalism; it reflects a heroic image of the courageous defender of the public interest, who acts out of personal virtue and conviction regardless of the consequences.

The more politically experienced legislator is more likely to assume the role of a trustee. There is some evidence that legislators who come to the office with little prior experience as public officials, and those with less service in the legislature, are more likely to respond in the manner of a "delegate," while their more experienced colleagues give "trustee" responses to interviewers.[58]

PARTY POLITICS IN STATE LEGISLATURES

One-Party States   The influence of parties in legislative decision making varies a great deal from state to state. First of all, it is obvious that the dominant party in a one-party state does not exercise tight party discipline over the voting of legislators. In terms of legislative behavior, one-party states are really no-party states.[59] Being a Democrat in the legislature of a one-party Democratic state does not influence roll-call voting behavior very much. Democratic governors in these states cannot depend upon party loyalty to win legislative support for their programs. However, the *minority* Republicans in the one-party Democratic state legislatures tend to stick together. Their cohesion increases their influence in legislative chambers where they are hopelessly outnumbered.

Emerging Legislative Party Organizations   As Republicans win more seats in the southern and border state legislatures, party organizations and party voting within the legislatures is increasing. When only a very few Republicans sat in these legislatures, they were more likely to see themselves as "loners" rather than a viable "opposition." Rather than organize a party caucus, these lonely legislators usually sought ways to integrate themselves into the factional politics of the dominant Democratic party. But as the number of minority Republican legislators grows, they are more likely to organize themselves into a party caucus, to develop a party legislative program, and to vote cohesively. The development of party cohesion in these formerly one-party Democratic states is aided when the governorship is captured by a Republican, even if only for a single term. The minority party's cohesiveness is usually greater than the dominant party's; the Democrats in these formerly one-party states may still be locked in factional battles. However, the

---

[58] Charles G. Bell and Charles E. Price, "Pre-Legislative Sources of Representational Roles," *Midwest Journal of Political Science,* 13 (May 1969), 254–70. See also Corey M. Rosen, "Legislative Influence and Policy Orientation in American State Legislatures," *American Journal of Political Science,* 18 (November 1974), 681–91.

[59] Nebraska, of course, is also a no-party state. The special conditions affecting legislative affairs in this nonpartisan legislature are discussed in Susan Welch and Eric H. Carlson, "The Impact of Party on Voting Behavior in a Nonpartisan Legislature," *American Political Science Review,* 67 (September 1973), 854–67. This research concludes, among other things, that in the nonpartisan Nebraska legislature there are no cohesive reference groups and the voting behavior of members is highly unpredictable. This makes it difficult for voters to make a rational choice at election time.

emerging "threat" of a Republican opposition usually spurs the Democrats into somewhat more cohesive legislative organization. Nonetheless legislative voting in these formerly one-party Democratic states rarely follows strict party lines, except on a vote that directly affects party fortunes, such as reapportionment or redistricting.[60]

Two-Party States   Within the competitive states, party divisions on roll-call votes are more frequent than any other divisions, including rural–urban divisions.[61] One common measure of party influence on voting is the percentage of nonunanimous roll-call votes on which a majority of Democrats voted against the majority of Republicans. Compilations by the *Congressional Quarterly* show that the proportion of roll calls in Congress in which the two parties have been in opposition has ranged from 35 to 50 percent over the years. Party voting may be even higher in the state legislatures of New York, Pennsylvania, Ohio, Delaware, Rhode Island, Massachusetts, and Michigan than it is in Congress.[62]

Party Issues   On what types of issues did the parties exercise great influence? Minor bills involving the licensing of water well drillers, beauticians, or barbers do not usually become the subject matter of party votes, and only infrequently will the parties divide over such matters as the designation of an official state bird. In the more urban and industrialized states, parties usually display the greatest cohesion on issues involving taxation and appropriations, welfare, and regulation of labor —in short, the major social and economic controversies that divide the national parties. Party influence in budgetary matters is particularly apparent, since the budget often involves issues of social welfare and class interest on which parties in urban states are split. In addition, the budget is clearly identified as the product of the governor and carries the label of the party of the governor. Another type of bill that is often the subject of party voting is one involving the party as an interest group. Parties often exhibit an interest in bills proposing to transfer powers from an office controlled by one party to an office controlled by the other, or bills proposing to create or abolish non–civil-service jobs. Parties display considerable interest in bills affecting the organization of local government, state administration, the civil service, registration and election laws, and legislative procedure.

Sources of Party Voting   What factors distinguish those states in which the party substantially influences legislative decision making from those states in which it does not? First of all, party cohesion is found in the competitive states

---

[60] See Robert Harmel and Keith E. Hamm, "Development of a Party Role in a No-Party Legislature," *Western Political Quarterly,* 39 (March 1986), 79–92. See also Cole Blease Graham and Kenny J. Whitby, "Party-Based Voting in a Southern State Legislature," *American Politics Quarterly,* 17 (April 1989) 181–93.

[61] See Glenn T. Broach, "A Comparative Dimensional Analysis of Partisan and Urban–Rural Voting in State Legislatures," *Journal of Politics,* 34 (August 1972), 905–21; Lance T. LeLoup, "Policy, Party and Voting in U.S. State Legislatures," *Legislative Studies Quarterly,* 1 (May 1976), 213–30.

[62] Hugh L. LeBlanc, "Voting in State Senates: Party and Constituency Influences," *Midwest Journal of Political Science,* 13 (February 1969), 33–57.

rather than in the noncompetitive states. Since the noncompetitive states are the rural nonindustrial states, party voting appears related to urbanism and economic development if all fifty states are considered.

Party cohesion is strongest in those urban industrial states in which the parties represent separate socioeconomic constituencies. Party voting occurs in those competitive states in which Democratic legislators represent central-city, low-income, ethnic, and racial constituencies, and Republican legislators represent middle-class, suburban, small-town, and rural constituencies. Party cohesion is weak in states where party alignments do not coincide with socioeconomic divisions of constituencies.

It is this division of constituencies that is the basis of party cohesion and influence in the legislature. One of the more rigorous investigations into the causes of party voting in a state legislature was Thomas A. Flinn's classic study of party voting in Ohio.[63] Flinn expressed the constituency basis of party cohesion as follows: "To the extent that parties find their support in contrasting constituencies, party responsibility is the consequence." Within each party, members from districts typical of their party in socioeconomic attributes support the party position more often than members from districts atypical of the party. Constituency characteristics, then, help to explain not only the outcome of elections but also the behavior of the elected.

Party Discipline   In a few states the party leadership sets the legislative agenda, determines committee assignments, and tries to bind legislators to vote for the position taken by the party caucus. But because of the weaknesses of the parties in the electoral process (see Chapter 5), party discipline in most state legislatures is very weak. Reformers in Colorado passed a constitutional referendum specifically designed to weaken the powers of party leaders and committees in the legislative process. It requires consideration "on its merits" of every bill referred to a committee, specifies that the full house can always bring a bill out of committee, and outlaws binding party caucuses, saying that legislators cannot "commit themselves or any other member or members, through a vote in a party caucus or any similar procedure, to vote in favor of or against any bill."[64]

ARE LEGISLATORS RESPONSIBLE POLICY MAKERS?

A classic dilemma of representative government is whether the legislator should vote his or her own conscience—"the trustee"—or vote the constituency's wishes —"the delegate." Good philosophical arguments can be found to support either of these guiding principles. Nearly 200 years ago the English political philosopher Edmund Burke confronted this question directly and urged representatives to vote their own conscience about what is right for society. Burke believed that the voters should elect wise and virtuous representatives to govern *for* them—to use their own judgment in deciding issues regardless of popular demands. Even today the

---

[63] Thomas A. Flinn, "Party Responsibility in the States: Some Causal Factors," *American Political Science Review,* 58 (1964), 60–71.

[64] *State Legislation,* August 1989, p. 16.

term *Burkean representation* refers to the willingness of a representative to ignore public opinion and decide public issues on the basis of one's own best judgment about what is right for society.

Other political philosophers stress *responsiveness* of representatives to the views of their constituents. Consider, for example, philosopher Hanna Pitkin's definition of representation: "Representation means acting in the interest of the represented, in a manner responsive to them."[65] Responsiveness connotes a deliberate effort by legislators to match their votes on public policy issues to their constituency's preferences. However, to be "responsive" to one's constituents, two conditions must be met: (1) the legislator must correctly perceive the constituents' views on the issues, and (2) the legislator must act in accord with these views.

Let us consider the first condition: Do legislators know the views of their constituents on public issues? Unfortunately, the evidence is mixed. When Iowa legislators were asked to predict whether their own district would vote for or against some proposed constitutional amendments, the resulting predictions were good on some issues but poor on others.[66] Interestingly, the poorest predictions came from legislators from poor districts, suggesting that legislators have less understanding of the views of poor constituents than affluent ones. In contrast, when Florida legislators were asked to predict how both their state and district would vote on referenda on school busing and school prayer, nearly all of them made accurate predictions for both their district and the state.[67] Perhaps one explanation for these apparently conflicting findings is that legislators know their constituents' views on well-publicized, controversial, emotionally charged issues, but that legislators are poor predictors of constituent opinion on other kinds of issues.

In a study of congressional voting behavior, Warren Miller and Donald Stokes constructed the model in Figure 6–4 to clarify the linkages between the constituency's attitude, the legislator's perception of his or her constituent's attitude, the legislator's own attitude, and his or her roll-call vote.[68] Their research suggested that constituency attitude, congressional perception of it, and congressional voting were closely linked on civil-rights issues, but *not* on foreign affairs or social-welfare issues.

State legislators may indeed vote their own attitude on *most* issues coming before the legislature. A careful study of voting on welfare, tax, and consumer issues in the Texas legislature revealed that "In both houses, in every issue-area examined, the path connecting the representative's attitude with his roll-call vote

[65] Hanna Pitkin, *The Concept of Representation* (Berkeley: University of California Press, 1967), p. 154.

[66] Ronald D. Hedlund and H. Paul Friesma, "Representatives' Perceptions of Constituency Opinion," *Journal of Politics,* 34 (August 1971), 730–52.

[67] Robert S. Erikson, Norman R. Luttbeg, and William V. Holloway, "Knowing One's District: How Legislators Predict Referendum Voting," *American Journal of Political Science,* 19 (May 1975), 231–41.

[68] See Warren E. Miller and Donald E. Stokes, "Constituency Influence in Congress," *American Political Science Review,* 57 (March 1963), 45–46.

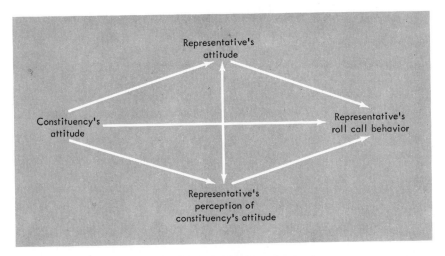

FIGURE 6–4   A Model of Constituency Influency

is far more important than the path linking his perceptions of his constituency's attitude with his voting."[69] The explanation offered was that activities of the governor and his or her staff, other legislators and legislative leaders, and outside interest groups, create "the din of the immediate legislative struggle" which "muffles" the voices from the home district. Even legislators from competitive districts were seemingly unaffected by their views of their constituents' attitudes. As expected, legislators who opted for the role of "delegate" voted what they believed to be their constituents' attitudes more than legislators who opted for the role of trustee.

In summary, the absence of direct evidence that (1) legislators know their constituents' views and (2) vote their constituents' views rather than their own views creates difficulties for the "responsiveness" theory of democracy. There is a great deal of "noise" along the lines from constituents' views to their legislator's roll-call vote.

Personal ideology rather than lobbying pressures or constituents' views is also a major factor in deciding legislative votes.

> None of this denies that legislators endeavor in some decisions to please interest groups or other actors. Cowed by threats, lured by enticements, legislators often make decisions they do not believe in. In most sessions, too, they confront a few highly publicized, controversial issues; their private policy views may matter little then. Nonetheless . . . representatives have the freedom on a range of issues to weigh priorities and evaluate policy options on their merits: to decide in accord with their own private conceptions of good public policy.[70]

---

[69] Bryan D. Jones, "Competitiveness, Role Orientations, and Legislative Responsiveness," *Journal of Politics*, 35 (November 1973), 924–47.

[70] Robert M. Entman, "The Impact of Ideology on Legislative Behavior," *Journal of Politics*, 45 (February 1983), 165.

However, the classic choice posed by Burke between district demands and personal judgment is an artificial issue to most legislators. They are products of their constituency, and they share its goals and values. Conflicts between their districts' views and their own are rare. We have seen that legislators have roots deep in their constituencies—many organizational memberships, lifetime residency, shared religious and ethnic affiliations, for example. The party with which the legislator identifies is also a creature of the constituency; it accedes to local interests, local political mores, local political style. Legislators are so much "of" their constituency that they need little direct prompting or supervision. As one discerning legislator commented: "Basically you represent the thinking of the people who have gone through what you have gone through and who are what you are. You vote according to that. In other words, if you come from a suburb you reflect the thinking of people in the suburbs; if you are of depressed people, you reflect that. You represent the sum total of your background."[71]

LOBBYING IN STATE LEGISLATURES

Lobbying in state capitals may be somewhat cruder—if not actually corrupt—than lobbying in Washington. In interviewing lobbyists and legislators in Washington, Lester Milbrath found that they considered state lobbying much more corrupt than national lobbying. "'Lobbying is very different before state legislators; it is much more individualistic. Maybe this is the reason they have more bribery in state legislatures than in Congress.' 'In the state legislatures, lobbying is definitely on a lower plane. The lobbyists are loose and hand out money and favors quite freely.' 'Lobbying at the state level is cruder, more basic, and more obvious.'"[72]

Needless to say, it is difficult to document such statements. However, it seems reasonable that state legislators are more subject to the pressures and appeals of organized interest groups than members of Congress. State legislators meet less often and for shorter periods of time than do members of Congress and, consequently, most state legislatures have not developed the formal and informal rules governing their behavior that exist in the U.S. Congress. Moreover, state legislators make less money than members of Congress and may therefore be more vulnerable to the appeals of interest groups offering financial support.

The influence of organized interest groups varies from state to state. Earlier (Chapter 4) we discussed interest groups in the fifty states and their involvement in public relations, campaign financing, and lobbying. We defined lobbying as any communication by someone acting on behalf of a group directed at a government decision maker with the hope of influencing decisions.

Narrow Issues   On what kinds of decisions are interest groups more likely to exercise influence? Party and constituency interests are most apparent on broad social and economic issues. On narrower issues parties are less likely to have either an interest or an opinion. The legislator is, therefore, freer to respond to the pleas

---

[71] Sorauf, *Party and Representation*, p. 253.

[72] Lester Milbrath, *The Washington Lobbyists* (Chicago: Rand McNally, 1963), pp. 241–43.

of organized groups on highly specialized topics than on major issues of public interest. The absence of both party and constituency influences on certain types of issues contributes to the effectiveness of organized interests. Economic interests seeking to use the law to improve their competitive position are a major source of group pressure on these specialized topics. Particularly active in lobbying are the businesses subject to extensive government regulation. The truckers, railroads, insurance companies, and liquor interests are consistently found to be among the most highly organized and active lobbyists in state capitals. Organized pressure comes from associations of governments and associations of government employees. State chapters of the National Education Association are persistent in presenting the demands of educational administrators and occasionally the demands of the dues-paying teachers as well.

Information Exchange   Legislators depend on lobbyists for much of their information on public issues. Legislators are aware of the potential bias in information given them by lobbyists. But the constant proximity of lobbyists to legislators facilitates information exchange.[73] Legislators *use* lobbyists, just as lobbyists use legislators:

> Whatever their image of lobbyists, legislators are more likely to look on them as service agents than as opinion manipulators. . . . Typically, legislators utilize lobbyists as sources of influence in three ways: by calling upon lobbyists to influence other legislators, by calling upon lobbyists to help amass public opinion in favor of the legislator's position, and by including lobbyists in planning strategy in an effort to negotiate a bill through the legislature.[74]

Threats   It is unwise for lobbyists to threaten legislators, for example, by vowing to defeat them in the next election. This is the tactic of an amateur lobbyist, not a professional. It usually produces a defensive response by the legislator. As one lobbyist put it: "Once you have closed the door you have no further access to the individual. Once you've threatened an individual, there is no possibility of winning in the future."[75] Even the publication of voting records of legislators by interest groups is considered an implied threat and is generally disregarded by legislators.

Getting the Message   Testimony at legislative committee hearings is a common form of information exchange between lobbyists and legislators. Often this testimony is the legislators' primary source of information about legislation. Direct meetings in legislators' offices are also frequent and effective. Social gatherings (where the liquor is usually furnished by the lobbyist) are more important in establishing friendships; professional lobbyists seldom bring up "business" on such occasions. Legislators are wined and dined so much during legislative sessions that

---

[73] Christopher A. Mooney, "Peddling Information in the State Legislature: Closeness Counts," *Western Political Quarterly*, 44 (June 1991), 433–44.

[74] Harmon Zeigler and Michael A. Baer, *Lobbying: Interaction and Influence in American State Legislatures* (Belmont, CA: Wadsworth, 1969), p. 107.

[75] Ibid., p. 121.

attendance at social functions is sometimes viewed as a chore. The least effective method of lobbying is the submission of long letters or reports.

Lobbying the Staff   One form of lobbying that is growing rapidly in importance is communication with legislative *staff* personnel. As state legislatures acquire more full-time staff for their standing committees, house and senate leaders, and majority and minority party caucuses, professional lobbyists are coming to recognize that these staff people can have as much or more to do with the specific content of bills as legislators themselves. Many of the more "modernized," "professional" state legislatures rely heavily on the advice of professional staffs. The wise lobbyist in these states cultivates friendships among staff personnel.

Regulation of Lobbying   The U.S. Constitution guarantees the right "to petition the government for redress of grievances." This First Amendment right protects individuals and groups in their attempts to communicate with and influence their lawmakers. Nonetheless, lobbying is regulated in some fashion in all of the states. Most state laws require lobbyists ("anyone receiving compensation to influence legislative action") to (1) register with the clerk or secretary of the house or senate and (2) file periodic reports of direct expenditures for lobbying activity. These regulations have relatively little impact on lobbying activity; many organizations claim that they are educational or religious in nature and not really lobbies, and they do not register. Many lobbies do not report all of their educational and public relations expenditures, but only a small portion, which they attribute directly to lobbying. Campaign contributions usually must be reported under state election laws. Of course, bribery and conspiracy may be prosecuted under criminal laws.

State legislatures and agencies charged with enforcement of lobbying regulations have traditionally been notorious for their neglect of their responsibilities. However, increasing professionalization of state legislatures appears to increase both their capacity and willingness to regulate lobbying.[76]

LEGISLATURES IN STATE POLITICS

At least three general propositions about state legislatures emerge from the discussions in this chapter. First of all, state legislatures reflect socioeconomic conditions of their states. These conditions help to explain many of the differences one encounters in state legislative politics: the level of legislative activity, the degree of interparty competition, the extent of party cohesion, the professionalism of the legislature, the nature of legislative conflict, the level of interest group activity and influence, and so on. Of course, there are some unique features of legislative politics in each of the fifty states based upon particular events, individuals, or historical experiences. Generally, however, the characteristics of a state's legislative system are closely linked to a state's social and economic climate.

---

[76] Cynthia Opheim, "Explaining the Differences in State Lobbying Regulation," *Western Political Quarterly,* 44 (June 1991), 405–21.

Second, it seems safe to say that most state legislatures function as "arbiters" of public policy rather than as "initiators." Policy initiation is the function of the governor, the bureaucrat, and the interest group. It is principally these elements that develop policy proposals in the first instance; legislatures are placed in the role of responding to the stimulus provided by these groups. The structure of legislatures clearly reflects their deliberative function. Their rules and procedures and their leadership and committee systems do not lend themselves to policy initiation so much as they lend themselves to deliberation, discussion, and delay. The size and complexity of state government has reached a scale where expert knowledge rather than lay enlightenment is the crucial ingredient in policy formation. The state budget, for example, perhaps the single most important policy-making document, is drawn up by bureaucrats subordinate to the governor and modified by the governor before submission to the legislature. Legislatures make further modifications, but seldom do they undertake to rewrite an executive budget. Legislatures are still critical obstacles through which appropriation and revenue measures must pass; they are still the scenes of bloody battles over the ends for which public money is to be spent.

Yet before legislative deliberation, the agenda for decision making has already been drawn up, the framework for conflict has already been established, and the issues have already been placed in particular bills. Sophisticated lawmakers are aware of their function as arbiters rather than as initiators of public policy. As one of them put it: "We're the policy-making body of the state government, and basically we should give leadership necessary to meet the problems the state faces. But in practice it comes from the executive branch."[77]

A third general proposition about legislatures is that they function to inject into public decision making a parochial influence. Legislatures function to represent locally organized interests, interests that are manifested in local rather than statewide constituencies. Legislators have deep roots in their local constituencies. They have the religious and ethnic affiliations of their constituents, they have lived among them for most of their lives, and they meet them frequently in their businesses and clubs. The process of recruiting legislators is carried on at the local level. State legislators clearly function to represent local interests in state politics.

---

[77] Wahlke et al., *Legislative System*, p. 255.

7

GOVERNORS IN STATE POLITICS

▲

THE MANY ROLES OF A GOVERNOR

Governors are central figures in American state politics. In the eyes of many citizens, governors are responsible for everything that happens in their states during their terms of office, whether or not they have the authority or the capacity to do anything about it. Governors are expected to bring industry into their states, prevent prison riots, raise teachers' salaries, keep taxes low, reduce unemployment, see that the state gets its fair share of grant money from Washington, provide disaster relief, and bring tourists into the state. Governors offer reassurance to citizens during crises and disasters—everything from floods, hurricanes, fires, and droughts, to toxic waste spills and nuclear plant accidents. These public expectations far exceed the powers of governors. In many ways the expectations placed upon the governor resemble those placed upon the president. But few governors have the power in state political systems that the president has in the national government. Like the president, governors are expected to be their state's chief administrator, chief legislator, leader of their party, ceremonial head of their government, chief ambassador to other governments, leader of public opinion, and chief crisis manager.

Chief Administrator As *chief administrator,* the governor must try to achieve co-ordination within the state's bureaucracy, oversee the preparation of the state's budget, and supervise major state programs. Governors must resolve conflicts within their administration and troubleshoot where difficulties arise. They must be concerned with scandal and endeavor to prevent it from becoming public, or act decisively to eliminate it if it does. The public will hold them responsible for any scandal in their administration, whether they were a party to it or not. The public will hold them responsible for the financial structure of the state, whether it was they or their predecessors who were responsible for the state's fiscal troubles.

Yet, as we shall see in this chapter, the formal administrative powers of a governor are severely restricted. Many of the governor's administrative agencies are headed by elected officials or independent boards or commissions, over which the governor has little or no control. Governors' powers of appointment and removal are severely restricted by state constitutions. Despite a generation of recommendations by political scientists and public administrators that governors' control over their administration should be strengthened, governors still do not have control over their administration that is commensurate with their responsibility for it.

Chief Legislator As *chief legislator,* the governor is responsible for the major statewide legislative programs. There is a general public expectation that every governor will put forward some sort of legislative program, even a governor committed to a "caretaker" role. The governor largely determines what public issues will be considered by the legislature. By sending bills to the legislature, governors are cast in the role of the "initiator" of public policy decisions. If they want to see their legislative proposals enacted into law, they must also persuade legislators to support them. In other words, they must also involve themselves directly in legislative decisions.

The veto power gives the governor bargaining power with the legislature. Few vetoes are overridden; in most states a two-thirds majority vote in both houses is required to override a veto. This means a governor needs only one-third plus one in either house to sustain his or her veto. So even the *threat* of a veto can force changes in a bill under consideration in the legislature. Moreover, in most states, the governor possesses the line-item veto, a power denied to the president of the United States. This allows the governor to veto specific items in an appropriations bill, including legislators' home district "pork" or "turkeys." The threat of vetoing these vote-winning projects gives the governor additional bargaining power with legislators. A governor can also call special sessions of the legislature, allowing the governor to spotlight specific issues and pressure the legislature to do something.

Party Leader Traditionally governors were regarded as the head of their party in the state. But with the general decline of party organization and discipline over the years, governors no longer rely much on their party role. Governors do not have the power to deny party nominations to recalcitrant legislators of their own party. Party nominations are generally won independently by legislators in their own districts. Governors have no formal disciplinary powers over members of their own party. And governors may choose to emphasize their own independence from their national party to further their own electoral ambitions.

However, within the legislature, parties still count. The governor usually receives greater support for his or her program from members of his or her own party. Legislators who run for office under the same party label as the governor have a stake in his or her success. Since all who run under the party's label share its common fortunes, and since its fortunes are often governed by the strength of its gubernatorial candidate, there will always be a tendency for loyal party members to support their governor. The organization of the legislature along party lines reinforces the party role of the governor. Legislative leaders of the governor's party —whether in the majority or minority—are expected to support the governor's program.

Ceremonial Head   *Ceremonial* duties occupy a great deal of a governor's time. A governor is seldom able to mobilize the symbolic and ceremonial power of the office on behalf of state goals in the same way that the president can mobilize the power of that office on behalf of national goals. Nonetheless, the skillful use of symbols and ceremonies can add to a governor's prestige and popularity. These assets can in turn contribute to political power.

Chief Negotiator   The governor is the *chief negotiator* with other governments in the American federal system, a variation of the diplomatic role of the president. Governors must negotiate with their local governments on the division of state and local responsibilities for public programs, and with other state governments over coordinating highway development, water pollution, resource conservation, and reciprocity in state laws. Increasingly, governors must undertake responsibility for negotiation with the national government as well. The governor shares responsibility with the state's United States senators in seeing to it that the state receives a "fair share" of federal contracts, highway monies, educational monies, poverty funds, and so on.

Opinion Leader   Governors are *leaders of public opinion* in their state. They are the most visible of state officials. Their comments on public affairs make news, and they are sought after for television, radio, and public appearances. They are able to focus public opinion on issues they deem important. They may not always be able to win public opinion to their side, but at least they will be heard.

Crisis Manager   Finally, governors may be called upon to *manage crises* in their states—hurricanes, floods, droughts, and other disasters. Indeed, a governor's performance in a crisis may determine his or her standing with the public.

THE MAKING OF A GOVERNOR

As the central position in American state politics, the governorship is a much sought-after office. The prestige of being called "governor" for the rest of one's life, and the opportunity to use the office as a steppingstone to the United States Senate, or even the presidency or vice-presidency of the United States, is extremely attractive to people of ambition in American politics.

Varieties of Background   Many governors have been the sons of families of great wealth, who have chosen public service as an outlet for their energies—the Roosevelts, the Harrimans, the duPonts, the Rockefellers, and the Scrantons. Others have been men who emphasized, or exaggerated, their humble beginnings —Huey Long of Louisiana, "Big Jim" Folsom of Alabama, "Pitchfork Ben" Tillman of South Carolina, "Old Gene" Talmadge of Georgia. The southern "populist" governors, however, were gradually replaced by more moderate and better educated men—Bob Graham of Florida, Bill Clinton of Arkansas, and Jimmy Carter of Georgia. George C. Wallace of Alabama may have been the last governor in the true populist tradition.

Governor Edmund G. "Jerry" Brown, Jr., of California won the office once held by his father "Pat" Brown, who defeated Richard M. Nixon in 1962. Nelson Rockefeller was elected to four consecutive four-year terms as governor of New York, holding that post longer than anyone in history. His brother, Winthrop Rockefeller, was governor of Arkansas, and his nephew, John D. Rockefeller IV, was governor of West Virginia. James B. Longley of Maine was the first independent candidate to win a governorship in modern history; he was followed by independent mavericks Walter Hickel of Alaska and Lowell Weicker of Connecticut. Governors have been movie actors (Ronald Reagan of California), restaurant owners (Lester Maddox of Georgia), truck drivers (Harold Hughes of Iowa), country music singers (Jimmie Davis of Louisiana who wrote "You Are My Sunshine"), and even party bosses (David Lawrence of Pennsylvania). However, the majority of governors have been *lawyers* by profession. (The predominance of lawyers in public office was explained in Chapter 6.)

Age   Television has accented youth and good looks among state governors. It helps "image-wise" to be tall, slim, handsome, fashionable, and smiling. The median beginning age of governors has declined over the last few decades to a youngish forty-seven. (Harold Stassen of Minnesota, who took office in 1938, was the nation's youngest governor at thirty-one.)

Race   Until Douglas Wilder's successful run for the Virginia statehouse in 1989 (see Chapter 14), no state had ever elected a black governor. California came close to doing so in 1982, when Democratic Mayor Thomas Bradley of Los Angeles lost to Republican George Deukmejian by less than 1 percent of the vote; Bradley tried again in 1986 but was badly beaten by Deukmejian. Black GOP candidate William Lucas was soundly defeated by incumbent Democrat James Blanchard in Michigan in 1986. Several Hispanics have been elected governor: Jerry Abodaca of New Mexico, Raul Castro of Arizona, Toney Anaya of New Mexico, and Bob Martinez of Florida.

Gender   Very few women have been elected governors of American states. Nellie Ross of Wyoming and Miriam "Ma" Ferguson of Texas both succeeded their husbands in office in the 1920s. Lurleen Wallace of Alabama replaced her husband, George C. Wallace, briefly in the 1960s, when he was constitutionally prohibited from another term in office. It was not until 1974 that Ella T. Grasso of Connecticut

TABLE 7–1 POLITICAL EXPERIENCE OF GOVERNORS

Last Public Office Prior to Election as Governor	1970–1990
State legislature	22%
Statewide office: lieutenant governor, secretary of state, treasurer, auditor, secretary of agriculture, public service commission	25
Attorney general or judicial office	15
Congressional	12
Administrative, federal and state	7
Local elective	5
Party office	3
Other office	5
No prior office	6

From *Politics in the American States: A Comparative Analysis,* 5/E by Virginia Gray et al. Copyright © 1985 by Virginia Gray, Herbert Jacobs, and Robert B. Albritton. Reprinted by permission of Harper Collins Publishers.

became the first woman governor whose husband had not previously held the office. Later the same year, Dixey Lee Ray of Washington accomplished the same feat. Martha Layne Collins was elected governor of Kentucky in 1983. In 1986 two women faced each other in the Nebraska governor's race, and Republican Kay Orr emerged the victor; Democrat Madeleine M. Kunin won a close race in Vermont. Lieutenant Governor Rose Mofford replaced the impeached Governor Evan Mecham of Arizona. Ann Richards's hard-fought victory in the Texas governor's race in 1990 demonstrated that women can triumph in rough, bitter personal campaigns. Two other women governors were also elected in 1990: Joan Finney in Kansas and Barbara Roberts in Oregon.

Political Experience   Governors usually come to their office with considerable experience in public affairs. Only about 6 percent come into the governor's chair without prior office holding (see Table 7–1). "Promotion" from a statewide elective office—lieutenant governor and attorney general, especially—is the most well-worn path to the governorship. Many governors have experience in state legislatures: Nearly half of all governors have previously served in the legislature and over one-fifth run directly from their legislative seats. Some members of Congress and some federal cabinet officers give up their seats to run for governor—an indication of the power and prestige of the office of governor. Pete Wilson of California was the first U.S. senator in modern times to leave that body to run for governor; Lawton Chiles of Florida left the U.S. Senate and later decided to run for governor.

GUBERNATORIAL POLITICS

Competition   Competition is usually strong, both in primary and general elections, for the governorship. Indeed, competition for the job has been increasing over time, especially in the southern states where Republican candidates now have a chance of winning governorships.[1] Yet overall the Democratic party has dominated state gubernatorial politics. In recent years Democratic governors have outnumbered Republican governors.

Getting Elected   What forces influence the outcome of gubernatorial elections? Are gubernatorial elections affected by national voting trends—"coattails"? Or are they more affected by conditions within the states, especially the performance of the state's economy? Or are gubernatorial elections primarily "candidate centered"—influenced mostly by the personal qualities of the candidates, their handling of state issues, the strength of their own political organizations, and their success in fund raising and campaigning?

Gubernatorial Vote Choice   If voters are asked "What mattered most in voting for governor?," they cite personal leadership qualities of the candidate more often than anything else (see Table 7–2). Party affiliation and agreement on issues follow in importance. Negative voting—dislike of the opponent—also plays a significant role in gubernatorial voting.

Voters do *not* usually hold a governor solely responsible for economic problems confronting the state. Most voters recognize that state economic conditions depend more on market factors, or on the actions of the national government, including the president, than on the governor. State (or local) officials may be held responsible for actions that make an already weak economy worse; they may expect a governor to do all that he or she can to ameliorate hard times. But few voters hold governors directly responsible for the state's economic well-being.[2]

While presidential and congressional elections are influenced by national economic conditions (recessions adversely affect the vote for candidates of the party in power, while prosperity generally helps), no similar influences can be seen in state legislative or gubernatorial elections. Political scientist John E. Chubb concludes: "Voters in state elections appear to hold politicians outside of the state, specifically the president and the president's party, responsible for economic conditions, and if conditions in a state should differ from those in neighboring states, to hold the governor only minimally responsible."[3]

---

[1] Republican southern governors over the last decade include: Alabama: Guy Hunt, 1987–; Arkansas: Winthrop Rockefeller, 1967–71 and Frank White, 1981–83; Florida: Claude R. Kirk, 1967–71 and Bob Martinez, 1987–; Louisiana: David C. Treen, 1980–84; North Carolina: James E. Holshouser, 1973–77 and James G. Martin, 1985–; South Carolina: James B. Edwards, 1975–79 and Carroll Campbell, 1987–; Tennessee: Winfield Dunn, 1971–75 and Lamar Alexander, 1979–86; Texas: William P. Clements, 1979–83 and 1987–; Virginia: Linwood Holton, 1970–74, Miles E. Godwin, 1974–78, and John N. Dalton, 1978–82.

[2] See Robert M. Stein "Economic Voting for Governor and U.S. Senator," *Journal of Politics,* 52 (February 1990), 29–53.

[3] John E. Chubb, "Institutions, the Economy and the Dynamics of State Elections," *American Political Science Review,* 82 (March 1988), 151. However, for contrary evidence showing that retrospective evaluations of a state's economy affects vote choice, see Craig J. Svoboda, "Modeling Gubernatorial Elections," paper presented at the American Political Science Association Meeting, Chicago, 1992.

TABLE 7–2   GUBERNATORIAL VOTE CHOICE

Q. "What mattered most in voting for governor?"	%	Q: "Who is to blame for the state's economic problems?"	%
Strong leadership	21.1	President	25.4
Management ability	19.7	Both president and governor	18.4
Political party	19.0	Governor	15.4
Agreement on issues	18.2	Neither	34.5
Dislike opponent	12.0		
Don't know/No answer	10.0		

Source: Adopted from Robert M. Stein, "Economic Voting for Governor and U.S. Senator," *Journal of Politics,* 52 (February 1990), 29–53. By permission of the author and the University of Texas Press. Based on *New York Times/ CBS News* election day surveys in 27 states in 1982, during a national economic recession.

Coattail Effects   There are some coattail effects in state gubernatorial and legislative elections. Gubernatorial candidates running on the same party ticket as popular presidential candidates enjoy a significant advantage. But most gubernatorial elections are held in "off-years"—years in which the nation is not electing a president. Off-year elections are deliberately designed to minimize the effects of presidential voting trends on state governors' elections. Nonetheless, there is some evidence that the electoral fate of gubernatorial candidates is affected by the popularity of the president. Gubernatorial candidates of the president's party attract more votes when the president's popularity in opinion polls is high. This is true whether the candidates are incumbents or aspirants.[4] Conversely, gubernatorial candidates of the president's party suffer when the president's popularity is low. Insofar as a president's popularity is affected by national economic trends, gubernatorial candidates of the president's party can suffer from national recessions and benefit from national prosperity.[5]

Candidate Effects   Despite these coattail effects, gubernatorial elections are mostly candidate centered. Governors are less closely tied to national policy issues than Congressional members; governors are not called upon by the media to explain their votes in support or opposition to the president's policy positions. The outcome of gubernatorial elections depends mostly on the personal qualities of the candidates, their ability to associate themselves with popular issues, the strength of their personal political organizations, their ability to raise campaign funds, and their skills in campaigning.

---

[4] Dennis M. Simon, "Presidents, Governors and Electoral Accountability," *Journal of Politics,* 51 (May 1989), 286–304; Thomas M. Holbrook-Provow, "National Factors in Gubernatorial Elections," *American Politics Quarterly,* 15 (October 1987), 471–83.

[5] Chubb, "Institutions."

Reelection   Incumbent governors who seek reelection are usually successful. In primary elections, incumbent governors usually face *little* serious opposition.[6] The overall success rate for incumbent governors seeking reelection has averaged about 80 percent in the twentieth century.[7] Yet occasionally governors are defeated, and it is interesting to try to understand these failures.

Political folklore includes the belief that any governor who raises taxes during his or her term will be defeated for reelection. But a careful study of this notion shows only a weak connection between tax increase and electoral defeat for governors.[8] Most governors who raise taxes and then seek reelection are successful! Frequently, however, those who are defeated *blame* their loss on raising taxes.

Economic conditions only occasionally hurt an incumbent governor seeking reelection. Although the national economy is an important factor in presidential and congressional elections, adverse economic conditions seldom harm incumbent governors.[9] Perhaps the economy is seen as a national issue and governors are not blamed for recessions. Political scientist Larry Sabato compiled a list of reasons for the defeat of governors seeking reelection.[10] These reasons, together with the percentage of elections in which these reasons were cited, are as follows: intraparty politics (splits within the governor's party) 31.8 percent; two-party politics (dominance of the opposition party) 21.7 percent; tax increases, 20.2 percent; scandal, 13.2 percent; administrative incompetence, 9.3 percent; race, 6.2 percent; environmental issues, 4.6 percent.

Campaigning   Modern gubernatorial campaigns are quite professional, and they usually involve professional public relations organizations, experienced mass media and television advertising firms, professional polling and political consultants, and sophisticated direct mail and fund-raising techniques. (See Chapter 5, "Professional Mass Media Campaigns.") Party organizations and amateur volunteers play a very limited role in most modern campaigns in the states. The traditional barnstorming, stump-speaking, hand-shaking, and door-to-door canvassing campaigns have largely disappeared. Candidates still do these things, but the focus of the campaign is on media advertising.

Of course, campaign themes and candidate "images" must be tailored to a state's political culture and tradition. Campaign "gimmicks" are increasingly popu-

---

[6] Andrew D. McNitt and Jim Seroka, "Intraparty Challenges of Incumbent Governors and Senators," *American Politics Quarterly,* 9 (July 1981), 321–40.

[7] Stephen Turrett, "The Vulnerability of American Governors," *Midwest Journal of Political Science,* 15 (February 1971), 108–32.

[8] Susan L. Kane and Richard F. Winters, "Taxes and Voting: Electoral Retribution in the American States," *Journal of Politics,* 55 (February 1993), 22–40.

[9] Patrick J. Kenney, "The Effect of State Economic Conditions on the Vote for Governor," *Social Science Quarterly,* 64 (March, 1983), 154–162.

[10] Larry Sabato, *Goodbye to Good-time Charlie,* 2nd ed. (Washington, DC: Congressional Quarterly Press, 1983), p. 109.

lar, particularly in state elections. Gimmicks can be as varied as the minds of advertising specialists. An example of an especially successful gimmick is the "working
days" of Governor Bob Graham of Florida. Graham is a Harvard-educated, millionaire lawyer and real estate developer from Miami, whose brief career in the Florida
legislature was generally perceived as unproductive and unsuccessful. But Graham
was ambitious for higher office, and he and his professional consultants realized
that he must develop an image with which working people could identify. So they
selected as the campaign theme for his gubernatorial race: "Bob Graham—Working for Governor," and Graham undertook during the campaign to work a full day
at each of 100 different jobs. Graham's television ads showed him collecting garbage, picking oranges, herding dairy cows, and so forth, and he garnered a great
deal of local television time with these colorful media events. Critics argued that
Graham's "working days campaign" were the only days of his life that he ever
worked. But this campaign gimmick was so successful that he continued his well-
publicized working days even after he won the governorship. After two terms in
the state capital, Graham easily won a seat in the U.S. Senate.

Money   Modern mass media campaigns—with professional media advertising,
opinion polls, direct mail persuasion, political consultants—are very costly. In the
1950s a typical gubernatorial campaign cost between $100,000 and $200,000;
today a typical gubernatorial campaign costs $2 million to $5 million in small
states and $10 million to $20 million in the larger states. Television advertising is
the major reason for increased costs. Candidates for governor should expect to
spend between $3 and $10 *per vote.*

Although money cannot buy a governorship, it is important to realize that (1)
no one can mount a serious gubernatorial campaign without either personal
wealth or strong financial backing by others, and (2) the heavier-spending candidate wins in two out of three elections. Most states require public reporting of
campaign contributions and expenditures, and most states place limits on contributions by individuals and groups. Nonetheless, individuals can spend what they
wish in order to express their personal political preferences separate from official
campaigns; fund-raising political action committees (PACs) can multiply in
number; and wealthy candidates can spend as much of their own money as they
wish on their own campaigns. (See Chapter 5.)

Political Ambitions   Historically, presidents were chosen from among the ranks
of America's state governors, particularly the governors of the larger states. During
the cold war, the importance of international affairs in American politics detracted
somewhat from the popular image of the governorship as the stepping stone to the
presidency. Governors tend to be associated with domestic rather than foreign policy questions. Men such as Truman, Nixon, McGovern, Humphrey, Kennedy,
Goldwater, and Johnson found the United States Senate a good place to promote
their campaigns for vice-presidential and presidential nominations. For a while,
scholars attributed the decline in the number of governors selected as presidential
candidates to a general decline in the popularity of governors.

But in recent years, distrust of "the government in Washington" and the low
esteem of Congress in the eyes of the general public have improved the presidential

fortunes of governors. Georgia governor Jimmy Carter skillfully exploited his image as an "outsider" in his successful 1976 presidential campaign. And Ronald Reagan, whose only political experience was his two terms as governor of California, reaffirmed the importance of governors in presidential politics. Massachusetts Governor Michael Dukakis lost to George Bush in 1988. (Bush had no experience in state government; he won election to Congress for two terms and then served in appointed federal posts—ambassador to China; UN ambassador, CIA director, vice-president.) But the end of the cold war brought domestic issues to the forefront of the nation's political agenda.

The focus on the economy in 1992, and continuing popular distrust of Congress, paved the way for Arkansas Governor Bill Clinton. He defeated several Democratic senators in the presidential primaries (former Massachusetts Senator Paul Tsongas, Iowa Senator Tom Harkin, Nebraska Senator Bob Kerry). George Bush's successes in foreign affairs, the victory in the Gulf War, and the collapse of the Soviet Union meant little to voters fearful about the nation's economic health. As governor of a small state, Clinton was well positioned to promise "change." He benefited from having *no* Washington experience; he could not be blamed for federal budget deficits. It is likely that governors will continue to dominate presidential politics as long as public confidence in Washington is low.

EXECUTIVE POWER IN STATE GOVERNMENT

Frequently we speak of "strong" and "weak" governors. Yet it is difficult to compare the power of one governor with that of another. To do so, one must examine the constitutional position of governors, their powers of appointment and removal over state officials, their ability or inability to succeed themselves, their powers over the state budget, their legislative influence, their position in their own party and its position in state politics, and their influence over public opinion in the state.

Governors, Weak and Strong   In many ways the organization of American state government resembles political thinking of one or two hundred years ago. This colonial experience emphasized "fear of the executive" and resulted in state constitutional restrictions on governors' terms of office, their ability to succeed themselves, their control over appointments and removals, the proliferation of separate boards and commissions to govern particular state programs, and long overlapping terms for the members of these boards and commissions. The Jacksonian era of "popular democracy" brought with it the idea that the way to ensure popular control of state government was to elect separately as many state officials as possible. The Reform movement of the late nineteenth and early twentieth centuries led to merit systems and civil service boards, which further curtailed the governor's power of appointment. Many important state offices are governed by boards or commissions whose members may be appointed by the governor with the consent of the state senate but for long overlapping terms, which reduces the governor's influence over members of these boards and commissions. Not all of these trends were experienced uniformly by all fifty states, and there are considerable variations from state to state in the powers that governors have over the state executive branch.

TABLE 7–3   STATES WITH ELECTED EXECUTIVE OFFICIALS

Governor	50
Lieutenant Governor	42
Attorney General	43
State Treasurer	38
Secretary of State	36
State Auditor	25
Superintendent of Education	16
Agriculture Commissioner	12
Public Service Commission	9
Controller	10
Insurance Commissioner	8
Land Commissioner	5
Labor Commissioner	4
University Regents	5
Education Board	11
Railroad Commission	2
Others	
Board of Education	California
Elections Commissioner	Louisiana
Highway Commissioner	Mississippi
Tax Commissioner	North Dakota
Adjutant	South Carolina

Source: Book of the States, 1992–93.

Executive Reorganization   Modern public administration generally recommends a stronger governor and more centralized state executive branch. Reform and reorganization proposals usually recommend (1) four-year terms for governors with the ability to succeed themselves; (2) the elimination of many separately elected state executive officials and limiting the statewide ballot to governor, lieutenant governor, and attorney general; (3) elimination of boards and commissions as heads of agencies and their replacement by single, removable gubernatorial appointees; and (4) the consolidation of many state agencies into larger departments reporting directly to the governor. However, states have been slow to adopt these reforms. Table 7–3 shows the variety of separately elected officials in the states.

Political Opposition to Reorganization   Even though the trend may be toward more streamlined state government organization, it is clear that separately elected officials and independent boards and officials will be around for a long time. Political parties and public officials develop a stake in the continued existence of separately elected public offices. Moreover, many interest groups prefer to be governed by boards and commissions that are independent of executive authority. They feel they have more influence over independent boards than those that come directly under a governor's authority. There is often the assumption that boards and commissions enable divergent interests to be represented in the governing of state agencies. Groups are thereby permitted to have a voice in state programs in which they are interested.

TABLE 7–4   TENURE PROVISIONS FOR GOVERNORS

Four-year Term, No Restrictions on Reelection

Arizona	Iowa	North Dakota
California	Massachusetts	Texas
Colorado	Michigan	Utah
Connecticut	Minnesota	Washington
Idaho	Montana	Wisconsin
Illinois	New York	Wyoming

Four-year Term, Restricted to Two Terms

Alabama	Maine	Oklahoma
Alaska	Maryland	Oregon
Arkansas	Missouri	Pennsylvania
Delaware	Nebraska	South Carolina
Florida	Nevada	South Dakota
Georgia	New Jersey	Tennessee
Hawaii	North Carolina	West Virginia
Kansas	Ohio	
Louisiana		

Four-year Term, Consecutive Reelection Prohibited

Kentucky	New Mexico
Mississippi	Virginia

Two-year Term, No Restrictions on Reelection

New Hampshire	Vermont
Rhode Island	

Source: Book of the States, 1992–93.

Tenure Power   Another component of a governor's influence is the ability or inability to succeed him- or herself in office. It is possible to rank the states according to the power that governors derive from their tenure in office. Governors with the highest "tenure power" are those who are elected for a four-year term and are permitted to succeed themselves indefinitely (see Table 7–4). Governors with the lowest "tenure power" are those who have only two-year terms. The Twenty-second Amendment to the U.S. Constitution restricts executive tenure at the presidential level to two terms, and many states have similar restrictions on their governors.

THE GOVERNOR'S MANAGERIAL POWERS

Governors are chief executives; they are supposed to manage state governmental bureaucracies. But aside from interviewing occasionally in response to a crisis, governors generally turn over their management chores to others. According to political scientist Alan Rosenthal, governors downplay their managerial role and avoid expending energy and power on management because "greater rewards derive from the pursuit of other functions—formulating policy, building popularity and support among the public, helping develop the state economy."[11] Managing the state bureaucracy is generally left to the governor's staff and department heads.

Appointment Powers   Perhaps the most important managerial power is the power to appoint subordinate officials. Personal appointment of subordinates does not guarantee their responsibility, but there is a greater likelihood that an official appointed by a governor will be someone whose values coincide with those of the governor. Of course, governors are subject to many different pressures in exercising their appointing power; often they must pay off political debts or win the support of a political faction by their selections. Salary limitations and the shortness of tenure make it exceedingly difficult to find capable people for positions of high responsibility in state government. However, it is safe to infer that governors who can name their major department heads are stronger than governors who cannot. Moreover, many department heads in state government are popularly elected, and many departments are headed by elected or appointed boards or commissions over whom the governor has relatively little control.

Comparing Appointive Powers   It is possible to compare the managerial powers of governors in the fifty states by observing how many department heads the governors themselves can appoint. The *Book of the States* lists forty-six managerial functions in state government and how the heads of these functions are selected. The functions are:

Adjutant general	Employment services	Parks and recreation
Administration	Emergency management	Personnel
Agriculture	Energy	Planning
Banking	Environment	Postaudit
Budget	Finance	Preaudit
Civil rights	Fish and game	Public library
Commerce	General services	Public utility regulation
Community affairs	Health	Purchasing
Comptroller	Highways	Revenue
Computer services	Historic preservation	Social services
Consumer affairs	Insurance	Solid waste
Corrections	Labor relations	State police
Economic development	Licensing	Tourism
Education, higher	Mental health	Transportation
Education, public schools	Natural resources	Welfare
Elections administration		

---

[11] Alan Rosenthal, *Governors and Legislatures: Contending Powers* (Washington: CQ Press, 1990), p. 170.

Not all states have separate agencies for each of these managerial functions; on the contrary, many functions are combined in larger departments.

If the agency head is separately elected by the people (as are most attorneys general, treasurers, and secretaries of state), then the governor has little direct control over them. If the governor can appoint an agency head *without* the need for legislative approval, we can say that the governor has stronger appointive powers than if legislative confirmation of appointment is required. Indeed, agency heads themselves tend to evaluate the governor's influence largely in terms of his or her ability to appoint them to office.[12]

We have classified the states according to the number of functions over which the governors have direct control (see Table 7–5). States that have had major constitutional revisions in recent years, such as New York and Illinois, tend to give their governor strong appointive powers. This is a reflection of the extent of management reform in these states.[13] At the other extreme, Florida's governor has weak appointive powers, not only because the secretary of state, attorney general, secretary of agriculture, superintendent of public instruction, treasurer and insurance commissioner, and controller are popularly elected, but also because major departments are headed by boards on which the governor has only one vote. Florida calls this its "cabinet system."

State Cabinets   State cabinets, composed of the heads of the major executive departments, advise the governors in over half of the states. Indeed, in Florida, Colorado, and New Jersey the cabinet is recognized in the state constitution and given more than just advisory powers. But most cabinets meet at the governor's discretion and function more or less in the fashion of the president's cabinet in the national government.

Removal Powers   Restrictions on governors' powers of appointment are further complicated by restrictions on their powers of removal. A common statutory or constitutional provision dealing with governor's removal powers states that removal must be "for cause only"; that is, governors must provide a clear-cut statement of charges and an opportunity for an open hearing to the employee they are trying to oust. This process is often unpleasant, and governors seek to avoid it unless they have strong evidence of incompetence, fraud, or mismanagement. When a governor's removal powers are limited "for cause only," it is next to impossible to remove a subordinate for policy differences. A governor may request an officeholder to resign, even when the governor's removal power is limited, and such a request may be honored by the officeholder in preference to continued unhappy relationships with the governor's office or in fear of the governor's ability to mobilize public opinion against him or her. As a final resort, a determined governor with influence in the legislature can always oust an official by a legislative act,

---

[12] F. Ted Hebert, Jeffrey L. Brudney, and Deil S. Wright, "Gubernatorial Influence and State Bureaucracy," *American Politics Quarterly,* 11 (April 1983), 243–64.

[13] See Keith J. Muller, "Explaining Variation and Change in Gubernatorial Power," *Western Political Quarterly,* 85 (September 1985), 424–31.

TABLE 7–5   APPOINTIVE POWERS OF GOVERNORS

Very Strong	Strong	Moderate	Weak	Very Weak
Connecticut	Arkansas	Georgia	Alaska	Florida
Delaware	California	Kansas	Arizona	Mississippi
Hawaii	Colorado	Louisiana	Alabama	South Carolina
Kentucky	Illinois	Maine	Idaho	Texas
Massachusetts	Indiana	Michigan	Missouri	
Minnesota	Iowa	Montana	Nevada	
New Jersey	Maryland	Nebraska	New Mexico	
New York	Ohio	New Hampshire	North Dakota	
North Carolina	South Dakota	Rhode Island	Oklahoma	
Pennsylvania		Utah	Oregon	
Tennessee			Washington	
Vermont			Wisconsin	
Virginia			Wyoming	
West Virginia				

Source: Calculated from information provided in *Book of States, 1992–93.*

which abolishes the office or agency the official heads and replaces it with another; this device is sometimes called a ''ripper bill.''

Competing Offices   Certain elected state officials, notably the lieutenant governor and the attorney general, often use their positions to advance their own candidacy for the governorship or the U.S. Senate, thus creating further problems for a governor, particularly when their ambitions are in competition with his or her own. Lieutenant governors, of course, have few substantive duties in state government, other than the ceremonial one of presiding over the state senate. However attorneys general have more influence—their legal opinions have great importance for a governor's program. Governors are often bound by statute to conform to the attorney general's legal opinion in interpreting state laws and constitutions.

Decline in Patronage   Patronage was once a major source of power for state governors. As late as the 1960s almost half of all state jobs were filled by the governor or the governor's patronage advisors from the ranks of ''deserving'' party workers. Party organizations were sustained with jobs in tax collection, licensing, parks, commerce, agriculture, welfare, and especially highways. The governor's office would ''clear'' appointments with party county chairpersons throughout the state, and patronage appointees were expected to work for the party organization at election time. Often state patronage employees held party posts themselves. Patronage was especially widespread in the older, two-party states of the East and Midwest.

However, patronage declined over the years; today more than three-quarters of all state jobs throughout the nation are covered by civil service or merit rules. In some states nearly all state workers are covered by civil service, and patronage is limited to boards, commissioners, policy-making offices, university trusteeships, and judicial posts. The patronage system was always awkward to administer; many lower-paid menial jobs were unattractive to party workers, and county chairpeople could not always find people to fill them.[14] As the influence of parties declined in electoral politics (see Chapter 5, "American Political Parties in Disarray"), governors themselves came to view patronage systems as more of a burden than a benefit to their administrations. Reform governors capitalized on the public's image of patronage as corrupt, and they gradually expanded civil service coverage. Federal law required civil service protection for state employees administering major federal grant programs in public assistance, unemployment insurance, and health care. Finally, the federal courts began to strike at patronage systems with decisions preventing governments from firing their employees for partisan political reasons.[15]

Civil Service   Civil service systems, particularly those administered by independent civil service commissions, significantly reduce executive control over program administration. There is a persistent tendency for civil service systems to be routine, mechanical, and unimaginative. Job classification schemes, to which recruitment, qualifications, and pay scales are closely tied, become so rigid with time that executives have little flexibility in recruiting really talented people to state government. Executives whose authority to promote, hire, and fire their employees is severely curtailed can hardly be expected to obtain maximum effort and cooperation from their employees. Even the public administration experts, who originally supported the civil service movement and the removal of state jobs from the governor's authority, are beginning to recommend that the power over personnel administration be returned to the governor.

Unionization   Unions among civil service employees further complicate executive control of the bureaucracy. Today, over half of all state and local government employees are unionized. The largest public employee union in the states is the American Federation of State, County, and Municipal Employees (AFSCME). Collective bargaining agreements usually stipulate salaries and wages, pensions and benefits, grievance procedures, and seniority. These restrict executive authority over dismissals, layoffs, reorganization, elimination of positions, merit and incentive pay plans, and other actions affecting personnel.

Unionization varies from state to state. Some state governments do not bargain collectively with their employees.[16] In these states union membership is small and state employees are not covered by labor–management contracts. Other states recognize employee unions and bargain collectively with them. In these states union membership may encompass up to 80 percent of all state employees (Hawaii,

---

[14] Frank J. Sorauf, "State Patronage in a Rural County," *American Political Science Review,* 50 (1956), 1046.

[15] *Elrod* v. *Burns,* 96 S. Ct. 2673 (1976); *Branti* v. *Finkel,* 445 U.S. 507 (1980).

[16] In 1992 the noncollective bargaining state governments were Alabama, Arizona, Colorado, Georgia, Idaho, Kentucky, Louisiana, Maryland, Mississippi, Nevada, North Carolina, North Dakota, Oklahoma, South Carolina, Tennessee, Texas, Utah, Virginia, West Virginia, Wyoming. Council of State Governments, *Book of the States, 1992–93,* p. 449.

New York, and Rhode Island), and most state employees are covered by labor–management contracts.

THE GOVERNOR'S FISCAL POWERS

The state budget is the most crucial policy document in state government. Governors' control over the state budget is perhaps their most formidable power. While the legislature must enact the state budget into law, and no state monies may be spent without a legislative appropriation, in practice the greatest amount of control over state governments rests with governors and their budget staff. The governor has full responsibility for the preparation of the budget and its submission to the legislature in all the states, except Louisiana, Mississippi, North Carolina, South Carolina, and Texas. In these states the governor shares budget responsibility with a commission composed of separately elected state officials and/or legislators.

Budget Making   Budget making involves bringing together the requests of all existing state agencies, calculating the costs of new state programs, estimating the probable income of the state, and evaluating these costs and income estimates in the light of program and policy objectives. The final budget document is submitted to the legislature for its adoption as an appropriations bill. No state monies can be spent without a legislative appropriation, and the legislature can make any alterations in the state budget that it sees fit. Potentially, then, a legislature can control any activity of the state government through its power over appropriations, but as a practical matter, the legislature seldom reviews every item of the governor's budget. In practice, budgets tend to reflect the views of those responsible for their preparation, namely the governor.

The most common budgetary behaviors in the states are:

Agency heads consistently request higher funds.

Governors' budget staffers consistently reduce agency requests.

The governor consistently pursues a balanced budget at higher expenditure levels than the previous year.

Legislatures approve higher appropriations but try to blame the governor if higher taxes are required.

Agency Pressure   The pressure for budget increases comes from the request of agency officials. Most agency officials feel compelled to ask for more money each year. Requesting an increase in funds affirms the significance and protects the status of agency employees, and it assures clientele groups that new and higher standards of service are being pursued aggressively. Requested increases also give the governor's office and the legislature something to cut that will not affect existing programs. The governor's budget staff generally recognizes the built-in pressure to expand budgets. The budget staff see themselves as "cutters." Agencies press for budgetary expansion with better programs in mind, while the governor's budget staff tries to reduce expenditures with cost cutting in mind.

Reliance on Staff   Governors must rely heavily on their budget staffs, which may be located in the governor's office or in a separate department. The budget staff may be directed by the governor's political appointee, but it should include some experienced, professional, merit employees. The budget staff must work closely with the governor in handling agency requests and developing the all-important annual budget submission to the legislature. The governor's budget makers may be the most influential group of bureaucrats in state government.

"Earmarking"   Governors have little influence over many items of state spending. Over 50 percent of state finances come from specially earmarked funds. It is quite common to earmark in state constitutions and laws certain funds for particular purposes, such as gasoline taxes for highways. The earmarking device provides certain agencies with an independent source of income, thus reducing the governor's control over operations. What is left, "general fund expenditures," is also largely committed to existing state programs, particularly welfare and education.

"Uncontrollables"   Governors typically campaign on platforms stressing both increased service and lower taxes. Once in office, however, they typically find it impossible to accomplish both and very difficult to accomplish either one. Often new programs planned by a governor must be put aside, because of "uncontrollable" growth in existing programs. For example, additional money may be required to educate more students who are entitled to an education under existing programs; or money must be found to pay the welfare benefits of additional clients or the Medicaid costs of additional patients "entitled" to care under existing laws. These entitlement programs constitute over three-quarters of state general fund appropriations.

Rating the Governors on Fiscal Conservatism   In 1992 the CATO Institute rated all the nation's governors on their fiscal conservatism—their success in holding down state taxing and spending (see Table 7–6). Republican Governor William Weld of Massachusetts ranked high for cutting spending and putting in jeopardy his state's reputation as "Taxachusetts." Democratic Governor Douglas Wilder of Virginia also rated high as a fiscal conservative by balancing the state's budget without tax increases. Republican Governor Mike Sullivan is credited with keeping taxing and spending in Wyoming *below* the rate of increase in personal income. At the other end of the scale (fiscal liberalism perhaps), Governor James Florio of New Jersey was credited in 1990 with the largest single tax hike—up to that time—in the history of American states. But Florio's tax increase record was broken in 1991 by Republican Governor Pete Wilson of California, who closed a $14 billion budget gap with $7 billion in new taxes. Independent Governor Lowell Weicker of Connecticut imposed an income tax on that state for the first time, paving the way for a rapid expansion of state spending.

Balancing the Budget   Unlike the federal government, state budgets must be balanced. This means that the governor must submit to the legislature a budget in which projected revenues are equal to recommended expenditures. And the legislature must not appropriate funds in excess of projected revenues. There are, of course, many accounting devices that allows governors and legislatures to get around the balanced budget limitation—devices known as "blue smoke and mirrors." These include "off-budget" special funds, separate state activities, capital

TABLE 7–6 GOVERNORS' FISCAL CONSERVATISM

Governor	Score	Grade	Governor	Score	Grade
William F. Weld (R., Mass)	85	A	John Ashcroft (R., Mo.)	55	C
Mike Sullivan (D., Wyo.)	75	A	William Donald Schaefer (D., Md.)	55	C
John Engler (R., Mich.)	73	B	Arne Carlson (R., Minn.)	54	C
David Walters (D., Okla.)	70	B	Mario M. Cuomo (D., N.Y.)	54	C
Douglas Wilder (D., Va.)	69	B	E. Benjamin Nelson (D., Neb.)	54	C
Evan Bayh (D., Ind.)	68	B	Ann W. Richards (D., Texas)	54	C
Joan Finney (D., Kan.)	68	B	Stan Stephens (R., Mont.)	54	C
George Mickelson (R., S.D.)	68	B	Cecil D. Andrus (D., Idaho)	51	D
Judd Gregg (R., N.H.)	67	B	James G. Marlin (R., N.C.)	50	D
Roy Romer (D., Colo.)	67	B	Barbara Roberts (D., Ore.)	50	D
Tommy Thompson (R., Wis.)	64	B	Bill Clinton (D., Ark.)	49	D
Ned McWherter (D., Tenn.)	62	B	Michael Castle (R., Del.)	48	D
Fife Symington (R., Ariz.)	62	C	Terry Branstad (R., Iowa)	46	D
Zell Miller (D., Ga.)	60	C	Lawton Chiles (D., Fla.)	46	D
Carroll A. Campbell (R., S.C.)	58	C	Booth Gardner (D., Wash.)	46	D
Robert P. Casey (D., Pa.)	58	C	Bruce Sundlun (D., R.I.)	40	D
Bruce King (D., N.M.)	58	C	Gaston Caperton (D., W.Va.)	38	F
John R. McKernan, Jr. (R., Maine)	58	C	Bob Miller (D., Nev.)	38	F
Jim Edgar (R., Ill.)	57	C	Pete Wilson (R., Calif.)	32	F
Horman H. Bangerter (R., Utah)	56	C	Lowell P. Weicker, Jr. (Ind., Conn.)	27	F
Guy Hunt (R., Ala.)	56	C	James J. Florio (D., N.J.)	25	F
George A. Sinner (D., N.D.)	56	C	John Waihee (D., Hawaii)	25	F
George V. Voinovich (R., Ohio)	56	C			

Note: Alaska, Kentucky, Louisiana, Mississippi and Vermont are excluded from the study.
Source: CATO Institute Washington DC.

budgets, and so on (see Chapter 18). Nonetheless the balanced budget requirement is a major restraint on state spending.

Economic Constraints   The most important force affecting the budget is the state's economy. When the economy is healthy, state revenues go up. Given a projected increase in revenues, governors can recommend new programs, expanded services, more aid to local government, and so on. Occasionally governors even recommend tax reductions, although spending increases are by far the favored response to projected revenue increases. In years of prosperity, governors and legislatures expand the activities of state government, without much concern about what to do when the economy takes a downturn: "Commitments are made and clienteles are created; however, should the economy take a turn for the worse, revenues will be insufficient to keep pace with promises and expectations."[17] Indeed, when the economy falters, governors must recommend tax increases, expenditure cuts, or some combination of both. Needless to say, these are very unpleasant choices for politicians.

The Governor's Legislative Powers

The responsibility for initiating major statewide legislative programs falls upon the governor. The governor's programs are presented to the legislature in various governor's messages and in the budget. While these instruments are only recommendations, the governor can set the agenda for debate with them, and "agenda setting" is an important power. The governor takes the initiative; legislators are on the defensive; if they do not act, they must explain why. Much of the governor's power over the legislature stems from his or her power over the policy agenda.

Setting Priorities   Governors are well advised to limit their policy agenda to a few priority issues each year, rather than sending the legislature a smorgasbord of items without any unifying goal or theme. A governor wants to develop a strong "batting average"—a reputation for getting a high percentage of his or her recommendations enacted by the legislature. Submitting multiple proposals increases the chances for defeat. Submitting only a few high-visibility proposals, and concentrating energy and power on securing their passage, usually increases the ratio of bills passed to bills submitted. But it is often difficult for governors to select their priority issues from the host of recommendations that come to them from interest groups and executive agencies. Governors can expand their policy agenda in good economic times when there are more revenues to pay for new initiatives. But in recessionary times, governors are constrained to few if any new initiatives.

Providing Leadership   "What does the governor want?" is a frequent question heard in legislative debate. Leadership requires the governor to do more than simply propose legislation. The governor must also "make it happen." Governors must rally public support, packaging their proposals in a way that people will understand and support. They must make speeches and public appearances and prepare news

---

[17] Rosenthal, p. 133.

releases highlighting their proposals. This "outside" strategy must be integrated with an "inside" strategy to persuade legislators to support the program. Governors must carefully steer their proposals through the legislative process—the committee system, floor proceedings, votes on amendments, conference committees, and final passage. They must develop good working relationships with the legislative leadership and then with the rank-and-file members. They must mobilize the support of interest groups behind their proposals. Finally, governors must be willing to compromise—to take "half a loaf" and declare victory. Governors must be flexible, accepting legislative amendments when necessary to preserve the major thrust of their program.

Special Sessions   Governors can increase pressure on legislatures to act on particular recommendations by calling special sessions. The governor can specify the topics that should be considered in the special session. This device can be particularly effective if the legislature has buried one of the governor's favorite programs in the regular session. Legislators do not like to be called back from their businesses to the state capitol for a special session, so even the threat of one may force them to pass the governor's program in the regular session. Of course, legislatures can defeat a governor's program even in special session, but their actions will be spotlighted.

Vetoes   The governor's veto power is a major source of power within the legislature. Only in North Carolina does the governor have no veto power at all. In some states, the veto power is restricted by giving the governor only a short time to consider a bill after it has passed the legislature, by permitting a simple majority of legislative members to override the veto, or by requiring vetoed bills to reappear at the next legislative session. And the North Dakota Constitution contains a unique provision that "Any governor . . . who menaces any member of the legislature by the threatened use of his veto power . . . shall be punished . . . by law. . . ." In other states, governors are given longer periods of time to consider a bill, and a two-thirds vote of both houses of the legislature is required to override a veto, rather than a simple majority. (See Table 7–7.)

The veto is often the governor's principal source of bargaining power in the legislature. Veto overrides by legislatures are rare. While the possibility of override gives the legislature "the last word" in theory, in practice few governors are so weak that they cannot garner at least one-third plus one of either house to sustain a veto. Only about 5 percent of bills passed by state legislatures are vetoed by governors, and governors are overridden on less than 10 percent of their vetoes. Of course vetoes are more common when a governor faces a legislature controlled by the opposition party.[18]

The *threat* of a veto is a more important bargaining tool than the actual exercise of the veto. A governor can threaten to veto a bill with objectionable provisions

---

[18] Charles Wiggins, "Executive Vetoes and Legislative Overrides in the American States," *Journal of Politics,* 42 (November 1980), 1110–17.

TABLE 7–7 GOVERNORS' VETO POWERS

Votes Required to Override Veto			Item Veto on Appropriations Bills	
2/3	3/5	MAJORITY	VETO	NO VETO
Alaska	Delaware	Alabama	Alabama	Indiana
Arizona	Illinois	Arkansas	Alaska	Maine
California	Maryland	Indiana	Arkansas	Maryland
Colorado	Nebraska	Kentucky	Arizona	Nevada
Connecticut	Ohio	Tennessee	California	New Hampshire
Florida	Rhode Island	West Virginia	Colorado	North Carolina
Georgia			Connecticut	Rhode Island
Hawaii			Delaware	Vermont
Idaho			Florida	
Iowa			Georgia	
Kansas			Hawaii	
Louisiana			Idaho	
Maine			Illinois	
Massachusetts			Iowa	
Michigan			Kansas	
Minnesota			Kentucky	
Mississippi			Louisiana	
Missouri			Massachusetts	
Montana			Michigan	
Nevada			Minnesota	
New Hampshire			Mississippi	
New Jersey			Missouri	
New Mexico			Montana	
New York			Nebraska	
North Dakota			New Jersey	
Oklahoma			New Mexico	
Oregon			New York	
Pennsylvania			North Dakota	
South Carolina			Ohio	
South Dakota			Oklahoma	
Texas			Oregon	
Utah			Pennsylvania	
Vermont			South Carolina	
Virginia			South Dakota	
Washington			Tennessee	
Wisconsin			Texas	
Wyoming			Utah	
			Virginia	
			Washington	
			West Virginia	
			Wisconsin	
			Wyoming	

Source: Book of the States, 1992–93.

before it reaches a floor vote. Governors can negotiate from a position of strength throughout the legislative process, shaping the bill to their preferences.

Occasionally legislatures may challenge governors to veto bills. This is more likely to occur with divided party control of state government—one party controls the legislature with a governor from the opposition party. The legislature can pass a popular bill opposed by the governor and then dare the governor to veto it. Even if the governor's veto is sustained, the majority party leaders in the legislature may feel they have created an issue for the next gubernatorial election. But this strategy usually guarantees a failure to get the bill enacted into law. Legislative leaders must decide whether they want the bill passed (for which they must bargain with the governor for his or her signature) or whether they want an issue for the next election.

Item Veto   Most governors also have the power to veto particular items in a larger appropriations bill. This allows them to pick out particular legislative spending proposals (frequently labeled "turkeys" by unsympathetic governors) and veto those proposals without jeopardizing the entire budget. In states *without* the item veto, governors may be forced to accept many legislative spending proposals in order to get a budget passed. The president of the United States does *not* have an item veto; presidents frequently complain that they have less power over the federal budget than most governors have over their state budgets.

The line item veto is also a powerful weapon in the governor's arsenal. The line item veto allows the governor to take legislators' pet budget items as hostage for their support on other unrelated legislation favored by the governor. Legislators who fail to support the governor risk losing their "turkeys." Trade-offs need not be explicit. Legislators who consistently oppose the governor's programs throughout the legislative session risk losing pork for their district when the governor goes through the appropriations acts line by line.

Governor–Legislature Relations   For most governors, working with the legislature is considered the most difficult and demanding part of their job.[19] "Practically all governors regard their legislature as a problem and are happy when the legislature leaves town."[20] About half of all governors have had some legislative experience before becoming governor. They may have some friends and acquaintances left over from their legislature days. And they may have greater respect for the legislative branch and greater empathy with the concerns of legislators. But many governors have little sympathy or patience with the slow and complicated legislative process.

Frequently legislators resent the exalted role of the governor. As a New York legislator remarked about Governor Cuomo: "Relating to the governor is like relating to the Pope, except that the only thing you have to kiss on the Pope is his

---

[19] Thad Beyle and Robert Dalton, *Being Governor: The View from the Office.* (Durham, NC: Duke University Press, 1983), p. 135.

[20] Rosenthal, p. 69.

ring."[21] Legislatures do not want to appear to be pushed around by governors. Many legislators develop a loyalty to the institution itself; they wish to preserve the independence of the legislature.

What works with the legislature? Political scientist Alan Rosenthal provides some pointers; governors should

> *Stand tall.* This entails not only the appearance of strength and decisiveness but a willingness to punish one's enemies.
>
> *Consult members.* Inform legislators of plans and programs and listen to their concerns.
>
> *Talk turkey.* Communicate in legislators' language of patronage and deals, give and take, reciprocity.
>
> *Rub elbows.* Stay in personal contact with legislators on a regular basis.
>
> *Massage egos.* Legislators like to share center stage with the governor, to be seen at bill signings, to be invited to the governor's mansion, to have the governor praise them in public.

DIVIDED GOVERNMENT: GOVERNOR VERSUS THE LEGISLATURE

Divided government, where one party controls one or both houses of the legislature and the other party controls the governorship, is increasingly frequent in American state politics. In recent years over half of the states have experienced divided party control (see Table 7–8). The election of Republican governors in southern states with heavily Democratic legislatures helps to explain increased occurrence of divided government in the states, as well as an increased tendency of voters everywhere to split their tickets. Republican governors are more likely to face Democratic-controlled legislatures than the reverse. But divided government itself has a major impact on executive–legislature relations.

Partisanship Cuts Both Ways   Party works to the advantage of governors when their party has a majority in the legislature. The governor and a legislature controlled by the same party have an incentive to produce results. This is especially true in a competitive two-party state. There is still institutional rivalry, wherein governors contend with legislatures for policy leadership. But both have an interest in compiling a record of success that the voters can attribute to everyone running under the party label in the next election. But when partisan differences are added to institutional rivalry, conflict rather than cooperation is more likely to characterize relations between governor and legislature.

Confronting Gridlock   A governor confronting opposition party control of the legislature must spend a great deal of time bargaining and compromising with legislative leaders of the opposition party. Governors must ensure that they keep their own party's legislators behind their proposals and then either work out accommo-

---

[21] Rosenthal, pp. 47, 294, 296–98.

TABLE 7–8   DIVIDED PARTY CONTROL OF STATE GOVERNMENT

	1987–1989	1989–1991	1991–1993	1993–1995
Unified				
Governor and majority of both houses, same party.	20	19	21	22
Divided				
Governor and majority of one or both houses, different parties	29	30	28	27
Total—49 states; Nebraska nonpartisan legislature excluded.				

dations with the opposition leadership or try to chip off enough votes from less loyal opposition members to win passage of their proposals. Neither is an easy task. Party activists, including legislators, differ on ideological grounds and policy issues. Moreover, the opposing party looks forward to defeating the governor in the next election. Often one or more opposition party aspirants for the governorship are sitting in the legislature. They seek to discredit the governor, not only during the election campaign, but during his or her entire term of office. Often the opposition party in the legislature will prefer that a needed bill go down to defeat just to hurt the governor's reputation. Only a very able governor can avoid gridlock with divided party control of state government.

 ## IMPEACHMENTS AND INVESTIGATIONS

Impeachment is a *political* process, not a legal process. While state constitutions, like the U.S. Constitution, usually define an impeachable offense as "treason, bribery, or other high crimes and misdemeanors," the political errors of impeached officials are usually more important than their legal offenses.

Impeachment, Trial, and Removal   All state constitutions, except Oregon's, provide for the impeachment of elected state officials by the legislature. Impeachment proceedings are initiated in the lower houses of forty-seven states, in the unicameral legislature of Nebraska, and the upper house in Alaska. Impeachment trials are held in the upper houses in forty-five states, in a special court of impeachment in Nebraska, in the lower house in Alaska, in a special commission in Missouri, and in the senate and court of appeals in New York. Most states require a two-thirds vote to convict and remove an official.

These impeachment provisions are rarely used. There appear to have been only eighteen gubernatorial impeachments since the nation's birth and eight trial convictions. When Arizona Governor Evan Mecham was impeached and convicted by the state legislature in 1988, it was the first such event in nearly sixty years. Several other governors have resigned when threatened with impeachment.[22]

---

[22] *Book of the States, 1988–89,* p. 27. Other twentieth-century impeachments and removals include New York Governor William Sulzer in 1913; Oklahoma Governor John Walton in 1923; and Oklahoma Governor Henry S. Johnson in 1929.

Criminal Investigations   Criminal investigations have led to the demise of several governors. Former Tennessee Governor Ray Blanton was convicted in 1981 for crimes committed while in office; former Maryland Governor Marvin Mandel was convicted and later pardoned for crimes committed while in office. Governor Edwin Edwards of Louisiana was acquitted in 1986 in a criminal trial; the racketeering charges temporarily undermined his support with voters and he lost a close vote in the next gubernatorial election. However, in 1991 Edwards was again elected governor in a run-off against former Ku Klux Klan member David Duke. In 1993 Republican Governor Guy Hunt of Alabama was convicted of misusing inauguration funds by the state's Democratic attorney general.

Evan Mecham of Arizona   Arizona's flamboyant Governor Evan Mecham managed to offend virtually every important political interest group in his state in his first few months in office. Mecham was a staunchly conservative Mormon, a successful Phoenix automobile dealer, and a political maverick who had perennially entered his name in governors' races with little chance of success. But in 1986 he surprised everyone by defeating an established Republican opponent in the primary and then squeaking out a victory with only 39 percent of the vote in a three-way race in the general election. His political troubles began with his inauguration day announcement that he was cancelling the state's Martin Luther King Jr. Day holiday.

Mecham's short-lived governorship was one long publicized "gaffe" after another. He publicly blamed working women for the high divorce rate; he told a Jewish audience that the United States was a Christian nation; and he ridiculed a petition by homosexuals to oust him. His appointments stirred additional controversy; they included a tax commissioner who had not filed his own state income tax and an education commissioner who testified that teachers should never contradict parents even if parents tell their children the world is flat. He embarrassed Republicans and enraged Democrats.

Less than a year after his election, a recall petition succeeded in getting the necessary 400,000 signatures, and a recall election was scheduled for 1988. In the meantime the state's attorney general indicted the governor on a series of campaign law violations. Before these charges came to trial, the state house of representatives initiated impeachment proceedings for "high crimes, misdemeanors, and maleficence in office." The state's senior Republican, former U.S. Senator Barry Goldwater, announced that "Mecham has got to go."

Mecham did not choose to go quietly, even after the house voted for impeachment. He defended himself at a bitter senate trial, during which he argued that he had committed no illegal acts and that the charges represented a vendetta against him by the press and his political enemies. Mecham was convicted by bipartisan votes (21–9 on one charge and 26–4 on another) in the senate and removed from office. The secretary of state, Rose Mofford, a Democrat, immediately succeeded him. The recall election was cancelled.

Later in criminal court, Mecham was acquitted of all of the charges of campaign law violations. The jury returned the verdict in less than three hours; several jurors reportedly hugged the ex-governor. There is little doubt that his impeachment and removal from office were political acts. Or, as the speaker of the Arizona house was quoted as saying, "if Ed Mecham had just kept his damn mouth shut and used his brain and not been so stubborn, he would still be governor today."

The Governor as Political Leader

The formal powers of governors—tenure, appointment and removal, budgetary, and veto powers—are not the equivalent of political influence. These formal powers can only be translated into control over public policy, legislative output, and bureaucratic performance through a governor's use of his or her own political "clout." A landslide election that carries the governor's party into control of both houses of the legislature can overcome many formal weaknesses in a governor's powers. A politically resourceful governor enjoying widespread public popularity who can skillfully employ the media to his or her advantage can overcome many constitutional weaknesses in the office.[23]

Media Access   Governors are the most visible figures in state politics. They command the attention of press, radio, and television. They have a greater opportunity than any other state official to exercise leadership by persuasion. An attractive governor who is skillful in public relations can command support from administrators, legislators, local officials, and party leaders through public appeals to their constituents. Politicians must respect the governor's greater access to the communications media and hence to the minds of their constituents. Effective governors not only understand the broad range of issues facing their states but also are able to speak clearly and persuasively about them.

Popularity   Media access and the visibility it produces provide governors with the opportunity to promote their personal popularity with the citizens of the state. The legislature is seldom as popular as the governor. Even if individual legislators are popular in their districts, the legislature as an institution is rarely very popular. (See Figure 7–1. Statewide opinion polls do not track governors' popularity as closely as national polls track the president of the United States. But opinion in most large states is regularly surveyed by private, university, and newspaper polls.) Most governors have press secretaries whose responsibility it is to develop and maintain a favorable media image for the governor. Many governors devote a great deal of their personal attention to this task—massaging the capital press, subsidizing media events, holding town meetings, traveling about the state, and so on. There may be some tendency for legislators and interest groups to avoid direct confrontations with a popular governor. Certainly a popular governor is in a better position to advance his or her program than an *un*popular governor. But the real problem is turning personal popularity into political power.

---

[23] See Lee Sigelman and Nelson C. Dometrius, "Governors as Chief Administrators: The Linkage Between Formal Powers and Informal Influence," *American Politics Quarterly,* 16 (April 1988), 157–70.

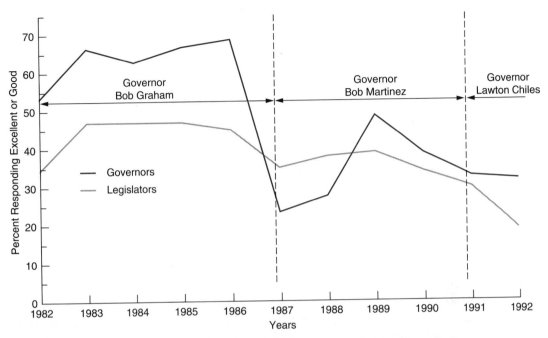

FIGURE 7–1   Governor and Legislatures: Popularity Ratings in Florida
Q. "How would you rate the job [governor] [the Florida Legislature] is doing?"
Percent saying excellent or good, versus fair or poor or don't know

Leadership   Governors' reputations as leaders, however, stem not only from what they say but also from what they do. Their reputations must include a capacity to decide issues and to persist in the decision once it is made. A reputation for backing down, for avoiding situations that involve them in public conflict, or for wavering in the face of momentary pressures invites the governors' adversaries to ignore or oppose them. A sense of insecurity or weakness can damage a governor's power more than any constitutional limitation. Governors can also increase their influence by developing a reputation for punishing their adversaries and rewarding their supporters. Once the reputation as an effective leader is established, cooperation is often forthcoming in anticipation of the governor's reaction.

Party   Governors are also the recognized leaders of their state parties. In a majority of states, it is the governor who picks the state party chairperson and who is consulted on questions of party platform, campaign tactics, nominations for party office, and party finances. The amount of power that a governor derives from the position of party leader varies from state to state according to the strength, cohesion, and discipline of the state parties. In urban industrial states, where party lines reflect socioeconomic, religious, and ethnic divisions, the governor can exercise power by an appeal to party loyalty. But in one-party states, particularly in the South and the West, the party mechanism is not really an effective instrument of gubernatorial power. Governors in one-party states must rely upon personal organizations or factional support. As we observed earlier, one-party states are really no-party states. The governor must negotiate with individuals and factions in the legislature on an issue-by-issue basis to accomplish his or her program.

Limitations   But even in two-party states there are limitations to the power that governors derive from their role as party leader. First of all, a governor cannot deny party renomination to disloyal members. Nominations are acquired in primary elections. Legislators must first consider constituency demands, not the voice of the governor. Second, the frequency of divided control, where governors face the legislature dominated by the opposition party, requires them to bargain with individuals and groups in the opposition party. If they have acquired a reputation for being too "partisan" in their approach to state programs, they will find it difficult to win over the necessary support of opposition party members. Finally, the use of patronage may make as many enemies as friends. There is an old political saying: "For every one patronage appointment, you make nine enemies and one ingrate."

Expectations   It is difficult to generalize about the power of fifty state governors, especially when changes over time affect every state. Powerful governors (judged in terms of their accomplishments in office) may be followed by weak governors, even in the same state. Nevertheless, it is possible to offer a few generalizations from our studies.

First of all, governors, unlike legislators, are expected to *initiate* public policies. These policy initiatives are developed in messages, speeches, news releases, press conferences, public appearances, bills drafted by the governor's office or other executive agencies, and, most of all, in the state budget. The public *expects* governors to take the lead in solving state problems, whether they are really able to do anything about them or not.

Indeed, our second generalization is that governors do not really have sufficient powers in state government to deal effectively with the demands and expectations placed upon them. State constitutions not only divide power between the governor and legislature, but also divide the executive itself, with many separately elected officials.

OTHER EXECUTIVE OFFICES

Lieutenant Governor   The lieutenant governor's office in many states is looked upon as a campaign platform for the governorship. Lieutenant governors are said to have a four-year head start for the top job. The lieutenant governor's formal duties are comparable to those of the vice-president of the United States; in other words, lieutenant governors have relatively little to do. The two basic functions of the office are to serve in direct line of succession to the governor and replace him or her in the event of a vacancy in that office, and to be the presiding officer of the state senate. Since lieutenant governors generally have political ambitions of their own, they seldom make good "assistant governors" who will submerge their own interests for the success of the governor's administration. Unlike the vice-president, lieutenant governors are separately elected in most states and are sometimes members of the governor's opposition party. Some efforts have been made to reduce the boredom of the lieutenant governors' office by assigning them membership on various boards and commissions.[24]

Attorney General The office of attorney general has more real powers and responsibilities than that of the lieutenant governor. Attorneys general are elected in forty-three states, and appointed in the other states, usually by the governor. Attorneys general are the chief legal counsel for their states. They represent the state in any suits to which it is a party. They act as legal counsel for the governor and for other state officials. The legal business of state agencies is subject to their supervision. The source of the attorney general's power comes from the quasi-judicial duty of rendering formal written opinions in response to requests from the governor, state agencies, or other public officials regarding the legality and constitutionality of their acts. These opinions have the power of law in state affairs unless they are successfully challenged in court. The governor and other officials are generally obliged to conform to the attorney general's legal opinion until a court specifies otherwise. Attorneys general render authoritative interpretations of state constitutions, laws, city ordinances, and administrative rulings.

The attorney general also has substantial law enforcement powers. Most states allow attorneys general to initiate criminal proceedings on their own motion, and nearly all states assign them responsibility for handling criminal cases on appeal to higher state courts or to federal courts. In some states the attorney general has supervisory powers over law enforcement throughout the state.

Treasurers, Auditors, and Comptrollers Most states have elected *treasurers,* and treasurers in other states are appointed by either the governor or the legislature. Treasurers are custodians of state funds: collecting taxes, acting as paymaster for the state, and administering the investment of state funds. The principal job of the treasurer is to make payments on departmental requisitions for payrolls and for checks to be issued to those who have furnished the state with goods and services. Generally, the department's requests for checks must be accompanied by a voucher showing the proper legislative authority for such payment. Requests for payment usually are accompanied by a statement from the auditor's or the comptroller's office that legislative appropriations are available for such payment. Thus, the treasurer's office works in close relation to another executive office of importance: that of auditor or comptroller.

The principal duty of the office of state *auditor* is that of assuring the legislature that expenditures and investment of state funds have been made in accordance with the law. This function is known as a "postaudit" and occurs after state expenditures have been made.

The primary duty of the office of the state *comptroller* is to ensure that a prospective departmental expenditure is in accordance with the law and does not ex-

---

[24] For a review of lieutenant governor's functions, see Daniel G. Cox, "The Subterranean Influence of Lieutenant Governors," paper presented at the Midwest Political Science Meeting, Chicago, 1993.

ceed the appropriations made by the legislature. This "preaudit" occurs before any expenditure is made by the treasurer. Public administration experts consider the comptroller's job of preaudit to be an executive function, and they urge that the comptroller be appointed by the governor. On the other hand, the job of postaudit is essentially a legislative check on the executive, and students of public administration generally feel that the auditor should be elected or appointed by the legislature. However, there is still some confusion in state organizations about the separate functions of auditors and comptrollers—some auditors do "preauditing" and some comptrollers do "postauditing."

Secretary of State   Another interesting state office is that of secretary of state. Thirty-six states elect secretaries of state. Like the lieutenant governor, the secretary of state has very little to do. Secretaries of state are the chief custodians of state records and, in the case of several states, "keepers of the great seal of the commonwealth." They keep many state documents filed in their office, including corporation papers. They also supervise the preparation of ballots and certify election results for the state. The keeping of documents and the supervision of elections does not involve much discretionary power, since these activities are closely regulated by law.

Personal Staff   All governors are permitted to maintain a small group of loyal, dedicated personal aides—the governor's staff. Many staff members previously worked in the governor's political campaign. Most work long hours in small offices for relatively low pay. Most are young. Most envision some sort of political career for themselves in the future; they believe the experience they are acquiring in the governor's office, and the contacts they are making, will help in their careers. The governor may have a chief of staff, an appointments secretary, a press secretary, a legal counsel, several speechwriters, one or more legislative aides, and perhaps some advisors in key policy areas—education, welfare, highways. These people are *not* civil service employees; their jobs depend directly on their value to the governor.

STATES AND CAPITALS

For each state we have listed the capital city and the largest city. You might try to identify these cities *without* first looking at their names.

State	*Capital*	*Largest City*
Alabama	Montgomery	Birmingham
Alaska	Juneau	Anchorage
Arizona	Phoenix	Phoenix
Arkansas	Little Rock	Little Rock
California	Sacramento	Los Angeles
Colorado	Denver	Denver
Connecticut	Hartford	Bridgeport

Delaware	Dover	Wilmington
Florida	Tallahassee	Jacksonville
Georgia	Atlanta	Atlanta
Hawaii	Honolulu	Honolulu
Idaho	Boise	Boise
Illinois	Springfield	Chicago
Indiana	Indianapolis	Indianapolis
Iowa	Des Moines	Des Moines
Kansas	Topeka	Wichita
Kentucky	Frankfort	Louisville
Louisiana	Baton Rouge	New Orleans
Maine	Augusta	Portland
Maryland	Annapolis	Baltimore
Massachusetts	Boston	Boston
Michigan	Lansing	Detroit
Minnesota	St. Paul	Minneapolis
Mississippi	Jackson	Jackson
Missouri	Jefferson City	St. Louis
Montana	Helena	Billings
Nebraska	Lincoln	Omaha
Nevada	Carson City	Las Vegas
New Hampshire	Concord	Manchester
New Jersey	Trenton	Newark
New Mexico	Santa Fe	Albuquerque
New York	Albany	New York
North Carolina	Raleigh	Charlotte
North Dakota	Bismarck	Fargo
Ohio	Columbus	Cleveland
Oklahoma	Oklahoma City	Oklahoma City
Oregon	Salem	Portland
Pennsylvania	Harrisburg	Philadelphia
Rhode Island	Providence	Providence
South Carolina	Columbia	Columbia
South Dakota	Pierre	Sioux Falls
Tennessee	Nashville	Memphis
Texas	Austin	Houston
Utah	Salt Lake City	Salt Lake City
Vermont	Montpelier	Burlington
Virginia	Richmond	Norfolk
Washington	Olympia	Seattle
West Virginia	Charleston	Charleston
Wisconsin	Madison	Milwaukee
Wyoming	Cheyenne	Casper

8

Courts, Crime, and Correctional Policy

▲

Politics and the Judicial Process

Courts are "political" institutions because they attempt to resolve conflicts in society. Like legislative and executive institutions, courts make public policy in the process of resolving conflict. Some of the nation's most important policy decisions have been made by courts rather than legislative or executive bodies. Federal courts have taken the lead in eliminating segregation in public life, ensuring the separation of church and state, defining relationships between individuals and law enforcers, guaranteeing individual voters an equal voice in government, and establishing the right of women to obtain abortions. These are just a few of the important policy decisions made by courts—policy decisions that are just as significant to all Americans as those made by Congress or the president. Courts, then, are deeply involved in policy making, and they are an important part of the political system in America. Sooner or later in American politics, most important policy questions reach the courts.[1]

---

[1] For a discussion of courts as political institutions, see Hebert Jacob, *Justice in America,* 3rd ed. (Boston: Little, Brown, 1978); Harold J. Spaeth, *Supreme Court Policy-Making* (San Francisco: Freeman, 1979); Henry R. Glick, *Courts, Politics and Justice* (New York: McGraw-Hill, 1983).

In resolving conflict and deciding about public policy, courts function very much like other government agencies. However, the *style* of judicial decision making differs significantly from legislative or executive decision making. Let us try to distinguish between courts as policy-making institutions and other legislative and executive agencies.

A "Passive" Appearance   First of all, courts rarely initiate policy decisions. Rather, they wait until a case involving a policy question they must decide is brought to them. However, the vast majority of cases brought before courts do not involve important policy issues. Much court activity involves the enforcement of existing public policy. Courts punish criminals, enforce contracts, and award damages to the victims of injuries. Most of these decisions are based upon established law. Only occasionally are important policy questions brought to the court. This "passive" character of the judicial process restricts the policy initiative of judges; neither legislators nor executives suffer from such restrictions.

Special Rules of Access   Courts also differ from other government agencies in that *access* to them is governed by a special set of requirements. An interested individual or group must have an attorney and sufficient money to bear the expense of the court suit. Courts must accept "jurisdiction," which means that a dispute must meet judicial criteria of a "case" or the courts cannot settle it. A case must involve two disputing parties, one of which must have incurred some real damages as a result of the action or inaction of the other. For example, an individual who objects to the state welfare program cannot take his or her objection to a court unless that person can show that the program inflicted some direct personal or property damage.

Legal Procedures   The *procedures* under which judges and other participants in the judicial process operate are also quite different from procedures in legislative or executive branches of government. Facts and arguments must be presented to the courts in the specified manner. Generally these communications are quite formal, and legal skills are generally required to provide written briefs or oral arguments that meet the technical specifications of the courts. While an interest group may hire a public-relations firm to pressure a legislature, they must hire a law firm to put their arguments into a legal context. Decorum in courtrooms is rigorously enforced in order to convey a sense of dignity; seldom do legislatures or executive offices function with the same degree of decorum.

Decisions on Specific Cases   Courts must limit their decisions to *specific cases.* While higher courts sometimes depart from particular cases and announce general policy positions, most courts refrain from general policy statements and limit their decisions to the particular circumstances of a case. Rarely do the courts announce a comprehensive policy in the way the legislature does when it enacts a law. Of course, the implication of a court's decision in a particular case is that future cases of the same nature will be decided the same way. This implication amounts to a policy statement; however, it is not as comprehensive as a legislative policy pronouncement, because future cases with only slightly different circumstances might be decided differently.

Appearance of Objectivity   Perhaps the most important distinction between judicial decision making and decision making in other branches of government is that judges must not appear to permit political consideration to affect their decisions. Judges must not appear to base their decisions on partisan considerations, to bargain, or to compromise in decision making. Legislators and governors may base their decisions on party platforms or on their estimate of what will win in the next election, but such considerations are not supposed to influence judges. The *appearance of objectivity* in judicial decision making gives courts a measure of prestige that other governmental institutions lack. While it is true that judges have fewer direct ties with political organizations than legislators or governors, they hold political views just as everyone else, and they would be less than human if these views did not affect their decision. However, it is important that a large portion of the American public perceive judges as unaffected by personal considerations. Court decisions become more acceptable to the public if they believe that the courts have dispensed unbiased justice.

These distinctive features of the judicial process—a passive appearance, special rules of access, specialized legal procedures, decorum, focus on particular cases, and appearance of objectivity in decision making—help to "legitimize" the decisions reached by the courts; that is, they help to win popular acceptance of these decisions.

Foundation of Common Law   Legal traditions are influential in court decisions. English common law has affected the law of all of our states except Louisiana, which was influenced by the Napoleonic Code. English common law developed in the thirteenth century through the decisions of judges who applied their notions of justice to specific cases. This body of judge-made law grew over the centuries and is still the foundation of our legal system today. *Laws passed by legislatures take precedence over common law,* but the common law is applied by the courts when no statutory provisions are relevant. The degree to which statutory law has replaced common law varies among the states according to the comprehensiveness of state statutes and codes. Common law covers both criminal and civil law, although the common law of crimes has been replaced by comprehensive criminal codes in the states.

THE LAWYERING OF AMERICA

The United States is the most litigious society in the world. We are threatening to drown ourselves in a sea of lawsuits. Virtually every petty conflict finds its way into the courts.

The rise in the number of lawsuits in the United States corresponds to a rise in the number of lawyers. There were 285,000 practicing lawyers in the nation in 1960; by 1990 this figure had grown to over 750,000 (compared to 645,000 practicing physicians). The continuing search for legal fees by these bright professional people has brought an avalanche of civil liability suits in federal and state courts—about 15 million per year.

Lawyers are in business, and their business is conflict. Generating business means generating conflict. Just as businesses search for new products, lawyers search for new legal principles upon which to bring lawsuits. Lawyers have been successful over the years in expanding *tort* liability, that is, liability for damages incurred in a civil wrongdoing. Negligence is the most common civil wrongdoing or tort.

Expanded Liability   Virtually any accident involving a commercial product can inspire a product liability suit. An individual who gets cut opening a can of peas can sue the canning company. Manufacturers must pay large insurance premiums to insure themselves against such suits and pass on the costs of the insurance in the price of the product. Municipal and state governments, once generally protected from lawsuits by citizens, have now lost most of their "immunity" and must purchase liability insurance for activities as diverse as recreation, street maintenance, waste collection, and police and fire protection. Real estate brokers may be sued by unhappy buyers and sellers. Homeowners and bar owners may be sued by persons injured by their guests. Hotels have paid damages to persons raped in their rooms. Coastal cities with beaches have been successfully sued by relatives of persons who drowned themselves in the ocean.

Contingency Fees   Many of these lawsuits are initiated by lawyers who charge fees on a contingency basis; the plaintiff pays nothing unless the attorney wins an award. Up to half of that award may go to the attorney in expenses and fees. Trial attorneys argue that many people could not afford to bring civil cases to court without a contingency fee contract.

Third-Party Suits   Defendants in civil cases are not necessarily the parties directly responsible for damages to the plaintiff. Instead, wealthier third parties, who may indirectly contribute to an accident, are favorite targets of lawsuits. For example, if a drunk driver injures a pedestrian, but the driver has only limited insurance and small personal wealth, a shrewd attorney will sue the bar that sold the driver the drinks, instead of the driver. Insurance premiums have risen sharply for physicians seeking malpractice insurance, as have premiums for recreation facilities, nurseries and day care centers, motels, and restaurants. Trial lawyers have been successful in coaxing ever-larger damage awards out of juries, especially against corporations, insurance companies, and governments. Many of these awards are reduced on appeal, but the trend in awards is unmistakably upward.

"Pain and Suffering" Awards   High jury awards in liability cases, sometimes running into tens of millions of dollars, cover much more than the doctor bills, lost wages, and cost of future care for injured parties. Most large damage awards are for *pain and suffering.* Pain and suffering awards are *added* compensation for the victim, beyond actual costs for medical care and lost wages.

"Joint and Several" Liability   Moreover, a legal rule known as *joint and several liability* allows a plaintiff to collect the entire award from any party that contributed in any way to the accident, if other defendants cannot pay. So if a drunk driver crosses a median strip and crashes into another car leaving its driver a cripple, the victim may sue the city for not placing a guard railing in the median strip. The rule encourages trial lawyers to sue the party "with the deepest pockets," that is, the wealthiest party rather than the party most responsible for the accident. Unsophisticated juries can be emotionally manipulated into granting huge damage awards, especially against businesses, municipalities, and insurance companies.

Liability Insurance   Insurance companies, facing unknown risks of high damage awards by courts, have canceled policies for small businesses, doctors, hospitals, child care centers, city recreational centers, and others; or renewed these policies only at exorbitant rates. The result has been an "insurance crisis" in the states. To be sure, this liability insurance crisis is not entirely the result of aggressive lawyers, law-creating judges, and sympathetic juries. The insurance industry itself in the 1970s lowered premiums and wrote many high-risk policies in order to obtain funds to invest at high interest rates. With a lowering of interest rates in the 1980s, the investment income of insurance companies was curtailed and many were forced to raise rates. Nonetheless, insurance companies cannot be expected to pay out in liability awards more than they take in on liability policy insurance premiums.

Tort Reform   Reforming the nation's liability laws is a major challenge confronting the nation's state governments. The most common reform proposals are capping the award for "pain and suffering" at $250,000 or $500,000; restricting the fees that lawyers can subtract from a victim's award; and ending the rule of "joint and several" liability. The reform movement can count on support from some normally powerful groups—the insurance companies, physicians and hospitals, and even municipal government. But a major obstacle remains—the trial lawyers who are disproportionately represented in state legislatures (see Chapter 6).

Unquestionably the threat of lawsuits is an important safeguard for society, compelling individuals, corporations and government agencies to behave responsibly toward others. And victims require compensation for *actual* damages incurred by the wrongdoing of others. Liability laws protect all of us. But we need to consider the social costs of unnecessary litigation, excessive jury awards, increased insurance premiums, and the exclusion of useful products (like vaccines or drugs) and services (day care, recreations) from the market place.

 ## THE NEW JUDICIAL FEDERALISM

The Supremacy Clause of the U.S. Constitution (Article VI) ensures that the federal constitution supercedes state constitutions and binds the judges in every state. But state constitutions cover many topics that are not addressed in the U.S. Constitution. More importantly, state constitutions may *add* individual rights that are not found in the U.S. Constitution, and state courts may interpret state constitutional language to *expand* individual rights beyond federal constitutional guarantees. We might think of the U.S. Constitution as a floor, providing minimum protection of individual rights for all persons in the nation. But state constitutions can build upon that floor, adding individual protections for persons within their state.

"Judicial federalism" refers to state courts' exercise of their authority to interpret their own state constitutions to guarantee protections to individual rights beyond those protected by the U.S. Constitution. While this authority has always existed under the American federal system, it was seldom exercised. The history of civil rights in America was written by the U.S. Supreme Court. Historically, the remedy to civil rights violations was to be found in federal court if it was to be found at all. Civil rights attorneys almost always turned to federal courts and the U.S. Constitution to seek protection for their clients. But the new activism of state courts in interpreting their own states' constitutional guarantees has begun to change this pattern. "Forum shopping" is a common strategy of lawyers; it involves the search for a court that will be most favorably disposed to one's argument. In the past, federal courts were almost always the forum of choice for civil rights claims. But recently state courts have become the forums of choice for such claims.

Many state constitutions contain rights not explicitly found in the U.S. Constitution. For example, various state constitutions guarantee rights to privacy, rights of political participation, rights of victims of crime, rights to public information, rights to work, rights to free public education, and equal gender rights (state ERAs).

These state constitutional guarantees can be very important. For example, the Florida Supreme Court decided that the state constitutional guarantee of the right of privacy struck down the state's laws restricting abortion. This *state* constitutional decision came only a few months after the U.S. Supreme Court's decision in *Webster* v. *Reproduction Health Services* (1989) that the U.S. Constitution did not prevent Missouri from enacting the same restrictions. Note that the Florida Supreme Court was adding to individual rights and that its decision affects only persons within the state of Florida. The Texas Supreme Court decided that the state constitutional guarantee of equality in public education required the system of local school finance to be replaced with statewide financing that equalized educational spending throughout the state. Years earlier the U.S. Supreme Court in *Serrano* v. *Priest* had decided that the U.S. Constitution did *not* include a right to equal educational funding across school districts.

State courts may also render independent interpretations of clauses in their own state bills of rights that are identical to clauses in the U.S. Constitution. For example, the California Supreme Court struck down the state's death penalty as a violation of the state constitutional prohibition of "cruel *or* unusual" punishment. Note that the California Supreme Court was adding to individual rights and that its decision affects only persons in the state of California.

THE STRUCTURE OF COURT SYSTEMS

State courts are generally organized into a hierarchy similar to that shown in Figure 8–1. The courts of a state constitute a single, integrated judicial system; even city courts, traffic courts, and justices of the peace are part of the state judicial system.

Minor Courts   At the lowest level are minor courts. These may be municipal courts, magistrates courts, police courts, traffic courts, family courts, and small claims courts. They are presided over by justices of the peace, magistrates, or police judges, not all of whom are trained in the law. These courts are concerned princi-

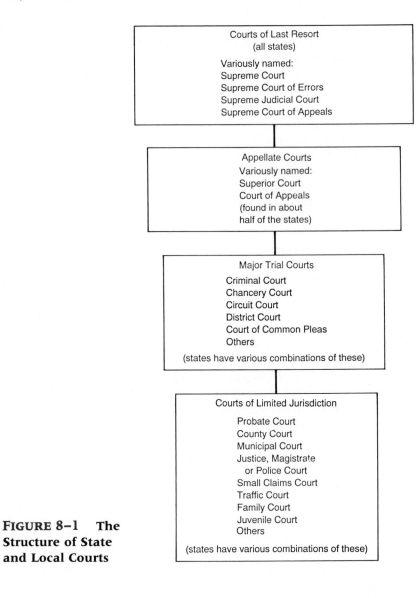

FIGURE 8–1 The Structure of State and Local Courts

pally with traffic cases, small claims, divorces and child custody, juvenile offenses, and misdemeanors, although they may hold preliminary hearings to determine whether a person accused of a felony shall be held in jail or placed under bond.

In many cities, municipal courts dispense justice in a "production line" style. Courtrooms are old, crowded, noisy, and confusing; witnesses, defendants, friends, relatives, all wait hours for their cases to be called. Most cases are handled informally at the bench in discussions with the judge. Leniency is the rule with most judges, unless the face of the defendant is very familiar to the judge; then thirty-, sixty-, or ninety-day sentences may be imposed very quickly.

The growth of small claims courts throughout the country has helped millions of people who could not afford an attorney to bring a civil claim into the court with simplicity and low cost. Proceedings in these courts are very informal: Both sides simply "tell it to the judge." Buyers and sellers, landlords and tenants, creditors and debtors, can get a resolution to their case quickly and easily.

Trial Courts   Major trial courts of general jurisdiction—sometimes called district courts, circuit courts, superior courts, chancery courts, county courts, criminal courts, or common pleas courts—handle major civil and criminal cases arising out of statutes, common law, and state constitutions. The geographic jurisdiction of these courts is usually the county or city; there are about 1500 major trial courts in the United States. Juries are used in these courts, and judges are generally qualified in the law. These courts handle criminal cases involving felonies and important civil suits. Almost all cases decided by state courts originate in these major trial courts; trial courts make the initial decisions in cases carried to appellate and supreme courts and may also handle some appeals from minor courts.

Supreme Courts   Every state has a court of last resort, which is generally called the supreme court. These courts consist of three to nine judges, and most of their work is devoted to cases on appeal from major trial courts, although some states grant original jurisdiction to supreme courts in special types of cases. Since they consider questions of law rather than questions of fact, they sit without jury. State supreme courts are the most important and visible judicial bodies in the states. Their decisions are written, published, and distributed like the decisions of the U.S. Supreme Court. Judges can express their views in majority opinions, dissenting opinions, or concurring opinions. These courts get the most controversial cases and those with the most at stake, since these cases are most likely to be appealed all the way to the state's highest court. To relieve supreme courts of heavy case burdens, many of the more populous states maintain intermediate courts of appeal between trial courts and courts of last resort.

Appeals from the state supreme courts may go directly to the U.S. Supreme Court on federal constitutional grounds. State supreme courts have the final word in the interpretation of *state* constitutions and laws. But many cases also raise federal constitutional questions, especially under the broad meaning of the "due process" clause and "equal protection" clause of the Fourteenth Amendment. So while most judicial appeals will end in state courts, the U.S. Supreme Court exercises general oversight through its power to accept appeals based on federal questions.

THE MAKING OF A JUDGE

Political debate over methods of selecting judges in the states has been going on for many years. In writing the federal Constitution, the Founding Fathers reflected conservative views in establishing an independent federal judiciary, whose members were appointed by the president for life terms and were not subject to direct popular control. Jacksonian views of popular election were strong in the states, however, and today a majority of state judges are directly elected by the people on partisan or nonpartisan ballots.

Five different methods of selecting judges are found in the fifty states: *partisan election, nonpartisan election, appointment by the governor, legislative selection,* and the *Missouri plan* (see Table 8–1). Many states use more than one method.

Most states elect their judges, some in partisan elections and some in nonpartisan elections in which candidates for the bench do not carry party labels. In four states, judges are chosen by their legislatures, and in eight states, they are appointed by the governor. Other states have adopted the so-called Missouri plan, in which governors appoint judges on the recommendation of a select committee, and after the judge has been in office for a year or more, the voters are given the opportunity to retain or oust the appointed judge.

Appointment   The argument for selecting judges by appointment rests upon the value of judicial independence and isolation from direct political involvement. Critics of the elective method feel that it forces judges into political relationships and compromises their independence on the bench. This is particularly true if judicial elections are held on a partisan rather than a nonpartisan ballot, where judges must secure nomination with the support of party leaders. Moreover, it is argued that voters are not able to evaluate "legal" qualifications—knowledge of the law, judicial temperament, skill in the courtroom, and so on. Hence, judges should be appointed, rather than elected by voters. Attorneys, bar associations, and judges themselves prefer an appointive method in which they are given the opportunity to screen candidates and evaluate legal qualifications prior to appointment.

Actually it is not possible to "take judges out of politics." Selection by ap-

TABLE 8–1   METHODS OF JUDICIAL SELECTION IN THE STATES[a]

Partisan Election	Selection by Legislature	Nonpartisan Election	Governor Appointment	Missouri Plan
Alabama	Connecticut	Florida	Delaware	Alaska
Arkansas	Rhode Island	Georgia	Hawaii	Arizona
Illinois	South Carolina	Idaho	Maine	California
Mississippi	Virginia	Kentucky	Maryland	Colorado
New Mexico		Louisiana	Massachusetts	Indiana
New York		Michigan	New Hampshire	Iowa
North Carolina		Minnesota	New Jersey	Kansas
Pennsylvania		Montana	South Dakota	Missouri
Tennessee		Nevada	Vermont	Nebraska
Texas		North Dakota		Oklahoma
West Virginia		Ohio		Utah
		Oregon		Wyoming
		Washington		
		Wisconsin		

[a] States are listed by method of selection used for supreme court. In some states different methods of selection are used for different courts.

Source: Book of the States 1992–93.

pointment or by the Missouri plan removes the selection of judges from *party* politics but simply places the selection in different political hands. Instead of party leaders, the governor or the bar association become the principal actors in judicial selection. Party leaders are assumed to be familiar with the wishes of attorneys. It is not clear which influence leads to "better" judges, or whether "better" judges are those more sensitive to community values or more trained in legal procedures. Interestingly, states with competitive two-party systems are not necessarily the same states that select their judges through partisan elections. Some of the competitive states appoint as well as elect their judges.

Interim Appointment   Although most states elect their judges, in practice many judges come to the bench in elective states through the appointment procedure. The apparent paradox comes about because even in elective states, governors generally have the power to make interim judicial appointments when a judgeship is vacant because of the retirement or death of a judge between elections. Interim-appointed judges must seek election at the next regular election, but by that time they have acquired the prestige and status of a judge, and they are unlikely to be defeated by an outsider. Many members of the judiciary in elective states deliberately resign before the end of their term, if they are not seeking reelection, in order to give the governor the opportunity to fill the post by appointment. It is interesting to note that over half of the supreme court judges in states that elect their judiciary come to the bench initially by means of appointment. In practice, then, the elective system of judicial selection is greatly compromised by the appointment of judges to fill unexpired terms.

Election   Another feature of the elective system of judicial selection, which often escapes attention, is that few incumbent judges are ever defeated in running for reelection. The majority of judges seeking reelection are unopposed by anyone on the ballot, and very few judges seeking reelection are ever defeated.[2] Voter interest in judicial elections is quite low.[3] Given a lack of information and interest in these elections, incumbent judges have an enormous advantage. They have the prestigious title "Judge" in front of their names and some name recognition. In states with partisan elections, judges are occasionally defeated if their party loses badly.[4] But even in these partisan elections judges are still separated from the normal political recruitment process. Judges enjoy more stability and independence from popular control than do legislators or governors.

Still another interesting note about the elective system of judicial selection: Very few voters know anything about judicial candidates. Indeed, one study suggests that fewer than 15 percent of the voters *coming from the polls* remembered the

---

[2] Jack Ladinsky and Alan Silver, "Popular Democracy and Judicial Independence," *Wisconsin Law Review* (1966), 132–33.

[3] Philip L. Dubois, "Voter Turnout in State Judicial Elections," *Journal of Politics,* 41 (1979), 865–87.

[4] Philip L. Dubois, "The Significance of Voting Cues in State Supreme Court Elections," *Law and Society Review,* 13 (Spring 1979), 759–79.

name of one candidate for the state supreme court, and fewer than 5 percent could remember the name of one candidate for county court.[5]

Missouri Plan   The *Missouri plan* combines the elective and appointive systems of selection. The Missouri plan calls for a select committee of judges, attorneys, and laypeople to make nominations for judicial vacancies. The governor appoints one of the committee's nominees to office. After the judge has served at least one year, the judge's name is placed on a nonpartisan ballot without any other name in opposition. "Shall judge (the name of the judge is inserted) of the (the name of the court is inserted) be retained in office? Yes___ No___." If voters vote yes, the judge is then entitled to a full term of office. If the voters vote no, the governor must select another name from those submitted by his nominating committee and repeat the whole process. In practice, a judge is hardly ever defeated under the Missouri plan, in part for the same reasons that make it difficult to defeat an incumbent judge (see preceding discussion). Moreover, since "you can't beat somebody with nobody," running under the referendum feature of the Missouri plan is the equivalent of being unopposed.[6] Less than 1 percent of Missouri plan judges are voted out of office.[7] The effect is to place judicial selection in the hands of the judges or attorneys who compose the nominating committee and the governor, with only a semblance of voter participation. Reformers argue that the plan removes judges from politics and spares the electorate the problem of voting on judicial candidates when they know little about their professional qualifications. Actually, the Missouri plan has *not* resulted in the selection of better-qualified judges,[8] although the plan remains very popular among reformers.

Whether the Selection Method Matters   There seems to be very little difference in the kinds of people who are elevated to judgeships by different judicial selection methods. One study comparing appointed, elected, and Missouri-plan judges concluded that among judges selected under different systems, there were few differences in their educational qualifications, experience, or social background (except that judges selected by state legislatures are more likely to have been state legislators).[9] More importantly, a careful study comparing decisions of state supreme courts selected by different methods shows no significant relation-

---

[5] Charles A. Johnson, Roger C. Schaefer, R. Neal McKnight, "The Salience of Judicial Candidates and Elections," *Social Science Quarterly,* 59 (September 1978), 371–78.

[6] Richard A. Watson and Rondal G. Downing, *The Politics of the Bench and Bar: Judicial Selection under the Missouri Nonpartisan Court Plan* (New York: John Wiley, Inc., 1969).

[7] William Jenkins, "Retention Elections: Who Wins When No One Loses," *Judicature,* 61 (August 1977), 79–86.

[8] Watson and Downing, *Politics of the Bench and Bar,* Chap. 6.

[9] Bradley Cannon, "The Impact of Formal Selection Processes on Characteristics of Judges—Reconsidered," *Law and Society Review,* 13 (May 1972), 570–93. An updated analysis showing that "no method of recruitment selects judges with substantially different credentials" is found in Craig F. Emmert and Henry R. Glick, "The Selection of State Supreme Court Judges," *American Politics Quarterly,* 16 (October 1988), 445–65.

ship between method of selection and judicial decision making.[10] Courts selected by partisan or nonpartisan elections, appointed by governors or legislators, or selected under the Missouri plan, show no clear and consistent trends in deciding for the state when it is a party to the case, or for criminal defendants, or for corporations, or for superior or inferior economic interests.

Race and Gender on the Bench   While women comprise over half of recent law school classes, they have not yet acceded to the bench in the same proportions as men. In some states as many as one-fourth of trial judges are women, but fewer have risen to state appellate or supreme courts.[11] Even fewer blacks have won election or appointment as state court judges. While many state appellate and supreme courts have a single black member, blacks are underrepresented among judges relative to their proportions of state populations. In California, Illinois, Maryland, Massachusetts, Michigan, New York, North Carolina and Tennessee, blacks were reported to hold over 5 percent of state court judgeships in 1985.

Judicial selection method—executive appointment, partisan or nonpartisan election, merit—has *no* effect on racial or gender representation in state judiciaries.[12]

Status   Judges are rarely recruited from among the most prestigious high-paying law firms. Judges at the trial level may earn $60,000 to $80,000 salaries, and appellate and supreme court judges $80,000 to $100,000 or more. These incomes exceed those of the average attorney, but they are paltry compared to salaries of senior partners at elite law firms. Moreover judges are restricted in investments and opportunities for outside income by judicial ethics codes. While a judge enjoys status in his or her courtroom, much of the work at the trial court level is tedious and repetitious. Finally, many elite lawyers do not relish the political tasks required to secure a judgeship—garnering the support of the bar association's judicial selection panel, or attracting the nod of the governor, or worse, campaigning for the office in an election.

Party Affiliation   Republicans have fared better in capturing judgeships than in winning legislative seats or governors' chairs. Of course, the one-party Democratic states have Democratic judges just as one-party Republican states have Republican judges; but Republicans do surprisingly well in winning judgeships in the competitive states, proportionately much better than Republican candidates for the legislature or governorship in these states.[13] Most of the judges selected in nonpartisan

---

[10] Burton M. Atkins and Henry R. Glick, "Formal Judicial Recruitment and State Supreme Court Decisions," *American Politics Quarterly,* 2 (October 1974), 427–49.

[11] See M. C. Henry, Jr. et al., *The Success of Women and Minorities in Achieving Judicial Office* (New York: Fund for Modern Courts, 1985); cited in Virginia Gray, Herbert Jacob, and Robert Albritten, eds., *Politics in the American States,* 5th ed. (Glenview, IL: Scott Foresman, 1990), p. 264.

[12] Nicholas O. Alozie, "Distribution of Women and Minority Judges," *Social Science Quarterly,* 71 (June 1990), 315–25.

[13] Stuart Nagel, "Unequal Party Representation in State Supreme Courts," *Journal of the American Judicature Society,* 44 (1961), 62–65.

elections refuse to identify themselves with a political party, as do nearly all the judges selected under the Missouri plan. Judges selected in partisan elections, of course, usually do not hesitate to identify themselves as Republicans or Democrats.

The Psychology of Judges   While most judges share a common background before coming to the bench—law school, practicing attorney, prosecutor—they are "not well-prepared for their jobs in the court."[14] The high esteem and prestige of the judiciary tend to obscure the negative aspects of the job: the requirement to remain aloof from courtroom battles, to isolate oneself, and to deal with the routines of judging.

> You come right out of a position of advocacy into where you have to be totally impersonal. It's tough to train yourself not to want to take part in a proceeding and the longer you stay on the bench, the less of a lawyer you become, the more you appreciate the constitutional provisions, the rights of people.[15]

Apparently it takes several years for attorneys to adjust fully to their new roles as judges. Coping with the social and political *isolation* appears to be the most difficult problem.

> The longer you stay on the bench, the fewer close friendships you have with lawyers. . . . As you go on it becomes more and more restrictive.

Most judges are not paid as much as successful attorneys. After five or ten years on the bench, judges must often decide whether to step down and try to improve their personal finances or stay on with a comfortable, but not high, salary until retirement. "It's not a job for an ambitious person."

THE REJECTION OF ROSE BIRD

Perhaps the most publicized judicial retention election in many years was the successful popular effort to oust California's Supreme Court Chief Justice Rose Bird in 1986. Justice Bird and two liberal colleagues on California's high court were the first members of that court ever to be rejected under the state's fifty-year-old retention procedure. Bird's defeat, by a thumping 66 percent margin, ended a controversial tenure on the California Supreme Court and reaffirmed democratic checks over state courts.

Rose Bird was appointed to the California Supreme Court by Governor Jerry Brown in 1977, even though she had never served in a prior judicial post. She had a B.A. from Long Island University, a law degree from the University of California, and a successful record as a county public defender. She was Jerry Brown's chauffeur in his 1974 gubernatorial campaign, and he later named her state secretary of agriculture, the first woman in a cabinet-level position in California history. Bird had no experience in agriculture, but the department also had responsibility for

---

[14] This material relies on an excellent essay by Lenore Alpert, Burton M. Atkins, and Robert C. Ziller, "Becoming a Judge: The Transition from Advocate to Arbiter," *Judicature,* 62 (February 1979), 325–35.

[15] Ibid.

consumer and occupational health and safety. The youthful and attractive secretary quickly captured media attention as an advocate of workers and consumers.

Under California law, a state supreme court justice must be approved by the electorate at the next gubernatorial election, which in Bird's case was November 1978. Critics attacked her lack of judicial experience, but the real issues were her liberal politics and her reputation as a champion of criminal defendants. A statewide "No on Bird" campaign portrayed her as "soft on crime," but she had the support of the California Bar Association, women's groups, and the state's leading newspapers. She won the confirmation vote with a slim 52 percent margin, the closest confirmation vote in the state's history.

Immediately after the confirmation vote, the *Los Angeles Times* reported that the supreme court had deliberately delayed a ruling overturning a state law mandating prison sentences for using a gun during a robbery in order to improve Justice Bird's chances at the polls. After several weeks of televised hearings, the state's Commission on Judicial Performance released a report stating that "no formal charges" of misconduct would be filed against Bird. But the investigation itself presented an unflattering picture of the court and its controversial chief justice.

During her nine-year tenure on the California Supreme Court, Bird led a successful liberal block in expanding the rights of criminal defendants. In a state in which four-fifths of the population favors the death penalty, Justice Bird voted to overturn every one of fifty-five death penalty sentences to come to the court on appeal. The court itself overturned all but three of the state's death sentences, and none were actually carried out during her tenure.

The public's frustration with a judicial system that failed to carry out death sentences mandated by law for heinous crimes eventually led to a successful recall campaign against Rose Bird and two other liberal state supreme court justices. A broad coalition formed behind the "bye bye Birdie" campaign: victims of crime and their families, parents and spouses of murder victims, police and prosecutors, and conservative groups. They were eventually joined by the state's popular Republican governor, George Deukmejian. Behind the scenes were strategists, consultants, and direct mail fund raisers who had earlier worked in Reagan gubernatorial campaigns and tax limitation efforts. Over $4 million was raised for the recall campaign. Despite Bird's claim that the money came from corporate interests opposed to her decisions on behalf of workers and consumers, official campaign spending reports show that most of the money came from individual contributors sending in less than one hundred dollars.[16]

As in other California political campaigns, most of the battle took place on television. A feature of the campaign against Bird was the sad face of a mother of a murdered twelve-year-old girl, sitting beside a framed picture of her daughter and asking voters to defeat the three justices who had voted to overturn the killer's death sentence.

Bird's campaign to retain her seat was also professionally managed and well funded. California liberal celebrities were called out to help raise funds; Warren

---

[16] *Los Angeles Times,* November 5, 1986, p. 24.

Beatty, Paul Newman, and television producer Norman Lear helped to put on fund raisers for her. Eventually she raised over $2 million for her campaign, and her two liberal colleagues raised $1 million each in their own defense. She led off her campaign claiming that U.S. Attorney General Edwin Meese and "right-wing bully boys" were behind the effort to oust her. Most of her money was spent on television commercials stressing her "backbone" and "integrity." She closed out her campaign charging that Governor George Deukmejian wanted to turn the California Supreme Court into a "house of death" to further his own political career. Indeed, the bitterness of her charges may have added to her defeat. The Democratic candidate for governor, Tom Bradley, and U.S. Senator Alan Cranston declined to come to her defense.

Bird's unpopularity apparently rubbed off on her fellow liberals on the court. On election day in 1986, voters rejected Rose Bird 66–34, and rejected Cruz Reynoso 60–40 and Joseph Grodin 57–43, while at the same time strongly approving two other justices. Bird was defiant in defeat: "I appreciate that some people within our state are impatient, impatient to see executions. . . . But I don't think anybody will sit easy if in fact this becomes a court that ensures nothing but executions to appease the overwhelming and insatiable appetite of ambitious politicians."[17]

If judges opt for the role of judicial activists, incorporating their own policy views into the constitutions and laws of a state, they must recognize that democratic voters have a right to reverse their policies by ousting them from office, just as democratic voters can oust governors and legislatures who do not reflect popular views. Judicial policy makers must be held accountable to the people.

 ## JUDICIAL DECISION MAKING: TRIAL COURTS

Social scientists know more about the behavior of federal court judges, and even state supreme court judges, than they know about the thousands of trial judges throughout the nation. This is largely because the decisions of higher courts are very visible and closely watched by lawyers and scholars. The actions of trial judges do not appear, at first glance, to have broad political impact. Nevertheless, trial court judges have enormous discretion in both civil and criminal cases. Perhaps the most dramatic and visible areas of trial judge discretion is *sentencing.*

Trial court judges display great disparities in the sentences they give out in identical cases. As most good attorneys know, as well as many defendants with long criminal records, it matters a great deal who sits as the judge in your case. The outcome of *most* criminal cases is decided in "plea bargaining" between prosecuting attorneys and defense attorneys, where defendants agree to plead guilty to a lesser offense and the prosecution agrees not to press more serious charges or ask for stiffer penalties. However, the bargain must be approved by the judge. Wise attorneys know in advance what kinds of bargains different judges are likely to accept. It is *not* the determination of guilt or innocence that concerns judges, so much as the processing of cases, the acceptance of pleas, and sentencing. One study pre-

---

[17] *Los Angeles Times,* November 5, 1986, p. 24.

sented forty-eight trial judges in Wisconsin with the same hypothetical case: breaking and entering, one count, in which the defendant was a twenty-five-year-old, employed, white male without any previous record. The sentences ranged from eleven months in jail to thirty days of unsupervised probation.[18]

Different trial court judges see their roles in different ways. Four separate roles can be identified which seem to motivate county court judges.[19]

1. The "game" judges: They perceive judging as difficult and challenging and get pleasure out of overcoming difficulties, meeting challenges, and presiding over a well-run courtroom. "I really enjoy conducting hearings and trials. . . . There is so much to do in this job; there is never a dull moment, handling motions, talking to lawyers, making sure the calendar is managed well."

   These "game" judges have held office longer than other judges; they are more active in court proceedings; their courtroom appears to be relaxed; they deny that they have much discretion; and they hand out the least severe penalties.

2. The "program" judges: They enjoy delving into substantive issues and pursuing specific policy objectives.

   "I think that judges are problem solvers at a personal level. A judge must be active in trying to get lawyers to settle without waiting until the investment in a case is so great that the parties feel they must have a trial."

   The "program" judges are younger; they perceive their role as passive umpires whose main job is to keep the courtroom functioning smoothly; they acknowledge that they have a great deal of discretion; and their sentences are also fairly light.

3. The "obligation" judges: They perceive their role in terms of duties, obligations, and ethical responsibilities.

   "Judges, unlike lawyers, are in a special position; they are under an obligation to do the right thing in every case, to determine, as best they can, the truth in a case and to apply the law.

   "You can't give away a little, just to get someone's approval. This isn't the legislature. You are dealing with people's lives, their future; you can't do less than what you believe to be right."

   Obligation judges are older; they have no future political ambitions; they run a formal and businesslike courtroom; they deny that they have much discretion; and they hand out fairly severe sentences.

4. The "status" judges: They are motivated by the special prestige and status associated with the office of judge.

   "When I go out to a restaurant it's 'Your Honor this' and 'Your Honor that.' It is nice to be respected and everybody respects a judge."

   "Most lawyers would stab their client for a fee and most of them would do anything to get this job."

---

[18] Austin Sarat, "Judging Trial Courts," *Journal of Politics,* 39 (May 1977), 368–98.

[19] Ibid. The quotations in this section were obtained from Wisconsin trial court judges by Sarat.

The status judges are young; they are ambitious for higher political or judicial office. They are very stiff in the courtroom, sometimes even nasty and abrasive (comment to an attorney during a case: "Based on your performance so far, it is no wonder that your practice is in the shape it is in."); and, finally, they hand out the stiffest sentences of any judges.

The trial court judges have a difficult yet vital job to perform. They must oversee the record of a case to prevent "reversible" error—that is, to see that no legal errors have been made that would result in a conviction being reversed or appealed. At the same time they must deal with human problems at an individual level. As one judge put it: "A trial judge is a pioneer; he approaches each case without any help. He is the first to deal with problems. . . . Sometimes I don't think that appellate judges understand that."

JUDICIAL DECISION MAKING: STATE SUPREME COURTS

Conflict in state supreme courts, as measured by the number of divided opinions, is less frequent than in the U.S. Supreme Court. Dissenting votes are reported on more than half of all U.S. Supreme Court decisions, but state judges dissent in very few cases. Public disagreement is somewhat more frequent in competitive party states where judges of both parties are represented on the court.

Issues   Criminal appeals account for nearly one-third of the work load of state supreme courts.[20] The largest proportion of state supreme court decision making involves economic interests. A large number of cases involving economic interests result from the important role of the states in the allocation of economic resources. All states regulate public utilities, including water, electrical companies, gas companies, and public transportation companies. The insurance industry is state regulated. Labor relations and worker's compensation cases are frequently found in state courts. Litigation over natural resources, real estate, small-business regulations, gas, oil, lumber and mining, alcoholic beverage control, racing, and gambling reflects the importance of state regulation in these fields. There is a correlation between the kinds of economic litigation decided by state supreme courts and the socioeconomic environment of the state. Supreme courts in poorer, rural states spend more time on private economic litigation (wills, trusts, estates, contracts, titles, and so on), while courts in urban industrial states wrestle with corporate law and governmental regulation of large economic interests. Judges are also called upon to make decisions in political controversies—disputes over elections, appointments to government positions, and jurisdictional squabbles between governments.

Party   What is the impact of the party affiliation of the judges in court decision making? Party affiliation probably has little impact in decisions in lower trial courts, where much of the litigation has little to do with policy making. However,

---

[20] Burton M. Atkins and Henry Glick, "Determinants of Issues in State Courts of Last Resort," *American Journal of Political Science,* 20 (February 1976), 97–115.

several studies have shown party affiliation to be an influence on state supreme court decision making.[21] Democratic judges tended to decide more frequently (1) for the administrative agency in business regulation cases; (2) for the claimant in unemployment compensation; (3) for the government in tax cases; (4) for the tenant in landlord–tenant cases; (5) for the consumer in sale-of-goods cases; and (6) for the employee in employee injury cases. There is no evidence that the party itself influences these judges. Rather, it is likely that the judges' social, economic, and political views influence both their decisions on the court and their decision to affiliate with the Democratic or Republican party.

Ethnicity   What is the effect of social and ethnic group membership on judges' decisions? Judges, like other decision makers, generally belong to higher social and economic groups; white, Anglo-Saxon Protestants are disproportionately represented among state judges. One study found that judges who were members of ethnic minority groups in America were more likely to decide (1) for the defense in criminal cases, (2) for finding a constitutional violation in criminal cases, and (3) for the wife in divorce cases than were judges with white, Anglo-Saxon backgrounds.[22] It also found a difference in the decisions of Catholic and non-Catholic judges. Catholic judges tended to decide (1) for the defense in criminal cases, (2) for the administrative agency in business regulation cases, (3) for the wife in divorce settlement cases, (4) for the debtor in debtor–creditor cases, and (5) for the employee in employee injury cases.

Judicial Activism Versus Restraint   The great debate of American jurisprudence centers about whether judges should make law in their decisions or whether they should limit themselves to interpreting the law. Great legalists have argued the merits of activism versus self-restraint in judicial decision making for more than a century.[23] The traditional restraint of state courts has been increasingly challenged in recent years by activism on the part of some state supreme courts. For example, some state supreme courts have decided to go beyond the U.S. Supreme Court in finding new constitutional rights for citizens. While the U.S. Supreme Court held that there is no constitutional right to taxpayer-funded abortions, courts in California, Connecticut, and Massachusetts have ruled that state medical aid programs must fund abortions under *state* constitutional interpretations. Although the U.S. Supreme Court ruled that variations among local school districts in property tax support of schools did not violate the Equal Protection Clause of the U.S. Constitution, several state supreme courts have held that equal protection clauses in their own state constitutions bar school financing formulas which favor pupils in

---

[21] Stuart Nagel, "Political Party Affiliation and Judges' Decisions," *American Political Science Association,* 55 (1961), 843–51; and Sidney Ulmer, "The Political Party Variable on the Michigan Supreme Court," *Journal of Public Law,* 11 (1962), 352–62.

[22] Stuart Nagel, "Ethnic Affiliation and Judicial Propensities," *Journal of Politics,* 24 (1962), 92–110.

[23] Jerome Frank, *Law and the Modern Mind* (New York: Coward-McCann, Inc., 1930); Benjamin N. Cardozo, *The Nature of the Judicial Process* (New Haven: Yale University Press, 1921); and Roscoe Pound, *Justice According to Law* (New Haven: Yale University Press, 1951).

affluent school districts over pupils in poorer school districts. And several state supreme courts have insisted on protections for criminal defendants that go beyond those provided by the U.S. Supreme Court.

Judicial Roles   Judicial decision making is influenced by judges' perceptions of their own role. Of course, popular debate about judicial activism is generally focused on the U.S. Supreme Court, but state court judges must also come to grips with this question. Henry Glick undertook to interview state supreme court judges in four states to ascertain their views of their roles in decision making.[24] About half of the judges interviewed opted for the more restrained role of "law interpreter":

> We interpret the law. That is our function. We're not authorized to write the law. We can only act in one way: that is to be solely interpreters of the law. The moment he steps out of the role of interpreter, he violates the Constitution which separates the legislative from the judiciary.

Less than one-quarter saw themselves as "lawmaker":

> Inevitably a judge makes law as does a legislative body. No matter how you decide a case you're making law. Whether you say yes or no in a case, you're making law. . . . Judges always make law and always will.

And some judges were characterized as "pragmatists":

> When you're a judge, you're part legislator, executive, and judge. You're a creature of all three branches of government when you make a decision. All sorts of things come into consideration.

Liberals, Conservatives, and Judicial Roles   Theoretically, activist and restraintist views of the judicial role are independent of liberal or conservative ideology. That is, judicial activism could be used in support of either liberal or conservative goals; or alternatively, judicial restraint could limit the lawmaking of judges disposed to either liberal or conservative ideas. However, there appears to be a tendency for liberal judges to be more activist than conservative judges. But the major impact of ideology is *through* the role orientation of judges. Self-restraint reduces the impact of ideology on judges' decisions. Activism greatly increases the impact of judges' ideologies. Activist judges are overtly ideological in reactions to criminal appeals—activist liberal judges vote for the defendant far more frequently than activist conservative judges who tend to support the prosecution.[25]

Summary   In summary, judicial decision making is influenced by interest group activity, political party affiliation, social and ethnic ties, religious affiliations, and the liberal and conservative views of judges. This does not mean that "judicial impartiality" is nonexistent or that judges are as free as legislators or governors to write their social and political views into the law. Judges participate in the game of

---

[24] Henry Glick, *Supreme Courts in State Politics* (New York: Basic Books, 1971). The quotations are from state supreme court judges, pp. 39–42; see John Patrick Hagan, "Patterns of Activism on State Supreme Courts," *Publius,* 18 (Winter 1988), 97–115.

[25] John M. Scheb, Terry Bowen, and Gary Anderson, "Ideology, Role Orientations and Behavior in State Courts of Last Resort," *American Politics Quarterly,* 19 (July 1991), 324–35.

politics as players as well as umpires, but they are limited by the rules of the game, the decisions of legislatures and governors, and public expectations about the way judges ought to behave.

CRIME IN THE STATES

Crime rates are the subject of a great deal of popular discussion. Crime rates are based upon the Federal Bureau of Investigation's *Uniform Crime Reports,* but the FBI reports are compiled from figures supplied by state and local police agencies. (See Table 8–2.) The FBI has established a uniform classification of the number of serious crimes per 100,000 people that are known to the police: murder and nonnegligent manslaughter, forcible rape, robbery, aggravated assault, burglary, larceny, and theft, including auto theft. However, one should be cautious in interpreting official crime rates. They are really a function of several factors: the tendencies of victims to report crimes to police, the adequacy of police departments in tabulating crime, and the amount of crime itself.

Trends in Crime Rates   The national crime rate has risen dramatically yet unevenly over the past few decades. From 1960 to 1975 the crime rate more than doubled, and "law and order" became an important political issue. In the early 1980s crime rates leveled off and even declined slightly from their record years. It was widely believed that the early rapid increase and later moderation was a product of age group changes in the population: The early baby boom had expanded the size of the "crime-prone" age group in the population, people fifteen to twenty-four; later, crime rates leveled off when this age group was no longer increasing as a percentage of the population. As late as 1983 many analysts were looking forward to gradual decreases in crime rates based on smaller crime-prone age groups. But in recent years crime rates have soared upward again. The new factor in the

TABLE 8–2   CRIME RATES IN THE UNITED STATES: OFFENSES KNOWN TO THE POLICE

	1960	1965	1970	1975	1980	1983	1990
Rates per 100,000 population							
Murder and nonnegligent manslaughter	5	5	8	10	10	8	9
Forcible rape	9	12	18	26	36	34	41
Robbery	60	172	172	209	244	214	257
Aggravated assault	85	110	162	215	291	273	424
Burglary	506	659	1,068	1,429	1,668	1,334	1,236
Larceny	1,028	1,321	2,066	2,473	3,156	2,866	3,195
Auto theft	182	256	454	461	495	429	658
Total crimes against person	160	199	360	459	581	529	732
Total crimes against property	1,716	2,235	3,599	4,363	5,319	4,630	5,088

Source: FBI, *Uniform Crime Reports,* reported in *Statistical Abstract of the United States, 1992.*

crime rate equation appears to be the widespread popularity of "crack" cocaine. Perhaps as many as one-half of all crimes today are drug-related.

Variation Among the States   Crime rates are related to urbanization and economic development in the states. Generally, the urban industrial high-income states have higher crime rates than the rural agricultural low-income states (see Figure 8–2). The high crime rate in Nevada suggests that crime is also related to gambling. The state has the most permissive gambling laws of any state in the nation.

Victimization   Official crime rates understate the real amount of crime. Citizens do not report many crimes to police. "Victimization" surveys regularly ask a national sample of individuals whether they or any member of their household has been a victim of crime during the past year. These surveys reveal that the actual amount of crime is greater than that reported to the FBI. The number of forcible rapes is more than three times the number reported, burglaries three times, aggravated assaults and larcenies more than double, and robbery 50 percent greater than the reported rate. Only auto theft statistics are reasonably accurate, indicating that most people call the police when their cars are stolen.[26]

Interviewees give a variety of reasons for their failure to report crime to the police. The most common reason is the feeling that police could not be effective in dealing with the crime. This is a serious comment about police protection in America today. Other reasons include the feeling that the crime was "a private matter," that the offender was a member of the family, or that the victim did not want to harm the offender. Fear of reprisal is mentioned much less frequently, usually in cases of assaults and family crimes.

Trends in Victimization   Surveys indicate that between 30 and 40 million people each year are victimized by crime; 6 million are victims of a violent crime. However, while victimization rates rose during the 1970s, they have *declined* over the past decade. Declining victimization rates, combined with an increasing official reported crime rate, suggest that citizen *reporting* of crime is increasing, even though the actual numbers of crimes committed may be decreasing.

THE WAR ON DRUGS

Public policy in the United States toward drug use is inconsistent. Alcohol and cigarettes are legal products, but Congress has banned their advertising on radio and television. Marijuana has been "decriminalized" in several states, making its possession a misdemeanor comparable to a traffic offense. Yet the production and sale of marijuana remain criminal offenses in every state. The use and possession of cocaine is a criminal offense everywhere in the United States. Heroin is a physically addictive drug, and its use in the United States may be declining somewhat.

---

[26] See Wesley G. Skogan, "The Validity of Official Crime Statistics: An Empirical Investigation," *Social Science Quarterly,* 55 (June 1974), 25–38.

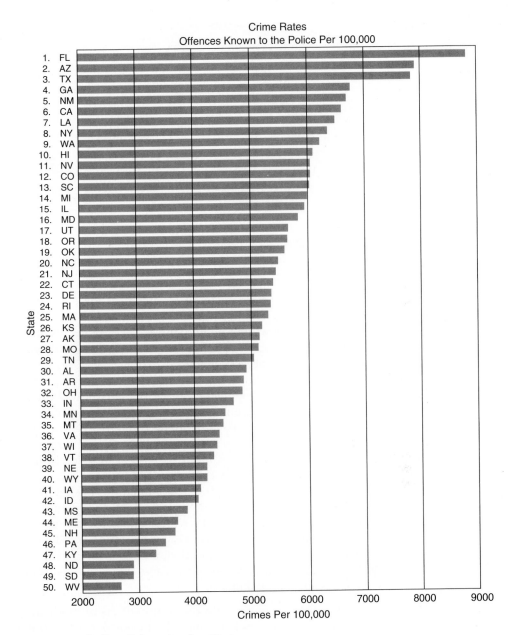

Crime Rates
Offences Known to the Police Per 100,000

FIGURE 8–2   Crime in the States

Alcohol   The United States government attempted to prohibit the manufacture and sale of alcohol for only thirteen years, during "Prohibition," 1920–1933. Today, the alcoholic beverage industry is a major component of our national economy, and nearly two-thirds of the adult population drink occasionally. But according to the U.S. National Institute on Drug Abuse, there are 12 million to 14 million

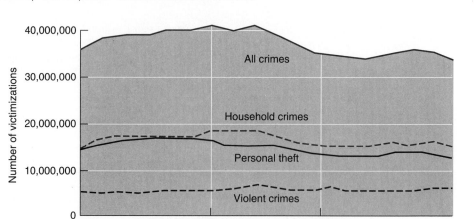

FIGURE 8–3 Victimization Trends, 1973–1990

Source: U.S. Department of Justice, Bureau of justice Statistics, "Criminal Victimization" Bulletin, October 1991.

"problem drinkers" in the nation—about 6 percent of the population.[27] These problem drinkers are not only dangers to themselves, but also to others, particularly on the highways. Almost half of all highway accident deaths are alcohol related. About 1.5 million people are arrested for driving while intoxicated (DWI) each year; this is the single largest category of arrests.[28]

Alcohol is controlled in the states primarily by laws dealing with the age of the purchaser. Immediately following the passage of the Twenty-sixth Amendment lowering the voting age to eighteen, most states dropped the legal drinking age to eighteen. But later the states reversed themselves, and today most states have returned the legal drinking age to twenty-one. In 1984 Congress required the U.S. Department of Transportation to withhold 10 percent of federal highway funds from any state that did not raise its drinking age to twenty-one (see "Congress Raises the Drinking Age" in Chapter 3). The argument for raising the legal drinking age generally centers around the higher automobile accident rate for young people and the dangers of "drinking and driving." The states have also tried to deal directly with the drunk driving by all age groups by setting specific blood alcohol concentration (BAC) standards for intoxication, usually 0.10; increasing the penalties for DWI; and even holding bars legally accountable if their patrons are found DWI (known as "dram shop liability").

Marijuana The medical evidence on the health effects of marijuana is mixed; conflicting reports have been issued about whether or not it is more dangerous than alcohol.[29] Estimates of the number of "regular" marijuana users are roughly

---

[27] See Richard C. Shroeder, *The Politics of Drugs,* 2nd ed. (Washington, DC: Congressional Quarterly Press, 1980), p. 80.

[28] *Statistical Abstract of the United States 1989,* p. 173.

[29] For a summary of this evidence and references to the relevant health literature, see Schroeder, *Politics of Drugs,* Chapter 4.

comparable to estimates of the number of problem drinkers—12 million. Marijuana users are younger than the general population. Decriminalizing marijuana use does not make its production or sale legal, but makes its possession (generally an ounce or less) a civil offense, much like a traffic offense.

Cocaine   The burgeoning market for cocaine currently challenges law enforcement efforts. Cocaine is not regarded as physically addictive, although the psychological urge to continue use of the drug is strong. It is made from coca leaves and imported into the United States. At one time, its high cost and use by celebrities made it the drug of choice in middle- and upper-class circles. In the 1980s a cheap yet potent version, "crack," spread rapidly in the nation's cities. The health problems associated with cocaine are fairly serious, as reported by the National Institute on Drug Abuse.[30] Death, although rare, can occur from a single ingestion.

Trafficking   Crime associated with drug trafficking is a serious national problem, whatever the health effects of various drugs. The world of drug trafficking is fraught with violence. Sellers rob and murder buyers and vice versa: Neither can seek the protection of police or courts in their dealing with the other. Although some citizens might wish to allow dealers to wipe each other out, the frequency with which innocent bystanders are killed must be considered.

It is very difficult to estimate the total size of the drug market, but $20 to $25 billion per year is a common figure.[31] This would suggest that the drug business is comparable in size to one of the ten largest U.S. industrial corporations. More important, perhaps, drugs produce huge profit margins: a kilo of cocaine purchased in Colombia may cost only $3,600; when sold in the United States, that kilo may retail for $80,000 to $120,000.[32] The price of smuggling a single, easily concealable kilo may run to $15,000. These huge profits allow drug traffickers to corrupt police and government officials as well as private citizens in the United States and other nations.

Drug Policy   Antidrug efforts can be divided into three categories: interdiction, enforcement, and education.

Interdiction: Efforts to seal U.S. borders against the importation of drugs have been frustrated by the sheer volume of smuggling. Each year increasingly large drug shipments are intercepted by the U.S. Drug Enforcement Administration, the U.S. Customs Service, the Coast Guard, and state and local agencies. Yet each year the volume of drugs entering the country seems to increase. Drug "busts" are considered just another cost of business to the traffickers. It is not likely that the use of U.S. military forces to augment other federal agencies can succeed in sealing our borders. American pressure against Latin American governments to destroy coca crops and assist in interdiction has already resulted in strained relationships. Our neighboring countries wonder why the U.S. government directs its efforts at the suppliers, when the demand for drugs arises within the United States itself.

---

[30] Ibid., p. 148.

[31] *Congressional Quarterly Weekly Report,* June 25, 1988.

[32] Ethan A. Nadelmann, "U.S. Drug Policy," *Foreign Policy* (Spring 1988), 83–108.

Enforcement: The FBI and state and local law enforcement agencies already devote great effort to combating drugs; an estimated 40 percent of all arrests in the United States are drug-related. Federal and state prisons now hold a larger percentage of the nation's population than ever before. Sentences have lengthened for drug trafficking, and prisons are overcrowded as a direct result of drug-related convictions. Drug testing in government and private employment is increasing, but unless it is random it is not very useful, and some courts have prevented random testing of individuals without their consent.

Education: Efforts at educating the public about the dangers of drugs have inspired many public and private campaigns, from former First Lady Nancy Reagan's "Just say no" to Jesse Jackson's "Up with hope, down with dope." But it is difficult to evaluate the effects of these efforts. The number of people prosecuted for drug offenses in U.S. district courts continues to rise each year (see Figure 8–4). Yet there appears to be no significant reduction in the availability of drugs on the street.

Federal Policy   Congress created a cabinet-level "drug czar," a National Drug Control Policy Director, in 1988 to develop and coordinate antidrug policy in the United States. The national "war on drugs" has included funds for federal prison construction and more courts and prosecutors; grants for state and local drug law enforcement; increased money for border control for the Coast Guard, Customs Service, Immigration and Naturalization Service; authorization for use of U.S. military in drug enforcement; and additional funds for the Drug Enforcement Administration. Congress added funds for treatment programs in states and cities.

Drugs and Crime   Police officials are convinced that drugs cause crime—not just violation of drug laws, but robbery, burglary, assault, and murder. Indeed, drug use among persons arrested for nondrug crimes is very high; reports from various cities indicate that half to two-thirds of all persons arrested for nondrug crimes test positive for drug use.[33] But this does not necessarily mean that drugs cause crime. A majority of criminals may use drugs, but the vast majority of drug users do not commit other crimes.

Who's Winning the War on Drugs?   The U.S. government's National Institute on Drug Abuse regularly surveys Americans to ask whether they have ever used particular drugs and whether they have used them in the past year or month. These surveys suggest that about 15 million people, or 6 percent of the U.S. population, have used an illicit drug in the previous thirty days (see Figure 8–5). Marijuana is the most commonly used illicit drug, followed by cocaine. There are an estimated 12 million regular users of marijuana, or almost 5 percent of the population, although many more have smoked it at least once.

According to the survey evidence, the numbers of people using elicit drugs has declined in recent years. However, the U.S. Drug Enforcement Administration (DEA) reports increase numbers of cocaine seizures and drug arrests each year. There appear to be no significant reductions in the volume of drugs entering the country or reaching the streets.

---

[33] *Statistical Abstract of the United States 1991,* p. 183.

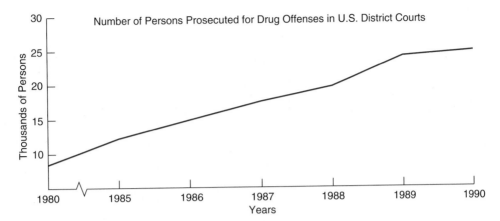

FIGURE 8–4   Federal Drug Prosecutions
Source: Bureau of Justice Statistics, U.S. Department of Justice, *Sourcebook of Criminal Justice Statistics, 1992*
(Washington: Government Printing Office), 1992.

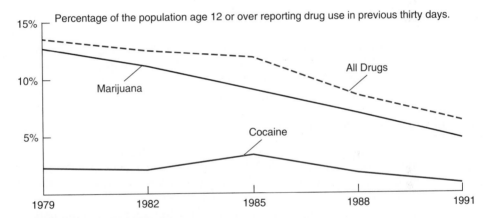

FIGURE 8–5   Reported Drug Use
Source: Bureau of Justice Statistics, U.S. Department of Justice, *Sourcebook of Criminal Justice Statistics 1992*
(Washington: Government Printing Office), 1992.

Educational campaigns against drugs may actually reduce the number of casual users, or these campaigns may signal that drug use is socially unacceptable and inhibit respondents from admitting use even in anonymous interviews. Perhaps the reported reduction in drug use over the years reflect both effects.

The most common interpretation of the poll results showing reduced drug use, and the law enforcement data showing continued volume of drug availability, is that *casual* use is down but daily use by *hard-core* addicted persons remains high.

Legalization?   The failure of antidrug policies to produce any significant reductions in drug supply or demand, coupled with the high costs of enforcement and the loss of civil liberties, has caused some observers to propose the legalization of drugs and government control of their production and sales. "Prohibition" failed earlier in the century to end alcohol consumption, and the crime, official corruption, and enormous cost of futile efforts to stop drinking eventually forced the nation to end Prohibition. Similarly it is argued that the legalization of drugs would end organized crime's profit monopoly over the drug trade, raise billions of dollars by legally taxing drugs, end the strain on relations with Latin American nations caused by efforts to eradicate drugs, and save additional billions in enforcement costs which could be used for education and treatment.[34] If drugs were legally obtainable under government supervision, it is argued that many of society's current problems would be aleviated: the crime and violence associated with the drug trade, the corruption of public officials, the spread of diseases associated with drug use, and the many infringements of personal liberty associated with antidrug wars.

But even the suggestion of drug legalization offends Americans who believe that legalization would greatly expand drug use in the country. Cheap, available drugs would greatly increase the numbers of addicted persons, creating a "society of zombies" that would destroy the social fabric of the nation. Cocaine and heroin are far more habit forming than alcohol, and legalization would encourage the development of newer and even more potent and addictive synthetic drugs. Whatever the health costs of drug abuse today, it is argued that legalization would produce public health problems of enormous magnitude.[35] Cocaine is very cheap to produce; the current $5 to $10 cost of a "hit" is mostly drug dealer profit; legalization even with taxation might produce a 50¢ "hit." Whatever the damages to society from drug-related crime and efforts to prohibit drugs, the damages to society from cheap, available drug usage would be far greater.

POLICE PROTECTION IN THE STATES

State, county, and municipal governments are all directly involved in law enforcement. Every state has a central law enforcement agency, sometimes called the state police, state troopers, state highway patrol, or even Texas Rangers. At one time, state governors had only the National Guard at their disposal to back up local law enforcement efforts, but the coming of the automobile and intercity highway traffic led to the establishment in every state of a centralized police system. In addition to patrolling the state's highways, these centralized agencies now provide expert aid and service for local police officers and strengthen law enforcement in sparsely populated regions. Three-quarters of the states have given their central police agencies full law enforcement authority in addition to highway duties: They may quell riots, cooperate with local authorities in the apprehension of criminals, or even intervene when local authorities are unable or unwilling to enforce the law. The size and influence of these agencies vary from state to state. On the whole, however, state police forces constitute a very small proportion of the total law en-

---

[34] Ethan A. Nadelmann, "The Case for Legalization," *The Public Interest* (Summer 1988), 3–31.

[35] John Kaplan, "Taking Drugs Seriously," *The Public Interest* (Summer 1988), 32–50.

forcement effort in America. Law enforcement in the nation is principally a *local* responsibility.

The County Sheriff   Historically, the county sheriff has been the keystone of law enforcement in the United States. Sheriffs and their deputies are still the principal enforcement and arresting officers in the rural counties and in the unincorporated fringe areas of many urban counties. In addition, the sheriff serves as an executive agent for county and state courts in both civil and criminal matters, and maintains the county jail for the retention of persons whose trials or sentences are pending or who are serving short sentences. The sheriff's office is a political one; in every state except Rhode Island the sheriff is an elected official. Reliance upon the sheriff's office for law enforcement is a characteristic of rural states. Since city police forces usually assume the sheriff's law enforcement duties within the boundaries of cities, the sheriff's office has seriously atrophied in most urban states; often the sheriff is reduced to a process server for the courts.

City Police   Urban police departments are the most important instruments of law enforcement and public safety in the nation today. City police officers vastly outnumber all other state and county law enforcement officers combined. The urban police department does more than merely enforce the law; it engages in a wide range of activities for social control. Police protection is heavier in urban states than rural states (see Figure 8–6).

The Police–Crime Ratio   The total number of police officers nationwide has grown to about 750,000. But the number of officers has *not* kept abreast of crime. On the contrary, the number of police officers relative to the number of reported crimes has declined steadily. This decline is unique to police personnel, as growth in the number of other state and local employees has generally exceeded the growth of their work load.

POLICE AND LAW ENFORCEMENT

Police perform at least three important functions in urban society—law enforcement, keeping the peace, and furnishing services. Actually, law enforcement may take up only a small portion of a police officer's daily activity, perhaps only 10 percent. The service function is far more common—attending accidents, directing traffic, escorting crowds, assisting stranded motorists, handling drunks, and so on. The function of peace keeping is also very common—breaking up fights, quieting noisy parties, handling domestic or neighborhood quarrels, and the like. It is in this function that police exercise the greatest discretion in the application of the law. In most of these incidents blame is difficult to determine, participants are reluctant to file charges, and police must use personal discretion in handling each case.

Police are on the front line of society's efforts to resolve conflict. Indeed, instead of a legal or law enforcement role, the police are more likely to adopt a peace-keeping role. Police are usually lenient in their arrest practices; that is, they use their arrest power less often than the law allows. Rather than arresting people, the police prefer first to reestablish order. Of course, the decision to be more or less lenient in enforcing the law gives the police a great deal of discretion.

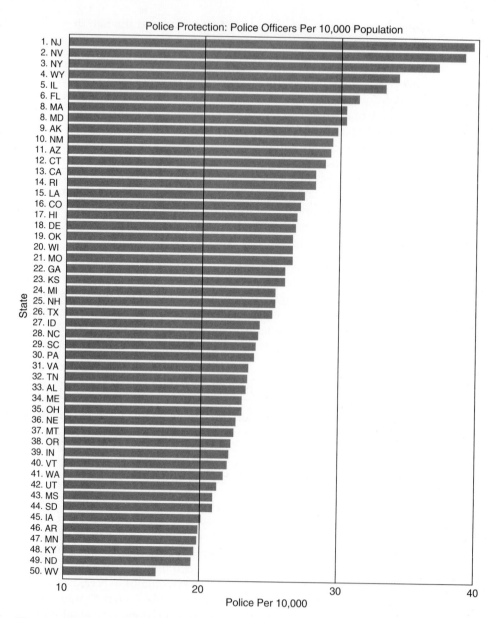

FIGURE 8–6   Police Protection in the States
Source: Statistical Abstract of the United States, 1992.

Police "Culture"   What factors influence police decision making? Probably the first factor to influence police behavior is the attitude of the other people involved in police encounters. If people adopt a cooperative attitude, display deference and respect for the officers, and conform to police expectations, they are much less likely to be arrested than those who show disrespect or use abusive language toward police.[36] One study neatly summarizes *police culture* in terms of attitudes that police bring to the streets.[37]

> People cannot be trusted; they are dangerous.
>
> Experience is better than abstract rules.
>
> You must make people respect you.
>
> Everyone hates a cop.
>
> Police make better decisions about guilt or innocence than courts do.
>
> People who are not controlled will break laws.
>
> Police must appear respectable.
>
> Police can accurately identify criminals.
>
> The major job of police is to prevent crime.
>
> Stronger punishment will deter crime.

Formal police training emphasizes self-control and caution in dealing with the public, but on-the-job experiences probably reinforce predispositions toward distrust of others. The element of danger in police work makes police officers naturally suspicious of others. They see many of the "worst kind" of people, and they see even the "best kind" at their worst.

Police in the Ghetto   The police officer's attitude toward blacks is often affected by the crime rates in ghetto areas. Police officers do not have the time or inclination to dwell on the social conditions associated with crime. Instead, most police officers adopt a working attitude which Jerome Skolnik refers to as the "rotten-apple" view of people: Crime is attributable to the intentions of bad individuals. Skolnik cites one police officer's simple summary: "Poverty doesn't cause crime, people do."[38] This attitude leads the wary police officer to quickly categorize persons on the street who are likely to create a danger to the officer and to society—"suspicious-looking persons"; emaciated persons who appear to be alcoholics or "junkies"; "known troublemakers"; persons who appear to avoid an officer or who are visibly "rattled" by an officer's presence; loiterers near rest rooms, playgrounds, shopping centers, and so forth. Many of these cues are automatically applied to blacks.

If police are overly suspicious of blacks, the attitudes of many ghetto blacks toward police are equally hostile. Black novelist James Baldwin wrote of police in the ghetto:

> Their very presence is an insult, and it would be, even if they spent their entire day feeding gumdrops to children. They represent the force of the white world, and that world's real intentions are simply, to keep the black man corralled up here, in his place. The badge, the gun and the holster and the swinging club make vivid what will happen should his rebellion become overt. . . .

---

[36] Stuart A. Scheingold, "Cultural Cleavage and Criminal Justice," *Journal of Politics,* 40, 865–97.

[37] Peter Manning, "The Police," in *Criminal Justice in America,* ed. Richard Quinney (Boston: Little, Brown, 1974).

[38] Jerome H. Skolnik, *The Politics of Protest* (New York: Ballantine Books, 1969), p. 259.

He has never himself done anything for which to be hated—which of us has? And yet he is facing, daily and nightly, people who would gladly see him dead, and he knows it.[39]

Police and Crime Reduction   Does increased police protection significantly reduce crime? The common assumption is that increased numbers of police officers and increased police expenditures can significantly reduce crime in cities. However, unfortunately, it is very difficult to produce firm evidence to support this assumption.[40] So many other factors may affect crime rates in cities—size, density, youth, unemployment, race, poverty, and so on—that police activity appears insignificant. An increase in police activity may even result in increased crime reporting, which shows up in official statistics as an *increase* in the crime rate.

Police Efficiency   Most crimes are never solved. This is particularly true of property crimes like burglary; these crimes seldom produce eyewitnesses or other useful information. On average across the nation police claim to solve about 14 percent of burglaries; this is their official "clearance rate." But some follow-up studies suggest that the real figure is closer to 5 percent.[41] Police "clear" only about 50 percent of all violent crimes, and 70 percent of murders. (See Table 8–3.) Most clearances occur in cases in which the victim and perpetrators know each other.

Over 12 million people are arrested each year, and many more millions of traffic citations are issued. But even this huge number is less than the 14 million crimes reported to police and the 30 to 40 million crimes estimated from victimization surveys.

TABLE 8–3   CRIME AND ARREST

CRIME	Percent of Crimes Cleared by Arrest	
	1950	1988
Murder	94.0	70.0
Rape	80.0	52.1
Robbery	44.0	25.6
Aggravated Assault	77.0	56.8
Burglary	29.0	13.5
Larceny/Theft	22.0	19.7

Source: Natural Center for Policy Analysis, "Crime Pays, But So Does Imprisonment" Dallas: National Center for Policy Analysis, 1992. Calculated from Federal Bureau of Investigation *Crime in the United States, Uniform Crime Reports,* annual issues (Washington: Government Printing Office).

---

[39] James Baldwin, *Nobody Knows My Name* (New York: Dell, 1962), pp. 61–62.

[40] E. Terrance Jones, "Evaluating Everyday Policies: Police Activity and Crime Incidence," *Urban Affairs Quarterly,* 8 (March 1973), 267–79.

[41] See Wesley G. Skogan, "Crime and Punishment," in Gray, Jacob, and Albritton, *Politics in the American States,* pp. 378–410.

THE POLITICS OF PROSECUTION

Prosecution is also part of the political process. Legislatures and governors enact policy, but its enforcement depends upon the decisions of prosecutors as well as judges. Political pressures are most obvious in the enforcement of controversial policies—gambling laws, Sunday closing laws, liquor rules, laws against prostitution, and other laws that are contrary to the interests of significant segments of the population. Prosecution also involves decision making about the allocation of law enforcement resources to different types of offenses—traffic violations, juvenile delinquency, auto theft, assault, burglary, larceny, and robbery. Decisions must be made about what sections of the city should be most vigorously protected and what segments of the population will be most closely watched. The public prosecutor, sometimes called the district attorney (D.A.) or state's attorney, is at the center of diverse pressures concerning law enforcement.

The political nature of the prosecutor's job is suggested by the frequency with which this job leads to higher political office. Prosecuting attorney is often a steppingstone to state and federal judgeships, congressional seats, and even the governorship. Ambitious D.A.s, concerned with their political future, may seek to build a reputation as a crusader against crime and vice, while at the same time maintaining the support and friendship of important interests in the community.

The political power of prosecutors stems from their discretion in deciding (1) whether or not to prosecute in criminal cases, and (2) whether prosecution will be on more serious or less serious charges. Prosecutors may decide simply to drop charges ("nol-pros") when they feel adequate proof is lacking or when they feel that police have committed a procedural error that infringed on the defendant's rights. Or prosecutors may engage in "plea bargaining"—reducing the charges from more serious to less serious crimes in exchange for defendants' promises to plead guilty. Or prosecutors may reduce charges because they believe it will be easier in court to obtain a guilty verdict on the lesser charge.

Are there any checks on the power of prosecutors? In principle, the *grand jury* is supposed to determine whether evidence presented to it by the prosecutor is sufficient to warrant the placing of a person on trial in a felony case. Ideally, the grand jury serves as a check against the overzealous district attorney, and as a protection for the citizen against unwarranted harassment. However, in practice, grand juries spend very little time deliberating on the vast majority of the cases.[42] A typical grand jury spends only five to ten minutes per case, primarily listening to the prosecutor's recommendation as to how the case should be decided. Over 80 percent of the cases may be decided on an immediate vote, without discussion among jurors, and almost always with unanimous votes. Finally, and most importantly, grand juries follow the recommendations of prosecutors in over 98 percent of the cases presented to them. The prosecutor controls the information submitted to grand

---

[42] The following discussion relies on evidence presented by Robert A. Carp, "The Behavior of Grand Juries: Acquiescence or Justice," *Social Science Quarterly,* 55 (March 1975), 853–70.

juries, instructs them in their duties, and is usually perceived by jurors as an expert and relied on for guidance. In short, there is no evidence that grand juries provide much of a check on the power of prosecutors.

 ## CRIME AND THE COURTS

We often believe that the central dilemma in law enforcement is the conflict between our *commitment to due process*—firmly embedded in the Bill of Rights in the U.S. Constitution—and our *determination to control crime*—through police, prosecution, courts, and prisons. This kind of thinking implies that we are faced with a continuing dilemma between limiting crime and maintaining civil liberty. However, increasingly it appears that *bureaucracy in the criminal justice system* is responsible for problems in both crime control and due process.

Typical problems in criminal courts include:[43]

- Major congestion on court dockets which delays the hearing of cases months or even years. Moreover, actual trials now average twice as long as they did a decade ago.
- Failure of courts to adopt modern management and administration practices to speed and improve justice.
- Increased litigation in the courts. Not only are more Americans aware of their rights, but more are using every avenue of appeal. Seldom do appeals concern the guilt or innocence of the defendant, but usually focus on procedural matters.
- Excessive delays in trials, "Defendants, whether guilty or innocent, are human; they love freedom and hate punishment. With a lawyer provided to secure release without the need for a conventional bail bond, most defendants, except in capital cases, are released pending trial. We should not be surprised that a defendant on bail exerts a heavy pressure on his court-appointed lawyer to postpone the trial as long as possible so as to remain free. These postponements—and sometimes there are a dozen or more—consume the time of judges and court staffs as well as lawyers. Cases are calendared and reset time after time while witnesses and jurors spend endless hours just waiting."
- Excessive delays in appeals. "We should not be surprised at delay when more and more defendants demand their undoubted constitutional right to trial by jury because we have provided them with lawyers and other needs at public expense; nor should we be surprised that most convicted persons seek a new trial when the appeal costs them nothing and when failure to take the appeal will cost them freedom. Being human a defendant plays out the line which society has cast him. Lawyers are competitive creatures and the adversary system encourages contention and often rewards delay; no lawyer wants to be called upon to defend the client's charge of incompetence for having failed to exploit all the procedural techniques which we have deliberately made available."

---

[43] Quotations from Chief Justice Warren E. Burger, address on the State of the Federal Judiciary to the American Bar Association, August 10, 1970.

- Excessive variation in sentencing. Some judges let defendants off on probation for crimes that would draw five-or-ten-year sentences by other judges. While flexibility in sentencing is essential in dealing justly with individuals, perceived inconsistencies damage the image of the courts in the public mind.
- Excessive "plea bargaining" between the prosecution and the defendant's attorney in which the defendant agrees to plead guilty to a lesser offense if the prosecutor will drop more serious charges.

RIGHTS OF DEFENDANTS

The Warren Court—the Supreme Court of the 1950s and 1960s, under the guidance of Chief Justice Earl Warren—greatly strengthened the rights of accused persons in criminal cases. Several key decisions were made by a split vote of the Court and drew heavy criticism from law enforcement officers and others as hamstringing police in their struggle with lawlessness. These decisions included:

Mapp v. *Ohio* (1961). Barring the use of illegally seized evidence in criminal cases in the states by applying the Fourth Amendment guarantee against unreasonable searches and seizures. Even if the evidence seized proves the guilt of the accused, the accused goes free because the police committed a procedural error.

Gideon v. *Wainwright* (1963). Ruling that equal protection under the Fourteenth Amendment requires that free legal counsel be appointed for all indigent defendants in all criminal cases.

Escobedo v. *Illinois* (1964). Ruling that a suspect is entitled to confer with counsel as soon as a police investigation focuses on him once "the process shifts from investigatory to accusatory."

Miranda v. *Arizona* (1966). Requiring that police—before questioning a suspect —must inform him or her of all constitutional rights including the right to counsel, appointed free if necessary, and the right to remain silent. Although the suspect may knowingly waive these rights, the police cannot question anyone who at any point asks for a lawyer or indicates "in any manner" that he or she does not wish to be questioned. If the police commit any error in these procedures, the accused goes free, regardless of the evidence of guilt.

It is difficult to ascertain to what extent these decisions have really hampered efforts to halt the rise in crime in America. The Supreme Court has not extended the rights of accused persons much beyond the Warren Court decisions, nor has it reversed any of these important decisions. Whatever progress is made in law enforcement will therefore have to be made within the current definition of the rights of defendants. It is important to note that most recommendations for judicial reform focus on the speedy administration of justice and not on changes in the rights of defendants.

CRIME AND DETERRENCE

Can punishment deter crime? This is a difficult question to answer. First of all, we must distinguish between *deterrence* and *incapacity*. *Incapacity* can be imposed by long terms of imprisonment, particularly for habitual offenders; the policy of "keeping criminals off the streets" does indeed protect the public for a period of time, although it is done at a considerable cost. The object of *deterrence* is to make the certainty and severity of punishment so great as to inhibit potential criminals from committing crimes.

Deterrence Theory   In theory, deterrence is enhanced by:

1. The *certainty* that a crime will be followed by costly punishment. Justice must be sure.
2. The *swiftness* of the punishment following the crime. Long delays between crime and punishment break the link in the mind of the criminal between the criminal act and its consequences. And a potential wrong-doer must believe that the costs of a crime will occur within a meaningful time frame, not in a distant, unknowable future. Justice must be swift.
3. The *severity* of the punishment. Punishment that is perceived as no more costly than the ordinary hazards of life on the streets which the potential criminal faces anyhow will not deter. Punishment must clearly outweigh whatever benefits might be derived from a life of crime in the mind of potential criminals. Punishment must be severe.

These criteria for an effective deterrent policy are ranked in the order of their probable importance. That is, it is most important that punishment for crime be certain. The severity of punishment is probably less important than its swiftness or certainty.[44]

An Economic View of Crime   Economists view crime as a product of rational calculations by people of the expected benefits and expected costs of their criminal acts. The reason we have so much crime is that crime pays—its benefits outweigh its costs. Economists believe that if you increase the cost of something (crime), less of it will be consumed (there will be fewer crimes). Their own studies confirm the deterrent effect of both the certainty and severity of punishment. Economist Gordon Tullock dismisses the notion that "crimes of passion" cannot be reduced by increasing the certainty and severity of punishment:

> The prisoners in Nazi concentration camps must frequently have been in a state of well-justified rage against some of their guards; yet this almost never led to their using violence against the guards, because punishment—which if they were lucky, would mean instant death, but was more likely to be death by torture—was so obvious and certain.[45]

Tullock argues that to increase the deterrent effect of punishment, potential criminals must be given information about it. Indeed, he suggests, governments

---

[44] See Maynard L. Erikson and Jack P. Gibbs, "The Deterrence Question," *Social Science Quarterly,* 54 (December 1973), 534–51; Jack P. Gibbs, "Crime, Punishment, and Deterrence," *Social Science Quarterly,* 48 (March 1968), 515–30; and Maynard L. Erikson and Jack P. Gibbs, "Specific versus General Properties of Legal Punishments and Deterrence," *Social Science Quarterly,* 56 (December 1975), 390–97.

[45] See Gordon Tullock, "Does Punishment Deter Crime?" *The Public Interest* (Summer 1974), 11.

might even lie—that is, pretend that punishment is more certain and severe than it is—in order to reduce crime.

Current Policies Do Not Deter However, virtually all social scientists agree that the current system of criminal justice in America is *not* a serious deterrent to crime. Punishment for crime is neither certain, swift, nor severe. Indeed, the criminal justice system itself, by failing to deter crime, is principally responsible for the fact that *crime in the United States is more common than in any other advanced industrial nation of the world.*

The best available estimates of the *certainty* of punishment for serious crime suggest that very few crimes actually result in jail sentences for the perpetrators. About 14 million serious crimes were reported to police in 1988; but only 2.3 million persons were arrested for these crimes (see Figure 8–7). Some of those arrested were charged with committing more than one crime, but it is estimated that police clear less than 20 percent of reported crimes by arresting the offender. Prosecutors do not charge about half of the persons arrested for serious offenses. Some offenders are handled as juveniles; some are permitted to plead guilty to minor offenses; others are released because witnesses fail to appear or evidence is weak or inadmissible in court. Of the persons charged with serious offenses by prosecutors, fewer than 20 percent receive jail sentences for their crimes. Convicted felons are three times more likely to receive probation instead of a prison sentence. Thus, even if punishment could deter crime, our current criminal justice system does *not* ensure punishment for crime.

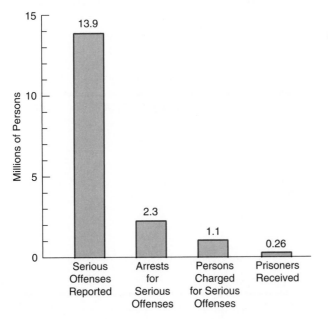

FIGURE 8–7 Crime and Punishment

Source: Statistical Abstract of the United States, 1991, pp. 176, 183, 193.

Social Heterogeneity Theory   Of course, there are many other conflicting theories of crime in America. For example, it is sometimes argued that this nation's high crime rate is a product of its social heterogeneity—the multiethnic, multiracial character of the American population. Low levels of crime in European countries, Japan, and China are often attributed to their homogeneous populations and shared cultures. Blacks in the United States are both victims and perpetrators of crime far more frequently than whites. While blacks constitute only about 12 percent of the population, they account for almost 30 percent of all of persons arrested for serious crimes (see Table 8–4). A larger segment of the black population is in the young crime-prone age (fifteen to twenty-four years), and these youths are more likely to live outside husband–wife families. It is argued that "the streets" of the nation's black inner cities produce a subculture that encourages crime.

"Crime of Passion" Theory   It is also argued that crime is irrational, that is, the criminal does not weigh benefits against potential costs before committing the act. Many acts of violence are committed by persons acting in blind rage—murders and aggravated assaults among family members, for example. Many rapes are acts of violence, inspired by hatred of women, rather than efforts to obtain sexual pleasure. More murders occur in the heat of arguments than in the commission of other felonies. These are crimes of passion rather than calculated acts. Thus, it is argued, no rational policies can be devised to deter these irrational acts.

Protecting Individual Liberty   Finally, we must recognize that the reduction of crime is not the overriding value of American society. Americans cherish individual liberty. Freedom from repression—from unlawful arrests, forced confession, restrictions on movement, curfews, arbitrary police actions, unlimited searching of homes or seizures of property, punishment without trial, trials without juries, unfair procedures, brutal punishments—is more important to Americans than freedom from crime. Many authoritarian governments boast of low crime rates and

TABLE 8–4   ARRESTS BY AGE, SEX, AND RACE

Percent of Total Arrests (1990)	
Male	81.6
Female	18.4
White	69.2
Black	28.9
Native American, Asian, other	1.9
Under 18	15.6
18–24	30.1
25–34	32.1
35–44	14.9
45–54	4.9
55 and over	2.5

Source: Sourcebook of Criminal Justice Statistics, 1992.

criminal justice systems that ensure certain, swift, and severe punishment, but these governments fail to protect the personal liberties of their citizens.

STATE PRISONS AND CORRECTIONAL POLICIES

The United States has experienced an explosive growth in its prison population in recent years. Over 8 million Americans each year are brought to a jail, police station, or juvenile home or prison. The vast majority are released within hours or days. There are, however, nearly a million inmates in state and federal prisons in the United States. These prisoners are serving time for serious offenses. Ninety percent had a record of crime before they committed the act that led to their current imprisonment. The rate of incarceration (prisoners per 100,000 population) in the United States is one of the highest in the world.

Why are so many people behind bars? Because they have committed so many crimes. The crime rate in the United States is also one of the highest in the world. Indeed, the number of prisoners in the United States *relative to the numbers of crimes* is no higher than in other industrialized nations.

Prisoners in the States   States differ a great deal in the number of prisoners and the proportion of their populations behind bars. (See Figures 8–8 and 8–9.) As might be expected, prisoner populations generally reflect the crime rate in the states; higher crime rate states have larger proportions of their population in prison.

Another cause of increased prison populations in the states is an increase in the length of criminal sentences. Throughout the 1980s many states attempted to "get tough on crime" by legislating longer sentences for particular crimes, specifying mandatory minimum sentences for crimes, eliminating judicial variation in sentences, adding years to the sentences given repeat or "habitual" criminals, and abolishing parole.

FIGURE 8–8   Growth in Prison Population

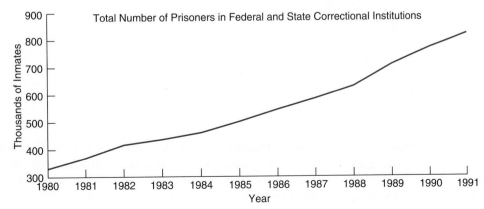

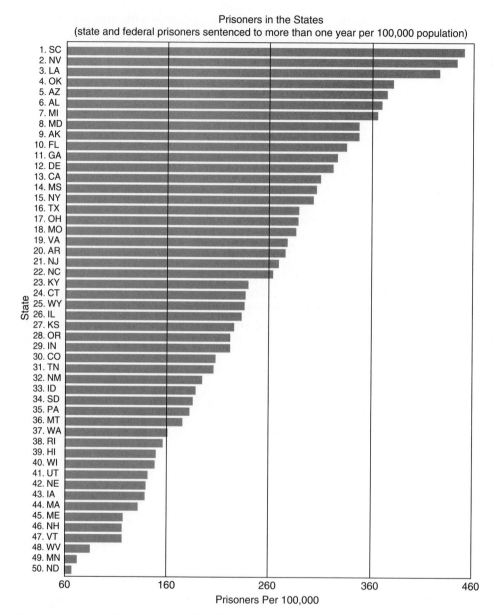

FIGURE 8–9   Prisoners in the States
Source: Statistical Abstract of the United States, 1992.

The Failure of Rehabilitation   For many years the prevailing philosophy in corrections was that of rehabilitation. In deciding sentences judges were free to consider not only the crime, but personal characteristics of the defendant. State criminal codes stated broad ranges of sentences for various crimes, for example, two to ten years. Moreover, judges in many states had the option of imposing "indeterminant" sentences (e.g., not less than one nor more than five years) and leaving the decision concerning how long a prisoner would serve to parole boards. While in prison, individuals were expected to "rehabilitate" themselves through education, job training, counseling, and other programs. Prisons were called "correctional institutions" to reflect their therapeutic value.

Over time it became increasingly difficult to maintain the fiction that prisons were designed to rehabilitate people. Eighty percent of all felonies are committed by repeaters—individuals who have had prior contact with the criminal justice system and were not corrected by it.[46] Penologists generally recommend more education and job training, more and better facilities, smaller prisons, halfway houses where offenders can adjust to civilian life before parole, more parole officers, and greater contact between prisoners and their families and friends. But as Daniel Glaser points out: "Unfortunately there is no convincing evidence that this investment reduces what criminologists call 'recidivism,' the offenders' return to crime."[47] In short, there is no evidence that people *can* be "rehabilitated," no matter what is done. Even the maintenance of order *within* prisons and the protection of the lives of guards and inmates have become serious national problems.

Prison life does little to encourage good behavior. "For the most part, the nation's adult and juvenile inmates spend their days in idleness punctuated by meals, violence, and weight lifting. Meaningful educational, vocational, and counseling programs are rare. Strong inmates are permitted to pressure weaker prisoners for sex, drugs, and money. Gangs organized along racial and ethnic lines are often the real 'sovereign of the cellblocks.'"[48]

Deterrence and Incapacitation   At least two other theories of punishment have competed with rehabilitation in guiding the criminal justice system. We have already described the theory of deterrence—punishment should be certain, swift, and severe, and it should be known and predictable. Clearly indeterminant sentencing and discretion given parole boards does *not* serve the goal of deterrence. Rather deterrence is served by making prison sentences predictable (certain) and long (severe). Potential law breakers are supposed to say to themselves, "If you can't serve the time, don't do the crime." Throughout the 1980s states enacted amendments to their criminal codes specifying *determinant sentences* for various crimes. The discretion of judges was restricted. Variation in sentencing was reduced (although not eliminated); judges were obliged by law to mete out sentences based on the crime and the number of previous convictions amassed by the defendant. Greater uniformity of sentencing also served the goal of reducing arbitrary, unfair, and discriminatory sentencing. For many crimes, deterrence was also strengthened by long *mandatory minimum* sentences. For example, many states enacted mandatory one-, two-, or three-year prison terms for the use of a gun in the commission of a felony.

---

[46] See Congressional Quarterly, *Crime and the Law* (Washington, DC: Congressional Quarterly Inc., 1971), p. 11.

[47] Daniel Glaser, *Effectiveness of a Prison and Parole System* (New York: Bobbs-Merill, 1969), p. 4.

[48] John J. DiIulio, Jr., "Punishing Smarter," *Brookings Review* (Summer 1989), 8.

Prison Overcrowding   But the effect of longer sentences, combined with higher crime rates and more prisoners, has been to create mammoth prison overcrowding. Overcrowding contributes directly to unsanitary and dangerous prison living conditions; overcrowding is associated with assaults, rapes, homicides, suicides, and riots. Prison staff are also placed at risk by overcrowding and the violence it produces.

Federal courts have determined that prison overcrowding is a violation of the U.S. Constitution's Eighth Amendment prohibition against "cruel and unusual punishments." (Simple crowding per se is not unconstitutional; federal courts must also find evidence of adverse effects of overcrowding.) Virtually all of the states confront federal court orders to reduce prison overcrowding at one or more of their prisons or their entire prison system. Most state prison system are near, at, or over their capacity to house prisoners

Early Releases   As a result of overcrowding, most states have had to resort to *early release* programs. Sentences of prisoners are automatically reduced and those near the end of their terms are let go first. Some states deny early release to certain violent offenders. Nonetheless, violent criminals on the average serve only half of their sentences, and nonviolent offenders less than one-third of their sentences. In some states, due to prison overcrowding, inmates serve only one-quarter of their sentences. In many states, early release programs have become institutionalized. The national average prison time actually served by convicted murderers is six years.[49]

Thus, the criminal justice system does not succeed in incapacitating criminals for very long. Indeed, it is estimated that about 20 percent of all violent crimes and 30 percent of property crimes are committed by *persons who would still have been in prison on an earlier conviction if they had served their full sentence.*[50] These "avertable" crimes are increasing over time as early release is used more and more to relieve prison overcrowding.

Building More Prisons   States have been compelled to build more prisons in recent years. But taxpayers are understandably upset with the prospects of spending $50,000 to $75,000 for each new prison bed, and $10,000 to $15,000 per year to keep a prisoner behind bars. But if the costs of incarceration are weighed against its benefits, taxpayers may feel better about prison construction and maintenance. A prisoner's "rap sheet" may list only three or four convictions and a dozen arrests. But interviews with offenders suggest the typical convict has committed hundreds of crimes. Various studies have attempted to estimate the dollars lost to society in the crimes committed by the typical convict in a year.[51] Estimates run from $200,000 to $400,000. This means that a year of crime may be ten to twenty times more costly to society than a year of incarceration.

---

[49] Richard B. Abell "Beyond Willie Horton: The Battle of the Prison Bulge," *Policy Review,* 47 (Winter 1989), 32–35.

[50] John J. DiIulio, Jr., "Punishing Smarter," *Brookings Review* (Summer 1989), 3–12.

[51] See Abell, "Beyond Willie Horton," pp. 32–35.

Efforts are now underway in many states to lower the cost of prison facilities. Not all prisoners need to be housed in maximum security institutions; nonviolent criminals can be safely housed in less costly minimum security facilities. "Privatization" can also dramatically lower the costs of maintaining prisoners. States and counties can contract with private companies to both build and maintain prisons at much lower costs than government itself requires to perform these functions. Moreover, initial evaluations suggest that conditions in private prisons are much better than in government prisons. Indeed, even the prisoners prefer privately run prisons.

The Failure of Probation and Parole   In addition to the nearly 1 million people behind bars, an additional 2 million are currently on probation or parole for serious crimes. But probation has been just as ineffective as prison in reducing crime. Even though persons placed on probation are considered less dangerous to society than persons imprisoned, studies indicate that nearly two-thirds of probationers will be arrested and over one-half will be convicted for a serious crime committed *while on probation.*

The function of parole and postrelease supervision is (1) to procure information on the parolee's postprison conduct and (2) to facilitate and graduate the transition between the prison and complete freedom. These functions are presumably oriented toward protecting the public and rehabilitating the offender. However, studies of recidivism indicate that up to three-quarters of persons paroled from prison will be rearrested for serious crimes. There is no difference in this high rate of recidivism between persons released under supervised parole and those released unconditionally. Thus, it does not appear that parole succeeds in its objectives.

THE DEATH PENALTY

One of the more heated debates in correctional policy today concerns capital punishment. Opponents of the death penalty argue that it is "cruel and unusual punishment" in violation of the Eighth Amendment of the U.S. Constitution. They also argue that the death penalty is applied unequally. A large proportion of those executed have been poor, uneducated, and nonwhite.

In contrast, there is a strong sense of justice among many Americans that demands retribution for heinous crimes—a life for a life. The death penalty dramatically signifies that society does not excuse or condone the taking of innocent lives. It symbolizes the value that society places on innocent lives. A mere jail sentence for murder devalues the life of the innocent victim. In most cases, a life sentence means less than ten years in prison under the current parole and probation policies of most states. Convicted murderers have been set free, and some have killed again. Moreover, prison guards and other inmates are exposed to convicted murderers who have "a license to kill," because they are already serving life sentences and have nothing to lose by killing again.

***Furman* v. *Georgia* and Unfair Application**   Prior to 1972, the death penalty was officially sanctioned by about half of the states. Federal law also retained the death penalty. However, no one had actually suffered the death penalty since 1967, because of numerous legal tangles and direct challenges to the constitutionality of capital punishment. In 1972, the Supreme Court ruled that capital punishment *as it was then imposed* violated the Eighth and Fourteenth Amendment prohibitions against cruel and unusual punishment and due process of law. The decision was made by a narrow 5–4 vote of the justices, and the reasoning in the case is very complex. Only two justices—Brennan and Marshall—declared that capital punishment itself is cruel and unusual. The other three justices in the majority—Douglas, White, and Stewart—felt that death sentences had been applied unfairly: A few individuals were receiving the death penalty for crimes for which many others were receiving much lighter sentences. These justices left open the possibility that capital punishment would be constitutional if it was specified for certain kinds of crime and applied uniformly.

The Death Penalty Reinstated   After *Furman* v. *Georgia,* most states rewrote their death-penalty laws to try to ensure fairness and uniformity of application.[52] Generally, these laws mandate the death penalty for murders committed during rape or robbery, hijacking or kidnapping; murders of prison guards; murder with torture; multiple murders; and so on. Two trials would be held: one to determine guilt or innocence and another to determine the penalty. At the second trial, evidence of "aggravating" and "mitigating" factors would be presented; if there were aggravating factors but no mitigating factors, the death penalty would be mandatory. In 1976, in *Gregs* v. *Georgia, Profit* v. *Florida,* and *Jurek* v. *Texas,* the Supreme Court upheld state laws that were carefully written to ensure fairness and due process in the application of the death penalty. The Court declared that capital punishment itself was not "cruel or unusual" within the meaning of the Eighth Amendment; that the authors of the Constitution did not consider it cruel or unusual; and that the reenactment of the death penalty by so many state legislators was evidence that the death penalty was not considered cruel or unusual by contemporary state lawmakers.

Few Executions   Despite these new laws, very few executions have been carried out. Over 2000 prisoners are awaiting execution on "death row" but fewer than 150 persons were executed in thirteen states through 1992 (Texas, Florida, Georgia, Louisiana, Virginia, North Carolina, Alabama, Indiana, Nevada, South Carolina, Missouri, Mississippi, Utah).

The reluctance of federal courts to permit executions has effectively curtailed the death penalty for all but a few unlucky individuals. Endless delays and court-ordered "stays" of execution have effectively reversed the decisions of state legislatures and state courts. With less than 1 percent of death sentences actually carried

---

[52] States *with* death penalty: Alabama, Arizona, Arkansas, California, Colorado, Connecticut, Delaware, Florida, Georgia, Idaho, Illinois, Indiana, Kentucky, Louisiana, Maryland, Mississippi, Missouri, Montana, Nebraska, Nevada, New Hampshire, New Jersey, New Mexico, North Carolina, Ohio, Oregon, Oklahoma, Pennsylvania, South Carolina, South Dakota, Tennessee, Texas, Utah, Vermont, Virginia, Washington, and Wyoming. States with *no* death penalty: Alaska, Hawaii, Iowa, Kansas, Maine, Massachusetts, Michigan, Minnesota, New York, North Dakota, Rhode Island, West Virginia, Wisconsin, and the District of Columbia. As of 1990.

out over the past decade, the death penalty cannot possibly be a deterrent to murder. Respect for the court system is eroded when the decisions of juries and judges are frustrated by convicted murderers.

The strategy of death row prisoners and their lawyers, of course, is to delay indefinitely the imposition of the death penalty with endless stays and appeals. So far the strategy has been successful for all but a few murderers. As trial judges and juries continue to impose the death penalty, and appellate courts continue to grant stays of execution, the number of prisoners on death row grows. The few who have been executed have averaged ten years' delay between trial and execution.

Racial Bias?   The U.S. Supreme Court is especially sensitive to arguments based on racial discrimination. Defense lawyers have challenged the death penalty in several states by attempting to prove that racial bias infects the application of capital punishment. While white murderers are just as likely to receive the death penalty as black murderers, there are statistical disparities in sentencing between killers of whites and killers of blacks. If the *victim* is white, there is a greater chance that the killer will be sentenced to death than if the victim is black. But in 1987 the U.S. Supreme Court ruled (in a 5–4 decision) that statistical disparities in the race of the victim do not by themselves bar the death penalty; there must be evidence of racial bias against a particular defendant in order for the Court to reverse a death sentence.[53]

Does the Death Penalty Deter?   The death penalty as it is employed today—inflicted on so few and so many years after the crime—has little deterrent effect. However, it gives prosecutors some leverage in plea bargaining with murder defendants. They may choose to plead guilty in exchange for a life sentence, when confronted with the possibility that the prosecutor may win a conviction and the death penalty in a jury trial.

Public Opinion and Capital Punishment   Much of the debate in the states over the death penalty, however, has *not* centered on the question of deterrence. Opponents of the death penalty call it "murder" and contend that it is morally indefensible for the state to take away life. Proponents of the death penalty say that the unwillingness of the state to impose capital punishment implies that little value is placed upon the lives of innocent victims. Public opinion now favors the death penalty by over 3 to 1. Only for a few years during the mid-1960s did public opinion oppose the death penalty, and then only by a small margin. With increases in the crime rate in the 1970s, heavy majorities swung back in favor of capital punishment. Public support for capital punishment remains high today.

---

[53] *McCluskey v. Kemp* 481 U.S. 279 (1987).

9

COMMUNITY POLITICAL SYSTEMS

▲

COMMUNITIES AS SETTINGS FOR POLITICS

American communities come in different shapes and sizes, and community politics come in a variety of styles. Generalizing about community politics is perhaps even more difficult than generalizing about American state politics. There are more than 86,000 local governments in the United States. These include cities, municipalities, townships, counties, and a host of other school districts and special districts. (See Table 9–1.) Two-thirds of the American people live in urban units of local government known as "municipalities," including "cities," "boroughs," "villages," or "towns." Other Americans are served by county or township governments. Moreover, there were 268 metropolitan areas in the United States in 1990, these are clusterings of people and governments around a core city of 50,000 or more residents. These metropolitan areas range in size up to the New York area, which has 600 local governments and 18 million people. In short, one may conceive of community political systems as rural counties, towns, and villages, cities of all sizes, or even sprawling metropolitan areas.

Community political systems serve two principal functions. One is that of supplying goods and services—for example, police protection or sewage disposal

TABLE 9–1   LOCAL GOVERNMENTS IN THE UNITED STATES

	1952	1962	1972	1982	1987	1992
Counties	3,052	3,043	3,044	3,041	3,042	3,043
Municipalities	16,807	17,997	18,517	19,076	19,200	19,296
Townships	17,202	17,144	16,991	16,734	16,691	16,666
School districts	67,355	34,678	15,781	14,851	14,721	14,586
Special districts	12,340	18,323	23,885	28,588	29,532	33,131
Total (including States and National Government)	116,756	91,185	78,269	82,341	83,186	86,743

Source: U.S. Bureau of the Census, *Census of Government, 1992.*

—that are not supplied by private enterprise. This is the "service" function. The other function is the "political" one, that of *managing conflict* over public policy. Of course, the "political" and the "service" functions of local governments are often indistinguishable in practice. A mayor who intervenes in a dispute about the location of a park is managing a local government service, namely recreation, at the same time that he or she is managing political conflict about whose neighborhood should get the most benefit from the new park. In the day-to-day administration of the service functions of local government, officials must decide a variety of political questions. Where are the facilities to be located? (Often the question is where *not* to locate facilities, since many neighborhoods avoid having public facilities for fear that they will displace families, attract "undesirables," or depress local property values.) How are public services to be paid for? Which agency or official will be in charge of a particular service? What policies or practices will govern the provision of this service? What level of service will be provided?

Occasionally, students are led to believe that local governments should be less "political" than state or national governments. Many people feel that it would be best to eliminate "politics" from local government. Historically, this attitude arose in conjunction with the municipal reform movement of the Progressive Era.[1] The reform movement involved a preference for nonpartisan elections, city-manager government, and an "antiseptic" style of local government, devoid of the stigma of "politics." A city without politics appealed to many idealists who were disenchanted with boss rule. However, politicians who respond to political considerations, in contrast to service considerations, are not necessarily sacrificing the welfare of their community. It is not necessarily true that the community is best served by treating the service function of government as if it were more important or more worthy of government attention than the political one. A politician who undertakes to arrange political compromises and balance competing interests in a community is performing a very important function. Helping people with different incomes, occupations, skin colors, religious beliefs, and styles of living to live together in a reasonably peaceful fashion is a vital task.

---

[1] See Richard Hofstadter, *The Age of Reform* (New York: Knopf, 1955); and Lorin Peterson, *The Day of the Mugwump* (New York: Random House, 1961.)

COPING WITH COMMUNITY CONFLICT

Government is best suited for managing *conventional* community conflicts—the adoption of the municipal budget, the periodic election of municipal officials, requests for rezoning, or complaints about municipal services. However, the real test of a political system's capacity to manage conflict occurs with the rise of *rancorous* conflict—street rioting, disruption over sex education, racial disputes, charges of police brutality, religious objections to school textbooks, and other emotionally charged issues. The distinction between conventional and rancorous conflict is based on the *intensity* of feelings aroused in the community, and not necessarily on the nature of the issue. Just as American communities come in different shapes and sizes, so do the conflicts that convulse their governments.

Sources of Conflict   What are the sources of community conflicts? Human diversity is the source of all political conflict—differences among people in wealth, occupation, education, ethnicity, race, religion, and style of living. In the United States, there are many rural communities, small towns and cities, and compact suburbs with very homogeneous populations. In these communities, there are few differences among citizens that create permanent lines of cleavage and none that run very deep. Some conflicts occur in these communities, of course, even rancorous ones, but groupings of forces are temporary. In contrast, in most large cities and metropolitan areas there are many different kinds of people living closely together, and there are more lasting cleavages, or "fault lines," which tend to open when controversial issues arise. These cleavages are readily recognized in disputes among upper-, middle-, and lower-income groups; races and ethnic groups; labor and management interests; property owners and nonproperty owners; families with children and those without; suburbanites and city dwellers; and traditional political party divisions.[2]

Coping with Dissatisfaction   How do individuals cope with community problems? If you are dissatisfied with the way things are going in your community, you have three choices: (1) resign yourself to the situation, do nothing, and just tolerate it; (2) move away and find a community that provides more satisfactions; (3) stay and make an attempt to change things. Political scientists tend to focus their attention on the people who try to change things, implying that this is the only way to respond rationally to community problems. However, economists have developed theories of residential mobility that focus on the individual's choice of community based on a rational calculation of personal costs and benefits.[3] (The theory is most applicable to metropolitan areas where many different kinds of communities are

---

[2] For some empirical support for these speculations, see Gordon S. Black, "Conflict in the Community: A Theory of the Effect of Community Size," *American Political Science Review,* 68 (September 1974), 1245–61; see also Timothy A. Almy, "Residential Locations and Electoral Cohesion," *American Political Science Review,* 67 (September 1973), 914–23, who argues that conflict is greater in communities where different social groups are residentially segregated.

[3] The widely cited source is Charles M. Tiebout, "The Pure Theory of Local Expenditure" *Journal of Political Economy,* 64 (October 1956), 416–24.

available.) There are recognized negative "push" factors—crime, congestion, noise, overcrowding, racial conflict—and positive "pull" factors—more space, larger houses, better schools, "nice" playmates for the children—both of which affect decisions to move. One might move to the suburbs "for the kids," or move to the city to be close to good restaurants, fine entertainment, cultural events, and specialty shops, or to reduce the trip to work. One can choose among suburbs by balancing residential amenities and services against land costs and taxes. In short, economists emphasize rational calculations and freedom of choice, which they assume most citizens possess.

Political scientists deal with the participants in urban politics, sometimes implying that nonparticipation or apathy is irrational, perhaps even unpatriotic. However, apathy *is* rational if the costs of organizing and mobilizing political support are high, and if the majority favors something you oppose. Furthermore, "moving out" may not always be possible—particularly for poor people, blacks, and the aged. Thus, apathy is rational if any other kind of action is a waste of time, energy, and money and is very unlikely to bring about significant change.

How do people actually respond to community dissatisfactions? There is some evidence to suggest that, in the face of community problems:[4]

1. Higher-status whites tend either to become politically active or to move out, with political activity somewhat more common.
2. Lower-status whites tend to move out rather than become politically active.
3. Blacks are more likely to become politically active than to move out, probably because of the increased difficulties most blacks face in residential relocation.
4. City residents are more likely to move out, whereas suburbanites are more likely to become politically active.

Additional evidence suggests that[5]

5. People who have been generally satisfied with the past performance of their local government, as well as people who have invested in home ownership or local businesses, are more likely to become politically active to solve a current problem, rather than to move out or do nothing.
6. Dissatisfied affluent residents may chose to "privatize" the community services that distress them. The most common example is the choice of private schools over the public school system, but occasionally residents and businesses also turn to private police protection, security services, garbage collection, and so on.

Overall, the tendency to "move away" from urban problems has greatly accentuated the difficulties of the nation's largest central cities. Many of these cities are actually declining in population—losing middle-class residents to their surround-

---

4 John M. Orbell and Toru Uno, "A Theory of Neighborhood Problem Solving: Political Action versus Residential Mobility," *American Political Science Review,* 66 (June 1972), 471–89.

5 For an extended discussion of this topic see William E. Lyons and David Lowery, "Citizen Response to Dissatisfaction in Urban Communities," *Journal of Politics,* 51 (November 1989), 841–68.

ing suburbs. We will return to this problem in Chapter 12, but it is important to know how individual citizens as well as governments cope with community problems.

EIGHTY-SIX THOUSAND GOVERNMENTS: WHAT THEY ALL DO

Local government is not mentioned in the U.S. Constitution. Although we regard the American federal system as a mixture of federal, state, and *local* governments, from a constitutional point of view, local governments are really parts of state governments. Communities have no right to self-government in the U.S. Constitution. All of their governmental powers legally flow from state laws and constitutions. Local governments—cities, townships, counties, special districts, and school districts—are creatures of the states, subject to the obligations, privileges, powers, and restrictions that state governments impose upon them. The state may create or destroy any or all units of local government. To the extent that local governments can collect taxes, regulate their citizens, and provide services, they are actually exercising *state* powers delegated to them by the state in either its constitution or its laws.

Different units of government are assigned different responsibilities by each of the states, so it is difficult to generalize about what each of these types of local governments is supposed to do. Indeed, even in the same state, there may be overlapping functions and responsibilities assigned to cities, counties, school districts, and special districts. Nevertheless, let us try to make some generalizations about what each of these types of government does, realizing of course that in any specific location the pattern of governmental activity may be slightly different:

Counties

—Rural: keep records of deeds, mortgages, births, marriages; assess and levy property taxes; maintain local roads; administer elections and certify election results to state; provide law enforcement through sheriff; maintain criminal court; maintain a local jail; administer state welfare programs.

—Urban: most of same functions as rural counties (except police and court systems which often become city functions), together with planning and control of new subdivisions; mental health; public health maintenance and public hospitals; care of the aged; recreation, including parks, stadiums, and convention centers; and perhaps some city functions.

Cities

—provide the "common functions" of police, fire, streets, sewage, sanitation, and parks; over half of the nation's large cities also provide welfare services and public education. (In other cities welfare is handled by county governments or directly by state agencies, and education is handled by separate school districts.)

School districts

—organized specifically to provide public elementary and secondary education; community colleges may be operated by county governments or by special districts with or without state support.

Townships

—generally subdivisions of counties with the same responsibilities as their county.

Special districts

—may be as large as the Port Authority of New York and New Jersey with billions in diversified assets. However, special districts are usually established for mass transit, soil conservation, libraries, water and irrigation, mosquito control, sewage disposal, airports, and so on.

The fifty states vary a great deal in the numbers of local governments they authorize. (See Figure 9–1.) Hawaii is the nation's most centralized state: There are only eighteen local governments in the Aloha State; fourteen of these are special districts without taxing power; three are counties; and one is the city of Honolulu. In contrast, there are 6627 local governments in Illinois, including 1279 cities, 102 counties, 1434 townships, 1029 school districts, and 2783 special districts.

COUNTY GOVERNMENTS: RURAL AND URBAN

All states, with the exception of Connecticut and Rhode Island, have organized *county* governments. In Louisiana, counties are called "parishes," and in Alaska they are called "boroughs." It is difficult to generalize about the powers of the nation's 3042 counties. The legal powers, organization, and officers of counties vary a great deal. Perhaps it would be best to begin a description of county government by distinguishing between *rural* and *urban* counties. Obviously there is a great deal of difference between Los Angeles County with 8.5 million people; Cook County, Chicago, with 5.2 million; and Harris County, Houston, with 2.8 million; and the 725 rural counties in the nation with populations of 10,000 or less.

Rural Counties   Traditionally, the rural county was the most important unit of local government: It handled such essential matters as law enforcement, courts, schools, roads, elections, poor relief, and the legal recording of property deeds, mortgages, wills, and marriages. Rural communities competed with each other for the location of the county seat, because the community named as county seat won social and political prestige, county jobs, a county fair, and preferential treatment in county roads and public buildings. Moreover, many rural dwellers identify themselves as "coming from" a particular county. The county seat attracted retail business: Farm markets were generally located in county seats, where a farmer could transact both public and private business. Rural county government provided an arena for a folksy, provincial, individualistic, "friends and neighbors" type of politics. Rural county government was the province of amateurs rather than experts or professionals. Decision making was personalized and informal. Often rural counties resemble urban counties about as much as the old-fashioned country store resembles a modern supermarket.

Urban Counties   County government in urban areas is acquiring many of the responsibilities of city governments. Urban counties may provide traditional "city services" to the unincorporated areas of the county, that is, to the areas not within

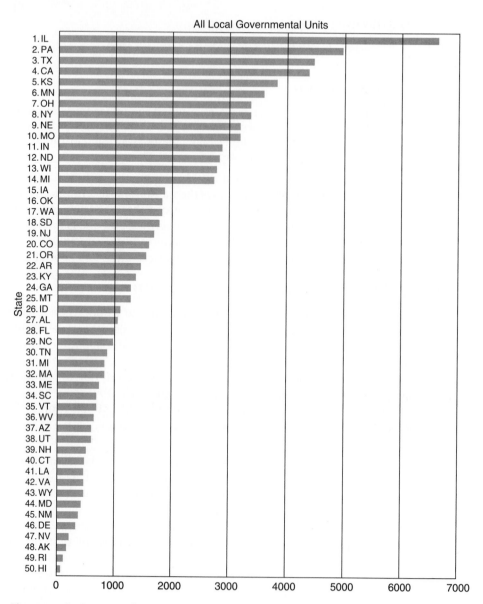

FIGURE 9–1   Local Governments in the States

Source: Statistical Abstract of the United States, 1992, p. 296.

the boundaries of cities, and occasionally to cities as well. This is particularly true of the county governments located in large metropolitan areas (see Table 9–2). Urban county governments generally provide all of the services of traditional rural counties together with a host of additional contemporary government services, from mass transit facilities and airports to sports stadiums and convention centers (see Table 9–3).

TABLE 9–2   URBAN COUNTIES OF ONE MILLION OR MORE PERSONS

County	Population (Millions)
Arizona	
Maricopa (Phoenix)	2.0
California	
Alameda (Oakland and Berkeley)	1.2
Los Angeles	8.6
Orange (South of Los Angeles)	2.3
San Diego	2.4
Santa Clara (San Jose)	1.4
Florida	
Broward (Ft. Lauderdale)	1.2
Dade (Miami)	1.8
Illinois	
Cook (Chicago)	5.3
Michigan	
Oakland (North of Detroit)	1.1
Wayne (Detroit)	2.1
Minnesota	
Hennepin (Minneapolis)	1.0
Missouri	
St. Louis	1.0
New York	
Bronx (part of New York City)	1.2
Kings (part of New York City)	2.3
Nassau (part of New York City)	1.3
New York (part of New York City)	1.5
Queens (part of New York City)	1.9
Suffolk (part of New York City)	1.3
Ohio	
Cuyahoga (Cleveland)	1.4
Pennsylvania	
Alleghenny (Pittsburgh)	1.4
Philadelphia	1.6
Texas	
Bexar (San Antonio)	1.2
Dallas	1.9
Harris (Houston)	2.8
Tarrant (Fort Worth)	1.1
Washington	
King (Seattle)	1.4

Source: U.S. Bureau of the Census.

TABLE 9–3   COUNTY FUNCTIONS

Traditional, Rural	Contemporary, Urban
Property tax assessment and collection	Mass transit
Election administration	Airports
Judicial administration, including civil and criminal courts, probate, etc.	Libraries
	Water supply and sewage disposal
Recording of deeds, mortgages, and other legal instruments	Water and air pollution control
	Building and housing code enforcement
Recording of vital statistics, including births, deaths, and marriages	Natural resource preservation
	Planning and land use control
Local roads and bridges, construction and maintenance	Community development and housing
	Parks and recreation
Law enforcement (sheriff and coroner)	Stadiums, convention and cultural centers
County jail maintenance	Public health, including clinics
Administer state welfare and social service programs	Public hospitals
	Disaster preparedness together with traditional functions
Other: county fairs, agricultural extension service	

THE STRUCTURE OF COUNTY GOVERNMENT

Although county governments may differ markedly in their organization, they generally have (1) a governing body variously called the "county commissioners," "county board," "board of supervisors," or even "judges," which is composed of anywhere from three to fifty elected members; (2) a number of separately elected officials with countywide jurisdictions, such as sheriff, county attorney, auditor, recorder, coroner, assessor, judge, treasurer, and so on; (3) a large number of special boards or commissions which have authority over various functions, whose members may be elected or appointed by the county commissioners or may even include the county commissioners in an ex officio capacity; and (4) an appointed county bureaucracy in planning, transportation, health, welfare, libraries, parks, and so on.

Traditional County Commission Structure   Traditionally county governments have been organized around the commission structure (see top of Figure 9–2). Over half of the nation's counties still operate under this structure. Typically there are three or five county commissioners, elected for overlapping four-year terms, and a large number of separately elected county officials. There is no single person responsible for administration of county functions. The commissioners may supervise some functions themselves and share supervision of other functions with other elected officials. Thus, for example, both the elected sheriff and the county commissioners share responsibility for the county jail, with the sheriff supervising day-to-day operations, but the commissioners deciding on its construction, repair, and financing. The commissioners usually decide on the property tax *rate* (or

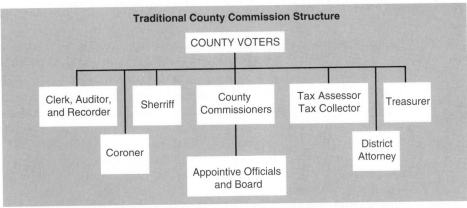

Traditional County Commission Structure

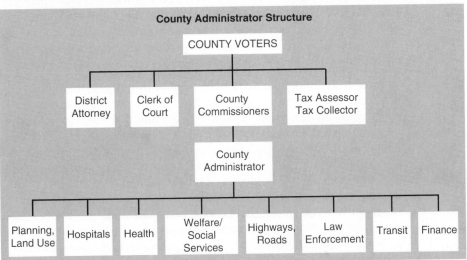

County Administrator Structure

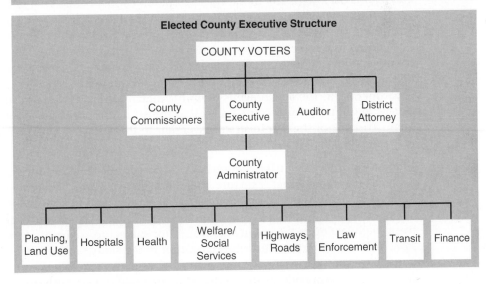

Elected County Executive Structure

FIGURE 9–2   Structures of County Government

"millage," with one mill equal to one-tenth of a percent) to be imposed on property owners (subject to maximums usually set by the state legislature). But the tax *assessor* determines the value of each parcel of property in the county against which the rate is to be applied. And in some counties a separate tax *collector* actually sends out the tax bills and undertakes to collect the revenue. A separate *treasurer* may maintain the county's financial accounts and write the checks. Thus, responsibility for county government is fragmented and dispersed.

Reformers view this traditional structure of county government as lacking in efficiency and accountability. Governmental functions are usually in the hands of untrained nonprofessional county officeholders. County jobs are awarded to "friends and neighbors and relatives." Few voters, even in small rural counties, know enough about what goes on in various offices in the "county courthouse" to hold individual officers responsible for their administration. Typically, independently elected county officials are returned to office term after term with little or no opposition. Only the sheriff's race in rural counties stirs up much interest.

County Administrator Structure   Urbanization and the proliferation of county functions usually result in demands for more professional administration of county government. When county commissioners find that they cannot cope with the volume and complexity of county business, they often seek professional assistance. The *county administrator* or county-manager structure of government offers a solution. It is based on the council-manager form of city government (see "Forms of City Government" later in this chapter). An appointed county administrator, responsible to the commission, is placed in charge of the various county departments and agencies. The commission makes policy and appoints the administrator to *implement* policy. The administrator prepares the budget for the commission's approval and then implements it; the administrator hires and fires department heads and reports back regularly to the commission on county business. It seldom works out as neatly as it appears on the organization chart, but the use of the county administrator plan has grown rapidly throughout the United States in recent years.

Voters lose some direct control over county functions with the adoption of the county administrator structure. And county commissioners themselves are usually obliged to go through the county administrator to influence activities in a county department. But the advantage is the professional leadership, administrative efficiency, and functional accountability that the structure brings to county government. The role of the administrator is similar to that of a city manager (see "City Managers in Municipal Politics" in Chapter 11).

Elected County Executive Structure   A few counties in the United States have adopted a governmental structure that features an *elected* "county executive." Voters elect *both* a county commission and a separate county executive officer, who exercises formal responsibility over county departments. The elected county executive usually appoints the county administrator subject to approval of the commission. This structure envisions the separation of legislative and executive powers, much like American state and national governments. The elected county executive, like the county administrator, has won approval in many urban counties over recent years.

County Officials   Typically, county officials have the following duties:

Commissioners: elected governing body with general responsibility for all county functions; most commissions have three to seven members with election by the county's voters at large.

Sheriff: maintains jail; furnishes law enforcement in unincorporated areas; carries out orders of the county court.

Auditor: maintains financial records; authorizes payment of county obligations.

County or district attorney: serves as chief prosecuting attorney; conducts criminal investigations and prosecutes law violators.

Coroner: conducts medical investigations to determine cause of death; maintains county morgue.

Tax collector: collects taxes.

Treasurer: maintains and disperses county funds; makes county fiscal reports.

Clerk: registers and records legal documents including deeds, mortgages, subdivision plats, marriages, divorces, births; certifies election returns.

Tax assessor: determines value of all taxable property in the county.

The many separately elected county officials are generally considered an obstacle to the emergence of strong executive leadership at the county level. The ability of county governments to assume more important functions and responsibilities, particularly in urban areas, probably hinges upon a reorganization of county government to provide for stronger executive leadership.

Townships   Another interesting unit of local government is the "township," which is found in about half of the states—the northern states from New England to the Midwest. Southern and western states have made little use of this unit of government. Townships are subdivisions of counties and perform many of the functions of county governments at a grass-roots level—elections, road repair, tax administration, fire protection, and even law enforcement through local justices of the peace. Townships are unincorporated, which means they do not have charters from state governments guaranteeing their political independence or authorizing them to provide many municipal services. The jurisdiction of townships may extend over many square miles of sparsely populated rural territory. About 40 million people, or one-fifth of the U.S. population, live under township governments today.

Township governments vary considerably in their powers and organization. Perhaps it would be best to classify them as "rural townships," and "urban townships." Rural townships outside of New England have lost much of their vitality in recent years. The school district consolidation movement (see Chapter 15) has centralized the control of public schools at the county level or in school districts that span villages and townships.

Some urban townships appear to have a brighter future as units of government than do rural townships. This is particularly true in certain suburban areas of larger cities where metropolitan growth has enveloped township governments. Some states, Pennsylvania for example, have authorized urban townships to exercise many of the powers and provide many of the services previously reserved to city governments.

The New England Town   In the New England states, the "town" is a significant unit of local government, with long traditions and deep roots in the political philosophy of the people of the region. In fact, the New England "town meeting" is often cited by political philosophers as the ideal form of *direct* democracy as distinguished from *representative* democracy. For the town meeting was, and to some extent still is, the central institution of "town" government. The New England town included a village and all of its surrounding farms. The town meeting was open to all eligible voters; it was generally an important social as well as political event. The town meeting would levy taxes, make appropriations, determine policy, and elect officers for the year. Between town meetings, a board of selected officials would supervise the activities of the town—schools, health, roads, care of the poor, and so on. Other officers include town clerk, tax assessors and collectors, justices of the peace, constables, road commissioners, and school board members. Although the ideal of direct democracy is still alive in many smaller New England towns, in the large towns, the pure democracy of the town meeting has given way to a representative system (representative town meeting government), in which town meeting members are elected prior to the town meeting. Moreover, much of the determination of the towns' financial affairs, previously decided at town meetings, has now been given over to elected officials, and many towns have appointed town managers to supervise the day-to-day administration of town services.

CITIES AS "MUNICIPAL CORPORATIONS"

Legally speaking, cities are "municipal corporations" that have received charters from state governments setting forth their boundaries, governmental powers and functions, structure and organization, methods of finance, and powers to elect and appoint officers and employees. The municipal *charter* is intended to grant the powers of local self-government to a community. Of course, the powers of self-government granted by a municipal charter are not unlimited. A state can change its charter or take it away altogether, as it sees fit. Cities, like other local governments, have only the powers that state laws and constitutions grant them. They are still subdivisions of the state. And, of course, state laws operate within the boundaries of cities. In fact, municipal corporations are generally responsible for the enforcement of state law within their boundaries. However, they also have the additional power to make local laws, "ordinances," which operate only within their boundaries. Perhaps the most serious limitation on the powers of cities is the fact that American courts have insisted upon interpreting the powers granted in charters very narrowly.

Dillon's Rule   The classic statement of this principle of restrictive interpretation of municipal powers was made by John F. Dillon over eighty years ago and is now well known as "Dillon's rule":

> It is a general and undisputed proposition of law that a municipal corporation possesses and can exercise the following powers, and no others: first, those granted in express words; second, those necessarily or fairly implied in or incident to the powers expressly granted; third, those essential to the accomplishment of the declared objects and purposes of the corporation—not simply convenient, but

indispensable. Any fair, reasonable, substantial doubt concerning the existence of power is resolved by the courts against a corporation, and the power is denied.[6]

Dillon's rule means that "a city cannot operate a peanut stand at the city zoo without first getting the state legislature to pass an enabling law, unless, per chance, the city's charter or some previously enacted law unmistakably covers the sale of peanuts."[7]

State Legislators Retain Local Powers   The restrictive interpretation of the powers of cities leads to rather lengthy city charters, since nearly everything a city does must have specific legal authorization in the charter. The city charter of New York, for example, is several hundred pages long. City charters must cover in detail such matters as boundaries, structure of government, ordinance-making powers, finances, contracts, purchasing, bonds, courts, municipal elections, property assessments, zoning laws and building codes, licenses, franchises, law enforcement, education, health, streets, parks, public utilities, and on and on. Since any proposed change in the powers, organization, or responsibilities of cities requires an act of a state legislature amending the city's charter, state legislatures are intimately involved in local legislation. This practice of narrowly interpreting city charters may appear awkward, but its effect is to increase the power of state legislators in city affairs. State legislators from cities acquire power because legislatures usually grant a local legislator the courtesy of accepting his or her views on local legislation that affects only that legislator's constituency.

Special Act Charters   State legislative control over cities is most firmly entrenched in *special act* charters. These charters are specially drawn for the cities named in them. Cities under special act charters remain directly under legislative control, and specific legislative approval for that city and that city alone must be obtained for any change in its government or service activities. Such charters give rise to local acts dealing with small details of city government in a specially named city, for example, "that Fall River be authorized to appropriate money for the purchase of uniforms for the park police and watershed guards of said city."[8] Under special act charters, laws that apply to one city do not necessarily apply to others.

General Act Charters   In contrast, *general act* charters usually classify cities according to their size and then apply municipal laws to all cities in each size classification. Thus, a state's municipal law may apply to all cities of less than 10,000 people, another law to all cities with populations of 10,000–25,000, another to cities with 25,000–50,000 people, and so on. These general act charters make it difficult to interfere in the activities of a particular city without affecting the activities of all cities of a similar size category. Yet in practice there are often exceptions and modifications to general act legislation. For example, since legislators know

---

[6] John F. Dillon, *Commentaries on the Laws of Municipal Corporations,* 5th ed. (Boston: Little, Brown, 1911), p. 448.

[7] Edward C. Banfield and James Q. Wilson, *City Politics* (Cambridge, MA: Harvard University Press, 1963), p. 65.

[8] Ibid., p. 66.

the populations of their cities, they can select size categories for municipal law that apply to only one city.

Optional Charters   *Optional charter* laws provide cities with some choice in the structure and organization of their governments. Such laws generally offer a choice of governmental forms: strong mayor and weak council, weak mayor and strong council, commission, city manager, or some modification of these.

Home Rule   *Home rule* charters are designed to give cities the power to adopt governmental forms and provide municipal services, as they see fit, without state legislative interference. Home rule charters may be given to cities by state constitutions or by legislative enactments; legislative home rule is considered less secure, since a legislature could retract the grant if it wished to do so. Beginning with Missouri in 1875, more than half the states have included in their constitutions provisions for the issuance of home rule charters. About two-thirds of the nation's cities with populations over 200,000 have some form of home rule.

The intended effect of home rule is to reverse "Dillon's rule" and enable cities to "exercise all legislative powers not prohibited by law or by charter." In other words, instead of preventing a city from doing anything not specifically authorized, home rule permits the city to do anything not specifically prohibited. The theory of home rule grants sweeping powers to cities; however, in practice, home rule has not brought self-government to cities.

Home rule provisions in state constitutions range from those that grant considerable power and discretion over local affairs, to provisions that are so useless that no city has ever made use of them. First of all, these constitutional provisions may be too cumbersome or vague for effective implementation. In some states, cities feel that it is easier to use the general law charters, particularly if they provide for optional forms of government, than to use the cumbersome procedures for obtaining home rule.

Another important limitation on home rule is the distinction between "self-enforcing" and "non–self-enforcing," or "permissive," home rule provisions in state constitutions. Non–self-enforcing home rule provisions merely permit the state legislature to grant home rule to its cities; cities cannot acquire home rule without legislative action. Only about a dozen states have "self-enforcing" home rule provisions, which enable cities to bypass the state legislature and adopt home rule for themselves.

Finally, home rule may be limited by court interpretations of the language of the constitutional provisions granting power to home rule in cities. Constitutional provisions may grant to home rule cities the power to make "all laws and ordinances relating to municipal concerns," or the "powers of local self-government," or all powers "in respect to municipal affairs." Of course, ordinances passed under home rule authority cannot be in conflict with state law. Courts must distinguish between municipal and statewide concerns. In cases where doubt exists, legal traditions of municipal law require that courts resolve the doubt in favor of the state and against local powers of home rule. State legislatures can intervene in local affairs in home rule cities by simply deciding that a particular matter is of statewide concern.

Politics of Home Rule   The politics of home rule often pits reform groups, city mayors, and administrators against state legislators and large municipal taxpayers. State legislators are generally wary of giving up their authority over cities. Rural legislators have little reason to support city home rule, and even city legislators seldom welcome proposals to give up their authority over local bills. Sometimes city employees with good access to the legislature will oppose giving a mayor or a city manager too much control over their employment. Taxpayer groups may fear that home rule will give the city the ability to increase taxes. Local bills may be pictured as a distraction to legislators by reformers, but many legislators enjoy the power that it brings them in local affairs and welcome the opportunity to perform legislative services for their constituents. And so, even with reapportionment adding to the number of urban legislators, the League of Women Voters, good-government groups, and mayors may still be frustrated in their attempts to achieve genuine home rule for American cities.

Courts Retain Local Powers   Courts figure prominently in municipal politics. This is because of the subordinate position of the municipal corporation in the hierarchy of governments, and legal traditions, such as Dillon's rule, which narrowly interpret the power of local governments. The power of courts over municipal affairs grants leverage to defenders of the *status quo* in any political battle at the local level. Proponents of a new municipal law or municipal service not only must win the battle over whether a city *ought* to pass the new law or provide the new service but also must win the legal battle over whether the city *can* pass the law or provide the service. Limitations and uncertainties abound about the validity of local enactments. Legal challenges to the authority of the city to pass new regulations or provide new services are frequent. The city attorney becomes a key official because he or she must advise the city about what it can or cannot do. Not only must the city obey the federal constitution, but it is also subject to the restraints of the state constitution, state laws, its municipal charter, and of course, Dillon's rule. The result is to greatly strengthen courts, attorneys, and defenders of the status quo.

FORMS OF CITY GOVERNMENT

American city government comes in various structural packages (see Figure 9–3). There are some adaptations and variations from city to city, but generally one can classify the form of city government as mayor-council, commission, council-manager, or town meeting. Approximately 41 percent of American cities have the mayor-council form of government; 3 percent have the commission form; 50 percent have the council-manager form; and 6 percent have town-meeting or representative town-meeting governments.[9]

Mayor-Council   The nation's largest cities tend to function under the *mayor-council* plan. This is the oldest form of American city government and is designed in the American tradition of separation of powers between legislature and execuve.

---

[9] International City Managers' Association, *Municipal Yearbook 1988* (Washington, DC: ICMA, 1988), p. 10.

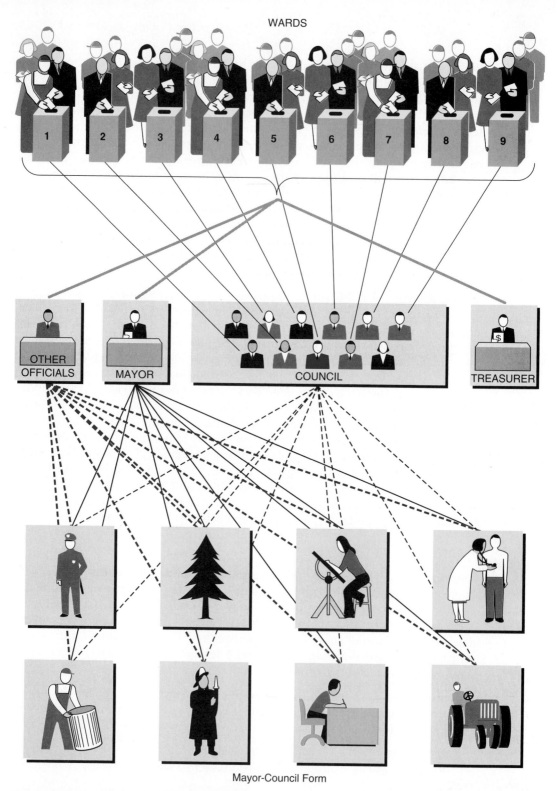

WARDS

OTHER OFFICIALS

MAYOR

COUNCIL

TREASURER

Mayor-Council Form

FIGURE 9–3 **Forms of City Government**

Source: National Municipal League. Reproduced by permission.

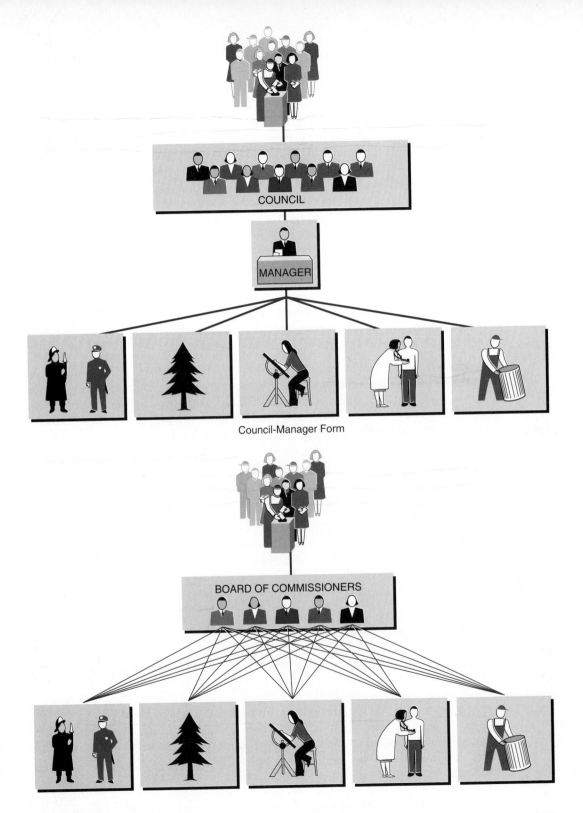

Council-Manager Form

BOARD OF COMMISSIONERS

FIGURE 9–3 *(continued)*

287

One may also establish subcategories of "strong" or "weak" mayor forms of mayor-council government. A strong mayor is one who is the undisputed master of the executive agencies of city government and who has substantial legislative powers in the form of budget making, vetoes, and opportunity to propose legislation. Only a few cities make the mayor the sole elected official among city executive officers; it is common for the mayor to share powers with other elected officials—city attorney, treasurer, tax assessor, auditor, clerk, and so on. Yet many mayors, by virtue of their prestige, persuasive abilities, or role as party leader, have been able to overcome most of the weaknesses of their formal office.

In recent years, large cities have been adding to the formal powers of their chief executives. Cities have augmented the mayors' role by providing them with direction over budgeting, purchasing, and personnel controls; and independent boards and commissions and individual councilmen have relinquished administrative control over city departments in many cities. Moreover, many cities have strengthened their mayors' position by providing them with a chief administrative officer, "CAO," to handle important staff and administrative duties of supervising city departments and providing central management services.

Commission   The *commission* form of city government gives both legislative and executive powers to a small body, usually consisting of five members. The commission form originated at the beginning of the century as a reform movement designed to end a system of divided responsibility between mayor and council. One of the commission members is nominally the mayor, but he or she has no more formal powers than the other commissioners. The board of commissioners is directly responsible for the operation of city departments and agencies. In practice, one commission member will become responsible for the management of a specific department, such as finance, public works, or public safety. As long as the council members are in agreement over policy, there are few problems; but when commissioners differ among themselves and develop separate spheres of influence in city government, city government becomes a multiheaded monster, totally lacking in coordination. The results of a commission form of government were generally so disastrous that the reform movement abandoned its early support of this form of government in favor of the council-manager plan.

Council-Manager   The *council-manager* form of government revived the distinction between legislative "policy making" and executive "administration" in city government. Policy-making responsibility is vested in an elected council, and administration is assigned to an appointed professional administrator known as a manager. The council chooses the manager who is responsible to it. All departments of the city government operate under the direction of the manager, who has the power to hire and fire personnel within the limits set by the merit system. The council's role in administration is limited to selecting and dismissing the city manager. The plan is based on the idea that policy making and administration are separate functions, and that the principal task of city government is to provide the highest level of services at the lowest possible costs—utilities, streets, fire and police protection, health, welfare, recreation, and so on. Hence, a professionally trained, career-oriented administrator is given direct control over city departments.

Town Meeting and Representative Town Meeting   Town-meeting or representative town-meeting governments are currently found in Connecticut, Maine, Massachusetts, New Hampshire, and Vermont. Most town meetings are held in response to the issuance of a warrant (agenda) by an elected town clerk and/or by the elected town council. The town meeting is open to all residents and it possesses full legislative authority. A town meeting may be called once or twice a year. In most town meetings, the passage of the annual budget is the most important item of business.

Town meetings usually choose a board to oversee business between meetings. Voters separately elect a town clerk, treasurer, assessor, constable, school board, and other officers. The town meeting may also elect a finance committee to prepare the budget.

While the town meeting has been celebrated by many political philosophers as "pure democracy," the reality is much less than full participatory democracy. Attendance at town meetings is usually less than 10 percent of the town's voters. In larger towns, the participation rate may be only 1 or 2 percent of the voters. The idealized town meeting democracy is really governance by a very small group of political activists. Special interest groups can easily pack a town meeting. Senior citizens attend these meetings in disproportionate numbers. And employees, members of the volunteer fire company, school teachers, and business and civic association members are also overrepresented. Of course, attendance increases when controversial items are on the agenda. And in many town-meeting governments, a decision can be overturned by citizen initiative and referendum.[10]

Representative town-meeting government (RTM) is a hybrid political institution that seeks to combine features of the open town meeting with representative government. In RTM the voters elect a relatively large number of persons to vote at meetings, yet voters retain the right to attend and speak at town meetings themselves. However, in practice the number of candidates for town-meeting members is frequently equal to or even smaller than the number of town-meeting members to be elected. Town clerks often must recruit people to become town-meeting members. In theory representative town-meeting members should be more attentive than townspeople because they accepted the responsibility of public office. But attendance is also a problem in RTM government.

TYPES OF CITIES AND FORMS OF GOVERNMENT

Let us examine the social, economic, and political forces shaping the structure of city government—that is, the conditions associated with the selection of one of the principal forms of government.

Size of City   First of all, city-manager government is closely associated with the *size* of cities. Large cities show a distinct preference for the more "political" form of mayor-council government in contrast to the more "efficient" form of council-

---

[10] See Joseph F. Zimmerman, "The New England Town Meeting: Pure Democracy in Action?" *Municipal Yearbook 1984* (Washington, DC: International City Managers Association, 1984), pp. 102–6.

manager government. (See Table 9–4.) All cities over 1 million population have the mayor-council form of government. Only a few large cities have council-manager government. The council-manager form of government is most popular in the middle-sized cities—those with populations of 25,000 to 250,000 people. Probably, cities with fewer than 10,000 residents do not have sufficient resources to justify hiring a trained professional city manager nor, in all probability, do they have the administrative problems requiring the expertise of such an individual. Thus, small cities, like large cities, tend to rely upon mayor-council government, although probably for different reasons.

Political Conflict   What explains the absence of city-manager government in large cities? A common explanation is that the political environment of large cities is so complex, with many competing interests, that these cities require strong *political* leadership that can arbitrate struggles for power, arrange compromises, and be directly responsible to the people for policy decisions. A large city requires a political form of government that can resolve the conflicting claims of diverse interests. This implies that in smaller cities there are fewer competing interests. A professional city manager would have less difficulty in accepting cues about correct behavior in a small city than in a large city with its complex political structure. There is a greater degree of consensus on policy direction in a smaller city; therefore, such a city requires a professional administrator rather than a political negotiator. The question is whether or not political skill or administrative expertise is more important in a city, and there is reason to believe that larger cities require political skills more than professional administration.

Growth Rate   Growing cities face more administrative and technical problems than cities whose population is stable. There is a strong relationship between population *growth* and council-manager government. A rapidly growing city faces many administrative problems in providing streets, sewers, and the many other services required by an expanding population. This creates a demand for a professional administrator.

In contrast, the mayor-council form of government is associated with cities having relatively stable populations, in which administrative and technical problems are not quite so pressing, and political conflict is more likely to be well defined and persistent. Council-manager government is more popular in the rapidly growing cities of the West and the South; mayor-council government is preferred in cities in the East and Midwest.

Social Class   Council-manager cities tend to be *middle-class* cities. Cities with large proportions of working-class residents, low-income families, and ethnic minorities prefer mayor-council government.[11]

Why is it that middle-class communities prefer the manager form of government while working-class communities prefer a mayor-council government? Middle-class citizens, those in white-collar jobs with good educations and reasonably

---

[11] Thomas R. Dye and Susan MacManus, "Predicting City Government Structure," *American Journal of Political Science,* 20 (May 1976), 257–72.

TABLE 9–4 FORMS OF GOVERNMENT IN AMERICAN CITIES

Population Size	Number of Cities Reporting	Council-manager		Mayor-council		Commission		Town-meeting	
		NUMBER	PERCENT	NUMBER	PERCENT	NUMBER	PERCENT	NUMBER	PERCENT
Over 1 million	6	0	0	6	100.0	0	0	0	0
500,000 to 1 million	17	5	29.4	12	70.6	0	0	0	0
250,000 to 500,000	34	15	44.1	17	50.0	2	5.9	0	0
100,000 to 250,000	113	67	59.3	41	36.3	5	4.4	0	0
50,000 to 100,000	280	162	57.9	104	37.1	9	3.2	5	1.8
25,000 to 50,000	616	340	55.2	226	36.7	30	4.9	20	3.2
10,000 to 25,000	1545	666	43.1	705	45.6	54	4.0	120	7.8
Under 10,000	4432	1295	29.2	2705	61.0	77	1.7	355	8.0

Source: International City Managers' Association, *Municipal Yearbook 1986.*

high incomes, are more likely to want government conducted in a businesslike fashion, with a council serving as a board of directors and a city manager as the president of a "municipal corporation." They are primarily concerned with efficiency, honesty, and saving their tax dollars. These values are not necessarily shared by labor, low-income, ethnic, and minority groups, which may prefer a government that grants small favors, dispenses patronage jobs, awards representation and "recognition" to minority groups, and can be held directly responsible by the voters at election time. In a campaign for city-manager government, one usually finds business leaders, newspapers, and civic associations supporting the plan, and labor unions and minority group organizations far less enthusiastic. Party organizations and professional politicians can usually be expected to oppose this plan. Its support generally comes from white-collar, high-income, well-educated, white neighborhoods, and its opposition from low-income, blue-collar, black, and ethnic neighborhoods.

Party Competition   Communities with well-organized *competitive party systems* are less likely to have manager government than one-party communities or communities in which the formal party organization is weak. States with the highest percentages of medium-sized cities with manager plans are Virginia, North Carolina, California, Texas, and Florida; in contrast, states with the highest percentages of mayor-council plans are Illinois, Connecticut, and Ohio. The former states are either one-party states or, in the case of California, states with relatively weak party organizations. The states with mayor-council cities are competitive two-party states. It is sometimes argued that the introduction of the manager plan decreases party activity in communities, but it is also true that the presence of strong party organizations may be a significant factor in the defeat of manager plans. Thus, manager government may depress party activity, or strong parties may kill off manager government, or both; but whatever the case, manager government appears incompatible with strong partisan politics in a community.

Region   Cities in the Northeast and Upper Midwest are more likely to have the mayor-council form of government as well as partisan elections. Cities in the South and West are more likely to have council-manager governments and nonpartisan elections. This regional pattern emerges as the strongest single correlate of local government structure.[12] This strong correlation between *region* and governmental structure is explained in part by the fact that southern and western cities are younger, growing cities without any history of strong party organizations; whereas northeastern and upper midwestern cities are older, stable cities with histories of strong party "machines." However, geographic region itself, apart from these other social and political factors, may also explain governmental form. In other words there may be some "imitation" effect within regions that is separate from the effects of other causal factors.[13]

---

[12] See Paul G. Farnhorn and Stephen N. Bryant, "Form of Local Government," *Social Science Quarterly,* 66 (June 1985), 386–400.

[13] See David Knoke, "The Spread of Municipal Reform," *American Journal of Sociology,* 87 (May 1982), 1314–39.

NONPARTISAN ELECTIONS

Most of America's cities use the nonpartisan ballot to elect local officials. Reformers believed that nonpartisanship would take the "politics" out of local government and raise the caliber of candidates for elected offices (see Chapter 10). They believed that nonpartisanship would restrict local campaigning to local issues and thereby rule out extraneous state or national issues from local elections. They also believed that by eliminating party labels, local campaigns would emphasize the qualifications of the individual candidates rather than their party affiliations.

Nonpartisanship is found in both large and small cities. Nonpartisanship is even more widespread than council-manager government. However, there is a tendency for these two forms to be related: 82 percent of all council-manager cities have nonpartisan ballots, while only 61 percent of all mayor-council cities are nonpartisan (see Table 9–5).

Party politics is still the prevailing style of local elections in eastern cities, 62 percent of which have partisan elections and only 38 percent of which have nonpartisan elections. Elsewhere in the nation nonpartisanship prevails. While nonpartisan cities are found in both one-party and two-party states, there is some tendency for competitive two-party states to have a smaller percentage of nonpartisan cities than one-party Democratic or Republican states. The nonpartisan ballot is also more likely to be adopted in homogeneous middle-class cities, where there is less social cleavage and smaller proportions of working-class and ethnic group members. There is a tendency for cities with large Catholic populations to retain the partisan ballot; there is also a tendency for cities with heavy factory employment to prefer partisan over nonpartisan elections. However, there are many exceptions: Cleveland, Detroit, and Boston are located in competitive party states and have large working-class populations, large Catholic populations, and deep social cleavages—yet they are officially nonpartisan cities.

To what extent has nonpartisanship succeeded in removing "politics" from local government? Of course, if "politics" is defined as conflict over public policy, then "politics" has certainly not disappeared with the elimination of party labels. There is no evidence that eliminating party ballots can reduce the level of community conflict. If we define "politics" to mean "partisanship," that is, *party* politics, then nonpartisanship can remove party influences from local government.

Apparently several types of political systems can be found in nonpartisan cities.[14]

---

[14] Classic literature on nonpartisan politics includes: Charles Adrian, "A Typology of Non-Partisan Elections," *Western Political Quarterly,* 12 (June 1959), 449–58; William H. Dutton and Alana Northrop, "Municipal Reform and the Changing Pattern of Urban Politics," *American Politics Quarterly,* 6 (October 1978), 429–52; Oliver P. Williams and Charles R. Adrian, "The Insulation of Local Politics under the Non-Partisan Ballot," *American Political Science Review,* 53 (1959), 1052–63; Robert Salisbury and Gordon Black, "Class and Party in Partisan and Non-Partisan Elections," *American Political Science Review,* 57 (September 1963), 587–97.

TABLE 9–5 TYPES OF ELECTORAL SYSTEMS IN AMERICAN CITIES

| | Nonpartisan Elections | | Electoral Districts | | | | | |
| | | | At-Large | | Districts | | Combination | |
	NUMBER	PERCENT	NUMBER	PERCENT	NUMBER	PERCENT	NUMBER	PERCENT
Total, all cities	2,851	72.6	2,354	60.4	497	12.8	1,044	26.8
Population size								
Over 500,000	11	84.6	2	15.4	3	23.1	8	61.5
250,000 to 500,000	16	69.6	8	34.8	4	19.4	11	47.8
100,000 to 250,000	71	76.3	35	37.6	24	17.2	42	45.2
50,000 to 100,000	177	77.3	121	53.3	16	10.6	82	36.1
25,000 to 50,000	353	74.3	264	55.9	54	11.4	154	32.6
10,000 to 25,000	691	68.8	575	58.3	114	11.6	297	30.1
Under 10,000	532	72.4	1,349	65.2	282	13.8	450	21.5
Form of government								
Mayor-Council	1,041	61.0	827	49.1	359	21.3	500	29.7
Council-Manager	1,722	81.9	1,427	68.1	132	6.3	536	25.6
Commission	88	74.6	100	87.7	6	5.3	8	7.0

Source: International City Manager's Association, *Municipal Yearbook 1988*, p. 17.

Disguised Party Politics   First of all, in some nonpartisan cities, parties continue to operate effectively behind the scenes in local affairs. This continuing party influence is most likely to be found in big cities of the Northeast and Midwest, in states where political parties are strong and competitive. In these cities persons who are known Democratic and Republican candidates run in officially "nonpartisan" elections.

Coalition Politics   Another type of nonpartisan political system is one in which the major parties are inactive, but clear *coalitions* of socioeconomic groups emerge that resemble the national Democratic and Republican parties. These opposing coalitions may involve liberal, labor, Catholic, and black groups on one side; and conservative, business, Protestant, middle-class groups on the other.

Group Politics   Nonpartisan systems may feature the activities of independent community *groups* and organizations. Frequently, these groups are civic associations led by newspapers, chambers of commerce, or neighborhood associations. These organizations may "slate" candidates, manage their campaigns, and even exercise some influence over them while they are in office. These organizations are not usually as permanent as parties, but they may operate as clearly identifiable political entities over the years.

Dispersed Politics   In still another type of nonpartisan political system, neither parties, nor coalitions, nor groups play any significant role, and there are no local slate-making associations. Individual candidates select themselves, collect their own money, and create their own temporary campaign organizations. Voting does not correlate with issues, or party identification, or socioeconomic groups, but instead tends to follow a "friends and neighbors" pattern. Indeed, voting in local nonpartisan elections often depends on factors such as incumbency, name recognition, position on the ballot (the first name on the list gets more votes), and very brief personal contacts (a handshake at the office or factory, or a door-to-door canvass, or even a telephone call).

Possible Republican Advantage   Does nonpartisanship increase Republican influence in city government? It is sometimes argued that the removal of party designations from local elections hurts Democrats by disengaging their traditional support from urban voters—the low-income, labor, ethnic, and black groups that traditionally vote the Democratic ticket. Moreover, the well-educated, high-income groups and interests that are normally Republican have a natural edge in organization, communication, and prestige in the absence of parties. Republicans also have better turnout records in nonpartisan elections. Surveys of local officials elected under partisan and nonpartisan systems tend to confirm that nonpartisanship results in the election of more Republicans.[15] However this Republican advan-

---

[15] Chester B. Rodgers and Harold D. Arman, "Nonpartisanship and Election to City Office," *Social Science Quarterly,* 51 (March 1971), 941–45.

tage in nonpartisan elections is very modest; it appears to be limited to smaller cities and cities that are dominated by Democrats.[16]

Nonpartisan Candidates   Does nonpartisanship result in "better-qualified" candidates winning public office? Of course, the answer to this question depends upon one's definition of better qualified. Nonpartisanship does result in more high-income, "respectable," older, white Anglo-Saxon Protestants with prestige jobs running for public office.[17] Working-class candidates are disadvantaged by nonpartisanship for several reasons. First, nonpartisanship reduces the turnout of labor, low-income, ethnic, Democratic voters and, consequently, increases the influence of well-educated, high-income, white, Anglo-Saxon, Protestant Republican voters who continue to come to the polls in nonpartisan elections. In addition, nonpartisanship means that recruitment of candidates will be left to civic associations, or ad hoc groups of one kind or another, rather than to Democratic or Republican party organizations. This difference in recruitment and endorsement practices tends to give an advantage to middle-class candidates. Candidates from the lower classes seldom receive the kind of public attention in private life that would make their names well known enough to place on a ballot, nor do they have the organizational ties or memberships that would bring them to the attention of civic associations that recruit in nonpartisan elections. In contrast, in partisan big-city politics, being a member of a working class, ethnic, or minority group may be a positive advantage. Parties traditionally try to "balance the ticket" with candidates who represent various groups in rough proportion to their voting strength. This practice of having a balanced party ticket with Irish, Italian, Polish, Jewish, and black names on the ballot is thought to add strength to the entire party ticket, since voters will be asked to vote for the party ticket rather than for the individual candidates.

Incumbent Advantage   Nonpartisanship contributes to the reelection of incumbent council members, particularly when nonpartisanship is combined with at-large elections.[18] Incumbent council members are reelected on the average about 80 percent of the time. When incumbents *are* defeated, they tend to suffer defeat in a group as a result of intensive community conflict.[19] Incumbents are more likely to have a name that is known to the voters. Incumbent council members in partisan cities are not reelected as often as incumbents in nonpartisan cities. Moreover, incumbent council members running at-large in the city were more likely to be reelected than incumbent council members running from districts. This

---

[16] Susan Welch and Timothy Bledsoe, "The Partisan Consequences of Nonpartisan Elections," *American Journal of Political Science,* 30 (February 1986), 128–39.

[17] Carol A. Cassel, "Social Background Characteristics of Nonpartisan City Council Members," *Western Political Quarterly,* 38 (September 1985), 495–501.

[18] Charles E. Gilbert and Christopher Clague, "Electoral Participation and Electoral Systems in Large Cities," *Journal of Politics,* 24 (1962), 323–30; James B. Jamison, "Some Social and Political Correlates of Incumbency in Municipal Elections," *Social Science Quarterly,* 51 (March 1971), 946–52.

[19] John J. Kirlen, "Electoral Conflict and Democracy in Cities," *Journal of Politics,* 37 (February 1975), 262–69.

suggests that it is difficult to hold public officials accountable in a nonpartisan election. The voter does not have the opportunity to hear organized criticisms of incumbent officeholders from an opposition party. When the only challenge to an incumbent officeholder is an unknown name on the ballot, he or she is more likely to be reelected than if he or she is challenged by a candidate backed by an opposition party. The higher rates of reelection in nonpartisan systems suggest that accountability is harder to achieve where party labels are absent.

AT-LARGE AND DISTRICT ELECTIONS

At-large elections are designed to promote a citywide approach to municipal problems among council members. Table 9–5 reveals that 60 percent of American cities elect their council members at-large, almost 13 percent by districts, and 27 percent by a combination of at-large and district constituencies. (There is always some confusion in counting cities as having at-large or ward elections, not only because some cities have "combination" elections with some council members elected by district and others at-large, but also because some cities *elect* council members at-large yet require that they *reside* in the districts they are supposed to represent.)

The Case for At-Large Elections   Traditionally reformers believed that district constituencies encourage parochial views, neighborhood interests, "log rolling," and other characteristics of "ward politics." These "undesirable" characteristics occur because council members are responsible to local majorities in the particular sections or wards from which they are elected. In contrast, council members elected at-large are responsible to citywide majorities; this should encourage impartial, cosmopolitan, and communitywide attitudes. Moreover, in council-manager cities, it is argued that the manager can be more effective in serving the "general good" of the whole community if the manager is responsible to council members elected at-large rather than by districts. (Of manager cities, 68 percent elect council members at-large, compared to only 49 percent of mayor-council cities.)

Minority Opposition   Minorities, who might be able to capture some council seats if these seats are elected by district, may oppose at-large elections if they feel unable to influence council members elected by communitywide majorities. Blacks especially have raised objections to at-large elections in predominantly white cities and counties. Council members and commissioners elected at-large by white majorities are perceived by many black voters as unresponsive to minority concerns.

Civil Rights Tests   The use of at-large elections to discriminate against racial minorities in their ability to participate in the political process and elect candidates of their own choice clearly violates the Equal Protection Clause of the Fourteenth Amendment and the federal Voting Rights Act. The U.S. Supreme Court in *Mobile* v. *Bolden* (1980) held that at-large elections are *not* unconstitutional in the absence of any evidence of discriminatory intent.[20] However, Congress amended the Voting

---

[20] *Mobile* v. *Bolden,* 446 U.S. 55 (1980).

Rights Act in 1982 to substitute a *results test* for the more difficult to prove *intent test* in assessing discrimination. But Congress stopped short of declaring all at-large elections discriminatory and illegal. Instead Congress established a "totality of circumstances" test to be used in deciding whether the at-large elections resulted in racial discrimination. The elements to be considered by the federal courts are:[21]

1. A history of official discrimination. (This test applies primarily to southern states.)
2. A record of racial polarization in voting.
3. Unusually large election districts.
4. The existence of candidate slating by parties or groups, and whether minority members have been slated.
5. The extent to which minorities have been adversely affected by local government decisions.
6. Whether political campaigns have been characterized by racial appeals.
7. The extent to which minority group members have been elected to office.

The federal courts are prepared to evaluate the use of at-large elections in each community by these tests.[22]

Federal Court Intervention　Federal court cases in recent years involving at-large elections suggest that it is becoming increasingly difficult for cities, counties, and even school districts to defend exclusive reliance on at-large elections. Civil rights groups have effectively utilized the "totality of circumstances" test to invalidate at-large elections across the country and especially in southern states. In some cases federal courts have ordered district elections for all officials, and in other cases federal courts have accepted combination plans—some council members elected by district and some at-large. The U.S. Supreme Court does *not* require proportional representation for minorities, that is, a council which is 20 percent black if the city's population is 20 percent black. However, lower federal courts have tended to compare the black proportion of the council with the black proportion of residents in determining whether the "totality of circumstances" suggests discrimination.

Trend Toward Mixed Districts　These constitutional challenges have led to a shift away from exclusively at-large electoral districts and toward greater reliance on a combination of at-large and district representation on city councils. Combination plans—for example, three council members elected at large and four by districts on a seven-member council—have been favorably received by federal courts. The percentage of all U.S. cities using combination electoral plans is rising rapidly; at-large plans, although still in use in a majority of cities, are being abandoned.[23]

---

[21] For a discussion of federal court applications of these tests, see Susan A. MacManus and Charles S. Bullock, "Racial Representation Issues," *PS,* 18 (Fall 1985), 759–69.

[22] *Thornburgh* v. *Gingles,* 106 S. Ct. 2752 (1986).

[23] International City Managers Association, *Baseline Data Report,* 19 (6) (Nov./Dec. 1987).

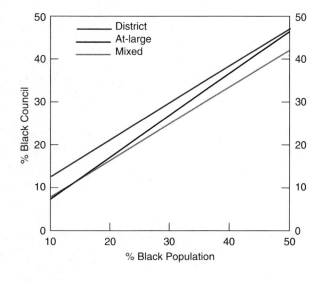

FIGURE 9–4
Black Representation on City Councils by Type of Electoral System

Source: Susan Welch, "The Impact of At-Large Elections on the Representation of Blacks and Hispanics," *Journal of Politics,* 52 (November 1990), 1063. By permission of the author and of the University of Texas Press.

Minority Representation Until recently, blacks were significantly *under-represented* on city councils that elected their members at-large. This notion of underrepresentation implies that blacks or other minorities should be represented on city councils in proportion to their percentage of the population—that representation means physical presence on the council and not just voter influence over council members. In the 1970s several studies reported that blacks won fewer than 50 percent of the seats they deserved (based on their percentage of a city's population) in *at-large* cities, compared to 85 to 100 percent of the seats they deserved in cities that elected council members *by districts.*[24] However, by the late 1980s, black representation on city councils throughout the nation had increased dramatically, and it no longer made much difference in black representation whether councils were elected at-large or by district.[25] Figure 9–4 shows the relationship between black representation on city councils (the "Y" or vertical axis) and black population percentage of cities (the "X" or horizontal axis). For cities with more than 10 percent and less than 50 percent black population, black representation on city councils is only slightly below black population percentages, and the difference between at-large and district elections is minuscule. For cities with black populations over 50 percent, "then it is whites who need district representation to obtain their proportion share of council seats."[26]

---

[24] Albert K. Karnig, "Black Representation on City Councils," *Urban Affairs Quarterly,* 12 (December 1976), 223–243; Thomas R. Dye and Theodore P. Robinson, "Reformism and Black Representation on City Councils," *Social Science Quarterly,* 59 (June 1978).

[25] Susan Welch, "The Impact of At-Large Districts on the Representation of Blacks and Hispanics," *Journal of Politics,* 52 (November 1990), 1050–1076. See also Charles S. Bullock and Susan M. MacManus, "Municipal Electoral Structure and the Election of Councilwomen," *Journal of Politics,* 53 (February 1991), 75–89.

[26] Welch, "The Impact of At-Large Districts," p. 1072.

10

STYLES OF COMMUNITY POLITICS

▲

 ## MACHINES AND BOSSES

Machine politics has gone out of style. Machines—tightly disciplined party organizations, held together and motivated by a desire for tangible benefits rather than by principle or ideology and run by professional politicians—emerged in the nation's large cities early in the nineteenth century. This style of city politics has historical importance. Between the Civil War and the New Deal, every big city had a machine at one time or another, and it is sometimes easier to understand the character of city politics today by knowing what went on in years past. A more important reason for examining the machine style of politics is to understand the style of political organization that employs personal and material rewards to control behavior. These kinds of rewards will always be important in politics, and the big-city machine serves as the prototype of a style of politics in which ideologies and issues are secondary and personal friendships, favors, and jobs are primary.

The political machine was essentially a large brokerage organization. It was a business organization, devoid of ideologies and issues, whose business it was to get votes and control elections by trading off social services, patronage, and petty favors to the urban masses, particularly the poor and the recent immigrants. To get the money to pay for these social services and favors, it traded off city contracts, protection, and privileges to business interests, which paid off in cash. Like other brokerage organizations, a great many middlemen came between the cash paid for a franchise for a trolley line or a construction contract and a Christmas turkey sent by the ward chairman to the Widow O'Leary. However, the machine worked. It performed many important social functions for the city.[1]

Personal Attention   First of all, it personalized government. With keen social intuition, the machine recognized the voter as a person, generally living in a neighborhood, who had specific problems and wants. The machine politician avoided abstract and remote public issues or ideologies and concentrated instead on the personal problems and needs of the constituents. The machine provided individual attention and recognition. As Tammany Hall boss George Washington Plunkitt, the philosopher king of old-style machine politics, explained:

> I know every man, woman, and child in the 15th district, except them that's been born this summer—and I know some of them, too. I know what they like and what they don't like, what they are strong at and what they are weak in, and I reach them by approachin' at the right side. . . . I don't trouble them with political arguments. I just study human nature and act accordin'.[2]

Welfare   The machine also performed functions of a welfare agency.

> What tells in holdin' your grip on your district is to go right down among the poor families and help them in the different ways they need help. I've got a regular system for this. If there's a fire in Ninth, Tenth, or Eleventh Avenue, for example, any hour of the day or night, I'm usually there with some of my election district captains as soon as the fire engines. If a family is burned out I don't ask whether they are Republicans or Democrats, and I don't refer them to the Charity Organization Society, which would investigate their case in a month or two and decide they were worthy of help about the time they are dead from starvation. I just get quarters for them, buy clothes for them if their clothes were burned up, and fix them up till they get things runnin' again. It's philanthropy, but it's politics, too—mighty good politics. Who can tell how many votes one of these fires bring me? The poor are the most grateful people in the world, and let me tell you, they have more friends in their neighborhoods than the rich have in theirs.[3]

Employment   The machine also functioned as an employment agency. In the absence of government unemployment insurance or a federal employment service, patronage was an effective political tool, particularly in hard times. Not only were city jobs at the disposal of the machine, but the machine also had its business contacts:

---

[1] See Robert K. Merton, *Social Theory and Social Structure* (Glencoe, IL: The Free Press, 1957), pp. 71–81.

[2] William L. Riordan, *Plunkitt of Tammany Hall* (New York: McClure, Phillips & Co., 1905), p. 46.

[3] Ibid., p. 52.

Another thing, I can always get a job for a deservin' man. I make it a point to keep on the track of jobs, and it seldom happens that I don't have a few up my sleeve ready for use. I know every big employer in the district and in the whole city, for that matter, and they ain't in the habit of sayin' no to me when I ask them for a job.[4]

Friendship   It was not so much the petty favors and patronage that won votes among urban dwellers, as it was the sense of friendship and humanity that characterized the "machine" and its "boss."[5] The free turkeys and bushels of coal were really only tokens of this friendship. As Jane Addams, the famous settlement house worker, explained:

On the whole, the gifts and favors were taken quite simply as evidence of genuine loving kindness. The alderman is really elected because he is a good friend and neighbor. He is corrupt, of course, but he is not elected because he is corrupt, but rather in spite of it. His standard suits his constituents. He exemplifies and exaggerates the popular type of a good man. He has attained what his constituents secretly long for.[6]

Assimilation   The machine also played an important role in educating recent immigrants and assimilating them into American life.[7] Machine politics provided a means of upward social mobility for ethnic group members, which was not open to them in businesses or professions. City machines sometimes met immigrants at dockside and led them in groups through naturalization and voter registration procedures. Machines did not keep out people with "funny" sounding names but instead went out of the way to put these names on ballots. Politics became a way "up" for the bright sons of Irish and Italian immigrants.

"Getting Things Done"   Finally, for businesses, and particularly for public utilities and construction companies with government contracts, the machine provided the necessary franchises, rights of way, contracts, and privileges. As Lincoln Steffens wrote: "You cannot build or operate a railroad, or a street railway, gas, water, or power company, develop and operate a mine, or cut forests or timber on a large scale, or run any privileged business, without corrupting or joining in the corruption of government."[8] The machine also provided the essential protection from police interference, which is required by illicit businesses, particularly gambling. In short, the machine helped to centralize power in large cities. It could "get things done at city hall."

---

[4] Ibid., p. 53.

[5] Edward C. Banfield and James Q. Wilson, *City Politics* (Cambridge, MA: Harvard-M.I.T. Press, 1963), Chap. 9.

[6] Jane Addams, *Democracy and Social Ethics* (New York: 1902), p. 254; also cited by Banfield and Wilson, *City Politics,* p. 118.

[7] See Elmer E. Cornwell, Jr., "Bosses, Machines, and Ethnic Groups," *Annals of the American Academy of Political and Social Science* (May 1964), 27–39.

[8] Lincoln Steffens, *Autobiography* (New York: Harcourt, Brace & World, 1931), p. 168.

The Decline of Machines   The era of the political machine has passed. Big-city political organizations have radically altered their style of operation. Federal and state welfare agencies now provide the basic welfare services that the bosses used to provide. Large-scale immigration has stopped, and there are fewer people requiring the kinds of services once provided by the machine. Patronage jobs do not look as attractive in an affluent economy, and today civil service examinations cover most governmental jobs anyhow. The middle class was excluded from machine politics, and much of the opposition to the machine came from the middle class. As the middle class grew in American society (today white-collar workers outnumber blue-collar workers), opposition to the machine has grown in every city. Middle-class voters supported reform movements and good-government crusades. They often succeeded in replacing the machine with professional city managers, civil service, and reorganized city government. They supported city administrations pledged to eliminate corruption and exercise economy and efficiency in government.

Political machines were never very efficient, even by their own standards. Machines frequently made poor use of their patronage and perquisites. Jobs were frequently handed out to personal friends and family members without regard to whether they worked hard in elections to produce additional votes for the machine.[9] Even the Daley organization in Chicago failed to allocate its "perks" according to strict vote-getting requirements.[10] In short, political machines were not always very good at machine politics—trading patronage and perks for votes and power.

MACHINE AND REFORM POLITICS IN CHICAGO

Daley: Last of the Bosses   For over two decades Mayor Richard J. Daley governed Chicago in the style of traditional politics. (When Mayor Daley himself was asked about his "machine," he replied, "Organization, not machine. Get that. Organization, not machine.") In Chicago, few others understood so well the labyrinths of formal and informal power. Daley won election to six four-year terms as mayor of Chicago, beginning in 1955. He remained the captain of his old Eleventh Ward Democratic committee, and he was chairman of the Cook County Democratic committee. He picked candidates' slates, ran the patronage machinery, and worked his will on nearly all of Chicago's city council. Illinois Democratic governors were usually responsive to his wishes, and Chicago's nine-member delegation to the U.S. House of Representatives also acted promptly on Daley's recommendations. The Cook County Democratic delegation to the Illinois legislature was firmly in his hands. No presidential candidate could ignore Daley's political "clout," either in the Democratic National Convention or in the general election. Daley may have

---

[9] Michael Johnson, "Patrons and Clients, Jobs and Machines: A Case Study of the Uses of Patronage," *American Political Science Review*, 73 (June 1979), 385–98.

[10] Kenneth R. Mladenka, "The Urban Bureaucracy and the Chicago Political Machine," *American Political Science Review*, 74 (December 1980), 991–98.

been the most successful mayor in America, not only for his political acumen, but also for his ability to manage a great metropolis.[11]

The Daley Style   In an era when successful politicians increasingly reflected a slick media image—tall, handsome, glamorous, articulate, at ease with television and press—Mayor Daley was a throwback to an earlier era of municipal politics. Daley looked like an old-time city boss—short and paunchy, with heavy jowls and deep-set eyes. He spoke with "deses" and "dems," but he was smart enough to limit his public appearances to ceremonial occasions.

Conflict Management   As a political broker, Daley was seldom the initiator of public policy. His approach to policy questions was more like that of an arbitrator between competing interests. When political controversies developed, Daley waited on the sidelines without committing himself, in the hope that public opinion would soon "crystallize" behind a particular course of action. Once the community was behind a project—and this determination Daley made himself after lengthy consultations with his political advisors—he then awarded his stamp of approval. This suggests that in policy matters many political "bosses" were not so much bosses as referees among interested individuals and groups. The boss was really "*a*political" when it came to policy matters. He was really more concerned with resolving conflict and maintaining his position and organization than he was with the outcome of public policy decisions. Boss Daley's politics: "Don't make no waves; don't back no losers."

The Machine Loses Clout   When Mayor Daley died in office in 1977, a lackluster machine replacement, Michael Bilandic, tried unsuccessfully to fill the shoes of the nation's most successful "boss." However, the once powerful Cook County Democratic committee gradually lost its direction, leadership, and "clout." Mayor Bilandic failed to hold together the coalition of white ethnic groups, blacks, Catholics, labor unions, and city employees, which were the backbone of the machine. In 1978 Bilandic fired a Daley appointee, Jane Byrne, from her post as the city's commissioner on consumer affairs. Byrne accused Bilandic of collusion in allowing taxi fare increases in the city, and she announced her intention to oppose Bilandic in the 1979 mayoralty race. Initially, observers gave her little chance of defeating the official machine candidate in the Democratic primary. However, a huge snowfall paralyzed the city for weeks, and Bilandic's administration was not very competent in handling the emergency. Perhaps more importantly, the machine itself seemed to fall apart without the leadership of Daley. On election day, Jane Byrne captured most of the city's predominantly black wards—traditionally machine strongholds. Byrne sounded like a reformer in public, but she privately reminded many old Daley supporters that she was an old and trusted friend of "hizzoner." Byrne

---

[11] For an excellent description of the functions of Mayor Daley's political organization in Chicago, see Edward C. Banfield, *Political Influence* (Glencoe, IL: The Free Press, 1961). For a hostile account of Mayor Daley by a liberal reformer, see Mike Royko, *Boss: Richard J. Daley of Chicago* (New York: E. P. Dutton, 1971).

emerged from the close contest as Chicago's first female mayor. Party regulars pledged to support her, and she promised to work with the Cook County Democratic committee. Nevertheless, it was clear to all that Chicago's once powerful machine was in disarray.

Blacks Split from the Machine   As the machine stumbled, the city's black voters became increasingly restless. Mayor Byrne's administration was attacked as unresponsive to black demands. Finally, in the 1983 Democratic mayoral primary the black community, under the leadership of Congressman Harold Washington, split from the Democratic machine. The machine went into the 1983 election hopelessly fractured. Mayor Byrne sought reelection and claimed control over city job holders; state attorney Richard M. Daley, son of the late mayor, challenged Byrne's control of the machine and called upon old loyalties to the family name; and Harold Washington worked hard to register and mobilize the city's black residents, 40 percent of Chicago's total population. The resulting split in the Democratic primary was: Washington, 37 percent; Byrne, 33 percent; Daley, 30 percent.

The general election campaign was a bitter one. The Republican candidate, businessman Bernard Epton, sensed an opportunity to become the city's first Republican mayor. He struck hard at Washington's weaknesses. Washington had once been convicted for failing to file federal income tax returns, and his license to practice law had once been suspended for accepting payments for services not performed. Several prominent white Democratic machine politicians deserted the Democratic candidate. Race dominated the campaign.

Voter turnout in Chicago's 1983 mayoral election was a record 82 percent of registration. Washington won with 51.4 percent. He had the near-unanimous support of black voters combined with just enough "Lakefront liberal" white voters to provide a thin margin of victory. But most white voters, including the white ethnic voters who provided the machine with its traditional base of support, cast their ballots against the black Democratic nominee.[12]

Harold Washington   Harold Washington was raised in Chicago machine politics. His father was a Democratic precinct captain, lawyer, and minister on Chicago's South Side. Young Harold emerged from the Army Air Corps after World War II and attended local Roosevelt College on the G.I. Bill. He graduated president of his (predominantly white) class and went on to Northwestern University Law School. When his father died in 1953, Harold inherited his law practice and his position in the Democratic party machine. Washington served in the Illinois state legislature for sixteen years prior to his election to Congress in 1980. Despite his background in machine politics, Washington battled endlessly with the white ethnic remnants of the machine. He pledged to end machine politics in Chicago and to "heal the divisions that have plagued us. . . . Chicago is one city."[13]

---

[12] Michael B. Preston, "The Election of Harold Washington," *P.S. Political Science* (Summer 1983), 486.

[13] *Time,* April 25, 1983, p. 24.

Racial Politics   The demise of the old Daley political machine allowed the city's racial divisions to surface as the major force in political life. Harold Washington faced formidable opposition among many white city workers, police officers and firefighters, and a majority of white council members elected from wards. The leader of white ethnic forces was Alderman Edward Vrdolyak, chairman of the Cook County Democratic committee, Mayor Daley's old post. Council meetings became scenes of bitter confrontations between Mayor Washington and Alderman Vrdolyak and his forces. Indeed, the struggle for power resulted in near paralysis of city business, as personnel appointments, election administration, and financial decisions were drowned in political controversy. As council meetings deteriorated from parliamentary pandemonium to near fistfights, the courts were called upon to resolve many city issues.

Mayor Washington's campaign theme, "It's our turn," was widely interpreted among white municipal job holders as a threat to replace them with blacks. But the dreams of blue-collar, white ethnics in Chicago to revive the old machine were dashed in 1987 when Mayor Washington defeated Edward Vrdolyak in the Democratic primary for mayor. Washington won with the support of almost all of the city's black voters combined with 15 percent of the white voters. Vrdolyak's blue-collar supporters also lost control of the city council.

Washington's Popularity   Harold Washington's personal popularity among blacks and Hispanics and a significant portion of affluent, liberal whites was a major factor in his success as mayor. The city itself was almost evenly divided between white and black residents, with Hispanics comprising a smaller but important constituency. Washington's popularity, together with the gradual decline of the white percentage of the city's population, led many observers to believe that Chicago had seen its last white mayor. But Washington's untimely death in 1988 brought a new administration to the city.

Old Name, New Style   Richard M. Daley is the eldest son of the former mayor and long-time boss of Chicago politics, Richard J. Daley. His father found him a job in the city attorney's office and later persuaded an incumbent state senator to give up his seat so that young "Richie" could start a political career. At the state capital, young Daley was unswervingly loyal to his father's machine. But after the mayor's death, and the personal tragedy of the death of a severely handicapped child, Richard M. Daley began to emerge as his own man.

Following Washington's death, Eugene Sawyer, another black former machine politician, became acting mayor. But black Alderman Timothy Evans won the support of most of the city's black political organizations. Sawyer came under intense pressure to drop out of the mayor's race in 1989 in order to avoid splitting the black vote. But Sawyer saw himself as the legitimate heir to Harold Washington's political coalition. Sawyer remained in the Democratic primary fight, while Evans announced that he would run as an independent in the general election and face the Democratic nominee. Everyone assumed that racial voting would predominate in both the primary and general elections, and Sawyer and Evans accused each other of destroying black unity.

Daley won the Democratic primary against Sawyer with 56 percent of the vote. He held on to white ethnic voters who had so long supported his father, won the Hispanic vote, and won back many white liberals who were convinced the younger Daley stood for reform.

Race also divided the voters in the general election. Daley won with 55 percent of the vote compared to 41 percent for Evans and 4 percent for Vrdolyak. But polls suggested that Daley won 91 percent of the white vote and Evans 95 percent of the black vote.[14] Very few voters crossed racial lines. Hispanics (16 percent of the population and about 7 percent of the electorate) supported Daley.

Daley, the Reformer   As mayor, Daley presented himself not as a "politician" but rather as a "manager" trying to reform a costly, unresponsive city bureaucracy. While critics claim that Daley's image as a reformer is only a cover for his political ambition, Daley's growing popularity in the job indicates that governmental reform is good politics. Chicago's voters seem to agree. Daley won the Democratic primary in 1991 with 63 percent of the vote (surpassing the best primary showing ever posted by his father), and then winning an overwhelming 71 percent of the vote in the general election.

Daley's efforts to reform the city bureaucracy present an ironic twist to the long history of machine and reform politics in Chicago. Daley's father had overstaffed city hall with patronage appointees who worked his precincts at election time. But over time, the courts had given most city workers civil service protection as a "reform" of patronage practices. The result was a bloated bureaucracy unresponsive to either the mayor or the council. "You get elected mayor to make decisions, and then you find out the bureaucracy is against you," complained Daley. "Their attitude is 'we're going to be here when you leave!'"[15] Daley has pushed to contract out to private firms—to "privatize"—many city functions, from janitorial services to towing of abandoned cars. And he has imposed modern data management and accounting practices on city agencies. Yet for all of his reform efforts, vestiges of the old patronage system remain.

REFORMERS AND DO-GOODERS

A reform style of politics appeared in the United States shortly after the Civil War to battle the "bosses." Beginning in 1869, scathing editorials in the *New York Times* and cartoons by Thomas Nast in *Harper's Weekly* attacked the "Tammany Society" in New York City, a political organization that controlled the local Democratic organization. William M. Tweed was president of the board of supervisors of New York County and undisputed boss of "Tammany Hall," as the New York County Democratic committee was called, after its old meeting place on Fourteenth Street. This early reform movement achieved temporary success under the brilliant leadership of Samuel J. Tilden, who succeeded in driving the "Tweed Ring" out of office and

---

[14] *New York Times,* April 5, 1989.

[15] Quoted in *U.S. News and World Report,* March 23, 1992, p. 41.

went on in 1876 to be the only presidential candidate ever to win a majority of popular votes and then be denied the presidency through the operation of the electoral college. George William Curtis, editor of *Harper's Weekly;* E. L. Godkin, editor of the *Nation;* and Senator Carl Schurz of Missouri laid the foundations for a style of reform politics that continues to have great influence in American cities.[16]

Early municipal reform is closely linked to the Progressive movement in American politics. Leaders such as Robert M. La Follette of Wisconsin, Hiram Johnson of California, Gifford Pinchot of Pennsylvania, and Charles Evans Hughes of New York backed municipal reform at the local level as well as the direct primary and direct election of senators and women's suffrage at the national level. In 1912 social worker Jane Addams, who labored in slums and settlement houses, sang, "Onward Christian Soldiers" at the Progressive party convention which nominated Teddy Roosevelt for president. Lincoln Steffens wrote in *The Shame of the Cities* ". . . St. Louis exemplified boodle; Minneapolis, police graft; Pittsburgh, a political industrial machine; and Philadelphia (the worst city in the country), general civic corruption."[17]

Social Bases of Reform   From its beginning, reform politics was strongly supported by the upper-class, Anglo-Saxon, Protestant, longtime residents of cities whose political ethos was very different from that which the new immigrants brought with them. The immigrant, the machine that relied upon his vote, and the businessman who relied upon the machine for street railway and other utility franchises, had formed an alliance in the nineteenth century that had displaced the native, old family, Yankee elite that had traditionally dominated northern cities. This upper-class elite fought to recapture control of local government through the municipal reform movement.

Richard Hofstadter described the social, ideological, and political clash between the new immigrants and the Anglo-Saxon Protestant upper class in the *Age of Reform:*

> Out of the clash between the needs of the immigrants and the sentiments of the natives, there emerged two thoroughly different systems of political ethics . . . one, founded upon the indigenous Yankee-Protestant political traditions, and upon middle class life, assumed and demanded the constant, disinterested activity of the citizen in public affairs, argued that political life ought to be run to a greater degree than it was in accordance to general principles, abstract laws, apart from the superior to personal needs. . . . The other system, founded upon the European background of the immigrants, upon their unfamiliarity with independent political action, their familiarity with hierarchy and authority, and upon the urgent needs that so often grew out of their migration, took for granted that the political life of the individual would arise out of family needs, interpreted political and civic relations, chiefly in terms of personal obligations, and placed strong personal loyalties above allegiance to abstract codes of law or morals.[18]

---

[16] See Richard J. Hofstadter, *The Age of Reform* (New York: Knopf, 1955); and Lorin Peterson, *The Day of the Mugwump* (New York: Random House, 1961).

[17] Lincoln Steffens, *The Shame of the Cities* (New York: Sagamore Press, 1957), p. 10.

[18] Hofstadter, *The Age of Reform,* p. 9.

This conflict can still be observed today in American politics. Machine politicians cater to ethnic groups, organized labor, blue-collar workers, and other white working-class elements of the city. The reform politician appeals to the upper- and middle-class affluent American who is well educated and public-service minded. Reform is popular among liberals, television and newspaper reporters, college professors, and others who consider themselves "intellectuals."

Reform Goals   Reform politics includes a belief that there is a "public interest" that should prevail over competing, partial interests in a city. The idea of balancing competing interests or compromising public policy is not part of the reformers' view of political life. Rather, the reform ethos includes a belief that there is a "right" and "moral" answer to public questions. Conflict and indeed even "politics" is viewed as distasteful. Enlightened people should agree on the public interest; municipal government is a technical and administrative problem rather than a political one. City government should be placed in the hands of those who are best qualified, by training, ability, and devotion to public service, to manage public business. These best-qualified people can decide on policy and then leave administration to professional experts. Any interference by special interests in the policies or administration of the best-qualified people should be viewed as corruption.

The objectives of early reform movements were:

1. *Eliminate corruption.* The elimination of corruption in public office, and the recruitment of "good people" (educated, upper-income individuals who were successful in private business or professions) to replace "politicians" (who were no more successful than their constituents in private life and who were dependent upon public office for their principal source of income).
2. *Nonpartisanship.* The elimination of parties from local politics by nonpartisan elections.
3. *Manager government.* The establishment of the council-manager form of government, and the separation of "politics" from the "business" of municipal government.
4. *At-large districts.* The establishment of at-large citywide constituencies in municipal elections in lieu of "district" constituencies in order to ensure that an elected official would consider the welfare of the entire city in public decision making and not merely his or her own neighborhood or "ward."
5. *Short ballot.* The reorganization of local government to eliminate many separately elected offices (the "short-ballot" movement) in order to simplify the voters' task and focus responsibility for the conduct of public affairs on a small number of top elected officials.
6. *Strong executive.* The strengthening of executive leadership in city government—longer terms for mayors, subordination of departments and commissions to a chief executive, and an executive budget combined with modern financial practices.
7. *Merit system.* The replacement of patronage appointments with the merit system of civil service.

8. *Home rule.* The separation of local politics from state and national politics by home-rule charters and the holding of local elections at times when there were no state and national elections.

All these objectives are interrelated. Ideally, a "reformed city" would be one with the manager form of government, nonpartisan election for mayor and council, a home-rule charter, a short ballot, at-large constituencies, a strong executive, a merit service personnel system, and honest people at the helm. Later, the reform movement added comprehensive city planning to its list of objectives—official planning agencies with professional planners authorized to prepare a master plan of future development for the city. The National Municipal League incorporated its program of reform into a *Model City Charter,* which continues to be the standard manual of municipal reform.[19] There is reason to believe that the early reformers also opposed immigration (which was very logical, of course, since the immigrant was the backbone of machine politics). Many persons active in municipal reform at the time supported the passage of the Immigration Act of 1921, reducing immigration to a trickle and establishing quotas heavily weighted in favor of Anglo-Saxon Protestant immigrants and against southern and eastern European Catholic immigrants.[20]

Reform Politics   Political divisions in American cities do not always take the form of upper classes versus lower classes. Increasingly in urban politics, one finds upper-class liberal reformers allied with minorities, notably blacks, in opposition to the white middle class and working class. Democratic reformers in municipal politics are generally liberal Democrats in national politics, while Republican reformers are frequently supporters of the progressive wing of that party.

Reformers are generally amateurs in politics, in contrast to the professional politicians who constitute the regular party organizations. The "amateur" is more motivated by the ideological and psychological rewards of mixing in government and public affairs; in contrast, the "professional" is interested in tangible rewards —jobs, contracts, public offices. Reformers do not deal with the personal problems

---

[19] National Municipal League, *Model City Charter* (Chicago: National Municipal League, 1961).

[20] Andrew D. White, first president of Cornell University, summarized early reform thinking when he wrote in 1890: "What is this evil theory? It is simply that the city is a political body; that its interior affairs have to do with national political parties and issues. My fundamental contention is that a city is a corporation; that as a city it has nothing whatever to do with general political interests; that party political names and duties are utterly out of place there. The questions in a city are not political questions. They have reference to the laying out of streets; to the erection of buildings; to sanitary arrangements, sewerage, water supply, gas supply, electrical supply; to the control of franchises and the like; and to provisions for the public health and comfort in parks, boulevards, libraries and museums. The work of a city being the creation and control of the city property, it should logically be managed as a piece of property by those who have created it, or a real substantial part in it, and who can therefore feel strongly their duty to it. Under our theory that a city is a political body, a crowd of illiterate peasants, freshly raked in from Irish bogs, or Bohemian mines, or Italian robber nests, may exercise virtual control."

Andrew D. White, "The Government of American Cities," in *Forum* (1890) reprinted in Edward C. Banfield, *Urban Government: A Reader in Administration and Politics* (Glencoe, IL: The Free Press, 1961).

confronting individuals but rather with the broad social problems confronting groups or classes. Reformers view government as an instrument for achieving broad social reforms and not merely as a source of jobs, buildings and civic improvements, or upward social mobility for gifted individuals from the lower classes. The politics of reform is frequently more ideological than pragmatic. Appeals are made to lofty principles, rather than material welfare. All of this, of course, is in direct contrast to the machine style of politics.

THE TRIUMPH OF REFORM?

The machine style of politics has largely disappeared from the urban scene.

Reasons for the Machine's Decline   Parties in general are losing their appeal to many Americans. Increasing proportions of voters are identifying themselves as "independents," rather than as Democrats or Republicans. (See Chapter 5.) Party offices (precinct committee, ward chairperson, county committee, and so on) are vacant in many cities and counties. The general decline in parties has contributed to the decline of machine politics. Several additional factors might be cited as contributing to the decline of machine politics:

1. The decline in immigration and the gradual assimilation of white ethnic groups—Irish, Italians, Germans, Poles, Slavs.
2. Federal social welfare programs, which undercut the machine's role in welfare work—unemployment insurance, workers' compensation, social security, and public assistance.
3. Rising levels of prosperity and higher educational levels, which make the traditional rewards of the machine less attractive.
4. The spread of middle-class values about honesty, efficiency, and good government, which inhibit party organizations in purchases, contracts, and vote buying, and other cruder forms of municipal corruption.
5. New avenues of upward social mobility that have opened up to the sons and daughters of ethnics, blacks, and working class families, and higher education which has allowed many to join the ranks of professionals, corporate executives, educators, and so on so that the party machine is no longer the only way "up" for persons at the bottom of the social ladder.
6. Structural reforms such as nonpartisanship, better voting procedures, city-manager government, and—most important of all—civil service, which have weakened the party's role in municipal elections and administration.

The Old Patronage   Patronage was once very useful in maintaining a party organization, attracting voters, financing the party, ensuring favorable government actions for party requests, and maintaining discipline within the party's ranks. But patronage jobs have been restricted over the years by the merit system in every state government and most large city governments as well. Many lower-level municipal jobs are not as valuable as they once were, as federal welfare programs and expanded opportunities for urban minorities provide alternatives to poor paying patronage jobs.

The New Patronage   However, if we define *patronage* to include a wide range of tangible benefits—construction contracts, insurance policies, printing and office supplies, architectural services, and other government contracts for goods or services—then patronage may still be important in many communities. Competitive bidding by potential government contractors is required in most states and cities, but it is not difficult to "rig" the process. The fact that the firms that do much of their business with government are also the largest contributors to political campaigns cannot be coincidence. Another source of patronage is the power of courts to appoint referees, appraisers, receivers in bankruptcies, and trustees and executors of estates; these plums require little work and produce high fees for attorneys who are "well connected." Few cities have ever been able to remove zoning from politics: Rezoning property from lower-value classifications (single-family residential) to higher-value classifications (apartments, commercial, industrial) is one of the most important "goodies" available to municipal governments. In addition, municipal construction permits, inspection, and licensing can be slow and cumbersome, or fast and painless, depending on the political resources of the builder-developer.[21]

Persistence of Material Rewards in Politics   Something resembling "machine" politics—political organizations held together and motivated by a desire for tangible benefits rather than principle or ideology—continues to thrive in many cities and rural counties. Most machines may not be as centralized, disciplined, or powerful as in a previous era, but as long as the need to personalize government exists—as long as individuals value small favors, appreciate personal intervention on their behalf with government agencies, need assistance in finding their way around city halls and county court houses, and require help in filing for benefits, obtaining bonds, registering complaints, dealing with the bureaucratic demands of government—political organizations will still have a role to play.

The Personalized Machines   Some big-city mayors have been successful in building personal political organizations centered on the mayor's office. They have expanded their supply of patronage jobs by enlarging the mayoral office staff and creating public authorities and agencies that are directly responsible to the mayor's office. Appointees to these fairly high-paying staff and administrative positions form the nucleus of the mayor's personal campaign organization. A resourceful mayor can augment his or her immediate staff people ("the palace guard") with appointments to city economic development authorities, community rehabilitation agencies, housing authorities, and other quasi-governmental bureaucracies. Many of these bureaucracies are federally funded and their top posts can be filled by an astute mayor using "creative" personnel practices.[22]

---

[21] See also Raymond E. Wolfinger, "Why Political Machines Have Not Withered Away and Other Revisionist Thoughts," *Journal of Politics*, 34 (May 1972), 365–98.

[22] See Alan D. Gaetano, "The Rise of the New Urban Political Machine," paper presented at Midwest Political Science Association meeting, 1986.

The Neighborhood Politician   In many large cities, elements of the old ward politics survive in particular neighborhoods. The neighborhood politician, perhaps a state senator or city council member, still strolls the sidewalks, glad-handing constituents, and promising to find a job for someone, fix a street light, and see about uncollected trash. Indeed, the modern neighborhood politician may enter each constituent's name in the office computer system and keep track of individual requests and favors rendered.[23] It still matters to many voters that their representative grew up in the neighborhood, still lives there, can be contacted day or night, knows their names, and gives personal attention to their problems.

REFORMISM AND PUBLIC POLICY

What are the policy consequences of reform government? Traditionally, political scientists assumed that the reform of city government would bring about changes in public policy. Reform was expected to result in better public services, lower tax rates, and more professional administration. However, *assumptions* regarding the impact of structural changes on public policy are not a substitute for *systematic investigation* of the actual linkages between political structures and public policies.

Sorting Out the Effect of Reform   It is not easy to distinguish *independent* effects of reform on public policy from the effects of other urban characteristics associated with reform—smaller size, southern and western regions, less ethnicity, more middle-class residents. Urban conditions such as population density, income, poverty, mobility, home ownership, and property value are *more* influential than the structure of government in determining levels of taxing and spending. However, despite the overriding importance of social and economic conditions in shaping municipal policy, the structure of government—reformed versus unreformed—does have *some* interesting effects on public policy.

Reform, Taxing, and Spending   The first important systematic study of the policy consequences of reformism found that reformed cities tended to tax and spend *less* than unreformed cities. Cities with manager governments were *less* willing to spend money for public purposes than cities with mayor-council governments.[24] But socioeconomic conditions had an even more important impact than reform on tax and spending policies. For example,

1. The more middle class the city, measured by income, education, and occupation, the lower the general tax and spending levels.
2. The greater the home ownership in a city, the lower the tax and spending levels.

---

[23] John F. Persimos, "Ward Politics 21st-Century Style," *Governing* (October 1989), 46–50.

[24] Robert L. Lineberry and Edmund P. Fowler, "Reformism and Public Policy in American Cities," *American Political Science Review,* 61 (September 1967), 701–16. See also David R. Morgan and John P. Pelissero, "Urban Policy: Does Political Structure Matter?" *American Political Science Review,* 74 (December 1980), 999–1005.

3. The larger the percentage of racial and ethnic minorities in the population, the higher the city's taxes and expenditures.

Reform and Responsiveness   What turned out to be an even more important finding was the difference in *responsiveness* of the two kinds of city governments—reformed and unreformed—to the socioeconomic composition of their populations. *Reformed* cities (cities with manager governments, at-large constituencies, and nonpartisan elections) appeared to be *un*responsive in their tax and spending policies to differences in income and educational, occupational, religious, and ethnic characteristics of their populations. In contrast, unreformed cities (cities with mayor-council governments, ward constituencies, and partisan elections) reflected class, racial, and religious composition in their taxing and spending decisions.

Reformism tends to reduce the importance of race, class, home ownership, ethnicity, and religion in city politics. It tends to minimize the role that social conflicts play in public decision making. In contrast, mayor-council governments, ward constituencies, and partisan elections permit social cleavages to be reflected in city politics and public policy to be responsive to socioeconomic factors. These findings suggest that reformed cities have gone a long way toward accomplishing the reformist goal—that is, "to immunize city governments from 'artificial' social cleavages—race, religion, ethnicity, and so on." Thus, political institutions seem to play an important role in policy formation:

> . . . a role substantially independent of a city's demography. . . . Nonpartisan elections, at-large constituencies, and manager governments are associated with a lessened responsiveness of cities to the enduring conflicts of political life.[25]

In short, reformism makes city governments less responsive to citizens' needs.[26]

Reform as an Obstacle to Civil Rights Groups   The assertion that reformism lessens the responsiveness of city governments was reinforced by an interesting study of the responses of cities to civil-rights-group activity. Political scientist Albert K. Karnig measured the strength of civil rights groups—the National Association for the Advancement of Colored People (NAACP), the National Urban League, the Congress of Racial Equality (CORE), and the Southern Christian Leadership Conference (SCLC)—in 417 cities.[27] He correlated the strength of these organizations with policies generally associated with the needs of poor and black people—low-rent housing, model cities, community-action programs, and neighborhood youth-corps programs. In general, he found the presence of civil rights organizations was related to increased community efforts in these areas. More importantly, however, he found that *reformed governments were less responsive* to civil rights groups in these policy areas than unreformed governments. The associations between

---

[25] Lineberry and Fowler, "Reformism and Public Policy," p. 715. See also William Lyons, "Reform and Response in American Cities," *Social Science Quarterly,* 59 (June 1978), 118–32.

[26] See also Susan Blackall Hansen, "Participation, Political Structure and Concurrence," *American Political Science Review,* 69 (December 1975), 1181–99.

[27] Albert K. Karnig, "Private Regarding Policy, Civil Rights Groups, and the Mediating Impact of Municipal Returns," *American Journal of Political Science,* 19 (February 1975), 91–106.

civil-rights-group activity and policies favoring the poor and the black were *lower* in cities with nonpartisan elections, manager governments, and at-large elections. This evidence suggests that blacks and other urban minorities have little to gain through reformism.

PRIVATIZATION AS REFORM

Conservatives have mounted their own reform movement in state and local government, centering on the notion of the "privatization" of public services. Traditionally conservatives have sought to restrain the growth of government:

> The bigger the government the greater the force for even bigger government. Budgets will expand, resulting in the appointment of more officials and the hiring of more workers. These will go to work at once to enlarge their budgets, do less work, hire still more workers, obtain better-than-average raises, and vote for more spending programs, while encouraging their constituents and beneficiaries to do the same. The forecast seems ominous: Sooner or later everyone will be working for government.[28]

Occasionally citizens revolt against the trend toward ever larger governments by voting for tax limitation proposals or threatening to move to lower tax jurisdictions. But according to the proponents of privatization, "a more educated, critical, and sophisticated" approach to controlling the growth of government is needed, namely the privatization of government services wherever and whenever possible.

Privatization   In the broadest sense privatization includes the shifting of many responsibilities *from* government *to* the private marketplace. "Load shedding" implies that government should sell off many of its enterprises—for example, housing projects, airports, stadiums—to private individuals or firms who would operate them more efficiently and effectively. But privatization has also generally come to mean greater reliance on private providers of governmental services functioning in a competitive marketplace and giving individuals greater choice in services.

Privatization recognizes a distinction between government *provision* of a service and government *production* of a service. Governments may decide to *provide* citizens with certain goods and services—for example, schools, police and fire protection, garbage collection, bus transportation, street maintenance, and so on —but not necessarily *produce* these services directly through government bureaucracies—public schools, municipal police and fire departments, municipal garbage collection, city-owed buses, city street maintenance departments, and so on. Rather, a variety of other methods of "service delivery" are available that rely more on private, competitive producers and individual choice.

How to Privatize   The following are among the more common methods of privatizing the provision of government services:

> *Contracting:* Governments contract with private organizations to provide a publicly funded service. Private firms compete to win and keep the contracts by providing quality services at low costs.

---

28 E. S. Savas, *Privatizing the Public Sector* (New York: Chatham House, 1982), p. 25.

Franchising: Governments grant exclusive contracts for a certain period of time to a private firm to provide a monopoly service—for example, cable television or garbage collection. The private firm collects fees directly from citizens under contractual terms agreed to by the government. The franchise firm may pay a fee to the government for the privilege. Government may terminate the franchise for poor performance or excessive fees charged to citizens.

Grants: Governments provide direct grants of money to private firms or nonprofit organizations conditioned on their providing low-cost services to citizens. Grants are typically made to hospitals and health facilities, libraries and cultural centers, and low-cost housing projects, among others.

Vouchers: Vouchers are given directly to citizens who qualify for them, allowing these citizens to exercise free choice in selecting the producers of the service. Unlike grants, in which the government chooses the producers of the service, vouchers give citizens the power to choose the producer. Producers compete to attract citizens who have vouchers; the vouchers are later turned in to the government by producers for cash. For example, rent vouchers to the poor or homeless allow them to select housing of their choice; grants to public housing organizations oblige the poor and homeless to seek shelter in specific projects. Education vouchers (see Chapter 14) would allow parents to choose any school, public or private, for their children. Schools would compete to attract pupils, cashing in their accumulated vouchers. The federal government's food stamp program is an already existing voucher system (see Chapter 17).

Interjurisdictional agreements: Governments may contract with other governments to provide certain services more efficiently and on a larger scale than they could provide for themselves. Strictly speaking, this is not privatization, but the idea of seeking the most efficient producers is offered as a reform.

Privatization proponents also recommend greater reliance on private market provision of services that government may require citizens to obtain (such as auto insurance), greater reliance on voluntary service and charitable organizations functioning with the cooperation of government; and finally the encouragement of individual self-help that might reduce the need for governmental services.

Surveys of the extent of privatization in city government services suggest that many cities have succeeded in contracting out services for

Vehicle towing and storage

Commercial solid waste disposal

Residential solid waste disposal

Day care facilities

Street light operation

Traffic signal installation/maintenance

Street repairs

Bus system operation

Ambulance service

Airport operation

Hospitals operations/management

roughly in that order of frequency.[29] A few cities and counties have even experimented with privatization of jail operations, building and grounds maintenance, data processing, tax billing, delinquency tax collection, and other functions traditionally performed by government employees.

The Politics of Privatization   Privatization is usually defended as a cost-saving measure—a way of reducing the waste, inefficiency, and unresponsiveness of "bloated municipal bureaucracies." It is argued that private contractors, operating in a competitive marketplace, can provide the same services at much lower costs than government bureaucracies. At the same time, privatization strengthens private enterprise.

Of course, privatization is usually opposed by powerful political groups—especially municipal employees and their unions and teachers' unions and public school administrators. They argue that the cost savings of privatization are often exaggerated and that the savings come at the price of reduced quality and/or a failure to serve all of the people. There is also concern about the loss of public control of services through privatization and a belief that government contractors and franchises can become at least as arrogant and unresponsive as government bureaucracies.

Some reformers acknowledge that privatization is not a cure-all. David Osborne writes that "privatization is one answer, but not *the* answer."

> The most important issue is not "public" vs. "private." It is monopoly vs.
> competition. Sometimes, when governments contract with private companies to
> pick up the garbage or run a prison, they wind up with monopolies, and their costs
> skyrocket. Private monopolies are just as inefficient as public monopolies. Defense
> contractors are an example. So are private utilities, which are in fact more
> expensive than publicly owned utilities.[30]

Government's job, according to Osborne, is to determine whether a particular function can best be produced by government employees; private contractors; or nonprofit, voluntary organizations. Governments cannot hand over the responsibility of *governance* to others; governments still make the policy decisions and provide the financing.

NEW REFORMS: "REINVENTING GOVERNMENT"

The current thrust of reform in government is focused on overcoming "the bankruptcy of bureaucracy"—the waste, inefficiency, impersonality, and unresponsiveness of large government organizations.[31] Today's reform efforts are largely devoted to overcoming the unanticipated results of the early Progressive reform

---

[29] *Municipal Yearbook 1987* (Washington: ICMA, 1988), pp. 43–53.

[30] David Osbourne, "Privatization: One Answer, Not *The* Answer," *Governing* (April 1992), 83.

[31] David Osbourne and Ted Gaebler, *Reinventing Government: How the Entrepreneurial Spirit Is Transforming the Public Sector* (New York: Addison-Wesley, 1992), p. 12.

movement that created the civil service and professionalized city and state and school administrations.

Entrepreneurial Government   People are angry at government at all levels. People believe governments are spending more but delivering less; they are frustrated with bureaucracies over which they have little control and tired of politicians who raise taxes and cut services. According to the new reformers: "Our fundamental problem today is not too much government or too little government . . . [but] the wrong kind of government. We do not need more government or less government, we need better government."[32]

The problem is perceived as one of overcoming "the routine tendency to protect turf, to resist change, to build empires, to enlarge one's sphere of control, to protect projects and programs regardless of whether or not they are any longer needed." The solution is the "entrepreneurial" government that "searches for efficient and effective ways of managing." The reform mayor of Indianapolis describes the entrepreneurial government:

> It is willing to abandon old programs and methods. It is innovative and imaginative and creative. It takes risks. It turns city functions into money makers rather than budget-busters. It eschews traditional alternatives that offer only life-support systems. It works with the private sector. It employs solid business sense. It privatizes. It creates enterprises and revenue-generating operations. It is market oriented. It focuses on performance measurement. It rewards merit. It says "Let's make this work," and it is unafraid to dream the great dream.[33]

Reinventing Government   How is the "entrepreneurial spirit" to be encouraged in government? In their widely read and cited book, *Reinventing Government*, the reformist authors set out ten principles of government entrepreneurialship:

1. *Steer rather than row.* Separate policy decisions (steering) from service delivery (rowing). Government should focus on steering while relying more on private firms to deliver services. Government should be a catalyst.

2. *Empower people rather than simply deliver services.* Governments should encourage communities and neighborhoods to undertake ownership and control of public services. Government should be community-owned.

3. *Inject competition into service delivery.* Competition between public and private agencies, among private contractors, or between different governments encourages efficiency, innovation, and responsiveness. Government should be competitive.

4. *Make government organizations mission-driven rather than rule-driven.* Do not prescribe how government organizations should go about doing things by prescribing rules, procedures, and regulations; but rather set goals and encourage government organizations to find the best ways to achieve them. Government should be mission-driven.

---

[32] Ibid., pp. 23–24.
[33] Quotes in ibid., p. 18.

5. *Encourage governments to be results oriented.* Government bureaucracies should be measured in terms of their results, not their size, numbers, or services. Government should fund outcomes, not inputs.

6. *Focus on the needs of customers, not the bureaucracy.* Governments should treat citizens as if they were customers, responding to their needs, "putting them in the driver's seat." Government should be customer-driven.

7. *Encourage governments to earn money through user charges.* Charging the users of government services, whenever possible, is fair; it raises revenues and balances demands for services. Governments should be enterprising.

8. *Practice prevention rather than cure.* Problems from fires to ill-health are cheaper to address through prevention than services. Government should be anticipatory.

9. *Decentralize government organizations.* Decentralization increases flexibility, effectiveness, innovation, morale, and commitment. Government should be decentralized.

10. *Use market incentives to bring about change rather than command and control.* Market mechanisms are preferred over regulations. Government should be market oriented.

Note that these are guiding principles, rather than recommendations for changes in the structure of state or local government. Unlike earlier reformers who focused on structural changes, today's reformers are more concerned about *how* governments go about their tasks.

Politics of Reinvention   The principles of "reinvention" are identified with the "neoliberal" ("new" liberals) and Democrats who acquired influence in state and local politics in the 1980s. A recognized leader of the movement was Arkansas Governor Bill Clinton who was widely praised for his innovative efforts in education and economic development in that state.[34] Clinton served for several years as chair of the Democratic Leadership Conference (DLC), designed to move the national Democratic party toward a more moderate, centrist position that could win back the support of white middle-class voters in presidential elections.

Political opposition to the new reform arises from many of the core constituency groups of the Democratic party—government employees, teachers' unions, environmental groups, and black leaders and organizations. Jesse Jackson once described the DLC derisively as "Democrats for the Leisure Class." Government employees and their unions are concerned about the antibureaucratic thrust of many of the new reforms; they fear a loss of their government sector jobs to private contractors. Likewise teachers' unions have been concerned with the reformers' focus on government performance, fearing that it means competence testing of students and teachers (see Chapter 15). Blacks and other minority groups fear that the focus on efficiency and productivity will overshadow concerns about equity. User fees and charges often place heavy burdens on the poor.

---

[34] See Thomas Osborne, *Laboratories of Democracy* (Boston: Harvard Business School, 1988), Ch. 3, "Arkansas: The Education Model."

POLITICAL CORRUPTION

Corruption is an ever-present theme in American political life. We all know that "politics is corrupt," but with the exception of some well-publicized cases, we really do not know *how* much corruption takes place. Corruption *may* be more widespread in state and local politics than in national politics, because state and local officials can avoid the spotlight of the national news media.

Defining Corruption   One major problem in studying corruption is defining the term. What is "corrupt" to one observer may be "just politics" to another or merely "an embarrassment" to someone else.

One attempt to sort out some of the ambiguities of "corruption" focused on four components:[35]

1. *The use of official position.* If officials use their public post in the illegal activity, it is considered *more* corrupt than if officials commit an illegal act outside of their official duties.

2. *The donor's relation to the official.* If the donor is a constituent, the favor performed is *less* likely to be perceived as corrupt than if the favor was performed for a nonconstituent. Using one's office to directly steal from the public treasury for one's own personal enrichment is "corrupt"; but using one's influence to obtain costly favors from other government agencies for one's hometown constituents is not.

3. *The favor rendered by the official.* If the favor rendered by the official is very special, it is more likely to be considered corrupt than if it is a routine type of constituent service. (Routine calls by legislators to executive agencies to check on the status of contracts for firms located in the legislator's district are not usually considered corrupt, even when the firms are large campaign contributors.)

4. *The size and nature of the payoff.* If the payoff is very large and occurs near the date of the favor, it is considered more corrupt than if the payoff is modest and is separated in time from the favor. Finally, money given for personal use is considered more corrupt than money given for campaign expenses.

For example, here is a list of hypothetical acts that state senators in twenty-four states were asked to rate as more or less corrupt, together with the percentage of senators who viewed each act as corrupt.[36]

1. The driveway of the mayor's home being paved by the city crew—95.9 percent.

2. A public official using public funds for personal travel—95.2 percent.

3. A state assembly member, while chairman of the public roads committee, authorizing the purchase of land he or she had recently acquired—95.1 percent.

---

[35] John G. Peters and Susan Welch, "Political Corruption in America: A Search for Definitions and a Theory," *American Political Science Review,* 72 (September 1978), 974–84.

[36] Ibid., p. 978.

4. A legislator accepting a large campaign contribution in return for voting "the right way" on a legislative bill—91.9 percent.

5. A judge with $50,000 worth of stock in a corporation hearing a case concerning that firm—78.8 percent.

6. A presidential candidate promising an ambassadorship in exchange for campaign contributions— 71.1 percent.

7. A secretary of defense owning $50,000 in stock in a company with which the Defense Department has a million-dollar contract—58.3 percent.

8. A member of Congress who holds a large amount of stock (about $50,000 worth) in Exxon working to maintain the oil depletion allowance—54.9 percent.

9. A member of Congress using seniority to obtain a weapons contract for a firm in his or her district—31.6 percent.

10. A public official using influence to get a friend or relative admitted to law school—23.7 percent.

The line between unethical behavior and criminal activity is a fuzzy one. Unethical behavior includes lying and misrepresentation; sexual exploitation and harassment; favoritism toward relatives, friends, and constituents; conflicts of interest, in which public officials decide issues in which they have a personal financial interest. Not all unethical behavior is criminal conduct. But bribery is a criminal offense—soliciting or receiving anything of value in exchange for the performance of a governmental duty.

How Much Corruption?   It is difficult to estimate the extent of corruption in American politics, in part because public officials do not usually volunteer information on their own corrupt behavior! The U.S. Justice Department reports on *federal* prosecutions of public officials for violations of criminal statutes (see Figure 10–1). These figures do not include state prosecutions, so they do not cover all of the criminal indictments brought against public officials each year. (And, of course, they do not tell us how much corruption went undetected.) Nonetheless, these figures indicate that now over one thousand public officials are indicted and convicted of criminal activity each year.

Explaining Corruption   Why do some government officials engage in corruption? We can think of at least three reasons: (1) for personal gain, that is, simply to enrich themselves; (2) to benefit friends, constituents, or ethnic groups with con-

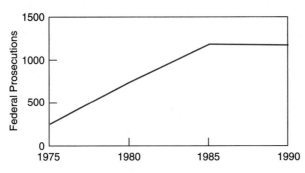

FIGURE 10–1   **Federal Prosecutions of Public Corruption**

Source: Statistical Abstract of the United States 1992, p. 195.

tracts, jobs, and aid; and (3) to bring coordination to fragmented government by exchanging favors simply "to get things done." Often we think of activities under these last two categories as less corrupt than efforts to achieve personal gain. Corruption for personal gain is less acceptable. Yet such corruption is almost an American tradition. Politicians over the years could echo Tammany Hall's George Washington Plunkitt, "I seen my opportunities and I took 'em."[37]

Political corruption is more common in some cities and states than in others. Generally corruption is measured by federal prosecutions because it is more common in large cities and larger states. Competitive parties tend to dampen corruption somewhat, suggesting that strong opposition parties perform a watchdog function. Gambling is closely associated with official corruption. But the size of government bureaucracies appears to be the strongest determinant of corruption: As government grows, so do the opportunities for corruption.[38]

Prosecuting Corruption   Investigating and prosecuting state and local government officials for corrupt activity was once the exclusive responsibility of the state attorney general's office using state laws. But today U.S. attorneys have largely taken over this responsibility. Acting under broad federal statutes—federal laws dealing with mail fraud, tax fraud, and the RICO Act (Racketeer Influenced and Corrupt Organizations)—federal prosecutors have largely displaced state prosecutors in dealing with official corruption.[39] Federal prosecutors have the vast resources of the FBI, the Internal Revenue Service, the Postal Inspection Service, and a myriad of other federal agencies to assist them in investigations. Moreover, U.S. attorneys have great discretion in their investigatory and prosecutory decisions. U.S. attorneys, unlike regional directors of other federal departments, are nominated by the president and confirmed by the U.S. Senate. They are not only free from state or local influence, they are also free from interference from federal elected officials. They can initiate lengthy and complex investigations, convene federal grand juries, obtain indictments, arrange plea bargains with defendants, and build "pyramid" cases against prominent officials. ("Pyramid building" consists of dropping or reducing charges against lower-level figures in exchange for their testimony implicating higher officials.) Federal prosecutors generally pride themselves on their ability to prosecute prominent state and local officials. And well-publicized successful prosecutions often provide a springboard for their own political ambitions.

The great discretion given U.S. attorneys, combined with partisan politics and their own personal ambitions, can lead to selective use of federal laws against prominent officials. Indeed, the possibility of "targeting" by a federal prosecutor should inspire caution in even the most honest state and local officials. Cleaning up

---

[37] Riordan, *Plunkitt of Tammany Hall*, p. 3.

[38] These findings are set forth in Kenneth J. Meier and Thomas M. Holbrook, "'I Seen My Opportunities and I Took 'Em': Political Corruption in the American States," *Journal of Politics*, 54 (February 1992), 135–55.

[39] See Arthur Maass, "Public Policy by Prosecution," *The Public Interest* (Fall 1987), 107–27.

political corruption in state and local government is *not* an enumerated or implied power of the federal government. This is one more activity that has shifted from the state to the national level and undermined earlier ideas of the American federalism (see Chapter 3). The states have a special interest in policing their own political processes. The principal responsibility for attacking corruption should rest with the states themselves and the people who elect state and local officials.

Voter Reaction   Do voters punish officials for corrupt activities? Not always. Voters sometimes reelect officials who have been convicted of criminal offenses. There are various reasons for the continued voter support of corrupt politicians. First of all, *charges* of corruption are so frequent in election campaigns that voters disregard information about improprieties in office. Or voters may perceive both candidates as more or less corrupt and simply make their voting choices on other factors. Second, if voters believe that officials' corrupt acts were designed to benefit their district or their race or their ethnic group, they may support them despite (or even because of) their corrupt acts. Third, corrupt politicians may be popular with their constituents, whether personally or because of their stand on issues; constituents may knowingly ignore corruption because they value the representation more. There are many other issues besides "honesty in government."[40]

THE RADICAL STYLE: POLITICS IN BERKELEY

Imagine a city council meeting held in a theater, with hundreds of enraged participants shouting political obscenities at each other, in a fierce debate over a resolution dealing with Israel's policy toward the Palestinians. Welcome to Berkeley, California, where a radical political style has displaced both traditional machine and liberal reform politics. If you believe that land reform in Nicaragua, or U.S. nuclear weapons policy, or hunger in Somalia might be beyond the scope of municipal government, you would be adjudged guilty of "sandbox politics" (thinking locally instead of globally) in Berkeley. Moreover, in dealing with garbage collection or traffic control, it is most important that you devise "environmentally correct, politically progressive solutions." For Berkeley thinks of itself as a beacon of "progressive" (radical) politics, an inspiring example for Madison, Wisconsin, and Burlington, Vermont, and eventually every other city in the world.[41]

Early in this century, Berkeley was a leader in reform politics, having adopted council-manager government in 1923. Home of the University of California, for many years Berkeley reflected the liberal reform politics so popular among academics. It developed fair housing laws, a school integration plan, public housing

[40] For some tests about voter reaction to corruption, see Barry S. Rundquist, Gerald S. Strom, and John G. Peters, "Corrupt Politicians and Their Electoral Support," *American Political Science Review*, 71 (September 1977), 954–63.

[41] See Joseph P. Lyford, "The Lessons of Berkeley," *The Center Magazine* (March 1980), 54–63; Peter Collier and David Horowitz, "Slouching Towards Berkeley: Socialism in One City," *The Public Interest* (Winter 1989), 47–68; Gail L. Zellman and Steven L. Schlossman, "The Berkeley Youth Wars," *The Public Interest* (Summer 1986), 29–41.

and citywide planning, all well in advance of other cities in the nation. But in the 1960s the Vietnam War "radicalized" politics in Berkeley. Anti-American and revolutionary romanticism replaced liberal politics; "revolutionary violence" was promoted as the path to "soulful socialism in Berkeley." Tom Hayden, now California state representative, organized the Berkeley Liberation Front, and in 1969 the first radical was elected to the Berkeley city council, Ronald Dellums, now a U.S. Congressman. By 1975 radicals had become the dominant force in Berkeley politics. They created a strongly disciplined organization, Berkeley Citizens' Action, renamed themselves "progressives," and set about the task of bringing socialism to Berkeley and the world.

One of their earliest programs centered on establishing "community control" over the police. A series of police department resignations and shakeups followed. Crime rates rose dramatically, as did drug sales and use. By the late 1980s Berkeley was challenging much larger American cities for the dubious honor of having the highest crime rate in the nation.

The radical agenda for Berkeley included a vigorous rent control program and stringent building regulation that virtually shut down private construction and real estate investment in the city. Wealth was to be "expropriated" in favor of "the people." The result was a disastrous decline in available housing and a rapid increase in homelessness. The radical response to these developments was to call for more public housing and to blame Washington when not enough funds were forthcoming for this purpose.

Berkeley's school system had once been regarded as one of California's finest. Berkeley had adopted a voluntary school desegregation plan in the early 1960s. But when radicals won control of the school board, they undertook to replace racial integration with "cultural nationalism"—the development of separate schools where black students would study black culture and Hispanic students would study Hispanic culture. These schools were eventually closed by the federal courts, but the resulting turmoil led one-quarter of Berkeley parents—black, white, and Hispanic—to send their children to private schools.

Distinguishing features of the radical political style include:

Diverting the community's attention from local to national and international political issues.

Abusing democratic processes by disruptive and violent behavior at public meetings under the guise of participating democracy.

Tolerating violent behavior by leftist and minority groups and rationalizing such behavior.

Stressing conflict rather than seeking consensus on the radical assumption that revolutions require continuing class struggle.

Elements of radical or "progressive" politics are identifiable in many cities.

It is no coincidence that the cities that have flirted with radical politics are university locations. Neither the faculty nor the students have a strong identification with real city problems—crime, garbage, streets, sewers, and so on. University life fosters abstract thinking about politics, and the temporary residential status of students and many faculty undermines responsibility for the long-term future of the community. Universities are independently funded; administrators, faculty, and students do not have to worry about the economic foundation of the community. And, of course, liberal to radical politics are popular among faculty, students, and the nonstudents who settle on the fringes of universities.

11

Participation in Community Politics

Voters in Municipal Elections

The influence of the voter is felt not only on election day but on every day that elected officials act to win voter support or avoid voter displeasure.

Voter turnout in local elections is substantially lower than in state or national elections. While 55 percent of the nation's eligible voters may cast ballots in a presidential election, voter turnouts of 25 to 35 percent are typical in local elections. Moreover, voter turnout in local elections has been declining over recent decades.

Nonpartisanship depresses voter turnout quite substantially. Voter turnout for municipal elections in nonpartisan cities averages closer to 25 percent, compared to over 35 percent for partisan cities. Partisan campaigns heighten voter turnout, in part because of the greater interest they generate and in part because of the role of party workers in getting out the vote.

Voter participation in local government can be further reduced by holding municipal elections at odd times of the year when no other state or national elections are being held. Approximately 60 percent of the nation's cities hold municipal elections that are completely independent of state or national elections. A common rationale for holding municipal elections at times other than state or national elections is to separate local issues from state or national questions, but the real effect of scheduling local elections independently is to reduce voter turnout and to increase the influence of groups who vote more regularly.

Voter turnout in cities with a mayor-council form of government is much higher than in cities with a council-manager plan. In summary, nonpartisanship, council-manager government, and separate municipal elections—all part of the municipal "reform" movement—operate to reduce voter turnout and probably strengthen the influence of middle-class voters at the polls.

Voter turnout in municipal elections is also affected by the social character of cities. Social cleavages, especially race, increase voter turnout. Mayoral elections in which the racial or ethnic backgrounds of the candidates are well publicized inspire heavy voter turnout. Social homogeneity, on the other hand, is associated with lower voter interest.

In summary, voter turnout in municipal elections can be described as follows:

Lower voter turnout is expected with:	*Higher voter turnout is expected with:*
• Nonpartisan electoral systems	• Partisan elections with competitive parties
• Council-manager form of government	• Strong mayor form of government
• City elections held separately from state or national elections	• City elections held concurrently with state and national elections
• Small or middle-sized cities	• Large cities
• Middle-class, homogeneous cities	• Ethnic, heterogeneous cities
• Midwestern, western, and southern cities	• Eastern cities

URBAN VOTER COALITIONS

The nation's large central cities tend to be Democratic, even when their suburbs are normally Republican. Working-class and ethnic whites in large cities may differ with blacks and white liberals over such issues as busing, affirmative action, and police activity. These issues, however, are more likely to cause splits *within* the Democratic party, and it is doubtful that the GOP can make any permanent inroads into Democratic control of the nation's large cities.

Referenda Voting   *Referenda voting* is an important aspect of local politics—an aspect not found at the national level. City charters frequently require that referenda be held on all proposals to increase indebtedness or to increase property taxation. Over three-quarters of American cities have referenda provisions in their charters. (See Table 11–1.) Citizen initiatives are permitted in over half of all council-manager cities but are permitted in only 37 percent of mayor-council and commission cities. Recall elections are permitted in over half of all American cities. (See Chapter 2 for definitions of initiative, referenda, and recall elections.)

Table 11-1   Cities with Initiative, Referendum, and Recall

Form of Government	Initiative	Referendum	Recall
Mayor-council	36.8%	71.4%	52.9%
Council-manager	58.8	82.9	70.4
Commission	36.5	76.1	59.4

Source: International City Managers' Association, *Municipal Yearbook 1989,* p. 10.

Home-Ownership   Referenda votes provide us with an excellent opportunity to examine the factors influencing voter attitudes toward local government and to test some theories about voting behavior on local issues. One theory is that voters in local referenda will try to maximize family income by weighing the benefits that will come to them from a bond issue against the amount of the tax that will fall on them as a result of the expenditure.[1] Non–property owners, having nothing to lose by the expenditure and something to gain, however small, can be expected to favor the passage of bond and expenditure referenda. (Renters seldom realize that landlords will pass the tax increase on to them in higher rent.) Homeowners are more likely to oppose public expenditures that are financed from property taxes than nonhomeowners.

"Public-Regardingness"   However, support for public expenditures may also be a function of a liberal, *public-regarding* ethic, which is rooted in an upper-class, white, Anglo-Saxon Protestant subculture in America. Public-regarding voters have a conception of the public interest that inspires them to support measures that benefit the whole community, whether or not they produce specific personal rewards. In contrast, *private-regarding* voters—mostly lower-income, working-class, Irish, Italian, Polish and other eastern European white voters—tend to vote against public expenditures that do not directly benefit them.[2] Blacks are much more likely to support public expenditures than low-income whites; although black homeowners are somewhat less enthusiastic than black renters.

Support for Public Spending   Whether one accepts the "public-regardingness" explanation or not, voting studies suggest: (1) Nonhomeowners give greater support to proposals for public spending than homeowners; (2) among homeowners, wealthy families support public expenditures more than middle- or low-income

---

[1] The following discussion of voter behavior on referenda relies upon James Q. Wilson and Edward C. Banfield, "Public Regardingness as a Value Premise in Voting Behavior," *American Political Science Review,* 58 (December 1964), 876–87; and "Political Ethos Revisited," *American Political Science Review,* 65 (December 1971), 1048–62.

[2] This explanation is disputed in Raymond E. Wolfinger and John Field, "Political Ethos and the Structure of City Government," *American Political Science Review,* 60 (June 1966), 306–26; and Roger Durand, "Ethnicity, Public-Regardingness and Referenda Voting," *Midwest Journal of Political Science,* 16 (May 1972), 259–68.

families; (3) white Anglo-Saxon Protestants, blacks, and Jews tend to support public expenditures more than Irish, Italian, Polish, or other eastern European ethnic voters.

The coalition between affluent, educated, upper-class, liberal whites and ghetto blacks is an important force in the politics of many big cities. Working-class ethnic whites see themselves increasingly threatened by both blacks and white liberals on the issues of busing, welfare, crime, and job preference. (See Chapter 13.)

GETTING INTO COMMUNITY POLITICS

Political ambition is the most distinguishing characteristic of elected officeholders at all levels of government. The people who run for and win public office are not necessarily the most intelligent, best-informed, wealthiest, or most successful business or professional people. At all levels of the political system, from presidential candidates, members of Congress, governors and state legislators, to city council and school board members, it is the most politically ambitious people who are willing to sacrifice time, family and private life, and energy and effort for the power and celebrity that comes with public office.

Most politicians publicly deny that personal ambition is their real motivation for seeking public office. Rather they describe their motives in highly idealistic terms—"civic duty," "service to community," "reform the government," "protect the environment." These responses reflect the norms of our political culture: People are not supposed to enter politics to satisfy *personal* ambitions, but rather to achieve *public* purposes. Many politicians do not really recognize their own drive for power—the drive to shape their community according to their own beliefs and values. But if there were no personal rewards in politics, no one would run for office.

Political Entrepreneurship   The talent required is that of *political entrepreneurship*—the ability to sell oneself to others as a candidate, to raise money from contributors, to organize people to work on one's behalf, to communicate and publicize oneself through the media. Political parties no longer recruit candidates; candidates recruit themselves. Interest groups do not recruit candidates; candidates seek out interest groups to win their support.

Professionalization   Politics is becoming increasingly professionalized. "Citizen-politicians"—people with business or professional careers who get into politics part time or for short periods of time—are being driven out of political life by career politicians—people who enter politics early in life as a full-time occupation and expect to make it their career.[3] Politics is increasingly demanding of time and energy. At all levels of governments, from city council to state legislatures to the U.S. Congress, political work is becoming full time and year-round. It is not only more demanding to *hold* office than it was a generation ago, but also far more de-

---

[3] Alan Ehrenhalt, *The United States of Ambition: Politicians, Power and the Pursuit of Office* (New York: Random House, 1991), p. 22.

manding to *run* for office. Campaigning has become more time-consuming, more technically sophisticated, and much more costly over time.

Occupations   Traditionally, city council members and county commissioners were local business people who were respected in the community and active in civic organizations. They were likely to own small businesses and to have many contacts among constituents—retail merchants, real estate brokers, insurance agents, and so on. (Seldom do executives of large corporations concern themselves with local affairs, although they may encourage lower-management personnel to do so.) The part-time nature of traditional community governance, combined with only nominal pay and few perks of office, made local office-holding a "community service." It attracted people whose business brought them into close contact with the life of the community and allowed them spare time to attend to community affairs.

These civic-minded small business people are still politically dominant in small towns and rural counties throughout the nation. But they are gradually being replaced by lawyers, government employees, teachers, and professional office-holders in medium to large cities. In these cities, council pay is higher, the work more time-consuming, greater celebrity attaches to council membership (television interviews, newspaper stories, deference, and respect), and greater opportunities exist for political advancement.

> Full-timers drive part-timers out of circulation. The city councilman who spends his days building political coalitions, meeting with constituents, and cultivating financial support sets a standard of political sophistication that colleagues pretty much have to meet if they are going to stay effective or even stay in office. Once a city council attracts its full-time members, it is on the way to becoming a de facto full-time institution, even if it does not think of itself as one.[4]

Political Bias in Recruitment   As a result of the increasing professionalization of local politics, liberals and Democrats are more likely to win office. Increasing demands of time and energy attract people for whom politics is more important and more rewarding than business or professional success. Older business and professional leaders, who once managed city affairs on a part-time basis while still tending to their businesses and professions, tended to be conservative and Republican. But these part-time, civic-minded business leaders are gradually being replaced by younger people for whom politics is a career.

> Serving in city government in Concord used to be easy work. Businessmen did it in their spare time. As the city grew, governing it became a demanding, time-consuming job. The Republican merchants and insurance brokers who used to do it no longer wanted to take the time. In their place came political professionals, and all the professionals, over an entire decade, were Democrats.[5]

---

[4] Ibid., p. 14.

[5] Ibid., p. 7.

City Councils: Terms and Elections   In most American cities, especially those with nonpartisan at-large elections, getting elected to city council is a do-it-yourself project. Most party organizations and civic associations are unreliable as sources of money and workers. Candidates must mobilize their own resources and create their own organizations. It is generally unwise to challenge an incumbent; over 80 percent of all incumbent council members seeking reelection are returned to office. When vacancies occur, there are likely to be many candidates in the race. Since local races lack the visibility of national or statewide races, most focus on the personality, style, or image of the candidate. Even when local issues divide the candidates, most voters in local elections will be unaware of the candidates' stands on these issues.

Winning Elections   In this fluid setting, electoral success depends on (1) the social acceptability of candidates relative to the community (especially their race and ethnic background); (2) their personal recognition in the community (name recognition, contacts from business, church, civic activity, etc.); and (3) their political resources (endorsements by newspapers and civic associations, access to political contributors, people willing to serve as volunteer workers, etc.). These factors are especially important for first-time candidates.[6] In subsequent campaigns, candidates develop more stable political followings.

Nonpartisanship   A majority of American cities elect their council members in nonpartisan elections (see Table 9–5). This reflects the success of the reform movement (described in Chapter 10) and the widespread acceptance of the idea of nonpartisanship in municipal government.

Council Size   Most city councils have five or seven members, but large city councils with up to twenty-two members are found in the larger, older cities of the Northeast and Midwest (see Table 11–2).

Council Terms   Four-year terms for council members are most frequent, but some council members are elected for two- or three-year terms. In most cities, council member terms overlap, so that some council seats are filled at every municipal election. Presumably overlapping terms ensure continuity in the deliberations of the council.

At-Large Versus District Elections   About two-thirds of American cities elect their council members at large and an additional 20 percent elect council members from a combination of at-large and district constituencies. At-large elections, where council candidates face the entire city electorate, are part of the package of "reform" government, together with nonpartisanship and manager government. However, at-large elections are increasingly coming under court scrutiny. Depending on the "totality of circumstances" in a community, at-large elections may adversely affect the voting rights of minorities. (See Chapter 9.)

---

[6] See Joel Lieske, "The Political Dynamics of Urban Voting Behavior," *American Journal of Political Science,* 33 (February 1989), 150–74.

TABLE 11–2   CITY COUNCILS

	Average Size of Council	Council Terms (%)		
		TWO YEARS	THREE YEARS	FOUR YEARS
Total	6.5	29.5	9.5	60.0
Size of city				
Over 1 million	22.0	50.0	0	50.0
500,000 to 1 million	13.3	40.0	0	60.0
250,000 to 500,000	10.2	33.3	0	66.7
100,000 to 150,000	8.0	19.5	2.6	77.9
50,000 to 100,000	8.0	28.1	2.6	68.4
25,000 to 50,000	6.8	25.8	6.2	65.6
10,000 to 25,000	6.5	28.0	12.5	57.5
5,000 to 10,000	6.2	29.1	11.8	57.6
Under 5,000	5.9	32.1	8.2	59.0

Source: International City Managers' Association, *Municipal Yearbook 1982,* pp. 182–83.

Runoff Elections   It has been alleged that majority runoff requirements in nonpartisan municipal elections pose a disadvantage for minority and women candidates. It is claimed that minority candidates who win a plurality of votes in the first-round election are later defeated in the runoff by a coalition of antiminority voters. But systematic studies of this issue fail to produce any evidence to support this minority disadvantage claim regarding runoff elections. Indeed, on the average, first-round front-runners win runoffs twice as often as they lose. (However, *incumbents* who are forced into runoffs lose more often than their challengers.) Blacks and women who win first-round elections are just as likely to win runoffs as white males.[7]

Friends at City Hall   A surprising number of council members are initially *appointed* to their office to fill the unexpired terms of resigning members. Those appointees are likely to be personal friends of council members or to have held some other city job. Finally, 80 percent of incumbents running for reelection are successful. Voluntary retirement is the most common exit from community politics. Political scientist Kenneth Prewitt observes that

> The election system provides advantages to those citizens who already have social and political resources; to those favorably located in the network of friendships which play such an important part in city politics; to those whose apprentice roles identify them as likely candidates for political office; to those who have natural

[7] See Charles S. Bullock and Loch K. Johnson, "Runoff Elections in Georgia," *Journal of Politics,* 47 (August 1985) 937–46; Arnold Fleischmann and Lana Stein, "Minority and Female Success in Municipal Runoff Elections," *Social Science Quarterly,* 68 (June 1987), 378–85.

organizational ties and support; and, finally, to those already in office if they choose to stand for reelection.[8]

WOMEN IN LOCAL POLITICS

Women's participation in local politics has risen dramatically in recent years. Today, of the approximately 19,000 municipal council members serving in cities with populations over 10,000, over 3700 or almost 20 percent are women.[9] As late as 1975 this figure was estimated to be only about 4 percent. Women have served as mayors of Chicago (Jane Byrne, 1979–1983), San Francisco (Diane Feinstein, 1978–1988), Dallas (Annette Strauss, 1987–1991), Houston (Kathy Whitmire, 1982–1992), Cincinnati (Bobbie Stern, 1975–1976, 1978–1979) and continue to serve in Pittsburgh (Sophie Masloff), San Diego (Maureen O'Conner), Washington, DC (Sharon Pratt Kelly), and many other major cities.

Why Local Politics?   Why have women taken a more active role in community politics? The increase in women's political participation has taken place at all levels of government, with more women serving in Congress[10] and in state legislatures (see Chapter 6). The movement of women into politics generally is attributed to the movement of women into the work force and the changing cultural values redefining women's role in American society. At the local level, women may find fewer obstacles to political office-holding than at the state or national level. Local offices do not require women to move away from their home communities to the state capital or to Washington. Women candidates, unlike men, are seldom relieved of all of their home responsibilities when running for or occupying political office.[11] Moreover, campaigns for local office do not require as much money as state or congressional campaigns. Fund raising has been a traditional obstacle to women candidates, although that barrier is diminishing relative to men over time. There is also a long tradition of women in volunteer community organizations, from hospitals and welfare agencies to cultural centers and neighborhood associations. Upon reexamining their traditional community roles, many women decided to use the knowledge and experience gained in volunteer work to move into elective politics:

> After devoting considerable time and energy to organizational life and civic activities, voluntary community service, or political party work, [a] woman sees it as only reasonable that she should be moving into elective or appointive positions of public responsibility.[12]

---

[8] Kenneth Prewitt, *The Recruitment of Political Leaders: A Study of Citizen-Politicians* (Indianapolis: Bobbs-Merrill, 1970), p. 148.

[9] Center for the American Woman in Politics, Eagleton Institute of Politics, Rutgers University, 1993.

[10] See Thomas R. Dye, *Politics in America* (Englewood Cliffs, NJ: Prentice Hall, 1994), Ch. 10.

[11] Ruth B. Mandel, *In the Running: The New Woman Candidate* (New Haven, CT: Ticknor and Fields, 1981), pp. 63–97.

[12] Ibid., p. 13.

Policy Consequences   What are the policy consequences of increased women's representation on city councils? The best available evidence suggests that there are no significant policy differences between men and women council members, even on feminist issues.[13] For example, political scientist Susan Gluck Mezey found that both men and women on Connecticut councils supported abortions, day care centers, and rape crisis centers. Typical liberal and conservative identifications were better predictors of how council members stood on issues than gender itself. Thus, increasing female representation in local government may not result in major policy changes.[14]

MINORITIES IN LOCAL POLITICS

Local politics is the entry level in the American political system for minorities as well as women. In 1992 over half of the largest cities in the United States had minority or women mayors (see Table 11–3). All but two of these twenty-two cities had minority or women mayors in the recent past.

Minority Mayors   Black mayors have served in many cities with majority white populations, including New York, Chicago, Los Angeles, and Philadelphia, as well as cities with majority black populations, including Detroit, Washington, DC, and New Orleans.

The success of blacks and Hispanics in city politics, especially in majority white and Anglo cities, suggests that race is becoming less important as a criterion in voter choice for municipal leadership. However, voting patterns in city elections in which black and white candidates face each other indicate a continuing residue of racial politics. Black voters continue to cast their votes solidly for black candidates in these elections; white voters continue to give majority support to white candidates. The swing vote in these black–white election confrontations usually rests with 30 to 40 percent of white voters who are prepared to support qualified black candidates.

Successful black candidates in majority white cities have generally emphasized racial harmony and conciliation. They have stressed broad themes of concern to all voters—regardless of race. They have built coalitions that cut across racial, ethnic, and economics lines; many have worked their way up the ranks of local organizations. They have avoided identification as "protest" candidates.

Minorities on Councils   Until recently blacks were generally underrepresented on city councils across the country. That is to say, blacks held a smaller proportion of seats on city councils than the black percentages of city populations. But the

---

[13] Susan Gluck Mezey, "Support for Women's Rights Policy," *American Politics Quarterly,* 6 (October 1978), 485–96. See also Albert K. Karnig and B. Oliver Walter, "Election of Women to City Councils," *Social Science Quarterly,* 56 (March 1976), 605–13.

[14] However, assertions of "gender cleavage" in municipal politics, based on observations of a single city where men supported economic development projects and women opposed them, can be found in Paul Schumaker and Nancy Elizabeth Burns, "Gender Cleavages and the Resolution of Local Policy Issues," *American Journal of Political Science,* 32 (November 1988), 1070–95.

TABLE 11-3   MINORITY AND WOMEN MAYORS

	Population (000)	Mayor	Percent Black	Percent Hispanic
New York	7,263	David Dinkins[a]	25	20
Los Angeles	3,259	Tom Bradley[a]	17	28
Chicago	3,010	Richard M. Daley	40	14
Philadelphia	1,643	Edward G. Rendell	38	4
Detroit	1,086	Coleman Young[a]	63	2
Houston	1,729	Bob Lanier	28	18
Washington, DC	626	Sharon Pratt Kelly[ab]	70	3
New Orleans	554	Sidney Barthelemy[a]	55	3
Boston	574	Raymond Flynn	22	6
Atlanta	422	Maynard Jackson[a]	67	1
St. Louis	426	Vincent Schoemehl	46	1
Dallas	1,004	Steve Bartlett	29	12
Minneapolis	357	Donald Frager	8	1
Baltimore	753	Curtis Schmoke[a]	55	1
San Diego	1,015	Maureen O'Conner[b]	9	15
Pittsburgh	387	Sophie Masloff[b]	24	1
Oakland	357	Lionel Wilson[a]	47	10
Cleveland	536	Mike White	44	3
Seattle	486	Norm Rice[a]	10	3
Miami	374	Xavier Suarez[c]	25	56
Denver	505	Fredrico Pena[c]	12	19
San Francisco	749	Frank Jordan	13	12

Office-holders January 1, 1993.

[a] Black.

[b] Women.

[c] Hispanic.

steady rise in the number of black city council members and county commissioners over the last twenty years (see Figure 11–1) has brought black representation to rough proportionality in most American cities. In cities in which blacks constitute 10 to 50 percent of the population, black representation on city councils generally reflects the black population percentage (see Figure 11–2). In cities in which the black population constitutes a majority (over 50 percent), black representation on city councils usually exceeds the black population percentage.[15]

In contrast, Hispanic representation on city councils is significantly below the Hispanic population percentages. Earlier we observed that Hispanic voter turnout was significantly lower than that for other social groups (see Chapter 4). Lower voter turnout among Hispanics is frequently attributed to cultural and language

---

[15] Susan Welch, "The Impact of At-Large Elections on the Representation of Blacks and Hispanics," *Journal of Politics*, 52 (November 1990), 1050–76.

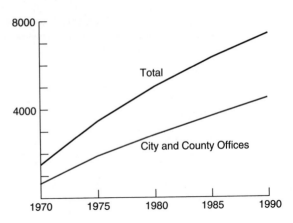

**FIGURE 11–1   Black
Elected Officials**

Source: Data from *Statistical
Abstract of the United States 1992,*
p. 267.

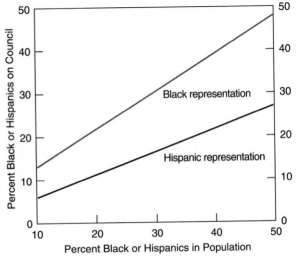

**FIGURE 11–2   Minority Population
and Representation
on City Councils**

Source: Data derived from Susan
Welch, "The Impact of At-Large
Elections on the Representation
of Blacks and Hispanics," *Journal
of Politics,* 52 (November 1990),
1050–76.

barriers and the resident alien status of many Hispanics. These factors together
with some structural features of reform government, including at-large elections,
continue to create barriers to political mobilization of Hispanics.[16]

Policy Consequences: Employment   What are the policy consequences of increasing black representation on city councils? Perhaps the most obvious consequence is increased black *employment* in city jobs. Black employment at all levels of
city administration—professional and managerial, police and fire, office and clerical, service and maintenance—tends to increase with increases in the black popu-

---

[16] See Rufus P. Browning, Dale Rodgers Marshall, and David H. Tabb, *Protest Is Not Enough*
(Berkeley: University of California Press, 1984); Rodney E. Hero, "Hispanics in Urban Government,"
Western Political Quarterly, 43 (June 1990), 403–14; Jerry L. Polinard, Robert D. Wrinkle, and Thomas
Longovia, "The Impact of District Elections on the Mexican American Community," *Social Science Quar-
terly,* 72 (September 1991), 609–14.

lation of the city, as we might expect.[17] But the single most important determinant of black employment in administrative and professional positions is the proportion of blacks elected to city councils.[18] The employment of blacks in service and maintenance jobs does not require political representation. However, to get important city jobs, blacks must first win political power.

Police Policies   Urban police departments have long been a focus of concern for minorities. Police policies have come under scrutiny for contributing to racial tensions, triggering riots, blocking minority aspirations, and shaping minority perceptions of justice. Many black mayors have campaigned on explicit pledges to reform police departments and adopt policies designed to make police responsive and sensitive to the concerns of minorities. The adoption of minority-oriented police policies, including increases in the number of minority police officers, has occurred with increases in black population percentages in cities, regardless of whether cities elect black mayors and council members. However, there is some evidence that the election of black mayors results in (1) accelerated recruitment of black police officers and (2) the adoption of citizen review boards to oversee police actions.[19]

Taxing and Spending   To date there is *no* evidence that cities with greater black representation on city councils, or even cities with black mayors, pursue significantly different taxing, spending, or service policies than do cities with little or no black representation.[20] This is really not surprising; black city leaders face the same problems as white city leaders in raising revenue, fighting crime, improving housing, reducing congestion, removing garbage, and so on. It is possible, of course, that black residents *feel* better about a city government that includes some black faces, and it is even possible that black neighborhoods might receive better *delivery* of urban services under black leadership. However, the overall problems of cities may remain unaffected by substituting black leadership for white leadership.

Attitudes at City Hall   The presence of blacks on city councils is important for city politics even if there is little impact on taxing and spending policies. Blacks in city government improve the image of that government among black residents; it helps to link minorities to city hall, to provide role models, and to sensitize white officials to minority concerns. "When minorities talk to the city council now, council members nod their heads rather than yawn."[21]

---

[17] Peter K. Eisinger, "Black Employment in Municipal Jobs," *American Political Science Review,* 76 (June 1982), 380–92.

[18] Thomas R. Dye and James Renick, "Political Power and City Jobs," *Social Science Quarterly,* 62 (September 1981), 475–86. See also Matthews Hutchins and Lee Sigelman, "Black Employment in State and Local Government," *Social Science Quarterly,* 62 (March 1981), 79–87.

[19] Grace Hall Saltzstein, "Black Mayors and Police Policies," *Journal of Politics,* 51 (August 1989), 525–44.

[20] Susan Welch and Albert K. Karnig, "The Impact of Black Elected Officials on Urban Social Expenditures," *Policy Science Journal,* 7 (Summer 1979), 707–14.

[21] Browning, Marshall, and Tabb, *Protest Is Not Enough,* p. 41.

COUNCIL MEMBERS: RESPONSIBLE POLICY MAKERS?

The policy-making role of council members varies a great deal from city to city. Council members have more formal power in commission or weak mayor forms of government, where the council itself sometimes appoints officials, prepares the budget, supervises departments, and performs other administrative tasks. However, in other cities—particularly strong mayor or manager cities—the council merely oversees city affairs. In these cities, the function of the council may be principally the representation of the interests of local constituents—forwarding complaints, making inquiries, pushing for new sidewalks or streetlights, and so forth.

Council members do *not* usually serve as either general policy innovators or general policy leaders. The role of the council is largely passive, granting or withholding approval in the name of the community when presented with proposals from a leadership outside of itself. The outside leadership is usually the manager, city departments, planning commission, citizen groups, or private enterprise.[22]

In confronting community problems, councils frequently appoint special study commissions, or contract with private consulting firms, in order to obtain their reports and recommendations. In many cases, the council knows what should be done about the problem even before the commission or the consultants render a report. But the council wants the support of independent and prestigious groups before initiating community projects.

Some council members have little interest in a political career and serve out of a sense of public service (frequently at considerable personal expense in time and energy). "Volunteerism" is probably most prevalent in suburban, small, and middle-class communities. Volunteers see their service as a sacrifice, and they are relatively immune from direct constituency pressure. Threats to oust them at the next election have little meaning. "I don't really give a damn whether I am reelected or not" is a common response. Moreover, the attitude of "volunteerism" results in councils that are "(a) more likely to vote against what they see as majority opinion; (b) less likely to feel under pressure from the public; (c) less likely to consider the upcoming election when choosing among policy alternatives; (d) less likely to facilitate group access to the council, and (e) less likely to perform services to constituents."[23]

The problem of political accountability in local politics is further aggravated by several factors:

1. *The frequency of appointment to elected office.* It is probable that as many as one-quarter of the nation's council members initially come into office by ap-

---

[22] Of course, council members themselves are not likely to agree that their role is a passive one. They like to think of themselves as policy innovators—people of vision and leadership—who follow their own convictions in public affairs regardless of what others want them to do.

[23] See Kenneth Prewitt, "Political Ambitions, Volunteerism, and Electoral Accountability," *American Political Science Review,* 64 (March 1970), 5–17.

pointment rather than election. They are appointed, usually by the mayor, to fill unexpired terms.

2. *The effective constituency is very small.* Given the low turnout in municipal elections, and the small constituencies served by a council member, only a very few votes are required to elect a person to office. (One estimate is that only 810 votes are required to elect an average council member in a city of 15,000.) A council member's personal friends, immediate neighbors, business associates, fellow church members, and acquaintances at the Rotary Club may be enough for election.

3. *Limited contact with citizens.* Few citizens know how to contact city officials, and even fewer citizens actually do so.[24] Moreover, citizen-initiated contacts are closely related to socioeconomic status, with higher-status individuals far more likely to contact city officials about a problem than middle- or lower-status persons.

4. *The infrequency of electoral defeat.* Incumbents running for reelection are hardly ever defeated. It is estimated that 80 percent of incumbent council members running for reelection are returned to office.[25] When they are defeated, it is frequently in groups, when several incumbents are turned out of office at once owing to a specific community controversy.

5. *The frequency of voluntary retirement from elected office.* The vast majority of council members voluntarily retire from office, over half of them after two terms. Officeholders simply conclude that the obligations of office exceed the rewards.

All these factors, together with the attitude of volunteerism, tend to remove municipal government from direct citizen control.

CITY COUNCILS AND PUBLIC POLICY

Despite this evidence of a lack of electoral accountability in local politics, some factors may compel council members to reflect the will of their constituents in policy making. First of all, volunteerism is becoming less prevalent over time, especially in large cities with competitive, partisan elections. We know that big-city council members are more likely to be attorneys and professional politicians, to aspire to higher office, and to spend more time on city affairs; we might infer from this that they would be more directly concerned with their constituents' views.

Shared Beliefs Moreover, council members tend to reflect, in their own socioeconomic background, the characteristics of their constituents. This does not *ensure* that council members share the same attitudes as their constituents on all matters; indeed, the experience of being a public official itself can help to shape a council member's views and give a different perspective on public affairs than the constituents'. However, if council members have deep roots in their communities (many

---

[24] Elaine B. Sharp, "Citizen-Initiated Contacting of Government Officials and Socio-Economic Status," *American Political Science Review,* 76 (March 1982), 109–15.

[25] John J. Kirlin, "Electoral Conflict and Democracy in American Cities," *Journal of Politics,* 37 (February 1975), 262–69.

social contacts and group memberships; shared socioeconomic, ethnic, racial, and religious characteristics with their constituents), they may reflect these in their policy making, whether they are consciously aware of these "constituency influences" or not. The effects of shared community life may be very influential in shaping decision making in small, homogeneous communities where uniformity of outlook may amount to compulsion. In short, although "electoral accountability" may have little direct influence over council members, "belief sharing" may still assure some congruence between the views of community residents and the views of their representatives.[26]

Common Community Environment   There are strong relationships between a community's socioeconomic environment, the perceptions and attitudes of its council members, and the public policies that are adopted. The "policy maps" of city council members (their perceptions of community conditions and goals for the future) are usually in accord with public-spending decisions.[27] In short, council members' attitudes seldom stray far from the constraints placed upon them by their communities' populations, needs, and resources.

CITY MANAGERS IN MUNICIPAL POLITICS

When council-manager government was first introduced as part of the municipal reform movement, managers were expressly admonished not to participate in community "politics." Early supporters of manager government believed in the separation of "politics" from "administration."[28] Politics, not only *party* politics but *policy* making as well, should be the exclusive domain of the elected city council. The manager was hired by the council to carry out its policy directives, and the manager could be removed by the council by majority vote at any time. This belief in the separation of policy making from administration was intended to produce "nonpolitical," efficient, and economical government, which middle-class supporters of the reform movement valued so highly. Popular control of government was to be guaranteed by making the manager's tenure completely dependent upon the will of the elected council.

However, after a few years of experience with manager government in America, it became increasingly apparent to the managers themselves that they could not escape responsibility for policy recommendations. It turned out to be very difficult in practice to separate policy making from administration. The first code of ethics of the International City Managers' Association (ICMA) stated flatly

---

[26] See David R. Morgan, "Political Linkage and Public Policy: Attitudinal Congruence Between Citizens and Officials," *Western Political Quarterly* (June 1973), 209–23.

[27] Heinz Eulau and Kenneth Prewitt, *The Labyrinths of Democracy* (Indianapolis: Bobbs-Merrill, 1973); Heinz Eulau and Robert Eyestone, "Policy Maps of City Councils and Policy Outcomes," *American Political Science Review,* 62 (March 1968), 143. Unfortunately, this work is difficult to understand because of the authors' use of obscure terms and elaborate classification schemes that do not fit well with the data. See Judith V. May, "Urban Legislators and Public Policy," a review essay in *Urban Affairs Quarterly,* 10 (June 1975), 487–96.

[28] Leonard D. White, *The City Manager* (Chicago: University of Chicago Press, 1927).

that "no manager should take an active part in politics." Managers agreed that they should stay out of partisan politics and election campaigns, but there was a great deal of debate about the role of managers in community policy making. In 1938, the ICMA revised its code of ethics to recognize the positive role of managers in policy leadership.[29]

Managers as Policy Leaders   Today, we are likely to find varying role orientations among city managers. Some see themselves as "policy managers," providing community leadership through their recommendations to their councils on a wide variety of matters. Others see themselves as "administrative managers," restricting themselves to the supervision of the municipal bureaucracy and avoiding innovative policy recommendations, particularly in controversial areas.

> Political types believe the manager should innovate and lead on policy matters. Further, they endorse direct participation on issues of community conflict and controversy, drawing back only on the question of political campaigning for city councilmen. In contrast, administrative types take a much more limited view of the manager's policy role. Ambivalent about innovation and leadership on policy matters, these managers readily reject involvement in community politics. Administrative managers prefer, in short, a neutral definition of the policy role.[30]

Probably a majority of professionally trained city managers see themselves as "policy managers." Better-educated managers who have had experience in different cities and who aspire to move to larger cities and assume greater responsibilities are unlikely to settle for a restricted, administrative role. However, managers without professional training in city administration or those with engineering degrees, who have lived most of their lives in their own communities and who expect to remain there, may be more likely to accept a fairly narrow administrative role.[31]

Managers as Administrators   While most managers see themselves as policy leaders, most council members see managers in their traditional role of administrators. This means that prudent managers will not wish to *appear* to be policy makers even when they are. They seek to have others present their policy proposals to the community and avoid the brasher methods of policy promotion. Like any successful politician, city managers try to avoid taking public stands on the more controversial issues facing the community. Their dependence upon the council for their jobs prevents them from being too extreme in policy promotion. Managers can push their councils, but they can seldom fight them with any success. Open disputes between the manager and the council are usually resolved by the dismissal of the manager. Managers who assume strong policy-leadership roles have shorter tenures than those who do not.

---

[29] See Harold A. Stone, Don K. Price, and Kathryn H. Stone, *City Manager Government in the United States* (Chicago: Public Administration Service, 1940).

[30] Robert O. Loveridge, *City Managers in Legislative Politics* (Indianapolis: Bobbs-Merrill, 1971), p. 110.

[31] See Timothy A. Almy, "Local-Cosmopolitanism and U.S. City Managers," *Urban Affairs Quarterly,* 10 (March 1975), 243–77.

Nevertheless, the manager is the most important policy initiator in most council-manager cities. Most managers determine the agenda for city council meetings. This permits them to determine the kinds of issues to be raised and the policy options to be considered. The council may not accept everything recommended by the manager, but the manager's recommendations will be given serious consideration. The city manager is the major source of information for most council members. The manager prepares the city budget; writes formal reports on city problems, defining the problems and proposing solutions; and advises and educates the council privately as well as publicly.

Managers in a Dual Role   Thus, managers really have two important roles in community politics: administration and policy making. The administrative role involves the supervision of the municipal bureaucracy; this role requires administrative skills and technical expertise. Managers direct their personal staff, develop and control the city budget, and appoint and remove department heads. In most council-manager cities, managers try to guard these powers from direct council interference; these powers are the managers' most important formal resources.

How Council Members View Managers   What kind of managers do mayors and council members want? Doubtlessly, some mayors and council members want to retain a larger policy role for themselves and resent a manager who wants to run the show. These elected officials might try to recruit "administrative managers" by avoiding applicants with forceful personalities, high professional qualifications, and experience in other cities. However, we have already suggested that many council members are "volunteers" who prefer a passive role in policy making—approving or disapproving proposals brought before them by the manager and others. A weak manager can lengthen council meetings and significantly increase the council's work load. So we should not be surprised to find many, if not most, council members welcoming policy leadership from the manager (as long as the manager avoids the appearance of dominating the council). Indeed, one study indicates that a majority of council members "expect the manager to take the lead" in budget decisions, hiring and firing personnel, reorganization of city departments, wage and salary negotiations, community improvements, and cooperative proposals with other communities.[32] Only in planning and zoning do council members say they want to retain leadership. Presumably these council members would try to recruit well-educated, professionally trained, experienced, and mobile managers to their community. However, past manager-council relations in a community may affect recruitment. Some communities may undergo cycles in council-manager relations: A council resentful of a strong manager replaces him or her with a weak one, only to find that their work load increases, decisions are postponed, complaints of inaction accumulate; and the council decides to find a new, stronger manager.

---

[32] Alan L. Saltzstein, "City Managers and City Councils: Perceptions of the Division of Authority," *Western Political Quarterly,* 27 (June 1974), 275–87.

Professionalism   Today, most city managers are professionals who have been trained in university graduate programs in public administration. They are familiar with budgeting and fiscal administration, public personnel management, municipal law, and planning. They tend to move from city to city as they advance in their professional careers. They may begin their careers as a staff assistant to a city official and then move to assistant city manager, then manager of a small town, and later perhaps of a larger city. About three-quarters of all city manager appointments are made from outside the city, and only about one-quarter are local residents, which indicates the professionalism of city management. The turnover rate among the nation's city managers is about 7.5 percent per year. The average tenure of managers who resigned or were removed from office has been about five years. The average city manager salary for 1992 was estimated at $65,000. Some larger cities paid their managers over $100,000 per year.

Social Backgrounds   The city management profession is still mostly male and mostly white. Some inroads have been made by women in the last decade: Women managers now account for 13 percent of the total. However, blacks have yet to make any significant inroads in the city manager profession; only a little over 1 percent of the nation's city managers are black.[33]

Frustrations   The many conflicting pressures on city managers create "25-hour a day workaholics," according to one overworked manager.[34] Managers regularly report putting in fifty to sixty hours per week at their jobs. At some point in their careers most managers give serious thought to leaving the profession, citing job pressures, lack of privacy, long hours, low pay, and job insecurity (see Table 11–4).

TABLE 11–4   FRUSTRATIONS OF CITY MANAGERS

Reasons for Considering Leaving the Profession, *Percent Citing*		Reasons for Which Managers Have Been Terminated, *Percent Citing*	
Total considered leaving	64	Poor working relationship with council	39
Pressure of the job	57	Politics	21
Lack of privacy	44	Change in council	15
Low pay	43	Left by choice	6
Long hours	43	Council-manager plan abandoned	6
Lack of job security	41	Budget problems	4
Pressure from family	24	No reason	2
Doubts about impact of job	15	Other	2
Other	22		

Source: Adopted from information in International City Managers' Association, *Municipal Yearbook 1982,* pp. 170–71.

---

[33] International City Managers' Association, *Municipal Yearbook 1992,* p. 19.

[34] Douglas Harmon, *On the Joys of Being a Manager* (Washington, DC: International City Managers' Association, 1973).

One in ten managers reports having been fired at least once. Most of these found another job within six months but reported using up their savings or severance pay to survive between jobs. The three principal reasons given for having been fired were "poor working relationships with council," "politics," and "change in the council." All of these reasons might be termed *political.*

 ## MAYORS IN CITY POLITICS

Today, more than ever before, the nation's cities need forceful, imaginative political leadership. The nation's major domestic problems—race relations, poverty, violence, congestion, poor schools, fiscal crisis—are concentrated in cities. Mayors are in the "hot seat" of American politics; they must deal directly with these pressing issues. No other elected official in the American federal system must deal face-to-face, eyeball-to-eyeball with these problems.

Limited Powers   The challenges facing big-city mayors are enormous; however, their powers to deal with these challenges are restricted on every side. Executive power in major cities is often fragmented among a variety of elected officials—city treasurer, city clerk, city comptroller, district attorney, and so on. The mayor may also be required to share power over municipal affairs with county officials. Many city agencies and functions are outside the mayor's formal authority: Independent boards and commissions often govern important city departments—for example, the board of education, board of health, zoning appeals board, planning commission, civil service board, library board, park commission, sewage and water board, and so on. Even if the mayor is permitted to appoint the members of the boards and commissions, they are often appointed for a fixed term, and the mayor cannot remove them. The mayor's power over the affairs of the city may also be affected by the many special district governments and public authorities operating within the city, including public housing, urban renewal, sewage and water, mass transit, port authority. Traditionally, school districts have been outside the authority of the mayor or city government. Mayors' powers over city finances may even be restricted—they may share budget-making powers with a board of estimate, and powers over expenditures with an elected comptroller or treasurer. Civil service regulations and independent civil service boards can greatly hamper mayors' control over their own bureaucrats. The activities of federal and state agencies in a city are largely beyond the mayor's control.

Selecting Mayors   The method of selecting mayors also influences their powers over city affairs. Some mayors are not directly elected by the people of their cities. (See Table 11–5.) These mayors are selected by their city councils or commissions and generally have little more power than other council members or commissioners. Their job is generally ceremonial: They crown beauty queens, dedicate parks, lay cornerstones, and lead parades. Larger cities and mayor-council cities generally elect their mayors. Mayors may be elected for anything from one to six years, but two-year and four-year terms are most common in American cities.

TABLE 11–5   THE MAYORS: METHOD OF SELECTION AND TERM OF OFFICE

	Method of Selection[a]		Term[b]		
	DIRECTLY ELECTED	SELECTED BY COUNCIL	ONE YEAR	TWO YEAR	FOUR YEAR
Total	77.7	20.9	11.1	41.4	44.7
By form of government					
Mayor-Council	98.0	1.9	2.1	33.9	62.5
Council-Manager	61.8	35.5	21.7	51.3	23.2
Commission	69.2	29.1	9.6	20.2	60.5

[a] Percentages do not equal 100 because 1.4% of cities reported selected their mayor by some other method, including rotation of council members and council members receiving most votes in election.

[b] Percentages do not equal 100 because 2.6% of mayors elected for three years and 0.2% for five or more years.

Source: International City Managers' Association, *Municipal Yearbook 1988.*

Legislative Powers   Mayors' legislative powers also vary widely. Of course, in all cities they have the right to submit messages to the council and to recommend policy. These recommendations will carry whatever prestige the mayor possesses in the community. Moreover, in council-manager and commission cities, mayors usually are themselves members of the council. In these cities where mayors are chosen by the council, they generally have voting power equal to that of other council members. In about one-third of mayor-council cities, the mayor also serves on the council; in about half of the mayor-council cities the mayor presides over meetings of the council and can cast a tie-breaking vote. In most cities where the mayor is *not* a member of the council, the mayor enjoys veto power over council-passed ordinances. The veto power distinguishes between ''strong-mayor'' and ''weak-mayor'' cities.

Administrative Powers   Another distinction between ''strong'' and ''weak'' mayors is made on the basis of their powers of administration. Weak mayors have very limited appointing powers and even more limited removal powers. They have little control over separately elected boards and commissions or separately elected offices, such as clerk, treasurer, tax assessor, comptroller, and attorney. The council, rather than the mayor, often appoints the key administrative officers. No single individual has the complete responsibility for law enforcement or coordinating city administration.

Political Powers   In summary, a mayor's ability to provide strong leadership in his or her city is limited by fragmented authority, multiple elected officials, limited jurisdiction over important urban services, civil service, state or federal interference, and constraints placed upon that power by ''reform'' and ''good-government'' arrangements. Nevertheless, even though it is recognized that mayors have few formal powers to deal with the enormous tasks facing them, it is frequently argued that mayors can and should exercise strong leadership as "political brokers"—mediating disputes, serving as a channel of communications, bringing conflicting groups together for reasonable discussions of their differences, and suggesting solutions that diverse groups can accept in coping with the city's problems. In other words, the "ideal" mayor overcomes limited formal powers by skill in persuasion, negotiation, and public relations. Each "success" in resolving a particular problem "pyramids" the mayor's prestige and influence, and he or she eventually accumulates considerable informal power. The mayor can then direct energy and power toward accomplishing one or more of the numerous goals set for mayors: reducing racial tensions, providing effective law enforcement, speeding redevelopment and renewal of downtown areas and the relocation of persons living there, improving public schools, constructing low-cost housing, cleaning up the urban environment, finding ways to move people and things about the city speedily and efficiently, and, most of all, finding ways to finance these goals.

But this "ideal" city leadership requires that the mayor possess certain minimum resources:[35]

1. Sufficient financial and staff resources in the mayor's office and in city government generally
2. City jurisdiction over social-program areas—education, housing, urban renewal, etc.
3. Mayor's jurisdiction within city government over these areas
4. A salary that enables the mayor to spend full time on the job
5. Friendly vehicles for publicity, such as newspapers or television stations supportive of the mayor and his or her goals
6. Political groups, including a political party, that the mayor can mobilize to attend meetings, parades, distribute literature, etc., on his or her behalf

Most mayors do not have the formal authority sufficient to deal with the many challenges facing city government. Successful mayors must rely chiefly upon their own personal qualities of leadership: their powers to persuade, to sell, to compromise, to bargain, and to "get things done." Mayors are not usually expected to initiate proposals for new programs or to create public issues. Nor is their primary concern the administration of existing programs, although they must always seek to avoid scandal and gross mismanagement, which would give their administrations a bad public "image." They must rely upon other public agencies, planners, citizens' groups, and private enterprise to propose new programs, and they can usually rely upon their department heads and other key subordinates to supervise the day-to-day administration of city government. Mayors are primarily pro-

---

[35] Jeffrey L. Pressman, "Preconditions of Mayoral Leadership," *American Political Science Review,* 66 (June 1972), 511–24.

moters of public policy: Their role is to promote, publicize, organize, and finance the projects that others suggest.

TOP BANANAS IN THE BIG APPLE

New York City, "The Big Apple," is the largest municipal government in the nation. Its annual expenditures ($38 billion) exceed those of forty-eight of the states (only the states of New York and California have larger budgets) as well as every other city in the nation. The mayoralty of New York may be the toughest executive job in the nation after the presidency itself.

Worms in the Big Apple   From the early days of the Tammany Hall machine, through the flamboyant mayoralties of Jimmy Walker and Fiorello LaGuardia, to the liberal visions of Mayors Robert Wagner and John Lindsay, the city's political organizations catered to the needs (and won the votes) of the city's large needy population. No other city provided such a range of free services and recreation: libraries, parks, and playgrounds; scores of city hospitals; museums and zoos; antipoverty programs and day care centers; drug-treatment programs; and a costly but tuition-free City University of New York, open to any high school graduate. No other city was as generous in salary and retirement benefits to such a large number of city employees. As a result of these many expensive services and benefits, the per capita cost of running New York City was, and still is, higher than any other city in the nation, except Washington, DC.

For years, under Mayors Robert Wagner and John Lindsay, the city's comptroller, Abraham Beame, managed to postpone fiscal disaster by budgeting gimmickry. Like many cities, New York is required by the state constitution to maintain a balanced budget—obviously an unenforceable requirement. Comptroller Beame simply shifted current expenses, salaries, and supplies to the capital construction budget, which covers long-term building projects for which the city can borrow money. Other strategies included deliberately overestimating revenues, establishing semi-independent city "authorities" that could borrow money, asking the state and federal governments for "advances" on grants-in-aid, and draining various trust funds. In 1973, Abraham Beame was elected mayor.

In early 1975, New York City banks insisted that the city balance its budget and undertake a long-range program to reduce its debts. The banks would no longer lend the city money unless the city displayed greater fiscal responsibility. New York Governor Hugh Carey succeeded in getting the New York State legislature to create a Municipal Assistance Corporation ("Big Mac") to convert short-term city debt into long-term debt and to sell to the public bonds that could be backed by specific city revenues. However, the response of the city's powerful municipal employees unions was predictable: Sanitation workers walked off the job to protest the firings and so did many police and firefighters. Garbage piled up on the streets, and "Fun City" was grimly relabeled "Fear City." The unions forced Mayor Beame to back down on his "crisis" budget. The unhappy result, of course, was that "Big Mac" was unable to persuade banks and investors that New York City was really serious about achieving a balanced budget.

Near Bankruptcy   The real financial crunch came in the fall of 1975. The city was unable to borrow money; outstanding debts were falling due, and there was not enough cash to pay city employees, welfare recipients, or bondholders. For several hours New York City teetered on the verge of default and bankruptcy until the city's teachers union agreed to lend the city enough money from its pension fund to struggle through for a few more weeks. Initially, New York's request for federal aid was met with strong presidential opposition. Republican President Gerald Ford quickly perceived a campaign issue for 1976—liberal Democratic fiscal irresponsibility leads to bankruptcy. The New York *Daily News* headlined the president's stand: "FORD TO CITY: DROP DEAD."

Eventually, all of the participants in New York's fiscal crisis were forced to come to an agreement. The federal government agreed to provide the city with over $2 billion in annual revolving credit; sales taxes in the city were increased to 8 percent (the highest in the nation); the banks, which were holding city bonds, were forced to accept delays in principal and interest payments; the city was obliged to make additional budget cuts, eliminating city jobs, holding down wages, and imposing tuition at the City University; the unions were obliged to accept additional work force cuts and to invest some of their pension funds in New York City bonds. But few observers really believed that New York could manage its problems.

Enter Ed Koch   Then in 1977 New York voters chose Ed Koch as mayor over the incumbent Abraham Beame and the flamboyant Bella Abzug. Ed Koch had worked his way through the City College of New York selling shoes. He fought in Germany in World War II and returned to New York University law school. He lived in the Greenwich Village section of the city and became active in liberal, reform Democratic politics. Koch served five terms in Congress before entering the mayor's race.

Ed Koch's approach to city government was simple enough: "Don't spend what you don't have." Despite his record as a big-spending, liberal Congressman, Koch cut city spending growth. To critics who charged that his spending cuts hurt the poor, he replied: "If you have a healthy city financially, who benefits? The *poor.* Because if you have an unhealthy city, who leaves? The middle-class. The poor *can't* leave."[36]

The mayor was concerned about crime in the city. He added to the police force and created new trial courts to reduce delays in judicial proceedings. He tried unsuccessfully to get pretrial jailing without bail of the most dangerous criminals. He tells the story of the judge who got mugged but announced that this would not affect his courtroom decisions. According to Koch, an old lady shouted, "Then mug him *again.*"

Like most mayors, Koch was frustrated by lack of direct authority over many government functions that directly affect life in the city. Of the New York City subway system, Koch says, "It stinks, but it's not my baby." The system is run by an independent Metropolitan Transit Authority (the MTA); the governor appoints its chairperson. About one-sixth of the city's budget comes from federal aid.

---

[36] *Time,* June 15, 1981, p. 26.

The Good Years   Before Ed Koch moved into Gracie Mansion, New York City had been described by scholars and journalists as "ungovernable." But whatever else his critics said about him, few would claim that Ed Koch did not govern New York City during his twelve years in office. In 1978 he presented the city's first balanced budget in many years. The Municipal Assistance Corporation gradually improved its standing in the financial community; later the city itself was able to sell its bonds again on the open market. The city became less dependent on federal aid throughout the 1980s.

"How'm I doin?" was Mayor Koch's trademark question. He used it on call-in talk shows, in public appearances, and in direct confrontation on the streets of New York with his constituents. Usually the reply was "Great!" and Koch's reelection votes confirmed that he was one of the nation's most popular mayors. In 1985 Koch was reelected by an unprecedented 78 percent of the vote.

But Mayor Koch made political enemies with his aggressive and outspoken approach to city government. He was defeated by Mario Cuomo in the 1982 Democratic primary race for governor, a defeat that reflected Koch's lack of popularity among traditionally powerful interest groups within the Democratic party. Koch attacked "the elitists," whom he described as "a very inbred group of very rich people who go around telling everybody what to do and how to suffer. They have an ideological leaning—it's radical left for everyone except themselves. They live high on the hog."[37] He referred to many in the welfare bureaucracy as "poverty pimps": "If we had given to the poor all of the money that we have appropriated for the poor over the last twenty years, the poor would be rich." Koch was described as the "first white man in New York in ten years to talk back to blacks."[38] Koch was unrepentant: "I speak for the middle classes. You know why? Because they pay the taxes; they provided jobs for poor people."

Like many of America's big cities, racial tension pervades virtually every urban problem in New York. Ed Koch boasted of a long record on behalf of civil rights and social justice. Yet blacks and Jewish leaders in New York, including Ed Koch, had frequently battled over affirmative action quota systems and racial set-asides. Koch did not hesitate to publicly attack blacks with whom he disagreed. He once said, "I'm not sure how to treat black reporters anymore. I want to treat them the same way I treat white reporters—like crap." He spoke out forcefully against racial injustice when incidents of discrimination and violence occurred in his city. He pleaded for calm and understanding during racially threatening periods, notably the highly publicized shooting of four black youths on a subway by Bernard Goetz, and the highway death of a black man trying to run from attacking white teenagers in the Howard Beach section of Queens. Yet his opposition to the presidential candidacy of Jesse Jackson in 1988 marked his final break with the city's black voters. In the heated New York Democratic presidential primary election, Koch lobbed insults at Jackson. Jews, he said, would have to be "crazy" to vote for

---

[37] Quotations from Edward I. Koch, *Mayor* (New York: Simon and Schuster, 1984).

[38] Gay Talese, "Ed Koch on His Honor," *New York Times Book Review,* February 12, 1984.

Jackson, given his opposition to Israel and the anti-Semitic comments of some of his backers.

David Dinkins: A Calming Voice   Perhaps after twelve years of aggressive, combative leadership, it was understandable that New York voters should seek a calm, reassuring, conciliatory voice. David Dinkins offered a marked contrast to the contentious Ed Koch. Always poised, impeccably dressed, soft-spoken and avuncular, David Dinkins promised a new era of calm in the tempest of New York politics and peace in the city's racial and ethnic wars.

Dinkins's father was a barber and later a realtor in Trenton, New Jersey, where young David went to public schools. Following a brief stint in the Marine Corps, he enrolled in Howard University in Washington, DC, and graduated cum laude in 1950 in mathematics. He returned to New York to attend Brooklyn Law School and quickly became involved in Harlem politics under the tutelage of his father-in-law, a New York state assemblyman, J. Raymond Jones, known as the "Harlem Fox." Dinkins practiced law and slowly worked his way up the patronage ladder. With Jones's support Dinkins was elected to the New York General Assembly in 1965 but served only one term. He replaced his father-in-law as Harlem party leader in 1967, a position he held for the next twenty years. He served as city clerk from 1975 to 1985, but lost two races for Manhattan Borough president before winning in 1985. He suffered a minor setback when an investigation revealed he had paid no city income taxes for four years. In a courageous talk in 1985 Dinkins challenged Louis Farrakhan, the controversial leader of the National Islam, for his attacks on Jews. After Farrakhan described Dinkins as a "traitor" to his race, Dinkins was assigned police protection.

Dinkins lived for many years in a rent-controlled apartment on Riverside Drive, overlooking the Hudson River; his children attended private schools and Yale and Case Western Reserve Universities.

Dinkins's calm demeanor appealed to New Yorkers after twelve years of boisterous irreverence from Ed Koch. More importantly, Dinkins avoided the confrontational racial style of Jesse Jackson. Dinkins reassured whites and Hispanics that he would represent *all* of the city, not just its black residents. Following a series of racially motivated acts of violence, many white New Yorkers came to believe that Dinkins would be better at managing racial tension than the volatile Koch.

Dinkins's reassuring style fit well with New York City's demographics—roughly 23 percent black, 17 percent Hispanic, and 60 percent white. In the hard-fought 1989 Democratic primary, Dinkins won virtually all of the black vote, a majority of the Hispanic vote, and one-third of the white vote in defeating Ed Koch's unprecedented bid for a fourth term as mayor. Koch took his loss in good grace, immediately endorsing Dinkins in the general election.

In the general election Dinkins confronted the first formidable candidate put forward by the Republican party in New York City in several decades—Rudolph W. Giuliani. Giuliani, a former federal prosecutor, had won fame by winning cases against drug lords and Wall Street financiers. During the campaign Giuliani launched hard-hitting personal attacks on Dinkins, especially citing his failure to pay city income taxes, but neither candidate raised racial issues. While Giuliani gathered more votes than any previous Republican candidate in the city, Dinkins won comfortably.

While Dinkins demonstrated his ability to bring together a broad coalition of blacks, Hispanics, white liberals, and union supporters to win office, actually governing the nation's largest city has proven more difficult. Faced with looming budget deficits, Dinkins raised city taxes and cut some services. Yet at the same time, he acquiesced to the teachers' union's demands for large salary increases. He has been equally ambivalent in handling the city's racial tensions, sometimes taking the lead in denouncing racism, while at other times seeming to ignore racial and ethnic conflicts. Some commentators praise his pragmatism; others criticize his lack of consistent direction.

INTEREST GROUPS IN CITY POLITICS

Interest group activity may be more influential in community politics than in state or national political affairs. Since the arena of local politics is smaller, the activities of organized interest groups may be more obvious at the local level. As one local councilman once said:

> Pressure groups are probably more important in local government than they are nationally or in the state, because they are right here. You see them and they see you, and what you do affects them. It's not like in Washington, where half the time a businessman doesn't really know what the result will be for him.[39]

The Civic Associations   At the local level, interest groups frequently assume the form of *civic associations*. Few communities are too small to have at least one or two associations devoted to civic well-being, and larger cities may have hundreds of these organizations. In a California study of local councils, 94 percent of the council members, who perceived group activity at the local level named civic associations (service clubs, citizens' commissions, improvement associations) as the most influential groups or organizations that were active and appeared before the council.[40] Only 28 percent of these council members named economic groups (merchants, realtors, unions, and so on), and 21 percent named taxpayer associations and reform groups. Actually, these results do not mean that economic interests or taxpayer associations are less active than civic associations, but probably that civic associations are the predominant style of organized interest group activity at the local level. Business people, reform groups, taxpayer associations, merchants, service clubs, developers, and so on organize themselves into civic associations for action at the local level. Civic associations generally make their appeals in terms of "the welfare of the community," "the public interest," "civic responsibility," "making Janesville a better place to live." In other words, civic associations claim to be community-serving rather than self-serving. Members belong to these groups

[39] Betty Zisk, Heinz Eulau, and Kenneth Prewitt, "City Councilmen and the Group Struggle," *Journal of Politics,* 27 (August 1965), 633. See also Betty Zisk, *Local Interest Politics: A One-Way Street* (Indianapolis: Bobbs-Merrill, 1973), p. 22.

[40] Zisk et al., "City Councilmen," p. 632.

as a hobby, because of the sense of prestige and civic participation they derive from membership. Occasionally, of course, participation in civic associations can be a stepping-stone to local office.

Taxpayer Groups   Organized *taxpayer groups* generally stand for lower taxes and fewer governmental activities and services. Their most enthusiastic support comes from the community's larger taxpayers, generally business people with large investments in commercial or industrial property in the community.

Environmental and "Growth-Management" Groups   Environmental groups and opponents of residential and commercial development have become major forces in community politics throughout the nation. These groups are generally opposed to community growth, although they employ the term "growth management" to imply that they do not necessarily oppose all growth. But they are generally opposed to highway construction, street widening, tree cutting, increased traffic, noise and pollution, commercial or industrial development, or anything else that offends their aesthetic preferences. These groups generally reflect liberal reformist views of upper–middle-class residents who are secure in their own jobs and own their own homes. Indeed, restrictions on new housing construction directly benefit them by increasing the value of existing property. Municipal government offers many tools to restrict growth—planning regulations, zoning laws, building permits, environmental regulations, developmental charges and restrictions, street and utility access, etc. (For further discussion, see Chapter 16.) Often environmental, "growth-management" groups combine with neighborhood associations to oppose specific developmental projects.

Neighborhood Groups   *Neighborhood associations* frequently spring up when residents perceive a threat to their property values. They may be formed to oppose a rezoning that would allow new business and unwanted traffic in their neighborhood, or to oppose a new mobile home park, or to petition for stoplights or sidewalks or pothole repairs. Sometimes neighborhood associations will fight to keep out "undesirables," whose presence they feel will reduce property values. Neighborhood groups may protest the location of low-income housing, halfway houses for parolees, or mental health facilities. Neighborhood associations may also lead the fight *against* development, where residents will be displaced or their life style threatened. They may oppose road building, urban renewal, or industrial and commercial development in or near their neighborhood. The NIMBY (not in my backyard) forces may be closely identified with "growth-management" efforts to slow or halt development. This posture places them in opposition to the local growth-oriented "power structure." (See Chapter 13.)

Business Groups   Traditionally *business interests* were the most influential of all groups in community politics. Many business people or "economic notables" occupied an important role in the structure of community decision making or "the power structure." (See Chapter 13.) Business interests are also represented in local politics by organized groups: The chamber of commerce and the junior chamber of commerce, or "Jaycees," are found in nearly every community, representing the general views of business. The program of the chamber of commerce is likely to be more general than the interests of particular sectors of the business community—banks, utilities, contractors, real estate developers, downtown merchants, or bar and club owners. The chamber or the Jaycees can be expected to support lower taxes and more economy and efficiency in government operations. They are also active "promoters" of community growth and business activity. They can be expected to back civic improvements so long as it does not raise the tax rate too much. "Service to the community" creates a "favorable image," which the chamber and business people are anxious to cultivate.

Generally, the active members of the chamber of commerce or the Jaycees are younger business owners in the community who are still on their way "up" in business. Owners of larger businesses, banks, utilities—the "big powers" in the community—are more likely to function informally in the community's power structure than to take an overt role in organized interest group activity.

The so-called service clubs—the Lions, Kiwanis, Rotarians, and others—are basically for business people. Their interests are likely to be more social than political, but their service projects often involve them in political activity and their meetings provide an excellent opportunity for speechmaking by political candidates.

The businesses most active in community affairs are those most directly affected by policies of local government, such as department stores, banks, utilities, contractors, real estate operators, bar and club owners, and television and newspaper interests.

Banks   Banks often own, or hold the mortgages on, downtown business property. They have an interest in maintaining business, commercial, and industrial property values. Banks are also interested in the growth and prosperity of the city as a whole, particularly large business enterprises who are their primary customers. Bankers are influential because they decide who is able to borrow money in a community and under what conditions. Banks are directly involved in local governments in financing municipal bond issues for public works, school buildings, and so on, and in pledging financial backing for urban renewal projects. Banks are also influential in land development, for they must provide the financial backing for real estate developers, contractors, businesses, and home buyers; hence they are interested in business regulation, taxation, zoning, and housing.

Contractors   Contractors are vitally interested in city government because the city has the power of inspection over all kinds of construction. Local governments enforce building, plumbing, electric, and other codes, which are of great interest to contractors. Some contractors, particularly road-grading and surfacing companies, depend on public contracts, and they are concerned with both city policy and the personnel who administer this policy. While municipal contracts are generally required by law to be given to the "low bidder" among "responsible" contractors, definitions about what is or is not a "low bid," and who is or who is not a "responsible" contractor, make it important for contractors to maintain close and friendly relationships with municipal officials. It is no accident that builders, contractors, and developers are usually the largest source of campaign contributions for local office seekers.

Real Estate Developers   Real estate developers are particularly interested in planning, zoning, and subdivision control regulations and urban renewal programs. (These are discussed at length in Chapter 16.) Developers of residential, commercial, and industrial property must work closely with city government officials to coordinate the provision of public services—especially streets, sewage, water, and electricity. They must also satisfy city officials regarding planning and zoning regulations, building codes, fire and safety laws, and environmental regulations. Today, real estate developers must be highly skilled in governmental relations.

Newspapers   Newspapers are an important force in community politics. The influence of the press would be relatively minor if its opinions were limited to its editorial pages. The influence of the press arises from its power to decide what is "news," thereby focusing public attention on the events and issues that are of interest to the press. Newspaper writers must first decide what proportion of space in the paper will be devoted to local news in contrast to state, national, and international news. A big-city paper may give local news about the same amount of space that it gives to national or foreign news. Suburban or small-town papers, which operate within the circulation area of a large metropolitan daily, may give a greater proportion of the news space to local events than to national and international affairs. Crime and corruption in government are favorite targets for the press. Editors believe that civic crusades and the exposure of crime and corruption help sell newspapers. Moreover, many editors and writers believe they have a civic responsibility to use the power of the press to protect the public. In the absence of crime or corruption, newspapers may turn to crusades on behalf of civic improvements—like a city auditorium or cultural center.

The politics of newspapers can be understood in part by some insight into the economics of the newspaper business. Newspapers get two-thirds of their revenue from advertising. Over the years the newspapers' percentage of all advertising dollars has declined in the face of stiff competition from television. Many big-city newspapers have either merged or gone out of business because of a lack of sufficient advertising revenue to offset increasing costs; it was not a lack of readers that brought about their collapse. Moreover, it is important to know that downtown department stores provide the largest source of advertising revenue. Big-city newspapers have been hurt by the flight of the middle class to the suburbs and the declining role of downtown department stores in retail sales in the metropolitan area. In metropolitan affairs, one can expect big-city newspapers to support the position of downtown interests. This means support for urban renewal, mass transit, downtown parking, and other pro–central-city policies in metropolitan affairs. On the other hand, suburban daily and weekly newspapers are supported by the advertising from suburban shopping centers, and they can be expected to take a pro-suburban position on metropolitan issues.

Newspapers are more influential in the absence of strong party organizations, which would compete with newspapers as channels of communication to the voters. Nonpartisanship, lengthy ballots, and numerous referenda all contribute to the influence of newspapers. Any situation that tends to obscure candidates or issues to the voter contributes to the power of newspapers, since the voter is obliged to rely upon them for information. Newspapers doubtlessly have more influence in local than in state or national politics because of (1) the relative importance in local politics of middle-class groups who read newspapers, (2) the relative obscurity of local politics to voters in their reliance upon newspapers for information about local affairs, and (3) the relative weakening of party affiliations in local politics.

Churches   Any listing of influential interest groups in local politics should include the community's churches and church-related organizations. Ministers, priests, rabbis, and leaders of religious lay groups are frequently participants in community decision making. The Catholic Church and its many lay organizations are vitally concerned with the operation of parochial schools. Protestant ministerial associations in large cities may be concerned with public health, welfare, housing, and other social problems. Ministers and church congregations in small towns may be concerned with the enforcement of blue laws, limitations on liquor sales, prohibitions on gambling, and other public policies relative to "vice" and public morality.

THE POWER OF MUNICIPAL UNIONS

No one has a greater personal stake in municipal government than municipal employees—police, firefighters, street crews, transit employees, welfare workers, sanitation workers, clerks, secretaries. There are over 15 million state and local government employees in the nation (4.5 million state employees, and 10.7 million employees of cities, counties, school districts, and special districts). Their rate of voter turnout in municipal elections is very high, and they are politically influential in small towns and suburbs whether they are organized into unions or not.

Municipal Employee Unions   Over one-third of the nation's state and local government employees are unionized. Municipal employee unions are more influential in large cities, where fragmentation of authority and public acceptance of union activity encourage unions to assert their employees' interests. In New York City, for example, associations of teachers, police, firefighters, transit workers, social workers, sanitation workers, and so on, have great political significance. Employee work stoppages and other forms of protest occur frequently, even though state law prohibits strikes of municipal employees. The American Federation of State, County, and Municipal Employees, the International Association of Fire Fighters, and the American Federation of Teachers, all AFL–CIO unions, are directly concerned with organization and collective bargaining in public employment. In addition, certain other unions, such as the Transport Workers Union, are organized to bargain on behalf of both public and private employees. In the absence of union representation, public employees may form "professional associations," such as the Fraternal Order of Police and, of course, the National Education Association.

Labor Relations   Most state laws today recognize the right of municipal employees to organize unions and bargain collectively with municipal officials over wages, hours, and conditions of work. However, in contrast to *private* employees, *public* employees are generally prohibited by law from striking. Instead, most state laws stipulate that public employee labor disputes are to go to arbitration—that is, be submitted to neutral third parties for decision. Decisions of arbitrators (or arbitration boards consisting of equal representation from employees and employers, together and with neutral members) may or may not be binding on both the city and union, depending on specific provisions of each state's laws. However, many public employee unions throughout the country have rendered "no-strike" laws practically useless in a heated labor dispute. Police, firefighters, teachers, sanitation workers, and others have struck in many large cities and there have been statewide strikes as well. Unions can nullify no-strike laws by simply adding another demand—no legal prosecution of strikers or union leaders—as a condition of going back to work.

Strikes   Strikes that threaten the health and safety of a community are qualitatively different from strikes that shut down private business enterprise and threaten only economic dislocation. Strikes of police, firefighters, hospital workers, or sanitation workers, for example, must be ended quickly for the safety of the community; this brings great pressure to bear on public officials to satisfy the demands of strikers, even at the risk of creating serious financial problems for the city. (Strikes by teachers, social workers, maintenance employees, clerks, and so forth may cause dislocations but do not immediately threaten the community's health or welfare.) Elected public officials are theoretically responsible to the majority of citizens who elected them. However, immediate pressure from vital municipal employees may force elected officials to sacrifice the long-run public interest.

Wages and Benefits   State and local employees, who for generations were paid wages below those for comparable jobs in private enterprise, now at least match private employees in salaries, benefits, pensions, and so on. Theoretically, public employee unions should be very effective in raising wages. It might be reasoned that: (1) Elected government officials are less constrained than private employers by profit and loss considerations, and more likely to grant union demands; and (2) unlike employees in the private sector, public employees participate in electing their own bosses, placing additional pressure on them to succumb to union demands. Empirical research does suggest that unionized municipal workers earn more than nonunionized municipal workers.[41] But unions may have even greater impact on raising fringe benefits (retirement, health benefits, vacations, etc.) of government employees.

---

[41] For a summary of research on this topic, see Gregory B. Lewis and Lana Stein, "Unions and Municipal Decline," *American Politics Quarterly,* 17 (April 1989), 208–22.

Political Clout   Unions in the *private* sector of the American economy have been in steep decline in recent decades; today less than 13 percent of the private work force is unionized. But unions in the *public* sector have grown dramatically; in 1990, 37 percent of all employees in federal, state, and local governments were union members. The American Federation of State County and Municipal Employees (AFSCME) is the nation's second largest union, after the Teamsters, and it adds members each year. Most of its membership is concentrated in ten states—New York, Ohio, Pennsylvania, Michigan, Illinois, Wisconsin, Massachusetts, Minnesota, Connecticut, and Hawaii.

Government employee unions can usually be counted on to lend strong support for tax increases at all levels of government: "The AFSCME protects the personnel levels, the bureaucrats and the budgets of government agencies. The union makes a good ally when you're lobbying for a tax increase or to retain public services."[42]

Government employee unions are vigorous opponents of privatization (see Chapter 10). The AFSCME objects strongly to the idea that private contractors can provide services more efficiently than municipal bureaucracies. Moreover, the union claims that privatization "diminishes government accountability to citizens."

---

[42] Quoted in John F. Persimos, "Can AFSCME Parley Its Savvy into Another Decade of Growth?" *Governing* (July 1989), 48.

12

Metropolitics: Conflict in the Metropolis

▲

The Metropolis: Setting for Conflict

Three out of every four Americans live in population clusters called *metropolitan areas*. What is a metropolitan area? The U.S. Census Bureau calls a metropolitan area a "Metropolitan Statistical Area" (MSA) and defines it as a city of 50,000 or more people together with adjacent counties that have predominantly urban populations with close ties to the central city. (See Figure 12–1.)

Some metropolitan areas adjoin each other, creating a continuous urban environment over an extended area. One such "megalopolis" is the New York–Northern New Jersey–Long Island area, encompassing parts of three states, nine MSAs, and 18 million people. The U.S. Census Bureau calls such an area a "Consolidated Metropolitan Statistical Area" (CMSA) and defines it as two or more adjoining MSAs with at least 1 million people in which a large number of workers commute between the MSAs. Nearly half of the nation's population lives in the thirty-seven metropolitan areas with 1 million or more people. (See Table 12–1.)

TABLE 12–1   METRO-AMERICA: METROPOLITAN AREAS WITH ONE MILLION OR MORE RESIDENTS

New York	18.0	St. Louis	2.4	Norfolk (VA)	1.4
Los Angeles	14.5	Seattle	2.6	Sacramento	1.5
Chicago	8.1	Minneapolis	2.5	New Orleans	1.3
San Francisco	6.3	Baltimore	2.4	Columbus (OH)	1.4
Philadelphia	5.9	Pittsburgh	2.2	San Antonio	1.3
Detroit	4.6	San Diego	2.5	Indianapolis	1.2
Boston	4.2	Tampa	2.0	Buffalo (NY)	1.2
Dallas	3.9	Phoenix	2.1	Providence (RI)	1.1
Washington, DC	3.9	Cincinnati	1.7	Charlotte (NC)	1.2
Houston	3.7	Denver	1.8	Hartford (CT)	1.1
Miami	3.2	Milwaukee	1.6	Salt Lake City	1.1
Cleveland	2.8	Kansas City	1.6	Orlando	1.1
Atlanta	2.8	Portland (OR)	1.5	Rochester	1.0

Source: U.S. Bureau of the Census, figures for July 1, 1990.

The states have become "metropolitanized." Today thirty-five states have more than half of their populations concentrated in metropolitan areas. (See Figure 12–2.)

Urban sociologists tell us that the very definition of metropolitan life involves *large numbers* of *different* types of people living *close together* who are socially and economically *dependent* upon one another.[1] *Numbers, density, heterogeneity,* and *interdependence* are said to be distinguishing characteristics of metropolitan life. It is not difficult to envision a metropolitan area as a large number of people living together; we can see these characteristics in metropolitan life from a map or an airplane window. However, it is more difficult to understand the heterogeneity and interdependence of people living in metropolitan areas.

Heterogeneity   The modern economic system of the metropolis is based upon a highly specialized and complex division of labor. Highly specialized jobs account for much of the heterogeneity in urban populations. Different jobs produce different levels of income, dress, and styles of living. People's jobs shape the way they look at the world and their evaluations of social and political events. In acquiring their jobs, people attain a certain level and type of education that also distinguish them from those in other jobs with different educational requirements. Differences in educational level in turn produce a wide variety of differences and opinions, attitudes, and styles of living. Metropolitan living concentrates people with all these different economic and occupational characteristics in a very few square miles.

Ethnic and Racial Diversity   Ethnic and racial diversity are also present. A few decades ago opportunities for human betterment in the cities attracted immigrants

---

[1] See especially Scott Greer, *Governing the Metropolis* (New York: John Wiley, 1961).

FIGURE 12–1   Standard Metropolitan Statistical Areas, 1992
Source: U.S. Bureau of the Census.

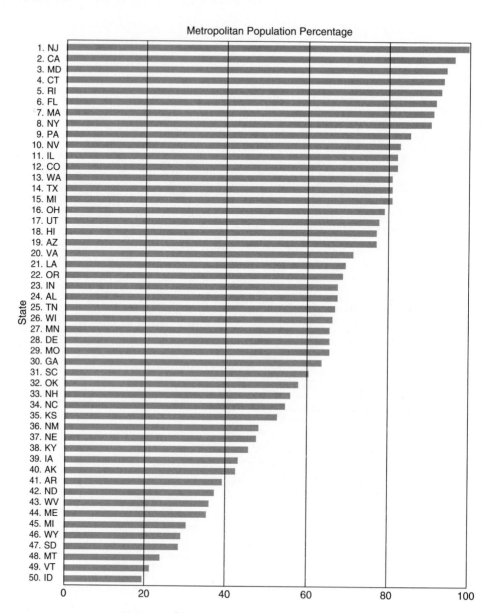

FIGURE 12–2   Metropolitanization in the States, 1992
Source: U.S. Bureau of the Census.

from Ireland, Germany, Italy, Poland, and Russia; today, the city attracts blacks, Hispanics, and rural families. Newcomers to the metropolis bring with them different needs, attitudes, and ways of life. The "melting pot" tends to reduce some of this diversity over time, but the pot does not "melt" people immediately, and there always seem to be new arrivals.

Ghettoization   The list of social, economic, and life-style differences among the people in a metropolitan area is almost endless. Scott Greer writes, "The city is a maze, a social zoo, a mass of heterogeneous social types."[2] Moreover, urban sociologists tell us that people with different social, economic, and life-style characteristics generally live in different parts of a metropolitan area. Physical separation of residences generally accompanies social and economic separation, and so there are "ghettos," "silk-stocking districts," "little Italys," middle-class suburbs, and so on. This physical separation tends to emphasize and reinforce differences among people in a metropolitan area.

Interdependence   Urban dwellers are highly dependent upon one another in their daily economic and social activities. Suburbanites, for example, rely upon the central city for food, clothing, newspapers, entertainment, hospitalization, and a host of other modern needs. More importantly, they rely upon the central city for employment opportunities. Conversely, the central city relies upon the suburbs to supply its labor and management forces. Downtown merchants look to the entire metropolitan area for consumers. This interdependence involves an intricate web of economic and social relationships, a high degree of communication, and a great deal of daily physical interchange among residents, groups, and firms in a metropolitan area. Just as specialization produces diversity among people, it also produces interdependence and the need for coordinated human activity.

Fragmented Government   Another characteristic of metropolitan areas is "fragmented" government. Suburban development, spreading out from central cities, generally ignored governmental boundaries and engulfed counties, townships, towns, and smaller cities. Some metropolitan areas even spread across state lines, and four metropolitan areas of the United States—Detroit, San Diego, El Paso, and Laredo—adjoin urban territory in Canada and Mexico. This suburbanization has meant that hundreds of governments may be operating in a single metropolitan area. Thus, while metropolitan areas are characterized by social and economic interdependence, and consequently require coordinating mechanisms, metropolitan government is generally "fragmented" into many smaller jurisdictions, none of which is capable of governing the entire metropolitan area in a unified fashion.

Governmental fragmentation in metropolitan areas is a function of size: The larger the metropolitan area, the more fragmented the governmental structure. Fragmentation is also related to the age of settlement and to income levels in the metropolis, although these factors are less influential than size. Apparently the older a metropolitan area, the more complex its governmental structure.

Potential for Conflict   The metropolis presents a serious problem in *conflict* management. Because a metropolitan area consists of a large number of different kinds of people living closely together, the problem of regulating conflict and maintaining order assumes tremendous proportions. Persons with different occu-

---

[2] Ibid., p. 5.

pations, incomes, and educational levels are known to have different views on public issues. The way that persons well equipped to compete for jobs and income in a free market view government housing and welfare programs may differ from the way that others not so well equipped view them. People at the bottom of the social ladder look at police—indeed, governmental authority in general—differently from the way those on higher rungs do. Persons who own their homes and those who do not regard taxation in a different light. Families with children and those without children have different ideas about school systems. And so it goes. Differences in the way people make their living, in their income and educational levels, in the color of their skin, in the way they worship, in their style of living—all are at the roots of political life in the metropolis.

CITIES VERSUS SUBURBS

Suburbs account for most of the growth of America's metropolitan areas. Very few large *central cities* are growing in size; on the contrary, many are losing population (see Table 12–2). Metropolitan areas are growing because their *suburbs* are growing.

Suburbanization   America's suburbanization is a product of technological advances in transportation—the automobile and the expressway. In the nineteenth century an industrial worker had to live within walking distance of his or her place of employment. This meant that the nineteenth-century American city crowded large masses of people into relatively small central areas, often in tenement houses and other high-density neighborhoods. However, modern modes of transportation —first the streetcar, then the private automobile, and then the expressway—eliminated the necessity of workers living close to their jobs. Now people can spend their working hours in a central business district office or industrial plant and spend their evenings in a residential suburb many miles away. The same technology that led to the suburbanization of residences has also influenced commercial and industrial location. Originally industry was tied to waterways or railroads for access to suppliers and markets. This dependence has been reduced by the development of motor truck transportation, the highway system, and the greater mobility of the labor force. Now many industries can locate in the suburbs, particularly light industries, which do not require extremely heavy bulk shipment that can only be handled by rail or water. When industry and people move to the suburbs, commerce follows. Giant suburban shopping centers have sprung up to compete with downtown stores. Thus, metropolitan areas are becoming decentralized over time as people, business, and industry spread themselves over the suburban landscape. As Lewis Mumford puts it: "The city has burst open and scattered its complex organs and organizations over the entire landscape."[3]

City–Suburban Differences   Social, economic, and racial conflict can be observed at all levels of government, but at the metropolitan level, it is most obvious in the conflict that occurs between central cities and their suburbs. At the heart of

---

[3] Lewis Mumford, *The City in History* (New York: Harcourt, Brace, & World, 1961), p. 34.

TABLE 12-2 CITIES WITH LARGEST PERCENTAGE LOSS IN POPULATION, 1980–1990

City	1990	1980	Change	City	1990	1980	Change
1. Gary, IN	116,646	151,968	-23.2%	16. Birmingham, AL	265,968	288,297	-7.7
2. Newark	275,221	329,248	-16.4	17. Richmond	203,056	219,214	-7.4
3. Detroit	1,027,974	1,203,369	-14.6	18. Chicago	2,783,726	3,005,072	-7.4
4. Pittsburgh	369,879	423,960	-12.8	19. Atlanta	394,017	425,022	-7.3
5. St. Louis	396,685	452,804	-12.4	20. Kansas City, KS	149,767	161,148	-7.1
6. Cleveland	505,616	573,822	-11.9	21. Baltimore	736,014	786,741	-6.4
7. Flint, MI	140,761	159,611	-11.8	22. Akron, OH	223,019	237,590	-6.1
8. New Orleans	496,938	557,927	-10.9	23. Toledo, OH	332,943	354,635	-6.1
9. Warren, MI	144,864	161,134	-10.1	24. Philadelphia	1,585,577	1,688,210	-6.1
10. Chattanooga, TN	152,466	169,514	-10.1	25. Dayton, OH	182,044	193,549	-5.9
11. Louisville, KY	269,063	298,694	-9.9	26. Knoxville, TN	165,121	175,045	-5.7
12. Peoria, IL	113,504	124,813	-9.1	27. Memphis	610,337	646,170	-5.5
13. Macon, GA	106,612	116,896	-8.8	28. Cincinnati	364,040	385,410	-5.5
14. Erie, PA	108,718	119,123	-8.7	29. Denver	467,610	492,694	-5.1
15. Buffalo	328,123	357,870	-8.3	30. District of Columbia	606,900	638,432	-4.9

Source: Bureau of the Census, U.S. Dept. of Commerce, 1990 Census.

city–suburban conflict are the differences in the kinds of people who live in cities and suburbs. City–suburban conflict is at the heart of "the metropolitan problem"; that is, the failure to achieve metropolitanwide consensus on public policy questions affecting the entire metropolitan area and the failure to develop metropolitan government institutions. Social, economic, and racial differences between cities and suburbs are major obstacles to the development of metropolitanwide policies and government institutions.[4]

Of course, generalizing about cities and suburbs is a dangerous thing. Although we will talk about some common characteristics of cities and suburbs, students are cautioned that individual suburbs may be quite different from one another (just as there are wide differences between social and economic groups living in central cities). There are, for example, industrial suburbs, residential suburbs, black suburbs, wealthy suburbs, working-class suburbs, and so forth.[5] Nevertheless, a clear perception of the social distance between cities and suburbs is important in understanding metropolitan politics.

Social Class   Cities and suburbs can be differentiated, first of all, on the basis of *social class*—the occupation, income, and educational levels of their population. The cultured class of an earlier era established "country" living as a symbol of affluence; widespread prosperity has made possible mass imitation of the aristocracy by an upwardly mobile middle-class population. The suburbs house greater proportions of white-collar employees, college graduates, and affluent families than any other sector in American life.

Status differentials in favor of suburbs are more pronounced in larger metropolitan areas; status differentials in smaller metropolitan areas are not as great as in larger areas, and sometimes even favor the city rather than the suburbs. However, on the whole, suburban living reflects middle-class values.

Familism   Cities and suburbs can also be differentiated on the basis of *"familism,"* or life style. Perhaps the most frequently mentioned reason for a move to the suburbs is "the kids." Family after family list consideration of their young as the primary cause for their move to suburbia. A familistic, or child-centered, life style can be identified in certain social statistics. A larger percentage of suburban families have children under eighteen than city families. In addition, the single-family, free-standing home has become symbolic of familistic living in an affluent society. The nonfamilistic life style is characteristic of the central city where there are proportionately fewer children and more apartment living.

Race   Perhaps the most important difference between cities and suburbs is their contrasting *racial composition.* The nonwhite percentage of all U.S. suburbs is about 6 percent, in contrast to a nonwhite percentage for all central cities of 22 percent. (See Table 12–3.)

---

[4] Richard Child Hill, "Separate and Unequal: Government Inequality in the Metropolis," *American Political Science Review,* 68 (December 1974), 1557–68.

[5] See Frederick M. Wirt et al., *On the City's Rim: Politics and Policy in Suburbia* (Lexington, MA: D.C. Heath, 1972).

Poverty   Low-income, low-education, unskilled populations are concentrated in the central cities. Social problems are also concentrated in central cities—racial imbalance, crime, violence, inadequate education, poverty, slum housing, and so on. By moving to the suburbs, white middle-class families not only separate themselves from blacks and poor people but also place physical distance between themselves and the major social problems that confront metropolitan areas. This permits them, for the time being, to avoid the problems associated with poverty.

Parties   In general, large cities are much more Democratic than their suburban rings, which generally produce more Republican votes. While temporary shifts may occur from one election to another, this general pattern of Democratic cities and Republican suburbs is likely to prevail for the near future. As long as the national Democratic party represents central-city, low-income, ethnic, labor, and racial constituencies, and the Republican party represents middle-class, educated, managerial, white, Anglo-Saxon Protestant constituencies, the political coloration of cities and suburbs is likely to be different.

Schools   City and suburban social differences are also reflected in the divergent public policies of city and suburban governments. First of all, there is some evidence that the child-centered character of suburban living produces higher educational expenditures in suburbs than in cities. Suburban parents with high hopes and plans for their children's occupational success tend to focus more concern upon the school system and spend more money on it per pupil than city residents. (Of course, in smaller metropolitan areas, where social and life-style differences between city and suburb are minimal, differences between city and suburb in educational expenditures are very slight and occasionally run opposite from the expected direction.)

TABLE 12–3   CITIES AND SUBURBS OF METROPOLITAN AREAS IN THE UNITED STATES

	Metropolitan Areas			Outside Metropolitan Areas
	TOTAL	CITIES	SUBURBS	
Total population (000)	192,726	77,844	114,882	55,984
Percent of U.S. total	76.2	31.5	44.7	23.8
Growth: percent population increase 1980–1990	11.6	7.5	15.7	2.2
Age: percent under 18	25.3	24.7	25.7	26.6
Race: percent black	13.0	22.1	6.9	8.7
Home ownership: percent owning home	58.4	49.1	68.1	80.6
Percent families with children	33.2	30.0	35.6	34.8
Median home value	$89,100	$71,600	$99,000	$50,100

Source: U.S. Bureau of the Census, 1990 Census of Population CP-1-1.

Costs of Government   Large central cities show substantially higher operating expenditures per capita than their suburbs. The maintenance of a large physical plant for the entire metropolitan area requires city residents to make higher per capita operating expenditures than those required for suburbanites. In addition, many living costs in suburban communities are shifted from public to private spending (private septic tanks instead of public sewers, private instead of public recreation, and so on). Differences in the public services provided by city and suburban governments are greatest in the area of police protection, recreation, and health. This reflects a concentration in the city of people who are likely to require these public services, in contrast to the suburbs.

Taxes   The tax bill in suburbs is only slightly lower than in central cities. Taxes had much to do with the migration of the "pioneer" suburbanites, those who moved to the suburbs in the 1930s and 1940s. At that time, suburban living offered a significant savings in property taxation over what were thought to be heavy city taxes. However, the tax advantage of the suburbs turned out partly to be a "self-denying prophecy": The more people who fled to the suburbs to avoid heavy taxes, the greater the demand for public services in these new suburban communities, and the higher suburban taxes became to meet these new demands. Yet, the tax bill in most suburbs remains lower than in central cities. The difference in tax burden between city and suburb would be even greater if suburbanites did not choose to spend more per pupil in education than city residents, which produces higher school taxes in the suburbs. The suburbs also manage to limit their indebtedness more than cities, and most of the indebtedness incurred by the suburbs is for school rather than municipal purposes.

Exceptions   Finally, it should be noted that differences between city and suburb in smaller metropolitan areas do not appear to be as great as differences between cities and suburbs in larger metropolitan areas. In fact, all these generalizations about cities and suburbs are, indeed, generalizations. Individual cities and suburbs can be found that do not conform to these national patterns.

◄ THE CASE FOR METROPOLITAN CONSOLIDATION

"The metropolitan problem" is often defined as a problem of "fragmented" government—that is, the proliferation of governments in metropolitan areas and the lack of coordination of public programs. The objective of the metropolitan reform movement of the last thirty years has been to reorganize, consolidate, and enlarge government jurisdictions. The goal is to rid metropolitan areas of "ineffective multiple local jurisdictions" and "governments that do not coincide with the boundaries of the metropolis."[6]

---

[6] Luther Gulick, *The Metropolitan Problem and American Ideas* (New York: Knopf, 1962); Walter A. Rosenbaum and Thomas A. Henderson, "Explaining Comprehensive Governmental Consolidation," *Journal of Politics,* 34 (May 1972), 428–57.

Public Service   Many advantages are claimed for metropolitan governmental reorganization. First of all, the reorganization and consolidation of metropolitan governments is expected to bring about *improved public services* as a result of centralization. Consolidation of governments is expected to achieve many economies of large-scale operations and enable government to provide specialized public services, which "fragmented" units of government cannot provide. For example, larger water treatment plant facilities can deliver water at lower per gallon costs, and larger sewage disposal plants can handle sewage at a lower per gallon cost of disposal.

The problem with this argument is that most studies show that larger municipal governments are *un*economic and fail to produce improved services. Only in very small cities (with populations under 25,000) can economies of scale be achieved by enlarging the scope of government; size does not seem to matter in cities of between 25,000 to 250,000 people; but in cities of over 250,000, further increases in size produce *dis*economies of scale and lower levels of public service per person.[7]

Coordination   Second, it is argued that metropolitan consolidation will provide the necessary *coordination of public services* for the metropolis. Study after study reported that crime, fire, traffic congestion, air pollution, water pollution, and so on do not respect municipal boundary lines. The transportation problem is the most common example of a coordination problem. Traffic experts have pleaded for the development of a balanced transportation system in which mass transit carries many of the passengers currently traveling in private automobiles. Yet mass transit requires decisive public action by the entire metropolitan area. Certainly, the city government is in a poor position to provide mass transit by itself without the support of the suburbanites who will be riding on it.

Equality   The third major argument for metropolitan consolidation stresses the need to eliminate *inequalities in financial burdens* throughout the metropolitan area. Suburbanites who escaped many city taxes continue to add to the cities' traffic and parking problems, use city streets and parks, find employment in the cities, use city hospitals and cultural facilities, and so on. By concentrating the poor, uneducated, unskilled minorities in central cities, we also saddle central cities with costly problems of public health and welfare, crime control, fire protection, slum clearance, and the like—all the social problems that are associated with poverty and discrimination. We concentrate these costly problems in cities at the same time that middle-class tax-paying individuals, tax-paying commercial enterprises, and tax-paying industries are moving into the suburbs. Thus, metropolitan-government fragmentation often succeeds in segregating financial needs from resources. The result is serious financial difficulty for many central cities.

---

[7] For a summary of these studies, see Elinor Ostrom, "Metropolitan Reform: Propositions Derived From Two Traditions," *Social Science Quarterly,* 53 (December 1972), 474–93.

Responsibility   It is also argued that metropolitan government will *clearly establish responsibility for metropolitanwide policy.* One of the consequences of "fragmented" government is the scattering of public authority and the decentralization of policy making in the metropolis. This proliferation in the number of autonomous governmental units reduces the probability of developing a consensus on metropolitan policy. Each autonomous unit exercises a veto power over metropolitan policy within its jurisdiction; it is often impossible to secure the unanimity required to achieve metropolitan consensus on any metropolitanwide problem. An opponent of any particular solution need only find, among the countless independent governmental bodies whose consent is required, one that can be induced to withhold its consent in order to obstruct action. The dispersion of power among a large number of governmental units makes it possible for each of them to reach decisions without concern for the possible spillover effects, which may be harmful to other governments or residents of the metropolis.

THE CASE FOR "FRAGMENTED" GOVERNMENT

Suburb "bashing" is a common theme among central-city politicians, city newspaper columnists, and many reform-minded scholars who would prefer centralized metropolitan government.[8] But the suburbs house nearly half of the nation's population and it is important to try to understand why so many suburbanites prefer "fragmented" government. Many citizens do not look upon "the optimum development of the metropolitan region" as a particularly compelling goal. Rather, there are a variety of social, political, and psychological values at stake in maintaining the existing "fragmented" system of local government.

Identity   First of all, the existence of separate and independent local governments for suburbs plays a vital role in developing and maintaining a sense of community *identity.* Suburbanities identify their residential community by reference to the local political unit. They do not think of themselves as residents of the "New York metropolitan region," but rather as residents of Scarsdale or Mineola. Even the existence of community problems, the existence of a governmental forum for their resolution, and the necessity to elect local officials heighten community involvement and identity. The suburban community, with a government small in scale and close to home, represents a partial escape from the anonymity of mass urban culture. The institutional apparatus of government helps the suburban community to differentiate itself from "the urban mass" by legislating differences in the size and design of buildings, neighborhood and subdivision plans, school policies, types and quality of public services, and tax expenditure levels.

Access   The political advantages of a fragmented suburbia cannot easily be dismissed. The existence of many local governments provides *additional forums* for the

---

[8] For an excellent analysis of the political values of scholars who study urban problems, see Brett W. Hawkins and Stephen L. Percy, "On Anti-Suburban Orthodoxy," *Social Science Quarterly,* 72 (September 1991), 478–90.

airing of public grievances. People feel better when they can publicly voice their complaints against governments, regardless of the eventual outcome of their grievance. The additional points of access, pressure, and control provided by a decentralized system of local government give added insurance that political demands will be heard and perhaps even acted upon. Opportunities for individual participation in the making of public policy are expanded in a decentralized governmental system.

Effectiveness   Maintaining the suburb as an independent political community provides the individual with a sense of *personal effectiveness* in public affairs. The individual can feel a greater sense of manageability over the affairs of a small community. A smaller community helps relieve feelings of frustration and apathy which people often feel in their relations with larger bureaucracies. Suburbanites feel that their votes, their opinions, and their political activities count for more in a small community. They cling to the idea of grass-roots democracy in an organizational society.

Influence   Fragmented government clearly offers a larger number of groups the opportunity to *exercise influence* over government policy. Groups that would be minorities in the metropolitan area as a whole can avail themselves of government position and enact diverse public policies. This applies to blacks in the central city as well as to whites in the suburbs. Fragmented government creates within the metropolitan area a wide range of government policies. Communities that prefer, for example, higher standards in their school system at higher costs have the opportunity to implement this preference. Communities that prefer higher levels of public service or one set of services over another or stricter enforcement of particular standards can achieve their goals under a decentralized governmental system. Communities that wish to get along with reduced public services in order to maximize funds available for private spending may do so.

Schools   Racial imbalance and the plight of central-city schools are important forces in maintaining the political autonomy of suburban school systems in the nation's large metropolitan areas. Many suburbanites left the central city to find "a better place to raise the kids," and this means, among other things, better schools. As we have already observed, suburbs generally spend more on the education of each child than central cities. Moreover, the increasing concentration of blacks in central cities has resulted in racial imbalance in center-city schools. Efforts to end de facto segregation within the cities frequently involve busing school children into and out of ghetto schools in order to achieve racial balance. In Chapter 14 we will discuss de facto segregation in greater detail. However, it is important to note here that independent suburban school districts are viewed by many suburbanites as protection against the possibility that their children might be bused to inner-city schools. Autonomous suburban school districts lie outside the jurisdiction of city officials. While it is possible that federal courts may some day order suburban school districts to cooperate with cities in achieving racial balance in schools, the political independence of suburban schools helps to assure that their children will not be used to achieve racial balance in city schools.

METROPOLITAN GOVERNMENT AS MARKETPLACE

Fragmented metropolitan government means many different mixes of municipal services, public schools, and tax levels in the same metropolitan area. So why can't people "shop around" among local communities and move into the community where the mix of services, schools, and taxes best suits their individual preferences?

The Tiebout Model   Economist Charles Tiebout argues that the existence of many local governments in the same area, all offering "public goods" (public schools, police and fire protection, water and sewer, refuse collection, streets and sidewalks) and various "prices" (taxes), provides a competitive and efficient government marketplace.[9] Families can choose for themselves what public goods they want at what price by simply moving to the community that best approximates their own preferences. Both families and businesses can "vote with their feet" for their preferred "bundle" of municipal services and taxes. Local governments must compete for residents and businesses by offering high-quality public services at the lowest possible tax rates. This encourages efficiency in local government.

Mobility?   The Tiebout model of efficient local government assumes that metropolitan residents have a high degree of *mobility,* that is, they can move anywhere in the metropolitan area anytime they wish. The major criticism of this model is that many metropolitan residents do not enjoy unlimited mobility. The poor are limited by meager financial resources from "shopping" for the best governmental services. And minorities often confront barriers to residential mobility regardless of their economic resources.

Equity?   Moreover, the Tiebout model in its original formulation ignores the interdependence of the metropolis. Many public services are metropolitanwide in scope—urban expressways, mass transit, clean air and water, public health and hospitals, for example. These services cannot be provided by small local governments. Suburbanites use public facilities and services of cities when they work in the city or go to the city for entertainment. If they do not share in the costs of these services and facilities, they become "free riders," unfairly benefiting from services paid for by others.

The major social problems of the city—poverty, racial tension, poor housing, crime and delinquency—are really problems of the entire metropolis. Political scientists John C. Bollens and Henry J. Schmandt, in *The Metropolis,* addressed this point very effectively:

> Some myopic defenders of suburbia go so far as to say that the major
> socioeconomic problems of urban society are problems of the central city, not those
> of the total metropolitan community. Where but within the boundaries of the core
> city, they ask, does one find an abundance of racial strife, crime, blight of housing,

---

and welfare recipients? Superficially, their logic may seem sound, since they are in general correct about the prevalent spatial location of these maladies. Although crimes and other social problems exist in suburbia, their magnitude and extent are substantially less than in the central city. But why in an interdependent metropolitan community should the responsibility of suburbanites be any less than that of the central city dwellers? Certainly no one would think of contending that residents of higher income neighborhoods within the corporate limits of the city should be exempt from responsibility for its less fortunate districts. What logic then is there in believing that neighborhoods on the other side of a legal line can wash their hands of social disorders in these sections?[10]

Satisfaction?   Yet the Tiebout model is correct in asserting that there is a great variety of life styles, housing types, governmental services and costs *within* large metropolitan areas, and that most families take these into account when choosing a place of residence. And judging by the subjective evaluations of residents, many different types of neighborhoods are judged satisfactory by the people living in them. Quality-of-life studies usually ask respondents how "satisfied" they are with their neighborhoods. These studies reveal that people living in *all* types of neighborhoods express satisfaction with them. Indeed, even lower-income people living in substandard housing or areas considered slums by outsiders report being satisfied. (However, attachment to friends and relatives is a major source of their satisfaction, rather than governmental services.)[11] The fact that residents of many different kinds of communities express satisfaction with them lends implicit support to the Tiebout model. There is also evidence that business locational decisions within the metropolis are influenced by the "bundle" of governmental services and taxes offered by local governments.[12]

"SOLUTIONS" TO THE METROPOLITAN PROBLEM

Let us examine various strategies for metropolitan governmental consolidation in connection with the values of suburban independence and the need for coordinating governmental activity in metropolitan areas.

Annexation   The most obvious method of achieving governmental consolidation in the metropolitan area would be for the central city to annex suburban areas. *Annexation* continues to be the most popular integrating device in the nation's metropolitan areas. Not all cities, however, have been equally successful in annexation efforts. Opposition to central-city annexation is generally more intense in the larger metropolitan areas. The bigger the metropolis, the more one can expect that suburbanites will defend themselves against being "swallowed up" or "sub-

10 John C. Bollens and Henry J. Schmandt, *The Metropolis* (New York: Harper & Row, 1965), pp. 249–50.

11 See Barrett A. Lee, "The Urban Unease Revisited: Perceptions of Local Satisfaction Among Metropolitan Residents," *Social Science Quarterly,* 62 (December 1987), 611–29; Craig St. John and Frieda Clark, "Race and Social Class Differences in the Characteristics Desired in Residential Neighborhoods," *Social Science Quarterly,* 65 (September 1984), 803–13.

12 See Mark Schneider, "Suburban Fiscal Disparities and the Location Decisions of Firms," *American Journal of Political Science,* 29 (August 1985), 587–605.

merged" by the central city. Central cities in smaller urbanized areas experience more success in annexing people than cities in large urbanized areas. Yet size does not appear to be the most influential factor affecting annexation success. Actually, the "age" of a city seems more influential than its size in determining the success of annexation efforts. Over three-fourths of the area and population annexed to central cities in the nation in the last two decades have been in newer cities of the West and South. City boundary lines in "older" metropolitan areas are relatively more fixed than in "newer" areas. Perhaps the immobility of boundaries is a product of sheer age. Over time, persons and organizations adjust themselves to circumstances as they find them. The longer these adjustments have been in existence, the greater the discomfort, expense, and fear of unanticipated consequences associated with change.[13]

City–County Consolidation   Three-quarters of the nation's metropolitan areas lie within single counties. From the standpoint of administration, there is much to be said for *city–county consolidation.* It would make sense administratively to endow county governments with the powers of cities and to organize them to exercise these powers effectively. Yet, important political problems—problems in the allocation of influence over public decision making—remain formidable barriers to strong county government. Suburbanites are likely to fear that consolidation will give city residents a dominant voice in county affairs. Suburbanites may also fear that city–county consolidation may force them to pay higher taxes to help support the higher municipal costs of running the city. Suburbanites may not welcome uniform, countywide policies in taxation or zoning or any number of other policy areas. Suburbanites who have paid for their own wells and septic tanks will hardly welcome the opportunity to help pay for city water or sewer services. Suburbanites with well-established, high-quality public school systems may be unenthusiastic about integrating their schools with city schools in a countywide system, and so on. A variety of policy differences may exist between city and suburb, which will reflect themselves in any attempt to achieve city–county consolidation.

Special Districts   One of the more popular approaches to metropolitan integration is the creation of *special districts or authorities* charged with administering a particular function or service on a metropolitanwide or at least an intermunicipal level, such as a park, sewage, water, parking, airport, planning, other district, or authority. (See Table 12–4.) Because the special district or authority leaves the social and governmental *status quo* relatively undisturbed, important integrative demands are met with a minimum of resistance with this device. The autonomy of suburban communities is not really threatened, loyalties are not disturbed, political jobs are not lost, and the existing tax structure is left relatively intact. Special districts or authorities may be preferred by suburban political leaders when they believe it will lessen the pressure for annexation by the central city. Special districts or

---

[13] See Arnold Fleischmann, "The Politics of Annexation," *Social Science Quarterly,* 67 (March 1986), 128–41; Gary J. Miller, *Cities by Contract: The Politics of Municipal Incorporation* (Cambridge, MA: MIT Press, 1981).

TABLE 12–4   SPECIAL DISTRICT GOVERNMENTS BY FUNCTION

Fire Protection	5070
Water Supply	3060
Soil and Water Conservation	2469
Housing and Community Development	3464
Drainage and Flood Control	2772
Cemeteries	1627
Sewage	1607
Education	713
Irrigation	854
Parks and Recreation	1004
Hospitals	783
Highways	621
Libraries	830
Natural Resources, Miscellaneous	265
Other Single Function	2342
Multiple Function	2051

Source: U.S. Bureau of the Census, *Census of Governments, 1987.*

authorities may also be able to incur additional debt after existing units of government have already reached their tax and debt limits. Thus, special districts or authorities may be able to operate in an area wider than that of existing units of governments and at the same time enable governments to evade tax or debt limits in financing a desired public service.

Yet, experience in cities that have relied heavily upon special districts or authorities has suggested that these devices may create as many problems as they solve. Many special districts and authorities are governed by a quasi-independent board or commission, which, once established, becomes largely immune from popular pressures for change. These agencies may be quite independent of other governmental jurisdictions in the metropolis; their concerns might be water, air or water pollution control, city planning, and so on. Remoteness from popular control or close political responsibility often results in the professional administrators of these authorities exercising great power over their particular function. While authorities and special districts are supposed to be nonprofit governmental agencies, they often act very much like private enterprises, concentrating their resources on those activities that produce revenue and ignoring equally important non–revenue-producing responsibilities. Independent authorities often borrow money, collect tolls and services charges, and otherwise control their own finances in a manner very much like a private business. The structure of these districts and authorities usually confuses the voters and makes it difficult for the average citizen to hold officials of these agencies responsible for their decisions. Moreover, since these special districts and authorities are usually created for a single purpose, they often come to define the public interest in terms of the promotion of their own particular function—recreation, mass transit, water, parks, and so on—without regard for other metropolitan concerns. This "single-mindedness" can lead to competition and conflict between authorities and other governmental agencies in the region. Sooner or later, the problem of coordinating the activities of these independent authorities of special districts arises. Thus, even from the point of view of administrative efficiency, it is not clear whether the special district or authority, with its maze of divided responsibility, reduces or compounds the problem of governmental coordination in the metropolis in the long run.

Interjurisdictional Agreements   Another approach to metropolitan integration is the *interjurisdictional agreement.* Voluntary cooperative agreements between governments in a metropolitan area are common. Agreements may take the form of *informal,* verbal understandings that might involve, for example, the exchange between welfare departments of information on cases, or cooperation among police departments in the apprehension of a lawbreaker, or agreements among local fire departments to come to the assistance of each other in the event of a major fire. Agreements may also be *formal* interjurisdictional agreements among governments, perhaps to build and operate a major facility such as a garbage incinerator or a sewage treatment plant. Interjurisdictional agreements may provide for (1) one government performing a service or providing a facility for one or more other governments on a contractual basis, (2) two or more governments performing a function jointly or operating a facility on a joint basis, or (3) two or more local governments agreeing to assist and supply mutual aid to each other in emergency situations.

One of the attractions of interjurisdictional agreements is that they provide a means for dealing with metropolitan problems on a voluntary basis while retaining local determination and control. Interjurisdictional agreements do not threaten the existence of communities or governments. They do not threaten the jobs of incumbent public officials. Yet at the same time they enable governments to achieve the economies and provide the specialized services that only a larger jurisdiction can make possible.

Councils of Government   Metropolitan councils of governments (COGs) are another form of integration in metropolitan areas. Metropolitan councils are associations of governments or government officials that provide an opportunity for study, discussion, and recommendations regarding common metropolitan problems. Not governments themselves, these COGs have no power to implement decisions but must rely instead upon compliance by member governments. Metropolitan councils provide an arena where officials of metropolitan governments can come together regularly, discuss problems, make recommendations, and, hopefully, coordinate their activities.[14]

---

[14] The best-known councils of government include the Metropolitan Regional Council (New York), Southern California Association of Governments (Los Angeles), Northeast Illinois Planning Commission (Chicago), Southeast Michigan Council of Governments (Detroit), Associated Bay Area Governments (San Francisco), Metropolitan Washington Council of Governments (Washington), East-West Gateway Council (St. Louis), Northeast Ohio Areawide Coordinating Agency (Cleveland).

Although COGs started slowly, the federal government provided the major stimulus to their acceptance by making federal planning funds available for metropolitanwide planning agencies. Today, most metropolitan areas have *some* organization functioning as a metropolitan council of government.[15]

Generally, COGs strive for unity in their decisions because their recommendations must be acted upon by member governments who are unlikely to implement proposals they oppose. The result, for the most part, is that studies and recommendations of COGs are likely to be rather bland. It is very difficult for these councils to deal with the really divisive issues in the metropolis. Since councils have no authority to act upon metropolitan problems, they may be, in the words of Bollens and Schmandt, a "toothless tiger or—even worse—a protector of the inadequate status quo."[16]

THE POLITICS OF METROPOLITAN CONSOLIDATION

City officials—mayors, managers, and council members—usually provide the public stimulus for annexation. Their immediate goal is to expand the tax base of the city; over the long run they seek growth and revenues. They do not want to see the city cut off from new residential, industrial, and commercial development on the rim of the metropolis. Their primary strategy is to cultivate political support for various annexation efforts by offering city services—especially water and sewer, fire and police protection, street lighting and sidewalks—at reasonable prices to residents of areas targeted for annexation. Sometimes builders and developers can be enticed to offer land for annexation in exchange for city water, sewer, or streets. Cities with active managers and planners are more likely to have continuous annexation programs.

City business interests, with capital already invested in downtown land, buildings, and enterprises, are usually strong supporters of annexation. These city power structures are growth oriented (see Chapter 13). If the city government is cut off from new sources of revenue, the costs of city government will increasingly fall on the shoulders of downtown business. The downtown Chambers of Commerce, the city newspaper, and the downtown civic (reform) organizations can all be expected to support the expansion of the city.

Political Opposition   Political opposition to annexation and city expansion is usually centered among suburban municipal officials and residents. They see continued value in "fragmentation"—a sense of community identity, access to government, personal influence in a smaller governmental setting, insulation from city dwellers whose life styles they do not share, and perhaps a desire to maintain

---

[15] Frances Frisken, "The Metropolis and the Central City," *Urban Affairs Quarterly,* 8 (June 1973), 395–422; Melvin B. Mogulof, "Metropolitan Councils of Government and the Federal Government," *Urban Affairs Quarterly,* 7 (June 1972), 489–507.

[16] See Bollens and Schmandt, *The Metropolis,* pp. 379–80. See Thomas M. Scott, "Metropolitan Governmental Reorganization Proposals," *Western Political Quarterly,* 21 (June 1968), 252–61; and Advisory Commission on Intergovernmental Relations, *Factors Affecting Voter Reactions to Governmental Reorganization* (Washington, DC: Government Printing Office, 1962).

racial isolation. They also fear higher tax rates in the city, and they may not feel that the additional services offered by city government are worth the added cost. County or township officials may take the lead in urging residents not to sign annexation petitions and to vote "no" if an election is held; they may also challenge annexation petitions and votes in the courts.

Political realities have frequently overwhelmed the "logic" of metropolitan consolidation. These political realities are deeply rooted in the social, economic, life-style, and racial differences between cities and suburbs described earlier. The record of consolidation referenda shows more defeats than victories.[17] Yet reformers have not been inhibited by the dismal record thus far, and consolidation proposals of various kinds are under discussion in a great many urban areas.

Consolidation involves considerable disruption for public officials—redesigning governmental structure, reordering the authority of various offices, combining offices and agencies, and enlarging the magnitude of government operations. Unless a *large* majority of community influentials are *very* dissatisfied with the current state of affairs and are motivated to actively support consolidation, there is little chance that consolidation efforts will be successful.[18]

Consolidation Commissions   Consolidation efforts usually begin with the formation of a charter commission to determine the form of the new consolidated government and write a charter for it. Usually the commission includes representatives of both the city and county governments to be consolidated, together with some "citizen" representatives. Sometimes the establishment of the commission itself is the subject of a referendum; interestingly, referenda to establish a commission tend to pass more often than not, even though the final vote on consolidation is likely to be negative. Establishing a charter commission is more easily obtainable than consolidation itself.

Consolidation Referenda   The critical point of the consolidation battle is the referenda vote on the acceptance of the new consolidated-government charter. The form of the vote depends on state law: A "double majority" vote requirement means that a majority "yes" vote must be obtained within the city *and* within the area outside of the city; a "double-count majority" vote requirement means that the vote of city residents is counted twice—once for the city and again for the county because they are also county residents. It is much easier for consolidation to win under the "double-count" requirement. Consolidation campaigns are usually managed by reform groups especially selected for the purpose. They are typically mass-media–oriented campaigns rather than the grass-roots organizational, ward- and precinct-level campaigns of party organizations. Voter turnout is only slightly

---

[17] Vincent L. Marando and Carl Whitley, "City-County Consolidation: An Overview of Voter Response," *Urban Affairs Quarterly,* 8 (December 1972), 181–203.

[18] For an interesting comparison of elite roles in successful (Jacksonville) and unsuccessful (Tampa) consolidation campaigns, see Thomas A. Henderson and Walter A. Rosenbaum, "Prospects for Consolidating Local Government: The Role of Elites in Electoral Outcomes," *American Journal of Political Science,* 17 (November 1973), 695–720.

heavier than that of ordinary municipal elections—ranging from 30 percent to 60 percent. Contrary to the public pronouncements of reformers, a high turnout does *not* help passage; indeed, there is a slightly better chance of success if turnout is low.

Most consolidation proposals are defeated by *county* residents, that is, suburbanites. The average voter turnout level of suburbanites is much higher than city dwellers, and the percentage of "no" votes is much greater in the suburbs than in the city. Thus, overall voter response to consolidation proposals tends to support the notion that suburbanites prefer to maintain their identity and autonomy, their own governmental institutions, and their insulation from city people and problems. They do *not* want the improved public services, coordinated policies, or shared financial burdens that reformers urge upon them. While fear of higher taxes plays a role in suburban opposition, there appear to be many other social and psychological factors at work in helping to preserve suburban autonomy.[19]

The fear of being "submerged" into a large, impersonal, unresponsive government is evidenced by the interesting fact that proposed consolidation charters that stipulate many elected representatives and separately elected administrators (sheriff, tax assessor, and so on) do better at the polls than the "streamline," governmental charters preferred by reformers. In other words, a "Jacksonian" consolidation charter has a better chance of passage than one with a small legislative body and single strong executive.

Race   Race is an increasingly important issue in consolidation campaigns. Most successful consolidation efforts have occurred in the South. A common appeal to suburbanites in the South is to vote to join the city in order to "save" it from black majority rule by "diluting" the black vote. However, the issue is complex and cuts both ways. Suburbanites may simply decide to stay out of a consolidated government precisely because it would include many central-city blacks. Blacks were traditionally expected to vote "yes" for economic reasons—to bring valuable suburban property into the tax base of the city. However, black support for consolidation will certainly turn to opposition if it appears that blacks will lose power in the outcome.[20]

Reform   Political support for consolidation is usually greatest among civic and business organizations and newspapers. Their arguments for consolidation are familiar—improved services, better coordination, more equal financial burdens, and clearer lines of responsibility. Moreover, consolidation offers an opportunity to reorganize local government: The new government may offer a manager form of government, a reduction in the number of elected officials, and a more orderly structure for the delivery of municipal services.

---

[19] It is unclear whether greater "social distance" between city and suburbs directly affects referenda voting. See Brett W. Hawkins, "Life-Style Distance and Voter Support of City-County Consolidation," *Social Science Quarterly,* 48 (December 1967), 325–28; Vincent L. Marando, "Life-Style Distances and Suburban Support for Urban Political Integration," *Social Science Quarterly,* 52 (June 1972), 155–60.

[20] See Richard L. Engstrom and W.E. Lyons, "Black Control or Consolidation: The Fringe Response," *Social Science Quarterly,* 53 (June 1972), 161–68.

The Tax Issue   Does city–county consolidation save the taxpayers' money? Reformers have been *unable* to produce any convincing evidence that consolidation either improves governmental services or reduces governmental costs.[21] Indeed, in careful study of this important question, employing a before-and-after research design in similar "experimental" and "control" cities, researchers found "no measurable impact" from consolidation on governmental costs of services.[22] This study focused on Florida's Jacksonville/Duval County which consolidated their governments, and Tampa/Hillsbourgh County which did not. Both metropolitan areas are similar in socioeconomic composition, both operate under the same state laws, and both have the same mayor-council form of government. Yet an examination of property taxes, total expenditures, and policy protection in both cities from 1955 through 1981 (Jacksonville/Duval County consolidated in 1969) showed *no* significant short-term or long-term differences between these two areas.

A Record of Failure   Most consolidation efforts fail. Only about one-quarter of the consolidation proposals that come to a vote are approved. These have all been single counties. Most have been in medium-size or smaller metropolitan areas. There have been no adoptions in the Northeast or Midwest; all consolidations have taken place in the South or West. Successful consolidations have always involved some unique political factors. Often it is necessary to allow some offices to remain separate in order to secure political support for consolidation, for example, retaining a separate sheriff's office and city police force, or retaining separate school districts.[23]

"Metro" Government   The American experience with federalism at the national level has prompted consideration of federated governmental structures for metropolitan areas. A "metro" government with authority to make metropolitan-wide policy in selected fields might be combined with local control over functions that are "local" in character. Metropolitan federation, in one form or another and at one time or another, has been proposed for many major metropolitan regions in the nation. Yet, with the exception of Toronto, Miami, and Nashville,[24] proposals for metropolitan federation have been consistently rejected by both voters and political leaders. While metropolitan federation promises many of the advantages of governmental consolidation listed earlier—administrative efficiency, economy of large-scale operation, elimination of financial inequalities, and public accountabil-

---

[21] Roy W. Bahl and Alan K. Campbell, *State and Local Government* (New York: Free Press, 1976).

[22] J. Edwin Benten, "City County Consolidation and Economics of Scale," *Social Science Quarterly,* 65 (March 1985), 190–98.

[23] See Vincent L. Marando, "City County Consolidation: Reform Regionalism Referenda and Requiem," *Western Political Quarterly,* 32 (December 1979), 409–21.

[24] See Edward Sofen, *The Miami Metropolitan Experiment* (Bloomington: University of Indiana Press, 1963); Edward Sofen, "The Politics of Metropolitan Leadership: The Miami Experience," *Midwest Journal of Political Science,* 5 (February 1961), 18–38; Brett W. Hawkins, *Nashville Metro* (Nashville, TN.: University of Vanderbilt Press, 1966); Brett W. Hawkins, "Public Opinion and Metropolitan Reorganization in Nashville," *Journal of Politics,* 28 (May 1966), 408–18.

ity for metropolitanwide policy—it seriously threatens many of the social, political, and psychological values in the existing "fragmented" system of local government in the metropolis. Metropolitan federation also poses a problem discussed earlier, that of deciding what is a "metropolitan" problem. In order to allocate functions to a "metro" government in a federation arrangement, one must first determine what is a metropolitan problem in which all the citizens of the area have a responsibility.

THE CONCENTRATION OF SOCIAL PROBLEMS IN THE INNER CITY

The nation's largest cities have become the principal location of virtually all of the social problems confronting our society—poverty, homelessness, racial tension, family instability, drug abuse, delinquency, and crime. (Some of these problems are discussed in other chapters—crime in Chapter 8, racial issues in Chapter 14, education in Chapter 16, and poverty and homelessness in Chapter 17.) But it is important to note here that these problems are all made worse by their concentration in the inner city. This concentration is a relatively recent occurrence; as late as 1970 there were higher rates of poverty in rural America than in the cities.

Joblessness   Why has the "inner city" become the locus of social problems? It has been argued that changes in the labor market from industrial goods-producing jobs to professional, financial, technical, and service jobs is increasingly polarizing the labor market into low-wage and high-wage sectors.[25] The decline in manufacturing jobs, together with a shift in remaining manufacturing jobs and commercial (sales) jobs to the suburbs, has left inner-city residents with fewer job opportunities. The rise in joblessness in the inner cities has in turn increased the concentration of poor people, added to the number of poor single-parent families, and increased welfare dependency.

Middle-Class Flight   At the same time, inner-city neighborhoods have experienced an out-migration of working-class and middle-class families. The number of inner-city neighborhoods in which the poverty rate exceeds 40 percent has risen sharply.[26] The loss of working- and middle-class families creates further social instability. In earlier decades most inner-city adults were employed, and they invested their income and time in their neighborhoods, patronizing churches, stores, schools, and community organizations. Their presence in the community provided "role models" for youth. But their out-migration has decreased contact between the classes, leaving the poorest members of the community isolated and "truly disadvantaged." Inner-city residents now lack not only nearby jobs, but also access to

---

[25] See William Julius Wilson, *The Truly Disadvantaged* (Chicago: University of Chicago Press, 1987).

[26] See Christopher Jencks and Paul E. Peterson, eds., *The Urban Underclass* (Washington, DC: Brookings Institution, 1991).

job information, social learning through working role models, and suitable (for example, employed) marriage partners.

The Truly Disadvantaged   It is argued that joblessness and poverty are much more demoralizing when concentrated in the inner city. Neighborhoods that have few legitimate employment opportunities, inadequate job information networks, and poor schools not only weaken the work ethic, but also give rise to illegal income-producing activities in the streets—drugs, crime, and prostitution. A jobless family living in a neighborhood where these ills are concentrated is influenced by the behaviors, beliefs, and perceptions of the people around them. These "concentration effects" make things worse. Moreover, the deterioration of inner-city neighborhoods saps the vitality of local businesses and public services, leading to fewer and shabbier movie theaters, restaurants, markets, parks, and playgrounds. Inner-city schools are particularly disadvantaged: As educational requirements for good jobs are rising, the quality of education available in the inner city is eroded by the concentration of children from poverty-impacted and disintegrating families. The fiscal burden on city governments increases: The cost of services to the inner city rises at the same time that the tax base is eroded by out-migrating businesses and working residents.

THE INNER CITY: RACIAL TENSIONS AND RIOTING

The concentration of social problems in the inner city not only adds to their severity, but also removes them from direct observation by most Americans. Only when the inner city erupts in rioting and violence do many Americans turn their attention to the racial tensions, family breakdowns, joblessness, welfare dependency, crime and drugs, poor schools, and hopelessness that permeate so many core areas of our nation's large cities. And often the attention of policy makers, the media, and the general public is fleeting—it is "politics as usual" after the rioting has been quelled, with inner-city dwellers left to pick up the charred pieces.

The Urban Riots of the Sixties   Domestic violence is not new to American cities. Three early riots—Watts in Los Angeles in 1965, and Newark and Detroit in 1967—were major civil disorders. Detroit was the worst of these outbreaks: A week of rioting left forty-three dead and more than 1000 injured. Whole sections of the city were reduced to charred ruins and smoke. Over 1300 buildings were totally demolished and 2700 businesses sacked. Detroit's upheaval began when police raided an after-hours club and arrested the bartender and several customers for selling and consuming alcoholic beverages after authorized closing hours. A force of 15,000 city and state police, National Guardsmen, and finally federal troops fought to quell the violence. Most of the looted retail businesses were liquor stores, grocery stores, and furniture stores. Many black merchants scrawled "Soul Brother" on their windows in an attempt to escape the wrath of the mobs. Eventually, home and shops covering a total area of fourteen square miles were gutted by fire. Firefighters were stoned and occasionally shot by ghetto residents. Of the forty-three persons who were killed during the riot, thirty-three were black and ten were white. Police officers killed 20 persons, and National Guard and Army troops an additional 10; one Guardsman, one firefighter, and one private security guard were among the dead.[27]

President Lyndon Johnson appointed a National Commission on Civil Disorder to study the nature and causes of urban rioting. Among the commission's conclusions were the following:

> Typically, rioting was a result of a complex relationship between underlying grievances and one or more "triggering" incidents. For example, grievances about allegedly abusive police practices . . . were often aggravated in the minds of many blacks by incidents involving the police, or the inaction of municipal authorities on complaints about police action.
>
> Many grievances in the black community resulted from discrimination, prejudice, and powerlessness which blacks often experience. . . .
>
> Characteristically, the typical rioter was not a hoodlum, habitual criminal, or riff-raff. . . . Instead, he was a teenager or young adult, a life-long resident of the city in which he rioted, a high school drop-out and almost invariably underemployed or employed in a menial job. He was proud of his race, extremely hostile to both whites and middle-class blacks, and highly distrustful of the political system and of political leaders.
>
> . . . Some rioters shared neither the conditions nor the grievance of their neighbors; some coolly and deliberately exploited the chaos created by others; some may have been drawn into the melee merely because they identified with, or wished to emulate, others.[28]

National Response   Many new "Great Society" social welfare programs were already underway at the time of these early riots. The War on Poverty produced a myriad of new federal programs in education, welfare, health care, and housing. While some of these programs were later abandoned, notably the federal Office of Economic Opportunity and its local antipoverty "community action" agencies, nonetheless many important policy innovations grew to become major programs today. Later, we will describe Headstart and other federal educational programs (Chapter 15); federal transportation and housing programs (Chapter 16); and Medicare, Medicaid, and welfare programs (Chapter 17).

But responsibility for the nation's "urban policy" remains divided between federal departments (for example, the Department of Health and Human Services, the Department of Education, the Department of Housing and Urban Development, the Department of Labor, the Department of Transportation, etc.) and between federal and state governments. Indeed, there is no clear agreement on what "urban policy" encompasses, inasmuch as the problems of cities include virtually every problem confronting the nation.

Despite the dramatic growth of federal social welfare programs and expenditures over the past three decades, there was little noticeable improvement in conditions in the inner city. The Detroit experience was particularly disillusioning: Its inner city is a more depressed and dangerous place today than when the riots

---

[27] National Advisory Commission on Civil Disorders, *Report* (Washington, DC: Government Printing Office, 1968), p. 107.

[28] Ibid., p. 4.

erupted in 1967. Its population plummeted from 1.6 million to 1 million as middle-class blacks and whites fled. Its crime rate soared 60 percent between 1976 and 1991, and it lost over one-third of its jobs. Efforts to stem the flight of the middle class and stabilize neighborhoods were largely ineffective. Thousands of abandoned apartments, stores, and business locations litter the inner city. If anything, the rioting accelerated the worsening of conditions.

The Los Angeles Riots—1992   The Los Angeles riots in 1992 were a bloody reminder that racial conflict and social misery in the nation's inner cities have not disappeared. The city's "Rodney King" riot was the nation's worst urban rioting of the twentieth century. It left over fifty people dead and many square miles of charred desolation in south-central Los Angeles. The triggering event was the not-guilty verdict rendered by a predominately white jury in suburban Simi Valley in the case of four white Los Angeles police officers accused of beating a black motorist, Rodney King. The case had attracted national attention owing to the fact that the beating had been videotaped and shown many times on national television. The verdict was regarded by both blacks and whites nationwide as a serious miscarriage of justice. Many blacks in the inner city regarded it as white support for continued police brutality and a signal to express their outrage. Within hours of the verdict black youth in south-central Los Angeles

> began throwing stones and bottles at passing cars. The mob swelled. They hauled two white motorists from their cars and stomped them. Then Reginald Oliver Denny, 36, a gravel-truck driver with long blond hair, drove into the melee. Five men grabbed him, kicked him, smashed him on the head with a fire extinguisher and stole his wallet. For nearly an hour panicked drivers drove around him. A news chopper filmed the assault, possibly even encouraged it. T.J. Murphy, 30, an aerospace engineer, saw the beating on TV and drove to the scene. He found Denny, eyes swollen shut, in the cab of his truck. With the help of three other African-Americans, Murphy shielded the critically injured trucker and got him to a hospital.
>
> . . . the violence rippled outward. Drivers jumped from cars and fled. Shouting kids smashed windows, tromped on hoods and roofs, torched the abandoned vehicles. They turned to a liquor store, small shops, a gas station. Before long, flames and black smoke engulfed the neighborhood. And the LAPD was nowhere in sight. . . .
>
> In the days of raw nerves before the verdict, Police Chief Daryl Gates—whose style of L.A. law had started the trouble in the first place—boasted of having a special contingency plan to cope with any trouble; . . . but [as the riots progressed] Gates was nowhere to be found. . . .
>
> The smoke from 1,000 fires grew up so dense that air-traffic controllers could keep open only one runway at Los Angeles International Airport. . . .
>
> Looters of all races owned the streets, storefronts and malls. Throughout the city black merchants spray-painted their doors and awnings or put signs in their windows to distinguish them from white and Asian shops. Sometimes it worked; mostly it didn't. . . .[29]

---

[29] *Newsweek,* May 11, 1992, pp. 30–38.

In the Ashes Despite a great deal of political rhetoric following urban rioting, neither Congress nor the president has responded with any clear solutions to the problems of the inner city. And it may be that these problems are largely beyond the reach of government policy: The breakdown of families, the drug culture, the loss of inner-city jobs, and racial and ethnic tensions have all proven to be highly resistant to anything government does. In later chapters we will examine government efforts in welfare, health, homelessness, housing, and education.

Rioting intensifies racial distrust and conflict. Black psychologist Halford Fairchild believes that "violence has laid bare the city's inter-ethnic competition and hostility. The potential exists for urban warfare where the battle lines are drawn according to skin color, language, and ethnicity."[30]

Governments may be more effecting in controlling riots than in ameliorating their underlying conditions. Police reforms may have a more direct effect on the outbreak of rioting than anything else cities can do. Police departments that maintain close relationships with minority communities, train officers in benign conflict-resolution tactics, vigorously investigate and publish charges of police brutality, and endeavor to anticipate and respond quickly to events that might trigger riots may minimize unrest in their cities.

---

[30] *New York Times,* November 11, 1992, p. 19.

13

COMMUNITY POWER STRUCTURES

▲

MODELS OF COMMUNITY POWER

Who runs this town? Do the elected public officials actually make the important decisions? Or is there a "power structure" in this community that really runs things? If so, who is in the power structure? Are public officials "gofers" who carry out the orders of powerful individuals who operate "behind the scenes"? Or are community affairs decided by democratically elected officials acting openly in response to the wishes of many different individuals and groups? Is city government of the people, by the people, and for the people? Or is it a government run by a small "elite," with the "masses" of people largely apathetic and uninfluential in public affairs? Do people who make the important decisions in business and finance also make the important decisions in urban renewal, public works, education, taxation, public charity, land development, and so on? Or are there different groups of people making decisions in each of these areas, with little or no overlap except for elected officials?

Social scientists have differed over the answers to these questions. Some social scientists, whom we shall refer to as "elitists," believe that power in American communities is concentrated in the hands of relatively few people, usually top business and financial leaders. They believe that this "elite" is subject to relatively little influence from the "masses" of people. Other social scientists, whom we shall refer to as "pluralists," believe that power is widely shared in American communities among many leadership groups who represent segments of the community and who are held responsible by the people through elections and group participation. Interestingly, both elitists and pluralists seem to agree that decisions are made by small minorities in the community. The idea of direct, individual citizen participation in decision making has suffered with the coming of organizational society and high levels of urbanization and industrialization. *Elitists describe a monolithic structure of power,* with a single leadership group making decisions on a variety of issues. *Pluralists describe a polycentric structure of power,* with different elite groups active in different issues and a great deal of competition, bargaining, and sharing of power among elites.[1]

Most "real" communities will probably fall somewhere in between—that is, along a continuum from the monolithic elite model of power to a diffused and polycentric pluralist model. Many social scientists are neither confirmed "elitists" nor "pluralists," but they are aware that different structures and power may exist in different communities. Yet these ideal models of community power may be helpful in understanding the different ways in which community power can be structured.

THE ELITE MODEL OF COMMUNITY POWER

European social theory has long been at odds with democratic political writers about the existence and necessity of elites. Gaetano Mosca, in his book *The Ruling Class,* wrote, "In all societies . . . two classes of people appear—a class that rules and a class that is ruled."[2] For Mosca, elitism is explained by the nature of social

---

[1] This literature on community power is so voluminous that it seems appropriate to cite only some of the major summary pieces: Thomas J. Anton, "Power, Pluralism, and Local Politics," *Administrative Science Quarterly,* 7 (March 1963), 425–57; Lawrence Herson, "In the Footsteps of Community Power," *American Political Science Review,* 55 (December 1961), 817–31; Peter Bachrach and Morton S. Baratz, "Two Faces of Power," *American Political Science Review,* 56 (December 1962), 947–53; Peter Bachrach and Morton C. Baratz, "Decisions and Nondecisions," *American Political Science Review,* 57 (September 1963), 632–42; Herbert Kaufman and Victor Jones, "The Mystery of Power," *Public Administration Review,* 14 (Summer 1954), 205–12; Nelson Polsby, *Community Power and Political Theory* (New Haven: Yale University Press, 1963); Robert Presthus, *Men at the Top* (New York: Oxford University Press, 1964); Robert Dahl, *Who Governs?* (New Haven: Yale University Press, 1961); Floyd Hunter, *Community Power Structure* (Chapel Hill: University of North Carolina Press, 1953); Robert Agger, Daniel Goldrich, and Bert Swanson, *The Rulers and the Ruled* (New York: John Wiley, 1965). Clarence N. Stone, "Systemic Power in Community Decision Making," *American Political Science Review,* 74 (December 1980), 978–90; G. William Domhoff, *Who Really Rules?* (Santa Monica, CA: Goodyear, 1978); Robert J. Waste (ed.), *Community Power: Directions for Future Research* (Beverly Hills, CA: Sage Publications, 1986); other citations are given in footnotes following.

[2] Gaetano Mosca, *The Ruling Class* (New York: McGraw-Hill, 1939), p. 50.

organization. Organization inevitably results in the concentration of political power in the hands of a few. Organized power cannot be resisted by an unorganized majority in which each individual ". . . stands alone before the totality of the organized minority. A hundred men acting uniformly in concert, with a common understanding, will triumph over a thousand men who are not in accord and can therefore be dealt with one by one."[3] Since organized power will prevail over individual effort in politics, sooner or later, organizations will come to be the more important actors in political life. And organizations cannot function without leaders. In Robert Michels's words, "He who says organization, says oligarchy."[4] The masses are permanently incapable of running or controlling political organizations. They must give that power to active, expert, and interested leadership groups. The idea that economic elites will tend to dominate in politics is also found in a great deal of social theory. Mosca wrote that the ruling class will possess ". . . some attribute real or apparent which is highly esteemed or very influential in the society in which they live." Needless to say, in a capitalist society, control over business and financial resources generally makes one "highly esteemed and very influential."

Power in "Middletown"   One of the earliest studies of American communities, the classic study of Middletown, conducted by sociologists Robert and Helen Lynd in the mid-1920s and again in the mid-1930s, confirmed a great deal of elitist thinking about community power.[5] The Lynds found in Muncie, Indiana, a monolithic power structure dominated by the owners of the town's largest industry. Community power was firmly entrenched in the hands of the business class, centering on, but not limited to, the "X family."[6] The power of this group was based upon its control over the economic life in the city, particularly its ability to control the extension of credit. The city was run by a "small top group" of "wealthy local manufacturers, bankers, the local head managers of . . . national corporations with units in Middletown, and . . . one or two outstanding lawyers." Democratic procedures and governmental institutions were so much window dressing for business control. The Lynds described the typical city official as a "man of meager calibre" and as "a man whom the inner business control group ignores economically and

---

[3] Ibid., p. 51.

[4] Robert Michels, *Political Parties* (Glencoe, IL: The Free Press, 1949).

[5] Robert S. Lynd and Helen M. Lynd, *Middletown* (New York: Harcourt Brace & World, 1929); and *Middletown in Transition* (New York: Harcourt Brace & World, 1937). Other classic community studies include W. Lloyd Warner et al., *Democracy in Jonesville* (New York: Harper & Row, 1949); and August B. Hollingshead, *Elmtown's Youth* (New York: John Wiley, 1949).

[6] The "X family," never identified in the Lynds' books, was actually the Ball family, glass manufacturers. As late as 1975 the Ball family exercised a controlling influence over the Ball Corporation, Ball Brothers Foundation, Ball Memorial Hospital, Muncie Aviation Corp., and Muncie Airport, Inc.; and E. F. Ball served as a director of American National Bank and Trust of Muncie, Borg-Warner Corp., Indiana Bell Telephone Co., Merchants National Bank of Muncie, and Wabash College. Ball State University in Muncie is named for the family.

socially and uses politically." Perhaps the most famous quotation from the Lynds' study was a comment by a Middletown man made in 1935:

> If I'm out of work, I go to the X plant; if I need money I go to the X bank, and if they don't like me I don't get it; my children go to the X college; when I get sick I go to the X hospital; I buy a building lot or house in the X subdivision; my wife goes downtown to buy X milk; I drink X beer, vote for X political parties, and get help from X charities; my boy goes to the X YMCA and my girl to their YWCA; I listen to the word of God in X subsidized churches; if I'm a Mason, I go to the X Masonic temple; I read the news from the X morning paper; and, if I'm rich enough, I travel via the X airport.[7]

Power in "Regional City"   One of the most influential studies of community politics was sociologist Floyd Hunter's *Community Power Structure,* a study of Atlanta, Georgia.[8] According to Hunter, no one person or family or business dominated "Regional City" (a synonym for Atlanta), as might be true in a smaller town. Instead, Hunter described several tiers of influentials, with the most important community decisions reserved for a top layer of the business community. Admission to the innermost circle was based primarily on one's position in the business world. These top decision makers were not formally organized but conferred informally and passed down decisions to government leaders, professional personnel, civic organizations, and other "figure heads." Hunter explained that the top power structure only concerned itself with major policy decisions; there were other substructures—economic, governmental, religious, educational, professional, civic, and cultural—that communicated and implemented the policies. (See Figure 13–1.) These substructures

> . . . are subordinate, however, to the interests of the policy makers who operate in the economic sphere of community life in Regional City. The institutions of the family, church, state, education, and the like draw sustenance from economic institutional sources and are thereby subordinate to this particular institution more than any other. . . . Within the policy forming groups the economic interests are dominant.[9]

Top power holders seldom operated openly. "Most of the top personnel in the power group are rarely seen in the meetings attended by the associational understructure personnel in Regional City."[10]

In Hunter's description of community decision making, decisions tended to flow *down* from top policy makers, composed primarily of business and financial leaders, to civic, professional, and cultural association leaders, religious and education leaders, and government officials, who implemented the program; and the masses of people had little direct or indirect participation in the whole process. Policy did not go *up* from associational groupings or from the people themselves. Ac-

[7] Lynd and Lynd, *Middletown in Transition,* p. 74.

[8] Floyd Hunter, *Community Power Structure* (Chapel Hill: University of North Carolina Press, 1969).

[9] Ibid., p. 94.

[10] Ibid., p. 90.

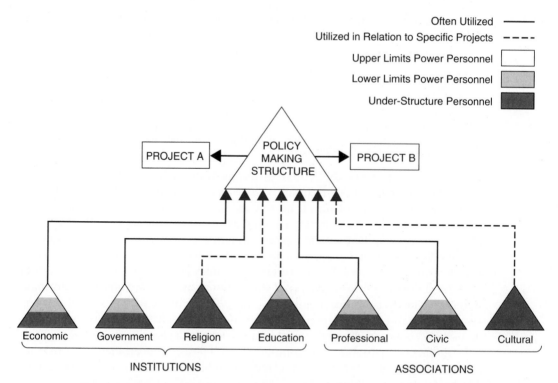

FIGURE 13–1   Power in "Regional City"

Source: Floyd Hunter, *Community Power Structure: A Study of Decision Makers* (Chapel Hill, University of North Carolina Press, 1953), p. 91. Reprinted by permission.

cording to Hunter, elected public officials are clearly part of the lower-level institutional substructure, which "executed" policy rather than formulated it. Finally, Hunter found that this whole structure was held together by "common interests, mutual obligations, money, habit, delegated responsibilities, and in some cases, by coercion and force."

THE PLURALIST MODEL OF COMMUNITY POWER

Political science had largely ignored the study of community power prior to the publication of Floyd Hunter's *Community Power Structure*. While sociologists had been developing an important body of literature on community power even before the Lynds' safari to darkest Indiana in the 1920s, community politics remained a "lost world" for political scientists.[11] Political science had been preoccupied with

---

[11] See Lawrence J. R. Herson, "The Lost World of Municipal Government," *American Political Science Review,* 51 (June 1957), 330–45.

the municipal reform movement, the structure of local government, and the administrative problems of economy and efficiency; they had largely ignored informal structures of power and decision making. Hunter's findings were very discomforting. They suggested that in reality American communities were not governed very democratically. Hunter's research challenged the notion of popular participation in "grass-roots" democracy and raised doubts as to whether or not the cherished values of Jeffersonian democracy were being realized in community life. While admitting that "none of us [political scientists] has moved in with such a study in dynamics of power in a metropolitan community," leading political scientists were willing to assert on the basis of their own "administrative experience" that Hunter's study as "at best . . . incomplete at worst . . . invalid."[12] Political scientists believed that much more competition, access, equality, and popular participation occurred in community politics than the work of the Lynds, Hunter, and others implied.

Multiple, Competitive, Interest Groups   Modern pluralism does not mean a commitment to "pure democracy," where all citizens participate directly in decision making. The underlying value of individual dignity continues to motivate contemporary pluralist thought, but it is generally recognized that the town-meeting type of pure democracy is not really possible in an urban industrial society. To modern pluralists, individual participation has come to mean membership in *organized groups.* Interest groups become the means by which individuals gain access to the political system. Government is held responsible, not directly by individuals, but by organized interest groups and political parties. Pluralists believe that competition between parties and organized groups, representing the interests of their citizen members, can protect the dignity of the individual and offer a viable alternative to individual participation in decision making.

The pluralist model of community power stresses the fragmentation of authority, the influence of elected public officials, the importance of organized group activity, and the role of public opinion and elections in determining public policy. Who rules in the pluralist community? "Different small groups of interested and active citizens in different issue areas with some overlap, if any, by public officials, and occasional intervention by a large number of people at the polls."[13]

Power in New Haven   Perhaps the most influential of the pluralist community studies was Robert A. Dahl's *Who Governs?,* a detailed analysis of decision making in New Haven, Connecticut. Dahl chose to examine sixteen major decisions on redevelopment and public education in New Haven and on nominations for mayor in both political parties for seven elections. Dahl found a polycentric and dispersed system of community power in New Haven, in contrast to Hunter's highly monolithic and centralized power structure. Influence was exercised from time to time

---

[12] Kaufman and Jones, "The Mystery of Power," pp. 205–12.

[13] Aaron Wildavsky, *Leadership in a Small Town* (Totowa, NJ: Bedminster Press, 1964), p. 8.

by many individuals, each exercising power over some issue but not over others. When the issue was one of urban renewal, one set of individuals was influential; in public education, a different group of leaders was involved. Business elites, who were said by Hunter to control Atlanta, were only one of many different influential groups in New Haven. According to Dahl,

> The economic notables, far from being a ruling group, are simply one of many groups out of which individuals sporadically emerge to influence the politics and acts of city officials. Almost anything one might say about the influence of the economic notables could be said with equal justice about a half dozen other groups in the New Haven community.[14]

The mayor of New Haven was the only decision maker who was influential in most of the issue areas studied, and his degree of influence varied from issue to issue:

> The mayor was not at the peak of a pyramid but at the center of intersecting circles. He rarely commanded. He negotiated, cajoled, exhorted, beguiled, charmed, pressed, appealed, reasoned, promised, insisted, demanded, even threatened; but he most needed support and acquiescence from other leaders who simply could not be commanded. Because he could not command them, he had to bargain.[15]

STUDYING COMMUNITY POWER

Social scientists have used different methods to study community power. To some extent these different methods explain the different *findings* of elitists and pluralists. Sociologists, including the elitists, study the entire social structure of the community, and they view power as a by-product of social and economic position. Persons in a position to control the social and economic life of the community are said to have political power whether they exercise it or not. In contrast, pluralists define power as participation in decision making. Persons are said to have power only when they participate directly in a particular community decision.

Pluralist Objections to Elitist Methods   Pluralists object to the presupposition that people who control economic resources are necessarily in positions of power:

> . . . nothing categorical can be assumed about power in any community. . . . If anything, there seems to be an unspoken notion among pluralist researchers that at bottom nobody dominates in a town, so that their first question is not likely to be, "Who runs this community?," but rather, "Does anyone at all run this community?" The first query is somewhat like, "Have you stopped beating your wife?," in that virtually any response short of total unwillingness to answer will supply the researchers with a "power elite" along the lines presupposed by the stratification theory.[16]

---

[14] Dahl, *Who Governs?*, p. 72.

[15] Ibid., p. 204.

[16] Nelson Polsby, "How to Study Community Power: The Pluralist Alternative," *Journal of Politics,* 21 (1960), 476.

Reputation Versus Reality   The pluralists also attack the use of certain socio-logical methods in community research. According to the pluralists, the interview technique, which was at the heart of Hunter's work, inquired about the *reputation* of power rather than about the *reality* of power. By asking people what they thought about power distributions in the community, Hunter was at best only con-ducting a public-opinion poll about power. Hunter was asking about beliefs and reputations; he paid little attention to actual behavior, preferring instead to rely on the ranking of knowledgeable people about how much power other people possessed.

Moreover, Hunter's concern for social structure, the persistence through time of power relations, led him to phrase his questions about influence and leadership in general terms rather than to tie them to particular issues or decisions. For exam-ple, Hunter asked the following question:

> Suppose a major project were before the community, one that required decision by a group of leaders whom nearly everyone would accept. Which persons would you choose to make up this group—regardless of whether or not you know them personally?

However, pluralists argue that general power rankings can be misleading:

> Most of the reputational researchers, by their failure to specify scopes in soliciting reputations for influence, assume that the power of their leader-nominees is equal for all issues. . . . This is an exceedingly dubious assumption. It is improbable, for instance, that the same people who decide which houses of prostitution are to be protected . . . also plan the public school curriculum.[17]

Power Potential Versus Exercise of Power   Pluralists argue that the "reputa-tional technique" results in confusing *status* with *power*. Respondents may offer names of persons who have high status and are well known in the community even though such persons may not actually wield power. A related problem confuses *po-tential for power* with the *exercise of power*. Respondents may nominate persons who occupy high formal positions in industry or government and could conceivably ex-ercise a great deal of power but who, as a matter of practice, do not. Pluralists be-lieve that the potential for power is not power itself, unless it is actually exercised over specific community decisions. Further, respondents may not have an accurate perception of the distribution of power in a community. The images people have of the decision-making process are more likely to be a product of their personal atti-tudes toward power than any real conditions prevailing in their communities.

Unity Versus Competition   Finally, the pluralists argue that Hunter's research did not adequately inquire about the existence of unity among the "elite." It is un-reasonable to expect that members of the elite *always* agree on everything and that they *always* impose their ideas on unwilling masses. On the other hand, a "ruling elite" should have some common attitudes and interests that are distinguishable

---

[17] Raymond E. Wolfinger, "Reputation and Reality in the Study of Community Power," *American Sociological Review,* 25 (1960), 636–44.

from the attitudes and interests of nonelites.[18] The question remains, however, *how much* unity among leaders is required in order to verify the existence of an elite? The fault in Hunter's methodology is that he never attempted to test for any commonality of attitudes or interests among his elite members. Instead, he inferred unity of interest from similarity in the class or status background of his elite members. Yet ample evidence is available that business and financial leaders disagree on many things.

Elitist Objections to Pluralist Methods   Pluralist methods of research, however, are not above criticism either. To the pluralists, power means participation in decision making; it means the activities of individuals in relation to other individuals. In Dahl's words: "*A* has power over *B* to the extent that he can get *B* to do something that *B* would not otherwise do."[19] Dahl conceives of power primarily in terms of the behavior of individuals at a specific point in time. His unit of analysis is the individual actor and not the social system. This is a very critical difference in conceptual starting places, and this difference leads directly to contrasting methodologies.

Because the pluralist defines power as a decision-making activity, it follows that pluralist research into power involves the "decisional technique," that is, a careful examination of a series of concrete public decisions. To study community power, pluralists first select a number of "key public decisions" that have received widespread publicity in the community. Then they identify the people who took an active part in making these decisions and obtain a full account of their actual behavior while these decisions were being made. The methodology involves reportorial techniques that have characterized case studies in political science for many years.

Noncomparable Case Study Method   But, like that of the elitists, the pluralists' definition of power and their methods of study help to determine their findings and conclusions.[20] First, the case study approach, to which the pluralists are committed, predisposes the researcher to regard each decision as unique. By examining power in relation to a particular decision, one's findings about power are likely to be tied to particular decisional situations. It is not surprising that the pluralist researchers, after compiling a series of separate case studies, conclude that the exercise of power is situational, that different people exercise power over different decisions, and that generalizations about the exercise of power in different issue areas are unwarranted. The case study method predisposes the researcher to see power in situational terms.

---

[18] Robert Dahl, "Critique of the Ruling Elite Model," *American Political Science Review,* 52 (December 1958), 463–69.

[19] Robert Dahl, "The Concept of Power," *Behavioral Science,* 2 (July 1957), 202.

[20] Anton, "Power, Pluralism, and Local Politics," pp. 425–57; Bachrach and Baratz, "Two Faces of Power," pp. 947–53.

Dahl himself is very pessimistic about the comparability of power studies and the likelihood of developing generalizations about power in communities: "We are not likely to produce—certainly not for some considerable time to come—anything like a single consistent coherent 'Theory of Power.' "[21] In short, the pluralist concept of power and the case study method assume the noncomparability of power relations even before the research has begun.

Non–Decision Making   The pluralist approach also implies that political power is completely reflected in open public decisions. No doubt power is exercised in resolving the well-publicized public issues, but is this the whole story of community power? Power is also exercised when social or political values or institutions limit public consideration to only those issues that are relatively unimportant to the power holders.[22] *A* is exercising power over *B* when *A* succeeds in suppressing issues that might in their resolution be seriously detrimental to *A*'s preferences. In other words, elites exercise power when they prevent issues from becoming public controversies. This exercise of power is known as "*non*–decision making."[23] The pluralist researcher who concentrates his or her attention on open "concrete decisions" may overlook the possibility that public decision making has been deliberately limited to relatively noncontroversial matters, notwithstanding the fact that there are serious latent conflicts in a community.

Public Versus Private Decisions   Pluralist methodology not only overlooks nondecisions, but also overlooks private decisions. Pluralist methodology assumes that the significant community decisions are made publicly; yet there is ample evidence that many of the most important decisions in a community are private decisions. Land use and development decisions, industrial-location and employment decisions, housing decisions, and many other important economic decisions that profoundly affect every aspect of community life are largely private decisions made with little public visibility. How can pluralists legitimately exclude these kinds of decisions from their analyses? They cannot claim that such decisions are not made. Their only recourse is to distinguish between *public* and *private* decisions and to claim that their interest is in *public* decisions. In other words, their only recourse is to narrow the scope of political science to public decision making. By arbitrarily limiting their subject matter, they can escape the responsibility for dealing with private decisions.

---

[21] Dahl, "The Concept of Power."

[22] Bachrach and Baratz, "Two Faces of Power," pp. 947–53; "Decisions and Nondecisions," pp. 632–42.

[23] For an interesting debate over the concept of non–decision making, see Geoffrey Debnam, "Nondecisions and Power: The Two Faces of Bachrach and Baratz," and Peter Bachrach and Morton S. Baratz, "Power and Its Two Faces Revisited," *American Political Science Review,* 69 (September 1975), 889–904; see also Richard M. Merelman, "On the Neo-Elitist Critique of Community Power," *American Political Science Review,* 62 (June 1968), 451–60; Raymond Wolfinger, "Nondecisions and the Study of Local Politics," *American Political Science Review,* 65 (December 1971), 1063–80.

Contrasting Interpretation of Findings   Even pluralist researchers report that very few people exercise influence in community affairs. Dahl and others acknowledge that the total number of people involved in concrete public decisions is a very small minority of the community. All pluralist researchers recognize that persons exercising leadership in each issue area are of higher social status than the rest of the community. These middle- and upper-class people possess more of the skills and qualities required of leaders in a democratic system.

In short, neither the elitist nor the pluralist model of community power is the equivalent of the American ideal of grass-roots democracy—a government of, by, and for the people, in which individuals decide their own future and all have an equal voice in the affairs of their communities.

SYSTEMIC POWER AND STRATEGIC ADVANTAGE

All known societies have some system of ranking their members. Sociologists use the term *stratification* to refer to the classification of individuals and their ranking along a superiority–inferiority scale. The United States Constitution guarantees legal and political equality of individuals, especially in its Equal Protection Clause; but in most other dimensions of society—income and wealth, occupation and institutional position, social status and life style—we recognize differences among individuals and rank these differences according to their desirability.

The American system of stratification tends to be diamond shaped: a small upper class, a large middle class, and a somewhat smaller lower class. The advantage of numbers—an important source of power in the electoral system—accrues to the middle class, not the lower class. All other sources of power are distributed unequally from top to bottom:

1. Economic power. The top stratum enjoys great wealth and income and control of corporations, banks, and other economic enterprises. The middle stratum has job skills, occupational positions, and moderate amounts of personal wealth and income. The lower stratum is largely economically dependent. Individuals in this stratum receive more governmental revenues than they produce.

2. Institutional position. The top stratum occupies positions of authority in institutions that organize society's resources—corporations, banks, utilities, television networks and stations, newspapers, foundations, universities, law firms, civic and cultural organizations. The middle stratum occupies middle- and lower-level positions in these same organizations and may also occupy key positions in government, unions, recreational associations, and churches. The bottom stratum is seldom organized at all. Indeed, most organizations claiming to represent the poor are run by middle- and upper-class people.

3. Social status and life style. The top stratum enjoys education, travel, leisure, clubs, and a social and cultural life that is widely envied. The middle classes try to emulate the upper-class life styles and succeed to a limited degree. But lower-class life style is restricted; goals are immediate and limited, and activities are protective or escapist.

Decision Making and Stratification   Community decision making takes place within a stratified social system. It defies common sense to argue, as pluralists do,[24] that community decisions are *unaffected* by the stratification of economic power, institutional position, and life style. Public officials—mayors, council members, commissioners, school board members, authority directors, and board members—as well as managers, administrators, and public employees, civic association officers, and interest group officers, all function within the larger stratified society. They must maintain and enhance their own income, position, and life style; and their behavior will be patterned by the system of stratification.

Power is exercised in open public decisions *and* in the distribution of advantages and disadvantages among individuals and groups within society. *Systemic power* refers to outcomes that are attributable to the stratification system's distribution of advantages and disadvantages. *Strategic advantage* refers to the power that the top stratum enjoys because of its income and wealth, positional authority, and status and life style.[25]

Anticipated Reactions   Systemic power may take many forms. Power is being exercised when public officials or administrators base their own behavior on the anticipated reactions of powerful people within the community. *A* has power over *B* if *B* modifies his or her conduct because of fear of *A*'s reaction or a need to stay in *A*'s good graces to obtain some future benefit. Note that *A* and *B* do not have to communicate directly. *A* may not even know what *B* is doing (or not doing) to win favor; there is no open public decision. The strength of this power relationship is determined by the distribution of wealth and income, position, and life style in the larger society, and the desire of public officials and administrators to maintain and enhance their share of these benefits now or in the future.

Agenda Setting   In agenda setting, power is being exercised in the selection of topics or problems to be addressed by government. Power is being exercised when someone suppresses an issue that might adversely affect their interests if it came up for a public vote on the council. This is a direct yet covert exercise of power. But power is also being exercised by groups who regularly succeed in getting their issues placed on a crowded agenda when there is competition for the space. Power is also being exercised when other groups are unable to attract public attention to their problems or articulate their problems and present their case for public action.

Opportunity Costs   With opportunity costs, power is being exercised when the costs of political success are higher for some groups than others. Persons in the top social stratum must expend a smaller proportion of their total resources than per-

---

[24] See Nelson W. Polsby, *Community Power and Political Theory* 2nd ed. (New Haven: Yale University Press, 1980).

[25] See Clarence N. Stone, "Systemic Power in Community Decision-Making: A Restatement of Stratification Theory," *American Political Science Review,* 74 (December 1980) 978–90.

sons in the bottom social stratum to achieve a political goal. "The weak must struggle while the strong have only to ask."[26] Public officials and administrators frequently ask business and community leaders "what things need doing?" The poor, by contrast, frequently need protests, marches, or direct action to call attention to their concerns. "The truly powerful are often able to achieve their aims with little effort, whereas those who are less powerful must make a much greater effort to achieve the same results."[27]

The disadvantaged in society often appear passive and quiescent. The pluralist researcher is obliged to conclude that they confront no serious problems or concerns. But quiescence may only signify that the poor are not well positioned to act on their grievances. With few resources, they cannot undertake costly battles that they are likely to lose. Indeed, when the poor *do* act politically, it is usually on behalf of some immediate and tangible benefit rather than long-range or fundamental change. It is logical for the poor to spend their limited political resources for short-term goals with some likelihood of success.

Mobilization of Bias   In a case of mobilization of bias, power is exercised in the way the political system is organized. Some forms of organization make it difficult for some issues to be raised and difficult for government to address some problems. For example, it is difficult for local governments to adopt policies that redistribute income from rich to poor; any community that taxed the rich heavily in order to generously support the poor would drive out its wealthy residents and attract large numbers of poor. Competition between communities and the ability of both rich and poor to move freely among communities prevent local governments from adapting highly redistributive policies.

It is true that the governmental system is based upon the principle of equality—equal protection of the laws, one-person–one-vote, and majority rule. This means that if an issue becomes a highly publicized, open public decision made by the elected governmental body, it is likely that public officials will be influenced by majority opinion. But the upper stratum enjoys an advantage when decisions have low public visibility, when public officials are least accountable to the general public, and when these officials are free to pursue their own private interests.

ECONOMIC POWER IN COMMUNITIES

Great power derives from control of economic resources. Most of the nation's economic resources are controlled by national institutions—industrial corporations, banks, utilities, insurance companies, investment firms, and the national government. Most of the forces shaping life in American communities arise outside of these communities; community leaders cannot make war or peace, or cause inflation or recession, or determine interest rates or the money supply.

---

[26] Ibid., p. 981.

[27] Ibid.

But there is one economic resource—land—which *is* controlled by community elites. Land is a valuable resource: Capital investment, labor and management, and production must be placed somewhere. Community power structures are composed primarily of interests whose goal is to intensify the use of community land and add to its value. Community elites seek to maximize land values, real estate commissions, builders' profits, rent payments, and mortgage interest, as well as to increase revenues to commercial enterprises serving the community. Community power structures are dominated by mortgage lending banks, real estate developers, builders, and landowners. They may be joined by owners or managers of local utilities, department stores, attorneys and title companies, and others whose wealth is affected by land use. Local bankers who finance the real estate developers and builders are probably at the center of the elite structure in most communities. Unquestionably these community elites compete among themselves for wealth, profit, power, and preeminence. But they share a consensus about intensifying the use of land. Corporate plants and offices, federal and state office buildings, and universities and colleges all contribute to the increased land values, not only on the parcels used by these facilities but also on neighboring parcels.

Growth is the shared elite value. The community elite is indeed a "growth machine."[28] Economic growth expands the work force and disposable income within the community. It stimulates housing development, retail stores, and other commercial activity. The landed elite understands that they all benefit, albeit to varying degrees, when economic growth occurs within the community.

The economic function of community elites is to prepare land for capital. Capital investment in the community will raise land values, expand the labor force, generate demand for housing as well as commercial services, and enhance the local tax base. The preparation of land for capital investment involves much more than just providing large tracts of level acreage. It involves the provision of good transportation facilities—highways, streets, rail access, and water and airport facilities. It involves the provision of utilities—water, gas and electrical power, solid waste disposal, and sewage treatment. It involves the provision of good municipal services, especially fire and police protection; the elimination of harassing business regulations and the reduction of taxes on new investments to the lowest feasible levels; the provision of a capable and cooperative labor force, educated for the needs of productive capital and motivated to work; and finally, the provision of sufficient amenities—cultural, recreational, aesthetic—to provide the corporate managers with a desirable life style.

Elites in different communities must compete with each other to attract capital investment. This competition is a constraint on the power of any particular community elite. Not only must a community compete for new investments, but it must also endeavor to prevent relocation of investments it already has.

---

[28] See Harvey Molotch, "The City as Growth Machine," *American Journal of Sociology,* 82 (September 1976), 309–30; and "Capital and Neighborhood in the United States," *Urban Affairs Quarterly,* 14 (March 1979) 289–312.

Community elites strive for consensus. They believe that community economic growth—increased capital investment, more jobs, and improved business conditions—benefit the entire community. According to Paul E. Peterson, community residents share a common interest in the economic well-being of the city:

> Policies and programs can be said to be in the interest of cities whenever the policies maintain or enhance the economic position, social prestige, or political power of the city as a whole.[29]

Community elites themselves would doubtlessly agree with Peterson. He adds that the interests of the city as a whole are closely bound to its export industries. These industries add net wealth to the community at large, while support and service industries merely transfer wealth within the community.

> Whatever helps them prosper redounds to the benefit of the community as a whole —perhaps four or five times over. It is just such an economic analysis (of the multiplier effect of export industries) that has influenced many local government policies. Especially the smaller towns and cities may provide free land, tax concessions, and favorable utility rates to incoming industries.[30]

The less economically developed a community, the more persuasive the argument on behalf of export industries.

Local government officials are expected to share in the elite consensus. Economic prosperity is necessary for protecting the fiscal base of local government. Growth in local budgets and public employment, as well as governmental services, depends upon growth in the local economy. Governmental growth expands the power, prestige, and status of government officials. Moreover, economic growth is usually good politics. Growth-oriented candidates for public office usually have larger campaign treasuries than antigrowth candidates. Growth-oriented candidates can solicit contributions from the community power structure. Finally, according to Peterson, most local politicians have "a sense of community responsibility." They know that if the economy of the community declines, "local business will suffer, workers will lose employment opportunities, cultural life will decline, and city land values will fall."[31]

COMMUNITY CONFLICT AND COUNTER-ELITES

But consensus on behalf of economic growth is sometimes challenged by other community interests. However much the "growth machine" elite may strive for consensus, some people do not like growth.

Indeed, it has become fashionable in upper–middle-class circles today to complain loudly about the problems created by growth—congestion, pollution, noise, unsightly development, or the replacement of green spaces with concrete slabs.

[29] Paul E. Peterson, *City Limits* (Chicago: University of Chicago Press, 1981), p. 20.

[30] Ibid., p. 23.

[31] Ibid., p. 29.

People who already own their houses and do not intend to sell them, people whose jobs are secure in government bureaucracies or tenured professorships, people who may be displaced from their homes and neighborhoods by new facilities, people who see no direct benefit to themselves from growth, and businesses or industries who fear the new competition that growth may bring to the community, all combine to form a potentially powerful *counter-elite.*[32]

No-growth movements (or, to use the current euphemism, "growth-management" movements) are *not* mass movements. They do *not* express the aspirations of workers for jobs or renters for their own homes. Instead, they reflect upper–middle-class life-style preferences of educated, affluent, articulate homeowners. Growth brings ugly factories, cheap commercial outlets, hamburger stands, fried chicken franchises, and "undesirable" residents. Even if new business or industry would help hold down local taxes, these affluent citizens would still oppose it. They would rather pay the higher taxes associated with no growth than change the appearance or life style of their community. They have secure jobs themselves and own their homes; they are relatively unconcerned about creating jobs or building homes for less affluent citizens.

No-growth movements challenge traditional economic elites in many large and growing cities in the West and South. The no-growth leaders may themselves have been beneficiaries of community growth only five or ten years ago, but they quickly perceive their own interest in slowing or halting additional growth. Now that they have climbed the ladder to their own success, they are prepared to knock the ladder down to preserve their own style of living.

Municipal government offers the tools to challenge the growth elite. (See Chapter 16.) Communities may restrict growth through zoning laws, subdivision control restrictions, utility regulations, building permits, and environmental regulations. Opposition to street widening, road building, or tree cutting can slow or halt development. Public utilities needed for development—water lines, sewage disposal facilities, fire houses, and so on—can be postponed indefinitely. High development fees, "impact fees," utility hookup charges, or building permit fees can all be used to discourage growth. Environmental laws, or even "historic preservation" laws, can be employed aggressively to halt development.

Not all of the opposition to growth is upper–middle-class in character. Students of community power have described the struggle of blacks and low-income neighborhood groups in opposing urban renewal and downtown city development. However, this literature suggests that traditional community elites are likely to be successful against this kind of opposition. We might speculate that the "growth machine" elites are more concerned about opposition from educated, affluent, upper–middle-class, "growth-management" homeowners than they are about opposition from minority, low-income neighborhood groups.

---

[32] For a parallel argument, see Heywood T. Sanders and Clarence N. Stone, "Developmental Politics Reconsidered," *Urban Affairs Quarterly,* 22 (June 1987), 521–39; and Mark Schneider, "Undermining the Growth Machine," *Journal of Politics,* 54 (February 1992), 214–30.

ELITISM: DEVELOPMENTAL AND REDISTRIBUTIVE POLICIES

Economic elites are most directly concerned with economic growth. The community "power structure"—the mortgage lending banks, real estate developers and builders, and landowners—are directly involved in developmental policies.

Developmental Policies   *Developmental policies* are those that directly enhance the economic position of the community. These include policies to attract industry, build streets and highways, improve transportation facilities, and renew depressed areas. Reputations for power in the community are made in developmental politics. This should not really surprise us. Job, home, and business are viewed by most people as the most important aspects of their lives. Those people in the community who are in a position to influence job opportunities, home building, and industrial and commercial developments are viewed by most residents as "powerful." So when residents are asked to make general judgments about power in their community, they name bankers, developers, builders, and business people. They do not usually name school board members, civic association officers, neighborhood activists, police or fire chiefs, minority group leaders, or even city council members. These persons may be active in other areas of policy making (allocational, redistributional, or organizational), but most citizens understand that the really important developmental policies—policies that directly affect jobs, houses, and business—will be largely determined by the community power structure.

Redistributional Policies   *Redistributional policies* are not designed to add to the net economic well-being of the whole community, but to benefit low-income residents by redirecting the economic resources of the community. Most redistributional policies in the United States—social security, welfare, medical care, unemployment compensation—are undertaken by state and national governments. Local governments are only occasionally called upon to decide redistributional questions. Many cities provide low-income housing, indigent hospital care, shelters for the homeless, and other services that are only partially covered by state or federal funds.

Redistribution policies seldom involve the community power structure directly. Community elites have an interest in keeping redistributional questions *out* of local politics, since their resolution may jeopardize members' wealth and income. Elites may manipulate the local policy agenda to exclude redistributional issues and ensure the "unpolitics" of local poverty, through the now familiar tactic of non–decision making. In addition, Peterson argues that the absence of redistributive issues in local politics "is seldom due to the suppressive activities of an organized economic elite," but rather a product of American federalism and the assignment of responsibility for health and income maintenance programs to state and neutral levels of governments.[33]

---

[33] Peterson, *City Limits,* p. 38.

Nonetheless, redistributive demands are likely to exist in any community. Class differences are potential fault lines in any community and latent sources of conflict. It is not unreasonable to assert that community elites would prefer to keep these redistributional issues and class conflicts off the political agenda. The theory of "nondecisions" suggests why community elites might not appear to be actively involved in redistributional politics yet be instrumental in their outcome.

Redistributive demands are occasionally raised in community politics, despite the structure of American federalism and the preferences of community elites.[34] Riots, protests, rent strikes, demonstrations, and other public manifestations of discontent are threatening to elites. If nothing else, unrest adversely affects the reputation of the community in its efforts to attract new industry. Economic elites cannot altogether ignore redistributive demands.

PLURALISM: ALLOCATIONAL AND ORGANIZATIONAL POLICIES

While community power structures concern themselves primarily with economic growth, there are many other issues in community politics. Some policy issues generate little direct interest among economic elites.

Allocational Policies   *Allocational policies* describe the broad range of traditional public services provided by local government—schools, streets, sewer, water and utilities, garbage collection, and parks and recreation, and so on. There are, of course, frequent distributional arguments over the provisions of these services. Occasionally the quality of these services becomes a developmental issue when potential investors express a concern about them. But, overall, these allocational policies are developmentally and distributionally neutral.

Pluralism in Allocational Decision Making   Community power structures are seldom directly interested or active in allocational policy. The allocational policy arena is pluralist in character. Decisions about police and fire protection, street maintenance, garbage collection, sewage disposal, school attendance boundaries, recreation, libraries, public buildings, and the like are usually made by elected public officials or professional managers employed by them. Council members, managers, school board members, and superintendents are responsive to the expressed demands of many varied and often competing groups within the community. Participation in decision making is open to anyone who attends public meetings, gathers petitions, or writes letters to the editor. Interest and activity rather than economic resources are the key to leadership in allocational policy. Access is based upon information about the issues, knowledge of the political proc-

---

[34] Paul K. Eisenger, "The Conditions of Protest Behavior in American Cities," *American Political Science Review,* 67 (March 1973), 11–29; Michael Lipsky, *Protest in City Politics* (Chicago: Rand McNally, 1970); Clarence Stone, *Economic Growth and Neighborhood Discontent* (Chapel Hill: University of North Carolina Press, 1976).

ess, and organizational and public relations skills. Community organizations are instruments by which individuals magnify their voices in public affairs. No single group of people dominates decision making in *all* of the service functions of a community's city, county, and school district governments. Elected officials are very sensitive to the opinions of their constituents on service questions. Allocational policies are material and divisable, so allocative policies can easily reflect compromises among competing groups. These are the familiar characteristics of pluralist politics.

Much of what takes place in local government—at commission meetings, public hearings, school board meetings, and in the offices of city managers and school superintendents—involves allocational policies. It is easy for pluralist scholars studying local government to mistake allocational politics for the whole of community politics. This error is facilitated by a narrow and traditional definition of political science as the study of *government* and the consequent exclusion of community social structure from the purview of pluralist studies. Allocational policies are the "key public decisions" studied by pluralist researchers, and governmental bodies are the locus of their studies.

Organizational Policies   *Organizational policies* encompass decisions about the structure of decision making in the community. These policies include the composition, terms, and legal activity of school boards, city and county commissions, city managers, school superintendents, independent authorities and boards, and other elected officials. Typical issues may include whether or not to have a city manager, a mayor-council, or a commission form of government, at-large or district elections, partisan or nonpartisan elections, an elected or appointed school superintendent, and so forth. Personnel and employment policies may also be considered organizational—that is, who gets elected to community office and who gets hired by the city. Sometimes these questions become redistributional when issues of minority or low-income representation are raised. Sometimes these questions are intertwined with allocational issues, as when incumbents are charged with poor performance on the job.

Community power structures are usually only interested bystanders in organizational politics. While it is true that their "class interests" would appear to place them on the side of the upper-class reformers, we know that bankers, developers, and builders had little difficulty in dealing with big city machines. Indeed, machines were often better in "getting things done at City Hall"—that is, moving growth projects to completion—than reformed administrations (see Chapter 10). There is no question that economic elites thrived under urban political machines.

Likewise, current disputes over organizational policies—the representation of blacks and other minorities in elected offices and municipal jobs—do not threaten economic interests. While the rhetoric of urban black politics frequently calls for massive income redistribution, the reality of black city administrations is quite different. Whatever fears white propertied elites may have had years ago about black power in the nation's cities should now be put to rest. There is no evidence that the nation's black mayors are hostile to economic growth and development. None has pursued redistributional policies to the point of alienating the business community or driving investment out of their cities. Indeed, the thrust of black redistributional demands—full employment, generous welfare, expanded medical care, publicly financed housing—falls largely on the federal government.

PLURALISM AND ELITISM RECONCILED?

Elitist and pluralist models of community power have inspired great debate in the social sciences over the years. But can these models be reconciled? Perhaps our best understanding of community power comes about through diversity in theories and methods of study. Students of community power are better advised to ask "What can each model tell us about community power?" rather than "What are the shortcomings of each model?" Elitist and pluralist models might be reconciled in several ways.

Different Models Describe Different Policies   First of all, elitist and pluralist models of community decision making may each be more accurate in separate policy areas. The influence of traditional community elite—mortgage bankers, real estate developers, builders and land owners—is more likely to be felt in *developmental policy*. The earliest studies of the activities of community power structures appear to describe developmental policy making. The elitist model of community power accurately describes the private and public influence of the community's economic leadership over developmental policy. Moreover, the community power structure is also very likely to employ the tactics of non–decision making in response to *redistributional policy* demands. Elitist notions about "the other face of power," about "agenda setting," and about "organizing issues out of local politics," all appear to describe redistributional policy making in communities.

In contrast, pluralist descriptions of community decision making best describe *allocational* and *organizational* policy making. Traditionally, pluralist studies focused on *governmental* decision making, ignoring decisions in the private market. Local governmental bodies concern themselves primarily with allocational issues: schools, buildings, teacher salaries, police and fire protection, garbage collection, street cleaning, and the like. Allocational policy making resembles the pluralist model, and pluralist studies of "key public decisions" made by governments provide the empirical support for this model. Likewise, most organizational issues—questions about the structure of government and minority representation in government—are decided in a pluralist fashion.

Different Models Portray Different Communities   Second, power structures may vary across communities. Some communities may have more concentrated, pyramidal structures of power, while others may be diffused and multicentered. For example, large communities with a great deal of social and economic diversity, a competitive party system, and a variety of well-organized competing interest groups tend to have *pluralist* decision-making systems. On the other hand, small communities with homogeneous populations, a single dominant industry, nonpartisan elections, and few competing organizations may have power structures resembling the *elite* model.

Different Models Combine for More Knowledge   Third, communities and policy decisions can be studied simultaneously from elitist and pluralist perspectives, and the results can be integrated so as to produce a deeper understanding of the various ways in which power is exercised. For example, the reputational method employed by elitists to identify the most powerful persons in the community helps to identify persons with high institutional positions in the community and control over economic resources, even though it provides little information about influence over specific decisions. The decision method employed by pluralists can identify key public decisions and active participants in these decisions even though it fails to specify issues that have been kept off the public agenda and who wins or loses in non–decision making. Each of these methods can provide information, that is, a "piece of the puzzle," in understanding community power.

Different Models for Public and Private Decisions   Finally, we ought to recognize that some community decisions are public, that is, made by governmental bodies, while others are private, made by real estate developers, banks and mortgage companies, builders and land owners, investors and business people. Private decisions may have as much or even more impact on life in a community than decisions made by government. The pluralist model may be best suited for understanding public decision making, while the elite model may better describe private decision making. Indeed, many pluralists now acknowledge that economic elites have a "privileged position" regarding decisions that are vital to society.[35] If we are to understand the full range of decisions that shape the community—public and private—we will have to consider both public and private power. This requires an integration of studies of governmental decision making with studies of systemic forces—economic power, institutional position, social status, and life style.

---

[35] Charles E. Lindbloom, *Politics and Markets* (New York: Basic Books, 1977), Chap. 13.

14

POLITICS AND CIVIL RIGHTS

▲

 FROM PROTEST TO POWER

Blacks and Hispanics have made significant progress in urban politics in recent years. The progress of these minorities in city government has important implications for the future of the American political system, because these are the two largest minority groups in the country. Minorities were almost totally excluded from significant influence in city politics prior to the 1960s. We have already discussed increases in black representation in city councils (Chapter 11) and state legislatures (Chapter 6), and black political power in the nation's largest cities is a recognized fact of American politics. As former Atlanta Mayor Andrew Young said, "It's like the old preacher says: we ain't what we oughta be; we ain't what we gonna be; but thank God we ain't what we was."[1]

---

[1] Quotation in Rufus P. Browning, Dale Rodgers Marshall, and David H. Tabb, *Protest Is Not Enough: The Struggle of Blacks and Hispanics for Equality in Urban Politics* (Berkeley: University of California Press, 1984), p. 17.

Variation in Responsiveness to Urban Minorities   One important test of a democratic system is its responsiveness to the demands of newly mobilized groups. Comparative studies of city governments suggest that there are significant variations in their responsiveness to the demands of newly mobilized minority groups. In an important study of ten California cities over a twenty-year period, appropriately titled *Protest Is Not Enough,* the authors observed that:

> In some cities, quite remarkable levels of responsiveness to minority interests were achieved, and minority representatives came to occupy positions of authority and respect.

> In other cities, relationships between white and minority leaders were more manipulative and co-operative, though significant concessions to minority interests were made.

> And in still other cities, established interests successfully resisted minority demands and efficiently excluded minority representation from influence.[2]

Conditions for Success   What determines the success or failure of minorities to gain influence in urban politics? The conditions associated with minority success were:

> The absolute size of minority groups in the city.

> The size of supportive groups, especially white liberals.

> A strategy of combining protests with a willingness to form electoral coalitions. Protests by themselves produced only limited results. Extreme protests delayed progress.

Protest alone is insufficient to bring about lasting political change. Protest must be accompanied by political mobilization, the formation of electoral coalitions, and winning public office.

> We know that protest is not enough. . . . Protest must be translated into electoral organizing, the traditional political activity of recruiting candidates, controlling the number who run, and developing support and coalitions.[3]

Policy Consequences   Do city government policies change as a result of minority incorporation into the political system? Black elected officials in cities perceive poverty and unemployment as more severe problems than do white officials in the same cities; and black office-holders are more likely to add race relations and racial balance in the distribution of city jobs and services to the policy agenda.[4] Another consequence of the election of blacks to public office, especially the mayor's office, is an increase in political participation among black citizens.[5]

---

[2] Ibid., p. 8

[3] Ibid., p. 213.

[4] Carmine Scavo, "Racial Integration of Local Government Leadership in Small Southern Cities," *Social Science Quarterly,* 71 (June 1990), 362–72.

[5] Lawrence Bobo and Franklin D. Gilliam, Jr., "Race, Sociopolitical Participation, and Black Empowerment," *American Political Science Review,* 84 (June 1990), 377–86.

But many city government policies, especially taxing and spending policies, are severely constrained by economic conditions and by limits and mandates set by the state and federal governments.[6] So it is unrealistic to expect major shifts in these policies to accompany the election of blacks or Hispanics to city office. The policies that respond to minority representation in city government are those that deal directly with minority presence in government. Broad taxing and spending policies are largely *un*affected by minority influence in government. Examples of the kind of policy changes directly attributable to minority representation in government include the creation of police review boards, the appointment of more minorities to city boards and commissions, increasing use of minority contractors, and a general increase in the number of programs oriented toward minorities. Perhaps the most significant policy impact of minority representation on city councils is an increase in the number of minorities in city employment and their employment in higher grade positions.[7]

THE STRUGGLE AGAINST SEGREGATION

The Fourteenth Amendment of the U.S. Constitution declares:

> All persons born or naturalized in the United States, and subject to the jurisdiction thereof, are citizens of the United States and of the State wherein they reside. No State shall make or enforce any law which shall abridge the privileges or immunities of citizens of the United States; nor shall any State deprive any person of life, liberty, or property, without due process of law; nor deny to any person within its jurisdiction the equal protection of the laws.

The language of the Fourteenth Amendment and its post–Civil War historical context leave little doubt that its original purpose was to achieve the full measure of citizenship and equality for American blacks. Some "radical" Republicans were prepared in 1867 to carry out the revolution in southern society that this amendment implied. Under military occupation, southern states adopted new constitutions that awarded the vote and full civil liberties to blacks, and southern states were compelled to ratify the Thirteenth, Fourteenth, and Fifteenth Amendments to the U.S. Constitution. Blacks were elected to southern state legislatures and to the Congress; the first black to serve in Congress, Hiram R. Revels, took over the U.S. Senate seat from Mississippi previously held by Confederate President Jefferson Davis.

However, by 1877 Reconstruction was abandoned. The national government was not willing to carry out the long and difficult task of really reconstructing society in the eleven states of the former Confederacy.[8] In what has been described as

---

[6] See Paul Peterson, *City Limits* (Chicago: University of Chicago Press, 1981).

[7] See Kenneth R. Mladenka, "Blacks and Hispanics in Urban Politics," *American Political Science Review,* 83 (March 1989), 165–91; Thomas R. Dye and James Renick, "Political Power and City Jobs: Determinants of Minority Employment, *Social Science Quarterly,* 62 (September 1981), 475–86.

[8] C. Vann Woodward, *Reunion and Reaction: The End of Reconstruction* (Boston: Little, Brown, 1951).

the "Compromise of 1877," the national government agreed to end military occupation of the South, give up its efforts to rearrange southern society, and lend tacit approval to white supremacy in that region. In return, the southern states pledged their support of the Union, accepted national supremacy, and agreed to permit the Republican candidate, Rutherford B. Hayes, to assume the presidency after the disputed election of 1876.

"Separate but Equal"   The Supreme Court adhered to the terms of the compromise. The result was an inversion of the meaning of the Fourteenth Amendment so that by 1896 it had become a bulwark of segregation. State laws segregating the races were upheld so long as persons in each of the separated races were treated equally. The constitutional argument on behalf of segregation under the Fourteenth Amendment was that the phrase "equal protection of the laws" did not prevent state-enforced *separation* of the races. Schools and other public facilities that were "separate but equal" won constitutional approval.[9] This separate but equal doctrine remained the Supreme Court's interpretation of the Equal Protection Clause of the Fourteenth Amendment until 1954.

As a matter of fact, of course, segregated facilities, including public schools, were seldom if ever equal, even with respect to physical conditions. In practice, the doctrine of segregation was "separate and *un*equal." The Supreme Court began to take notice of this after World War II. While it declined to overrule the segregationist interpretation of the Fourteenth Amendment, it began to order the admission of individual blacks to white public universities, where evidence indicated that separate black institutions were inferior or nonexistent.[10]

NAACP   Leaders of the newly emerging civil rights movement in the 1940s and 1950s were not satisfied with court decisions that examined the circumstances in each case to determine if separate school facilities were really equal. The National Association for the Advancement of Colored People (NAACP), led by Roy Wilkins, its executive director, and Thurgood Marshall, its chief counsel, pressed for a court decision that segregation itself meant inequality within the meaning of the Fourteenth Amendment, whether or not facilities were equal in all tangible respects. In short, they wanted a complete reversal of the "separate but equal" interpretation of the Fourteenth Amendment, and a holding that laws *separating* the races were unconstitutional.

The civil rights groups chose to bring suit for desegregation in Topeka, Kansas, where segregated black and white schools were equal with respect to buildings, curricula, qualifications and salaries of teachers, and other tangible factors. The legal strategy was to prevent the Court from ordering the admission of a black because *tangible* facilities were not equal and to force the Court to review the doctrine of segregation itself.

---

[9] *Plessy* v. *Ferguson,* 163 U.S. 537 (1896).

[10] *Sweatt* v. *Painter,* 339 U.S. 629 (1950); *McLaurin* v. *Oklahoma State Regents,* 339 U.S. 637 (1950).

Brown v. Topeka   On May 17, 1954, the Court rendered its decision in *Brown* v. *Board of Education of Topeka, Kansas:*

> Segregation of white and colored children in public schools has a detrimental effect upon the colored children. The impact is greater when it has the sanction of law, for the policy of separating the races is usually interpreted as denoting the inferiority of the Negro group. A sense of inferiority affects the motivation of a child to learn. Segregation with the sanction of law, therefore, has a tendency to retard the educational and mental development of Negro children and to deprive them of some of the benefits they would receive in a racially integrated school system.[11]

The symbolic importance of the original *Brown* v. *Topeka* decision cannot be overestimated. While it would be many years before any significant number of black children would attend formerly segregated white schools, the decision by the nation's highest court undoubtedly stimulated black hopes and expectations. Black sociologist Kenneth Clark writes:

> This [civil rights] movement would probably not have existed at all were it not for the 1954 Supreme Court school desegregation decision which provided a tremendous boost to the morale of Negroes by its *clear* affirmation that color is irrelevant to the rights of American citizens. Until this time the Southern Negro generally had accommodated to the separatism of the black from the white society.[12]

STATE RESISTANCE

The Supreme Court had spoken forcefully in the *Brown* case in 1954 in declaring segregation unconstitutional. From a constitutional viewpoint, any state-supported segregation of the races after 1954 was prohibited. Article VI of the Constitution declares that the words of that document are "the supreme law of the land . . . anything in the constitution or laws of any state to the contrary notwithstanding." From a political viewpoint, however, the battle over segregation was just beginning.

Segregation in the States   In 1954 the practice of segregation was widespread and deeply ingrained in American life. Seventeen states required the segregation of the races in public schools. These seventeen states were:

Alabama	North Carolina	Delaware
Arkansas	South Carolina	Kentucky
Florida	Tennessee	Maryland
Georgia	Texas	Missouri
Louisiana	Virginia	Oklahoma
Mississippi		West Virginia

---

[11] *Brown* v. *Board of Education of Topeka, Kansas,* 347 U.S. 483 (1954).

[12] Kenneth B. Clark, *Dark Ghetto* (New York: Harper & Row, 1965), pp. 77–78.

The Congress of the United States required the segregation of the races in the public schools of the District of Columbia.[13] Four additional states—Arizona, Kansas, New Mexico, and Wyoming—authorized segregation upon the option of local school boards. (See Figure 14–1.)

Thus, in deciding *Brown* v. *Topeka,* the Supreme Court struck down the laws of twenty-one states and the District of Columbia in a single opinion. Such a far-reaching decision was bound to meet with difficulties in implementation. The Supreme Court did not order immediate nationwide desegregation, but instead it turned over the responsibility for desegregation to state and local authorities under the supervision of federal district courts.

The six border states with segregated school systems—Delaware, Kentucky, Maryland, Missouri, Oklahoma, and West Virginia—together with the school districts in Kansas, Arizona, and New Mexico that had operated segregated schools, chose not to resist desegregation. The District of Columbia also desegregated its public schools the year following the Supreme Court's decision.

Resistance   Resistance to school integration was the policy of the eleven states of the Old Confederacy. Refusal of a school district to desegregate until it was faced with a federal court injunction was the most common form of delay. Other schemes included state payment of private school tuition in lieu of providing public schools, amending compulsory attendance laws to provide that no child shall be required to attend an integrated school, requiring schools faced with desegregation orders to cease operation, and the use of pupil-placement laws to avoid or minimize the extent of integration.[14] State officials also attempted to delay desegregation on the grounds that it would endanger public safety.[15] On the whole, those states that chose to resist desegregation were quite successful in doing so during the ten-year period from 1954 to 1964. Ten years after *Brown* v. *Topeka,* only about 2 percent of the black schoolchildren in the eleven southern states were attending integrated schools.

Federal Funds   In the Civil Rights Act of 1964, Congress finally entered the civil rights field in support of court efforts to achieve desegregation. Among other things, the Civil Rights Act of 1964 provided that every federal department and agency must take action to end segregation in all programs or activities receiving federal financial assistance. It was specified that this action was to include termina-

---

[13] The Supreme Court also ruled that Congress was bound to respect the equal protection doctrine imposed upon the states by the Fourteenth Amendment as part of the due process clause of the Fifth Amendment. *Bolling* v. *Sharpe,* 347 U.S. 497 (1954).

[14] State laws that were obviously designed to evade constitutional responsibilities to end segregation were struck down in federal courts; but court litigation and delays slowed progress toward integration.

[15] The Supreme Court declared that the threat of violence was not sufficient reason to deny constitutional rights to black children and again dismissed the ancient interposition arguments. *Cooper* v. *Aaron,* 358 U.S. 1 (1958).

Segration Required

Local Option on Segration

No Legislation

Segregation Prohibited

FIGURE 14–1   Segregation Laws in the United States in 1954

tion of financial assistance if states and communities receiving federal funds refused to comply with federal desegregation orders. Acting under the authority of Title VI, the U.S. Office of Education (now the Department of Education) required all school districts in the seventeen formerly segregated states to submit desegregation plans as a condition of federal assistance. Progress toward desegregation was speeded up.

Unitary Schools   The last vestige of legal justification for delay in implementing school desegregation collapsed in 1969 when the Supreme Court rejected a request by Mississippi school officials for a delay in implementing school desegregation plans in that state. The Supreme Court declared that every school district was obligated to end dual school systems "at once" and "now and hereafter" to operate only unitary schools.[16] The effect of the decision—fifteen years after the original Brown case—was to eliminate any further legal justification for the continuation of segregation in public schools.

---

[16] *Alexander* v. *Holmes County Board of Education,* 396 U.S. 19 (1969).

Busing and Racial Balancing in Schools

In *Brown* v. *Board of Education of Topeka, Kansas,* the Supreme Court found that segregation had "a tendency to retard the educational and mental development of Negro children and to deprive them of some of the benefits they would receive in a racially integrated school system." The U.S. Civil Rights Commission reported that even when segregation was "de facto," that is, a product of segregated housing patterns and neighborhood schools rather than direct discrimination, the adverse effects on black students were still significant.[17] In northern urban school districts, the commission reported, predominantly black schools were less likely to have good libraries or advanced courses in sciences and languages than predominantly white schools and more likely to have overcrowded classrooms, poorly trained teachers, and teachers who were dissatisfied with their school assignments. Therein lies the essential argument for ending de facto segregation in school systems throughout the nation.

Racial Balance   Ending racial isolation in the public schools frequently involves busing schoolchildren into and out of segregated neighborhoods. The objective is to achieve a racial "balance" in public schools, so that each has roughly the same percentages of blacks and whites as are found in the total population of the entire school district. Indeed, in some large cities where blacks comprise the overwhelming majority of public school students, desegregation may require city students to be bused to the suburbs and suburban students to be bused to the core city.

White Flight   However, social science research suggests that busing does not always accomplish its intended effects. Black students who are bused out of their neighborhoods to predominantly white schools do not improve their educational performance relative to white students.[18] Moreover, in some cities where extensive busing is employed, "white flight" from the public schools is so widespread that the schools end up more segregated than before busing was imposed.[19] Black pupils now comprise the overwhelming majority of public school pupils in Detroit, Philadelphia, Boston, Atlanta, Chicago, Baltimore, Cleveland, Gary, Memphis, New Orleans, Newark, Richmond, St. Louis, and almost all of the public school pupils in Washington, DC.

Critics of the notion of white flight argue that there are many other reasons besides desegregation that encourage white migration out of the city—poor schools, crime, high city taxes, and so on. A controversy over school desegregation may be the final factor that compels a family to move *now,* but many other condi-

---

[17] United States Commission on Civil Rights, *Racial Isolation in the Public Schools,* 2 vols. (Washington, DC: Government Printing Office, 1967). See also James S. Coleman, *Equality of Educational Opportunity* (Washington, DC: Government Printing Office, 1966).

[18] See David J. Armor, "The Evidence on Busing," *The Public Interest* (Summer 1972), 90–120.

[19] Michael W. Giles, Everett F. Cataldo, and Douglas S. Gatlin, "White Flight and Percent Blacks: The Tipping Point Re-examined," *Social Science Quarterly,* 56 (June 1975), 85–92; and "The Impact of Busing on White Flight," *Social Science Quarterly,* 55 (September 1974), 493–501.

tions in the nation's large central cities suggest that the family will move eventually.

Busing in Boston   The experience with busing in Boston indicated the extent of mass resistance to busing and how white flight defeated the original policy objective. In 1974 U.S. Federal District Court Judge W. Arthur Garrity found that Boston school authorities had knowingly endeavored to keep their schools racially segregated. He ordered massive busing throughout the city. When the Boston School Committee refused to cooperate, he took over the governance of the school system himself. Serious racial conflict accompanied early attempts to bus students to and from high schools in working-class white neighborhoods. But Judge Garrity stuck to his plans: "No amount of public or parental opposition will excuse avoidance by school officials, of constitutionally imposed obligations."[20]

In 1973, prior to Judge Garrity's busing orders, Boston had 94,000 public school students, 57 percent of whom were white. When Judge Garrity finally removed himself from the case in 1985 and returned control of the schools to elected city officials, only 57,000 students remained in Boston's schools, and only 27 percent of them were white.[21] There was no creditable evidence that black students had improved their performance on standard test scores. Most white students in the Boston area attended either suburban schools or private schools (Judge Garrity lived in suburban Wellesley). Yet over time racial conflict in Boston subsided. The most vocal anti-busing politicians were eventually voted out of office.

Federal Court Supervision   Federal district judges enjoy wide freedom in fashioning remedies for past or present discriminatory practices by governments. If a federal district court anywhere in the United States finds that any actions by governments or school officials have contributed to racial imbalances (e.g., in drawing school district attendance lines), the judge may order the adoption of a desegregation plan to overcome racial imbalances produced by official action. A large number of cities have come under federal district court orders to improve racial balances in their schools through busing.

In the important case of *Swan* v. *Charlotte-Mecklenburg Board of Education,* the Supreme Court upheld (1) the use of racial balance requirements in schools and the assignment of pupils to schools based on race, (2) "close scrutiny" by judges of schools that are predominantly of one race, (3) gerrymandering of school attendance zones as well as "clustering" or "grouping" of schools to achieve equal balance; and (4) court-ordered busing of pupils to achieve racial balance.

> Absent a constitutional violation there would be no basis for judicially ordering assignment of students on a racial basis. All things being equal, with no history of discrimination, it might well be desirable to assign pupils to schools nearest their homes. But all things are not equal in a system that has been deliberately constructed and maintained to enforce racial segregation. The remedy for such

---

[20] George M. Metcalf, *From Little Rock to Boston: The History of School Desegregation* (Westport, CT: Greenwood Press, 1983), p. 202.

[21] *New York Times,* September 15, 1985, p. A-10.

segregation may be administratively awkward, inconvenient, and even bizarre in some situations and may impose burdens on some; but all awkwardness and inconvenience cannot be avoided when remedial adjustments are being made to eliminate the dual school system.[22]

The Court was careful to note, however, that racial imbalance in schools is not itself grounds for ordering these remedies, unless it is also shown that some present or past governmental action contributed to the imbalance.

Cross-District Busing   In the absence of any governmental actions contributing to racial imbalance, states and school districts are *not* required by the Fourteenth Amendment to integrate their schools. Thus, for example, where central-city schools are predominantly black, and suburban schools are predominantly white, owing to residential patterns, cross-district busing is not required, unless it is shown that some official action brought about these racial imbalances. The Supreme Court threw out a lower federal court order for massive busing of students between Detroit and fifty-two suburban school districts. Although Detroit city schools are 70 percent black, none of the Detroit-area school districts segregated students within their own boundaries. Chief Justice Burger, writing for the majority, said:

> The constitutional right for the Negro respondents residing in Detroit is to attend a unitary school system in that district. Unless petitioners drew the district lines in a discriminatory fashion, or arranged for the white student residing in the Detroit district to attend schools in Oakland or Macomb counties, they were under no constitutional duty to make provision for Negro students to do so.[23]

In a strong dissent, Justice Thurgood Marshall wrote:

> In the short run it may seem to be the easiest course to allow our great metropolitan areas to be divided up each into cities—one white, the other black— but it is a course, I predict, our people will ultimately regret.

This important decision means the largely black central cities, surrounded by largely white suburbs, will remain de facto segregated because there are not enough white students living within the city to achieve integration.

When Is Desegregation Complete?   Many school districts in the South and elsewhere have operated under federal court supervision for many years. How long should court supervision continue, and what standards are to be used in determining when desegregation has been achieved once and for all? In recent years the Supreme Court under Chief Justice Rehnquist has undertaken to free some school districts from direct federal court supervision. Where the last vestiges of state-sanctioned discrimination have been removed "as far as practicable," the Supreme Court has allowed lower federal courts to dissolve racial balancing plans even though imbalances due to residential patterns continue to exist.[24]

---

[22] *Swan v. Charlotte-Mecklenburg County Board of Education,* 402 U.S. 1 (1971).

[23] *Milliken v. Bradley,* 418 U.S. 717 (1974).

[24] *Oklahoma City Board of Education v. Dowell,* 498 U.S. 237 (1991).

Martin Luther King, Jr., and the Civil Rights Movement

The initial objective of the civil rights movement in America was to prevent discrimination and segregation as practiced by or supported by *governments*, particularly states, municipalities, and school districts. However, even while important victories for the civil rights movement were being recorded in the prevention of discrimination by governments, particularly in the *Brown* case, the movement began to broaden its objectives to include the elimination of discrimination in all segments of American life, private as well as public.

The Constitution does not govern the activities of private individuals. It is the laws of Congress and the states that govern the conduct of private individuals. When the civil rights movement turned to combating private discrimination, it had to carry its fight into the legislative branch of government. The federal courts could help restrict discrimination by state and local governments and school authorities, but only Congress, state legislatures, and city councils could restrict discrimination practiced by private owners of restaurants, hotels and motels, private employers, and other individuals who were not government officials.

Martin Luther King, Jr.   The leadership in the struggle to eliminate discrimination and segregation from private life was provided by a young black minister, Martin Luther King, Jr. King's father was the pastor of one of the South's largest and most influential congregations, the Ebenezer Baptist Church in Atlanta, Georgia. Martin Luther King, Jr., received his doctorate from Boston University and began his ministry in Montgomery, Alabama. In 1955 the black community of Montgomery began a year-long boycott with frequent demonstrations against the Montgomery city buses over segregated seating practices. The dramatic appeal and the eventual success of the boycott in Montgomery brought nationwide attention to its leader and led to the creation in 1957 of the Southern Christian Leadership Conference.

Nonviolent Direct Action   Under King's leadership the civil rights movement developed and refined political techniques for minorities in American politics, including *nonviolent direct action*. Nonviolent direct action is a form of protest that involves breaking "unjust" laws in an open, "loving," nonviolent fashion. The general notion of civil disobedience is not new; it played an important role in American history from the Boston Tea Party to the abolitionists who illegally hid runaway slaves, to the suffragettes who demonstrated for women's voting rights, to the labor organizers who formed the nation's major industrial unions, to the civil rights workers of the early 1960s who deliberately violated segregation laws. The purpose of nonviolent direct action is to call attention, or to "bear witness," to the existence of injustice. In the words of Martin Luther King, Jr., civil disobedience "seeks to dramatize the issue so that it can no longer be ignored."

There should be no violence in true civil disobedience, and only "unjust" laws are broken. Moreover, the law is broken "openly, lovingly," with a willingness to accept the penalty. Punishment is actively sought rather than avoided, since punishment will help to emphasize the injustice of the law. The object is to stir the conscience of an elite and win support for measures that will eliminate the injustices. By willingly accepting punishment for the violation of an unjust law, one demonstrates the strength of one's convictions. The dramatization of injustice makes news; the public's sympathy is won when injustices are spotlighted; and the willingness of demonstrators to accept punishment is visible evidence of their sincerity. Cruelty or violence directed against the demonstrators by police or others plays into the hands of the protesters by further emphasizing the injustices they are experiencing.

Martin Luther King, Jr., in his famous "Letter from Birmingham City Jail," explained:

> In no sense do I advocate evading or defying the law as the rabid segregationist would do. This would lead to anarchy. One who breaks an unjust law must do it *openly, lovingly* (not hatefully as the white mothers did in New Orleans when they were seen on television screaming, "nigger, nigger, nigger") and with a willingness to accept the penalty. I submit that an individual who breaks a law that conscience tells him is unjust, and willingly accepts the penalty by staying in jail to arouse the conscience of the community over its injustice, is in reality expressing the very highest respect for law.[25]

Marches in Birmingham and Washington   Perhaps the most dramatic confrontation between the civil rights movement and the southern segregationists occurred in Birmingham, Alabama, in the spring of 1963. In support of a request for desegregation of downtown eating places and the formation of a biracial committee to work out the integration of public schools, Martin Luther King, Jr., led several thousand Birmingham blacks in a series of orderly street marches. The demonstrators were met with strong police action, including fire hoses, police dogs, and electric cattle prods. Newspaper pictures of blacks being attacked by police and bitten by dogs were flashed all over the world. More than 25,000 demonstrators, including Dr. King, were jailed.

The Birmingham protest set off demonstrations in many parts of the country; the theme remained one of nonviolence, and it was usually whites rather than blacks who resorted to violence in these demonstrations. The culmination of the nonviolent philosophy was a giant, yet orderly, march on Washington, held on August 28, 1963. More than 200,000 blacks and whites participated in the march, which was endorsed by various labor leaders, religious groups, and political figures. The march ended at the Lincoln Memorial where Martin Luther King, Jr., delivered his most eloquent appeal, "I Have a Dream":

> I have a dream. It is a dream deeply rooted in the American dream. I have a dream that one day this nation will rise up and live up and live out the true meaning of its creed: "We hold these truths to be self-evident; that all men are created equal."
>
> I have a dream that one day on the red hills of Georgia the sons of former slaves and the sons of former slaveowners will be able to sit down together at the table of brotherhood.
>
> I have a dream that one day even the state of Mississippi, a desert state sweltering with the heat of injustice and oppression, will be transformed into an oasis of freedom and justice.

---

[25] Martin Luther King, Jr., "Letter from Birmingham City Jail," April 16, 1963.

I have a dream that my four little children will one day live in a nation where they will not be judged by the color of their skin but by the content of their character. . . .[26]

It was in response to this march that President John F. Kennedy sent a strong civil rights bill to Congress, which was passed after his death—the famous Civil Rights Act of 1964.

THE CIVIL RIGHTS ACT OF 1964

The Civil Rights Act of 1964 passed both houses of Congress by better than a two-thirds favorable vote; it won the overwhelming support of both Republican and Democratic members of Congress. It was signed into law on July 4, 1964. It ranks with the Emancipation Proclamation, the Fourteenth Amendment, and *Brown* v. *Topeka* as one of the most important steps toward full equality for blacks in America. Among other things, the Civil Rights Act of 1964 provides:

- That it is unlawful to discriminate or segregate persons on the grounds of race, color, religion, or national origin in any place of public accommodation, including hotels, motels, restaurants, movies, theatres, sports areas, entertainment houses, and other places which offer to serve the public. This prohibition extends to all establishments whose operations affect interstate commerce or whose discriminatory practices are supported by state action. (Title II)
- That each federal department and agency shall take action to end discrimination in all programs or activities receiving federal financial assistance in any form. This action shall include termination of financial assistance. (Title VI)
- That it shall be unlawful for any employer or labor union with twenty-five or more persons after 1965 to discriminate against any individual in any fashion in employment, because of his race, color, religion, sex, or national origin, and that an Equal Employment Opportunity Commission shall be established to enforce this provision by investigation, conference, conciliation, persuasion, and, if need be, civil action in federal court. (Title VII)[27]

---

[26] Martin Luther King, Jr., August 28, 1963, at the Lincoln Memorial, Washington, DC.

[27] Opponents of the Civil Rights Act of 1964 argued that Congress unconstitutionally exceeded its delegated powers when it prohibited discrimination and segregation practiced by *privately owned* public accommodations and *private* employers. Nowhere among the delegated powers of Congress in Article I of the Constitution, or even in the Fourteenth or Fifteenth Amendments, is Congress specifically given the power to prohibit discrimination practiced by *private* individuals. In reply, supporters of the act argued that Congress has the power to regulate interstate commerce. Instead of relying upon the Fourteenth Amendment, which prohibits only *state-supported* discrimination, Congress was relying on its powers over interstate commerce. In unanimous opinions in *Heart of Atlanta Motel* v. *United States* and *Katzenbach* v. *McClung* in December 1964, the Supreme Court upheld the constitutionality of the Civil Rights Act. The Court held that Congress could, by virtue of its power over interstate commerce, prohibit discrimination in any establishment that serves or offers to serve interstate travelers or that sells food or goods previously moved in interstate commerce. This power over commerce included not only major establishments, like the Heart of Atlanta Motel, but also the family-owned Ollie's Barbecue serving a local clientele. *Heart of Atlanta Motel* v. *United States,* 379 U.S. 241 (1964); *Katzenbach* v. *McClung,* 379 U.S. 294 (1964).

Fair Housing   For many years "fair housing" had been considered the most sensitive area of civil rights legislation. Discrimination in the sale and rental of housing was the last major civil rights problem on which Congress took action. Discrimination in housing had not been mentioned in any previous legislation; even the comprehensive Civil Rights Act of 1964 made no reference to housing. Prohibiting discrimination in the sale or rental of housing affected the constituencies of northern members of Congress more than any of the earlier, southern-oriented legislation. The prospects for a fair housing law were not very good at the beginning of 1968. When Martin Luther King, Jr., was assassinated on April 4, however, the mood of the nation and of Congress changed dramatically, and many felt that Congress should pass a fair housing law as a tribute to the slain civil rights leader. The Civil Rights Act of 1968 prohibited the following forms of discrimination:

- Refusal to sell or rent a dwelling to any person because of race, color, religion, or national origin.
- Discrimination against a person in the terms, conditions or privileges of the sale or rental of a dwelling, or advertising the sale or rental of a dwelling indicating a preference or discrimination based on race, color, religion or national origin.

The act applied to all apartments and houses, rented or sold by either real estate developers or by private individuals who used the services of real estate agents. It exempted private individuals who sold their own home without the services of a real estate agent, provided they did not indicate any preference or discrimination in advertising in the sale or rental of a house.

 ## AFFIRMATIVE ACTION

Although the gains of the civil rights movement were immensely important, they were primarily gains in *opportunity,* rather than in *results.* The civil rights movement of the 1960s did not bring about major changes in the conditions under which most blacks lived in America. Racial politics today center around the actual inequalities between blacks and whites in incomes, jobs, housing, health, education, and other conditions of life.

Continuing Inequalities   The issue of inequality is often posed today as differences in the "life chances" of blacks and whites. Figures can reveal only the bare outline of the life chances in American society (see Table 14–1). The average income of a black family is less than 60 percent of the average white family's income. Nearly 32 percent of all black families are below the recognized poverty line, while less than 11 percent of white families live in poverty. The unemployment rate for blacks is over twice as high as that for whites. Blacks are less likely to hold prestigious white-collar jobs in professional, managerial, clerical, or sales work. They do not hold many skilled craft jobs in industry but are concentrated in operative, service, and laboring positions. The civil rights movement opened up new opportuni-

TABLE 14–1   MINORITY LIFE CHANCES

Median Income of Families

	1975	1980	1985	1990
White	14,268	21,904	29,152	36,915
Black	8,779	12,674	16,786	21,423
Hispanic	9,551	14,716	19,027	23,431

Percentage of Persons Below Poverty Level

	1975	1980	1985	1990
White	9.7	10.2	11.4	10.7
Black	31.3	32.5	31.3	31.9
Hispanic	26.9	25.7	29.0	28.1

Percentage of Persons Over 25 Completing

	HIGH SCHOOL	COLLEGE
White	79	22
Black	65	11
Hispanic	51	9

Unemployment Rate

	1980	1985	1990
White	6.3	6.2	4.7
Black	14.3	15.1	11.3
Hispanic	10.1	10.5	8.0

Source: Statistical Abstract of the United States, 1992.

ties for black Americans. But equality of *opportunity* is not the same as *absolute* equality.

Policy Choices   What public policies should be pursued to achieve equality in America? Is it sufficient that government eliminate discrimination, guarantee "equality of opportunity," and apply "color-blind" standards to both blacks and whites? Or should government take "affirmative action" to overcome the results of past unequal treatment of minorities—that is, preferential or compensatory treatment to assist minority applicants for university admissions and scholarships, job hiring and promotion, and other opportunities for advancement in life?

The early emphasis of government policy, of course, was nondiscrimination. This approach began with President Harry Truman's decision to desegregate the armed forces in 1946 and was carried through to Title VI and Title VII of the Civil Rights Act of 1964 to eliminate discrimination in federally aided projects and private employment. Gradually, however, policy shifted from the traditional aim of equality of opportunity through nondiscrimination alone to affirmative action to establish "goals and timetables" to achieve greater equality of results between blacks and whites. While avoiding the term *quota,* the notion of affirmative action tests the success of equal opportunity by observing whether minorities achieve admissions, jobs, and promotions in proportion to their numbers in the population.

Constitutional Issues—The Bakke Case   The constitutional question posed by "affirmative action" programs is whether or not they discriminate against whites in violation of the Equal Protection Clause of the Fourteenth Amendment. A related question is whether or not affirmative action programs discriminate against whites in violation of the Civil Rights Act of 1964, which prohibits discrimination "on account of race," not just discrimination against blacks.

In the absence of a history of racial discrimination by an employer or university, the Supreme Court appears to be willing to scrutinize affirmative action programs to ensure that they do not directly discriminate against whites. In *Regents of the University of California* v. *Bakke* (1978), the Supreme Court struck down a special admissions program for minorities at a state medical school on the grounds that it excluded a white applicant because of his race and violated his rights under the Equal Protection Clause.[28] Allan Bakke applied to the University of California Davis Medical School two consecutive years and was rejected; in both years black applicants with significantly lower grade point averages and medical aptitude test scores were accepted through a special admissions program that reserved sixteen minority places in a class of one hundred.[29] The University of California did not deny that its admission decisions were based on race. Instead, it argued that its racial classification was "benign," that is, designed to assist minorities, not to hinder them. The special admissions program was designed (1) to "reduce the historical deficit of traditionally disfavored minorities in medical schools and the medical profession," (2) to "counter the effects of societal discrimination," (3) to "increase the number of physicians who will practice in communities currently underserved," and (4) to "obtain the educational benefits that flow from an ethnically diverse student body."

The Supreme Court held that these objectives were legitimate and that race and ethnic origin *may* be considered in reviewing applications to a state school without violating the Equal Protection Clause. However, the Court also held that a *separate* admissions program for minorities with a specific quota of openings that were unavailable to white applicants violated the Equal Protection Clause. The Court ordered Bakke admitted to medical school and the elimination of the special

---

[28] *Regents of the University of California* v. *Bakke,* 438 U.S. 265 (1978).

[29] Bakke's overall grade point average was 3.46, while the average for special admission students was 2.62. Bakke's MCAT scores were verbal–96, quantitative–94, science–97, general information–72; while the average MCAT scores for special admissions students were verbal–34, quantitative–30, science–37, general information–18.

admissions program. It recommended that California consider an admissions program developed at Harvard that considered disadvantaged racial or ethnic background as a "plus" in an overall evaluation of an application but did not set numerical quotas or exclude any persons from competing for all positions.[30]

Affirmative Action as a Remedy for Past Discrimination   The Supreme Court generally approves of affirmative action programs when there is evidence of past discriminatory practices. In *United Steelworkers of America* v. *Weber* (1979), the Supreme Court approved a plan developed by a private employer and a union to reserve 50 percent of higher paying, skilled jobs for minorities. Kaiser Aluminum Corporation and the United Steelworkers Union, under federal government pressure, had established a program to get more blacks into skilled technical jobs; only 2 percent of the skilled jobs were held by blacks in the plant where Weber worked, while 39 percent of the local work force was black. When Weber, a white male, was excluded from the training program, and blacks with less seniority and fewer qualifications were accepted, he filed suit in federal court claiming that he had been discriminated against because of his race in violation of Title VII of the Civil Rights Act of 1964. But the Supreme Court held that Title VII "left employers and unions in the private sector free to take such race-conscious steps to eliminate manifest racial imbalances in traditionally segregated job categories. We hold that Title VII does not prohibit such . . . affirmative action plans."[31]

The changing membership of the Supreme Court over time has *not* resulted in any significant alteration of the Court's policy regarding affirmative action as a remedy for past discrimination. In 1987 in *United States* v. *Paradise,* the Court upheld a rigid 50 percent black quota system for promotions in the Alabama Department of Safety, which had excluded blacks from the ranks of state troopers prior to 1972 and had not promoted any blacks higher than corporal prior to 1984. In a 5–4 decision, the majority stressed the long history of discrimination in the agency as a reason for upholding the quota system. Whatever burdens were imposed on innocent parties were outweighed by the need to correct the effects of past discrimination.[32]

Cases Questioning Affirmative Action   Yet the Supreme Court has continued to express concern about whites who are directly and adversely affected by government action solely because of their race. In *Firefighters Local Union* v. *Stotts* (1984), the Court ruled that a city could not lay off white firefighters in favor of black fire-

---

[30] The Bakke case did *not* affect overall minority enrollments in law schools and medical schools. Black and Hispanic enrollments continued to rise until the 1980s, when economic conditions appeared to have an adverse effect on minority enrollments. See John Gruhl and Susan Welch, "The Impact of the Bakke Decision on Black and Hispanic Enrollments in Medical and Law Schools," *Social Science Quarterly,* 71 (September 1990), 458–73.

[31] *United Steelworkers* v. *Weber,* 443 U.S. 193 (1979).

[32] *United States* v. *Paradise,* 480 U.S. 149 (1987).

fighters with less seniority.[33] In *Richmond* v. *Crosen* (1989), the Supreme Court held that a minority set-aside program in Richmond, Virginia, which mandated that 30 percent of all city construction contracts must go to "blacks, Spanish-speaking, Orientals, Indians, Eskimos, or Aleuts" violated the Equal Protection Clause of the Fourteenth Amendment.[34]

It is important to note that the Supreme Court has never adopted the color-blind doctrine first espoused by Justice John Harlan in his *dissent* from *Plessy* v. *Ferguson*—that "our constitution is color-blind and neither knows nor tolerates classes among citizens." If the Equal Protection Clause required that the laws of the United States and the states be truly color-blind, then *no* racial guidelines, goals, or quotas would be tolerated. This view has occasionally been expressed in recent minority dissents.[35]

The Absence of a Clear Constitution Principle   The Supreme Court's decisions on affirmative action have not provided the nation with a clear and coherent interpretation of the Constitution. There is no clear rule of law, or legal test, or constitutional principle that tells us what is permissible and what is prohibited in the way of racially conscious laws and practices. Each affirmative action program must be judged separately.

Nonetheless, over time some general tendencies in Supreme Court policy can be identified. Affirmative action programs are *more likely to be found constitutional* when

- They are adopted in response to past history of discrimination.
- They are "narrowly tailored" to remedy the effects of previous discrimination.
- They do not absolutely bar whites or men from competing or participating.
- They serve an important social or educational objective.

State–Local AA Plans   Today all states and most cities have affirmative action plans. Numerical goals are a common component of these EEO/AA (Equal Employment Opportunity/Affirmation Action) plans.[36] Virtually all plans designated blacks, Hispanics, and women as beneficiaries; many add handicapped persons, Native Americans, homosexuals, older workers, ex-offenders, and rehabilitated alcoholics and drug abusers.

Congressional Action   The battle over affirmative action has been waged in the Congress as well as the courts. Members of Congress are very much aware of sur-

---

[33] *Firefighters Local Union* v. *Stotts,* 465 U.S. 561 (1984).

[34] *Richmond* v. *Crosen,* 109 S. Ct. 706 (1989).

[35] See Justice Anton Scalia's dissent in *Johnson* v. *Transportation Agency of Santa Clara County,* 480 U.S. 616 (1987).

[36] See Evelina R. Moulder, "Affirmative Action in Local Governments," *Municipal Yearbook, 1986* (Chicago: International City Managers Association, 1986), pp. 24–28.

vey results that show most Americans favor "affirmative action" when it is expressed in the abstract. But they are equally aware that the poll results are much different when "preferences" or "quotas" are mentioned. So Congress, ever mindful of the polls, has tried to find a way to advance affirmative action while avoiding direct reference to preferences or quotas.

In the Civil Rights and Women Equity Act of 1991, Congress sought to deflect criticism of affirmative action by specifically including an antiquota provision: Nothing in the bill is to be "construed to require, encourage, or permit an employer to adopt hiring or promotion quotas on the basis of race, color, religion, sex or national origin, and the use of such quotas shall be deemed to be an unlawful employment practice."[37]

However, the act went on to state that statistical imbalance in an employer's work force may be evidence of employment practices (rules, requirements, academic qualifications, tests) that have a "disparate impact" on minorities or women. Employers must bear the burden of proof that any practice that has a "disparate impact" is necessary and has "a significant and manifest relationship to the requirements for effective job performance." The act provides both compensating money awards (usually back pay and attorney's fees) as well as punitive money awards for victims of discrimination.

WILDER OF VIRGINIA: PUTTING RACE TO REST

Race has been a central domestic issue in American politics over the long history of the nation. It is the only issue over which the nation fought a civil war. No one claims that racism in America has been eliminated. But failure to recognize progress can be self-defeating. If people believe that America is "hopelessly racist," then constructive efforts to combat discrimination are undermined.

Virginia was the capital of the Confederacy. For a century after the Civil War it was a symbol of resistance to racial equality. It harbored one of the nation's most narrow-minded statewide political machines well into the 1960s. Blacks were excluded from public office, discouraged from voting by the state poll tax, and denied educational equality through "massive resistance" to school integration. Yet two decades later Virginia became the first state to elect a black governor. Douglass Wilder, grandson of slaves, governs a state with an 80 percent white population from the domed capitol where Jefferson Davis once presided over the Confederacy.

Wilder grew up in segregated Richmond, one of eight children whose father worked as an insurance agent. He waited tables while attending a local black college; as a U.S. Marine, he fought in the Korean War, winning a Bronze Star in combat; he returned to earn a law degree from Howard University. He was financially successful in a Richmond law practice, although a court reprimand for mal-

---

[37] *Congressional Quarterly Weekly Report,* June 8, 1991, p. 1501.

practice would tarnish his record and haunt him in later political campaigns. He became the first black elected to the Virginia state senate in 1969. His early political style was confrontational, but experience and success in the legislature brought greater maturity and moderation in his relations with his white colleagues. By 1985 Virginia newspapers were ranking him among the state's most effective legislators. He had broadened his interests from racial affairs to a wide range of state issues. He embraced rather than ridiculed his state's historical symbols. Yet he was known as a tough negotiator within Democratic party circles.

When Democratic gubernatorial aspirant Gerald Baliles faced an uphill battle in 1985, Wilder maneuvered his way onto the ticket by threatening the party with the loss of black votes. He was an effective campaigner for lieutenant governor, touring all of the state's 95 counties and running TV ads showing support by rural conservative white police officers. He won the post with 52 percent of the vote.

In contrast to Jesse Jackson's often divisive politics of race, Douglass Wilder projected an image of statewide consensus and progress. "As a boy when I would read about an Abe Lincoln or a Thomas Jefferson . . . when I would read that all men are created equal . . . I knew it meant me."[38] With soft tones and a reassuring manner, Wilder moved to the center of Democratic politics in his state, becoming tough on crime and supporting the death penalty. Even while waging a successful battle to create a state holiday in honor of Martin Luther King, Jr., he solicited the support of moderate and conservative forces in Virginia. In 1989, with Baliles unable to succeed himself, Wilder easily captured the Democratic nomination for governor.

In winning the Virginia governorship, Douglass Wilder did more than any other elected public official to put race to rest as a political issue. Throughout the campaign Wilder insisted, "Race is not an issue."[39] He declined offers of help from Jesse Jackson. His Republican opponent attacked his earlier liberal record, charging that he had flipflopped on the issues. It was a tough campaign: Wilder's millionaire legal and business interests, including his ownership of slum property, were the subject of negative TV ads. Wilder hit back hard and won support using conservative rhetoric. He won "pro-choice" votes on the abortion issue with the slogan "Keep politicians out of your personal life." A Labor Day riot of black students at Virginia Beach almost upset his mainstream campaign. But when the votes were counted, Wilder emerged with a razor-thin 50 percent margin of victory. He won over 40 percent of the white vote in the state and 90 percent of the black vote. His white running mate for lieutenant governor won 54 percent of the vote, suggesting perhaps that some white Democratic voters could not bring themselves to support Wilder.

Wilder's victory in a predominantly white southern state provides the model for successful statewide biracial politics. Political moderation, mainstream views,

---

[38] *Time,* November 20, 1989, p. 54.

[39] *New York Times,* September 16, 1989.

and a reassuring image can prevail where passionate rhetoric, left-leaning politics, and a flamboyant image will fail. Race can be put to rest by able and effective politicians.

HISPANIC POWER

The term *Hispanic* refers to persons of Spanish-speaking ancestry and culture, including Mexican-Americans, as well as Puerto Ricans and Cubans. In 1990 there were over 22 million Hispanics in the United States, comprising 9 percent of the U.S. population. (There were 30 million blacks, making up 12.1 percent of the population.) The largest subgroup of Hispanics are Mexican-Americans, some of whom are descendants of citizens living in the Mexican territory that was annexed to the United States in 1848. (See Figure 1–6 in Chapter 1.) Most of them, however, have come to the United States in accelerating numbers in recent years. The largest Mexican-American populations are found in Texas, Arizona, New Mexico, and California. (See Figure 14–2.) The second largest subgroup are Puerto Ricans, many of whom retain ties to the commonwealth and move back and forth from the island to the mainland, especially New York City. The third largest subgroup are Cubans, most of whom have fled from Castro's Cuba. They live mainly in the Miami metropolitan area. While these groups have different experiences, they share a common language and culture, and they have encountered similar difficulties in making government responsive to their needs.

In recent years Hispanics have served as governors in Florida, Arizona, and New Mexico, and as mayors in Miami, Denver, San Antonio, and several other large cities. However, overall Hispanic political influence in state and local politics does not match Hispanic population percentages.[40] Hispanic voter turnout is lower than for other ethnic groups in America. Many Hispanics are still resident aliens and therefore not eligible to vote. Language barriers may also present an obstacle to full participation. Finally, Hispanic voters divide their political loyalties. The largest Hispanic groups, Mexican-Americans, tend to vote Democratic; their power is concentrated in California, Texas, Arizona, and New Mexico. Cuban-Americans and other political refugees from Marxist guerrilla wars in Central and South America tend to vote Republican. These groups are economically very successful; they are concentrated in the Miami area, and they are now a major force in city and state politics in Florida. In Miami, Los Angeles, and other cities with large Hispanic populations *and* large black populations, competition and conflict, rather than minority coalition building, have often characterized relations between these groups.[41]

---

[40] See F. Chris Garcia, ed., *Latinos in the Political System* (Notre Dame, IN: Notre Dame University Press, 1988).

[41] See Paula D. McClain and Albert K. Karnig, "Black and Hispanic Political Competition," *American Political Science Review,* 84 (June 1990), 535–45.

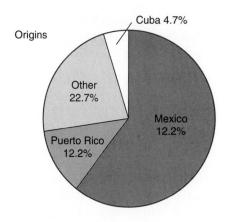

Origins

Cuba 4.7%

Other
22.7%

Mexico
12.2%

Puerto Rico
12.2%

States with Hispanic Population over 10 Percent

New Mexico	38.2%	Colorado	12.9%
California	25.8	New York	12.3
Texas	25.5	Florida	12.2
Arizona	18.8	Nevada	10.4

Cities with Majority Hispanic Populations

East Los Angeles CA	94.7%	Miami FL	62.5%
Laredo TX	93.9	San Antonio TX	55.6
Hialeah FL	87.6	Oxnard CA	54.4
El Monte CA	72.5	Pomona CA	51.3
El Paso TX	69.0	Corpus Christi TX	50.4
Santa Ana CA	65.2	Salinas CA	50.6

Median family income, 1991 U.S. average $35,353

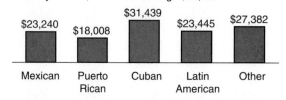

$23,240	$18,008	$31,439	$23,445	$27,382
Mexican	Puerto Rican	Cuban	Latin American	Other

Persons below poverty level 1991, U.S. average 12.1%

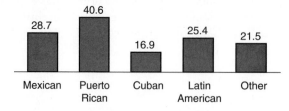

28.7	40.6	16.9	25.4	21.5
Mexican	Puerto Rican	Cuban	Latin American	Other

**FIGURE 14–2   Hispanic Americans:
                 Social and Economic Characteristics**

Source: Statistical Abstract of the United States 1992.

GENDER EQUALITY

Until recently, gender issues had been determined largely by *state* laws, particularly laws governing marriage, divorce, employment, and abortion. State laws frequently differentiated between the rights and responsibilities of men and women. Women had many special protections in state laws, but often these protections limited opportunities for advancement and encouraged dependence upon men.

Employment   Traditionally, state laws governing employment considered women as frail creatures in need of special protections against long hours, heavy work, night work, and so on. Moreover, states did not guarantee equal pay and promotion opportunities for women or bar sexual discrimination in employment. However, Title VII of the federal Civil Rights Act of 1964 prevents sexual (as well as racial) discrimination in hiring, pay, and promotions. The Equal Employment Opportunity Commission, which is the federal agency charged with eliminating discrimination in employment, has established guidelines barring stereotyped classifications of "men's jobs" and "women's jobs." State laws and employer practices that differentiate between men and women in hours, pay, retirement age, and so on have been struck down.

Gender Classifications   The Supreme Court has ruled that states can no longer set different ages for men and women to become legal adults[42] or purchase alcoholic beverages;[43] women cannot be barred from police or firefighting jobs by arbitrary height and weight requirements;[44] insurance and retirement plans for women must pay the same monthly benefits even though women on the average live longer;[45] and schools must pay coaches in girls' sports the same as coaches in boys' sports.[46] However, all-male and all-female schools are still permitted;[47] and Congress may draft men for military service without drafting women.[48] Gender protection under the Equal Protection Clause also extends to men: The Supreme Court struck down a state law that allowed wives to obtain alimony from husbands but did not permit husbands to obtain alimony from wives.[49]

Credit   The Federal Equal Credit Opportunity Act of 1974 prohibits sex discrimination in credit transactions. Federal law prevent banks, credit unions, savings and loan associations, retail stores, and credit card companies from denying credit because of sex or marital status. However, these businesses may still deny credit for a

---

[42] *Stanton* v. *Stanton*, 421 U.S. 7 (1975).

[43] *Craig* v. *Boren*, 429 U.S. 191 (1976).

[44] *Dothland* v. *Raulinson*, 433 U.S. 321 (1977).

[45] *Arizona* v. *Norvis*, 103 S. CT. 3492 (1983).

[46] *E.E.O.C.* v. *Madison Community School District*, 55 U.S.L.W. 2644 (1987).

[47] *Vorcheheimer* v. *Philadelphia School District*, 430 U.S. 703 (1977).

[48] *Rostker* v. *Goldberg*, 453 U.S. 57 (1981).

[49] *Orr* v. *Orr*, 440 U.S. 268 (1979).

poor or nonexistent credit rating, and some women who have always maintained accounts in their husband's name may still face credit problems if they apply in their own name.

Education   Title IX of the Federal Education Act Amendment of 1972 deals with sex discrimination in education. This federal law bars discrimination in admissions, housing, rules, financial aid, faculty and staff recruitment, pay, and—most troublesome of all—athletics. The latter problem has proven very difficult because men's football and basketball programs have traditionally brought in the money to finance all other sports and have received the largest share of school athletic budgets.

The Earnings Gap   Women's earnings on average are substantially below men's earnings. In 1990, for example, women earned only about 72 percent of what men earned. Despite federal laws barring direct gender discrimination in employment, the existence of a "dual" labor market, with male-dominated "blue-collar" jobs distinguishable from female-dominated "pink-collar" jobs, continues to be a major obstacle to economic equality between men and women. A study sponsored by the National Academy of Sciences concluded that most of the differences in men's and women's earnings could be attributed to sex segregation in occupations.[50] These occupational differences were attributed to cultural stereotyping, social conditioning, and training and education that narrow the choices available to women. While significant progress has been made in recent years in reducing occupational sex segregation, nonetheless, many observers doubt that sexually differentiated occupations will be eliminated soon.

Comparable Worth   As a result of a growing recognition that the wage gap is more a result of occupational differentiation than direct discrimination, some feminist organizations have turned to a new approach—the demand that pay levels in various occupations be determined by "comparable worth" rather than by the labor market. *Comparable worth* means *more* than paying men and women equally for the same work; it means paying the same wages for jobs of comparable value to the employer. It means that traditionally male and female jobs would be evaluated by governmental agencies or courts to determine their "worth" to the employer, perhaps by considering responsibilities, effort, knowledge, and skill requirements. Jobs adjudged to be comparable would have equal wages. Government agencies or the courts would replace the labor market in the determination of wage rates.

To date the U.S. Equal Employment Opportunity Commission has rejected the notion of comparable worth and declined to recommend wages for traditionally male and female jobs. And so far the federal courts have refused to declare that different wages in traditionally male and female occupations are evidence of sexual discrimination in violation of federal law. However, some state governments and private employers have undertaken to review their own pay scales to determine if traditionally female occupations are underpaid.

---

[50] National Research Council, National Academy of Sciences, *Women's Work, Men's Work* (Washington, DC: National Academy Press, 1985).

THE BATTLE OVER ABORTION

Arguments over abortion touch on fundamental moral and religious principles. Proponents of legalized abortion, who often refer to themselves as "pro-choice," argue that a woman should be permitted to control her own body and should not be forced by law to have unwanted children. They cite the heavy toll in lives lost in criminal abortions and the psychological and emotional pain of an unwanted pregnancy. Opponents of abortion, who often refer to themselves as "pro-life," generally base their belief on the sanctity of life, including the life of the unborn child, which they believe deserves the protection of law—"the right to life." Many believe that the killing of an unborn child for any reason other than the preservation of the life of the mother is murder.

Early State Laws   Historically, abortions for any purpose other than saving the life of the mother were criminal offenses under state law. About a dozen states acted in the late 1960s to permit abortions in cases of rape or incest, or to protect the physical health of the mother, and in some cases her mental health as well. Relatively few legal abortions were performed under these laws, however, because of the red tape involved—review of each case by several concurring physicians, approval of a hospital board, and so forth. Then, in 1970, New York, Alaska, Hawaii, and Washington enacted laws that in effect permitted abortion at the request of the woman involved with the concurrence of her physician.

Roe v. Wade   The U.S. Supreme Court's decision in *Roe* v. *Wade* was one of the most important and far-reaching in the Court's history.[51] The Supreme Court ruled that the constitutional guarantee of "liberty" in the Fifth and Fourteenth Amendments included a woman's decision to bear or not to bear a child. The Supreme Court ruled that the word *person* in the Constitution did not include the unborn child. Therefore, the Fifth and Fourteenth Amendments to the Constitution, guaranteeing "life, liberty and property," did not protect the "life" of the fetus. The Court also ruled that a state's power to protect the health and safety of the mother could not justify *any* restriction on abortion in the first three months of pregnancy. Between the third and sixth months of pregnancy, a state could set standards for abortion procedures in order to protect the health of women, but a state could not prohibit abortions. Only in the final three months could a state prohibit or regulate abortion to protect the unborn.

Reactions in the States   The Supreme Court's decision did not end the controversy over abortion. Congress declined to pass a constitutional amendment restricting abortion or declaring that the guarantee of life begins at conception. However, Congress banned the use of federal funds under Medicaid (medical care for the poor) for abortions except to protect the life of a woman. The Supreme Court upheld the constitutionality of federal and state laws denying tax funds for abortions. While women retained the right to an abortion, the Court held that there was

---

[51] *Roe* v. *Wade*, 410 U.S. 113 (1973).

no constitutional obligation for governments to pay for abortions;[52] the decision about whether to pay for abortions from tax revenues was left to Congress and the states.[53] However, efforts by the states to directly restrict abortion ran into Supreme Court opposition.[54]

Abortions in the States   About 1.6 million abortions are performed each year in the United States. This is about 44 percent of the number of live births. About 85 percent of all abortions are performed at abortion clinics; others are performed in physicians' offices or in hospitals, where the cost is significantly higher. Most of these abortions are performed in the first three months; about 10 percent are performed after the third month. Abortion is more frequent in some states (New York, Nevada, New Jersey, California) than in other states (Utah, Idaho, West Virginia, Wyoming, South Dakota).

Why are abortions more frequent in some states than in others? A careful study of this question by political scientist Susan B. Hansen revealed that abortion rates were *not* related to unwanted pregnancies, that is, the "demand" for abortions.[55] Rather, abortion rates were related to state policies affecting the availability of abortion services, that is, to government policies affecting the "supply" of abortions. Among the reported findings were that abortion rates are higher in states that permitted abortion before *Roe* v. *Wade;* states with the lowest abortion rates (Utah and Idaho) have large Mormon populations; and greater state legislative support for abortion facilities and health services leads to higher abortion rates.

State Restrictions   Opponents of abortion won a victory in the *Webster* case in 1989 when the Supreme Court upheld a Missouri law sharply restricting abortions.[56] The right to abortion under *Roe* v. *Wade* was not overturned, but narrowed in application. The effect of the decision was to return the question of abortion restrictions to the states for decision.

The Court held that Missouri could deny public funds for abortions that were not necessary for the life of the woman and could deny the use of public facilities or employees in performing or assisting in abortions. More important, the Court upheld the requirement for a test of "viability" after twenty weeks and a prohibition of an abortion of a viable fetus except to save a woman's life. The Court recognized the state's "interest in the protection of human life when viability is possible."

---

[52] *Harris* v. *McRae,* 448 U.S. 297 (1980).

[53] For a review of state funding of abortions, see Kenneth J. Meier and Deborah R. McFarlane, "The Politics of Funding Abortion," *American Politics Quarterly,* 21 (January 1993), 81–101.

[54] *Planned Parenthood of Missouri* v. *Danforth,* 428 U.S. 52 (1976); *Bellotti* v. *Baird,* 443 U.S. 622 (1979); *Akron* v. *Akron Center for Reproductive Health,* 103 S. Ct. 2481 (1983).

[55] Susan B. Hansen, "State Implementation of Supreme Court Decisions: Abortion Rates Since *Roe* v. *Wade,*" *Journal of Politics,* 42 (1980), 372–95.

[56] *Webster* v. *Reproductive Health Services,* 492 U.S. 490 (1989).

Abortion Battles in the States   The effect of the *Webster* decision was to rekindle contentious debates over abortion in virtually all state capitals.[57] Various legal restrictions on abortions have been passed in the states, including (1) *public financing:* prohibitions on public financing of abortions; (2) *viability tests:* requirements for a test of viability and prohibitions on the abortion of a viable fetus; (3) *conscience laws:* laws granting permission to doctors and hospitals to refuse to perform abortions; (4) *fetal disposal:* laws requiring humane and sanitary disposal of fetal remains; (5) *informed consent:* laws requiring physicians to inform patients about the development of the fetus and the availability of assistance in pregnancy, (6) *parental notification:* laws requiring that parents of minors seeking abortion be informed; (7) *spousal verification:* laws requiring spouses to be informed; (8) *hospitalization requirement:* laws requiring that late abortions be performed in hospitals; (9) *clinic licensing:* laws setting standards of cleanliness and care in abortion clinics; (10) *gender selection:* laws prohibiting abortion based on the gender of the fetus.

Reaffirming *Roe* v. *Wade*   Abortion has become such a polarizing issue that pro-choice and pro-life groups are generally unwilling to search out a middle ground. Yet the current Supreme Court appears to have chosen a policy of affirming a woman's right to abortion while upholding modest restrictions.

Pennsylvania is a state where pro-life forces won the support of the governor and legislature for a series of restrictions on abortion—physicians must inform women of risks and alternatives; a twenty-four–hour waiting period is required; minors must have consent of parents or a judge; spouses must be notified. These restrictions reached the Supreme Court in the case of *Planned Parenthood of Pennsylvania* v. *Casey* in 1992.[58]

Justice Sandra Day O'Connor took the lead in forming a moderate, swing bloc on the Court; her majority opinion strongly reaffirmed the fundamental right of abortion:

> Our law affords constitutional protection to personal decisions relating to marriage, procreation, contraception, family relationships, child rearing and education . . . These matters, involving the most intimate and personal choices a person may make in a lifetime, choices central to personal dignity and autonomy, are central to the liberty protected by the Fourteenth Amendment. . . . A woman's liberty is not so unlimited, however, that from the outset the State cannot show its concern for the life of the unborn, and at a later point in fetal development the State's interest in life has sufficient force so that the right of the woman to terminate the pregnancy can be restricted. We conclude the line should be drawn at viability, so that before that time the woman has a right to choose to terminate her pregnancy. . . .

Justice O'Connor went on to establish a new standard for constitutionally evaluating restrictions: They must not impose an "undue burden" on women seeking

---

[57] See Malcolm L. Goggin, "Understanding the New Politics of Abortion," *American Politics Quarterly,* 21 (January 1983), 4–30.

[58] *Planned Parenthood* v. *Casey,* 112 S. Ct. 2791 (1992).

abortion or place "substantial obstacles" in her path. All of Pennsylvania's restrictions were upheld except spousal notification.

Supporters of abortion rights are endeavoring to have Congress intervene by passing a law striking down state restrictions on abortion. A Freedom of Choice Act, if passed, would invalidate most state restrictions on abortion. And the Clinton administration has urged Congress to repeal the "Hyde Amendment" that prevents states from providing public funds for abortion under Medicaid.

15

THE POLITICS OF EDUCATION

▲

GOALS IN EDUCATIONAL POLICY

The primary responsibility for public education rests with the fifty state governments and their subdivisions. It is the largest and most costly of state functions.

In 1647 the Massachusetts colonial legislature first required towns to provide for the education of children out of public funds. The rugged individualists of earlier eras thought it outrageous that one person should be taxed to pay for the education of another person's child. They were joined in their opposition to public education by those aristocrats who were opposed to arming the common people with the power that knowledge gives. However, the logic of democracy led inevitably to public education. The earliest democrats believed that the safest repository of the ultimate powers of society was the people themselves. If the people make mistakes, the remedy was not remove power from their hands, but to help them in forming their judgment through education. Congress passed the Northwest Ordinance in 1787 offering land grants for public schools in the new territories and giving succeeding generations words to be forever etched on grammar school cornerstones: "Religion, morality, and knowledge being necessary to good govern-

435

ment and the happiness of mankind, schools and the means for education shall ever be encouraged." When American democracy adopted universal suffrage, it affected every aspect of American life, and particularly education. If the common people were to be granted the right of suffrage, they must be educated to the task. This meant that public education had to be universal, free, and compulsory.

If there ever was a time when schools were only expected to combat ignorance and illiteracy, that time is far behind us. Today, schools are expected to do many things: resolve racial conflict and build an integrated society; improve the self-image of minority children; inspire patriotism and good citizenship; offer various forms of recreation and mass entertainment (football games, bands, choruses, cheerleaders, and the like); teach children to get along well with others and appreciate multiple cultures; reduce the highway accident toll by teaching students to be good drivers; eliminate unemployment and poverty by teaching job skills; end malnutrition and hunger through school lunch and milk programs; produce scientists and other technicians to continue America's progress in science and technology; fight drug abuse and educate children about sex and sexually transmitted diseases; and act as custodians for teenagers who have no interest in education but are not permitted to work or roam the streets unsupervised. In other words, nearly all the nation's problems are reflected in demands placed on schools. And, of course, these demands are frequently conflicting.

EDUCATIONAL PERFORMANCE MEASUREMENT

Too often educational reports focus on "inputs"—measures of resources expended on education—rather than "outputs"—measures of an educational system's performance. Professional educators frequently resist performance measurement, especially comparisons between states or school districts. (The National Education Association's popular "Rankings of the States" focuses exclusively on enrollment, staff, and expenditure measures.) It is true that many performance measures, especially test scores, are controversial; many commentators argue that they do not measure the qualitative goals of education or that they are biased in one fashion or another. Certainly all interested citizens will welcome future refinements in educational performance measurement. But we cannot ignore performance simply because our measures are unrefined. We need to make reasoned use of the best available comparative measures of educational performance.

The Dropout Rate　Certainly one measure of an educational system's performance is its ability to retain and graduate its students. National studies have consistently shown that high school dropouts tend to experience more unemployment and earn less over a lifetime than high school graduates. Yet often schools fail to convince young people that staying in school is a worthwhile endeavor.

The conflict over dropouts begins with arguments over how to measure the dropout rate. The U.S. Department of Education currently counts high school dropouts in two ways:

1. Persons who are recorded by the schools as having stopped attending during the tenth, eleventh, and twelfth grades in a single year, as a percentage of total attendance.

This measure produced an annual figure of about 4 percent in 1992, down from 6 percent in 1980. This measure is preferred by professional educators because it is low and because educators themselves collect the data.

2.   Persons age sixteen to nineteen years old who are not attending school and have not graduated from high school, as a percentage of all sixteen- to nineteen-year-olds.

This measure produced an annual figure of 12.1 percent in 1992, down from 14 percent in 1980. This measure is often overlooked by school administrators because it is so high. Another figure that is seldom mentioned by school administrators is the 26 percent of nineteen-year-olds who have not graduated from high school.

The good news is that high school dropout rates are declining over time, however they are measured. Even so, dropout rates differ by race and ethnicity; the percentage of white sixteen- to nineteen-year-olds not attending or not graduated from school is about 9 percent; for blacks it is about 13 percent, and for Hispanics about 32 percent.[1] Dropout rates are higher than the national average in southern states and states with large Hispanic populations.

Controversies over Testing   Performance testing of students is another controversial issue in educational circles. Professional educators argue that the acquisition of verbal and quantitative skills is not the only, or even perhaps the most important, product of public education. Educators often criticize the tests as culturally biased, unfair to minorities, or otherwise flawed. Nonetheless, public sentiment is strongly in favor of testing students' basic skills. Governors and state legislators have pressured educational administrators to engage in more testing. Cross-national studies have attempted to evaluate the performance of American students over time, and to compare their performance with that of students of other nations (Table 15–1). The results of these tests, showing U.S. students ranking well below students of other advanced nations, has added urgency to calls on the national and state levels for added emphasis on basic skills.

SAT Scores   For many years critics of modern public education cited declining scores on standardized tests, particularly the Scholastic Aptitude Test (SAT) required by many colleges and universities, as evidence of the failure of the schools to teach basic reading and mathematics skills. SAT scores declined dramatically during the 1960s and 1970s, ironically during a period in which per pupil educational spending was rising and the federal government initiated federal aid to education. (See Figure 15–1.) When the decline ended in 1982, it was attributed to increasing emphasis on basic skills and standardized testing. But changes in these test scores are also a function of how many students take the test. During the declining years, increasing numbers of students were taking the test—students who never aspired to college in the past and whose test scores did not match those of the earlier,

---

[1] *Statistical Abstract of the United States, 1992,* p. 160.

TABLE 15–1   INTERNATIONAL PROFICIENCY SCORES IN SCIENCE AND MATHEMATICS

	Science			Mathematics	
RANK	NATION	PERCENT CORRECT	RANK	NATION	PERCENT CORRECT
1	South Korea	78	1	South Korea	73
2	Taiwan	76	2	Taiwan	73
3	Switzerland	74	3	Switzerland	71
4	Hungary	73	4	Russia	70
5	Russia	71	5	Hungary	68
6	Slovenia	70	6	France	64
7	Italy	70	7	Italy	64
8	Israel	70	8	Israel	63
9	Canada	69	9	Canada	62
10	France	69	10	Scotland	61
11	Scotland	68	11	Ireland	61
12	Spain	68	12	Slovenia	57
13	**United States**	**67**	13	Spain	55
14	Ireland	63	**14**	**United States**	**55**
15	Jordan	57	15	Jordan	40

Note: Scores for thirteen-year-old students on International Assessment of Educational Progress test in 1992 made as comparable as possible. Notable nonparticipating nations, Germany and Japan, are likely to have ranked high.
Source: U.S. Department of Education, *Learning Mathematics and Learning Science, 1992.*

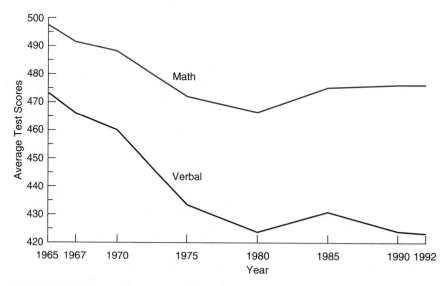

FIGURE 15–1   SAT Score Trends
Source: Statistical Abstract of the United States, 1992, p. 159, updated by author.

smaller group of college-bound test takers. In recent years SAT scores have remained fairly stable, but no significant improvements have been recorded.

Professional educators and school administrators generally oppose efforts to evaluate state educational performance by comparing average SAT scores. In addition to the objections to testing previously mentioned, educators argue that only college-bound students usually take the test, rather than all of the students in a school system. In some states over 75 percent of graduating students take the test, while in twenty-two states fewer than 20 percent do so. Average scores are higher when only a small select group takes the test. Table 15–2 ranks those states in which more than 20 percent and less than 20 percent of graduating students took the SAT, by average combined verbal and quantitative scores. (The percentages of students taking the test are shown in parentheses.) Oregon and New Hampshire are ranked highest among states with 50 percent or more students taking the test.

TABLE 15–2   EDUCATIONAL PERFORMANCE BY STATE

	Dropout Rate[a]			Average SAT Scores[b]	
RANK	STATE	RATE	RANK	STATE	SCORE (PERCENT TAKING)
1	Nevada	14.9	1	Montana	988 (24)
2	Arizona	14.3	2	Colorado	960 (29)
3	California	14.3	3	Ohio	951 (23)
4	Florida	14.2	4	Arizona	937 (27)
5	Georgia	14.1	5	Oregon	925 (55)
6	Tennessee	13.6	6	New Hampshire	923 (76)
7	North Carolina	13.2	7	Nevada	922 (27)
8	Kentucky	13.0	8	Washington	916 (50)
9	Rhode Island	12.9	9	Alaska	908 (42)
10	Alabama	12.6	10	Maryland	907 (66)
11	Texas	12.5	11	Massachusetts	902 (80)
12	Missouri	12.2	12	Connecticut	900 (29)
13	Louisiana	11.9	13	California	900 (46)
14	South Carolina	11.9	14	Vermont	897 (69)
15	Mississippi	11.7	15	Delaware	895 (66)
16	Indiana	11.4	16	Virginia	893 (63)
17	Delaware	11.2	17	New Jersey	891 (75)
18	Maryland	11.0	18	Florida	884 (50)
19	Oregon	11.0	19	Maine	882 (66)
20	Arkansas	10.9	20	New York	882 (75)
21	New Mexico	10.8	21	Rhode Island	881 (70)
22	West Virginia	10.6	22	Hawaii	878 (56)
23	Illinois	10.4	23	Pennsylvania	877 (68)
24	Virginia	10.4	24	Texas	876 (44)
25	Washington	10.2	25	Indiana	868 (58)
26	New York	10.1	26	North Carolina	855 (57)
27	Michigan	9.9	27	Georgia	842 (65)
28	New Hampshire	9.9	28	South Carolina	831 (59)

TABLE 15–2 EDUCATIONAL PERFORMANCE BY STATE *(Continued)*

	Dropout Rate[a]			Average SAT Scores[b]	
RANK	STATE	RATE	RANK	STATE	SCORE (PERCENT TAKING)
29	Oklahoma	9.9			
30	Alaska	9.6		**States with less than 20 percent taking SAT**	
31	Colorado	9.6			
32	Idaho	9.6		STATES	SCORE (PERCENT TAKING)
33	Massachusetts	9.5		Iowa	1096 (5)
34	Pennsylvania	9.4		North Dakota	1068 (6)
35	New Jersey	9.3		Minnesota	1053 (10)
36	Connecticut	9.2		Utah	1041 (5)
37	Ohio	8.8		South Dakota	1040 (6)
38	Vermont	8.7		Kansas	1033 (10)
39	Kansas	8.4		Wisconsin	1029 (11)
40	Maine	8.4		Nebraska	1018 (11)
41	Utah	7.9		Tennessee	1013 (13)
42	Montana	7.1		Illinois	1010 (15)
43	South Dakota	7.1		Oklahoma	1007 (9)
44	Hawaii	7.0		Mississippi	1004 (4)
45	Wisconsin	6.9		Missouri	1004 (11)
46	Nebraska	6.6		Alabama	996 (8)
47	Iowa	6.5		New Mexico	996 (12)
48	Wyoming	6.3		Arkansas	990 (6)
49	Minnesota	6.1		Louisiana	990 (9)
50	North Dakota	4.3		Kentucky	988 (11)
				Michigan	987 (11)
				Wyoming	978 (13)
				Idaho	963 (17)
				West Virginia	924 (17)

[a] Percentage of sixteen- to nineteen-year-olds not attending and not graduated from high school 1992.
Source: U.S. Department of Education.
[b] Combined verbal and quantitative scores.
Source: College Board.

EDUCATIONAL REFORM

How can the quality of education be improved? Systematic research over the last two decades has made it clear that money alone does not guarantee good educational performance. The early landmark work of sociologist James Coleman *Equality of Educational Opportunity* (popularly known as the Coleman report), demonstrated that pupil expenditures, teacher salaries, classroom size, facilities and materials, were *un*related to student achievement.[2] Student success is more closely related to characteristics of the home environment than to those of the schools.

---

[2] James S. Coleman et al., *Equality of Educational Opportunity* (Washington, DC: Government Printing Office, 1966).

However, Coleman later demonstrated that student achievement levels are higher in schools in which there is a high expectation for achievement, an orderly and disciplined learning environment, an emphasis on basic skills, frequent monitoring of student progress, and teacher–parent interaction and agreement on values and norms.[3] These factors help explain why students from the same family backgrounds perform better in private and Catholic schools than in public schools.[4]

A Nation At Risk   Educational reform was given impetus by an influential 1983 report by the National Commission on Excellence in Education entitled "A Nation At Risk."[5]

> Our nation is at risk. Our once unchallenged prominence in commerce, industry, science, and technological innovation is being overtaken by competitors throughout the world. . . .
>
> If an unfriendly foreign power had attempted to impose on America the mediocre educational performance that exists today, we might well have viewed it as an act of war.

The commission cited the following as evidence of the nation's decline in educational achievement: international comparisons of student achievement among industrialized nations which often rank American students last and never first; marked declines in student achievement over the preceding twenty years; declining high school enrollments in courses in science, mathematics, and foreign language; declining amounts of school homework; rising grades for pupils despite declining achievement scores.

Reform Recommendations   The commission's recommendations set the agenda for educational policy debate in the states. Among the many recommendations were these:

- A minimum high school curriculum of four years of English, three years of mathematics, three years of social science, and one-half year of computer science.
- Four to six years of foreign language study beginning in the elementary grades.
- Standardized tests for achievement for all of these subjects.
- More homework, a seven-hour school day, and a 200- to 220-day school year.
- Reliable grades and standardized tests for promotion and graduation.
- "Performance-based" salaries for teachers and rewards for "superior" teaching.[6]

---

[3] James S. Coleman et al., *High School Achievement* (New York: Basic Books, 1982).

[4] James S. Coleman and Thomas Hoffer, *Public and Private High Schools* (New York: Basic Books, 1987).

[5] National Commission on Excellence in Education, *A Nation At Risk* (Washington, DC: Government Printing Office, 1983).

[6] For a review of state implementation of these reforms, see Dennis P. Doyle and Terry W. Hartle, *Excellence in Education: The States Take Charge* (Washington, DC: American Enterprise Institute, 1985), p. 53.

Performance Testing   Many state legislatures responded to the commission's report and the demand for greater achievement in basic skills by requiring minimum competence testing (MCT) in the schools. MCTs may be used as diagnostic tools to determine the need for remedial education, or minimum scores may be required for promotion or graduation. Currently, about half of the states require students to pass a minimum competence test to receive a high school diploma. These tests usually require performance at an eighth- or ninth-grade level.

Minimum competence tests force schools and teachers to place greater emphasis on the "basics." Professional educators have been less enthusiastic about testing than citizen groups and state legislators. Educators contend that testing leads to narrow "test-taking" education rather than broad preparation for life. Testing requires teachers to devote more time to coaching students on how to pass an exam rather than preparing them for productive lives after graduation.

But the most serious opposition to testing has come from minority group leaders who charge that the tests are racially biased. Average black student scores are frequently lower than average white student scores, and a larger percentage of black students than white students are held back from promotion and graduation by testing. Some black leaders charge that racial bias in the examination itself, as well as racial isolation in the school, contributes to black–white differences in exam scores. Denying a disproportionate number of black students a diploma because of the schools' failure to teach basics may be viewed as a form of discrimination. However, to date, federal courts have declined to rule that testing itself is discriminatory, as long as sufficient time and opportunity have been provided to all students to prepare for the examination.

Testing Teacher Competency   Professional education groups have opposed teacher competency tests on the grounds that standardized tests cannot really measure competency in the classroom. The National Education Association has opposed all testing of teachers; the American Federation of Teachers is willing to accept competency testing only for new teachers. The Education Testing Service (which prepares the GRE, LSAT, and other standardized national examinations) offers a National Teacher Examination (NTE), which measures general knowledge, basic comprehension, and mathematical skills. Today, only a few states have adopted teacher competency tests, but the results have been disquieting. Large numbers of experienced teachers have failed the tests.

Pay and Recruitment   Another concern of the National Commission on Excellence in Education was the inability of the teaching profession to attract quality students. The average SAT scores of education majors are lower than the average scores of other students. It should not be surprising that education fails to attract many top students when average starting salaries for teachers nationwide are less than 75 percent of the average starting salaries for other graduates. Years ago, when women were excluded from many other professions, teaching attracted women of high ability even though salaries were low. But today, with expanded opportunities for women, the teaching profession cannot expect to attract quality graduates without offering competitive salaries.

Merit Pay   Few state legislators are willing or able to raise all teachers' salaries to the level of other professionals. The adoption of "merit pay" provides a less costly option, yet one that promises to reward good teaching. Ideally, merit pay would help retain exceptional teachers and encourage quality teaching, without rewarding mediocrity through general (across-the-board) salary increases to all teachers. But the professional education groups fear that merit pay will become a substitute for adequate teachers' salaries. They also argue that there are no objective criteria for measuring "merit" in classroom teaching. Using student test scores would unfairly penalize teachers who taught disadvantaged students. And teacher scores on "pencil-and-paper" tests do not really measure classroom performance. And of course, the subjective allocation of merit pay by principals and superintendents is potentially arbitrary. In short, merit pay plans often founder on an age-old question: What is good teaching?

Master Teachers   Another proposal to recruit and retain the best among our nation's teachers centers on identification of master teachers, and a system of promotions, rewards, and responsibilities that encourages professional development. Exceptional classroom teachers might look forward to the designation "master teacher" with professional recognition and salary; they might undertake additional responsibilities in assisting other teachers. But, as with merit pay, problems of implementing a master teacher program abound: What objective criteria exist for identifying master teachers? Is the possession of a master's or Ph.D. degree evidence of effective teaching? Who should make the selection?

Educational Goals   The president and the nation's governors have generally agreed on the *goals* for American education. In 1991 President George Bush and the nation's governors, including Arkansas Governor Bill Clinton, agreed in *America 2000* to strive toward the following goals by the year 2000.[7]

- All children in America will start school ready to learn.
- The high school graduation rate is to increase to at least 90 percent. (This is the percent of nineteen-year-olds who have graduated from high school, currently at 76 percent.)
- American students will leave grades four, eight, and twelve having demonstrated competency in challenging subject matter, including English, mathematics, science, history, and geography. (This recommendation endorses the National Assessment of Educational Progress, emphasizing standardized testing of basic skills.)
- U.S. students will be first in the world in science and mathematics achievement. (See Table 15–3.)
- Every adult American will become literate.
- Every school in America will be free of drugs and violence and will offer a disciplined environment conducive to learning.

---

[7] U.S. Department of Education, *America 2000* (Washington, DC: Government Printing Office, 1991).

RADICAL REFORM, PARENTAL CHOICE

It is unlikely that the United States will reach its educational goals without a comprehensive and "radical" restructuring of education. Simply spending more money on the current system of public education in the nation does not promise much in terms of improved performance. Nor do the imposition of tougher standards, more required courses, more hours in schools, and other top-down mandates from states to the schools.[8] Rather, good performance is associated with the sharing of high expectations among parents, teachers, and pupils; a mutual determination of goals, methods, and disciplinary standards among teachers, administrators, and parents; close monitoring of student progress by teachers and parents; and frequent interaction between parents and principals and teachers.[9] But the problem is how to bring about these conditions.

Parental Choice   "Choice" is a key word in the movement to restructure public education. Parental choice among schools is designed to do more than benefit only those parents who take the time and effort to choose the best schools for their children. It is also designed to foster competition for pupils among schools and thereby improve education for everyone. It sends a message to educators to structure their schools to give parents what they want for their children or risk losing enrollment and funding.

Parental choice involves open enrollment among public schools, with district and state educational funds flowing to those schools on the basis of the enrollment they attract. Competition involves magnet school programs with freedom for principals and teachers to determine goals, curriculum, discipline, and structure in their schools. No school would be guaranteed students or funds; enrollments and financing would come only when students and parents choose to go to particular schools. Parents could choose any school in a district, or perhaps even across districts; pupils would *not* be assigned on the basis of attendance boundaries. The "best" schools would have excess demand and might have to turn pupils away; parents would have second and third choices. Some schools might end up with very few students; they would be forced to either improve or close. Over time, high schools would tend to specialize, some emphasizing math and science, others the fine arts, others business, and still others vocational training. Some schools might be "adopted" by businesses, professional organizations, or universities.

Educational Vouchers   An even more controversial version of choice involves educational vouchers that would be given to parents to spend at any school they

---

[8] See John E. Chubb and Terry M. Moe, "Politics, Markets, and the Organization of Schools," *American Political Science Review,* 82 (December 1988), 1065–87; and their *Politics, Markets, and America's Schools* (Washington, DC: Brookings Institution, 1990).

[9] James S. Coleman and Thomas Hoffer, *Public and Private High Schools* (New York: Basic Books, 1987).

choose, public or private. State governments would redeem the vouchers submitted by schools by paying specified amounts—perhaps the equivalent of the state's per pupil educational spending (the U.S. average was over $5000 in 1992). All public and private schools would compete equally for students, and state education funds would flow to those schools that enrolled more students. Competition would encourage all schools to satisfy parental demands for excellence. Racial or religious or ethnic discrimination would be strictly prohibited in any private or public school receiving vouchers. Providing vouchers for private school education would be most effective for children from poor or disadvantaged homes. These children currently do not have the same options as children from more affluent homes of fleeing the public schools and enrolling in private academies.

Experiments   Several states and school districts have experimented with choice plans. Minnesota is the first state to allow parents to decide which *public* school district their children will attend. Funding follows the student, and transportation is provided for low-income students. Parents can opt for any public school in the state. Other earlier parental-choice plans were carried out within school districts. An especially noteworthy plan was devised for East Harlem in New York City, where the school superintendent argued that low-income parents should have a choice of schools just as high-income parents have through private schools.

> Parental choice can provide the catalyst for educational reform by introducing a market mechanism to the public educational system—a marketplace for ideas, innovations, and investments. It also increases a sense of ownership for parents, teachers and administrators, providing a framework for improvement efforts. . . .
>
> Inner city minority parents are no less concerned than their middle class counterparts to see their children educated in stimulating, orderly, vigorous schools and no less capable of choosing those schools when information is made available to them.[10]

Opposition   Yet there is strong opposition to the choice idea. The most vocal opposition comes from professional school administrators and state educational agencies. They argue that giving parents the right to move their children from school to school disrupts educational planning and threatens the viability of schools that are perceived as inferior. It may lead to a stratification of schools into popular, magnet schools that would attract the best students, and the less popular schools that would be left with the task of educating students whose parents were unaware or uninterested in their children's education. Other opponents of choice plans fear that public education might be undermined if the choice available to parents includes the option of sending their children to private, church-related schools. Public education groups are fearful that vouchers will divert public money from public to private schools. As governor of Arkansas, Bill Clinton endorsed the notion of choice, but only *within* the public school system.[11]

---

[10] Sy Fliegel, "Parental Choice in East Harlem," *Florida Policy Review,* 5 (Summer 1989), 27–28.

[11] Bill Clinton and Al Gore, *Putting People First* (New York: Times Books, 1992), p. 86.

THE LIMITED FEDERAL ROLE IN EDUCATION

Traditionally, education in America was a community responsibility. But today state governments have taken major responsibility for public education. The federal government remains largely an interested spectator in the area of educational policy. While it has taken the lead in guaranteeing racial equality in education, and separating religion from public schools, it has never assumed any significant share of the costs of education. The federal share of educational spending has never exceeded 10 percent. (See Table 15–3.)

Early Federal Aid   The federal government's role in education, however, is a longstanding one. In the famous Northwest Ordinance of 1787, Congress offered land grants for public schools in the new territories. Then in 1862 the Morrill Land Grant Act provided grants of federal land to each state for the establishment of colleges specializing in agricultural and mechanical arts. These became known as "land-grant colleges." In 1867 Congress established a U.S. Office of Education, which became the Department of Education in 1979. The Smith-Hughes Act of 1917 set up the first program of federal grants-in-aid to promote vocational education and enabled schools to provide training in agriculture, home economics, trades, and industries. In the National School Lunch and Milk programs, begun in 1946, federal grants and commodity donations are made for nonprofit lunches and milk served in public and private schools. In the Federal Impacted Areas Aid Program, begun in 1950, federal aid is authorized in "federally impacted" areas of the nation. These are areas where federal activities create a substantial increase in school enrollments or a reduction in taxable resources because of federally owned property.

In response to the Soviet Union's success in launching "Sputnik," the first satellite into space in 1957, Congress became concerned that the American educational system might not be keeping abreast of advances made in other nations, particularly in science and technology. In the National Defense Education Act (NDEA) of 1958, Congress provided financial aid to states and public school districts to improve instruction in science, mathematics, and foreign languages; to

TABLE 15–3   SOURCES OF FUNDS FOR EDUCATION IN THE UNITED STATES

	Percentage of Educational Expenditures by Source			
	1965	1975	1985	1990
Federal	9.4	10.0	8.6	8.5
State	29.5	33.8	38.8	38.7
Local	35.1	30.8	25.6	25.3
Private	26.0	25.3	27.0	27.5

Source: Statistical Abstract of the United States, 1992, p. 141.

strengthen guidance counseling and testing; and to improve statistical services—in addition to establishing a system of loans to undergraduates, fellowships to graduate students, and funds to colleges—all in an effort to improve the training of teachers in America.

Educational Block Grants   The Elementary and Secondary Education Act of 1965 marked the first large breakthrough in federal aid to education. Yet even ESEA was not a *general* aid-to-education program—one that would assist all public and private schools in school construction and teachers' salaries. The main thrust of ESEA is in "poverty-impacted" schools, instructional materials, and educational research and training. The Education Consolidation and Improvement Act of 1981 consolidated ESEA and related education programs into a single "block grant" allowing the states greater discretion in how federal educational funds can be spent.

Federal Aid and Educational Quality   It is difficult to demonstrate that federal aid programs improved the quality of education in America. Indeed, during the years in which federal aid was increasing, student achievement scores were *declining* (see Figure 15–1).

In its report "A Nation At Risk," the National Commission on Excellence in Education reaffirmed that "state and local government officials, including school board members and governors, and legislators, have *the primary responsibility* for funding and governing the schools." Raising the educational achievement levels of America's youth depends less on the amount spent than on how it is spent.

Directions from Washington   Presidents and Congress are often tempted to direct state educational policies from Washington. To date, however, the goals set forth at national conferences have not been enacted into law, although Congress has considered proposals to make instruction in basic subjects and national testing a prerequisite to federal educational aid to the states.

Organizing and Financing Public Schools

The fifty state governments, by means of enabling legislation, establish local school districts and endow them with the authority to operate public schools. There are about 15,000 local school boards, and 85,000 board members, who are chosen usually, but not always, by popular election. State laws authorize these boards to levy and collect taxes, borrow money, engage in school construction, hire instructional personnel, and make certain determinations about local school policy. Yet, in every state, the authority of local school districts is severely limited by state legislation. State law determines the types and rates of taxes to be levied, the maximum debt that can be incurred, the number of days schools shall remain open, the number of years of compulsory school attendance, the minimum salaries to be paid to teachers, the types of schools to be operated by the local boards, the number of grades to be taught, the qualifications of teachers, and the general content of curricula. In addition, many states choose the textbooks, establish course outlines, recommend teaching methods, establish statewide examinations, fix minimum teacher–pupil ratios, and stipulate course content in great detail. In short, the responsibility for public education is firmly in the hands of state governments.

State responsibility for public education is no mere paper arrangement. States ensure local compliance with state educational policy through (1) bureaucratic oversight, involving state boards of education, state commissioners or superintendents of education, and state departments of education, and (2) financial control through state allocation of funds to local school districts.

State Boards of Education   Traditionally state control over education was vested in state boards of education. In most states these boards are appointed by the governor; in some states they are composed of state officials; and in eleven states (Alabama, Colorado, Hawaii, Kansas, Louisiana, Michigan, Nebraska, Nevada, New Mexico, Ohio, and Texas) they are directly elected by the voters. These boards generally have the formal power to decide everything from teacher certification to textbook selection. However, in practice these boards rely heavily on the recommendations of the state commissioner of education and the state department of education.

State Commissioners of Education   All states have chief education officers, variously entitled commissioner of education, state school superintendent, or superintendent of public instruction. In sixteen states this official is elected (Arizona, California, Florida, Georgia, Idaho, Indiana, Kentucky, Montana, North Carolina, North Dakota, Oklahoma, Oregon, South Carolina, Washington, Wisconsin, and Wyoming). In other states they are appointed by the governor or the state education board. The chief education officer may exercise the most important influence over education in the state, as public spokesperson for education, in testimony before the legislature, and as the head of the state department of education.

State Departments of Education   State educational bureaucracies have greatly expanded in size and power over the years. They disburse state funds to local schools, prepare statewide curricula, select textbooks and materials, determine teacher qualifications, establish and enforce school building codes, and supervise statewide testing. Their principal tool in enforcing their control over local schools is the allocation of state educational money.

State Financing   States ensure the implementation of state educational policies through state grants of money to local school districts. Every state provides grants in one form or another to local school districts to supplement locally derived school revenue. This places the superior taxing powers of the state in the service of public schools operated at the local level. In every state, an equalization formula in the distribution of state grants to local districts operates to help equalize educational opportunities in all parts of the state. Equalization formulas differ from state to state as do the amounts of state grants involved, but in every state, poorer school districts receive larger shares of state funds than wealthier districts. This enables the state to guarantee a minimum "foundation" program in education throughout the state. In addition, since state grants to local school districts are administered through state departments of education, state school officials are given an effective tool for implementing state policies, namely, withholding or threatening to withhold state funds from school districts that do not conform to state standards. The growth of state responsibility for school policy was accomplished largely by the use of money—state grants to local schools.

School District Consolidation   One of the most dramatic reorganization and centralization movements in American government in this century was the successful drive to reduce, through consolidation, the number of local school districts in the United States. In a thirty-year period (1950–1980), three out of every four school districts were eliminated through consolidation. Support for school district consolidation came from state school officials in every state. Opposition to consolidation was local in character.

EXPLAINING EDUCATIONAL POLICIES IN THE STATES

Public elementary and secondary schools enroll about 40 million students. Nationwide about $5200 per year is spent on the public education of each child.[12] Yet national averages can obscure as much as they reveal about the record of the states in public education. Fifty state school systems establish policy for the nation, and this decentralization results in variations from state to state in educational policy. Only by examining public policy in all fifty states can the full dimension of American education be understood.

Variation Among States   In 1992, for example, public school expenditures for each pupil ranged from $2993 in Utah to $9159 in New Jersey. (See Figure 15–2.) Why is it that some states spend more than twice as much on the education of each child as other states? Economic resources are an important determinant of a state's willingness and ability to provide educational services. Urbanization, education, and, especially, income, correlate significantly with variations among the states in per pupil expenditures for public education. The results are the same even if the southern states are excluded from analysis. Clearly, wealth is the principal determinant of the amount of money to be spent on the education of each child.

Variation Within States   A central issue in the struggle over public education is that of distributing the benefits and costs of education equitably. Most school revenues are derived from *local* property taxes. In every state except Hawaii, local school boards must raise money from property taxes to finance their schools. This means that communities that do *not* have much taxable property cannot finance their schools as well as communities that are blessed with great wealth. Frequently, wealthy communities can provide better education for their children at *lower* tax rates than poor communities can provide at *higher* tax rates, simply because of disparities in the value of taxable property from one community to the next.

Disparities in educational funding among school districts *within* states can be quite large. A Congressional Research Service study reported disparities in excess of two to one (e.g., $8000 versus $4000) in per pupil spending among school districts in eleven states in the late 1980s (New York, New Jersey, Ohio, Pennsylvania,

---

[12] *Statistical Abstract of the United States, 1992.*

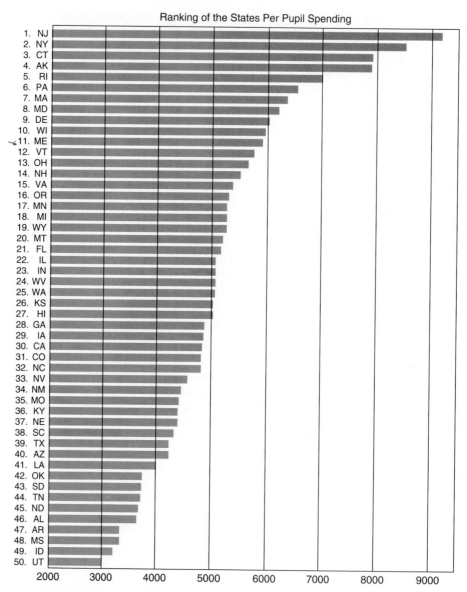

Ranking of the States Per Pupil Spending

FIGURE 15–2   **Rankings of the States Per Pupil Spending**
Source: Statistical Abstract of the United States, 1992.

Texas, Montana, Missouri, Michigan, Indiana, Illinois, and Georgia).[13] It is argued that these disparities deny equality of educational opportunity and pose constitutional questions under both the Fourteenth Amendment of the U.S. Constitution and similar guarantees of equality found in most state constitutions.

---

[13] *Congressional Quarterly Weekly Report,* March 27, 1993, p. 752.

The United States Supreme Court has declined to intervene in this struggle over educational financing. In 1973 the Court ruled that disparities in property values between jurisdictions relying on property taxes to finance education did *not* violate the equal protection clause of the Fourteenth Amendment.[14] But increasingly *state courts* have intervened in school financing to ensure equality across school districts based on their interpretation of *state* constitutional provisions. Following a California state court precedent in *Serrano* v. *Priest*,[15] state courts have pressured legislatures to come up with equalization plans in state grants that overcome disparities in fiscal revenues among school districts within a state. Since 1989, five state supreme courts have ruled that their states' educational finance systems violate their state constitutions' equal opportunity provision (Texas, Kentucky, Montana, New Jersey, and Tennessee).

GOVERNING LOCAL SCHOOLS

Responsibility for many basic decisions in public education lies with the fifteen thousand separate school districts in America. In theory, these school districts are under local control. The people of the local school district are supposed to exercise that control through an elected *school board* and an elected or appointed *superintendent* who acts as the chief executive of the community schools. There is some variation to that pattern—in approximately a quarter of the nation's school districts, the boards are appointed rather than elected, usually by city councils, county commissions, mayors, or even judges. In theory, school boards exercise control over curriculum (that is, what should be taught in the schools), buildings and facilities, personnel (including both administrators and teachers), and perhaps most important of all, financing. In practice, however, as we have already seen, the concept of local control over education is heavily circumscribed by both state and federal laws.

Who Governs Our Schools?   American schools face a dilemma in determining who should govern.[16] Aside from the interference of federal and state administrative agencies, there is the recurring problem of "democracy" versus "professionalism." Is a democratically elected board, responsible to the citizens, an appropriate model of governance for the schools? Or should technical and policy issues be determined by professional educators who possess the necessary technical competence? Or should we continue to attempt to combine these two conflicting notions of governance?

Democratic theory assumes that schools are public institutions that should be governed by the local citizenry through their elected representatives. This was the original concept in American public education developed in the nineteenth century. However, as school issues became more complex, the knowledge of citizen school boards seemed insufficient to cope with the many problems confronting the

---

[14] *Rodriquez* v. *San Antonio Independent School District,* 411 U.S. 1 (1973).

[15] *Serrano* v. *Priest,* 5 Cal. 584 (1971).

[16] For a comprehensive study of local school politics see Harmon Zeigler and M. Kent Jennings, *Governing American Schools: Political Interaction in Local School Districts* (Boston: Duxbury Press, 1974).

schools—teaching innovations, curricular changes, multi–million-dollar building programs, special educational programs, and so forth. In the twentieth century, school superintendents and their administrative assistants came to exercise more and more control over day-to-day operations of the schools. Theoretically, superintendents only implement the policies of the board, but in practice they have assumed much of the policy making in local school districts. Superintendents keep in touch with the university schools of education; devote full time to their job; receive direct advice from attorneys, architects, accountants, and educational consultants; and generally set the agenda for school board meetings.

Professionalism Versus Democracy   The resulting "professionalism" in education tangles directly with the "democratic" notion of control of schools. There are few meetings of local school boards that do not involve at least some tug-of-war between board members and the superintendent. (It is interesting to note that in European countries education has long been under the control of professionals, with little or no direct citizen participation in school governance.) Professional educators are frequently disdainful of the laypeople who compose the school board: The professionals must patiently explain matters of curriculum, faculties, personnel, and finance to citizen board members who are untrained in the matters about which they must decide. Professional educators often support the idea that "politics" should be kept out of education; to them, this means that nonprofessionals, even elected school board members, should not interfere in educational decisions.

The School District Superintendents

The school district superintendents are usually professionally trained educators, either appointed by the local school board or separately elected on a nonpartisan ballot. The superintendent is responsible for the management of the public schools —hiring and supervising teachers and principals, planning and organizing the schools, preparing budgets and overseeing expenditures, and recommending policy to the board.

Professional Dominance?   Superintendents are expected to bring professional expertise to the schools. But if citizen boards were once easily intimidated by professionally trained superintendents, such is seldom the case today:

> The American school superintendent, long the benevolent ruler whose word was law, has become a harried, embattled figure of authority. . . . Browbeaten by once subservient boards of education, teachers' associations and parents, the superintendent can hardly be blamed if he feels he has lost control of his destiny.[17]

School superintendents stress their professional expertise and rely heavily on their educational credentials to give weight to their policy recommendations. One

---

[17] Harmon Zeigler, Ellen Kehoe, and Jane Reisman, *City Managers and School Superintendents* (New York: Praeger, 1985), p. 21.

study reports that 73 percent of school superintendents in large metropolitan areas hold doctoral degrees.[18] Those without doctorates have at least a master's degree. Most superintendents earned their graduate degree *after* they had been employed several years as teachers.

Responsibilities   School superintendents have three major responsibilities. First, the superintendents set the agenda for school board decisions. About 75 percent of agenda items are placed there by the superintendent. Second, the superintendent makes policy recommendations. Most agenda items will carry a recommendation. Third, the superintendent implements board decisions. In performing these responsibilities, superintendents, even more than city managers, provide strong leadership—advocating policy changes and selling programs to the community. Moreover, many superintendents, in contrast to city managers, involve themselves in school board elections, providing encouragement to candidates whom they respect.

Leadership   Training in educational administration stresses the authority of the superintendent. A typical textbook in the field proclaims:

> The board must rely for leadership on its chief administration officer, the superintendent. . . . the board may be regarded in much the same light as a board of directors of a business corporation and the superintendent as the president in immediate charge of operations. . . . Legislation must be guided by what administration knows about schools. . . . a superintendent may be expected to be in advance of the board's thinking. . . . It is perfectly correct for him to participate in policy making because of his special knowledge and preparation.[19]

Professional superintendents do not expect to be overruled by their boards. Many of them have a "trust me or fire me" attitude that often makes compromise difficult. Nonetheless, the average tenure of appointed school superintendents is fairly long, about eight years. This is slightly longer than the average tenure of city managers (seven years).

A dominant role for school superintendents in educational policy, a role claimed on the basis of professional expertise and educational credentials, tends to minimize citizen participation in education decision making. But this role may be increasingly challenged. As one school superintendent acknowledged:

> The job of superintendent has changed radically over the past twenty years. . . . Now I have to deal with teacher militancy, closing schools, firing teachers, being more accountable for costs, and working with more active parents and citizens.[20]

However, school board members and interested citizens generally believe that popular control of education is a vital component of democracy. Schools

---

[18] Ibid., p. 40.

[19] Calvin Greider, *Public School Administration* (New York: Ronald Press, 1961), p. 113; also cited by Zeigler et al., *City Managers*, p. 59.

[20] Zeigler et al., *City Managers*, p. 158.

should be "responsive" to community needs and desires. Frequently, citizen criticism has focused on the schools' failure to teach basic skills—reading, writing, and arithmetic. Another frequent source of citizen concern is the perceived retreat of the schools from traditional moral values. These issues have in turn raised the underlying question—who should govern our schools, professional educators or interested citizens?

SCHOOL BOARDS: RESPONSIBLE POLICY MAKERS?

Even if we accept the notion that schools should be governed by a democratically elected board, how can we know whether board members are accurately reflecting their constituents' desires and aspirations? Like most decision makers, the nation's 85,000 school board members are unrepresentative of their constituents in socio-economic background. Specifically, board members are more often male, white, middle-aged, better educated, more prestigiously employed, Republican, and Protestant and have lived in the county longer than their constituents.[21] They come disproportionately from "educational families"; three-fifths of all school board members have relatives in education, usually their spouse. Moreover, at least three-fifths of school board members report that they were first prompted to run for the school board by friends already on the board; this suggests a perpetuation of similar kinds of people on school boards. Most school board elections are nonpartisan. One-quarter of the nation's school boards are appointed, not elected; but even in elected boards at least one-quarter of the members originally came to the board as appointees to replace individuals who left the board with unexpired terms. Seldom are incumbents defeated for reelection; two-thirds of the board members who leave office do so voluntarily. The average tenure of board members is about five years, compared to over eight years for superintendents. School board members do not ordinarily aspire to, or gain, higher political office. All of this suggests "volunteerism" among board members and difficulty in holding members accountable through the threat of electoral defeat.

Responsiveness   However, it appears that in more politically competitive school districts, school board members have closer ties to their constituents, they listen more closely to citizen groups, and they are more likely to challenge the dominance of the superintendent. Board members are more "responsive" to citizen demands when elections are partisan and competitive and when there is a history of forced turnover. These conditions are more likely to be found in large cities with elected boards than in small towns or suburbs. In short, a "politicized" board is more responsive to citizen demands, while a "depoliticized" board is more easily dominated by the superintendent.

Yet the real dilemma remains unsolved: Can democratically elected, responsi-

---

[21] Zeigler and Jennings, *Governing American Schools,* p. 27. Based on a national sample of school board members. See also Trudy Haffron Bers, "Local Political Elites: Men and Women on Boards of Education," *Western Political Quarterly,* 31 (September 1978), 381–91.

ble school boards do a better job of educating America's youth than a professional educational bureaucracy? Political scientists Zeigler and Jennings conclude:

> In spite of the obvious perils, political decisions are—as long as we remain committed to democracy—logically superior to technical decisions.[22]

However, educationist C. A. Bowers writes:

> When a school's moral responsibility to the student is not sacrificed to political expediency, education can become a humanizing process . . . as long as the "conventional wisdom" legitimizes control of the schools through political strife . . . is it possible to define the purpose of education in terms that elevate and enhance the well-being of the individual and not in terms of the self-proclaimed need of contending interest groups?[23]

Black Representation   Black membership on the nation's large central city school district boards reflects fairly accurately the black population in central cities.[24] About 20 percent of these board members are black, and about 20 percent of the population of these cities is black. Black representation on school boards has been linked to a variety of school policies: increased employment of black teachers; fewer black students disciplined, suspended, or dropping out; fewer black students assigned to special education classes, and more black students in gifted programs.

Teachers' Unions   The struggle for power over the schools between interested citizens, school board members, and professional educators has now been joined by still another powerful force—the nation's teachers' unions. Most of the nation's 2 million teachers are organized into either the older, larger National Education Association (NEA) or the smaller American Federation of Teachers (AFT), an affiliate of the AFL–CIO. Since its origin, the AFT has espoused the right to organize, bargain collectively, and strike, in the fashion of other labor unions. The AFT is small in numbers, but its membership is concentrated in the nation's largest cities, where it exercises considerable power. Traditionally, the NEA was considered a "professional" organization of both teachers and administrators. However, today state and district chapters of the NEA are organized as labor unions, demanding collective bargaining rights for their members and threatening to strike to achieve them. Both AFT and NEA chapters have shut down schools to force concessions by superintendents, board members, and taxpayers—not only in salaries and benefits, but also in pupil–teacher ratios, classroom conditions, school discipline, and other educational matters. As the teachers' unions grow stronger, the traditional question of whether citizens or professional administrators should run the schools will be made more complex: What role should teachers' unions have in determining educational policy?

---

[22] Zeigler and Jennings, *Governing American Schools*, p. 253.

[23] C.A. Bowers, *Education and Social Policy: Local Control of Education* (New York: Random House, 1970), pp. 4–5.

[24] Kenneth J. Meier and Robert E. England, "Black Representation and Educational Policy," *American Political Science Review*, 78 (June 1984), 393–403.

THE POLITICS OF HIGHER EDUCATION

States have been involved in public higher education since the colonial era. State governments in the Northeast frequently made contributions to support private colleges in their states. The first university to be chartered by a state legislature was the University of Georgia in 1794. Before the Civil War, northeastern states relied exclusively on private colleges, and the southern states assumed the leadership in public higher education. The early curricula at southern state universities, however, resembled the rigid classical studies of the early private colleges—with heavy emphasis on Greek and Latin, history, philosophy, and literature.

Early Federal Support   It was not until the Morrill Land Grant Act of 1862 that public higher education began to make major strides in the American states. Interestingly, the eastern states were slow to respond to the opportunity afforded by the Morrill Act to develop public universities; eastern states continued to rely primarily on their private colleges and universities. The southern states were economically depressed in the post–Civil War period, and leadership in public higher education passed to the midwestern states. The philosophy of the Morrill Act emphasized agricultural and mechanical studies, rather than the classical curricula of eastern colleges, and the movement for "A and M" education spread rapidly in the agricultural states. The early groups of midwestern state universities were closely tied to agricultural education, including agricultural extension services. State universities also took over the responsibility for the training of public school teachers in colleges of education. The state universities introduced a broad range of modern subjects in the university curricula—business administration, agriculture, home economics, education, engineering. It was not until the 1960s that the eastern states began to develop public higher education (notably the State University of New York multicampus system).

Public Higher Education   Today, public higher education enrolls three-quarters of the nation's college and university students. Perhaps more importantly, the nation's leading state universities can challenge the best private institutions in academic excellence. The University of California at Berkeley and the University of Michigan are deservedly ranked with Harvard, Yale, Princeton, Stanford, and Chicago.

Higher education in America is mass education. No other nation sends so large a proportion of its young people to college. Nearly 14 million Americans are enrolled in colleges and universities. Over half of all high school graduates enroll in college. (See Table 15–4.)

Economic Value of Education   An education may be its own reward, enhancing one's life regardless of economic circumstances. But there is also ample evidence that education improves one's earning potential. (See Figure 15–3.) At each level of advanced education, earnings are significantly enhanced.

Community Colleges   In most states, community colleges are separate from state colleges and universities; the community colleges are really part of local gov-

TABLE 15–4   HIGHER EDUCATION IN AMERICA

	1970	1980	1990
Institutions			
Total	2,556	3,231	3,535
Four-year colleges and universities	1,665	1,957	2,127
Two-year colleges	891	1,274	1,408
Faculty (thousands)	474	686	824
Enrollment (thousands)			
Total	8,581	12,097	13,457
Four-year colleges and universities	6,290	7,571	8,374
Two-year colleges	1,630	4,526	5,083
Public	5,800	9,457	10,515
Private	2,120	2,640	2,942
Graduate	1,031	1,343	1,518
Undergraduate	7,376	10,495	11,666

Source: Statistical Abstract of the United States, 1992, p. 165.

ernment. They receive revenue from local property taxes as well as grants from the state and federal government. They are usually governed by a local board, whose members are elected or appointed from the communities served by the college.

Community colleges are the fastest growing sector of American higher education. (See Table 15–4.) These colleges are designed to reflect the local area's requirements for higher education, and they usually offer both a general undergraduate curriculum that fulfills the first two years of a baccalaureate degree, and vocational and technical programs that fulfill community needs for skilled workers. Moreover, community colleges usually offer special programs and courses in adult higher education often in association with community groups. It is estimated that about 45 percent of community college students are enrolled in baccalaureate programs.[25]

University Governance   The organization and governance of public higher education varies a great deal from state to state. Most states have established boards of trustees (or "regents") with authority to govern the state universities. One of the purposes of the boards is to insulate higher education from the vicissitudes of politics. Prominent citizens who are appointed to these boards are expected to champion higher education with the public and the legislature, as well as set overall policy guidelines for colleges and universities. In the past, there were separate boards for each institution and separate consideration by the governor's office and the legislature of each institution's budgetary request. However, the resulting competition caused state after state to create unified "university system" boards to coordinate higher education. These university system boards consolidate the

---

[25] Trudy Haffron Bers, "Politics Programs and Local Governments: The Case of Community Colleges," *Journal of Politics*, 40 (February 1980), 150–64.

THE ECONOMIC VALUE OF EDUCATION
Average Monthly Earnings, 1990

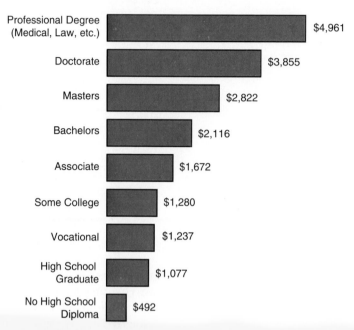

Professional Degree (Medical, Law, etc.)	$4,961
Doctorate	$3,855
Masters	$2,822
Bachelors	$2,116
Associate	$1,672
Some College	$1,280
Vocational	$1,237
High School Graduate	$1,077
No High School Diploma	$492

FIGURE 15-3　The Economic Value of Education
Source: Bureau of the Census, *What's It Worth?*, Washington, DC: Government Printing Office, 1993.

budget requests of each institution, determine systemwide priorities, and present a single budget for higher education to the governor and the legislature. The stronger and more independent the university system board, the less likely that university and college funding will be distributed in a pork-barrel fashion by legislators seeking to enhance their local constituencies.

The Presidents　The key figures in university politics are the presidents. They are the chief spokespersons for higher education, and they must convince the public, the regents, the governor, and the legislature of the value of state universities. The presidents' crucial role is one of maintaining support for higher education in the state; they frequently delegate administrative responsibilities for the internal operation of the university to the vice-presidents and deans. Support for higher education among the public and its representatives can be affected by a broad spectrum of university activities, some of which are not directly related to the pursuit of knowledge. A winning football team can stimulate legislative enthusiasm and win appropriations for a new classroom building. University service-oriented research —developing new crops or feeds, assessing the state's mineral resources, advising state and local government agencies on administrative problems, analyzing the state economy, advising local school authorities, and so forth—may help to convince the public of the practical benefits of knowledge. University faculty may be interested in advanced research and the education of future Ph.D.s, but legislators and their constituents are more interested in the quality and effectiveness of undergraduate teaching.

The Faculty   The faculty traditionally identified themselves as professionals with strong attachments to their institutions. The historic pattern of college and university government included faculty participation in policy making—not only in determining academic requirements but also in budgeting, the hiring and firing of personnel, building programs, and so forth. However, government by faculty committee has proven cumbersome, unwieldy, and time-consuming in an era of large-scale enrollments, multi–million-dollar budgets, and increases in the size and complexity of academic administration. Increasingly, concepts of public "accountability," academic "management," cost control, centralized budgeting and purchasing have transferred power in colleges and universities from faculty to professional academic administrators.

The Unions   The traditional organization for faculty was the American Association of University Professors (AAUP); historically, this group confined itself to publishing data on faculty salaries and officially "censoring" colleges or universities that violated longstanding notions of academic freedom or tenure. (*Tenure* ensures that faculty members who have demonstrated their competence by service in a college or university position for three to seven years cannot thereafter be dismissed except for "cause"—a serious infraction of established rules or dereliction of duty, provable in an open hearing.) In recent years, some faculty have become convinced that traditional patterns of *individual* bargaining over salaries, teaching load, and working conditions in colleges and universities should be replaced by *collective* bargaining in the style of unionized labor. The American Federation of Teachers of the AFL–CIO, as well as the National Education Association and the AAUP have sought to represent faculty in collective bargaining. Many states now authorize collective bargaining with the faculty of public colleges and universities if the faculty votes for such bargaining. Faculty collective bargaining is complicated by the fact that faculty continue to play some role in academic government—choosing deans and department heads, sitting on salary committees, and so forth.

Financing   The costs of public higher education are borne largely by taxpayers. Rarely does tuition at state colleges and universities pay for more than one-quarter of the costs of providing an education. Public higher education spending per capita ranges from approximately $175 to $500 per year in the states (see Figure 15–4).

Federal Role   Federal aid to colleges and universities comes in a variety of forms. Historically, the Morrill Act of 1862 provided the groundwork for federal assistance in higher education. In 1890 Congress initiated several federal grants to support the operations of the land-grant colleges, and this aid, although very modest, continues to the present. Federal support for scientific research has also had an important impact on higher education. In 1950 Congress established the National Science Foundation (NSF) to promote scientific research and education through direct grants to university faculty and departments. (In 1965 Congress established a

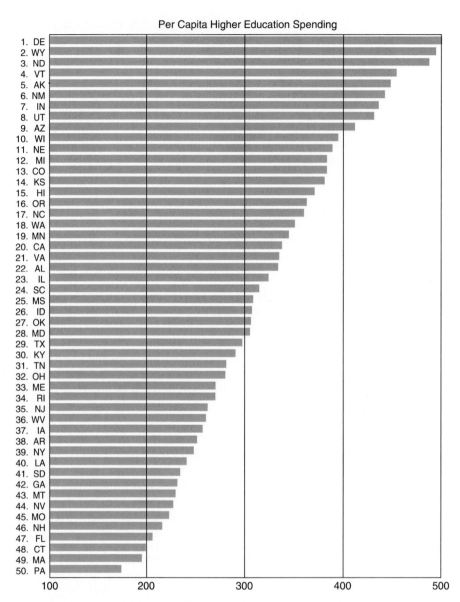

FIGURE 15–4   Per Capita Higher Education Spending

National Endowment for the Arts and Humanities, but these fields receive only a fraction of the amounts given to NSF.) In addition to NSF, many other federal agencies—the Department of Defense, the Department of Education, the U.S. Public Health Service, the Department of Health and Human Services, the Department of Housing and Urban Development, and so forth—grant research contracts to universities for specific projects. Thus, research has become a very big item in university life.

The federal government directly assists institutions of higher education through federal grants and loans for construction and improvement of both public and private higher educational facilities. It directly assists students through Basic Educational Opportunity Grants, commonly called "Pell Grants" for its sponsor Senator Claiborne Pell (D.–Rhode Island). The program offers college students in good standing a money grant each year that is based on the amount their families could reasonably be expected to contribute to their educational expenses. The Stafford guaranteed student loan program encourages private banks to make low-interest loans to students. The federal government pays the interest charges while the student is in school and guarantees repayment in the event the student defaults on the payment after graduation. The Perkins national direct student loan program allows students to borrow from the financial aid offices of their own universities. Again, no interest is charged while the student is in college; repayment is delayed until after the student leaves school. Finally, a national work-study program uses federal funds to allow colleges and universities to employ students part-time while they continue to go to school.

READING, WRITING, AND RELIGION

The First Amendment to the Constitution of the United States contains two important guarantees of religious freedom: (1) "Congress shall make no law respecting an establishment of religion . . . ," and (2) "Or prohibiting the free exercise thereof." The Due Process Clause of the Fourteenth Amendment made these guarantees of religious liberty applicable to the states and their subdivisions as well as to Congress.

"Free Exercise" and Private Religious Schools   Most of the debate over religion in the public schools centers around the *No Establishment Clause* of the First Amendment rather than the *Free Exercise Clause.* However, it was respect for the Free Exercise Clause that caused the Supreme Court in 1925 to declare unconstitutional an attempt on the part of a state to prohibit private religious schools and to force all children to attend public schools. In the words of the Supreme Court: "The fundamental theory of liberty upon which all governments in this Union repose excludes any general power of the state to standardize its children by forcing them to accept instruction from public teachers only. The child is not the mere creature of the state."[26] It is this decision that protects the entire structure of private religious schools in this nation.

The Meaning of "No Establishment"   A great deal of religious conflict in America has centered around the meaning of the *No Establishment Clause,* and the public schools have been the principal scene of this conflict. One interpretation of the clause holds that it does not prevent government from aiding religious schools or encouraging religious beliefs in the public schools, so long as it does not discriminate against any particular religion. Another interpretation of the No Establishment Clause is that it creates a "wall of separation" between church and state in

---

[26] *Pierce* v. *The Society of Sisters,* 268 U.S. 510 (1925).

America, which prevents government from directly aiding religious schools or encouraging religious beliefs in any way.

Support for Public Aid to Religious Schools   The Catholic Church in America enrolls over half of all private school students in the nation, and the Catholic Church has led the fight for an interpretation of the No Establishment Clause that would permit government to aid religious schools. As Catholic spokespeople see it, Catholic parents have a right to send their children to Catholic schools; and since they are taxpayers, they also expect that some tax monies should go to the aid of church schools. To do otherwise, they argue, would discriminate against parents who choose a religious education for their children. Those who favor government aid to religious schools frequently refer to the language found in several cases decided by the Supreme Court, which appears to support the idea that government can *in a limited fashion* support the activities of church-related schools. In *Cochran* v. *Board of Education* (1930), the Court upheld a state law providing free textbooks for children attending both public and parochial schools on the grounds that this aid benefited the *children* rather than the Catholic Church and hence did not constitute an "establishment" of religion within the meaning of the First Amendment.[27] In *Everson* v. *Board of Education* (1947), the Supreme Court upheld the provision of school bus service to parochial school children at public expense on the grounds that the "wall of separation between church and state" does not prohibit the state from adopting a general program which helps *all* children, regardless of religion, to proceed safely to and from schools.[28] These cases suggest that the Supreme Court is willing to permit some forms of aid to parochial school *children* that indirectly aids religion, so long as this is not directly used for the teaching of religion.

Proponents of public aid for church schools argue that these schools render a valuable public service by instructing millions of children who would have to be instructed by the state, at additional expense, if church schools were not available. Moreover, there are many precedents for public support of religious institutions: Church property has always been exempt from taxation; church contributions are deductible from federal income taxes; federal funds have been appropriated for the construction of religiously operated hospitals; chaplains are provided in the armed forces as well as in the Congress of the United States; veterans' programs permit veterans to use their educational subsidies to finance college educations in Catholic universities; federal grants and loans for college construction are available to Catholic as well as to public colleges, and so on.

Opposition to Public Aid to Religious Schools   Opponents of aid to church schools argue that free public schools are available to the parents of all children regardless of religious denomination. If religious parents are not content with the type of school that the state provides, they should expect to pay for the establishment and operation of special schools. The state is under no obligation to finance the religious preferences in education of religious groups. In fact, they contend that

---

[27] *Cochran* v. *Board of Education*, 281 U.S. 370 (1930).

[28] *Everson* v. *Board of Education*, 330 U.S. 1 (1947).

it is unfair to compel taxpayers to support religion directly or indirectly; furthermore, the diversion of any substantial amount of public education funds to church schools would weaken the public school system.

The Supreme Court has also voiced the opinion that the No Establishment Clause of the First Amendment should constitute a "wall of separation" between church and state. In the words of the Court:

> Neither a state nor the federal government can set up a church. Neither can pass laws which aid one religion, aid all religions, or prefer one religion over another. Neither can force nor influence a person to go to or to remain away from church against his will, or force him to profess a belief or disbelief in any religion. No person can be punished for entertaining or professing religious beliefs or disbeliefs, for church attendance or nonattendance. No tax in any amount, large or small, can be levied to support any religious activities or institutions, whatever they may be called, or whatever form they may adopt to teach or practice religion. Neither a state nor the federal government can openly or secretly, participate in the affairs of any religious organizations or groups, and vice versa.[29]

The Supreme Court held in 1971 that it was unconstitutional for a state to pay the costs of teachers' salaries or instructional materials in parochial schools.[30] The Court acknowledged that it had previously approved the provision of state textbooks and bus transportation directly to parochial school children. Nevertheless, the Court held that state payments to parochial schools involved "excessive entanglement between government and religion" and violated both the establishment and free exercise clauses of the First Amendment. State payments to religious schools, the Court said, would require excessive government controls and surveillance to ensure that funds were used only for secular instruction. Moreover, the Court expressed the fear that state aid to parochial schools would create "political divisions along religious lines . . . one of the principal evils against which the First Amendment was intended to protect." However, in *Roemer* v. *Maryland* (1976) the Supreme Court upheld government grants of money to church-related *colleges and universities:* "Religious institutions need not be quarantined from public benefits which are neutrally available to all."[31]

Prayer in the Schools   Religious conflict in public schools also centers around the question of prayer and Bible-reading ceremonies conducted by public schools. The practice of opening the school day with prayer and Bible-reading ceremonies was once widespread in American public schools. Usually the prayer was a Protestant rendition of the Lord's Prayer, and Bible reading was from the King James version. To avoid the denominational aspects of these ceremonies, the New York State Board of Regents substituted a nondenominational prayer, which it required to be said aloud in each class in the presence of a teacher at the beginning of each school day:

> Almighty God, we acknowledge our dependence upon Thee, and we beg Thy blessings upon us, our parents, our teachers, and our country.

---

[29] Hugo Black, majority opinion in *Everson* v. *Board of Education,* 330 U.S. 1 (1947).

[30] *Lemon* v. *Kurtzman,* 403 U.S. 602 (1972).

[31] *Roemer* v. *Maryland,* 415 U.S. 382 (1976).

New York argued that this prayer ceremony did not violate the No Establishment Clause, because the prayer was denominationally neutral and because student participation in the prayer was voluntary. However, in *Engle* v. *Vitale* (1962), the Supreme Court stated that "the constitutional prohibition against laws respecting an establishment of a religion must at least mean in this country it is no part of the business of government to compose official prayers for any group of the American people to recite as part of a religious program carried on by government."[32] The Court pointed out making prayer voluntary did not free it from the prohibitions of the No Establishment Clause; that clause prevented the *establishment* of a religious ceremony by a government agency, regardless of whether the ceremony was voluntary or not:

> Neither the fact that the prayer may be denominationally neutral, nor the fact that its observance on the part of the students is voluntary can serve to free it from the limitations of the establishment clause, as it might from the free exercise clause, of the First Amendment, both of which are operative against the states by virtue of the 14th Amendment. . . . The establishment clause, unlike the free exercise clause, does not depend on any showing of direct governmental compulsion and is violated by the enactment of laws which establish an official religion whether those laws operate directly to coerce nonobserving individuals or not.[33]

One year later, in the case of *Abbington Township* v. *Schempp,* the Court considered the constitutionality of Bible-reading ceremonies in the public schools.[34] Here again, even though the children were not required to participate, the Court found that Bible reading as an opening exercise in the schools was a religious ceremony. The Court went to some trouble in its opinion to point out that they were not "throwing the Bible out of the school," for they specifically stated that the study of the Bible or of religion, when presented objectively as part of a secular program of education, did not violate the First Amendment, but religious *ceremonies* involving Bible reading or prayer, established by a state or school, did so.

State efforts to encourage "voluntary prayer" in public schools have also been struck down by the Supreme Court as unconstitutional. When the state of Alabama authorized a period of silence for "meditation or voluntary prayer" in public schools, the Court ruled that this was an "establishment of religion." The Court said the law had no secular purpose, that it conveyed "a message of state endorsement and promotion of prayer," and that its real intent was to encourage prayer in public schools.[35] In a stinging dissenting opinion, Chief Justice Warren Burger noted that the Supreme Court itself opened its session with a prayer, that both houses of Congress opened every session with prayers led by official chaplains paid by the government. "To suggest that a moment of silence statute that includes the word *prayer* unconstitutionally endorses religion, manifests not neutrality but hostility toward religion."

---

[32] *Engle* v. *Vitale,* 370 U.S. 421 (1962).

[33] Ibid.

[34] *Abbington Township* v. *Schempp,* 374 U.S. 203 (1963).

[35] *Wallace* v. *Jaffree,* 105 S. Ct. 2479 (1986).

16

THE POLITICS OF PLANNING, HOUSING, AND TRANSPORTATION

▲

CONTROLLING THE USE OF LAND

The most significant and far-reaching powers of local governments in the United States center on their control of land use. Land is a scarce and valuable resource. Historically, its use was determined by private owners responding principally to free market economic forces—putting their land to its most productive and most remunerative use. But over time, land use decisions have been largely removed from private property owners and placed in the hands of local government agencies. Local governments respond to both economic and political forces in determining how land within their communities is to be used.

Early City Planning   City planning began in antiquity with the emergence of the first cities. Governing authorities have long determined the location of streets, squares, temples, walls, and fortresses. Most early American cities were planned as

465

a gridiron of streets and squares in the fashion of William Penn's plan for Philadelphia in 1682. A notable exception to the gridiron pattern was Pierre L'Enfant's 1791 plan for Washington, DC, with radial streets slashing through the gridiron.[1] Until the early twentieth century, city planning was focused almost exclusively on the layout of streets and the location of public buildings and parks. A city's "master plan" was a map showing the location of present and future streets and public facilities. There was relatively little regulation of the use of private property.

Comprehensive Planning   But the reform movement of the early twentieth century (see "Reformers and Do-Gooders" in Chapter 10) brought with it a much broader definition of planning. "Comprehensive planning" involves not only the determination of the location of *public* facilities but also the control of *private* land uses.

Comprehensive planning involves the identification of community goals, the development of plans to implement these goals, and the use of governmental tools to influence and shape private and public decision making to serve these goals. Community goals are identified not only in land use and physical development policies, but also in those for population growth, health and safety, housing and welfare, education, transportation, economic development, culture, life style and beautification, historic preservation, and environmental protection. According to the American Institute of Planners (AIP), planning is "a comprehensive, coordinated and continuing process, the purpose of which is to help public and private decision makers arrive at decisions which promote the common good of society."[2] Obviously this extended definition of planning plunges the planner deep into the political life of the community.

Constitutional Concerns   How far can government go in regulating the use of property without depriving individuals of their property rights? The U.S. Constitution (Fifth Amendment) states clearly: "nor shall private property be taken for public use without just compensation." Taking land for highways, streets, and public buildings, even when the owners do not wish to sell, is known as *eminent domain*. A city or state must go to court and show that the land is needed for a legitimate public purpose; the court will then establish a fair price (*just compensation*) based on testimony from the owner, the city or state, and impartial appraisers. Eminent domain is a constitutional protection to American citizens against arbitrary government seizure of their land.

But what if a government does not "take" ownership of the property, but instead restricts the owner's use of it through regulation? Zoning ordinances, subdivision regulations, environmental regulations, or building and housing codes may reduce the value of the property to the owner. Should the owner be compensated for loss of uses?

---

[1] See Anthony J. Catanese and James C. Snyder, *Urban Planning,* 2nd ed. (New York: McGraw Hill, 1988).

[2] American Institute of Planners, *AIP Planning Policies* (Washington DC: Author, 1977).

Courts have always recognized that governments can make laws to protect the health, safety, and general welfare of its citizens. Owners of property have never been entitled to any compensation for obeying laws or ordinances with a clear public purpose. But it was not clear that zoning restrictions were legitimate public purposes until 1926 when the U.S. Supreme Court upheld city zoning ordinances as "a proper exercise of police powers."[3] Cities are *not* required to compensate owners for lost value as a result of zoning regulations. Yet it was still argued that some planning and zoning provisions, especially those designed for beauty and aesthetics, had no relation to public health, safety, and welfare. They simply enacted somebody's taste over that of their neighbor. But in 1954 the U.S. Supreme Court upheld a very broad interpretation of the police power: "It is within the power of the legislature to determine that the community should be beautiful as well as healthy, spacious as well as clean, well-balanced as well as carefully patrolled."[4] So it is difficult to challenge the constitutionality of planning and zoning as a "taking" of private property without compensation. However, the U.S. Supreme Court has held that a regulation that denies a property owner all economically beneficial use of land (e.g., a state coastal zone management regulation preventing any construction on a beach lot) was a "taking" that required just compensation to the owner to be constitutional.[5]

PLANNERS IN POLITICS

State laws authorize and often mandate that cities develop comprehensive plans. Traditionally the comprehensive plan was prepared by semi-independent *planning commissions* composed of private citizens appointed by the mayor and approved by the city council. These commissions rely heavily on *professional planners* to prepare the comprehensive plan. Professional planners are mostly university graduates in city planning. They are organized into the American Institute of Planners (AIP), which publishes its own journal and grants professional credentials to planners. Over time however, independent, citizen planning commissions are gradually being replaced with planning departments within city government that are directly responsible to the mayor and council.

Developing Support   Citizen planning commissions are still retained in many communities to facilitate citizen input into the planning process and to develop political support for the comprehensive plan. Planning commissions often hold public hearings on the comprehensive plans and proposed changes to it.

The decisions of professional planners and planning commissions are officially considered advisory. That is, the comprehensive plan must be enacted by the city council to become law. The recommendations of the planning commission can be overturned by the city council. But the advice of a prudent planning staff, with

---

[3] *Village of Euclid, Ohio* v. *Amber Realty Company,* 272 U.S. 365 (1926).

[4] *Berman* v. *Parker,* 348 U.S. 26 (1954).

[5] *Lucas* v. *South Carolina Coastal Council,* 112 Sup.Ct. 2886 (1992).

the support of influential private citizens on the planning commission, cannot be easily ignored.

Policy-Making Roles   Planners, like reformers generally, claim to represent the welfare of the community as a whole. They are usually hostile to what they perceive to be narrow, self-serving interests in the community, especially business people and real estate developers

Planners can play a variety of roles in the policy-making process.[6] One role is that of the pure "technician," who develops plans strictly on the basis of professional planning theory, avoiding political entanglements and remaining aloof from struggles over the acceptance or implementation of plans. The technician-planner emphasizes neutral expertise. Another role is that of the "broker," who acts as confidential advisor to policy makers and considers the political "marketability" of the plans and recommendations. A third role is the "mobilizer," who actively seeks community support for the plans and enlists the backing of civic, business, professional, and service clubs. Yet another role is that of "advocate." Advocacy planning assumes that the poor and minority groups are largely unrepresented in community decision making, and therefore it is the responsibility of planners to represent them in the comprehensive planning process.

The Influence of Planners   While the formal role of planners is advisory, they can have a substantial influence on community policy. In smaller cities, planners may be preoccupied with the day-to-day administration of the zoning and subdivision control ordinances. They may have insufficient time or staff to engage in genuine long-range comprehensive planning. In large cities, the planning staff may be the only agency that has a comprehensive view of community development. Although they may not have the power to "decide" about public policy, they can "initiate" policy discussions through their plans, proposals, and recommendations. The planners can project the image of the city of the future and thereby establish the agenda of community decision making. Their plans can initiate public discussion over the goals and values to be implemented in the community. The comprehensive plan can be a tool for mobilizing public interest in community development.

Limits on Planning   There are, of course, some limitations on the influence of planners. First of all, many important decisions in community development are made by private enterprise rather than by government. Real estate interests, developers, builders, and property owners make many of the key decisions that shape the development of the community. Their actions are often determined by the economics of the marketplace. Property owners will try to find a way to make the most profitable use of their land, the ideas of the planners notwithstanding. Second, the planners can only advise policy makers; they are just one voice among many attempting to influence public decisions about land use and physical development. A somewhat cynical view of planning was once expressed as follows: "In older cities it ratifies what the market did before planning and land use control were estab-

---

[6] See John M. Levy, *Contemporary Urban Planning* (Englewood Cliffs, NJ: Prentice Hall, 1988).

lished. In suburban and newly developing areas it sanctions what the market will do anyway."[7]

Opposition to Planning   The free market usually does a better job of allocating resources in a society than does government. Opponents of government planning and land use control argue that the decisions of thousands of individual property owners result in a better allocation of land than the decisions of government bureaucrats. The decentralization of marketplace decisions allows more rapid adjustment to change and satisfies the preferences of more people than centralized bureaucratic decision making. Marketplace prices signal the most appropriate uses of land, just as they do the most appropriate uses of other resources.

Opponents also argue that requiring government permits for land uses—for new commercial, industrial, or residential developments and for new homes, buildings, or other structures—adds to the time and costs of development and the size of government bureaucracy. By adding to the costs of housing, planning places owning homes beyond the reach of many middle-class families. By adding to the costs of industry, or banning new industrial development altogether, planning limits the number of jobs created in a community. By empowering local officials to describe how land will be used, individual citizens are deprived of an important individual freedom.

PLANNING: INSTRUMENTS OF CONTROL

What formal powers do local governments have to control land use? Cities that choose to implement comprehensive planning and control land use have a variety of legal tools available to them: (1) zoning ordinances, (2) subdivision regulations, (3) an official map, (4) building and construction codes, (5) a capital improvement program, including locational decisions on public facilities and buildings, (6) environmental regulations, and (7) moratoriums on new construction. Planning agencies often have an important role in all these activities, even though the principal responsibility for these tools of implementation rests with the mayor and council.

Zoning   Planning agencies usually prepare the *zoning ordinance* for the approval of the city council. The zoning ordinance divides the community into districts for the purpose of regulating the use and development of land and buildings. Zoning originated as an attempt to separate residential areas from commercial and industrial activity, thereby protecting residential property values. The zoning ordinance divides the community into residential, commercial, and industrial zones, and perhaps subdivisions within each zone, such as "light industrial" and "heavy industrial," or "single-family residential" and "multifamily residential." Owners of land in each zone must use their land in conformity with the zoning ordinance; however, exceptions are made for people who have used the land in a certain way before the adoption of the zoning ordinance. An ordinance cannot prevent a person

[7] William Wheaton, "Metropolitan Allocation Planning," *Journal of American Institute of Planners,* 33 (March 1967), 103. Also cited by John C. Bollens and Henry J. Schmandt, *The Metropolic,* 4th ed. (New York: Harper & Row, 1982).

from using the land as one has done in the past; thus, zoning laws can only influence land use if they are passed prior to the development of a community. Many new and rapidly expanding communities pass zoning ordinances too late—after commercial and industrial establishments are strung out along highways, ideal industrial land is covered with houses, good park and recreational land has been sold for other purposes, and so on.

Since the planning agency prepares the zoning ordinances as well as the comprehensive plan, the ordinance is expected to conform with the plan. In many communities, the role of the planning agency is strengthened by the requirement that a city council *must* submit all proposed changes in the zoning ordinance to the planning agency for its recommendation before any council action.

Changes in the zoning ordinance usually originate at the request of property owners. They may wish to change the zoning classification of their property to enhance its value—for example, to change it from single-family to multifamily residential, or from residential to commercial. Usually the planning agency will hold a public hearing on a proposed change before sending its findings and recommendation to the city council. The city council may also hold a public hearing before deciding on the change.

City councils can and sometimes do ignore the recommendations of their planning agencies when strong pressures are exerted by neighborhood groups or environmentalists opposed to rezoning, or by developers and property owners supporting it. However, the recommendations of planning agencies prevail in the vast majority of rezoning cases, indicating the power of the planners in community affairs.[8]

A *zoning variance* is a request for a limited and specific variation from the strict standards in a zoning ordinance as applied to a particular piece of property. Some cities create special boards to hear requests for zoning variances, and other cities allow their planning agency to grant zoning variances. The zoning variance may be the most abused of all zoning procedures. It is not intended to encourage "spot" zoning, grant special privileges, or circumvent the interest of the zoning ordinance, but this is frequently what happens.

In addition to specifying land *use,* the zoning ordinance includes many *restrictions* designed to protect the health, safety, recreation, and convenience of residents, as well as the aesthetic beauty of the city. Examples of these restrictions include minimum lot sizes (one-quarter, one-half, or even one acre) for single-family residences; minimum lot widths (25, 50, or 75 feet of street frontage); minimum densities of units for apartment buildings (10, 20, 30 units per acre); uniform set-back requirements (distance from the street to the building); height and bulk requirements for buildings; minimum distances between houses and buildings; off-street parking requirements; and fire and explosive material, noise, smoke, odor, and outdoor storage regulations. Some cities specify "historic preservation districts" which require the preservation of structures and building styles; the Vieux Carre (French Quarter) in New Orleans is a leading example.

---

[8] See Arnold Fleischmann and Carol A. Pierannunzi, "Citizens, Development Interests, and Local Land-Use Regulation," *Journal of Politics,* 52 (August 1990), 838–53.

Subdivision Control   Another means of implementing the master plan is *subdivision regulations,* which govern the way in which land is divided into smaller lots and made ready for improvements. Subdivision regulations, together with the zoning ordinance, may specify the minimum size of lots, the standards to be followed by real estate developers in laying out new streets, and the improvements developers must provide, such as sewers, water mains, parks, playgrounds, and sidewalks. Often planning agencies are given direct responsibility for the enforcement of subdivision regulations. Builders and developers must submit their proposed "plats" for subdividing land and for improvements to the planning commission for approval before deeds can be recorded.

Official Map   The planning agency also prepares the *official map* of the city for enactment by the council. The official map shows proposed, as well as existing, streets, water mains, public utilities, and the like. Presumably, no one is permitted to build any structures on land that appears as a street or other public facility on the official map. Many cities require the council to submit to the planning agency for their recommendation any proposed action that affects the plan of streets or the subdivision plan and any proposed acquisition or sale of city real estate.

Building and Construction Codes   Most cities have building codes designed to ensure public health and safety. These codes are lengthy documents specifying everything from the thickness of building beams and the strength of trusses, to the type of furnaces, electric wiring, ventilation, fireproofing, and even earthquake resistance that must be incorporated into buildings. No construction may be undertaken without first obtaining a building permit which must be prominently displayed at the building site. Building inspectors are then dispatched periodically to the site to see if work is progressing in conformance with the building codes. The planning agency does not usually administer the code (that is normally the function of a building or housing department), but the planners are usually consulted about proposed changes in the building code.

Housing codes are designed to bring existing structures up to minimum standards. They set forth minimum requirements for fire safety, ventilation, plumbing, sanitation, and building condition. As with building codes, enforcement is the responsibility of city government, but the planning commission is normally consulted about changes in the code.

Capital Improvements   Comprehensive planning can also be implemented through a *capital improvement program.* This program is simply the planned schedule of public projects by the city—new public buildings, parks, streets, and so on. Many larger cities instruct their planning agencies to prepare a long-range capital improvement program for a five- or ten-year period. Of course, the council may choose to ignore the planning commission's long-range capital improvement program in its decisions about capital expenditures, but at least the planning commission will have expressed its opinions about major capital investments.

Environmental Regulations   Planners have increasingly turned to environmental laws and regulations to assert control over community development. State laws or local ordinances may designate "areas of critical concern" in an effort to halt development. Designation of such areas is usually very subjective; they may be swamps, forests, waterfront, or wildlife habitats, or even historic, scenic, or archeological sites. "Critical" may also refer to flood plains or steep hillsides or any other land on which planners wish to halt construction.

States and cities are increasingly requiring developers to prepare "environmental impact statements"—assessments of the environmental consequences of proposed construction or land-use change. These statements are usually prepared by professional consultants at added cost to builders and developers.

Moratoriums   Moratoriums are temporary freezes on building or development pending the completion of a comprehensive plan or the construction of necessary public facilities—sewers, roads, and so on—to support the new development. Moratoriums are perhaps the most drastic action available to city and county governments to halt growth.

PLANNING PRACTICES

The formal instruments of land use control are often considered too inflexible for optimum planning. Local governments and private property owners frequently seek ways to avoid the rigidities of zoning and subdivision ordinances and construction codes. These regulations, when applied strictly and uniformly, often limit the freedom of architects and developers, produce a sterile environment through separation of land uses, and lead to excessive court litigation. So planners have increasingly turned to a variety of practices intended to minimize some of the worst consequences of land use regulation.

PUDs   One technique that has grown in popularity in recent years is planned urban development (PUD). PUD ordinances vary but typically they allow developers with a minimum number of acres (e.g., ten, twenty, or more) to have the option of abiding by conventional zoning, subdivision, and building codes, or alternatively submitting an overall site plan for the approval of the planning agency and council. PUD designs usually incorporate mixed residential and commercial uses, perhaps with single-family homes and apartments or condominiums, retail shops, hotels and restaurants, parks and open spaces, all included. Planners and councils often exercise considerable discretion in approving or rejecting or forcing modifications in PUDs, depending on their own preferences.

Exactions and Impact Fees   Many communities require developers to pay substantial fees or give over land to local government in exchange for approval of their land use plans. This practice, known as "exaction," is often defended as a charge to pay the local government's costs in connection with the new development, for example, additional roads or sewers needed or additional schools or parks required for new residents. A closely related practice is that of charging developers "impact fees" that are supposed to compensate the community for increased costs imposed by the development *beyond* the added tax revenues that the development will generate when completed. But it is virtually impossible to accurately calculate impact costs, if indeed a development actually does impose more costs on a community than the revenues it produces. So impact fees become just another cost to developers that are passed on to homebuyers and (through commercial tenants) to consumers.

Developer Agreements   Often conflict between local governments and developers are settled through developer agreements. Some states (e.g., California) specifically authorize municipalities to enter into such agreements, bypassing zoning, subdivision, and construction ordinances. In other states, often lawsuits, or the threat of lawsuits, by developers force municipalities into such agreements. The municipality benefits by being able to specify the details of a project. The developer benefits by obtaining a legally binding contract that cannot be changed later by the municipality as the project proceeds to completion.

NO-GROWTH POLITICS

"No-growth" movements in communities are citizen efforts to halt or restrict population growth and economic development. Generally, no-growthers prefer the phrase "growth management" to "no-growth," implying that not all growth or development is undesirable. However, these movements generally support restrictive zoning laws, costly requirements placed on builders and developers, strong environmental regulations, high "impact fees" on new housing or commercial developments, protection of trees, green spaces, historic cities, and so on. Unrestricted growth threatens the aesthetic preferences of upper-middle-class homeowners. It brings congestion, noise, pollution, ugly factories, cheap commercial outlets, hamburger stands, fried chicken franchises, and "undesirable" residents.

Who Are the No-Growthers?   Opposition to growth is generally concentrated among well-educated, upper-middle-class, white residents who own their own homes and whose income does not directly depend upon the economic health of the community. College and university faculty are fertile grounds for antigrowth movements. Home-owning, elderly persons on Social Security or retirement income often join in opposition to community change.[9] Restrictions on development help inflate the prices of existing homes. Hence it is in the economic interest of homeowners, once they have acquired their own homes, to oppose further development. While the rhetoric of "growth management" usually cites environmental, scenic, or historic rationales for limiting growth, the deliberate inflation of existing property values provides an economic interest in opposition to new development.

Generally, the traditional "community power structure" supports growth (see Chapter 13). Real estate developers, builders, mortgage bankers, and retail merchants generally seek to encourage economic development. However, occasionally larger, better-financed developers may support costly and cumbersome planning restrictions as a means of forcing smaller developers out of the local real estate market.

---

[9] See Charles E. Connerly and James E. Frank, "Predicting Support for Local Growth Controls," *Social Science Quarterly*, 67 (September 1986), 572–86.

Tactics of No-Growthers   "No-growth" movements are influential in many large and growing cities—for example, Denver, Phoenix, San Francisco, San Jose, and Tucson. More importantly, *many upper-middle-class suburban communities* (even those in metropolitan areas with declining core cities) view growth restrictions as in their own interest. These cities may restrict growth through zoning laws, subdivision-control restrictions, utility regulations, building permits, environmental regulations, and even municipal land purchases. Zoning laws can rule out multifamily dwelling or specify only large expensive lot sizes for homes. Zoning laws can exclude heavy or "dirty" industrial development, or restrict "strip" commercial development along highways. Opposition to street widening, road building, or tree cutting can slow or halt development. Public utilities needed for development—water lines, sewage disposal, fire houses, and so on—can be postponed indefinitely. High development fees, utility hookup charges, or building permit costs can all be used to discourage growth. Unrealistic antipollution laws can also discourage growth. If all else fails, a community can buy up vacant land itself or make it a "wildlife refuge."

Note that the burden of these policies falls not only on builders and developers (who are the most influential opponents of "no-growth" policies), but also on the poor, the working class, and non–property owners. These groups need the jobs that business and industry can bring to a community, and they need reasonably priced homes in which to live.

When suburban communities restrict growth, they are often distributing population to other parts of the metropolitan area.[10] The people kept out do not cease to exist; they find housing elsewhere in the metropolitan area. They usually end up imposing greater costs on other municipalities—central cities or larger, close-in suburbs—which are less able to absorb these costs than the wealthier upper-middle-class communities that succeeded in excluding them. What appears to be a local "growth" issue may be in reality a metropolitan "distribution" issue.

The Nimby Syndrome   Opponents of growth can usually count on help from community residents who will be directly inconvenienced by particular projects. Even people who would otherwise support new commercial or housing developments or new public facilities may voice the protest, "Not in my back yard!" earning them the Nimby label. Many Americans want growth; they just do not want it near them.[11]

Nimbys may be the noisiest of protest groups. They are the homeowners and voters who are most directly affected by a private or public project. They can organize, sue, petition, and demonstrate to block projects. And virtually every project inspires Nimby opposition. Nimbys are particularly active regarding waste disposal

---

[10] For discussions of why suburban communities adopt growth controls, see Mark Baldasarre, *Trouble in Paradise* (New York: Columbia University Press, 1986); John R. Logan and Min Zhou, "The Adoption of Growth Controls in Suburban Communities," *Social Science Quarterly,* 71 (March 1990), 118–29.

[11] See Kent E. Portney, "Allaying the NIMBY Syndrome," *Hazardous Waste,* 1 (1984), 411–21; and "Coping in the Age of Nimby," *New York Times,* June 19, 1988.

sites, incinerators, highways, prisons, mental health facilities, low-income public housing projects, power plants, pipelines, and factories.

Nimbys are formidable opponents. While they may constitute only a small minority of the community, they have a very large stake in defeating a project. They have a strong motivation to become active participants—meeting, organizing, petitioning, parading, demonstrating. The majority of the community may benefit from the project, but because each person has only a small stake in its completion, no one has the same strong motivation to participate as the Nimbys. Government agencies and private corporations seeking to locate projects in communities are well advised to conduct professional public relations campaigns well in advance of ground breaking. When the power of the Nimbys is added to that of "no-growth" forces, economic development can be stalemated.

HOUSING AND COMMUNITY DEVELOPMENT POLICY

For nearly a half century, the federal government has pursued a national goal of "a decent home and suitable living environment for every American family." And the nation has made impressive strides toward achieving that goal. Today nearly two-thirds of all Americans own their own homes. Yet problems remain. Low-cost housing is in short supply. Home ownership is declining, especially among younger families. Indeed, liberals and conservatives alike agree that "affordability" is the principal problem facing American housing today.

The national effort in housing is centered in the U.S. Department of Housing and Urban Development (HUD). HUD is the federal department concerned primarily with mortgage insurance, public housing, community development, and related programs.

Mortgage Insurance   The federal government began as early as 1934 to guarantee private mortgages against default by the individual home buyer. The Federal Housing Administration (FHA), now a part of HUD, insures home mortgages and thereby helps banks, savings and loan associations, and other lending agencies to provide long-term, low–down-payment mortgages for Americans wishing to buy their own homes. After checking the credit rating of the prospective buyer, FHA assures the private mortgage lender—bank, savings and loan company, or insurance company—of repayment of the loan in case the home buyer defaults. This reduces the risk and encourages mortgage lenders to offer more loans, lower down payments, and longer repayment periods. While these advantages in borrowing assist middle-class home buyers, note that the direct beneficiaries of mortgage insurance are the banks and mortgage-lending companies who are insured against losses. The Department of Veterans Affairs also provides VA insurance for veterans seeking mortgages.

FHA and VA mortgage insurance has been extremely successful in promoting home ownership among millions of middle-class Americans who have financed their homes through federally insured mortgages.

A great many of these mortgages financed suburban homes. In fact, the success of mortgage insurance programs may have contributed to the deterioration of the nation's central cities by enabling so many middle-class white families to acquire their cherished homes in the suburbs and leave the city behind. The FHA's mortgage insurance program is an entirely federal program, but its impact on city and suburban governments should not be underestimated.

HUD also subsidizes and insures apartment projects for low- and moderate-income families and housing projects for the elderly and handicapped. It also provides flood insurance and risk insurance in areas where private insurance is difficult to obtain.

Fraud and Mismanagement   Federal subsidies and insurance guarantees offer many opportunities for fraud and mismanagement. Real estate developers with "connections" at HUD have succeeded in the past into winning approval for mortgage insurance guarantees for large projects that banks would otherwise consider too risky for mortgage loans. But with government guarantees of payback in event of default by developers or owners, banks have proceeded to grant mortgages for poorly planned projects and unqualified buyers. When default occurs, HUD must pay the banks with taxpayers' money. Because both developers and banks do not fully share the risk in a project—HUD mortgage insurance assumes the risk—they may not exercise the same sound fiscal judgment they would if their own money was fully at risk. Moreover, the opportunities for fraud are many: HUD officials have been bribed to approve projects that are known to be unsound; credit checks and appraisals have been deliberately inflated; high-priced luxury projects have been approved under low-income or elderly assistance programs; political associates and campaign contributors have obtained preference for their projects over those that might better serve the community. Many of these problems have been uncovered in recent years.

The Troubled History of Public Housing   The Housing Act of 1937 initiated federal public housing programs to provide low-rent public housing for the poor who could not afford decent housing on the private market. The public housing program was designed for people without jobs or incomes sufficient to enable them to afford home ownership, even with the help of FHA mortgage insurance. HUD does not build, own, or operate public housing projects; rather, it provides the necessary financial support to enable local communities to provide public housing for their poor if communities chose to do so. HUD makes loans and grants to *local public housing authorities* established by local governments to build, own, and operate low-cost public housing. These housing authorities keep rents low in relation to their tenants' ability to pay. This means that local housing authorities operate at a loss and the federal government reimburses them. No community is required to have a public housing authority; it must apply to Washington and meet federal standards in order to receive federal financial support.

Public housing functioned fairly well in its early years. Its tenants were mostly working poor who sought temporary housing, could pay some rent, and moved on to the private housing market once their economic status improved. These were the people Congress intended to help when the program was originated during the Great Depression of the 1930s.

But by the 1950s the occupants of most big city public housing projects were the chronically unemployed, female-headed households whose only source of income were welfare payments. These occupants could not afford any rent, even for building maintenance costs, and public housing across the country deteriorated. Some public housing projects became uninhabitable.

Very often, the concentration of large numbers of poor persons with a great variety of social problems into a single, mass housing project compounded their problems. The cost of central-city land required many big cities to build high-rises of ten to twenty stories. These huge buildings frequently became unlivable—with crime in the hallways, elevators that seldom worked, drugs and human filth in halls and stairways, and families locking themselves in and alienating themselves from community life. Huge housing projects were impersonal and bureaucratic, and they often failed to provide many of the stabilizing neighborhood influences of the old slums. Children could be raised in public housing projects and never see a regularly employed male head of a household going to and from work. The behavior and value patterns of problem families were reinforced.

Moreover, removing thousands of people from neighborhood environments and placing them in the institution-like setting of large public housing developments very often increased their alienation or separation from society and removed what few social controls existed in the slum neighborhood. A family living in public housing that successfully found employment and raised its income level faced eviction to make room for more "deserving" families. Finally, black groups often complained that public housing was a new form of racial segregation, and, indeed, the concentration of blacks among public housing dwellers does lead to a great deal of de facto segregation in housing projects.

Efforts at Public Housing Reform   Federal housing policy shifted somewhat under the "Great Society" banner of President Lyndon Johnson. The cabinet-level Department of Housing and Urban Development was created in 1965, and efforts began to move federal policy away from large publicly owned housing projects toward subsidies for private developers as well as local public housing agencies to build scatter site low-income housing. Moreover, recognizing the fact that most public housing residents could not afford rents sufficient to maintain buildings adequately, HUD began subsidizing maintenance and operating costs, as well as capital expenditures, of local housing authorities. HUD limited rents to 25 percent (later raised to 30 percent) of tenants' income. To encourage the private market to provide low-income housing, a subsidy program known as "Section 8" paid rental vouchers to private apartment owners to house the poor. Some Section 8 money went directly to developers for new construction, but scandals eventually led to the elimination of construction subsidies, except for housing for the elderly and disabled.

During the Reagan and Bush presidencies, federal housing policy tilted toward "privatization"—greater efforts to encourage private developers to provide affordable low-income housing, as well as encouragement to tenants in public housing to manage their own developments and eventually purchase their own units. HUD Secretary Jack Kemp developed Home Ownership for People Everywhere (HOPE) to help public housing residents buy their units; but relatively few units were sold under HOPE, as residents confronted the problem of paying future maintenance costs of their purchased units. The Clinton administration and HUD Secretary Henry Cisneros are phasing out the HOPE program.

Public Housing Today   Today there about 3200 local public housing authorities nationwide. They house about 3.4 million residents who pay no more than 30 percent of their income in rent. These residents are among the nation's poorest citizens; in 1992 the average *family* income in public housing was $7394.[12] Most of this income is in the form of government welfare payments; only about one-quarter of public housing residents depend primarily on earned income. Over 1 million eligible families are on the waiting list of public housing authorities for units to become available. While former HUD Secretary Jack Kemp is widely credited with having reduced fraud and mismanagement, many "troubled" local housing authorities and projects remain.

Community Development   In the original Housing Act of 1937, the ideal of "urban renewal" was closely tied to public housing. Slums were to be torn down as public housing sites were constructed. Later in the Housing Act of 1949, the urban renewal program was separated from public housing, and the federal government undertook to support a broad program of urban redevelopment to help cities fight a loss in population and to reclaim the economic importance of the core cities. After World War II, the suburban exodus had progressed to the point where central cities faced slow decay and death if large public efforts were not undertaken. Urban renewal could not be undertaken by private enterprise because it was not profitable; suburban property was usually cheaper than downtown property, and it did not require large-scale clearance of obsolete buildings. Moreover, private enterprise did not possess the power of eminent domain, which enables the city to purchase the many separately owned small tracts of land needed to ensure an economically feasible new investment. For many years, the federal government provided financial support for specific renewal projects in cities.

Community Development Block Grants   In the Housing and Community Development Act of 1974, federal development grants cities were consolidated into *community development block grant* (CDBG) programs. Cities and counties were authorized to receive these grants to assist them in eliminating slums; increasing the supply of low-income housing; conserving existing housing; improving health, safety, welfare, and public service; improving planning; and preserving property with special value. Community development block grants are based on a formula that includes population, housing overcrowding, and extent of poverty. No local "matching" funds are required. Communities are required to submit an annual application that describes their housing and redevelopment needs, and a comprehensive strategy for meeting those needs.

To ensure that the CDBG program remains targeted on the poor, the legislation requires localities and states to certify that not less than 60 percent of their CDBG funds are spent on activities that benefit low and moderate income persons. Low- and moderate-income persons are defined as those persons whose income

---

[12] *Congressional Quarterly Weekly Report,* April 10, 1993, p. 970.

does not exceed 80 percent of the median income for the area. CDBG program funds are currently allocated as follows: 70 percent to cities and 30 percent to state-administered small cities and rural communities.

Community development block grants can be used by local authorities to acquire blighted land, clear off or modernize obsolete or dilapidated structures, and make downtown sites available for new uses. When the sites are physically cleared of the old structures, they can be resold to private developers for residential, commercial, or industrial use, and the difference between the costs of acquisition and clearance and the income from the private sale to the developers is paid for by the federal government. In other words, local authorities sustain a loss in their redevelopment activities, and this loss is made up by federal grants.

No city is required to engage in redevelopment, but if cities wish federal financial backing, they must show in their applications that they have developed a comprehensive program for redevelopment and the prevention of future blight. They must demonstrate that they have adequate building and health codes, good zoning and subdivision control regulations, sufficient local financing and public support, and a comprehensive plan of development with provisions for relocating displaced persons.

Economics of Development   Urban redevelopment is best understood from an economic standpoint. The key to success is to encourage private developers to purchase the land and make a heavy investment in middle- or high-income housing or in commercial or industrial use. In fact, before undertaking a project, local authorities frequently "find a developer first, and then see what interests that developer." The city cannot afford to purchase land, thereby taking it off the tax rolls, invest in its clearance, and then be stuck without a buyer. A private developer must be encouraged to invest in the property and thus enhance the value of the central city. Over time a city can more than pay off its investment by increased tax returns from redeveloped property and hence make a "profit." Thus, many people can come out of a project feeling successful—the city increases its tax base and annual revenues, the private developer makes a profit, and mayors can point to the physical improvements in the city that occurred during their administrations.

Relocation   Relocation is the most sensitive problem in redevelopment. Most people relocated by redevelopment are poor and black. They have no interest in moving simply to make room for middle- or higher-income housing, or business or industry, or universities, hospitals, and other public facilities. Even though relocated families are frequently given priority for public housing, there is not nearly enough space in public housing to contain them all. They are simply moved from one slum to another. The slum landowner is paid a just price for the land, but the renter receives only a small moving allowance. Redevelopment officials assist relocated families in finding new housing and generally claim success in moving families to better housing. However, frequently the result is higher rents, and redevelopment may actually help to create new slums in other sections of the city. Small business owners are especially vulnerable to relocation. They often depend on a small, well-known neighborhood clientele, and they cannot compete successfully when forced to move to other sections of the city.

Politics of Development   Political support for redevelopment has come from mayors who wish to make their reputation by engaging in large-scale renewal activities that produce impressive "before" and "after" pictures of the city. Business owners wishing to preserve downtown investments and developers wishing to acquire land in urban centers have provided a solid base of support for downtown renewal. Mayors, planners, the press, and the good-government forces have made urban redevelopment politically much more popular than public housing.

NATIONAL TRANSPORTATION POLICY

Few inventions have had such a far-reaching effect on the life of the American people as the automobile. Henry Ford built one of the first gasoline-driven carriages in America in 1893, and by 1900 there were 8,000 automobiles registered in the United States. The Model T was introduced in the autumn of 1908. By concentrating on a single unlovely but enduring model, and by introducing the assembly line processes, the Ford Motor Company began producing automobiles for the masses. Today, there are nearly 200 million registered motor vehicles in the nation and 3.5 million miles of paved roads.

Highway Politics   Highway politics are of interest not only to the automotive industry and the driving public, but also to the oil industry, the American Road Builders Association, the cement industry, the railroads, the trucking industry, the farmers, the outdoor advertising industry, and the county commissioners, taxpayer associations, ecologists and conservationists, and neighborhood improvement associations. These political interests are concerned with the allocation of money for highway purposes, the sources of funds for highway revenue, the extent of gasoline and motor vehicle taxation, the regulation of traffic on the highways, the location of highways, the determination of construction policies, the division of responsibility among federal, state, and local governments for highway financing and administration, the division of highway funds between rural and urban areas, and many other important outcomes in highway politics.

Early Federal Aid   It was in the Federal Aid Road Act of 1916 that the federal government first provided regular funds for highway construction under terms that gave the federal government considerable influence over state policy. For example, if states wanted to get federal money, they were required to have a highway department, and to have their plans for highway construction approved by federal authorities. In 1921, federal aid was limited to a connected system of principal state highways, now called the "federal aid primary highway system." Uniform standards were prescribed and even a uniform numbering system was added, such as "US 1," or "US 30." The emphasis of the program was clearly rural. Later, the federal government also designated a federal aid "secondary" system of farm-to-market roads and provided for "urban extensions" of primary roads, in addition to the federal aid for the primary highway system.

The Interstate System   Congress authorized a national system of interstate and defense highways in 1956 ("I" highways). The interstate system is the most important feature of the federal highway policy. Costs are allocated on the basis of 90

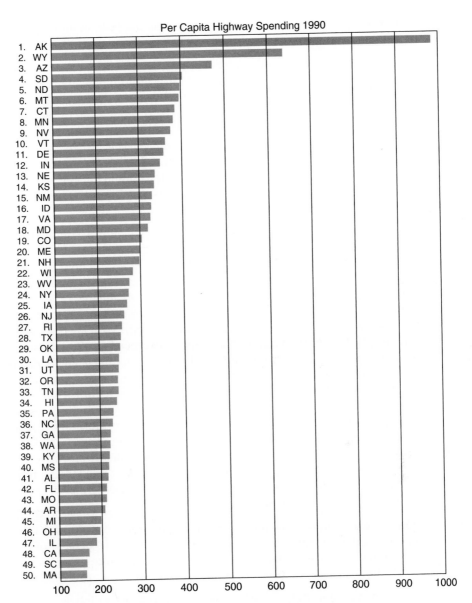

FIGURE 16–1   Per Capita Highway Spending, 1990

percent federal and 10 percent state. The Federal Highway Act of 1956, as amended, authorized 42,500 miles of highway, designed to connect principal metropolitan areas and industrial centers and thereby shifted the emphasis of federal highway activity from rural to urban needs. Although the system constitutes less than 2 percent of the total surfaced roads in the nation, it carries over 20 percent of all highway traffic. The U.S. Department of Transportation has been given strong supervisory powers, including the selection of routes, but administration and execution are still left to state highway departments. Federal monies are paid to the states, not to the contractors, as the work progresses.

Federal Highway Money   Revenue from the federal gasoline tax has long been "earmarked" for the Federal Highway Trust Fund. For many years this was the principal source of federal highway aid to the states. Although the current federal gasoline tax is now nine cents per gallon, the revenue from this tax alone is insufficient to repair and maintain the nation's highway system. (Since 1970, federal highway trust fund money has also been allocated to urban mass transit.) Additional revenues must now come from other federal taxes.

Congress generally recognizes the need to rebuild the nation's highways. The real political fireworks center on requirements that Congress attaches to the receipt of federal highway funds.

The National Speed Limit   An example of the controversies generated by federal highway policy was the long battle over the 55-miles-per-hour speed limit. Prior to 1974 most states had speed limits of 70 miles per hour on interstate highways. A national speed limit of 55 was enacted by Congress during the Arab oil embargo as a means of saving gasoline. Congress mandated that a state be denied 10 percent of its federal highway aid if it failed to enact and enforce a 55-mile-per-hour speed limit. The U.S. Department of Transportation checked speeds on state highways; if more than half of the vehicles exceeded the limit, a state could lose federal highway funds. But truckers and others who drive a great deal, particularly over long open stretches of interstate highway in the western United States lobbied hard to eliminate the 55-miles-per-hour national speed limit. They argued that the costs in billions of additional hours spent on the road were unreasonable, that the 55-miles-per-hour speed limit was widely ignored anyway, and that it eroded respect for the law. The national speed limit was also seen as symbolic of federal intrusion in state affairs and a threat to American federalism. However, insurance companies and consumer safety groups lobbied hard to keep the 55-miles-per-hour speed limit. In 1987 Congress finally relented; the speed limit on rural portions of interstate highways was raised to 65-miles-per-hour.

The Twenty-One-Year-Old Drinking Age   Currently federal law also mandates that the Department of Transportation withhold 10 percent of a state's highway funds if it fails to enact a twenty-one-year-old minimum age for the purchase of alcoholic beverages. (See Chapter 3, "Congress Raises the Drinking Age.")

Mandating Seat Belts   The Secretary of Transportation is authorized to set standards of auto safety for manufacturers. For years insurance and consumer lobbies pressed for federally mandated air bags in all automobiles. But the automobile manufacturers argued that air bags were very costly, and that when air bags were offered as an option, very few auto buyers chose to pay for them. In 1984 the Secretary of Transportation Elizabeth Dole ruled that auto makers would have to install air bags unless states with two-thirds of the nation's population passed tough mandatory seat-belt-use laws by 1989. While many states passed seat belt laws, not all of these laws meet the original tough standards. Most are limited to "secondary enforcement,'' which means that police will ticket motorists for failing to wear a seatbelt only if their car is stopped for another infraction.

Auto Safety   Under pressure from consumer lobbies and the U.S. Department of Transportation, auto manufacturers gradually improved the safety of their products. The traffic death rate in the United States (the number of deaths from motor vehicle accidents per 100 million miles traveled) was 4.7 in 1970. This rate dropped significantly to 3.2 in 1975 following the federally mandated 55-mile-per-hour speed limit. But the traffic death rate continued to drop during the 1980s even as average highway speeds returned to previous levels. The number of accidents, about 34 million per year, remained the same, but the death rate dropped to 2.2 by 1990. These figures suggest that auto safety improvements are allowing more people to survive accidents. There is additional evidence that *state* traffic safety regulations, mandated seat belt use, and drunk driving prosecution reforms have also been influential in reducing the highway death toll.[13]

STATE TRANSPORTATION POLITICS

The states retain the principal responsibility for building and maintaining the nation's highways. State regulations govern the licensing of drivers and vehicles. State and local governments also operate airports, port facilities, and mass transit.

Highway Politics   For many years, rural interests in state legislatures, together with representatives of the automobile, trucking, and oil industries, dominated transportation politics. Farmers wanted roads to move themselves and their products to cities; and auto, trucking, and oil interests wanted the states to build roads to subsidize their industries. The only opposition came from the railroads, which objected to the subsidization of their competitors, the truckers. But the railroads were an industry in decline, and the highway interests won most of the battles.

Highway interests in the states sought to separate highway departments from general state government and to separate gasoline tax revenues from general state revenues. Highway interests believed that their road-building programs would fare better when organization and funding were not in competition with other state programs. They succeeded in most states in obtaining (1) the creation of separate highway boards and commissions and (2) the establishment of separate highway trust funds to receive gasoline tax revenues "earmarked" for highway construction and maintenance. Indeed, some states passed constitutional amendments preventing the "diversion" of gasoline taxes for nonhighway purposes. These policies guaranteed a continual flow of road-building funds and gave highways preferential treatment over other public programs. Today some southern and western states retain these special organizational and funding arrangements for highways.

---

[13] Jerome S. Legge, "Policy Alternatives and Traffic Safety," *Western Political Quarterly,* 43 (September 1990), 597–612; Jerome S. Legge, "Reforming Highway Safety in New York," *Social Science Quarterly,* 71 (June 1990), 373–82.

Highway and Economic Growth   Highway construction, and infrastructure development generally, is widely recognized as a key component of economic development.[14] Nonetheless, while overall government spending has skyrocketed in recent decades, spending for public infrastructure (highways, bridges, ports, airports, sewers, etc.) has stagnated. Despite evidence that spending for highways is linked to economic development,[15] state and local government spending for highway construction and maintenance has declined from about 20 percent of total spending in 1962 to less than 7 percent in 1990. Even the share of national income devoted to highways has declined, from 2.3 percent in 1962 to 1.3 percent in 1990.[16] These figures suggest not only that the nation is failing to invest in *new* public infrastructure, but also that older existing highways, bridges, sewers, and water mains are deteriorating over time.

Urban Mass Transit Politics   In recent years mass transit interests have gained political influence in both Congress and most state legislatures. The creation of the U.S. Department of Transportation in 1966 merged the old Federal Highway Administration with the Federal Transit Administration (charged with distributing federal mass transit funds) and the Maritime Administration and U.S. Coast Guard, the Federal Railroad Administration, the Federal Aviation Administration, and the National Highway Traffic Safety Administration. This integrated transportation organization became a model for the creation of comprehensive transportation departments in most states, with the urban states leading the way. This organizational structure suggested that highway interests would no longer dominate bureaucratic decision making in transportation policy. More important, perhaps, Congress and many other states began diverting gasoline taxes to mass transit.

METROPOLITAN TRANSPORTATION

City planners and transportation specialists argue that the only way to relieve traffic congestion and preserve central cities is to get people out of private automobiles and onto public transit, that is, "to move people, not cars." Automobiles on expressways can move about 2,000 people per lane per hour; buses can move between 6,000 and 9,000; rail systems can carry up to 60,000 people per hour. In other words, one rail line is estimated to be equal to twenty or thirty expressway lanes of automobiles in terms of its ability to move people.

Commuting to Work   However, the average citizen has a large investment in the automobile. Few Americans want to see their financial investment sit in a garage all day. Americans clearly prefer private automobile transportation and costly expressways to mass transit, regardless of the arguments of transportation experts.

---

[14] Governing's Special Report, "The Public's Capital: A Forum on Infrastructure Issues," *Governing,* July 1992.

[15] See Thomas R. Dye, "Taxing, Spending, and Economic Growth in the States," *Journal of Politics,* 42 (November 1980), 1085–1087.

[16] Advisory Commission on Intergovernmental Relations, *Significant Features of Fiscal Federalism 1992* (Washington, DC: Author, 1992), Table 55.

Only 6 percent of Americans use buses or trains to commute to work. The result is that mass transit facilities almost always lose money.

Changing Commuting Patterns   Almost all cities now experience heavy expressway congestion at rush hour and a resulting increase in time and cost to the average automobile commuter. But predictions about future expressway "gridlock" may prove inaccurate. The proportion of daily commuters who drive from the suburbs to work in central cities is gradually decreasing as more businesses move to the suburbs. Intersuburban commuting is increasing over time; circumferential expressways circling cities now carry more traffic than expressways leading into central cities.[17]

Rail-based mass transit facilities are usually designed for city-suburban commuting. As the central city fades as a center for employment and shopping, and more people travel from suburb to suburb, the ridership for mass transit decreases.[18]

The Case for Subsidies   It is necessary to provide public subsidies to commuter-rail companies or to have governments operate these facilities at a loss if commuter service is to be maintained. Only a small portion of the costs of public transit come from the fares charged riders. However, it is argued that the cost of mass transit subsidies is very small in comparison with the cost of building and maintaining expressways. Thus, mass transit is considered cost-effective for many cities, even if fares do not meet operating expenses. Moreover, new, speedier, more comfortable, air-conditioned, high-capacity trains with fewer stops and more frequent trips may lure many riders back to public transportation.

Mass transit facilities are very costly, particularly for cities that do not already have commuter rail service. Proponents of greater federal aid for mass transit argue that cities and states do not have sufficient resources to build mass transit facilities. They argue that mass transit is cheaper than expressway construction and that expressways can never handle predicted traffic increases anyhow. They emphasize the costs of traffic jams in time and wages lost and their economic impact on central cities. Opponents of federal aid for mass transit object to the idea that the entire nation, including rural areas, should be asked to contribute to solving transportation problems of the nation's cities. Moreover, they are doubtful about the feasibility of convincing Americans that they should give up the convenience of their automobiles for mass transit.

Federal Mass Transit Aid   For many years the federal government has subsidized the building of highways, particularly the interstate highways, where the federal government assumed 90 percent of the costs. It was not until the 1970s that the federal government showed any comparable interest in mass transit. (Indeed, the *interstate* highway system, despite its name, has carried a major share of *intra-*

---

[17] U.S. Department of Transportation, *Demographic Change and Worktrip Travel Trends* (Washington, DC: Government Printing Office, 1985).

[18] See Peter Gordon and Harry Richardson, "Notes from the Underground: The Failure of Mass Transit," *The Public Interest* (Winter 1989), 77–86.

metropolitan city–suburban traffic.) The energy crisis accelerated federal efforts in mass transit. In the Urban Mass Transit Act of 1974, the U.S. Department of Transportation was authorized to make grants to cities for both construction and operation of mass transit systems. In many cities, this simply meant the creation of a local mass transit authority and the purchase of buses. However, in some cities, massive new mass transit programs were developed with federal funds.

Among the most striking efforts in mass transit were San Francisco's BART (Bay Area Rapid Transit), Washington, DC's METRO, and Atlanta's MARTA (Metropolitan Atlanta Rapid Transit Authority). These are large projects into which the cities and the federal government pumped hundreds of million of dollars. They incorporated all of the latest features of modern, pleasant, rapid, convenient, and efficient mass transit. Nonetheless, ridership cannot pay for continuing operating costs, let alone the enormous costs of construction. Perhaps the worst example of federally subsidized mass transit is Miami's Metrorail. The costs were so great and the ridership so small that critics estimated it would have been cheaper for the federal government to buy every regular rider a Rolls-Royce.

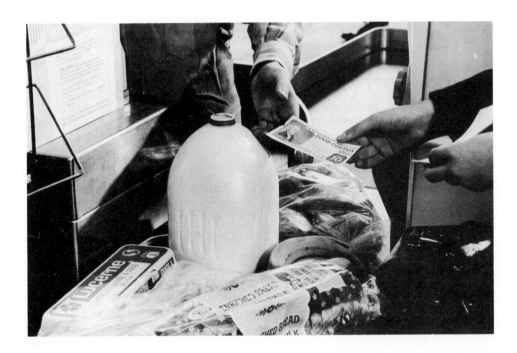

17

THE POLITICS OF POVERTY, WELFARE, AND HEALTH

▲

POVERTY IN AMERICA

Political conflict over poverty in America begins with disagreements over its nature and extent, and then it proceeds to disputes over its causes and remedies.

How Many Poor?   How much poverty really exists in America? According to the U.S. Bureau of the Census, there were about 34 million poor people in the United States in 1990. This was approximately 13.5 percent of the population. This official definition of poverty is estimated to include all those Americans whose annual cash income falls below that which is required to maintain a decent standard of living. This definition of the poverty line is derived by calculating "thrifty" food costs for families of various sizes and then multiplying these costs by three, on the assumption that poor families spend one-third of their income on food. The dollar amounts of these lines are flexible to take into account the effect of inflation, and they rise each year with the rate of inflation. In 1990 the poverty line for an urban family of four was $13,359 per year. The median income for all families for the nation in that year was $35,353.[1]

Liberal Criticism   This official definition of poverty has many critics. Some liberals believe poverty is underestimated because (1) the official definition does not take into account regional differences in the cost of living, climate, or accepted styles of living; (2) the "thrifty" food budget on which the poverty level is based is too low for good nutrition and health; (3) the official definition includes cash income from welfare and Social Security (without this government assistance, the number of poor would be much higher, perhaps 25 percent of the total population); and (4) the official definition does not count the many "near poor"; there are 45 million Americans or 18.0 percent of the population living below 125 percent of the poverty level.

Conservative Criticism   Some conservatives also challenge the official definition of poverty: (1) It does not consider the value of family assets. People (usually older people) who own their own mortgage-free homes, furniture, and automobiles may have current incomes below the poverty line yet not suffer hardship; (2) there are many families and individuals who are officially counted as poor but who do not think of themselves as "poor people"—students, for example, who deliberately postpone income to secure an education; (3) many persons (poor and nonpoor) underreport their real income and this leads to overestimates of the number of poor; (4) more importantly, the official definition of poverty excludes "in kind" (noncash) benefits given to the poor by governments. These benefits include, for example, food stamps, free medical care, public housing, and school lunches. If these benefits were "costed out" (calculated as cash income), there may be only half as many poor people as shown in official statistics.

Three Definitions of Poverty   Thus in addition to the "official" government definition of poverty, we can also consider "latent poverty"—the number of people who would be poor if there were no government welfare or Social Security programs—and "net poverty"—the number of people who fall below the poverty line after costing out the value of in kind government benefits. It is estimated that the "net poverty" rate was only about 9 percent in 1990. The official poverty rate, the latent poverty rate, and the net poverty rate are shown on Figure 17–1.

WHO ARE THE POOR?

Poverty occurs in many kinds of families and in all races and ethnic groups. However, some groups experience poverty in greater proportions than the national average.

---

[1] U.S. Bureau of the Census, *Statistical Abstract of the United States, 1992,* p. 460.

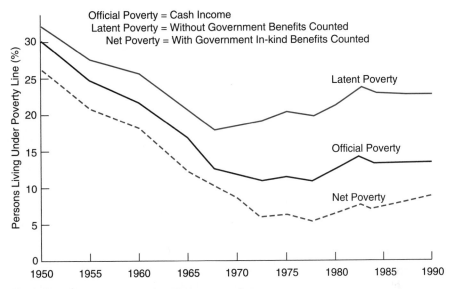

FIGURE 17–1   Three Definitions of Poverty

Family Structure   Poverty is most common among female-headed families. The incidence of poverty among these families in 1990 was 49.9 percent, compared to only 8.6 percent for married couples (see Table 17–1). These women and their children comprise over two-thirds of all of the persons living in poverty in the United States. These figures describe "the feminization of poverty" in America. Clearly, poverty is closely related to family structure. Today the disintegration of the traditional husband–wife family is the single most influential factor contributing to poverty.

TABLE 17–1   POVERTY IN AMERICA

Poverty definition 1990	$13,359
(Nonfarm family of four)	
Number of poor	33.6 million
Poverty percentage of total population	13.5
Race (% poor)	
White	10.7
Black	31.9
Hispanic	28.1
Age (% poor)	
Over 65	12.2
Family (% poor)	
Married couple	8.6
Single parent, mother only	49.9

Source: Statistical Abstract of the United States, 1992. p. 458.

Race   Blacks experience poverty in much greater proportions than whites. Over the years the poverty rate among blacks in the United States has been about three times higher than the poverty rate among whites. Poverty among Hispanics is also significantly greater than among whites.

Age   The aged in America experience *less* poverty than the nonaged. The aged are not poor, despite the popularity of the phrase "the poor and the aged." The poverty rate for persons over sixty-five years of age is *below* the national average. Moreover, the aged are much wealthier than the nonaged. They are more likely than younger people to own homes with paid mortgages. A large portion of their medical expenses is paid by Medicare. With fewer expenses, the aged, even with relatively smaller cash incomes, experience poverty in a different fashion than young mothers with children. The lowering of the poverty rate among the aged is a relatively recent occurrence. Continuing increases in Social Security benefits over the years are largely responsible for this singular "victory" in the war against poverty.

Wealth   Wealth is the net worth of all one's possessions—home value minus mortgage, auto value minus loan, business value minus debts, money in bank accounts, savings, stocks and bonds, and real estate. All calculations of poverty consider *income,* not *wealth.* It is theoretically possible for persons to have considerable wealth (e.g., to own a mortgage-free home and a loan-free automobile and have money in savings and investments), yet fall within the official definition of poverty because current cash income is low. Indeed, many of the *aged* who are counted as poor because their incomes are low have substantial accumulations of wealth. The U.S. Census Bureau estimates that in 1990 the net worth of the median family over age 65 was $91,300, compared to a net worth of only $4,000 for householders under age 35.[2] This suggests that the elderly are twenty times wealthier than the young!

POVERTY AS INEQUALITY

It is also possible to define poverty as "a state of mind"—some people think they have less income or fewer material possessions than most Americans, and they believe they are entitled to more. Their sense of deprivation is not tied to any *absolute* level of income. Instead, their sense of deprivation is *relative* to what most Americans have and what they, therefore, believe they are entitled to. Even fairly substantial incomes may result in a sense of relative deprivation in a very affluent society; commercial advertising and the mass media portray the life of the "average American" as one of high levels of consumption and material well-being.

Inequality in the States   Economists have provided us with a way of measuring income inequality within political systems. Income inequality is measured by a Gini coefficient or a Gini index, which ranges from a plus 1.00 (theoretically perfect inequality) to 0.00 (theoretically perfect equality). Income inequality is greatest in Mississippi and least in Utah. (See Figure 17–2.) In general, income

---

[2] *Statistical Abstract of the United States, 1992,* p. 462.

General Income Inequality: Gini Index

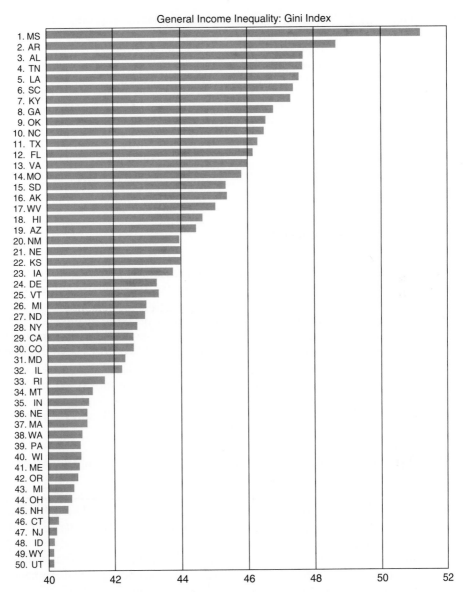

FIGURE 17-2   Rankings of the States: Inequality

inequality is greater in the southern, rural, and poorer states. Income distributions are more equalized in the wealthy, urban, industrialized states.

Inequality in the Nation   Inequality in America is decreasing over time. However, the rate of decrease is not very rapid. Certainly poverty as relative deprivation is not disappearing at the same rate as absolute poverty. Table 17–2 divides all American families into five groups—from the lowest one-fifth of personal income to the highest one-fifth—and shows the percentage of total family personal income

TABLE 17–2   DISTRIBUTION OF FAMILY INCOME BY QUINTILES AND TOP 5 PERCENT, SELECTED YEARS, 1929–1990

Quintiles	1929	1947	1954	1968	1974	1980	1990
Lowest	3.5	5.0	4.8	5.7	5.4	5.1	4.6
Second	9.0	11.0	11.1	12.4	12.0	11.6	10.8
Third	13.8	16.0	16.4	17.7	17.6	17.5	16.6
Fourth	19.3	22.0	22.5	23.7	24.1	24.1	23.8
Highest	54.4	46.0	45.2	40.6	41.0	41.6	44.3
Total	100	100	100	100	100	100	100
Top 5 percent	30.0	20.9	20.3	14.0	15.3	15.3	17.4

Source: U.S. Bureau of the Census, *Current Population Reports,* series P-60

received by each of these groups over the years. (If perfect income equality existed, each fifth of American families would receive 20 percent of all family personal income, and it would not be possible to rank fifths from highest to lowest.) The poorest one-fifth received 3.5 percent of all family personal income in 1929; by 1947, however, this group had increased its percentage of all family personal income to 5.0. (Most of this increase occurred during World War II.) The highest one-fifth received 54.5 percent of all family personal income in 1929; by 1947, however, this percentage had declined to 46.0. Another measure of income equalization over time is the decline in the percentage of income received by the top 5 percent in America. The top 5 percent received 30.0 percent of all family personal income in 1929, but only 15.3 percent in 1980.

Recent Increases in Inequality   While income differences in America have declined over the long run, inequality increased in the 1980s. This reversal of historical trends has generated both political rhetoric and serious scholarly inquiry about its causes. The political argument that inequality increased because of miserly federal social welfare payments in the 1980s is untrue. Aggregate government social welfare transfer payments did *not* decline, either in real dollars or as a percent of gross national product. It is true that the *rate of increase* in social welfare spending declined in the 1980s, but total social welfare spending by governments remained at approximately 18.5 percent of GNP throughout the 1980s.

Recent increases in inequality in the United States are a product of several social and economic trends: (1) the decline of the manufacturing sector of the economy with its relatively high-paying blue-collar jobs, and the ascendancy of the communications, information, and service sectors of the economy with a combination of high-paying and low-paying jobs; (2) a rise in the number of two-wage families, making single-wage female-headed households relatively less affluent; and (3) demographic trends, which include larger proportions of aged and female-headed families.

PUBLIC POLICY AS A CAUSE OF POVERTY

Does government itself create poverty by fashioning social welfare programs and policies that destroy incentives to work, encourage families to break up, and condemn the poor to social dependency? Does the current social welfare system sentence to a life of poverty many millions of people who would otherwise form families, take low-paying jobs, and perhaps with hard work and perseverance gradually pull themselves and their children into the mainstream of American life?

Poverty in America steadily *declined* from 1950, when about 30 percent of the population was officially poor, to about 11 percent in 1970. (See Figure 17–1.) During this period of progress toward the elimination of poverty, government welfare programs were minimal. There were small AFDC (Aid to Families with Dependent Children) programs for women with children who lived alone; eligibility was restricted and welfare authorities checked to see if an employable male lived in the house. There were also federal payments for aged, blind, and disabled poor. Welfare roles were modest; only about 1 to 2 percent of American families received AFDC payments.

However, with the addition of many new Great Society welfare programs, the downward trend in poverty ended. Indeed, the numbers and proportion of the population living in poverty began to move upward in the 1970s and early 1980s. This was a period in which AFDC payments were significantly increased and eligibility rules were relaxed. The Food Stamp program was initiated in 1965 and became a major new welfare benefit. Medicaid was initiated in the same year. Federal aid to the aged, blind, and disabled was merged into a new SSI (Supplement Security Income) program, which quadrupled in numbers of recipients.

Did poverty increase in spite of, or because of, these new social welfare programs? Poverty remained high in the 1970s despite a reasonably healthy economy. Discrimination did not become significantly *worse* during this period; on the contrary, the civil rights laws enacted in the 1960s were creating many new opportunities for blacks. Finally, poverty was reduced among the aged due to generous increases in social security benefits. The greatest increases in poverty occurred in families headed by *working-age persons.* In short, it is difficult to find alternative explanations for the rise in poverty. We are obliged to consider the possibility that *policy* changes—new welfare programs, expanded benefits, and relaxed eligibility requirements—contributed to increased poverty.

According to Charles Murray, the persons hurt most by current welfare policies are the poor themselves.[3] Murray argues that current welfare policy provides many disincentives to family life. The breakup of the family, nearly everyone agrees, is closely associated with poverty. The effect of generous welfare benefits and relaxed eligibility requirements on employment has been argued for centuries. Surveys show that the poor prefer work to welfare, but welfare payments may pro-

---

[3] Charles Murray, *Losing Ground* (New York: Basic Books, 1983).

duce subtle effects on the behavior of the poor. Persons unwilling to take minimum wage jobs may never acquire the work habits required to move into better-paying jobs later in their lives. Welfare may even help to create a dependent and defeatist subculture, lowering personal self-esteem and contributing further to joblessness, illegitimacy, and broken homes.

Murray's policy prescription is a drastic one:

> . . . scrapping the entire federal welfare and income-support structure for working age persons, including AFDC (Aid to Families with Dependent Children), Medicaid, Food Stamps, Unemployment Insurance; workers compensation, subsidized housing, disability insurance, and the rest. It would leave the working-age person with no recourse whatever except the job market, family members, friends, and public or private locally funded services. . . . cut the knot, for there is no way to untie it.[4]

The result, he argues, would be less poverty, less illegitimacy, more upward mobility, freedom and hope for the poor. "The lives of large numbers of poor people would be radically changed for the better." According to Murray, the obstacle to this solution is not only the army of politicians and bureaucrats who want to keep their dependent clients, but more importantly the vast majority of generous and well-meaning middle-class Americans who support welfare programs because they do not understand how badly these programs injure the poor.

SOCIAL INSURANCE

State and local welfare activities are greatly influenced by federal policies. In the Social Security Act of 1935, the federal government undertook to establish the basic framework for welfare policies for all levels of government. Table 17–3 summarizes the nation's major social welfare programs by degree of federal and state responsibility.

OASDI   One of the key features of the Social Security Act is the Old-Age, Survivors, and Disability Insurance (OASDI) program; this is a compulsory social insurance program financed by regular deductions from earnings, which gives individuals a legal right to benefits in the event of certain occurrences that cause a reduction of their income—old age, death of the head of the household, or permanent disability.[5] OASDI is based on the same principle as private insurance—the sharing of a risk of the loss of income—except that it is a government program that is compulsory for all workers. OASDI is not public *charity,* but a way of compelling people to provide *insurance* against a loss of income. Both employees and employers must pay equal amounts toward the employees' OASDI insurance. Upon retirement, an insured worker is entitled to monthly benefit payments based upon age at retirement and the amount earned during his or her working years. OASDI also ensures benefit payments to survivors of an insured worker, including the spouse if

---

[4] Ibid., pp. 227–28.

[5] The original act did not include disability insurance; this was added by amendment in 1950. Health insurance for the aged, "Medicare," was added by amendment in 1965.

TABLE 17-3   FEDERALISM AND MAJOR SOCIAL WELFARE PROGRAMS

Income Maintenance	Federal	Federal/State	State
Social Security (OASDI)	X		
Aid to Families with Dependent Children (AFDC)		X	
Supplemental Security Income (SSI)	X		
General assistance			X
Unemployment compensation		X	
Nutrition			
Food stamps		X	
School lunches		X	
Women and Infants and Children (WIC)		X	
Health			
Medicare (aged)	X		
Medicaid (poor)		X	
Public health			X
Social Services			
Mental health			X
Drug and alcohol abuse			X
Child protection			X
Social services for the elderly			X
Social services for the disabled			X
Housing assistance			X

there are dependent children. However, if the spouse has no dependent children, benefits will not begin until he or she reaches retirement age. Finally, OASDI ensures benefit payments to people who suffer permanent and total disabilities that prevent them from working more than one year.

OASDI is a completely federal program, administered by the Social Security Administration in the Department of Health and Human Services. However, OASDI has an important indirect effect on state and local welfare programs, by removing people in whole or in part from welfare roles. By compelling people to insure themselves against the possibility of their own poverty, Social Security has doubtlessly reduced the welfare problems that state and local governments would otherwise face.

Unemployment Compensation   The second feature of the Social Security Act was that it induced states to enact unemployment compensation programs through the imposition of the payroll tax on all employers. A federal unemployment tax is levied on the payroll of employers of four or more workers, but employers paying into state insurance programs that meet federal standards may use these state payments to offset most of their federal unemployment tax. In other words, the federal government threatens to undertake an unemployment compensation program and tax if the states do not do so themselves. This federal program succeeded in inducing all fifty states to establish unemployment compensation programs. However, the federal standards are flexible, and the states have some freedom in shaping their own unemployment programs. In all cases, unemployed workers must report in person and show that they are willing and able to work in order to receive unemployment compensation benefits, and states cannot deny workers benefits for refusing to work as strikebreakers or refusing to work for rates lower than prevailing rates.

PUBLIC ASSISTANCE

A third major feature of the Social Security Act was its public assistance provisions. The OASDI and unemployment compensation programs were based upon the insurance principle, but the federal government also undertook to help the states provide assistance payments to certain needy persons.

Cash Programs: SSI and AFDC   Today, the federal government directly aids three categories of welfare recipients—the aged, the blind, and the disabled—under a program called Supplemental Security Income (SSI). The federal government also provides *grants to the states* to assist the fourth and largest category—families with dependent children. Within broad outlines of the federal policy, states retain some discretion in the Aid to Families with Dependent Children (AFDC) program in terms of the amounts of money appropriated, benefits to be paid to recipients, and rules of the program, such as rules of eligibility. Each state may choose to grant assistance beyond the amounts supported by the national government. Each state establishes its own standards to determine "need." As a result, there is a great deal of variation among the states in ease of access to welfare rolls and in the size of welfare benefits. (See Figure 17–3.)

Federal Oversight   Federal standards for state AFDC programs are established as a prerequisite to receiving federal aid. Federal law requires the states to make financial contributions to their public assistance programs and to supervise these programs either directly or through local agencies. Whatever standards a state adopts must be applicable throughout the state, and there must be no discrimination in these welfare programs. The federal Department of Health and Human Services demands periodic reporting from the states, insists that states administer federally supported programs under a merit system of employment, and prevents the states from imposing unreasonable residence requirements on recipients. However, in questions of administration, standards of eligibility, types of assistance, and amounts of payments, the states are free to determine their own welfare programs.

Food Stamps   The Food Stamp Program now distributes billions in federal monies to improve food and nutrition among the poor. Eligible persons may receive food stamps, generally from county welfare departments, which may be used to purchase food at supermarkets. This program has mushroomed very rapidly since its origins, with expansions in eligible population and increases in the costs of food. Eligibility for food stamps now extends to many people who are not poor enough to qualify for public assistance. Federal expenditures for food stamps are

AFDC Average Monthly Payments Dollars Per Family: 1990

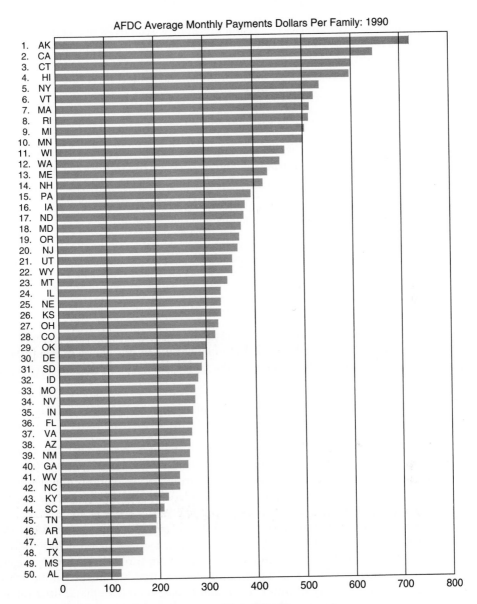

**FIGURE 17–3   AFDC Average Monthly Payments
in Dollars per Family, 1990**

rapidly approaching federal expenditures for the AFDC program, making food stamps a major subsidy for low-income families.

Housing Assistance   Housing assistance is also a major in kind benefit program for the poor. An estimated 6 million people live in 2 million housing units in the nation that benefit from various federal housing subsidies.

Other Social Programs   Public assistance recipients are generally eligible for participation in a variety of other social programs. These include school lunch and milk; job training; various educational and child care programs and services; special food programs for women, infants, and children (WIC); home heating and weatherization assistance; free legal services; and more.

WELFARE POLITICS IN THE STATES

Political conflict over welfare policy arises in part from a clash of values over individual responsibility and social compassion. As Harvard sociologist David Ellwood explains:

> Welfare brings some of our most precious values—involving autonomy, responsibility, work, family, community and compassion—into conflict. We want to help those who are not making it but in so doing, we seem to cheapen the efforts of those who are struggling hard just to get by. We want to offer financial support to those with low incomes, but if we do we reduce the pressure on them and their incentive to work. We want to help people who are not able to help themselves but then we worry that people will not bother to help themselves. We recognize the insecurity of single-parent families but, in helping them, we appear to be promoting or supporting their formation.[6]

While the social insurance programs (Social Security, Medicare, and unemployment compensation) are politically popular and enjoy the support of large numbers of active beneficiaries, the public assistance programs (AFDC, SSI, and Medicaid) are far less popular.

Welfare Controversies   A variety of controversies surround public assistance programs in the states:

Work Disincentives   In most states, if a recipient of assistance takes a full-time job, assistance checks are reduced or stopped. If the former recipient is then laid off, it may take some time to get back on welfare. In other words, employment is uncertain, while assistance is not. The jobs available to most recipients are very low-paying jobs that do not produce much more income than does assistance, particularly when transportation, child care, and other costs of working are considered. Moreover, a family on the welfare rolls is generally entitled to participate in the Food Stamp Program, to receive health care through Medicaid, to gain access to free or low-rent public housing, to receive free lunches in public schools, and to receive a variety of other social and educational benefits at little or no cost to themselves. These benefits and services are available to the poor and are not counted as income, yet the nonpoor must pay for similar services out of their own earnings. If a family head on welfare takes a job, he or she not only loses welfare assistance, but, more important perhaps, becomes ineligible for food stamps, Medicaid, public housing, and many other social services.

---

[6] David Ellwood, *Poor Support: Poverty in the American Family* (New York: Basic Books, 1988), p. 6.

The Working Poor   Many of the nation's poor do not receive public assistance. Of the 34 million poor people in the United States in 1990, perhaps 10 million received no federal or state welfare benefits at all. Many of these poor are working poor who are ineligible for welfare assistance because they hold jobs, even though these jobs pay very little.

Cash Versus In Kind Assistance   The merits of cash versus goods and services as a form of public assistance have long been debated. It is frequently argued that cash payments are ineffective in alleviating poverty because recipients are often unable to manage household money. They fall prey to advertising that encourages them to spend money for nonessential items and to overlook the food and clothing needs of themselves and their children. Assistance in the form of goods (e.g., food stamps that can only be used to purchase basic food items) and services (e.g., health care, day care for children, home management counseling) might represent a more effective approach. However, recipients themselves resent the goods and services approach, charging that it is paternalistic, that it curtails flexibility in family spending, and that it implies irresponsibility on the part of the recipient.

Welfare Costs   Welfare benefits to recipients are very modest. The median benefit across the nation in 1992 (cash assistance plus food stamps) was about 75 percent of the poverty level. Even adding noncash benefits (Medicaid, school lunches, etc.) fails to lift welfare families out of poverty. The problem is not that we are spending too much on the poor, but that too little of what we spend on welfare actually finds its way to the poor.

Much of the spending is absorbed by an expanding bureaucracy for delivering social services that eats up a disproportionate amount of the funds available for fighting poverty. For instance in 1984 a study found that two-thirds of every dollar spent by Cook County (which includes Chicago) went to social service providers rather than to the poor.[7]

Workfare   In the Family Support Act of 1988, liberals and conservatives joined in an effort to reform the largest cash assistance program, Aid to Families with Dependent Children. The goal was to end long-term dependence on welfare. The fact that most nonpoor mothers work convinced many liberals that welfare mothers have no special claim to stay at home. And conservatives acknowledged that some transitional aid—education, job training, continued health care, and day care for children—might be necessary to move welfare mothers into the work force.

The Family Support Act requires that states

- Develop a federal job training program (JOBS) for most adults receiving AFDC payments; AFDC recipients who are not exempt because of age, illness, or disability may be required to participate.
- Provide child care for JOBS participants.

---

[7] Will Marshall and Elaine Ciulla Kamark "Replacing Welfare with Work," in *Mandate for Change,* Will Marshall and Martin Schran, eds. (New York: Berkeley Books, 1993), p. 224.

- Furnish transitional child care and Medicaid for 12 months after a participant leaves AFDC to take a job.
- Strengthen its child support enforcement programs.

But the states have been slow to fully implement the program; neither the federal government nor the states have fully funded the JOBS or child care provisions of the act; and a recession in 1991 increased welfare rolls beyond expectations. More importantly, moving people from welfare rolls to private employment has proven to be very difficult.

Clinton's Reforms   Like earlier welfare reform efforts, the Clinton administration proposes to "empower people with the education, training, child care they need for up to two years, so they can break the cycle of dependency." However, Clinton proposes to go one important step further: "After two years, require those who can work to go to work, either in the private sector or in community service."[8] But a two-year limit to welfare payments is viewed as "punitive" by many liberal groups, even with education, training, child care, and continuing Medicaid benefits. Conservatives note that the extensive benefits and supports required to end welfare dependency will end up costing taxpayers even more than continued welfare payments. Many long-term welfare recipients will be unable to find private employment; the "community service" alternative may turn out to be costly make-work. Yet the Clinton reforms imply a social compact—the responsibility of welfare recipients to strive for self-sufficiency in return for community support.

Variations in Benefits Among States   What accounts for differences among the states in welfare policy? A state's income is the single most important determinant of the level of welfare benefits. In terms of welfare payments, it is far better to be poor in a wealthy state than in a poor one.

Poorer states have larger proportions of their populations on public assistance rolls and lower welfare benefit payments. This means they pay smaller amounts of money to larger numbers of people. The federal government pays a large share of public assistance costs in poorer states, while requiring richer states to share a greater portion of their public assistance costs. Federal percentages of the total public assistance expenditures *decline* with increases in state income levels.

Party Competition and Welfare Policy   What effect does party competition have on welfare policies in the states? The traditional assumption in the political science literature was that competition would make governments more responsive to the interests and needs of the have-nots. And, indeed, it is true that welfare benefits are higher in those states with greater party competition. However, these states are also the more economically developed states with higher income and education levels. It is difficult to sort out the effect of party competition from the effect of economic development on welfare benefits. Nonetheless, the evidence supports the view that economic development is *more* influential than party competition in determining welfare policies. In other words, states devote more money

---

[8] Bill Clinton and Al Gore, *Putting People First* (New York: Times Books, 1992), p. 165.

to helping have-nots because they have more economic resources to do so, and not necessarily because of political competition. Competition, however, does have *some* independent effect on liberalizing welfare benefits.[9]

HEALTH CARE POLICY

America spends more of its resources on health care than any other nation. Currently over 12 percent of the nation's GNP is devoted to health care. Americans spend nearly twice as much per capita on health than the Japanese or Europeans. Nonetheless, the United States ranks well *below* other advanced democracies in key measures of the health of its people, including average life spans and infant death rates. (See Table 17–4.) Moreover, unlike most other advanced democracies that make provision for health care for all citizens, there are an estimated 35 million people in the United States, nearly 15 percent of the population, who have no medical insurance—governmental or private—and who therefore have no guarantee of access to medical care. In short, the American health care system is the most expensive and least universal in its coverage in the world.

TABLE 17–4   HEALTH AND HEALTH CARE COSTS IN ADVANCED DEMOCRACIES

	Health Costs as Percentage of GNP	Life Expectancy	Infant Death Rate
United States	12.4	75.7	10.3
Australia	7.5	78.7	7.9
Austria	8.4	78.9	5.4
Belgium	7.4	78.8	5.5
Canada	9.0	79.2	7.2
Denmark	6.2	78.0	6.1
France	8.9	79.3	6.1
Germany	8.1	77.9	7.1
Greece	5.3	79.3	10.0
Italy	7.7	79.6	6.0
Japan	6.5	80.8	4.4
Spain	6.6	78.3	6.2
Sweden	8.7	77.8	5.9
Switzerland	7.7	79.1	4.7
United Kingdom	6.2	76.5	7.2

Source: Statistical Abstract of the United States, 1992, p. 825.

---

[9] For a full discussion of the problems of assessing the relative effects of political and economic forces on public policy, see Thomas R. Dye, *Understanding Public Policy,* 7th ed. (Englewood Cliffs, NJ: Prentice Hall, 1992), Chap 2.

The Health of Americans   Good health correlates best with factors over which doctors and hospitals have no direct control: heredity, life style (smoking, eating, drinking, exercise, stress), and the physical environment. Historically, most of the reductions in death rates have resulted from public health and sanitation improvements, including immunization against smallpox, clean public water supplies, sanitary sewage disposal, improved diets, and increased standards of living. Many of the leading causes of death today, including heart disease, stroke, cirrhosis of the liver, accidents, and suicides, are closely linked to personal habits and life styles and are beyond the reach of medicine. Thus, the greatest contribution to better health is likely to be found in altered personal habits and life styles, rather than in more medical care.

Community Public Health and Hospitals   Public health and sanitation are among the oldest functions of local government. Keeping clean is still one of the major tasks of cities today, a task that includes street cleaning, sewage disposal, garbage collection, and the provision of a clean water supply. Very often these services are taken for granted in the United States, but in many underdeveloped countries of the world, health and sanitation are still major concerns.

Local public health departments are directly concerned with the *prevention* of disease. They engage in compulsory vaccination, immunization, and quarantine, as well as regulatory activity in the processing of milk and the safeguarding of water supplies.

In addition to the preventive activities of the public health departments, state and local governments also provide extensive, tax-supported hospital care. State and local governments provide both general and specialized hospitals, health centers, and nursing homes and very often subsidize private hospitals and medical facilities as well. New York City operates the nation's largest city hospital system, but almost every community subsidizes hospital facilities in some way. City and county hospitals and heavily subsidized private hospitals are expected to provide at least emergency care to indigent patients.

Medicare   The federal government added *Medicare* to the Social Security program in 1965. Medicare provides for prepaid hospital insurance for the aged, and low-cost voluntary medical insurance for the aged under federal administration. Medicare includes (1) a compulsory basic health insurance plan covering hospital costs for the aged, which is financed through payroll taxes collected under the Social Security system; and (2) a voluntary but supplemental medical program that will pay doctors' bills and additional medical expenses, financed in part by contributions from the aged and in part by the general tax revenues. Only aged persons are covered by Medicare.

Medicaid   The federal government also provides federal funds under *Medicaid* to enable states to guarantee medical services to the poor. Each state operates its own Medicaid program. Unlike Medicare, Medicaid is a welfare program designed for needy persons; no prior contributions are required, and recipients of Medicaid services are generally welfare recipients. States can extend coverage to other medically needy persons if they choose to do so.

Paying the Health Care Bill   Government pays about 41 percent of all health care costs—through Medicare for the aged, Medicaid for the poor, and other government programs including military and veterans care. Private insurance pays for 32 percent of the nation's health costs; direct patient payments count for only 25 percent. (See Figure 17–4.)

Health Care Inflation   The costs of health care in the United States have risen much faster than prices in general. Medical costs have nearly tripled over the last ten years, and they consume an increasingly larger percentage of the nation's total output. Advances in medical technology have produced elaborate and expensive equipment. Hospitals that have made heavy financial investment in this equipment must use it as often as possible. Physicians trained in highly specialized techniques and procedures wish to use them. Physicians and hospitals are forced by the threat of malpractice litigation to use the most advanced tests and treatments.

Coping with Costs   Various efforts have been made to counter rising costs. Private insurers have negotiated discounts with groups of physicians and with hospitals (so-called "preferred provider organizations") and have implemented rules to guide physicians about when patients should and should not receive costly diagnostic and therapeutic procedures (so-called "managed care"). The government has replaced payments to hospitals under Medicare based on costs incurred, with payment of fixed fees based on primary and secondary diagnoses at the time of admission (the diagnosis related group, or DRG system). Government and private insurers have encouraged the expansion of health maintenance organizations (HMOs) that promise to provide a stipulated list of services to patients for a fixed fee and that are able to provide care at lower total costs than can other providers.

FIGURE 17–4   Who Pays the Health Care Bill?
Source: Statistical Abstract of the United States, 1992

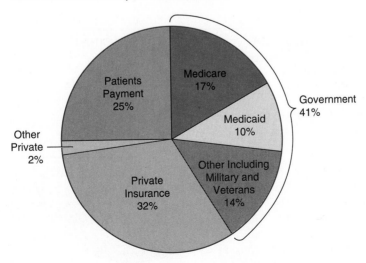

Nonetheless, health care costs continue to rise. Whether this trend reflects the failure of cost control efforts or the strength of forces driving up costs is not clear. What is increasingly obvious is that payers, private and public, are finding health care costs increasingly burdensome and even insupportable.

Medicaid in the States   Medicaid is the costliest of all public assistance programs. States must pay about 43 percent of Medicaid's costs, with the federal government paying the remainder. Medicaid is the most rapidly growing item in the budget of most states.

Medicaid is increasingly becoming the last resort for people who have no medical insurance and for those whose insurance does not cover long-term illness or nursing home care. People confronted with serious or "catastrophic" illness who exhaust their private insurance or Medicare coverage are often forced to impoverish themselves in order to qualify for Medicaid. (Medicare pays for only 60 days of hospital care and 100 days of nursing home care.) Moreover, as the number and proportion of the very old in society rise (those 80 years and over comprise the nation's fastest growing age group), the need for long-term nursing home care grows. Medicaid is the only program that covers nursing home care, but middle-class people must first "spend down" their savings or transfer their wealth to others in order to qualify for Medicaid. Nursing home care is now the largest item in Medicaid spending. (See Figure 17–5.)

POLITICS AND HEALTH CARE REFORM

Health care reform centers on two central problems: controlling costs and expanding access. These problems are related: Expanding access to Americans who are currently uninsured and closing gaps in coverage require increases in costs, even while the central thrust of reform is to bring down overall health care costs.

No system of health care provides as much care as people want. Each individual, believing his or her health and life are at stake, will want the most thorough

FIGURE 17–5   Medicaid Expenditures

Source: Statistical Abstract of the United States, 1992.

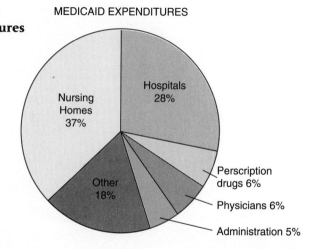

MEDICAID EXPENDITURES

Nursing Homes 37%
Hospitals 28%
Other 18%
Perscription drugs 6%
Physicians 6%
Administration 5%

diagnostic testing, the most constant care, the most advanced treatment. Physicians have no strong incentive to save on costs; they want the most advanced diagnostic and treatment facilities available for their patients. Any tendency for physicians to limit testing and treatment is countered by the threat of malpractice suits. So both patients and physicians push up the costs of health care when public and private insurance, "third party payers," foot the bill.

Rationing—The Oregon Plan   Oregon is the only state to have confronted the problem of limits to health care in a direct fashion. In reforming its Medicaid program, Oregon sought to expand coverage to everyone at or below the poverty line, yet at the same time to limit costs. It did so by engaging a panel of citizens and medical groups to draw up a list of 709 medical services ranked from highest to lowest priority, based on both the seriousness of the condition to be treated and the likelihood that treatment would be effective. High priorities were awarded to treatments to prevent death in patients likely to recover (appendectomy, medications for heart disease) and to effective preventative care (mammograms, blood pressure screening). Low on the priority list were conditions that get better by themselves (head colds, flu) and conditions where treatment is generally futile (severe brain injuries, end-stage cancer). Medicaid patients are eligible for as many treatments as the state legislature decides to fund in any year. Thus, in the first year, legislature appropriations covered 587 of the 709 treatments (with low-back pain as the cutoff point at 588).

State innovations in Medicaid, as well as many other federal aid programs, usually require waivers from the federal government. The Bush administration initially denied the Oregon plan a waiver, but the Clinton administration did so, thereby encouraging a new approach to health care reform.

"Play or Pay"   States have also experimented with various methods of expanding health insurance coverage to those currently uninsured, including persons working for employers who do not provide insurance and persons who are unemployed. A "play or pay" approach requires all employers to either provide health insurance to all their workers and their dependents or alternatively pay into a state fund that would purchase insurance for uncovered workers. Rules are usually established concerning the proportion of premium costs paid by employers and employees and the range of services covered. While this approach expands coverage, it does little to control costs.

Managed Competition   Some states have experimented with managed competition as an approach to health care cost containment. Management competition is an arrangement in which health insurance purchasing organizations (HIPOs) are organized to pool health insurance purchasers (employers and individuals) in order to improve their bargaining power with insurers and providers. HIPOs are usually required to accept all applicants, including those with preexisting conditions. They receive government subsidies for members of groups expected to generate especially high costs. They negotiate costs either with insurance companies or directly with hospitals and physicians. Because of their size they are better able to collect information and identify providers that supply high-quality care at reasonable prices.

The Interest Group Battle   While there is widespread public support for the general goals of health care reform—expanding coverage and reducing costs—there is no agreement among the principal interest groups on health care politics about the details of reform. *Insurance companies* are unhappy with the notion of health insurance purchasing organizations that would bargain down insurance premiums or even bypass insurance companies altogether and deal directly with hospitals and physicians' groups. *Physicians* strongly oppose price controls and treatment guidelines; they also oppose any program that takes away patient choice of physicians. *Hospitals,* both public and private profit making, oppose government payment schedules. *Drug companies* want to see prescription drugs paid for by government-sponsored insurance, but they vigorously oppose price controls on drugs. All of these groups have strong lobbying organizations in state capitals and in Washington, DC, and all have PAC's that contribute heavily to state and national political campaigns.

National Health Care Reform   President Bill Clinton campaigned on the promise to reform the nation's health care system—both expanding access and containing costs.

> The American health-care system costs too much and does not work. It leaves 60 million Americans without adequate health insurance and bankrupts our families, our businesses, and our federal budget. . . .
> Health care should be a right, not a privilege.[10]

A comprehensive national program incorporates much of the knowledge gained from experimentation in the states.

---

[10] Clinton and Gore, *Putting People First.*

18

THE POLITICS OF BUDGETING AND TAXATION

▲

AN OVERVIEW OF GOVERNMENT FINANCES

Governments do many things that cannot be measured in dollars. Nonetheless, government expenditures are the best available measure of overall government activity. The expenditure side of a government's budget tells us what public funds are being spent for, and the revenue side tell us how these funds are being raised.

Government Finances and the GNP   Dollars figures in government budgets are often mind-boggling. The federal government spends over $1.5 *trillion* each year, and all state and local governments combined spend an additional $1 *trillion*. To better understand what these dollar figures mean, it is helpful to view them in relation to the nation's gross domestic product (GDP), the sum of all the goods and services produced in the United States in a year.[1] (See Figure 18–1)

Over time governmental spending in the United States has grown faster than the economy. In 1929 total governmental spending—federal, state, and local combined—amounted to only about 10 percent of the GDP. Today total governmental spending amounts to nearly 37 percent of GDP. *Federal* spending accounts for about 23 percent of GDP, and spending by all *state and local* governments adds another 14 percent.

State and Local Government Spending   State and local governments direct most of their spending toward education, social services (welfare and health), public safety (police and fire), and transportation.

Education is the most costly of these functions; health costs are rising more rapidly than any other function.

FIGURE 18–1   Growth of Government Spending Expenditures as a Percentage of GDP

Source: Advisory Commission on Intergovernmental Relations. *Significant Features of Fiscal Federalism 1992*

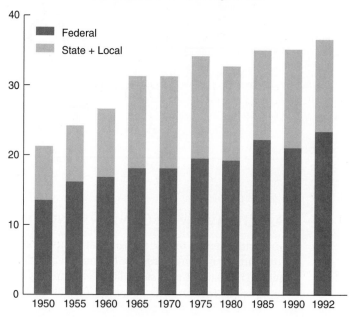

GROWTH OF GOVERNMENT SPENDING
Expenditures as a Percentage of GNP

[1] The gross domestic product is replacing the gross national product (GNP) as a measure of national economic activity. The GDP and GNP are roughly equivalent in dollars.

State and Local Government Revenues   State and local governments in the United States derive revenue from a variety of sources. Of course, taxes are the largest source of revenue, accounting for nearly 60 percent of all state and local revenue. Federal grants are another major source of state and local government revenue (see Chapter 3), accounting for over 16 percent of total revenues. User charges of various kinds, from water and sewer, liquor store and electric utility revenues, to transit fares and admission fees, account for about 14 percent of all state–local revenue. Lotteries now bring in about 2 percent of all state–local revenue, and the remainder is derived from insurance premiums, licenses, fines, and miscellaneous sources.

TYPES OF TAXES AND TAX POLITICS

The politics of taxation often center about the question of who actually bears the burden or "incidence" of a tax, that is, which income groups must devote the largest proportion of their income to taxes. Taxes that require high-income groups to pay a larger percentage of their incomes in taxes than low-income groups are said to be *progressive,* while taxes that take a larger share of the income of low-income groups are said to be *regressive.* Taxation at equal percentage rates, regardless of income level, is said to be *proportional.*

Local Property Taxes   Property taxes are the largest source of revenue for local governments in the United States. (See Figure 18–2.) However, property taxes are usually regressive. This conclusion is based on the assumption that renters actually pay their property taxes through increased rentals levied by the landlord, and the further assumption that high-income groups have more wealth in untaxed forms of property. Since the property tax is the foundation of local tax structures in every state, it is reasonable to conclude that states that rely largely upon local governments for taxes and services are relying more upon regressive tax structures. Yet, in defense of property taxation, it is often argued that no other form of taxation is really feasible for local governments. Local sales and income taxes force individuals and businesses to leave the communities levying them; real estate, on the other hand, is less easy to move about and hide from local tax assessors. Real estate taxes are the only type of taxes that can be effectively collected by relatively untrained local tax officials.

Revenues from property taxation depend upon the property wealth of a community. Dependence upon property taxation means that wealthier communities will be able to raise more funds with less burden on taxpayers than communities without much property wealth. In other words, reliance on property taxation results in inequalities in burdens and benefits between wealthier and poorer communities.

The burden of property taxes depends on (1) the ratio of assessed value of property to the fair market value of the property; (2) the rate at which assessed property is taxed, which is usually expressed in mills, or tenths of a percent; and finally, (3) the nature and extent of tax exemptions and reductions for certain types of property. The ratio of assessed value to full market value may vary from one

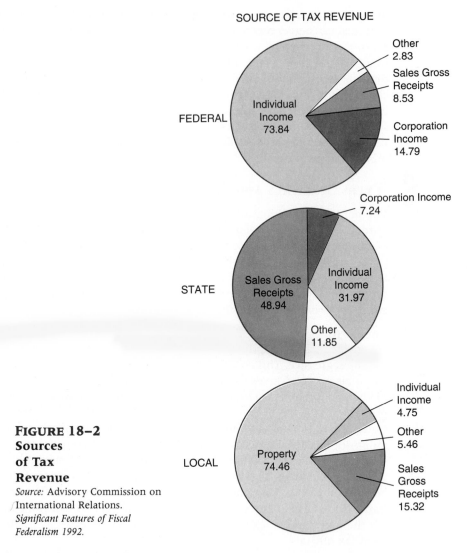

SOURCE OF TAX REVENUE

**FIGURE 18–2
Sources
of Tax
Revenue**
Source: Advisory Commission on
International Relations.
*Significant Features of Fiscal
Federalism 1992.*

community to the next, even in states with laws requiring uniform assessment ratios throughout the state. The failure of communities to have periodic and professional tax evaluation means that taxes continue to be levied on old assessment figures, even while market values go up. The result, over time, is a considerable lowering of assessment ratios, and therefore taxes, on older homes and businesses and industries. Newer residents, whose sale price is generally known to tax assessors, must therefore pay taxes on the uniform assessment ratio. There are very few communities in which a suggestion of a reevaluation will not set off a heated debate between those who are enjoying a low assessment and those who are not. When a community tampers with reevaluation or a change in the ratio of assessed to market value, it threatens to change the incidence or distribution of tax burdens within a community. If new tax revenues are needed, it is much easier to simply increase the rate or millage to be applied against the assessed value of property. Many communities face state restrictions on maximum tax rates, or they are required to submit any proposed increase in tax rates to the voters in a referendum. These restrictions are usually favored by low-tax forces, which have succeeded in obtaining legislation at the state level that impairs the taxing abilities of local governments.

Some categories of property are exempt from taxation; these usually include properties that are used for nonprofit, charitable, religious, educational, and other public purposes. Occasionally, such exemptions are attacked by those who feel that they are, in effect, subsidies to the exempted organizations; this is particularly true regarding exemptions for religious property. Exemptions for educational or public properties sometimes work a hardship on communities in which large public facilities or educational institutions are located. However, the exemptions that arouse the greatest controversy are usually those given by state or local governments to new business and industry, in an effort to induce them to locate in the state or community granting the exemption.

State Sales Taxes   While the property tax is the most important source of revenue for local communities, *the general sales tax is the most important source of tax revenue for state governments.* Consumers are a notoriously weak pressure group. It is difficult for them to count pennies dribbled away four or five at a time; the tax does not involve obvious payroll deductions, as in income taxation, or year-end bills, as in property taxation. As of 1992 only five states did *not* impose a general sales tax (Alaska, Delaware, Montana, New Hampshire, and Oregon).

State and local *sales and excise taxes* are generally considered regressive, but not as regressive as property taxes. The regressivity of sales taxation is based upon the assumption that low-income groups must devote most, if not all, of their income to purchases, while high-income groups devote larger shares of their income to savings. However, many states exclude some of the necessities of life from sales taxation, such as packaged food, rent, and medical expenses, in order to reduce the burden of sales taxation on the poor. Because of these exclusions, sales taxes in many states are proportional.

States generally rely more heavily on sales taxation than on income taxation. However, reliance upon one or the other type of tax varies from state to state. The decision to place primary reliance upon sales or income taxation is one of the most important policy choices facing state government. The yield from both types of taxation can be quite large.

There are several arguments on behalf of sales taxation in the states. The first is that sales taxation is the only major source of revenue left to the states—local governments must rely on property taxes, and the federal government has placed such a heavy tax burden on incomes that taxpayers will not countenance an additional state bite out of their paychecks. Moreover, sales taxes are not as visible as income or property taxes, since sales taxes are paid pennies at a time. Generally, the customer considers the sales tax as part of the price of an item. Taxpayers never add up the total they have paid in sales taxes, so sales taxation appears to be a relatively "painless" form of taxation. In addition, sales taxes ensure that low-income groups who benefit from public services will share in the costs of government. Actual hardships for the poor from sales taxes can be reduced by excluding food and other necessities from taxation, but the poor will pay taxes when purchasing other consumer items. Finally, sales taxes are useful in reaching mobile populations, that is, tourists, commuters, and transients—people who derive benefits from a host state but who would not otherwise help pay for these benefits.

State Income Taxes   Wisconsin enacted the first modern, enforceable state income tax in 1911, and more than half the states had adopted income taxation by 1940. Today forty-one states tax all forms of individual income and two additional states tax nonwage income. But seven states eschew income taxation altogether, and two additional states do not tax wage income. (See Table 18–1.) Connecticut

TABLE 18–1   INCOME TAXATION IN THE STATES, 1992

States Without Income Taxes	States Taxing Interest, Dividends, and Capital Gains Only
Alaska	New Hampshire
Florida	Tennessee
Nevada	
South Dakota	
Texas	
Washington	
Wyoming	

States Taxing Adjusted Gross Income (rate ranges in parentheses)

Alabama (2.0–5.0)	Kansas (4.5–6.0)	New York (4.3–7.9)
Arizona (3.8–7.0)	Kentucky (2.0–6.0)	North Carolina (6.0–7.7)
Arkansas (1.0–7.0)	Louisiana (2.0–6.0)	North Dakota (2.6–12.0)
California (1.0–11.0)	Maine (2.0–8.6)	Ohio (0.7–6.9)
Connecticut (4.5)	Maryland (2.0–5.0)	Oklahoma (0.5–7.0)
Colorado (5.0)	Massachusetts (5.0–12.0)	Oregon (5.0–9.0)
Delaware (3.2–7.7)	Michigan (4.6)	Pennsylvania (3.1)
Georgia (1.0–6.0)	Minnesota (6.0–8.5)	Rhode Island (27.5% federal)[a]
Hawaii (2.0–10.0)	Mississippi (3.0–5.0)	South Carolina (2.5–7.0)
Idaho (2.0–8.2)	Missouri (1.5–6.0)	Utah (2.6–7.2)
Illinois (3.0)	Montana (2.0–11.0)	Vermont (25–34% federal)[a]
Indiana (3.4)	Nebraska (2.4–6.9)	Virginia (2.0–5.8)
Iowa (0.4–10.0)	New Jersey (2.0–7.0)	West Virginia (3.0–6.5)
	New Mexico (1.8–8.5)	Wisconsin (4.9–6.9)

[a] State income taxes determined as a percentage of federal income tax liability.

Source: Data from Council of State Governments, *Book of the States 1992–93* (Lexington: Council of State Governments, 1992) pp. 400–401.

was the most recent state to enact an income tax in 1991. Fiscal pressures on state government continue to stir debate in the non–income tax states over the adoption of the tax.

State *income taxes* are usually defended on the principle of "ability to pay"; that is, the theory that high-income groups can afford to pay a larger percentage of their income into taxation at no more of a sacrifice than that required of low-income groups who devote a smaller proportion of their income to taxation. The principle of a graduated income tax based on ability to pay, a principle accepted at the federal level in 1913 with the passage of the Sixteenth Amendment, together with the convenience, economy, and efficiency of income taxes, is generally cited by proponents of income taxation.

Personal income taxes in a few states are "flat rate" taxes of 3 percent (Illinois) or 5.0 percent (Colorado) of personal income. In other income tax states, the rates are "progressive"—rising from 2 to 3 percent, to 10 or 11 percent, with increases in income levels. A handful of states tie their *state* personal income tax to the *federal* income tax, by specifying that state taxes will be a specific percentage of federal taxes. Most states also have their own systems of exemptions.

Corporate Taxes   In addition to property taxes paid to local governments, corporations in forty-six states pay a corporate income tax. (Nevada, Texas, Washington, and Wyoming do not tax corporate income.) These taxes range from a 5 percent flat rate to sliding scales of 3 to 12 percent of net profits. Raising corporate taxes is popular with voters; individuals do not pay corporate taxes directly; but these taxes may be passed along to consumers in higher prices. The greatest barrier to higher state corporate taxes is the possibility that such taxes will cause corporations to locate in another state. It is difficult for a state to maintain a "good business climate" if its corporate taxes are high. Most studies find that industrial-location decisions are influenced by many factors other than taxes—for example, access to markets, raw materials, skilled labor, and energy. However, businesses expect their taxes to be kept in line with those of their competitors. In addition to corporate profits taxes, business looks at unemployment compensation and worker's compensation "premiums" (taxes) and the costs of environmental regulations.

Lottery and Gambling Revenue   More than half the states receive income from horse racing, gambling, or lotteries. Nevada leads the way with nearly a quarter of its revenue coming directly from gambling taxes. Nevada allows casino gambling throughout the state; New Jersey permits casino gambling in Atlantic City. Most states restrict gambling to parimutuel betting on the racetrack. The total revenues raised from such sources, however, make up less than 0.5 percent of all state–local revenues.

Over half of the states now have public lotteries as a means of raising money. However, lotteries bring in less than 2 percent of all state–local government revenue. The administrative costs, including prize money, run about 50 percent of the gross revenue. This compares very unfavorably with the estimated 5 percent cost of collecting income taxes, and with the only slightly higher cost of collecting sales taxes.

User Charges   User charges are currently the fastest growing source of state and local government revenue. Today charges and miscellaneous revenues constitute nearly 25 percent of state–local revenue. (This figure is really a combination of user charges, utility and liquor store revenues, and miscellaneous revenues.) User charges directly link the benefits and costs of public goods in the fashion of the marketplace. Only those persons who actually use the government service pay for it. User charges include charges for water and sewer, garbage collection, electricity supplied by municipalities, transit fares, toll roads, airport landing fees, space rentals, parking meters, stadium fees, admissions to parks, zoos, swimming pools, and so on.

EXPLAINING STATE TAX SYSTEMS

What accounts for differences in tax policy among the states? Total state–local tax revenues in 1990 varied from a high of over $3,200 per person in New York, to a low of $1,264 in Mississippi (see Figure 18–3). This means that per capita tax levels of some states are over twice as high as those of other states. (Alaska and Wyoming receive most of their tax revenues from *severance taxes* on oil, gas, and coal extracted from the land. The burden of these taxes falls on consumers throughout the nation rather than directly on these states' residents.) Tax burdens, that is, taxes in relation to personal income, also vary considerably among the states (see Figure 18–3).

First of all, let us examine the effect of economic development on levels of taxation in the states. There is little doubt that the ability of the states to raise tax revenue is a function of their level of economic development.

The concept of tax *burden* generally refers to taxes paid in relation to personal income; because of differences among the states in income levels, states with the highest *levels of taxation* (see Figure 18–3) are not necessarily the same states with the highest *tax burdens* (see Figure 18–3). The total tax burden in a state is measured by "total state and local tax revenues as a percentage of personal income." The state–local tax burden averages 11.5 percent of personal income in the United States.

Among the fifty states, high levels of economic development usually reduce the burdens of taxation. Wealthy states can collect a great deal of tax monies without taking a very large percentage of personal income. High tax burdens are not necessarily a product of high tax levels, although, of course, there is some relationship between these variables (e.g., New York). Yet, high tax levels in an urbanized, industrialized, high-income state may not necessarily be accompanied by a heavy tax burden (e.g., Connecticut). It is possible to have low tax levels that, because of the lack of industry and low income levels, may be very burdensome—that is, quite high in relation to low incomes (e.g., West Virginia).

Another important difference between richer and poorer states is in the degree of decentralization in state and local finance and administration. Local governments tend to play a greater role in the collection of taxes and the provision of public services in urban, high-income states, while state governments collect a greater portion of revenue and provide more services in rural, low-income states. Earlier, we observed that state governments in poorer rural states undertake more

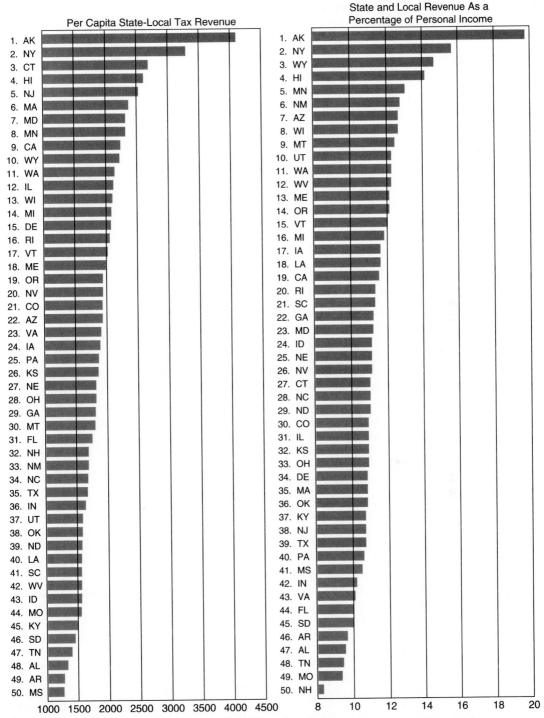

FIGURE 18–3 Per Capita State–Local Tax Revenue and State and Local Revenue as a Percentage of Personal Income

Source: *Statistical Abstract of the United States, 1992.*

direct responsibilities in education, welfare, and highways. Low levels of economic development tend to force decentralization upon these states. Wealthy urban states can afford to let local governments shoulder more responsibilities.

REVOLTING AGAINST TAXES

The United States is the land of tax revolts. The national tradition of revolting against taxes includes the Boston Tea Party in 1773, a leading event in the movement toward independence; Shay's Rebellion in 1786, an important stimulus to creating the Constitution of the United States; and the Whisky Rebellion of 1794, forcefully extinguished by President George Washington. The political culture of the nation has always reflected a distrust of government power. The total tax burden in the United States is less than most other advanced industrialized nations of the world. Yet opinion polls regularly show that most Americans believe their taxes are "too high."

Public Opinion About Taxes   Much of the popular grievance about tax burdens is directed (accurately) against *federal* taxation. The federal income tax is most often mentioned as "the worst tax . . . the least fair" (see Table 18–2). Local property taxes are not very popular either; they were perceived as "the worst tax" in the 1970s.

The "tax revolt" that swept the nation in the 1980s and inspired federal tax reform got its start in the states. Indeed it might be traced to a 1978 California referendum, known as "Proposition 13." California citizens were sufficiently aroused to ignore the pleas and warnings of business, labor, and government leaders and pass a property-tax–cutting citizen referendum by a two-to-one margin. (See Chapter 2.)

However, despite predictions of a *national* tax revolt, voters were not stampeded into slashing taxes at every opportunity, regardless of the consequences. While some states voted to limit state and local taxing and spending, other states voted down identical taxing and spending limitations. Opinion polls that confront respondents with a *direct trade-off* between reducing taxes or cutting public services

TABLE 18–2   TAX ATTITUDES

"Which do you think is the worst tax—that is, the least fair?"					
	1992	1985	1982	1975	1972
Federal income tax	30	36	36	28	19
State income tax	16	10	11	11	13
State sales tax	17	15	14	17	13
Local property tax	23	29	30	33	45
Don't know	14	10	9	11	11

Source: Advisory Commission on Intergovernmental Relations. *Changing Public Attitudes on Government and Taxes 1992.*

show pluralities favoring keeping taxes "about the same," rather than "increasing" or "reducing" them. In other words, the largest group of voters seems willing to accept current tax levels if they are convinced that these burdens are directly tied to services—education, police, fire, sanitation, highways, and even welfare for the "truly deserving."

Tax Limitation Proposals   Tax limitation proposals fall into several general categories. Of course, any specific plan may vary in details from the outlines described here:

Property-Tax Limits   Some proposals are specifically directed at property taxes. These proposals may limit allowable tax rates to 10 or 15 mills of full value of property, limit annual assessment increases, and/or allow reassessments only when the property is sold. This form of limitation applies mainly to local governments and school districts and may actually increase state taxes if state governments simply take over local services.

Personal-Income Limits   A somewhat more complex scheme promises to limit state taxes to a certain percentage of the state's personal income. For example, if state taxes currently amount to 7 percent of a state's total personal income, a constitutional amendment could be offered to voters that limits all future state and local taxes to a total of no more than 7 percent of personal income. This prevents state government from growing at a faster rate than personal income, but it does allow tax revenues to rise.

Expenditure Limits   Similar restrictions can be placed on total state *expenditures*—limiting spending to a certain percentage of a state's total personal income. Presumably expenditure limits would hold down taxes over the long run, and therefore expenditure limits can be considered as an indirect form of tax limitation.

Prohibitions on Specific Taxes   State constitutions can be written or amended to prohibit certain types of taxes or require specific types of exemptions. For example, if the state constitution bars an income tax, this is a very effective tax limitation. States may also exempt specific items from sales taxes; some common exemptions include groceries, medicines, rents, and purchases by religious, educational, or charitable organizations.

Exemptions and Special Treatments   The *homestead exemption* is an increasingly popular method of excluding some part of the value of owner-occupied homes from property taxes. Homestead exemptions go only to homeowners, not to businesses; these exemptions may be expressed in dollar amounts of assessed value (where the first $5,000 or $10,000 of assessed value of a home is nontaxable), or in terms of percentages of assessed value (where the first 25 or 50 percent of assessed value of a home is nontaxable). *Personal property*-tax exemptions are common—exemptions of automobiles, boats, furniture, stocks and bonds, and the like—in part because of the difficulty in identifying and assessing the true value of these types of property. Some states have adopted *circuit-breaker* programs that exempt property from taxation for individuals who are poor, aged, disabled, and so forth.

Impact of Limits   What impact have tax limits had on the state and local government operations? The consequences of tax limits have been greater for *local* than for state governments. Constitutional provisions limiting state government taxing or spending have generally failed to have any discernible effect on state taxing or spending levels.[2] However, local property tax limits have had the effect of increasing reliance of local governments on state aid as well as fees and charges.[3]

EXPLAINING TAX REVOLTS

Why do people support tax limitation measures? A variety of explanations have been offered and tested in opinion polls, but no single explanation seems to explain why people vote for or against tax limitations.[4]

The Self-Interest Explanation   People who benefit most from government spending should oppose tax limitation measures, while people whose tax burdens are heaviest should support these measures. Despite the popularity of "rational" theory, this explanation finds only limited support in opinion surveys; high-income homeowners are only slightly more supportive of tax limits than beneficiaries of government services.

The High-Tax Explanation   People who pay high taxes should support tax limitations, while people who pay modest taxes should show little interest in the tax revolt. Again, there is very little solid evidence to support this theory. Although people who say taxes are "high" tend to vote in favor of tax limitations, the states that have passed limitations are not necessarily the high-tax-burden states.

The "Waste-in-Government" Explanation   People who think government wastes a lot of money should support tax limitation proposals. Opinion polls do show a relationship between perceived waste and support for tax limits. This implies that tax limitation referenda can be defeated if people can be convinced that tax dollars are not wasted.

The Ideological Explanation   According to this explanation, conservatives should support tax limits, while liberals should oppose them. Indeed, according to this rationale, the tax revolt itself is a product of increasing conservatism of the electorate in the late 1970s and early 1980s. There is some support for this explana-

---

[2] James Cox and David Lowery, "The Impact of the Tax Revolt Era State Fiscal Caps," *Social Science Quarterly,* 71 (September 1990), 492–509.

[3] Phillip G. Joyce and Daniel R. Mullins, "The Changing Fiscal Structure of State and Local Public Sector: The Impact of Tax and Expenditure Limits," *Limit Administration Review,* 51 (May/June 1991), 240–53.

[4] The following discussion relies on the theoretical concepts and reports of opinion surveys in David Lowery and Lee Sigelman, "Understanding the Tax Revolt: Eight Explanations," *American Political Science Review,* 75 (December 1981), 963–74; James M. Buchanan, "The Potential for Taxpayers Revolt in American Democracy," *Social Science Quarterly,* 59 (March 1979), 691–96; Paul Allen Beck and Thomas R. Dye, "Sources of Public Opinion on Taxes," *Journal of Politics,* 44 (February 1982), 172–82; Carl Ladd, "The Polls: Taxing and Spending," *Public Opinion Quarterly,* 43 (Spring 1979), 126–35; Susan Hansen, *The Politics of Taxation* (New York: Praeger, 1983).

tion in opinion polls: Conservatives and Republicans tend to support tax limitation measures more than liberals or Democrats.

The Fairness Explanation   People who perceive the tax system as "unfair" should be more likely to vote for tax limitations than people who do not. Again, there is some limited evidence in opinion polls to support this explanation.

The Alienation Explanation   This explanation views the tax revolt as a reflection of declining confidence in government. Negative feelings about government go beyond perceptions of waste, or fairness, or burdensome taxation, and tap deeply felt resentment and alienation from the political system. Again, there is some limited support for this explanation in opinion polls.

It is not surprising that no single explanation of the tax revolt can be offered. Indeed, even a combination of all of the explanations mentioned here does not fully explain voting on tax proposals. Other explanations may be derived from *the specific characteristics of politics in the states* in which tax limitation referenda have been voted on. Still other explanations may focus on *the specific provisions of the tax limitation amendments* being voted upon.

CITY FISCAL STRESS AND CUTBACK MANAGEMENT

Fiscal stress does *not* refer to the annual struggle to balance the budget without raising taxes or cutting services. This struggle occurs in every city. Fiscal stress refers to a financial condition so unfavorable as to impair borrowing ability, require reduction of municipal services, pose a threat to public health and safety, and thus diminish the quality and satisfaction of urban life.[5] Fiscal stress occurs when cities have large municipal payrolls, large socially dependent populations, and heavy tax burdens, yet an eroding tax base, a weak or declining economy, and population loss.

Fiscal stress has widespread impact.[6] As a city tries to solve its budget problems, it raises taxes; imposes fees; reduces its work force; cuts back on maintenance of streets, bridges, buildings, and parks; and postpones capital construction projects. These measures further hurt the local economy. Businesses move away and cancel plans to expand. Unemployment increases as well as demands for help from government. As a city's deficits grow, its bonds become hard to sell to banks and investors. This forces up interest costs that further hurt the city's budget.

Fiscal stress imposes new administrative tasks for mayors and managers. These tasks have been labeled as "cutback management." Managing organizational decline—cutting back on spending and organizational activity, deciding

---

[5] David T. Stanley, "Cities in Trouble," in *Managing Fiscal Stress,* ed. Charles H. Levine (Chatham, NJ: Chatham, 1980).

[6] Various measures of fiscal stress have been devised and applied to American cities. See Richard P. Nathan and Charles Adams, "Understanding Central City Hardship," *Political Science Quarterly,* 91 (Spring 1976), 51–61; David T. Stanley, "Cities in Trouble," in *Managing Fiscal Stress,* ed. Charles H. Levine (Chatham, NJ: Chatham, 1980); Terry N. Clark and Lorna Crowley Ferguson, *City Money* (New York: Columbia University Press, 1983).

who will be let go, what programs will be scaled down or terminated, and what citizens will be asked to make sacrifices—is not as much fun as managing an expanding organization.

Difficult Decisions   Cutback management presents a host of problems for government officials. These include the following considerations:

Resist cutting or smooth the decline. Should officials resist cutting by claiming it cannot be done without great injury to the city? Should they cut vital and popular programs first in order to stir opposition to the cut? By taking police and firefighters off the streets or closing the schools? By refusing to cut back until paydays are missed and loans are defaulted? Or should officials try to smooth the cutback by cutting low-prestige programs, administrative personnel, social programs, and less vital services?

Take one deep gouge or a series of decrements. Should officials try to improve city finances with a single very difficult year by making one set of deep cuts in the budget? Or should they plan a series of smaller cuts over several years to minimize the impact of the cuts and hope that the financial condition of the city may turn around and the cutting can stop?

Share the pain or target the cuts. Should city officials cut all programs "across the board" in order to minimize pain, avoid conflict, maintain morale, and build team spirit in the organization? Or should they make hard decisions about what programs are not really necessary? Targeting cuts requires officials to identify and rank priorities; it generates intense political conflict and tends to be avoided until things get very bad and across-the-board cuts are no longer feasible.

Promote efficiency or equity. Should city officials favor the most efficient programs, usually police and fire protection, streets and sanitation, over the more costly social-service programs? Or should city officials act to protect the most dependent elements of the population?

Cutback Strategies   What strategies can be employed by cities facing retrenchment? We have attempted to summarize some general strategies available to governments in confronting cutbacks:[7]

The no-change strategy: Across-the-board cuts, seniority retention, and hiring freezes. Across-the-board cuts appear to be popular. They distribute the pain of budget reductions equally across agencies and among services. However, eventually across-the-board strategies must be abandoned "as officials become aware that the reductions are permanent . . . that equal cuts are not fair, as some programs are more important than others."[8] A hiring freeze is also a convenient and pop-

---

[7] For an argument that strategies change over time, see Stephen C. Brooks, "Urban Fiscal Stress: A Decade of Difference," Midwest Political Science Association Meeting, Chicago, 1993.

[8] Gregory B. Lewis, "Municipal Expenditures Through Thick and Thin," *Publius,* special issue (May 1984), 380–90.

ular short-run strategy to minimize the pain of cutbacks. Hiring freezes rely on "natural attrition" through resignations and retirements to cut down the size of the work force. It does not require politically difficult decisions about which employees are most essential. If natural attrition does not occur fast enough to meet budget deficits, the next strategy is seniority retention. A "last-in–first-out" rule in layoffs may be viewed by most employees as fair, although it may result in disproportionate harm to women and minorities if they were recruited to government more recently.

A hierarchy of community-needs strategy. An alternative strategy is for cities to set priorities for essential services. Decisions about what services are essential may differ from city to city, but in general we can expect a ranking (from most essential to least essential): public safety (police and fire), public works (streets, sewers, sanitation), administrative services, human services, leisure services.

A "privatizing" strategy. Some city services are "priceable"—users can be charged for them. Cities can charge users for garbage collection, water supply, ambulance service, special police services, transit, licensing, libraries, recreation, and so forth. So one retrenchment strategy is to increase the number and types of user charges for city services. A related strategy is to transfer these services to private enterprise, which can usually perform them cheaper than can the city government. User charges are politically popular because citizens can "see" what they are buying and they are not forced to buy anything they do not want.

A reduction in capital spending strategy. When tough times hit, one of the first responses is to cut back on capital spending—canceling or postponing new equipment purchases, new construction, major repairs. There are short-term advantages to this strategy; city employees can keep their jobs and service levels can be maintained. But over the longer term, this strategy can produce costly results, as streets, bridges, buildings, and equipment fail. Some capital investments can save money over the long run if they improve productivity and reduce labor costs.

A reduction in labor strategy. Cities may finally confront the necessity to reduce personnel costs—hiring freezes, layoffs, renegotiated labor contracts. The most labor-intensive city functions are police and fire protection, together with hospitals and schools in those cities that have these responsibilities. Cutbacks in police and fire personnel are politically unpopular. Indeed, city officials may threaten such cutbacks to force a reconsideration of the rollbacks.

POLITICS AND FISCAL CRISIS

Do political styles influence the way in which cities confront fiscal crisis? Urban sociologist Terry N. Clark thinks so, and he has constructed a typology of fiscal responses based upon a city political style. The table that follows is adapted from Clark and Ferguson.[9]

---

[9] See also Cal Clark and B. Oliver Walter, "Urban Political Cultures, Financial Stress, and City Fiscal Austerity Strategies," *Western Political Quarterly,* 44 (September 1991), 676–97.

RESPONSE TO FISCAL STRESS BY DOMINANT POLITICAL STYLE

	Democrats, Municipal Employees, Blacks	Machines, White Ethnics	Republicans, Businessowners, Taxpayers	Reformers, "New Fiscal Populists," Technocrats
General policies	Find new revenues; increase taxes; borrow money; defer hard decisions; cut capital spending first; cut emloyee compensation last.	Similar to Democrats but with emphasis on retaining ethnic group members on city payroll and continuing services and projects important to ethnic neighborhoods.	Cut taxes; reduce services if necessary; make no special effort to protect city employees; cut social service programs most; perhaps pursue productivity improvement program.	Emphasize productivity improvement; maintain symbolic responsiveness to disadvantaged (visit ghettos, etc.) then make cuts similar to Republicans.
Personnel policies	Keep high compensation for city employees and keep number high.	Restrict compensation of city employees but keep number high.	Reduce both number and compensation of city employees.	Reduce both number and compensation of city employees.
User charges	No user charges for city services.	Occasional user charges.	Heavy reliance on user charges for city services.	Selective user charges with exemptions to protect disadvantaged.
Decision making	Decision making by mayor and council with heavy input from municipal employee unions, black leaders, service recipients.	Decision making by mayor and council with heavy input from dominant ethnic groups and party organization.	Decision making based on reports by taxpayer, civic, business, and citizen groups, with reliance on professional staff.	Decision making same as Republicans but symbolic stress on individual citizen participation; use of polls, public meetings, etc. to solicit citizen input.

Source: Adapted from Terry N. Clark and Lorna Crowley Ferguson, *City Money* (New York: Columbia University Press, 1983). By permission.

THE POLITICS OF BUDGETING

Too often we think of budgeting as the dull province of clerks and statisticians. Nothing could be more wrong. Budgets are political documents that record the struggles over "who gets what." The budget is the single most important policy statement of any government. There are very few government activities or programs that do not require an expenditure of funds, and no public funds may be spent without budgetary authorization. The budget sets forth government programs, with price tags attached. The size and shape of the budget is a matter of serious contention in the political life of any state or community. Governors, mayors, administrators, legislators, interest groups, and citizens all compete to have their policy preferences recorded in the budget. The budget lies at the heart of the political process.

The Executive Budget　The budgetary process begins with the governor or mayor's budget office sending to each governmental agency and department a budget request form, accompanied by broad policy directives to agency and department heads about the size and shape of their requests. Very often these budget requests must be made six to twelve months prior to the beginning of the fiscal year for which the requests are made; state and local governmental fiscal years usually run from July 1 to June 30.[10] After all requests have been submitted to the budget office, the serious task of consolidating these many requests begins. Individual department requests are reviewed, revised, and generally scaled down; often departments are given more or less formal hearings on their budget request by the budget director. The budget agency must also make revenue estimates based upon information it obtains from the tax department.

Governors or mayors must decide whether their budget is to be balanced or not; whether particular departmental requests should be increased or reduced, in view of the programs and promises important to their administrations; whether economies should involve overall "belt tightening" by every agency or merely the elimination of particular programs; or finally, whether they should recommend the raising of new taxes or the incurring of additional debt. These decisions may be the most important that mayors or governors make in their terms of office, and they generally consult both political and financial advisors—budget and tax experts, party officials, interest group representatives, and legislative leaders. Ordinarily, these difficult decisions must be made before governors or mayors present their budget message to the legislature. This budget message explains and defends the final budget presented by the chief executive to his legislative branch.

The Legislative Appropriation　The governor's budget generally appears in the legislature as an appropriations bill, and it follows the normal path of any bill. It is assigned to an appropriations committee, which often holds hearings on the bill and occasionally reshapes and revises the executive budget. The fate of the governor's budget in the legislature generally depends upon his or her general political power, public reactions to recommendations, the degree of support he or she receives from department heads, who are often called to testify at legislative budget hearings, his or her relationships with key legislative leaders, and the effectiveness of interest groups that favor or oppose particular expenditures.

---

[10] The federal government's fiscal year is October 1 to September 30.

After it is passed in identical form by both houses, the final appropriations measure is sent to the governor for signature. If the governor has an item veto, he or she can still make significant changes in the budget at that time.

"Incrementalism" in Budgeting   What forces are actually involved in the budget-making process? Invariably, the forms provided by the budget office require departments to prepare budget requests alongside the previous year's expenditures. Decision makers generally consider the last year's expenditures as a base. Consequently, active consideration of budget proposals is generally narrowed to new items or requested increases over the last year's base. The attention of governors and legislators, and mayors and councils, is focused on a narrow range of increases or decreases in a budget. A budget is almost never reviewed as a whole every year, in the sense of reconsidering the value of existing programs. Departments are seldom required to defend or explain budget requests that do *not* exceed current appropriations; but requested increases in appropriations require extensive explanation, and they are most subject to downward revision by higher political officials.[11]

The "incremental" nature of budgeting creates some interesting informal rules of the budget game:

1. Spend all of your appropriation. A failure to use up an appropriation indicates that the full amount was unnecessary in the first place, which in turn implies that your budget should be cut next year.

2. Never request a sum less than your current appropriation. It is easier to find ways to spend up to current appropriation levels than it is to explain why you want a reduction. Besides, a reduction indicates your program is not growing and this is an embarrassing admission to most government administrators.

3. Put top priority programs into the base, that is, that part of the budget that is within current appropriation levels. Budget offices, governors and mayors, and legislative bodies will seldom challenge programs that appear to be part of existing operations.

4. Increases that are desired should be made to appear small and should appear to grow out of existing operations. The appearance of a fundamental change in a budget should be avoided.

5. Give the budget office, chief executive, and the legislature something to cut. Normally it is desirable to submit requests for substantial increases in existing programs and many requests for new programs, in order to give higher political authorities something to cut. This enables them to "save" the public untold millions of dollars and justify their claim to promoting "economy" in government. Giving them something to cut also diverts attention away from the basic budget with its vital programs.

---

[11] For a discussion of the budgetary process at the federal level, see Aaron Wildavsky, *The New Politics of the Budgetary Process* (Boston: Little, Brown, 1988).

Politics in Budgeting   Budgeting is very *political.* Being a good politician involves (1) the cultivation of a good base of support for one's requests among the public at large and among people served by the agency, (2) the development of interest, enthusiasm, and support for one's program among top political figures and legislative leaders, and (3) skill in following strategies that exploit one's opportunities to the maximum. Informing the public and one's clientele of the full benefit of the services they receive from the agency may increase the intensity with which they will support the agency's request. If possible, the agency should inspire its clientele to contact governors, mayors, legislators, and council members and help work for the agency's request. This is much more effective than the agency's trying to promote for its own requests.

Constraints in Budgeting   As we have already seen, socioeconomic conditions further reduce the alternatives for budgetary action. Very often, local governments *begin* the budgetary process by estimating the amount of revenues that can reasonably be expected from the existing tax base, various service charges, and intergovernmental revenues; this estimate then becomes the ceiling for all budget requests. This practice, together with the conservative tendency of accepting past expenditure levels, seriously curtails policy change. This may be part of the reason why governors and mayors have a difficult time bringing about significant policy changes, and it contributes to the public's view of "politics as usual" and a feeling that nothing can be done, regardless of who is elected.

Fragmented Budgeting   Budgeting is also quite *fragmented.* In most of the states there is a great deal of constitutional and statutory "earmarking" of revenues. A common example is the earmarking of gasoline tax revenues for highway purposes. This practice fragments the budget and reduces executive control over the allocation of public funds.

Nonprogrammatic Budgeting   Finally, budgeting is *nonprogrammatic.* For reasons that accountants have so far kept to themselves, an agency budget typically lists expenditures under ambiguous phrases: "personnel services," "contractual services," "travel," "supplies," "equipment." Needless to say, it is impossible to tell from such a listing exactly what programs the agency is spending its money on. Obviously, such a budget obscures policy decisions by hiding programs behind meaningless phrases. Even if these categories are broken down into line items (for example, under "personnel services," the line item budget might say, "John Doaks, Assistant Administrator $35,000"), it is still next to impossible to identify the costs of various programs. Reform-oriented administrators have called for budgeting by programs for many years; this would present budgetary requests in terms of end products or program packages, like aid to dependent children, vocational rehabilitation, administration of fair employment practices laws, highway patrolling, and so on. Many chief executives favor program budgeting because it will give them greater control over the policy. However, very often administrative agencies are hostile toward program budgeting; it certainly adds to the cost of bookkeeping, and many agencies feel insecure in describing precisely what it is they do. Moreover, there are some *political* functions served by nonprogram budgeting. Compromise comes much more readily when the items in dispute can be treated in dollars instead of differences in policy. Political bargaining and logrolling are made easier when discussions focus on increases and decreases in budgets rather than the desirability of whole programs.

WHEN ENDS DON'T MEET: STATE AND LOCAL DEBT

What happens when revenues fail to match expenditures in state and local government budgets? Most state constitutions require the operating budget of the state government, and those of local governments as well, to be balanced. In other words, most state constitutions prohibit deficits in *operating budgets*. Revenue estimates must match authorized expenditures in the appropriation act. If actual revenues fail to meet the estimates during the fiscal year, expenditures must be cut so that no deficit occurs at the end of the year.

Capital Financing   However, state constitutions generally permit state and local governments to borrow funds for capital improvements, with provision for repayment of the debt during the useful life of the project. State and local governments may sell bonds to finance traditional "essential functions"—roads, schools, parks, libraries, prisons, and government office buildings. These governments may also sell bonds to finance water and sewer systems, airports, ports, mass transportation facilities, solid waste disposal plants, hazardous waste disposal, single- and multi-family housing projects, and hospitals. In the world of municipal finance, these are referred to as "nonessential functions," even though we might argue that they are essential to a community. Finally, government may sell bonds to finance "private activities"—industrial development projects, trade and convention centers, sports arenas.

Constitutional Restrictions   State constitutions may place restrictions on these debts in the form of *debt ceilings,* limiting the total amount of money that a government can borrow (usually expressed as a percentage of the total assessed value of taxable property in the community); and *bond referenda* provisions requiring that any bonded indebtedness (and the taxes imposed to pay off this indebtedness) be approved by the voters in a referendum. These restrictions usually apply only to general obligation bonds.

General Obligation Versus Revenue Bonds   Bonds issued by state and local government may be either general obligation bonds or revenue bonds. *General obligation bonds* are backed by "the full faith and credit" of the government that issues them. This pledges the full taxing powers of the government to pay both the principal and interest due on the bonds. Because these bonds are more secure, lenders are willing to accept lower interest rates on them. This saves the government (and the taxpayer) money in interest payments. *Revenue bonds* are not guaranteed by the issuing government but instead backed by whatever revenues the project itself generates. Both the interest and principal of revenue bonds are paid from fees, and charges or rents ("revenues") generated by the project, rather than tax revenues of the government. Because these bonds are not backed by the full taxing powers of the government, lenders face greater risks and therefore require higher interest payments. Revenue bonds are not usually subject to constitutional debt ceilings or referendum requirements.

Industrial Development Bonds   Competition between municipalities for economic development has led to a vast expansion in industrial development bonds. These are revenue bonds issued by a municipality to obtain funds to purchase land and build facilities for private businesses. Pollution control revenue bonds are issued by municipalities to obtain funds to provide industries with air and water pollution control facilities. Municipalities sometimes issue single-family mortgage revenue bonds to assist home buyers, builders, and developers. Municipalities may issue hospital revenue bonds to assist private as well as public hospitals in the community. These types of revenue bonds blur the distinction between public and private business. At one time most state and local indebtedness was in the form of general obligation bonds. But industrial development, pollution control, mortgage revenue, and hospital bonds, have become so popular that these nonguaranteed revenue bonds now constitute well over half of the outstanding municipal debt in the nation.

Municipal Bond Interest Deductibility   Traditionally the federal government did not levy individual or corporate income taxes on the interest that lenders received from state and local government bonds. All municipal bond interest income was deductible from gross income for federal tax purposes. The original rationale for this deductibility was based on the federal ideal: The national government should not interfere with the operations of state governments and their subdivisions. "The power to tax is the power to destroy,"[12] and therefore neither level of government should tax the instrumentalities of the other. Later this rationale was replaced by more practical considerations: By not taxing municipal bond interest, the federal government was providing an incentive for investment in public infrastructure—schools, streets, hospitals, sewers, airports. Because the federal government forgoes taxing municipal bond income, we might consider these lost federal revenues as a subsidy to state and local governments and the people who lend money to them.

The deductibility of municipal bond interest from federal income taxation makes these bonds very attractive to high-income investors. This attraction allows state and local governments to pay out less interest on their tax-free bonds than corporations must pay out on comparable taxable corporate bonds. Thus, for example, if average *corporate* AAA-rated 30-year bonds were paying 8 percent interest (taxable), average *municipal* AAA-rated 30-year bonds might only pay 6 percent interest (tax free). Many investors would prefer the lower rate because it was tax free. In short, federal deductibility allowed state and local governments to borrow money relatively cheaply.

---

[12] *McCullogh* v. *Maryland,* 4 Wheaton 316 (1819).

Public Bonds for Private Uses   But controversy arose over the years as more and more private businesses asked municipal governments to issue revenue bonds on their behalf—bonds that business used to finance everything from the purchase of single-family homes and the development of luxury apartments, to the building of industrial plants and commercial offices. Business preferred municipal revenue bond financing over its own direct financing because municipal bond interest rates were cheaper owing to federal deductibility. In other words, the issuance of municipal "private purpose" revenue bonds was really a device to obtain cheaper interest rates for business at the expense of lost revenues to the federal government.

Federal Tax Reform and Municipal Finance   The Federal Tax Reform Act of 1986 distinguished between "essential function" bonds (bonds issued for roads, schools, parks, libraries, prisons, and government buildings), "nonessential function" bonds (bonds issued for water and sewer, transportation, multifamily housing, hazardous waste disposal, and health and education facilities), and "private activities" bonds (bonds for industrial development, pollution control, parking facilities, and sports and convention centers). Only essential function bond income is completely free of all federal income taxation. Nonessential bond income is subject to the federal alternate minimum tax (AMT), which means it may be taxable if the taxpayer has a large amount of tax-free income. And income from "private purpose" municipal bonds no longer enjoys tax-free status. These separate treatments complicate the municipal bond market for both governments and investors.

City Debt Patterns   In examining total municipal indebtedness, we should consider both general obligation and revenue indebtedness. General obligation indebtedness of a city may range up to $1000 per resident or more (New York City). Revenue indebtedness can range even higher, to over $3000 per resident. Of course some cities avoid debt altogether. Indebtedness appears to be greater in cities in the Northeast, cities that undertake a wide variety of functions and services, and cities under fiscal strain.[13]

---

[13] See Elaine B. Sharp, "The Politics and Economics of the New City Debt," *American Political Science Review*, 80 (December 1986), 1241–58.

PHOTO CREDITS

INDEX

▲